PROCEEDINGS OF THE SECOND SCANDINAVIAN LOGIC SYMPOSIUM

STUDIES IN LOGIC

AND

THE FOUNDATIONS OF MATHEMATICS

VOLUME 63

NORTH-HOLLAND PUBLISHING COMPANY
AMSTERDAM · LONDON

PROCEEDINGS OF THE SECOND SCANDINAVIAN LOGIC SYMPOSIUM

Edited by

J. E. FENSTAD

University of Oslo

1971

NORTH-HOLLAND PUBLISHING COMPANY
AMSTERDAM · LONDON

Library of Congress Catalog Card Number 71-153401

International Standard Book Number 0 7204 2259 0

PUBLISHERS:

NORTH-HOLLAND PUBLISHING COMPANY – AMSTERDAM
NORTH-HOLLAND PUBLISHING COMPANY, LTD. – LONDON

PRINTED IN THE NETHERLANDS

PREFACE

The Second Scandinavian Logic Symposium was held at the University of Oslo, June 18–20, 1970. The Symposium was recognized as a meeting of the Association for Symbolic Logic and received financial support from the International Union of the History and Philosophy of Science and from the Norwegian Research Council. About 50 persons attended the meeting.

The program consisted mainly of one hour or half hour invited papers, but there were also sessions for contributed papers. This volume contains 13 of the papers presented at the meeting. Of the three remaining papers included two replace papers originally presented. These are the contribution of Tait and the joint paper by Boone, Collins and Matijasevič. One paper, P. Martin-Löf *Hauptsatz for the theory of species,* was written after the Symposium but is included since it is closely related to some of the other papers. It should also be noted that the authors have been free to revise their papers after the Symposium, and this has in several cases (as noted individually by the authors concerned) led to subsequent important extensions of the results as originally reported. This has caused some overlap, see e.g. the contributions of Girard, Prawitz and Martin-Löf which all contain a proof of the full cut-elimination theorem for second order logic (and type theory). However, since these results were obtained independently, we have decided to publish the papers without any editorial interference.

Finally we note one difficulty faced by every editor of the proceedings of a meeting like this Symposium. The papers do not all belong to the same field, hence there is no obvious choice of title for the book. Various editors have tried various combinations of words such as "set", "model", "recursion theory", "formal system", etc. We have not succeeded in finding a sufficiently novel combination of these words, so we are left with a somewhat tame, but precise title of our book.

Oslo, October 1970 Jens Erik Fenstad

CONTENTS

ON THE DECISION PROBLEM FOR FORMULAS IN WHICH ALL DISJUNCTIONS ARE BINARY*

Stal O. AANDERAA
University of Oslo

Abstract

Let Z_1 be the class of closed formulas of the form $\exists a \forall y Kay$ & $\forall x \exists u \forall y Mxuy$ where Kay and $Mxuy$ are conjunctions of binary disjunctions of signed atomic formulas of the form $F\alpha\beta$ or $\neg F\alpha\beta$ where F is a binary predicate symbol, and α and β are one of the variables a, x, u and y. We prove in our paper that there is no recursive set which separates the non-satisfiable formulas in Z_1 from those satisfiable in a finite domain.

1. Introduction

In order to state the result of this paper, it is convenient first to introduce some definitions.

Definition 1. For any class of formulas X let $N(X)$, $I(X)$ and $F(X)$ be the subclasses of X which contain all formulas in X which have respectively, no model, only infinite models, finite models.

Note that $N(X)$ and $F(X)$ are r.e. (recursive enumerable) if X is r.e.

Definition 2. A class of formulas X is a *Trachtenbrot class* if $N(X)$ and $F(X)$ are recursively inseparable. (Two disjoint sets A_0 and A_1 are recursively inseparable if there exists no recursive set B such that $A_0 \subseteq B$ and $A_1 \cap B = \phi$.)

Note that if X is a Trachtenbrot class, then neither $N(X)$ nor $F(X)$ nor $I(X)$ are recursive.

* The first draft of this paper was written when the author was guest investigator at Rockefeller University, New York, March-May 1970.

Trachtenbrot (1953) proved that the class of all formulas in first order predicate calculus is a Trachtenbrot class.

We shall here deal with formulas which are in prenex normal form or which are a conjunction of formulas in prenex normal form.

Definition 3. Let $Q_1, Q_2, ..., Q_n$ (n=1,2,...) be a sequence of strings of quantifiers. Then a formula S is a Q_1 & Q_2 & ... & Q_n-formula if S is a closed formula in first order predicate calculus of the form Q_1M_1 & Q_2M_2 & ... & Q_nM_n where M_i (i=1,2,...,n) is quantifier-free and contains neither the equality sign nor function symbols. The Q_1 & Q_2 & ... & Q_n-class is the class of all Q_1 & Q_2 & ... & Q_n-formulas. If X is a class of formulas then a Q_1 & Q_2 & ... & $Q_n \cap X$-formula is a formula which is both a Q_1 & Q_2 & ... & Q_n-formula and a formula in X. The Q_1 & Q_2 & ... & $Q_n \cap X$-class is the intersection of the classes Q_1 & Q_2 & ... & Q_n and X.

Hao Wang 1962 has proved that both the ∀∃∀ class and the ∀∀∀∃ class are Trachtenbrot classes. But I(∃∃...∃∀∀...∀-class) and I(∃∃...∃∀∀∃∃...∃-class) are empty classes. Hence the classes N(∃∃...∃∀∀...∀-class), F(∃∃...∃∀∀...∀-class), N(∃∃...∃∀∀∃∃...∃-class) and F(∃∃...∃∀∀∃∃...∃-class) are all recursive. This shows that the ∃∃...∃∀∀...∀-classes and the ∃∃...∃∀∀∃∃...∃-classes are not Trachtenbrot classes. Hence the problem of deciding whether a prefix class is a Trachtenbrot class is solved. These problems are in fact also solved for such classes as Q_1 & Q_2 & ... & Q_n-classes.

If we also put some restrictions on the matrix, then new cases occur. Some of these cases have been solved. We may classify the formulas according to the atomic subformulas. See Dreben, Kahr and Wang 1962 and Wang 1962, and Aanderaa 1966.

Melvin R.Krom and S.Ju Maslov have studied formulas in which the matrices consist of conjunctions of binary disjunctions. See Krom 1962, 1967a, 1967b, 1968, 1970 and Maslov 1964. The aim of this paper is also to investigate such formulas. It is therefore convenient to introduce the following definition.

Definition 4. Let A be a formula in first-order predicate calculus and let A' be the result of deleting the quantifiers in A. Then A is a *Krom formula* if A' consists of a conjunction

$$C_1 \ \& \ C_2 \ \& \ ... \ \& \ C_m \tag{2}$$

of binary disjunctions $C_i = D_{1i} \vee D_{2i}$ of signed atomic formulas* D_{1i}, D_{2i},

* A signed atomic formula is a formula of the form B or $\neg B$ where B is an atomic formula.

$i = 1, 2, ..., m$. Each term C_i in (2) is called a conjunct of A'. The class of Krom formulas is denoted by Kr.

Note that to each Krom formula A, there corresponds a Krom formula B in prenex normal form such that $\vdash A \equiv B$.

The main theorem of the first part of this paper is:

Theorem 1. *The* $\exists\forall$ & $\forall\exists\forall \cap$ Kr-*class is a Trachtenbrot class.*

From theorem 1 follows immediate the following corollaries.

Corollary 1. *The decision problem for the* $\exists\forall$ & $\forall\exists\forall \cap$ Kr-*class is recursively unsolvable.*

Corollary 2. *The* $\exists\forall\exists\forall \cap$ Kr-*class is a Trachtenbrot class.*

Corollary 3. *The* $\forall\exists\exists\forall \cap$ Kr-*class is a Trachtenbrot class.*

Corollary 4. *The decision problem for the* $\exists\forall\exists\forall \cap$ Kr-*class is recursively unsolvable.*

Corollary 5. *The decision problem for the* $\forall\exists\exists\forall \cap$ Kr-*class is recursively unsolvable.*

Krom 1970 has proved a weaker form of corollary 5. He proved that the decision problem for the class of Krom formulas in prenex normal form with a prefix of the form $\forall\exists\exists \ldots \exists\forall$ is recursively undecidable.

We shall also prove the following theorem in the first part of this paper:

Theorem 2. *The classes* $\exists\forall$ & $\forall\exists\forall \cap$ Kr, $\exists\forall\exists\forall \cap$ Kr *and* $\forall\exists\exists\forall \cap$ Kr *are reduction classes.*

It turns out, however, that the classes $N(\forall\exists\forall \cap$Kr-class) and $F(\forall\exists\forall \cap$Kr-class) are recursive. See §4 in this paper.

Maslov 1964 has proved that the class $N(\exists\exists \ldots \exists\forall\forall \ldots \forall\exists\exists \ldots \exists \cap$Kr-class) is recursive.

We shall give the proofs of theorems 1 and 2 in detail; and our intention is that the proofs should be elementary. We shall reduce an output problem for register machines to the problem of deciding whether $\exists\forall$ & $\forall\exists\forall$-formulas are consistent or have a finite model.

We shall only define register machines and state the result we need from the theory of register machines. Two-register machines are called 2-type non-writing machines in Minsky 1961. n-register machines are called program machines in Minsky 1967, pp. 199–215, and two-register machines are studied on pp. 255–258. Register machines are also some times called counter machines. By using an appropriate coding, 2-register machines may be used to define recursive functions. See for instance Fischer 1966, Minsky 1962, Minsky 1967, Shepherdson 1965, or Shepherdson and Sturgis 1963.

We shall first establish a lemma about register machines and recursively inseparable sets in §3. We shall prove the theorems 1 and 2 in §3. Finally, we shall state some further new results in §4. But since these results seem to be of lesser importance we shall in §4 only sketch the proofs.

2. The n-register machine

An n-register machine R_n consists of n registers (or also called counters) $T_1, T_2, ..., T_n$, capable of storing arbitrarily large natural numbers, R_n is programmed by a numbered sequence $I_1, I_2, ..., I_r$ of instructions. An instantaneous description (abbreviated ID) of R_n is denoted by

$$(i, x_1, x_2, \ldots, x_n)$$

(where $1 \leqslant i \leqslant r$ and $x_1, x_2, ..., x_n \geqslant 0$) and describes R_n ready to execute instruction I_i, with registers $T_1, T_2, ..., T_n$ containing $x_1, x_2, ..., x_n$, respectively. The instructions are all chosen from the instruction repertoire,

$$\mathrm{H}_0, \mathrm{H}_1, \mathrm{P}(h), \mathrm{DJ}(h,j) (h=1,2,\ldots,n, j=1,2,\ldots,r) \quad .$$

Here

H_0	means: halt and output zero.
H_1	means: halt and output 1.
$\mathrm{P}(h)$	means: add 1 to the contents of register number h. Go on to next instruction.
$\mathrm{DJ}(h,j)$	means: If contents of register number h is not zero, decrease it by 1 and jump to instruction number j. If contents of register number h is zero, go on to next instruction.

A register machine R is defined when its program

$$I_1, I_2, I_3, \ldots, I_r \tag{3}$$

is defined. In order to deal with computations we shall introduce relations $\vdash_R$ and $\vdash_R^*$ between ID's (see table 1). We shall often write $\vdash$ and $\vdash^*$ for $\vdash_R$ and $\vdash_R^*$ when no confusion results. From now on we shall deal mainly with 2-register machines.

Table 1

Case	If $I_i =$	then the relation $\vdash$ is defined to satisfy	and the following binary disjunction is added
0	$= I_1$	$\vdash (1,0,0)$	$F_1aa \vee F_2aa$
1	= P(1)	$(i,\alpha,\beta) \vdash (i+1,\alpha+1,\beta)$	$\neg F_ixy \vee F_{i+1}uy$
2	= P(2)	$(i,\alpha,\beta) \vdash (i+1,\alpha,\beta+1)$	$\neg F_iyx \vee F_{i+1}yu$
3	= D(1,j)	$(i,\alpha+1,\beta) \vdash (j,\alpha,\beta)$	$\neg F_iuy \vee F_jxy$
4	= D(1,j)	$(i,0,\beta) \vdash (i+1,0,\beta)$	$\neg F_iay \vee F_{i+1}ay$
5	= D(2,j)	$(i,\alpha,\beta+1) \vdash (j,\alpha,\beta)$	$\neg F_iyu \vee F_jyx$
6	= D(2,j)	$(i,\alpha,0) \vdash (i+1,\alpha,0)$	$\neg F_iya \vee F_{i+1}ya$
7	$= H_0$	$(i,\alpha,\beta) \vdash 0$	$\neg F_ixy \vee \neg F_ixy$
8	$= H_1$	$(i,\alpha,\beta) \vdash 1$	$\neg F_ixy \vee F_ixy$

We shall use i, j with or without subscript to denote numbers of the set $\{1,2,\ldots,r\}$ and α and β with or without subscript to denote non-negative integers. Then $\vdash (i,\alpha,\beta)$ means that (i,α,β) is the initial ID. In §3 $\vdash (i,\alpha,\beta)$ if $(i,\alpha,\beta) = (1,0,0)$. $(i_1,\alpha_1,\beta_1) \vdash_R (i_2,\alpha_2,\beta_1)$, according to the program (3). If $z = 0$ or $z = 1$ then $(i,\alpha,\beta) \vdash z$ means that (i,α,β) is a halting state with output z, 0 and 1 are called improper instantaneous descriptions, (proper instantaneous description are of the form (i,α,β) where i, α, β are non-negative integers and $1 \leqslant i \leqslant r$). Suppose that the relation $\vdash$ is defined. Then we define $\vdash^*$ as follows.

Definition 5. $b \vdash_R^* c$ means that either $b = c$ or there exist ID's $d_0, d_1, \ldots, d_n$ ($n \geqslant 0$) where $d_0 = b$ and $d_n = c$ and $d_k \vdash_R d_{k+1}$ ($k=0,1,\ldots,n-1$). Moreover, $\vdash_R^* c$ if there exists an a such that $a \vdash_R^* c$ and $\vdash_R a$. We shall say that c is an *immediate successor* of b if $b \vdash_R c$. Moreover, c is a *successor* of b if $b \vdash_R^* c$.

We shall in the next section give a precise definition of the relation $\vdash$ and at the same time associate a formula to each 2-register machine R.

3. Reduction to 2-register machines

To each 2-register machine R with program (3) we shall associate a first order language L_R and a formula S_R in L_R. To each instruction I_i we associate a binary predicate letter F_i. The intended interpretation of F_i is an interpretation over the non-negative integers such that $F_i\alpha\beta$ is true if $\vdash^*(i,\alpha,\beta)$.

We shall now define the relation $\vdash_{\overline{R}}$ describing R's operation on its ID's. At the same time we shall define the Krom formula of the form

$$\exists a\forall yKay \;\&\; \forall x\exists u\forall yMxuy \tag{4}$$

which correspond to R, by listing its binary disjunctions. Each binary disjunction C is a conjunct in Kay if neither x nor u occurs in C and C is a conjunct in $Mxuy$ if a does not occur in C.

Then $\vdash_{\overline{R}}$ and (4) are defined according to table 1 above, which is constructed according to the numbered sequence of instruction (3).

Note that in case 8 in table 1, the binary disjunction is a tautology. Hence we may in this case add no binary disjunction as well.

Definition 6. $b \overset{*}{\vdash} c$ means that ID's $d_0, d_1, \ldots, d_n$ ($n \geqslant 0$) exist where $d_0 = b$, $d_n = c$ and $d_0 \vdash d_1 \vdash \ldots \vdash d_n$. Moreover, $\overset{*}{\vdash} c$ if $(1,0,0) \overset{*}{\vdash} c$. We shall say that c is an *immediate successor* of b if $b \vdash c$. Moreover, c is a *successor* of b if $b \overset{*}{\vdash} c$.

Definition 7. A *finite computation* (or a converging computation) is a finite sequence of ID's $d_1, d_2, \ldots, d_{m-1}, d_m$ such that $d_i \vdash d_{i+1}$ ($i=1,2,\ldots,m-1$) and d_{m-1} is terminal and d_m is an improper ID.

An *infinite computation* (or a diverging computation) is an infinite sequence of ID's $d_1, d_2, d_3, \ldots$ such that $d_i \vdash d_{i+1}$ ($i=1,2,3,\ldots$)

We shall in §3 consider computations where d_1 is $(1,0,0)$.

Example 1. Consider the following 2-register machine R_1 and its corresponding formulas. $\exists a\forall yK_1ay \;\&\; \forall x\exists u\forall yM_1xuy$

I_1	DJ(1,6)	$F_1aa \vee F_1aa, \neg F_1uy \vee F_6xy, \neg F_1ay \vee F_2ay$
I_2	P(1)	$\neg F_2xy \vee F_3uy$
I_3	DJ(2,1)	$\neg F_3yu \vee F_1yx, \neg F_3ya \vee F_4ya$
I_4	H_0	$\neg F_4xy \vee \neg F_4xy$
I_5	P(2)	$\neg F_5yx \vee F_6yu$
I_6	H_1	$\neg F_6xy \vee F_6xy$

Hence K_1ay is

$$(F_1aa \vee F_1aa) \,\&\, (\neg F_1ay \vee F_2ay) \,\&\, (\neg F_3ya \vee F_4ya)$$

and M_1xyu is

$$(\neg F_1uy \vee F_6xy) \,\&\, (\neg F_2xy \vee F_3uy) \,\&\, (\neg F_3yu \vee F_1yx)$$

$$(\neg F_4xy \vee \neg F_4xy) \,\&\, (\neg F_5yx \vee F_6yu) \,\&\, (\neg F_6xy \vee F_6xy) \,.$$

The following is the computation from empty registers in example 1: (1,0,0), (2,0,0), (3,1,0), (4,1,0), 0.

Consider the following examples

	Example 2	Example 3
I_1	DJ(1,6)	P(1)
I_2	P(1)	P(1)
I_3	P(2)	DJ(1,1)
I_4	DJ(2,1)	H_0
I_5	H_0	H_1
I_6	H_1	

The computation according to example 2 from empty registers is:

$$(1,0,0), (2,0,0), (3,1,0), (4,1,1), (1,1,0), (6,0,0), 1 \,.$$

The computation from empty registers according to example 3 is infinite, and the first seven ID's are

$$(1,0,0), (2,1,0), (3,2,0), (1,1,0), (2,2,0), (3,3,0), (1,2,0), (2,3,0), \ldots$$

Let $d_1, d_2, \ldots, d_m$ be a finite computation. The *output* of the computation from d_1 is then d_m. If a computation diverges, then the output is not defined.

Consider now computation where the initial ID is $(1,2^i,0)$ for some i. Then each register machine R as defined above defines a partial recursive function ψ such that range $\psi \subseteq$ 0,1 and such that

$$(1,2^i,0) \vdash_R^* 0 \Leftrightarrow \psi(i) = 0 \tag{5}$$

$$(1,2^i,0) \vdash_R^* 1 \Leftrightarrow \psi(i) = 1 \,. \tag{6}$$

Moreover, given a partial recursive function ψ such that range $\psi \subseteq$ 0,1 there exists a register machine R such that (5) and (6) are satisfied. (See Minsky 1967, p. 257 or Hopcroft and Ullman 1969, p. 100 or Fischer 1966, p. 377).

The following lemma is then easily proved by standard methods in recursion theory. (See Rogers 1967, p. 94).

Lemma 1. *Let N^+, I^+ and F^+ be the set of 2-register machines such that the output of the computation from empty registers are* 0, *not defined and* 1, *respectively. Then N^+ and F^+ are recursively inseparable.*

Proof. Suppose that there exists a recursive set A such that $F^+ \subseteq A$ and $N^+ \cap A = \phi$. (We shall prove lemma 1 by obtaining a contradiction from this assumption.) Then there exists a recursive function f such that range $f = \{0,1\}$ and such that

$$R_x \in A \Rightarrow f(x) = 0 \,.$$

$$R_x \notin A \Rightarrow f(x) = 1 \,.$$

Here R_x is the 2-register machine with gödel number x. Hence

$$R_x \in F^+ \Rightarrow f(x) = 0$$

$$R_x \in N^+ \Rightarrow f(x) = 1 \,.$$

There exists a recursive function h such that

$$(1,2^x,0) \vdash^*_{R_x} 1 \Leftrightarrow (1,0,0) \vdash^*_{R_{h(x)}} 1$$

and

$$(1,2^x,0) \vdash^*_{R_x} 0 \Leftrightarrow (1,0,0) \vdash^*_{R_{h(x)}} 0 .$$

Let $g(x) = f(h(x))$. Then g is a recursive function and range $g = \{0,1\}$. Then

$$(1,2^x,0) \vdash^*_{R_x} 1 \Rightarrow g(x) = 0 \tag{7}$$

$$(1,2^x,0) \vdash^*_{R_x} 0 \Rightarrow g(x) = 1 . \tag{8}$$

Choose z such that

$$(1,2^x,0) \vdash^*_{R_z} 1 \Leftrightarrow g(x) = 1 \tag{9}$$

$$(1,2^x,0) \vdash^*_{R_z} 0 \Leftrightarrow g(x) = 0 . \tag{10}$$

Substituting z for x in (7), (8), (9) and (10) we obtain a contradiction. This proves lemma 1.

Lemma 2. *The effective mapping* Π_1 *of 2-register machines into the* $\exists\forall$ & $\forall\exists\forall \cap$ Kr-*class of formulas defined by* (4) *and table 1, satisfies the following conditions*

$$R \in N^+ \Rightarrow \Pi_1(R) \in N(\exists\forall\&\forall\exists\forall\cap\mathrm{Kr}) \tag{11}$$

$$R \in F^+ \Rightarrow \Pi_1(R) \in F(\exists\forall\&\forall\exists\forall\cap\mathrm{Kr}) . \tag{12}$$

(Here N^+ and F^+ are defined as in lemma 1.)

Proof. We shall first prove (11).

Suppose that $R \in N^+$, and suppose that $\Pi_1(R)$ is consistent. We shall prove that this is a contradiction. Since $R \in N^+$ we have that $\vdash^*_R 0$ i.e. $(1,0,0) \vdash^*_R 0$.

The formula $\Pi_1(R)$ is of the form

$$\exists a \forall y K a y \;\&\; \forall x \exists u \forall y M x u y . \tag{4}$$

We can now use either a model-theoretic argument or a syntactical argument. Since (4) has a model, there exist elements in $a_0, a_1, a_2, \ldots, a_n$ such that

$$\forall y K a_0 y \ \& \ \forall y M a_0 a_1 y \ \& \ \forall y M a_1 a_2 y \ \& \ \ldots \ \& \ \forall y M a_{n-1} a_n y \tag{13}$$

is true. Here we choose n larger than the maximum of the content of the registers in the computation

$$d_0, d_1, \ldots, d_t, \ldots, d_{m-1}, d_m \tag{14}$$

where $d_0 = (1,0,0)$ and $d_m = 0$.

Hence we have that

$$K a_0 a_\beta \ \& \ M a_0 a_1 a_\beta \ \& \ M a_1 a_2 a_\beta \ \& \ \ldots \ \& \ M a_{n-1} a_n a_\beta \tag{15.β}$$

for $\beta = 0, 1, \ldots, n$.

We shall now prove that if $d_t = (j,\alpha,\beta)$ in (14) (t=0,1,2,...,$m-1$), then $F_j a_\alpha a_\beta$ is true. The proof is by induction on t. If $t = 0$, then $d_t = d_0 = (1,0,0)$, since $a_0 = a$ we have according to case 0 in table 1 that $F_1 a_0 a_0$ is true. Suppose that $d_{t-1} = (i,\alpha,\beta)$ and $d_t = (j,\gamma,\delta)$ and that $F_i a_\alpha a_\beta$ is true. We shall prove that $F_j a_\gamma a_\delta$ is true. We have 6 cases according to table 1. Suppose that I_i is the instruction P(1) (case 1). Then $d_t = (i+1,\alpha+1,\beta)$. We shall prove that $F_{i+1} a_{\alpha+1} a_\beta$. $M a_\alpha a_{\alpha+1} a_\beta$ is true according to (15.β). According to case 1 $\neg F_i xy \vee F_{i+1} uy$ is a binary disjunction (conjunct) $Mxuy$. Hence $\neg F_i a_\alpha a_\beta \vee F_{i+1} a_{\alpha+1} a_\beta$ is a conjunct in $M a_\alpha a_{\alpha+1} a_\beta$. Hence $\neg F_i a_\alpha a_\beta \vee F_{i+1} a_{a+1} a_\beta$ is true. Moreover, $F_i a_\alpha a_\beta$ is true by induction hypothesis, since $d_t = (i,\alpha,\beta)$. Hence $F_{i+1} a_{\alpha+1} a_\beta$ is true. This completes the induction proof in the case $d_{t-1} = (i,\alpha,\beta)$ and I_i is P(1). The case I_i is P(2) (case 2) is proved in the same way. If I_i is D(1,j) then we have to distinguish between the case 3 where $d_{t-1} = (i,\alpha,\beta)$ and $\alpha > 0$ and the case 4 where $\alpha = 0$. In case 3 we have that $\neg F_i a_\alpha a_\beta \vee F_j a_{\alpha-1} a_\beta$ is a conjunct of $M a_{\alpha-1} a_\alpha a_\beta$. In case $\alpha = 0$ (case 4) we have that $\neg F_i a_0 a_\beta \vee F_{i+1} a_0 a_\beta$ is a conjunct of $K a_0 a_\beta$ in (15.β). Otherwise the proof if as before. Hence we have in particular that if $d_{m-1} = (j,\alpha,\beta)$ then $F_j a_\alpha a_\beta$ is true. But I_j is H_0. Hence we have that $F_j a_\alpha a_\beta \vee \neg F_j a_\alpha a_\beta$ is true since $\neg F_j a_\alpha a_\beta$ is a conjunct in $M a_\alpha a_{\alpha+1} a_\beta$, which is true according to (15.β). Then $F_j a_\alpha a_\beta$ is false, which is a contradiction. This completes the proof of (11).

Note that we can easily obtain a syntactical proof by proving that (4) implies the existential closure of (13) which in turn implies the existential closure of the conjunction

$$(15.0) \ \& \ (15.1) \ \& \ \ldots \ \& \ (15.n) \,.$$

Then the argument is as before, except for replacing "true" by "provable".

To prove (12) let

$$d_0, d_1, ..., d_t, ..., d_{m-1}, d_m \tag{16}$$

be a computation where $d_0 = (1,0,0)$ and $d_m = 1$. Let n be larger than the maximal content of the registers in the computation (16). It is easy to verify that the formula $\Pi_1(R)$ of the form (4) is satisfiable in an infinite domain $\{a_0,a_1,a_2,...\}$ where $F_i a_\alpha a_\beta$ is true if (i,α,β) occurs in (16). To see this we choose $a = a_0$ in $\exists a \forall y Kay$ and if x in $\forall x \exists u \forall y Mxuy$ has the value a_α, then we pick the value $a_{\alpha+1}$ for u. Since n was larger than the maximal content of the registers, we have that $F_i a_\alpha a_\beta$ is false if $\alpha \geqslant n+1$ or $\beta \geqslant n+1$. Hence we have that $F_i a_\alpha a_\beta \equiv F_i a_n a_\beta$ and $F a_\beta a_\alpha \equiv F a_\beta a_n$ if $\alpha \geqslant n$. Hence (4) is satisfiable in the domain $\{a_0,a_1,a_2,...,a_n\}$, where $F_i a_\alpha a_\beta$ is true if (i,α,β) occurs in (16).

This proves (12) and the proof of lemma 2 is complete.

To prove theorem 1, suppose that theorem 1 is false. Then there exists a recursive set Y_1 which separates $N(Z_1)$ and $F(Z_1)$*, i.e. $F(Z_1) \subseteq Y_1$ and $N(Z_1) \cap Y_1 = \phi$. Let Π_1 be the mapping mentioned in lemma 2. Let S be the set $\Pi_1^{-1}(Y_1)$ i.e.

$$R \in S \Leftrightarrow \Pi_1(R) \in Y_1 \,. \tag{17}$$

Let N^+ and F^+ be as in lemma 1. Then $N^+ \cap S = \phi$ since suppose that $R \in N^+$, then $\Pi_1(R) \in N(Z_1)$ by (11). But $\Pi_1(R) \in N(Z_1)$ and $N(Z_1) \cap Y_1 = \phi$. Hence $\Pi_1(R) \notin Y_1$ and therefore $R \notin S$ by (17). Hence $N^+ \cap S = \phi$. Moreover, $F^+ \subseteq S$, since suppose $R \subseteq F^+$. Then $\Pi(R) \in F(Z_1)$ by (12). Hence $\Pi(R) \in Y_1$ since $F(Z_1) \subseteq Y_1$, hence $R \in S$. This shows that $F^+ \subseteq S$. But S is recursive since the set Y_1 is recursive and the mapping Π_1 is recursive. Hence S is a recursive set which separates N^+ and F^+, which is impossible according to lemma 1. This proves theorem 1.

To prove theorem 2, we use the following familiar fact in logic: (see H.Wang 1962).

Lemma 3. *There is an effective partial procedure by which, given a formula in first order predicate calculus, we can test whether it has no model, a finite model, or only infinite models. The procedure terminates in the first two cases, but does not terminate in the last case.*

* Z_1 is the class of $\exists\forall \,\&\, \forall\exists\forall \cap$ Kr-formulas.

Hence, given a formula S in first order predicate calculus, we can effectively construct a 2-register machine $R(S)$, which gives output 0 if S has no model, and output 1 if S has a finite model, and diverges otherwise. Then by lemma 2, $\Pi_1(R(S))$ is consistent if S is consistent. Hence $\exists\forall$ & $\forall\exists\forall \cap$ Kr is a reduction class. This proves theorem 2.

4. Further results

We shall state some further results which may be proved by refinement of the technique used so far. Since the result seems to be of less importance than the earlier results we shall only sketch the proof. First we shall here consider other computations started on empty registers. The initial values of the registers are called input. In the construction of the formulas, input may be taken care of by adding new monadic predicate letters G_i and H_i. Intuitively, G_ix means $x = i$ and H_ix means $x = 2^i$. Binary disjunctions of the form $G_0a \vee G_0a$ and $\neg G_ix \vee G_{i+1}u$, $G_{i+1}u \vee \neg G_ix$, $\neg G_jx \vee H_ix$ and $G_jx \vee \neg H_ix$ where $j = 2^i$ will take care of the input.

As far as model theory is concerned, we shall partly follow Shoenfield with respect to notions and notations. See Shoenfield 1967, p. 14–23. Let $\mathfrak{A}$ be a structure for a first-order language L. $|\mathfrak{A}|$ is the *universe* of $\mathfrak{A}$ and the elements of $|\mathfrak{A}|$ are called the *individuals* of $\mathfrak{A}$. Then $L(\mathfrak{A})$ is the first-order language obtained from L by adding all the names of individuals of $\mathfrak{A}$. If A is a closed formula in $L(\mathfrak{A})$, let $\mathfrak{A}(A) = T$ mean that A is true in $\mathfrak{A}$. This is also often expressed by $\mathfrak{A} \models A$ or $\models_{\mathfrak{A}} A$. Let Γ^+ be the set of atomic formulas in $L(\mathfrak{A})$ and let Γ^- be the set of negations of formulas in Γ^+. Following Robinson 1963, p.24, we define *the positive diagram* $D^+(\mathfrak{A})$ of $\mathfrak{A}$ to be the set of formulas A in Γ^+ such that $\mathfrak{A}(A) = T$, and *the negative diagram* $D^-(\mathfrak{A})$ of $\mathfrak{A}$ is the set of formulas A in Γ^- such that $\mathfrak{A}(A) = T$. The *diagram* $D(\mathfrak{A})$ of $\mathfrak{A}$ is the set $D^+(\mathfrak{A}) \cup D^-(\mathfrak{A})$. If $\Gamma = \Gamma^+ \cup \Gamma^-$, note that $D^+(\mathfrak{A})$, $D^-(\mathfrak{A})$ and $D(\mathfrak{A})$ in the sense of Robinson 1963, p. 24 correspond to $D_{\Gamma^+}(\mathfrak{A})$, $D_{\Gamma^-}(\mathfrak{A})$ and $D_\Gamma(\mathfrak{A})$, respectively, in the sense of Shoenfield 1967, p. 74.

Definition 8. Let Z be a class of formulas where each formula in Z is no more complex than

$$\exists a \forall x \exists u \forall y Maxuy \tag{18}$$

or a conjunction of formulas of the form (18) or simpler. Here $Maxuy$ is quantifier-free. A *Buchi model* for the class Z is a model $\mathfrak{A}$ such that

$|\mathfrak{A}| = \{0,1,2,...\}$ and such that for each part of the form (18), we have that $\mathfrak{A}(M0nn'm) = T$ where $n' = n + 1$, for each number n and m.

The main theorem in this section is:

Theorem 3. *Let A_0 and A_1 be two disjoint r.e. sets. Then there exist two sequences of Krom formulas $B_i(A_0,A_1)$ and $B_i'(A_0,A_1)$ of the forms*

$$B_i = B_i(A_0,A_1) = \exists a\forall yN_1ay \,\&\, \forall x\exists u\forall y(N_2xuy\&M_ixu)$$

$$\&\,\forall x(\neg P_ix\vee F_0x) \tag{19}$$

$$B_i' = B_i'(A_0,A_1) = \exists a_0\exists a_1...\exists a_j\forall y(N_1a_0y\&N_2a_0a_1y\&N_2a_1a_2y\&...$$

$$\&N_2a_{j-1}a_jy\&F_0a_j)\,\&\,\forall x\exists u\forall yN_2xuy\,, \qquad (j=2^i) \tag{20}$$

where M_ixu is an initial segment of an infinite conjunction Mxu. Moreover, Mxu contains only monadic predicates. N_1ay and N_2xuy are also quantifier-free and contain only monadic and dyadic predicate symbols. The sets $\{B_0,B_1,B_2,...\}$ and $\{B_0',B_1',B_2',...\}$ are denoted by $Z(A_0,A_1)$ and $Z'(A_0,A_1)$ respectively. The relation between A_0, A_1, B_i, and B_i' is as follows:

(i) $\vdash B_i \supset B_i'$.

(ii) *Every model $\mathfrak{A}'$ of B_i' can be extended to a model $\mathfrak{A}$ of B_i, such that $|\mathfrak{A}| = |\mathfrak{A}'|$.*

(iii) $i\in A_0 \Leftrightarrow B_i \in N(Z(A_0,A_1))$ *(inconsistent).*

(iv) $i\in A_1 \Leftrightarrow B_i \in F(Z(A_0,A_1))$.

(v) *The class $\{B_i|i\notin A_0\}$ is a consistent class.*

(vi) *Let A_4 be a finite subset of A_1. Then the class of formulas $\{B_i|i\in A_4\}$ is satisfiable in a finite domain.*

(vii) *Let A_2 be a r.e. set of natural numbers such that $A_2 \cap A_0 = \phi$. Then there exists a Buchi model $\mathfrak{A}_2$ for the class $\{B_i|i\in A_2\}$ whose diagram is r.e. Moreover, we also have that $i\in A_2 \Leftrightarrow \mathfrak{A}_2(B_i) = T$.*

(viii) *Let A_3 be a recursive set of natural numbers such that $A_3 \cap A_0 = \phi$. Then there exists a Buchi model $\mathfrak{A}_3$ for the class A_3 such that the diagram of $\mathfrak{A}_3$ is recursive and such that $i\in A_3 \Leftrightarrow \mathfrak{A}_3(B_i) = T$.*

(ix) *There exists a Krom formula $B'' = B''(A_0,A_1)$ of the form*

$$\exists a\forall yN_1''ay \,\&\, \forall x\exists u\forall yN_2''xuy \tag{21}$$

such that

$$i \in A_1 \Leftrightarrow \vdash B'' \supset B'_i$$

and

$$i \in A_0 \Leftrightarrow \vdash B'' \supset \neg B'_i \,.$$

Hence if A_0 and A_1 are recursively inseparable, then B'' is an essentially undecidable theory.
(x) *If A_0 and A_1 are recursively inseparable, then B'' has no recursive Buchi model.*

In theorem 3 we have written $B_i = B_i(A_0,A_1)$, $B'_i = B'_i(A_0,A_1)$ and $B'' = B''(A_0,A_1)$ to emphasize that B_i, B'_i and B'' depend on A_0 and A_1. Note also that all B_i contain a fixed number of dyadic predicates, but the number of monadic predicates increases by the order of 2^i in B_i. All B'_i contain a fixed number of predicate symbols.

Sketch of a proof of theorem 3. In order to define input we use monadic predicates in $M_i xu$. F_0 is the only monadic predicate which occurs both in M_i and N_1. N_2 does not contain monadic predicates. $F_0 x$ means x is an input. $N_1 ay$ contains the disjunction $\neg F_0 y \vee F_1 ya$. In the formulas B'_i (i=0,1,2,...) input is defined by $F_0 a_j$ where $j = 2^i$. The reason why this will work is that the part $\forall y(N_1 a_0 y \& N_2 a_0 a_1 y \& ... \& N_2 a_{j-1} a_j y \& F_0 a_j)$ of the formula B'_i forces $a_0, a_1, a_2, ..., a_j$ to be an initial segment of a Buchi model for $\exists a \forall y N_1 ay$ & $\forall x \exists u \forall y N_2 xuy$. Then theorem 3 (i), (ii), (iii), (v), (vi) and (viii) is easy to prove. In order to prove theorem 3 (iv) we have to modify the construction somewhat. It is easy to prove that

(iv′) $\qquad i \in A_1 \Rightarrow B_i \in F(Z(A_0,A_1))$

but

(iv″) $\qquad B_i \in F(Z(A_0,A_1)) \Rightarrow i \in A_1$

may not be true in general. Suppose that $i \notin A_1$. If $i \in A_0$ then $B_i \notin F(Z(A_0,A_1))$. Hence suppose that $i \notin A_0$ also. If the register machine R with input 2^i cycles (goes into a finite loop) we would have that $B_i \in F(Z(A_0,A_1))$. But it is easy to construct the register machine in such a way that it never cycles. It is still difficult to prove that $B_i \notin F(Z(A_0,A_1))$. We can solve the problem by adding some new binary disjunctions to $N_2 xay$. Let G be a new binary predicate. The new disjunctions are $\neg Gxx \vee \neg Gxx$, $\neg Gyx \vee Gyu$, $\neg F_i xy \vee Gxu$, $\neg F_i yx \vee Gxu$, where $i = 1, 2, ..., r$. In order to prove theorem 3 (iv), we use the fact that the formula

$$\forall x \exists u \forall y ((\neg Gxx \vee \neg Gxx) \& (\neg Gyx \vee Gyu) \& Gxu)$$

is consistent but that it has no finite models.

In order to prove theorem 3 (ix) and (x) we shall construct the formula (21) using the same binary predicate letters as in $N_1 ay$ and $N_2 xuy$ in (19) and (20).

Let A be a set of natural numbers, such that $A \cap A_0 = \phi$. Then we may define a structure $\mathfrak{A}$ satisfying all formulas B_i and B'_i where $i \in A$, and where $F_j \alpha\beta$ is true $\Leftrightarrow (\exists i)(i \in A$ and $(1, 2^i, 0) \overset{*}{\vdash} (j, \alpha, \beta))$. The intended model $\mathfrak{A}''$ for (21) is such that

$$F_j \alpha\beta \text{ is true} \Leftrightarrow (\exists i)(\exists \alpha_1)(\exists \beta_1)((j, \alpha, \beta) \overset{*}{\vdash} (i, \alpha_1, \beta_1) \text{ and } I_i \text{ is } \mathrm{H}_1).$$

Hence in case 1 when I_i is H_1 we add $F_i xy \vee F_i xy$ and for each binary disjunction in table 1 of the form $\neg P \vee Q$ where P and Q are atomic formulas, we also add $P \vee \neg Q$. In this way we obtain $P \equiv Q$, which are what we want, since if $(j_1, \alpha_1, \beta_1) \overset{*}{\vdash} (j_2, \alpha_2, \beta_2)$ then each of the following statements implies the other:

$$(\exists i)(\exists \alpha_3)(\exists \beta_3)((j_1, \alpha_1, \beta_1) \overset{*}{\vdash} (i, \alpha_3, \beta_3) \text{ and } I_i \text{ is } \mathrm{H}_1),$$

$$(\exists i)(\exists \alpha_3)(\exists \beta_3)((j_2, \alpha_2, \beta_2) \overset{*}{\vdash} (i, \alpha_3, \beta_3) \text{ and } I_i \text{ is } \mathrm{H}_1).$$

We also add $F_0 y \vee \neg F_1 ya$ to $N_1 ay$ to obtain $N''_1 ay$. These are the main steps in the proof of theorem 3 (ix). Suppose that A_0 and A_1 are recursively inseparable. Then the set $\{\alpha | F_0 \alpha \text{ is true}\}$ is not a recursive set in a Büchi model for B''. This proves theorem 3 (x). This completes the outline of the proof of theorem 3.

From theorem 3 we obtain the following corollaries.

Corollary 6. *The formula*

$$\exists a \forall y N''_1 ay \;\&\; \forall x \exists u Hxu \;\&\; \forall x \forall z \forall y (\neg Hxz \vee N''_2 xzy)$$

where N''_1 and N''_2 are as in (21) *and H is a new predicate letter, has no recursive model.*

Definition 9. A class Z of formulas in first order predicate calculus is called a *conservative reduction class* if there exists an effective procedure by which, when an arbitrary formula S in first order predicate logic is given, a corresponding formula S_Z of the class Z can be found such that
(i) S is satisfiable $\Leftrightarrow S_Z$ is satisfiable
(ii) S is satisfiable in a finite domain $\Leftrightarrow S_Z$
is satisfiable in a finite domain.

From lemma 3 and theorem 3, we obtain the following improvements of theorem 2.

Corollary 7. *The classes* $\exists\forall$ & $\forall\exists\forall \cap$ Kr *and* $\forall\exists\exists\forall \cap$ Kr *are conservative reduction classes.*

Theorem 4. *The classes* $N(\forall\exists\forall\cap\mathrm{Kr})$, $F(\forall\exists\forall\cap\mathrm{Kr})$ *and* $I(\forall\exists\forall\cap\mathrm{Kr})$ *are all non-empty and recursive.*

In order to prove theorem 4 we first prove that we reduce the case to consider formulas

$$\forall x \exists u \forall y Mxuy \tag{22}$$

which contain atomic parts of the forms

$$Fxy,\ Fyx,\ Fuy,\ Fyu \tag{23}$$

and

$$Fxx,\ Fyy,\ Fuu\ , \tag{24}$$

only, where F is a binary predicate symbol.

We shall here first consider the set $N(\forall\exists\forall\cap\mathrm{Kr})$. If (22) is satisfiable, then (22) has models whose domain is the integers $\{...-1,0,1,2,...\} = Z$ and such that $M\alpha(\alpha+1)\beta$ is true for every pair of integers α, β.

Let $M'xay$ be the formula obtained by deleting all disjunctions which contain atomic parts of the form (24). We shall now consider sets of pairs of integers (α_1,β_1) satisfying

$$(\forall\alpha)(\forall\beta)M'a(\alpha+1)\beta \supset (G_1\alpha_0\beta_0 \supset G_2(\alpha_0+\alpha_1)(\beta_0+\beta_1)) \tag{25}$$

where $G_i xy$ is Fxy, or $\neg Fxy$ or Fyx or $\neg Fyx$ for some binary predicate Fxy. As in the theory of bounded languages in Ginsburg 1966 we regard Z^n instead of N^n where $N = \{0,1,2,...\}$, to be a subset of the space $\mathcal{R}^n$. Moreover, given subsets C and P of Z_n, let $L(C;P)$ denote the set of all elements in Z^n which can be represented by the form

$$c_0 + x_1 + x_2 + ... + x_m$$

for some c_0 in C and some (possibly empty) sequence $x_1, ..., x_m$ of elements of P. C is called the set of constants and P the set of periods of $L(C;P)$.

$L \subseteq Z^n$ is said to be a *linear set* if C consists of exactly one element, say $C = \{c\}$, and P is finite, say $\{p_1,...,p_n\}$. A subset of Z_n is said to be *semilinear* if it is a finite union of linear sets.

Note that we consider here subsets of Z^n instead of N^n as used in the theory of bounded languages.

We can now prove the following lemma.

Lemma 4. *The set of pairs* (α,β) *satisfying* (25) *is a semilinear set. There exists an effective procedure by which a representation of the semilinear sets can be obtained from* $M'xuy$.

Next we prove the following lemma:

Lemma 5. *The set of integers* α *satisfying*

$$(\forall\alpha)(\forall\beta)M\alpha(\alpha+1)\beta \supset (\mathrm{H}_1\alpha_0 \supset \mathrm{H}_2(\alpha_0+\alpha))$$

is a semilinear set. Here $\mathrm{H}_i x$ *is* Fxx *or* $\neg Fxx$ *for some binary predicate F. There exists an effective procedure by which a representation of the semilinear sets can be obtained from* $Mxuy$.

The lemmas 4 and 5 are proved almost in the same way as Parikh's theorem which says that if $L \subseteq a^*b^*$ is a contextfree language, then the set $\{(i,j) | a^i b^j \in L\}$ is semilinear. See Ginsburg 1966, pp. 146–149.

The theorem 4 now follows easily.

References

Aanderaa, S.O., A new undecidable problem with application in logic, Doctoral thesis (Harvard University, Cambridge, Mass., U.S.A., 1966).

Büchi, J.R., Turing Machines and the Entscheidungsproblem, Math. Ann. 148 (1962) 201–213.

Chang, C.C. and H.J.Keisler, An improved prenex normal form. J. Symbolic Logic 27 (1962) 317–326.

Dreben, B., A.S.Kahr and H.Wang, Classification of AEA formulas by letter atoms, Bull. Amer. Math. Soc. 68 (1962) 528–532.

Fischer, P.C., Turing machines with restricted memory access, Information and Control 9 (1966) 364–379.

Ginsburg, S., The mathematical theory of context-free languages (McGraw-Hill, New York, 1966).

Hopcroft, J.E. and J.D.Ullmann, Formal languages and their relation to Automata (Addison-Wesley, Reading, Mass., U.S.A., 1969).

Kahr, A.S., E.F.Moore and H.Wang, Entscheidungsproblem reduced to the AEA case, Proc. Nat. Acad. Sci. U.S.A. 48 (1962) 365–377.

Krom, M.R., A property of sentences that define quasiorder, Notre Dame J. Formal Logic 7 (1966) 349–352.

Krom, M.R., The decision problem for a class of first-order formulas in which all disjunctions are binary, Z. Math. Logik Grundlagen Math. 13 (1967a) 15–20.

Krom, M.R., The decision problem for segregated formulas in first-order logic, Math. Scand. 21 (1967b) 233–240.

Krom, M.R., Some interpolation theorems for first-order formulas in which all disjunctions are binary, Logique et Analyse 43 (1968) 403–412.

Krom, M.R., The decision problem for formulas in prenex conjunctive normal form with binary disjunctions, J. Symbolic Logic 35 (1970) 210–216.

Maslov, S.Ju., An inverse method of establishing deducibilities in the classical predicate calculus, Dokl. Akad. Nauk SSSR 159 (1964) 1420–1424.

Minsky, M.L., Recursive unsolvability of Post's problem of tag and other topics in the theory of Turing machines, Ann. of Math. 74 (1961) 437–455.

Minsky, M.L., Computation: finite and infinite machines (Prentice-Hall, 1967).

Rogers, H.Jr., Theory of recursive functions and effective Computability (McGraw-Hill, 1967).

Robinson, A., Introduction to model theory and to the metamathematics of algebra (North-Holland, Amsterdam, 1963).

Shepherdson, J.C., Machine configuration and word problems of given degree of unsolvability, Z. Math. Logik Grundlagen Math. 11 (1965) 149–175.

Shepherdson, J.C. and H.E.Sturgis, Computability of recursive functions, J. Assoc. Comput. Mach. 10 (1963) 217–255.

Shoenfield, J.R., Mathematical Logic (Addison-Wesley, 1967).

Trachtenbrot, B.A., O.Rekurajonoj Otdelimosti, Dokl. Akad. Nauk SSSR 88 (1953) 953–955.

Wang, H., Proving theorems by pattern recognition, II. Bell System Tech. J. 40 (1961) 1–41.

Wang, H., Domino and the AEA case of the decision problem, Proc. Symposium on Mathematical Theory of Autcmatic, Polytechnic Institute of Brooklyn (1962) 23–55.

THE IMMORTALITY PROBLEM FOR NON-ERASING TURING MACHINES

Dag BELSNES
University of Oslo

Introduction

Σ is an alphabet, i.e. a finite set of symbols. An infinite word $x_1x_2 \ldots x_n \ldots$ from Σ is called *ultimately periodic* if there exist integers $n_0, n_1 \geqslant 1$ such that $x_{n+n_1} = x_n$ for every $n \geqslant n_0$. Σ^* denotes the set of all finite words from Σ (also the empty word Λ). Σ^∞ denotes the set of ultimately periodic infinite words. Let $L = x_1x_2 \ldots x_n \epsilon \Sigma^*$. The length n of L is written $|L|$. ${}_iL_j$ where $1 \leqslant i \leqslant j \leqslant |L|$ denotes the subword $x_ix_{i+1} \ldots x_j$ of L.

Let M be a Turing machine (TM). In the sequel Σ will denote the alphabet of M, K the set of internal states of M, and we let $s = \# \Sigma$ and $k = \#K$. M operates on an one-way (towards the right) infinite tape T where every square stores a symbol from Σ. The squares of T is numbered 1, 2, ... from the left. ${}_iT_j$, where $1 \leqslant i \leqslant j$, denotes the squares of T with numbers $i, i+1, \ldots, j$. An *instantaneous description* (ID) of M is a triple $\langle q,X,n \rangle$ where $q \epsilon K$, $X \epsilon \Sigma^\infty$ and $n \geqslant 1$. $\langle q,X,n \rangle$ describes that M is in state q with the read-write head scanning square no. n and that the tape T contains X. M is to stop if M tries to go off the tape at the left end.

Let α and β be two ID-s. $\alpha \vdash^* \beta$ ($\alpha \vdash \beta$) means that β is an (immediately) successor of α. α is a *terminal* ID if there is no ID β such that $\alpha \vdash \beta$. Each ID with a terminal successor is called a *mortal* ID, opposite to an *immortal* ID (IID) which is the start of an infinite execution.

M is called a *non-writing* TM if it contains no write-instructions. One element of Σ is called the *blank* symbol. M is non-erasing if M writes only on squares containing a blank.

The *immortality problem* (IP) associated with a set of TM-s is the problem of deciding, for a given TM in the set, whether or not there exists an IID. P.K.Hooper [1] has shown that the IP for the set of all TM-s is recursively undecidable. In this paper we show that IP for non-erasing TM-s is decidable, if the tape is allowed to contain ultimately periodic words. If, however, the tape is restricted to contain only a finite number of non-blanks, then the IP for the set of non-erasing TM-s is recursively undecidable (of degree $0''$).

IP for non-writing TM-s

Let M be an arbitrary TM. A relation $\sim$ on Σ^* is defined by for every $L, J \epsilon \Sigma^*$

$$L \sim J \Leftrightarrow (\forall X \epsilon \Sigma^\infty)(\forall q \epsilon K)(\forall i>0)$$

$$[\langle q, LX, |L|+1\rangle \vdash^* \langle\ ,\ , |L|+i\rangle \Leftrightarrow$$

$$\langle q, JX, |J|+1\rangle \vdash^* \langle\ ,\ , |J|+i\rangle] \ .$$

Here $\langle q, LX, |L|+1\rangle \vdash^* \langle\ ,\ , |L|+i\rangle$ is a shorthand for

$$(\exists p \epsilon K)(\exists Y \epsilon \Sigma^\infty)\langle q, LX, |L|+1\rangle \vdash^* \langle p, Y, |L|+i\rangle \ .$$

It is easily shown that $\sim$ is an equivalence relation. For $L \epsilon \Sigma^*$ we denote by $\tilde{L}$ the equivalence class containing L.

Lemma 1. *Let M satisfy*

(i) $\#\{\tilde{L} \mid L \epsilon \Sigma^*\} = r < \infty$ *and*

(ii) $(\exists E \epsilon \Sigma^\infty)(\exists p \epsilon K)\langle p, E1\rangle \vdash^* \langle\ ,\ , rk+1\rangle \ .$

$(k=\#K)$. *Then M has an* IID.

Proof. For $j = 1, 2, 3, \ldots, rk+1$ let q_j be the state of M the *first* time M arrives at square no. j after starting at $\langle p, E, 1\rangle$ (see condition (ii)). Denote by J_j the content of ${}_1T_{j-1}$ at the same moment. ($q_1 = p$ and $J_1 = \Lambda$.) By notation we have

$$\langle q_1, {}_1E_{j-1}X, 1\rangle \vdash^* \langle q_j, J_jX, j\rangle \text{ for all } X \epsilon \Sigma^\infty$$

$$\text{and } j = 1, 2, \ldots, rk+1 \ . \tag{1}$$

(i) implies that $\#\{\langle q, \tilde{J}\rangle \mid q \epsilon K \ \&\ J \epsilon \Sigma^*\} = rk$. Therefore there exist integers g and h such that $1 \leqslant g < h \leqslant rk+1$ and $\langle q_g, \tilde{J}_g\rangle = \langle g_h, \tilde{J}_h\rangle$. Since $J_g \sim J_h$, it can be established without difficulties that

$$(\forall X \epsilon \Sigma^{\infty})(\forall i \geqslant 0)[\langle q_1, {}_1E_{g-1}X, 1\rangle \vdash^* \langle\ ,\ , g+i\rangle$$

$$\Rightarrow \langle q_1, {}_1E_{h-1}X, 1\rangle \vdash^* \langle\ ,\ , h+i\rangle] \ . \tag{2}$$

Letting $X = {}_gE_{h-1}^{\infty}$ $(= {}_gE_{h-1} \cdot {}_gE_{h-1} \ldots)$ we have ${}_1E_{h-1}X = {}_1E_{g-1} \cdot {}_gE_{h-1}X$ $= {}_1E_{g-1}X$, and for $i = m \cdot (h-g)$ where $m \geqslant 0$, (2) implies

$$\langle q_1, {}_1E_{g-1}X, 1\rangle \vdash^* \langle\ ,\ , g+m(h-g)\rangle \Rightarrow$$

$$\langle q_1, {}_1E_{g-1}X, 1\rangle \vdash^* \langle\ ,\ , g+(m+1)(h-g)\rangle \ . \tag{3}$$

From (1) with $j = g$ it follows that

$$\langle q_1, {}_1E_{g-1}X, 1\rangle \vdash^* \langle\ ,\ , g+0\cdot(h-g)\rangle \ . \tag{4}$$

Using (3) and (4) we have by induction that for every $m \geqslant 0$

$$\langle q_1, {}_1E_{g-1}X, 1\rangle \vdash^* \langle\ ,\ , g+m(h-g)\rangle \ .$$

Since $h - g > 0$ this means that $\langle q_1, {}_1E_{g-1} \cdot {}_gE_{h-1}^{\infty}, 1\rangle$ is an IID.

Definition. Let M be an arbitrary TM, and let $d \notin K$. For every $L \epsilon \Sigma^*$ a function $f_L : K \to K \cup \{d\}$ is defined as follows. If $L = \Lambda$, then $f_L(q) = d$ for every $q \epsilon K$. If $L \neq \Lambda$, then let $q \epsilon K$ and start M at $\langle q, LX, |L|\rangle$ where $X \epsilon \Sigma^{\infty}$. If M arrives at square no. $|L| + 1$, first time in state q', we set $f(q) = q'$. If, on the contrary, M halts or loops on ${}_1T_{|L|}$, then $f(q) = d$.

Let L be the content of the $|L|$ first squares of T, and let the read-write head of M be posed at a square with a number greater than $|L|$. If M later enters ${}_1T_{|L|}$, first time in state q, then $f_L(q)$ tells whether M returns or not, and if returning, $f_L(q)$ is the return-state. If M is non-writing, f_L contains the same information about every visit into ${}_1T_{|L|}$. We therefore have:

Lemma 2. *If M is a non-writing* TM, *then*

$$(\forall L, J \epsilon \Sigma^*)[f_L = f_J \Rightarrow L \sim J] \ .$$

From lemma 2 it follows that if M is non-writing, then $\#\{\widetilde{L} | L \epsilon \Sigma^*\} \leqslant (k+1)^k$.

Lemma 3. *Let M be an arbitrary* TM. *If* $(\exists E\epsilon\Sigma^{\infty})(\exists p\epsilon K)[\langle p,E,1\rangle \vdash^{*} \langle E,k(k+1)^{k}+1\rangle$ *without using a write-instruction*], *then M has an* IID *where M never writes*.

Proof. Using lemma 1 and lemma 2 on the submachine of M obtained by removing every write-instruction, the lemma follows immediately.

Proposition 4. *Let M be an arbitrary* TM. *The question "has M an* IID *where M never writes?" can be answered effectively*.

Proof. Let $i = k(k+1)^{k}$ and $X\epsilon\Sigma^{\infty}$. For every of the s^{i} different $L\epsilon\Sigma^{\infty}$ of length i and every $q\epsilon K$, M is started at $\langle q,LX,1\rangle$. We can effectively decide whether

1) M leaves ${}_1T_i$ before $ik + 1$ instructions are executed without having written on ${}_1T_i$, or

2) M writes or stops on ${}_1T_i$ before $ik + 1$ instructions are executed without first having left ${}_1T_i$, or

3) M will continue for ever on ${}_1T_i$ without writing.

If every combination yields case 2), then the question is answered with no. If case 3) applies for a combination, then the concerned ID is an IID, and in case 1) the answer is also yes by lemma 3.

IP for non-erasing TM-s

Let M be a non-erasing TM and let ${}_1T_{|L|}$ contain L. f_L gives us return-information about the first visit into ${}_1T_{|L|}$ from the right. If, however, M alters the content of ${}_1T_{|L|}$ before leaving ${}_1T_{|L|}$, then f_L may not contain the return-information about the next visit. This leads to the following definition.

Definition. Let M be a non-erasing TM where $K = \{a_1,...,a_k\}$. To every $L\epsilon\Sigma^{*}$ we associate a finite tree-structure TR_L. To each node except the root, there is associated a state in K. From each node goes either one branch for each element of K or none. TR_L is defined inductively with respect to the number n of blanks in L.

$n = 0$.

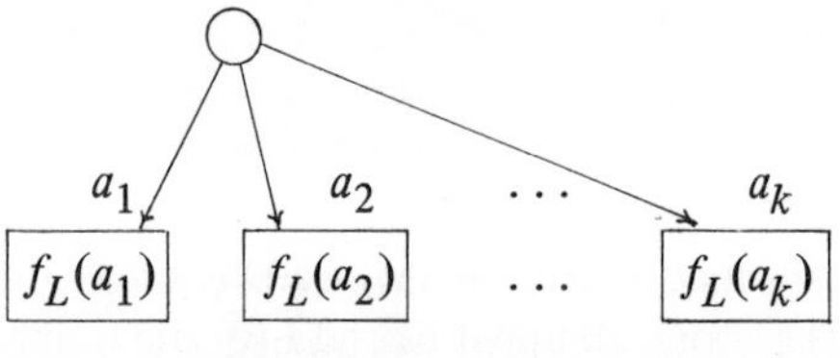

TR_L for $n = 0$.

$n > 0$. Define the first ramification from the root of TR_L as for $n = 0$. If $f_L(a_i) = d$, then the a_i-branch terminates. $f_L(a_i) \neq d$ means that M starting at $\langle a_i, LX, |L|\rangle$, eventually will leave ${}_1T_{|L|}$ towards the right in the state $f_L(a_i)$. If ${}_1T_{|L|}$ still contains L, then the a_i-branch terminates. If, however, M has changed the content to L', then, since M is non-erasing, L' contains less than n blanks, and we let the node at the end of the a_i-branch be the root of the subtree given by $\mathrm{TR}_{L'}$.

If ${}_1T_{|L|}$ contains L, then TR_L contains information about the return-states for every sequence of visits into ${}_1T_{|L|}$ from the right. Thus, if $\mathrm{TR}_L = \mathrm{TR}_J$, then, ${}_1T_{|L|}$ containing L and ${}_1T_{|J|}$ containing J seem identically from the right. Without difficulties we then have:

Lemma 5. *Let M be a non-erasing* TM. *Then*

$$(\forall L,J \in \Sigma^*)[\mathrm{TR}_L = \mathrm{TR}_J \Rightarrow L \sim J] .$$

Definition. A TM M is called a *Q-machine* if M is non-erasing and M has no IID where M never writes.

Proposition 4 yields that we effectively can decide whether any given TM M is a Q-machine or not. Every non-erasing TM which is not a Q-machine, has by definition an IID, and IP for this set is trivially solvable. A main point in the demonstration of the decidability of IP for the set of all non-erasing TM-s, is that given a Q-machine M there is an effectively computable upper bound for the number of different TR_L when L runs through Σ^*. We have:

Lemma 6. *Let M be a Q-machine. Then for every integer $i \geqslant 1$ the operation "M into ${}_1T_i$, then write on ${}_1T_i$ and thereafter leave ${}_1T_i$" can at most be repeated $k \cdot (k+1)^k$ times.*

Proof. Follows from lemma 3 since M is a Q-machine.

Lemma 7. *To every given Q-machine M there is an integer i effectively computable from the number k of states of M, such that if*

$$(\exists E \epsilon \Sigma^{\infty})(\exists p \epsilon K)\langle p,E,1\rangle \vdash^{*} \langle\ ,\ ,i\rangle\ ,$$

the M has an IID.

Proof. From lemma 6 it follows that no path in TR_L can be longer than $k(k+1)^k + 1$ for any $L \epsilon \Sigma^*$. Therefore, an upper bound r for the number of elements in $\{TR_L | L \epsilon \Sigma^*\}$ can be calculated from k. Using lemma 5 and lemma 1 we have that $i = rk + 1$ satisfies the lemma.

Theorem 8. IP *for the set of non-erasing* TM-s *is effectively decidable. (The tape contains ultimately periodic words.)*

Proof. Proposition 4 tells that we effectively can decide whether a TM M is a Q-machine or not. If M is not a Q-machine, M has an IID. Suppose therefore that M is a Q-machine. We calculate an integer i as mentioned in lemma 7. For every of the s^i different $L \epsilon \Sigma^*$ with $|L| = i$, and for every $q \epsilon K$ M is started at the ID $\langle q,LX,1\rangle$ (X arbitrary element of Σ^{∞}). Because M is a Q-machine, M cannot loop on ${}_1T_i$. Hence, M must, before $ik + 1$ orders are executed, either

1) stop on ${}_1T_i$ without having left ${}_1T_i$, or

2) reach square no. $i + 1$.

If every combination of L and q gives case 1), then M have no IID. If, howevery, case 2) is obtained for a combination, lemma 7 ensures that M has an IID.

We observe that the proof of theorem 8 is constructive such that not only the existence of an algorithm is demonstrated, but also an algorithm for solving the IP for non-erasing TM-s is indicated explicitely.

An ID for M is so defined that the content of the tape always is an infinite ultimately periodic word (the tape contains only a finite amount of information). Let an ID^{∞} be a triple $\langle q,X,n\rangle$ where $q \epsilon K$, $n \geqslant 1$ and X is an arbitrary infinite sequence of symbols from Σ. The corresponding immortality problem for non-erasing TM-s is also decidable because we have that M has an $IID^{\infty} \Leftrightarrow M$ has an IID. For suppose that M has an IID^{∞}. If M is not a Q-machine, then we know that M has an IID. Is M a Q-machine, we obtain by use of lemma 7 that M also has an IID. The converce is obvious since any IID also is an IID^{∞}.

Tapes containing a finite number of non-blanks

Let an ID^n be an ID where the tape contains only a finite number of non-blanks. Considering ID^n-s only, then the IP for non-erasing TM turns out to be undecidable. In [3] it is shown that for any given recursive predicate $R(x,y,z)$, there are effective procedures for constructing tag systems T_z, words w_x and integers $u_{z,w}$ such that

$$(\forall y)R(x,y,z) \Leftrightarrow w_x \text{ is a } T_z\text{-IID, and} \quad (1)$$

$$w \text{ is a } T_z\text{-IID} \Leftrightarrow [u_{z,w} \neq 0 \ \& \ (\forall y)R(u_{z,w}-1,y,z)] \ . \quad (2)$$

For definition of a tag system see Post [2]. With any given tag system T we associate a non-erasing TM M_T which simulates T. Next we show that M_T starting at an arbitrary ID^n α, M_T either halts or transforms α into a M_T-ID^n β which represents a T-ID b. A corresponding result to that above then applies for non-erasing TM-s. Let a tag system T be given by alphabet $\Sigma = \{S_1,S_2,\ldots,S_s\}$, deletion number P and productions $S_i \rightarrow W_i \ (\epsilon\Sigma^*)$ for $i = 1,2,\ldots,s$. The alphabet of the associated TM M_T is $\Sigma_M = \Sigma \cup \{B,1\}$ where B is the blank symbol $(B,1 \notin \Sigma)$.

A T-ID $b_1b_2\ldots b_n \ \epsilon\Sigma^*$ is represented by any M_T-ID^n of the form $\langle a_1, L1b_1Bb_2\ldots Bb_mB^\infty, |L|+1\rangle$ where $L\epsilon\Sigma^*$ is arbitrary and a_1 is a fixed state of M_T.

Instead of writing explicitly the instructions of M_T, we will imitate M_T's manner of operation by the following flow-diagram.

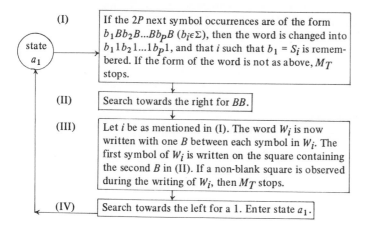

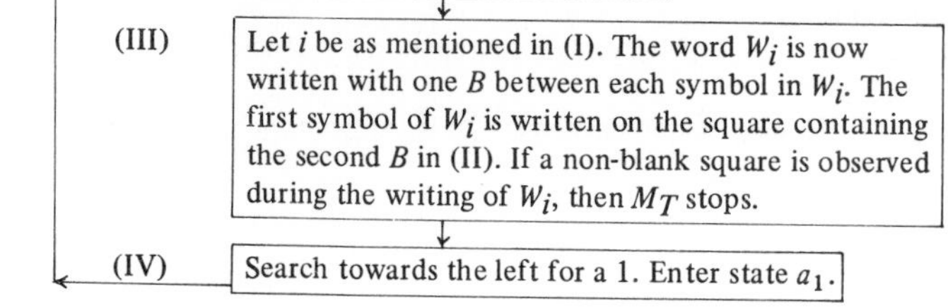
(I)
state a_1
If the $2P$ next symbol occurrences are of the form $b_1Bb_2B\ldots Bb_PB$ $(b_i\epsilon\Sigma)$, then the word is changed into $b_11b_21\ldots1b_P1$, and that i such that $b_1 = S_i$ is remembered. If the form of the word is not as above, M_T stops.
(II)
Search towards the right for BB.
(III)
Let i be as mentioned in (I). The word W_i is now written with one B between each symbol in W_i. The first symbol of W_i is written on the square containing the second B in (II). If a non-blank square is observed during the writing of W_i, then M_T stops.
(IV)
Search towards the left for a 1. Enter state a_1.

M_T is so constructed that if $L_1 \overset{*}{\underset{T}{\vdash}} L_2$ where $L_1, L_2 \epsilon \Sigma^*$, and α is a M_T-ID^n representing L_1, then there exists a M_T-ID^n β such that β represents L_2 and $\alpha \overset{*}{\underset{M_T}{\vdash}} \beta$. Furthermore, if L_1 is terminal (i.e. $|L_1| < P$), then, because of (I), $\alpha \overset{*}{\underset{M_T}{\vdash}} \gamma$ where γ is a terminal ID^n. Hence M_T simulates T.

We can set up the instructions of M_T such that there is no possibility of an infinite execution within any of the instruction-groups (I), (II), (III) or (IV). (The search in (II) always succeeds when M_T starts at an ID^n.) Hence, M_T either stops or continually enters state a_1. We therefore have that if M_T starts at a given ID^n $\langle q,LB^\infty,m\rangle$, then M_T either stops or there exist $L' \epsilon \Sigma_M^*$ and $b_1, b_2, ..., b_i \epsilon \Sigma$ such that

$$\langle q,LB^\infty,m\rangle \overset{*}{\underset{M_T}{\vdash}} \langle a_1,L'1b_1B...Bb_iB^\infty,|L'|+1\rangle .$$

The last ID^n represents the T-ID $b_1b_2...b_i$.

Theorem 9. *Given any recursively predicate* $R(x,y,z)$, *there are effective procedures for constructing non-erasing* TM M_z, ID^n-s α_x *and integers* $u_{z,\alpha}$ *such that*

$$(\forall y)R(x,y,z) \Leftrightarrow \alpha_x \text{ is a } M_z\text{-IID}^n, \text{ and} \qquad (1)$$

$$\alpha \text{ is a } M_z\text{-IID}^n \Leftrightarrow [u_{z,\alpha} \neq 0 \;\&\; (\forall y)R(u_{z,\alpha}-1,y,z)] \;. \qquad (2)$$

Corollary 10. *The* IP *for the set of non-erasing* TM-s *is recursively undecidable of degree* 0″. *(Finite number of non-blanks on the tape.)*

Corollary 11. *For each recursively enumerable degree* **d**, *there is a non-erasing* TM *whose halting problem is of degree* **d**.

References

[1] P.K.Hooper, The undecidability of the Turing machine immortality problem, J. Symbolic Logic 2 (1966) 31.

[2] E.L.Post, Formal reductions of the general combinatorial decision problem, Amer. J. Math. 2 (1943) 65.

[3] S.Aanderaa and D.Belsnes, Decision problems for tag systems, J. Symbolic Logic (to appear).

EMBEDDINGS INTO SEMIGROUPS WITH ONLY A FEW DEFINING RELATIONS

W.W.BOONE*
University of Illinois at Urbana - Champaign

D.J.COLLINS
Queen Mary College, University of London

and

Yu. V.MATIJASEVIČ
Leningrad Branch Steklov Institute of Mathematics, Academy of Sciences of the U.S.S.R.

Introduction

In [4] the third author constructed a Thue system (finitely presented semigroup or associative calculus) $\mathfrak{N}$ with three defining relations and unsolvable word problem. This was achieved by defining an encoding function θ from words of a given Thue system $\mathfrak{T}$, known to have unsolvable word problem, to words of $\mathfrak{N}$ and then verifying that for any two words X and Y of $\mathfrak{T}$, $X = Y$ in $\mathfrak{T}$ if and only if $X^\theta = Y^\theta$ in $\mathfrak{N}$. The function θ does not, however, define a homomorphism so that $\mathfrak{T}$ is not in fact embedded in $\mathfrak{N}$.

In the present paper we consider the question of establishing a similar sort of result when we impose the condition that $\mathfrak{T}$ actually be embedded in the Thue system we construct. We shall give two techniques, the first of which is due to the first two authors and the second to the third author.

§1

In this section we give the first technique.

Theorem 1. *There is a uniform construction applicable to any Thue system* $\mathfrak{T}$

* Supported by U.S. National Science Foundation contract GP-23907.

with n generators yielding a Thue system $\mathfrak{D}$, *depending on* $\mathfrak{T}$, *with* $n^2 + 5n + 4$ *defining relations in which* $\mathfrak{T}$ *can be embedded via the identity mapping.*

The proof of Theorem 1 is based on methods of G.S.Cějtin [1] and V.L.Murskii [5]. Theorem 1 can be considerably sharpened in that the number of defining relations of the embedding Thue system can be reduced if we employ the ideas in [4] and we indicate later how this may be done. However, none of the later Thue systems used for embedding will have the simplicity of the present $\mathfrak{D}$, taking into account the length of the defining relations, the nature of the mapping which gives the embedding and the explicitness with which the system is given.

We sketch the proof of Theorem 1 for the case $n = 2$. The proof is similar for other values of n.

We use the following notation:

1 denotes the empty word;

$\equiv$ denotes graphical equality, i.e. identity as words;

$=_{\mathfrak{T}}$ denotes equality in the Thue system $\mathfrak{T}$;

defining relations will be written in the form $F = G$;

$X \underset{\mathfrak{T}}{\to} Y$ means that the word X can be transformed into the word Y by an application of a defining relation of $\mathfrak{T}$.

Let the given Thue system $\mathfrak{T}$ have presentation:

$$x, y\ ; \qquad E_i = F_i,\ i = 1, 2, ..., t\ .$$

We require a "copy" of $\mathfrak{T}$ on the symbols a and b, which we shall call $\mathfrak{A}$ and write as:

$$a, b\ ; \qquad A_i = B_i,\ i = 1, 2, ..., t\ .$$

Then $\mathfrak{D}$ has presentation:

$$a, b, c, d, e_1, e_2, f, h_L, h_R, x, y\ ;$$

$$ac = ca \quad ad = da \quad af = fa \quad ag = ga$$

$$bc = cb \quad bd = db \quad bf = fb \quad bg = gb$$

$$ce_1 = e_1 ca \quad de_1 = e_1 db \quad e_2 c = cae_2 \quad e_2 d = dbe_2$$

$$e_1 g = ge_2 \quad f = fe_1 \quad e_2 f = f$$

$$h_L S_{\mathfrak{A}} h_R = 1 \quad xh_L = h_L a \quad yh_L = h_L b$$

where $S_{\mathfrak{A}} = f\bar{A}_1 g\bar{B}_1 f \ldots f\bar{A}_t g\bar{B}_t f$ and $\bar{A}_i$ and $\bar{B}_i$ are obtained from A_i and B_i by replacing a and b by c and d respectively. With this notation we restate Theorem 1.

Theorem 1. *If X and Y are any two words of* $\mathfrak{T}$, *then* $X =_{\mathfrak{T}} Y$ *if and only if* $X =_{\mathfrak{D}} Y$.

In proving Theorem 1 we must examine the Thue system $\mathfrak{C}$ obtained from $\mathfrak{D}$ by deleting the generators x, y, h_L and h_R and the three relations involving these symbols. The system $\mathfrak{C}$ is a modification of a system due to Céjtin in [1] (see also D.Scott [6]).

Lemma 1.1. *Let U and V be any two words of* $\mathfrak{A}$. *Then* $U =_{\mathfrak{A}} V$ *if and only if* $US_{\mathfrak{A}} =_{\mathfrak{C}} VS_{\mathfrak{A}}$.

Proof. A detailed account of the system $\mathfrak{C}$ appears in [2]. This lemma is essentially a restatement of the theorem proved in [2].

Lemma 1.2. *Let X and Y be any two words of* $\mathfrak{T}$. *If* $X =_{\mathfrak{T}} Y$, *the* $X =_{\mathfrak{D}} Y$.

Proof. Let U and V be obtained from X and Y by the mapping $x \to a$ and $y \to b$. Then $X =_{\mathfrak{D}} h_L US_{\mathfrak{A}} h_R$ and $Y =_{\mathfrak{D}} h_L VS_{\mathfrak{A}} h_R$. Since $U =_{\mathfrak{A}} V$ and the defining relations of $\mathfrak{C}$ are among the defining relations of $\mathfrak{D}$, the lemma follows from Lemma 1.1.

For the converse of Lemma 1.2 we shall define a "projection" function π with the property that if $X =_{\mathfrak{D}} W$, X a word of $\mathfrak{T}$, then $X =_{\mathfrak{T}} W^{\pi}$; moreover it will be the case that $Y^{\pi} \equiv Y$ for any word Y of $\mathfrak{T}$.

We first require the notion of a normal word. If we regard the symbols h_L and h_R as left and right brackets respectively, then we call a word W of $\mathfrak{D}$ *normal* if it is properly bracketed, i.e., the symbols h_L and h_R appearing in W are paired in such a way that each h_L lies to the left of the corresponding h_R and no two pairs split one another.

A more rigorous definition of normality is given in the following manner. Let $W \equiv \alpha_1 \alpha_2 \ldots \alpha_m$; we shall assign to each symbol occurrence α_i in W an integer which we shall call the signature of α_i in W and denote by $\sigma_W(\alpha_i)$.

Firstly we define

$\lambda_W(\alpha_i)$ = number of occurrences of h_L lying strictly to the left of α_i in W and
$\mu_W(\alpha_i)$ = number of occurrences of h_R lying strictly to the left of α_i in W.
Then

$$\sigma_W(\alpha_i) = \begin{cases} \lambda_W(\alpha_i) - \mu_W(\alpha_i) & \text{if } \alpha_i \not\equiv h_L \\ \lambda_W(\alpha_i) + 1 - \mu_W(\alpha_i) & \text{if } \alpha_i \equiv h_L . \end{cases}$$

In this terminology $W \equiv d_1 d_2 \ldots d_m$ is normal if and only if W satisfies
(a) for each i, $\sigma_W(\alpha_i) \geqslant 0$;
(b) if α_i is h_L or h_R, then $\sigma_W(\alpha_i) \geqslant 1$;
(c) if α_m is h_R, then $\sigma_W(\alpha_m) = 1$ and otherwise $\sigma_W(\alpha_m) = 0$.

The first step in the definition of π is as follows. If W is a normal word then we define W^ρ to be the word obtained from W by deleting
(i) all symbol occurrences of signature greater than 1,
(ii) all occurrences of x and y of signature 1.

Clearly W^ρ is a word of the form

$$R_0 h_L Z_1 h_R R_1 \ldots h_L Z_p h_R R_p \tag{*}$$

where Z_i, $i = 1, 2, \ldots, p$ is a word of $\mathfrak{C}$.

We now recall a definition from [2]. A word Z of $\mathfrak{C}$ is called *$\mathfrak{A}$-regular* if

$$Z \equiv Y_0 f X_1 g Y_1 f \ldots f X_t g Y_t f X_{t+1}$$

where
(i) each X_i and Y_i is free of f and g,
(ii) the projection (or skeleton) of Z on the symbols c, d, f and g is $S_{\mathfrak{A}}$,
(iii) each X_i is free of e_2 and each Y_i is free of e_1.

Then Lemma 4 of [2] gives a procedure for obtaining from an A-regular word Z a word $Z^{\sim}$ of $\mathfrak{A}$ such that $Z =_{\mathfrak{C}} Z^{\sim} S_{\mathfrak{A}}$. It is useful to note that Z is A-regular if and only if aZ and bZ are $\mathfrak{A}$-regular and that $(aZ)^{\sim} \equiv aZ^{\sim}$ and $(bZ)^{\sim} \equiv bZ^{\sim}$ whenever these are defined. Also $S_{\mathfrak{A}}^{\sim} \equiv 1$.

A word W of $\mathfrak{T}$ is called *fully normal* if W is normal and W^ρ, written as in (*), satisfies
(a) each R_i is a word of $\mathfrak{T}$,
(b) each Z_i is $\mathfrak{A}$-regular.

Then if W is fully normal, we define

$$W^\pi \equiv R_0 (Z_1^{\sim})^+ R_1 \ldots (Z_p^{\sim})^+ R_p$$

where $(Z_i^{\sim})^+$ is obtained from $Z_i^{\sim}$ by the map $a \to x$ and $b \to y$.

Lemma 1.3. *Let X be a word of $\mathfrak{T}$, W a word of $\mathfrak{T}$ and suppose $X =_{\mathfrak{T}} W$. Then*

(i) *W is fully normal;*
(ii) $X =_{\mathfrak{T}} W^{\pi}$.
In particular if Y is also a word of $\mathfrak{T}$ *and* $X =_{\mathfrak{D}} Y$, *then* $X =_{\mathfrak{T}} Y$.

Proof. This is proved by a rather messy but basically straightforward induction on the number of applications of defining relations of $\mathfrak{D}$ which are required to transform X into W. The argument uses the properties of the various concepts we have defined, Lemmas 3 and 5 of [2] and the facts about $\mathfrak{A}$-regular words specifically noted above.

The converse of Lemma 1.2 follows immediately from (ii) and the fact that $Y^{\pi} \equiv Y$.

Remark. It is of interest to note that since $\mathfrak{C}$ is also embedded in $\mathfrak{D}$ (as may be shown by a similar sort of argument) the degree of the word problem for $\mathfrak{D}$ is the highest possible. The embedding, in regard to $\mathfrak{T}$, does not, therefore, preserve the degree of the word problem.

The following is the sharpened version of Theorem 1 referred to earlier.

Theorem 2. *There is a uniform construction applicable to any Thue system* $\mathfrak{T}$ *with n generators yielding a Thue system* $\mathfrak{G}$, *depending on* $\mathfrak{T}$, *with* $n + 4$ *defining relations in which* $\mathfrak{T}$ *can be embedded via the identity mapping.*

If we drop the condition that the embedding be effected via the identity mapping then the following seems to be the sharpest possible result obtainable with the present technique.

Corollary. *There is a uniform construction applicable to any Thue system* $\mathfrak{T}$ *yielding a Thue system* $\mathfrak{F}$, *depending on* $\mathfrak{T}$, *with six defining relations in which* $\mathfrak{T}$ *can be embedded.*

Proof. It is well-known – see, M Hall Jr. [3] – that every Thue system can be embedded, in a uniform manner, in a two-generator Thue system.

Remark. Using the results of V.L.Murskii [5] it is even possible to construct a single fixed Thue system $\mathfrak{U}$ with six defining relations in which every Thue system – indeed every recursively presented semigroup – is embedded.

We now outline the proof of Theorem 2, again taking $n = 2$. The method of [4] permits us to define, from $\mathfrak{C}$, a Thue system $\mathfrak{N}$ with generators α and σ and three defining relations, and an encoding function κ from words of $\mathfrak{C}$ to words to $\mathfrak{N}$ so that the following holds (*).

Lemma 1.4. *Let U and V be words of* $\mathfrak{A}$. *Then*
(i) $(UV)^\kappa \equiv U^\kappa V^\kappa$
(ii) $U =_{\mathfrak{A}} V$ *if and only if* $U^\kappa S^\kappa_{\mathfrak{A}} \sigma\alpha^{2d} =_{\mathfrak{N}} V^\kappa S^\kappa_{\mathfrak{A}} \sigma\alpha^{2d}$
for a certain fixed integer d.

The system $\mathfrak{E}$ is then obtained by adding to $\mathfrak{N}$ the generators h_L, h_R, x, y and the relations $h_L S^\kappa_{\mathfrak{A}} \sigma\alpha^{2d} h_R = 1, xh_L = h_L a^\kappa, yh_L = h_L b^\kappa$.

The analogue of Lemma 1.2 now follows easily from Lemma 1.4. The analogue of Lemma 1.3 is proved in the same manner as Lemma 1.3 but with a few alterations. These are
(1) clause (ii) in the definition of fully normal should read: each Z_i is a word of $\mathfrak{N}$ for which there exists an $\mathfrak{A}$-regular word P_i of $\mathfrak{C}$ such that $Z_i =_{\mathfrak{N}} P_i^\kappa \sigma\alpha^{2d}$.
(2) W^π is then defined as before except that Z_i is replaced by P_i.

Details of the type of calculation necessary to decode κ in the manner required by (1) may be found in §2.

§2

Here we present the second technique, and obtain a sharper result than the Corollary of §1.

Theorem 3. *There is a uniform construction applicable to any Thue system* $\mathfrak{A}$ *yielding a Thue system* $\mathfrak{N}$, *depending on* $\mathfrak{A}$, *with four defining relations in which* $\mathfrak{A}$ *can be embedded.*

Remark. Just as in §1, the result of Murskii [5] shows that it is possible to construct a single fixed Thue system with four defining relations in which every recursively presented semigroup can be embedded.

Let the Thue system $\mathfrak{A}$ have presentation:

(*) κ is essentially the composition of ψ and τ as defined in §2 below.

$$a_1, a_2, \ldots, a_n\ ;$$

$$A_i = B_i, i = 1, 2, \ldots, m.$$

We shall define some auxiliary Thue systems. Let $l(A_i)$ and $l(B_i)$ denote the lengths of A_i and B_i respectively and let h be an integer greater than $\max\{l(A_i), l(B_i); i = 1, 2, \ldots, m\}$. Then our first auxiliary system is $\mathfrak{B}$ presented as:

$$a_0, a_1, a_2, \ldots, a_n\ ;$$

$$A_i a_0^{h+2-l(A_i)} = B_i a_0^{h+1-l(B_i)} \qquad i = 1, 2, \ldots, m.$$

$$a_0 a_j a_0^h = a_0 a_j a_0^h, \quad j = 0, 1, 2, \ldots, n.$$

We shall embed $\mathfrak{A}$ in $\mathfrak{B}$ via the mapping $\varphi : U \to U a_0^{h+2}$.

Lemma 2.1. (i) *Let U be a word of $\mathfrak{A}$ and r a positive integer. Then $U a_0^{h+2} =_{\mathfrak{B}} a_0^r U a_0^{h+2}$.*
(ii) *If U and V are any words of $\mathfrak{A}$, then $(UV)^\varphi =_{\mathfrak{B}} U^\varphi V^\varphi$.*

Proof. (i) This is proved by induction on the length of U.
(ii) By part (i), $V a_0^{h+2} =_{\mathfrak{B}} a_0^{h+2} V a_0^{h+2}$.

Lemma 2.2. *Let U and V be any two words of $\mathfrak{A}$. Then $U =_{\mathfrak{A}} V$ if and only if $U^\varphi =_{\mathfrak{B}} V^\varphi$.*

Proof. This is proved by two simple inductive arguments, using Lemma 2.1 (i) in one of them.

Remarks. It is convenient to observe, for later use, that if $U =_{\mathfrak{A}} V$ then U^φ can be transformed into V^φ using the relations of $\mathfrak{B}$ in such a way that if $W_1 F W_2 \to W_1 G W_2$ is a step in the transformation process, applying the relation $F = G$, then W_2 is non-empty. The choice of the power $(h+2)$ in the definition of φ is designed to ensure that the above is the case.

Our second auxiliary Thue system is denoted by $\mathfrak{C}$ and has generators β and γ. We define an encoding function ψ from words of $\mathfrak{B}$ to words of $\mathfrak{C}$ by

$$1 \to 1$$

$$\psi : a_j \to \beta\beta\gamma^{j+1}\beta\gamma^{n+1-j},\ j = 0, 1, 2, \ldots, n\ .$$

$$UV \to U^\psi V^\psi\ .$$

Then let $C_i = D_i$, $i = 1, 2, \ldots, m + n + 1$ be the relations in β and γ obtained by encoding the relations of $\mathfrak{B}$ via ψ. Then the formal presentation of $\mathfrak{C}$ is:

$$\beta, \gamma; \qquad C_i = D_i, i = 1, 2, \ldots, 2^d$$

where d is a positive integer such that $m + n + 1 \leqslant 2^d$ and $C_i = D_i$ for $i > m + n + 1$ is simply a repetition of, say, $C_1 = D_1$.

For technical reasons, we require the number of relations of C to be a power of 2.

Lemma 2.3. *Let U and V be any two words of* $\mathfrak{B}$. *Then* $U =_{\mathfrak{B}} V$ *if and only if* $U^\psi =_{\mathfrak{C}} V^\psi$.

Proof. The type of argument required is well-known (see, for example, [3]).

We now start to cut down the number of relations in the systems we consider. Our third auxiliary system is denoted by $\mathfrak{M}$. Before giving its presentation we require some notation. Let $p_{i,j}$ denote the i-th letter of C_j and $q_{i,j}$ the i-th letter of D_j, $j = 1, 2, \ldots, 2^d$. Also let $k = 2^d$, $r = (h+2)(n+5) = l(C_j)$, and $s = (h+1)(n+5) = l(D_j)$. We define

$$M \equiv p_{1,1}p_{1,2} \cdots p_{1,k}p_{2,1} \cdots p_{2,k} \cdots p_{r,1} \cdots p_{r,k}$$

and

$$N \equiv q_{1,1}q_{1,2} \cdots q_{1,k}q_{2,1} \cdots q_{2,k} \cdots q_{s,1} \cdots q_{s,k}\ .$$

Then $\mathfrak{M}$ has presentation:

$$\beta, \gamma, \epsilon, \rho\ ;$$

$$\beta\epsilon = \epsilon\beta\beta \quad \beta\epsilon = \epsilon\gamma\beta \qquad \gamma\epsilon = \epsilon\beta\gamma \quad \gamma\epsilon = \epsilon\gamma\gamma$$

$$M = N \quad \epsilon^d = \epsilon^d\rho\epsilon^d\ .$$

We pass from the system $\mathfrak{C}$ to the system $\mathfrak{M}$ via the function χ: $P \to P\epsilon^d\rho$, P any word of $\mathfrak{C}$.

Lemma 2.4. (i) *For any word P of* $\mathfrak{C}$ *there is a word* P' *of* $\mathfrak{C}$ *such that* $P\epsilon^d =_{\mathfrak{M}} \epsilon^d P'$.
(ii) *If P and Q are any two words of* $\mathfrak{C}$ *then* $(PQ)^\chi =_{\mathfrak{M}} P^\chi Q^\chi$.

Proof. (i) This follows by induction on the length of P, using the first four relations of $\mathfrak{M}$.
(ii) $PQ\epsilon^d\rho =_{\mathfrak{M}} P\epsilon^d Q'\rho =_{\mathfrak{M}} P\epsilon^d\rho\epsilon^d Q'\rho =_{\mathfrak{M}} P^\chi Q^\chi$.

Lemma 2.5. *Let* $1 \leqslant j \leqslant 2^d$. *Then*
(i) $\epsilon^d\beta^{2^d-j}M =_{\mathfrak{M}} C_j\epsilon^d\gamma^{2^d-j}$;
(ii) $\epsilon^d\beta^{2^d-j}N =_{\mathfrak{M}} D_j\epsilon^d\gamma^{2^d-j}$.

Proof. A simple induction argument shows that when ϵ^d is passed from left to right across a word it leaves behind it every 2^d-th symbol of the word. The lemma follows from a careful examination of M and N.

Lemma 2.6. *Let U and V be any two words of* $\mathfrak{A}$. *If* $U =_{\mathfrak{A}} V$, then $(Ua_0^{h+2})^\psi\epsilon^d\rho =_{\mathfrak{M}} (Va_0^{h+2})^\psi\epsilon^d\rho$, *i.e.* $U^{\varphi\psi\chi} =_{\mathfrak{M}} V^{\varphi\psi\chi}$.

Proof. If $U =_{\mathfrak{A}} V$, then $(Ua_0^{h+2})^\psi =_{\mathfrak{C}} (Va_0^{h+2})^\psi$. Using induction, we need only consider the situation when $(Ua_0^{h+2})^\psi \equiv U_1^\psi C_j U_2^\psi$ and $(Va_0^{h+2})^\psi \equiv U_1^\psi D_j U_2^\psi$. By our remark after Lemma 2.2, U_2^ψ is non-empty and may therefore be written as βP.

Then

$$U_1^\psi C_j U_2^\psi \epsilon^d\rho =_{\mathfrak{M}} U_1^\psi C_j\beta\epsilon^d P'\rho$$

$$=_{\mathfrak{M}} U_1^\psi C_j\epsilon^d\gamma^{2^d-1}\beta P'\rho$$

$$=_{\mathfrak{M}} U_1^\psi \epsilon^d\beta^{2^d-j}M\gamma^{j-1}\beta P'\rho\ .$$

Since $U_1^\psi D_j U_2^\psi \epsilon^d\rho =_{\mathfrak{M}} U_1^\psi\epsilon^d\beta^{2^d-j}N\gamma^{j-1}\beta P'\rho$, in the same way, the lemma is proved.

We now show that $\mathfrak{A}$ is embedded in $\mathfrak{M}$. For our final result we do not, strictly speaking, need this fact. We do, however, need most of the machinery developed for its proof. For the sake of completeness we include the additional argument necessary to verify that $\mathfrak{A}$ is embedded in $\mathfrak{M}$.

Our first lemma shows that we can essentially disregard the relation $\epsilon^d = \epsilon^d \rho \epsilon^d$.

Lemma 2.7. *Let U and V be words of* $\mathfrak{B}$ *such that* $U^\psi \epsilon^d \rho =_{\mathfrak{M}} V^\psi \epsilon^d \rho$. *Then* $U^\psi \epsilon^d \rho$ *can be transformed into* $V^\psi \epsilon^d \rho$ *without applications of the defining relation* $\epsilon^d = \epsilon^d \rho \epsilon^d$.

Proof. Let $U^\psi \epsilon^d \rho \equiv R_1 \underset{\mathfrak{M}}{\rightarrow} R_2 \underset{\mathfrak{M}}{\rightarrow} \cdots \underset{\mathfrak{M}}{\rightarrow} R_p \equiv V^\psi \epsilon^d \rho$. We call an application of $\epsilon^d \to \epsilon^d \rho \epsilon^d$ an *insertion of* ρ and argue by induction on the number of insertions of ρ in the above sequence.

Let u be the greatest integer such that $R_u \underset{\mathfrak{M}}{\rightarrow} R_{u+1}$ by an insertion of ρ. Then $R_u \equiv R_{u1} \epsilon^d R_{u2}$ and $R_{u+1} \equiv R_{u1} \epsilon^d \rho \epsilon^d R_{u2}$. Now it is clear that every R_i has final symbol ρ and that this last occurrence of ρ is unaffected by the applications of the defining relations of $\mathfrak{M}$. The occurrence of ρ which makes its first appearance in R_{u+1} must disappear at some subsequent stage.

Using the maximality of u, we deduce that there exists $v > u$ such that

(a) $R_v \equiv R_{v1} \epsilon^d \rho \epsilon^d R_{v2}$ and $R_{v+1} \equiv R_{v1} \epsilon^d R_{v2}$;

(b) $R_{u1} \epsilon^d$ can be transformed into $R_{v1} \epsilon^d$ without insertions of ρ;

(c) $\epsilon^d R_{u2}$ can be transformed into $\epsilon^d R_{v2}$ without insertions of ρ.

It is then obvious that R_u can be transformed into R_{v+1} without insertions of ρ. By induction we conclude that $U^\psi \epsilon^d \rho$ can be transformed into $V^\psi \epsilon^d \rho$ without insertions of ρ and the lemma follows from this.

Let $\mathfrak{M}_0$ be the Thue system:

$$\beta, \gamma, \epsilon\ ;$$

$$\beta\epsilon = \epsilon\beta\beta \quad \beta\epsilon = \epsilon\gamma\beta$$

$$\gamma\epsilon = \epsilon\beta\gamma \quad \gamma\epsilon = \epsilon\gamma\gamma$$

$$M = N\ .$$

Lemma 2.8. *If U and V are words of* $\mathfrak{B}$ *such that* $U^\psi \epsilon^d \rho =_{\mathfrak{M}} V^\psi \epsilon^d \rho$, *then* $U^\psi \epsilon^d =_{\mathfrak{M}_0} V^\psi \epsilon^d$.

Proof. This follows obviously from Lemma 2.7.

We define a decoding function λ from words of $\mathfrak{M}_0$ to words of $\mathfrak{C}$ by:

$$1^\lambda \equiv 1$$

$$(\beta R)^\lambda \equiv \beta R^\lambda \quad (\gamma R)^\lambda \equiv \gamma R^\lambda$$

$$(\epsilon R)^\lambda \equiv x_2 x_4 \ldots x_{2n} \quad \text{where} \quad R^\lambda \equiv x_1 x_2 \ldots x_{2n+i}\,, \quad i = 0, 1$$

$$(\text{and } (\epsilon 1)^\lambda \equiv 1).$$

Lemma 2.9. *Let R and S be any two words of $\mathfrak{M}_0$. Then $(RS)^\lambda \equiv (RS^\lambda)^\lambda$.*

Proof. This is easily proved by induction on the length of R.

Lemma 2.10. *If $F = G$ is a relation of $\mathfrak{M}_0$ other than $M = N$ and R and S are any two words of $\mathfrak{M}_0$, then $(RFS)^\lambda \equiv (RFS)^\lambda$.*

Proof. $(RFS)^\lambda \equiv (R(FS^\lambda)^\lambda)^\lambda$ and $(RGS)^\lambda \equiv (R(GS^\lambda)^\lambda)^\lambda$. It is easy to see that $(FS^\lambda)^\lambda \equiv (GS^\lambda)^\lambda$.

Lemma 2.11. *Let U be a word of $\mathfrak{B}$ and R and S words of $\mathfrak{M}_0$ such that*
(a) *RMS (respectively RNS) contains d occurrences of ϵ;*
(b) *$(RMS)^\lambda \equiv U^\psi$ (respectively $(RNS)^\lambda \equiv U^\psi$).*
Then there exists a word V of $\mathfrak{B}$ such that
(i) *$(RNS)^\lambda \equiv V^\psi$ (respectively $(RMS)^\lambda \equiv V^\psi$);*
(ii) *$U =_{\mathfrak{B}} V$.*

Proof. We firstly remark that M has a subword $\beta 2^{d+1}$. The definition of λ is such that if R contains p occurrences of ϵ, $p \leqslant d$, then $(RMS)^\lambda$ will contain a subword $\beta 2^{d+1-p}$. Since $(RMS)^\lambda \equiv U^\psi$, $p = d$. Moreover, it follows from the definitions of λ and ψ that $(RMS)^\lambda \equiv U_1^\psi C_j U_2^\psi$.

Since $l(M) - l(N) = 2^d$, we deduce, in the same way, that $(RNS)^\lambda \equiv U_1^\psi D_j U_2^\psi$.

The argument is similar in the alternative case and the lemma follows from the relationship between $\mathfrak{B}$ and $\mathfrak{C}$.

Lemma 2.12. *Let U be a word of $\mathfrak{B}$ and R a word of $\mathfrak{M}_0$ such that $U^\psi \epsilon^d =_{\mathfrak{M}_0} R$. Then there exists a unique word W of $\mathfrak{B}$ such that*

(i) $R^{\lambda} \equiv W^{\psi}$.
(ii) $U =_{\mathfrak{B}} W$.
In particular if V is any word of $\mathfrak{B}$ *and* $U^{\psi}\epsilon^{d} =_{\mathfrak{M}_0} V^{\psi}\epsilon^{d}$, *then* $U =_{\mathfrak{B}} V$.

Proof. This follows from Lemmas 2.10 and 2.11 by an obvious induction argument.

Finally we construct the Thue system $\mathfrak{N}$ of Theorem 3, with generators α, σ, ρ. We pass from $\mathfrak{M}$ to $\mathfrak{N}$ via the function τ defined by:

$$\tau: \quad \begin{array}{l} 1 \to 1 \\ \beta \to \sigma\alpha \\ \gamma \to \sigma\ ; \\ \epsilon \to \alpha\alpha \\ \rho \to \rho \end{array} \qquad \text{and} \quad (RS)^{\tau} \equiv R^{\tau}S^{\tau}$$

Then $\mathfrak{N}$ has presentation:

$$\alpha, \sigma, \rho\ ;$$

$$\sigma\alpha\alpha = \alpha\alpha\sigma\alpha\sigma \quad \sigma\alpha\alpha = \alpha\alpha\sigma\sigma$$

$$M^{\tau} = N^{\tau} \quad \alpha^{2d} = \alpha^{2d}\rho\alpha^{2d}\ .$$

Lemma 2.13. *Let R and S be any two words of* $\mathfrak{M}$. *If* $R =_{\mathfrak{M}} S$, *then* $R^{\tau} =_{\mathfrak{N}} S^{\tau}$.

Proof. It is easy to verify that if $F = G$ is a defining relation of M, then $F^{\tau} =_{\mathfrak{N}} G^{\tau}$.

Lemma 2.14. *Let U and V be any two words of* $\mathfrak{B}$ *such that* $(U^{\psi}\epsilon^{d}\rho)^{\tau} =_{\mathfrak{N}} (V^{\psi}\epsilon^{d}\rho)^{\tau}$. *Then* $(U^{\psi}\epsilon^{d}\rho)^{\tau}$ *can be transformed into* $(V^{\psi}\epsilon^{d}\rho)^{\tau}$ *without applications of the defining relation* $\alpha^{2d} = \alpha^{2d}\rho\alpha^{2d}$.

Proof. The argument required is virtually identical to that given for Lemma 2.7.

Let $\mathfrak{N}_0$ be the Thue system:

$$\alpha, \sigma;$$

$$\sigma\alpha\alpha = \alpha\alpha\sigma\alpha\sigma \quad \sigma\alpha\alpha = \alpha\alpha\sigma\sigma$$

$$M^\tau = N^\tau.$$

Lemma 2.15. *Let U and V be any two words of* B *such that* $(U^\psi \epsilon^d \rho)^\tau =_{\mathfrak{N}} (V^\psi \epsilon^d \rho)^\tau$. *Then* $(U^\psi \epsilon^d)^\tau =_{\mathfrak{N}_0} (V^\psi \epsilon^d)^\tau$.

Proof. This follows easily from the previous lemma.

Lemma 2.16. *Let U be a word of* $\mathfrak{B}$ *and Z a word of* $\mathfrak{N}_0$ *such that* $(U^\psi \epsilon^d)^\tau =_{\mathfrak{N}_0} Z$. *Then there exists a word V of* $\mathfrak{B}$ *and a word R of* $\mathfrak{M}_0$ *such that*
(i) $R^\tau \equiv Z$
(ii) *R contains d occurrences of* ϵ,
(iii) $V^\psi \equiv R^\lambda$,
(iv) $U =_{\mathfrak{B}} V$.

Proof. We note firstly that it is easy to see that any word of $\mathfrak{N}_0$ is either of the form αS^τ or of the form S^τ for some word S of $\mathfrak{M}_0$.

Our second observation is that it is also easy to see that if a relation of $\mathfrak{N}_0$ other than $M^\tau = N^\tau$ is applied to a word S^τ then the result is a word of the form T^τ and that S can be transformed into T by an application of a relation of $\mathfrak{M}_0$ (other than $M=N$).

To examine applications of $M^\tau = N^\tau$, suppose that $(U^\psi \epsilon^d)^\tau =_{\mathfrak{N}_0} Z_1 M^\tau Z_2$ and there exist S and W such that
(i) $S^\tau \equiv Z_1 M^\tau Z_2$
(ii) S contains d occurrences of ϵ
(iii) $W^\psi \equiv S^\lambda$
(iv) $U =_{\mathfrak{B}} W$.

If $Z_2 \equiv S_2^\tau$, for some S_2, then clearly there exists S_1 such that $Z_1 \equiv S_1^\tau$ and $Z_1 M^\tau Z_2 \equiv (S_1 M S_2)^\tau$. It follows that $Z_1 N^\tau Z_2 \equiv (S_1 N S_2)^\tau$ and hence, by Lemma 2.11, that $(S_1 N S_2)^\lambda \equiv V^\psi$ and $W =_{\mathfrak{B}} V$.

If on the other hand $Z_2 \equiv \alpha S_2^\tau$, for some S_2, we argue a little differently. Let M' (respectively N') be obtained from M (respectively N) by replacing the final occurrence of γ by β. Then $S \equiv S_1 M' S_2$ and $Z_1 N^\tau Z_2 \equiv (S_1 N' S_2)^\tau$. The argument of Lemma 2.11 is still valid and the desired conclusion obtained *except* in the situation in which the displayed occurrence of M' in S gives rise to the subword $p_{1,k}p_{2,k}\cdots p_{r-1,k}\beta$ in $(S_1M'S_2)^\lambda$. However this last possibility is inconsistent with the fact that $(S_1M'S_2)^\lambda \equiv W^\psi$.

The argument is similar when N^τ is replaced by M^τ and the lemma follows by an obvious induction.

Theorem 3. *Let X and Y be any two words of $\mathfrak{A}$ and let θ be the composition of φ, ψ, χ and τ. Then*
(i) $(XY)^\theta =_{\mathfrak{N}} X^\theta Y^\theta$,
(ii) $X =_{\mathfrak{A}} Y$ *if and only if* $X^\theta =_{\mathfrak{N}} Y^\theta$.

Proof. (i) This follows from Lemma 2.1, the definition of ψ, Lemma 2.4 and the definition of τ.
(ii) If $X =_{\mathfrak{A}} Y$, then by Lemmas 2.6 and 2.13, $X^\theta =_{\mathfrak{N}} Y^\theta$. Conversely, supose $X^\theta =_{\mathfrak{N}} Y^\theta$; by Lemma 2.15 $(X^{\varphi\psi}\epsilon^d)^\tau =_{\mathfrak{N}_0} (Y^{\varphi\psi}\epsilon^d)^\tau$. Applying Lemma 2.16 we deduce that $X^\varphi =_{\mathfrak{B}} Y^\varphi$ and hence, by Lemma 2.1, $X =_{\mathfrak{A}} Y$,

In conclusion we should like to note that the construction of §2 is similar to the construction given in [4]. We have taken the opportunity to give here details which were not included in [4].

References

[1] G.S.Cejtin, An associative calculus with an insoluble problem of equivalence (Russian), Trudy. Mat. Inst. Steklov 52 (1958) 172–189.
[2] D.J.Collins, A universal semigroup, to appear in Algebra i Logika.
[3] M.Hall Jr., The word problem for semigroups with two generators, J. Symb. Logic 14 (1949) 115–118.
[4] Ju.V.Matijasevič, Simple examples of undecidable associative calculi, Soviet Math. 8 (1967) 555–557.
[5] V.L.Murskii, Isomorphic embedding of a semigroup with an enumerable set of defining relations in a finitely presented semigroup (Russian), Matem. Sametki 1 (1967) 217–224.
[6] D.Scott, A short recursively unsolvable problem (abstract), J. Symb. Logic 21 (1956) 111–112.

THE AXIOM OF DETERMINATENESS

Jens Erik FENSTAD
University of Oslo

1. The games

We shall consider certain infinite games with perfect information.

Let X be a set, – we are mostly going to consider the case where $X = N$, the set of natural numbers, or $X = \{0,1\}$. Let A be a subset of X^N. In the *game* $G_X(A)$ there are two players I and II who successively chooses elements from X, player I starting.

A *play*, x, is an element $x \in X^N$, and I wins the play x if $x \in A$, otherwise II wins.

A *strategy* σ is a map from finite sequences of X to elements of X. If player I is using the strategy σ and II is using a strategy τ, let us denote the resulting play by $\sigma^*\tau$.

A more formal definition of $\sigma^*\tau$ is as follows: Let in general $\alpha_0(n) = \alpha(2n)$ and $\alpha_1(n) = \alpha(2n+1)$, then define inductively

$$(\sigma^*\tau)_0(n) = \sigma((\sigma^*\tau)_1 | n)$$

$$(\sigma^*\tau)_1(n) = \tau((\sigma^*\tau)_0 | n+1)\ .$$

Thus we see that if $x \in X^N$ is the play produced by I using σ and II τ, then the element x_{2n} of x is obtained by applying σ to the sequence $\langle x_1, x_3, \ldots, x_{2n-1} \rangle$, i.e. the the preceeding choices of II (we have perfect information), and x_{2n+1} is obtained by applying τ to the previous choices of I, i.e. to the sequence $\langle x_0, x_2, \ldots, x_{2n} \rangle$.

A *winning strategy* for I in the game $G_X(A)$ is a strategy σ such that $\sigma^*\tau \in A$ for all counterstrategies τ, and a winning strategy τ for II satisfies $\sigma^*\tau \notin A$ for all σ.

A game $G_X(A)$ is *determinate* if either I or II has a winning strategy, i.e. if

(*) $\qquad \exists\sigma\forall\tau(\sigma^*\tau\in A) \vee \exists\tau\forall\sigma(\sigma^*\tau\notin A)\ .$

A set A is called *determinate* if the game $G_N(A)$ is determinate.

It is a mathematically interesting problem to decide which games are determinate. But the topic has an interest beyond this purely mathematical question. On a very general level we can make the following remark.

The assumption (*) involves a non-trivial switch of quantifiers. We may rewrite (*) as

$$\forall\tau\exists\sigma(\sigma*\tau\in A) \rightarrow \exists\sigma\forall\tau(\sigma*\tau\in A)\,,$$

i.e. the existence of "local" counterstrategies implies the existence of a "global", i.e. winning, strategy. Usually implications of the type $\forall\exists \rightarrow \exists\forall$ require some assumptions of finiteness, compactness, uniformly boundedness, or the like.

An unrestricted assumption of the type that games $G_X(A)$ are always determinate, seems like cheating. Instead of *proving* the existence of a "uniformizing" element, we simply *postulate* that it exists.

The assumption is non-trivial. As a first example we shall derive the countable axiom of choice from (*).

Let $F = \{X_1, X_2, ...\}$ be a countable family of sets $X_i \subseteq N^N$. (We need only assume that $\mathrm{card}(\bigcup\{X|X\in F\}) \leqslant 2^{\aleph_0}$.) We shall show that (*) implies that there is a choice function for F, i.e. a map f such that $f(X) \in X$, for all $X \in F$.

The proof follows by considering a suitable game: Player II wins if and only if whenever n_0 is the first choice of I and $\langle n_1, n_3, ...\rangle$ is the sequence of choices of II, then $\langle n_1, n_3, ...\rangle \in X_{n_0}$.

More formally let $N^N - A = \{x | \langle x_1, x_3, ...\rangle \in X_{x_0}\}$. One sees at once that

$$\forall\sigma\exists\tau(\sigma*\tau\notin A)\,,$$

hence by determinateness we obtain

$$\exists\tau\forall\sigma(\sigma*\tau\notin A)\,.$$

But this is nothing but an unfamiliar way of asserting the implication

$$\forall n\exists f(f\in X_n) \rightarrow \exists f\forall n(\lambda y\cdot f(y,n)\in X_n)\,,$$

the winning strategy for II is the desired choice function.

Thus determinateness is a strong assumption. Perhaps a bit too strong in view of our next example which is due to Stål Aanderaa:

Let D be a non-principal ultrafilter on N. Define a set X_D by the following requirement:

$$h \in X_D \text{ iff } \{i | \mu j[h(j) \geqslant i] \text{ is even}\} \in D$$

(here μ is as usual the "least-number"-operator).

Consider the following game: Let I use a strategy σ and II a strategy τ. Let $h = \sigma * \tau$, so that I has chosen $h(0), h(2), \ldots$ and II has chosen $h(1), h(3), \ldots$.

We let I win the play $h = \sigma * \tau$ if either the first $n+1$ such that $h(n) = h(n+1)$ is odd, or h is strictly increasing and $h \in X_D$.

We let II win the play $h = \sigma * \tau$ if either the first $n+1$ such that $h(n) = h(n+1)$ is even, or h is strictly increasing and $h \notin X_D$.

As shown by Aanderaa this game is not determined: The idea of the game is that both I and II have to bound large segments of N with their choices of the numbers $h(n)$. But since N is unbounded, anything one of the players can do in this respect, the other can do at least as well. So the game turns out to be non-determined. (Warning: The formal proof requires a little work. The idea is to verify that if the range of the function h_1 is unbounded and $h_1(i+1) = h_2(i)$ for all i, then $h_1 \in X_D$ iff $h_2 \notin X_D$. Further one observes that given any "reasonable" strategy σ for I (i.e. a σ such that $(\sigma * \tau)(2n) > (\sigma * \tau)(2n-1)$ for all τ and $n > 1$) there are strategies τ_1 and τ_2 for II such that $(\sigma * \tau_1)(i+1) = (\sigma * \tau_2)(i)$ for all i. Since the game is essentially symmetric, this shows that X_D is not determinate.

What this example shows is that determinateness of the games $G_N(A)$ implies that there are no non-principal ultrafilter on N, i.e. *the Boolean Prime Ideal theorem fails*.

It is well known that the uncountable axiom of choice is inconsistent with determinateness. It does not seem to have been noticed earlier that the BPI also fails.

In this connection let us add a remark of interest to the logician. To prove the general completeness theorem for first order logic one needs the BPI. And without the general completeness theorem little will be left of model theory.

Remark. We shall on occasions refer to games $G_X^*(A)$ and $G_X^{**}(A)$. In games of type G^* I may choose arbitrary finite (including empty) sequences from X

and II chooses single elements. In games of type G^{**} both I and II may choose arbitrary (non-empty) finite sequences from X.

Infinite games of the above type was apparently first considered in Poland in the 1920's, but not much seems to have been published on the topic.

In 1953 Gale and Stewart wrote a paper *Infinite games with perfect information* [6], proving among other things that open sets (in the games G_N) are determined. Using the axiom of choice they also produced a fairly simple non-determined game. They also gave a series of examples showing that the class of determinate sets has very few desireable algebraic closure properties.

Their work was continued in a game-theoretic context by P.Wolfe and M.Davis, the latter author showing in a paper [5] from 1964 that every set belonging to the class $F_{\sigma\delta} \cup G_{\delta\sigma}$ are determined, – this result still being the best obtained, unless large cardinal assumptions are added to set theory.

Independently some work was also done on infinite games in Poland. In 1962 a short paper by J.Mycielski and H.Steinhaus, *A mathematical axiom contradicting the axiom of choice* [13], suggested a new approach. They noted that assumptions of determinateness had remarkable deductive power, and although contradicting the unrestricted axiom of choice, led to a mathematics in some respects more satisfying than the usual one, e.g. determinateness implies that every subset of the real line is Lebesgue measurable. They also noted that analysis when confined to separable spaces, would exist unchanged, i.e. "positive" results such as the Hahn-Banach theorem, the compactness of the Hilbert cube, etc., would still be true (whereas the general Hahn-Banach theorem and the general Tychonoff theorem would fail in the non-separable case).

The 1964 paper of Mycielski, *On the axiom of determinateness* [11], gives a very complete survey of what was known about determinateness at the time.

Already Mycielski had remarked in [11], using previous work of Specker, that the consistency of **ZF** (not including AC, the axiom of choice) and AD (= axiom of determinateness) implies the consistency of **ZF** + AC and the assumption that strongly inaccessible cardinals exists. In 1967 R.Solovay (in a still unpublished paper [19]) showed that the consistency of **ZF** + AC + MC (where MC = there exists measurable cardinals) follows from the consistency of **ZF** + AD. This result gives an indication of the strength of the axiom of determinateness.

In 1967 D.Blackwell published a short note, *Infinite games and analytic sets* [4], where he showed that the reduction principle for co-analytic (i.e.

$\mathbf{\Pi}_1^1$) sets follows from the basic result of Gale and Stewart that open sets are determined.

His observation was independently extended by D.Martin [7] and by J.Addison and Y.Moschovakis [3] in 1968. In these papers it was shown that determinateness of certain games had deep consequences for the analytic and projective hierarchies in Bairespace and Cantorspace.

At the same time (but, however, first published in 1970) D.Martin [8] showed that adding MC to **ZF** implies that every analytic set (i.e. $\mathbf{\Sigma}_1^1$ set) is determinate.

This concludes our brief "historical remarks". The present paper is a survey paper. There might be a few refinements to existing results and some new details added, but the aim has been to give an exposition of those parts of the theory which are closely related to "ordinary" mathematics (here: descriptive set theory and real analysis). In this respect we aim at bringing the 1964 survey of J.Mycielski [11] up to date. (However, since there is a large "unpublished literature" on the topic, our survey is probably incomplete.)

We believe that determinateness is an interesting and important topic. As we shall argue in the concluding section of this paper, some form of determinateness assumption might be a reasonable addition to the current set theoretic foundation of mathematics.

Remark on notation. Our notation is standard. We assume that the reader has some basic knowledge of set theory and real analysis. Example: We do not explain the Gödel notion of "constructible set". But since we are giving very few proofs, only a rudimentary knowledge of constructibility is necessary for following the exposition. From recursion theory we use the standard notation (as e.g. $\mathbf{\Sigma}_n^1, \mathbf{\Pi}_n^1$ and $\mathbf{\Delta}_n^1$ for sets on the n-th level of the projective hierarchy) and occasionally we refer to some basic fact about "finite path trees", or the like. And in discussing the Lebesgue measurability of various subsets of the real line we assume that the reader know what Lebesgue measure is, but very little beyond that.

2. Determinacy and the analytic and projective hierarchies

Reduction principles play a central role in the study of hierarchies. Let us recall the basic definitions. A class Q of sets satisfies the *reduction principle* if for all $X, Y \in Q$ there are sets $X_1, Y_1 \in Q$ such that $X_1 \subseteq X$, $Y_1 \subseteq Y$, $X_1 \cap Y_1 = \phi$, and $X_1 \cup Y_1 = X \cup Y$. The main point here is, of course, that

X_1 and Y_1 also belong to Q, i.e. is of the same kind of complexity as X and Y.

It is classical that in **ZF** + AC we have Red($\mathbf{\Pi}_1^1$) and Red($\mathbf{\Sigma}_2^1$), where Red(Q) means that Q satisfies the reduction principle.

Assuming the axiom of constructibility, V = L, Addison [1] extended this to Red(Σ_k^1) for all $k \geqslant 3$. The idea behind the proof is quite simple. Using V = L one can show that there is a Δ_2^1 well ordering of N^N with ordinal ω_1. Now any set in Σ_k^1 is obtained by taking a union over N^N, which by V = L has a "nice" well ordering where all initial segments are countable. So given any element in $X \cap Y$, put it in X_1 if it is generated "earlier" in X than in Y, otherwise put it in Y_1.

Both Martin [7] and Addison, Moschovakis [3] observed that reduction principles obtains in the higher levels of the hierarchies, if one adds suitable assumptions of determinateness. We shall give a brief exposition of the latter author's work (returning to Martin's ideas in the next section).

The basic result is a "prewellordering theorem". A prewellordering on a set is a total, transitive and well-founded binary relation on the set. (Note: If $\leqslant$ is a pre-wellordering, then we do not assume that $x \leqslant y$ and $y \leqslant x$ imply $x = y$. By passing to equivalence classes, $x \sim y$ if $x \leqslant y$ and $y \leqslant x$, we get a true well-ordering and hence an associated ordinal.)

Observe the following simple example: If $A \in \Sigma_1^0$, i.e. $A = \{x \mid \exists n R(x,n)\}$, where x may be any (finite) sequence of function and number variables, then the relation

$$x \leqslant_0 y \quad \text{iff} \quad x, y \in A \quad \text{and} \quad \mu n R(x,n) \leqslant \mu m R(y,m)$$

is a prewellordering of A.

To explain the general result announced by Addison and Moschovakis we need some further terminology. Let E_k^1 be $\mathbf{\Sigma}_k^1$ if k is even and $\mathbf{\Pi}_k^1$ if k is odd. A subset C of $N \times X$, where X may be any finite product of N and N^N, is called E_k^1-universal for X if C is E_k^1 and for every E_k^1-subset A of X there is some $n \in N$ such that $x \in A$ iff $\langle n,x \rangle \in C$.

Prewellordering theorem. *Let X be as above, let l be an even number, and let k be l or $l+1$. If every $\mathbf{\Delta}_l^1$ subset of N^N is determinate, then there is a subset $W_k \subseteq N \times X$ which is E_k^1-universal for X, and a prewellordering $\leqslant_k$ of W_k whose initial segments are uniformly $\mathbf{\Delta}_k^1$.*

We shall briefly indicate the basic ideas of the proof. The proof goes by induction. In the basis the simple example $\leqslant_0$ above will serve.

In the induction step one must distinguish between the case where $k = l$ is even or $k = l + 1$ is odd. In the former case we pass from a $\mathbf{\Pi}$ to a $\mathbf{\Sigma}$ class, hence we get by taking infima of wellorderings, just as in the "absolute" case, i.e. from $\mathbf{\Pi}_1^1$ to $\mathbf{\Sigma}_2^1$. In detail: let $z \in W_k$ iff $\exists\alpha(z,\alpha) \in W_{k-1}$ and define $z <_k w$ if $z, w \in W_{k-1}$ and the $\leqslant_{k-1}$ – least (z,α) is $\leqslant_{k-1}$ – less than the $\leqslant_{k-1}$ – least (w,β).

In the odd case one has to go from a $\mathbf{\Sigma}$ to a $\mathbf{\Pi}$ class. This means that one has to take suprema of wellorderings in order to get $\mathbf{\Delta}_k^1$ definitions of the segments of $\leqslant_k$. But this cannot be done using ordinary function quantifiers, a fact which has obstructed the passage from $\mathbf{\Sigma}_2^1$ to $\mathbf{\Pi}_3^1$ in "absolute" recursion theory. Assuming V = L Addison gave one "solution" to the problem. Assuming determinacy of projective sets gives another, and perhaps in some respects, more satisfactory "solution" to the problem.

A required E_k^1-universal set has the form $W_k = \{x | \forall\alpha(x,\alpha) \in W_{k-1}\}$. Given $x, y \in W_k$ define a set $B_{x,y}$ by setting

$$B_{x,y} = \{\alpha \in N^N | (x,\alpha_0) \leqslant_{k-1} (y,\alpha_1)\},$$

where α_0 and α_1 are defined from α as in the first section of this paper. One sees that $B_{x,y} \in \mathbf{\Delta}_l^1$, hence is determinate by assumption. The ordering $\leqslant_k$ on W_k is now defined by

$$x \leqslant_k y \equiv x, y \in W_k \quad \text{and} \quad \exists\tau\forall\sigma(\sigma^*\tau \in B_{x,y}).$$

The definition is "natural" which is seen by considering the case $k = 1$ and $l = 0$. In this case W_1 has the form: $W_1 = \{x | \forall\alpha\exists n R(x,\bar{\alpha}(n))\}$, and $\alpha \in B_{x,y}$ iff $\mu n R(x,\bar{\alpha}_0(n)) \leqslant \mu m R(y,\bar{\alpha}_1(n))$. (Note that in this case $B_{x,y}$ is provably determinate by the main result of Gale, Stewart [6].)

Consider now the usual sequence trees T_x and T_y associated with R, x and y. If $x, y \in W_1$, the trees are well-founded, so let $O(T_x)$ and $O(T_y)$ denote the corresponding ordinals. The so-called "basic tree lemma" (see e.g. Rogers [16]) asserts that $O(T_x) < O(T_y)$ if (except for degenerate cases) there exists a branch tree T_y' of T_y such that for all branch trees T_x' of T_x, $O(T_x') < O(T_y')$. The existence of a winning strategy τ, as required in the definition of $\leqslant_1$ thus follows from the basic tree lemma, and a proof of the prewellordering theorem is easily obtained in this case. But in order to generalize one needs a proof within a game-theoretic context.

We shall not prove in detail that $\leqslant_k$ has the required properties. As quite typical for the proof we shall verify that the relation is total: Assume that $x, y \in W_k$ and $\neg(x \leqslant_k y)$, i.e.

$$\neg\exists\tau\forall\sigma(\sigma*\tau\in B_{x,y}) .$$

By the suitable assumption of determinateness this implies

$$\exists\sigma\forall\tau(\sigma*\tau\notin B_{x,y}) ,$$

which means that

$$\exists\sigma\forall\tau((y,(\sigma*\tau)_1) \leqslant_{k-1} (x,(\sigma*\tau)_0)) .$$

But since player II always can imitate player I, one easily infers that

$$\exists\tau\forall\sigma((y,(\sigma*\tau)_0) \leqslant_{k-1} (x,(\sigma*\tau)_1)) ,$$

i.e. $y \leqslant_1 x$.

Transitivity and well-foundedness is obtained by simultaneously playing several games. In the verification of well foundedness one also needs the axiom of dependent choices (DC).

Using the prewellordering theorem one may now lift all theorems of "abstract" or "generalized" recursion theory to every level of the hierarchy. Many of these results are listed in the announcement of Addison and Moschovakis [3].

Remark. Our understanding of the prewellordering theorem has greatly benefitted from many discussions with T.Ottesen, who in a seminar at Oslo has worked out the various consequences of the pwo theorem and also added several refinements.

In conclusion let us return to the reduction principles. Assuming V = L one has the series

$$\mathrm{Red}(\mathbf{\Pi}^1_1),\ \mathrm{Red}(\mathbf{\Sigma}^1_2),\ \mathrm{Red}(\mathbf{\Sigma}^1_3),\ \mathrm{Red}(\mathbf{\Sigma}^1_4),\ \ldots$$

The prewellordering theorem gives the series

$$\mathrm{Red}(\mathbf{\Pi}^1_1),\ \mathrm{Red}(\mathbf{\Sigma}^1_2),\ \mathrm{Red}(\mathbf{\Pi}^1_3),\ \mathrm{Red}(\mathbf{\Sigma}^1_4),\ \ldots$$

More precisely one proves that DC (= axiom of dependent choices) and determinateness of $\mathbf{\Delta}^1_{2k}$ sets imply $\mathrm{Red}(\mathbf{\Pi}^1_{2k+1})$ and $\mathrm{Red}(\mathbf{\Sigma}^1_{2k+2})$. The proof is straight forward since we can use the prewellordering theorem to separate elements in the intersection.

One sees that AD and V = L both give answers, but conflicting ones. Note that it is AD which continues the pattern of the classical, or "absolute" case.

The next topic would be the extension of uniformization principles using AD. There is one paper by Martin and Solovay, *A basis theorem for* Σ^1_3 *sets of reals* [9], which makes a one-step extension (going by way of measurable cardinals), but the field seems to be wide open. Reduction principles and "generalized" recursion theory seems to need very little beyond the assignment of ordinals (existence of prewellorderings). Uniformization princples seem to lie much deeper.

3. Determinacy and the real line

It is a standard fact of measure theory that there are subsets of the real line which are not Lebesgue measurable. One remarkable consequence of AD is the following result of Mycielski and Swierczkowski [14].

Theorem. AD *implies that every subset of the real line is Lebesgue measurable.*

We shall give a brief sketch of the proof and indicate some refinements. Rather than working on the real line we shall consider the space 2^N and the usual product measure μ on 2^N (i.e. $\mu(\{\alpha\in 2^N | \alpha(n)=0\}) = \mu(\{\alpha\in 2^N | \alpha(n)=1\}) = \frac{1}{2}$ for all $n\in N$).

Let $X \subseteq 2^N$ and let $r = \langle r_n \rangle$ be a sequence of numbers of the form $r_n = 2^{-t_n}$ where each t_n is a natural number and $2 < t_1 < t_2 < \ldots$. Associated with X and r there will be a game $G(X,r)$, and the assumption that these games are determinate will imply that every subset of 2^N is μ-measurable.

Let J_k be the class of subsets $S \subseteq 2^N$ which satisfy the following requirements:

(i) Each S is a union of basic neighborhoods.

(ii) Each S is contained in a basic neighborhood of diameter $\leqslant 2^{-k}$.

(iii) The μ-measure of S is

$$\mu(S) = r_1 r_2 \ldots r_k = 2^{-(t_1+\ldots+t_k)} .$$

The game $G(X,r)$ is played as follows:

Move 1 : Player I chooses a set $S_1 \in J_1$.

Move 2 : Player II chooses a set $S_2 \in J_2$ such that $S_2 \subseteq S_1$.
Move 3 : Player I chooses a set $S_3 \in J_3$ such that $S_3 \subseteq S_2$. etc.

Note that because of (i) and (ii)

$$\bigcap_{n=1}^{\infty} S_n$$

reduces to one point. If the point determined by the play $S_0 = 2^N, S_1, S_2, \ldots$ belongs to X, then I wins. If the point belongs to $2^N - X$, then II wins.

Let μ_* denote the inner measure on 2^N associated with μ. Mycielski and Swierczkowski obtained the following estimates for $\mu_*(X)$ and $\mu_*(2^N - X)$:

(a) If I has a winning strategy in the game $G(X,r)$, then

$$\mu_*(X) \geqslant r_1 \cdot \prod_{n=1}^{\infty} (1-2 \cdot r_{2n}) .$$

(b) If II has a winning strategy in the game $G(X,r)$, then

$$\mu_*(2^N - X) \geqslant \prod_{n=1}^{\infty} (1-2 \cdot r_{2n-1}) .$$

(To be accurate: Mycielski and Swierczkowski worked with the interval $[0,1]$. An analysis of their proof shows that it works as well for the space 2^N, some extra care being needed to obtain the sets S_n^j, see the sketch below.)

We indicate how (a) and (b) are proved: Let I be using a strategy σ. Let

$$S_0 = 2^N, S_1, \ldots, S_{2n-1}$$

be a position in a play of the game. One observes that there is a finite number of sets $S_{2n}^1, \ldots, S_{2n}^m \in J_{2n}$ such that the sets

$$\hat{S}_{2n}^i = \sigma(\langle S_0, \ldots, S_{2n-1}, S_{2n}^i \rangle)$$

are disjoint for $n = 1, \ldots, m$, and such that

$$\mu\left(\bigcup_{i=1}^{m} \hat{S}_{2n}^i\right) \geqslant \mu(S_{2n-1}) \cdot (1-2r_{2n}) .$$

Let A_m be the union of all possible such sets at move $2m+1$ in plays where I has been using the strategy σ and II at each of his moves has picked one of the sets S^i_{2n}. One proves that $A_{m+1} \subseteq A_m$ and, using the above inequality, that

$$\mu(A_m) \geqslant r_1 \cdot \prod_{n=1}^{m} (1-2r_{2n}) .$$

If

$$x \in \bigcap_{m=1}^{\infty} A_m ,$$

there exists a strategy τ_x for II such that the play $\sigma * \tau_x$ produces the point x, viz. II always chooses the unique set S^i_{2n} such that $x \in \sigma(\langle S_0,\ldots,S^i_{2n}\rangle)$, the latter sets being disjoint.

If σ is a winning strategy for I, then the argument shows that $\bigcap A_m \subseteq X$, hence the estimate above on the μ-measure of A_m gives the inequality of (a). In a similar way one proves (b).

The theorem is an immediate consequence: If there are non-measurable sets, then by standard measure theory there will be a set $X \subseteq 2^N$ such that $\mu_*(X) = 0$ and $\mu_*(2^N - X) = 0$. But by (a) and (b) this is impossible, – if every game $G(X,r)$ is determined.

To obtain a refinement we choose a particular type of sequence $r = \langle r_n \rangle$, viz. we set

$$r_{2n-1} = 2^{-(K \cdot n+1)} \qquad \text{for} \quad n \geqslant 1 ,$$

and

$$r_{2n} = 2^{-K \cdot (n+1)} \qquad \text{for} \quad n \geqslant 0 ,$$

where K is some natural number > 1. We then see that

$$\prod_{n=1}^{\infty} (1-2r_{2n-1}) = \prod_{n=1}^{\infty} (1-2^{-K n}) \geqslant e^{-2/2^K-1}$$

and we observe that $e^{-2/2^K-1} \to 1$ from below when $K \to \infty$.

Assume now that every game $G(X,r)$ is determined, where X is a $\mathbf{\Pi}_n^1$ subset of 2^N and r is a sequence of the type considered above.

To derive a contradiction let X_1 be a non-measurable $\mathbf{\Pi}_n^1$ subset of 2^N. Standard measure theory (needing nothing more than a countable version of the axiom of choice) shows that there is a Borel set $F \subseteq X_1$ such that $\mu_*(X_1) = \mu(F)$. Hence if we set $X = X_1 - F$, then X is $\mathbf{\Pi}_n^1$ and $\mu_*(X) = 0$.

Since X also must be non-measurable, we see that $\mu_*(2^N - X) < 1$. Choose K such that

$$e^{-2/2^K - 1} > \mu_*(2^N - X) .$$

By assumption the game $G(X,r)$ is determinate, where r is the particular sequence determined by K. So either (a) or (b) should obtain. But both are impossible, hence the given $\mathbf{\Pi}_n^1$ subset X_1 of 2^N must be μ-measurable.

The game $G(X,r)$ is not in standard form. But we see from the "effectiveness" of the clauses (i) – (iii) in the definition of the class J_k, and from the fact that the sequence r depends upon a single number parameter K, that it can – without too much effort – be recast as a game of the type G_N, and further that determinateness of the associated $\mathbf{\Pi}_n^1$ game G_N gives the determinateness of the considered $G(X,r)$ game. Thus our analysis yields the following corollary to the theorem of Mycielski and Swierczkowski:

Theorem. *If the game $G_N(A)$ is determined for every $\mathbf{\Pi}_n^1$ set A, then every $\mathbf{\Pi}_n^1$ subset of 2^N is μ-measurable.*

Remark. AD also implies further "nice" properties of the real line or the space 2^N, e.g. every non-denumerable subset contains a perfect subset and every subset has the property of Baire (i.e. there is some open set such that the symmetric difference of the given set and the open set is a set set of first category). We return to these properties in the next section.

Not every consequence of AD with respect to the real line is "nice". From results we have mentioned it follows that the uncountable axiom of choice fails. Further we get incomparability of many cardinal numbers, e.g. $\aleph_1$ and $2^{\aleph_0}$ will be incomparable. And we may conclude that there is no well-ordering of the real line.

But we can still consider prewellorderings of the continuum. Let

$\boldsymbol{\delta}_n^1$ = the least ordinal not the type of a $\mathbf{\Delta}_n^1$ prewellordering of the real line.

It is a classical result that $\delta_1^1 = \omega_1$. We have the recent results of Moschovakis [10]:

Theorem. *Assume* AD *and* DC. *Then each* δ_n^1 *is a cardinal and* $\delta_n^1 \geqslant \omega_n$. *(If n is odd, then* δ_n^1 *is regular).*

It is tempting to formulate the conjecture: $\delta_n^1 = \omega_n$, which according to Moschovakis [10], ought to be true on notational grounds alone. D.Martin (unpublished) proved that $\delta_2^1 \leqslant \omega_2$ is a theorem of **ZF** + AC, so that the conjecture is verified for $n = 1, 2$. Recently he is reported to have settled the conjecture in the negative by showing that AD implies that ω_3 is a singular cardinal. Thus AD gives a rather complicated and unfamiliar theory of cardinals. The reader must judge for himself whether this is an argument for or against AD. In this connection he may also contemplate the following noteworthy result.

Theorem. AD *implies that* ω_1 *is a measurable cardinal.*

This means that there is a countably additive, two-valued measure defined on the powerset of ω_1 such that ω_1 has measure 1 and each point has measure 0.

The theorem is due to Solovay [19], but it is now possible to give a very different and much simpler proof based on a result of Martin [7].

Theorem. *Let D be the set of all degrees of undecidability and let E be an arbitrary subset of D. Then there exists a degree* d_0 *such that either* $d \in E$ *for all* $d \geqslant d_0$, *or* $d \in D - E$ *for all* $d \geqslant d_0$.

The proof is simple and worth repeating: Let E^* be the set of all sequences in 2^N whose degree belongs to E. Assume that I has a winning strategy in the game $G_2(E^*)$, and let d_0 be its degree. Let $d \geqslant d_0$ and let α be a sequence of degree d. If II plays according to α and I plays according to his winning strategy, the sequence produced will have degree d. Hence $d \in E$.

From this one gets a countably additive 0–1 measure on the set of degrees D. Let $E \subseteq D$, we define

$$\lambda(E) = \begin{cases} 1 & \text{if } (\exists d_0)(\forall d \geqslant d_0)[d \in E] \\ 0 & \text{ow.} \end{cases}$$

And using the map $f: D \to \omega_1$ defined by $f(d) = \omega_1^d$ where ω_1^d is the least (countable) ordinal not recursive in d, we get a measure μ on ω_1 by the formula

$$\mu(A) = \lambda(f^{-1}(A)) ,$$

for A an arbitrary subset of ω_1.

Remark. Martin in [7] used the measure λ to lift many of the results of general recursion theory (such as reduction principles) to all levels of the analytic and projective hierarchies. The use of λ to get a measure μ on ω_1 was noticed later.

We have now an immediate proof of the following theorem of Solovay [19]:

Theorem. Con(ZF+AD) *implies* Con(ZF+AC+MC).

Let μ be the measure constructed above. The inner model L_μ will then be the required model.

Stronger results are known. We have e.g. the following result of Solvay:

Theorem. Con(ZF+AD+DC) *implies* Con(ZF+AC+$\forall\alpha\exists$M (*M is an inner transitive model with* α *measurable cardinals*)).

We shall conclude this part of our survey by relating AD to Souslin hypothesis.

Let L be a totally ordered set without a first or last element which is connected in the usual interval topology. Souslin conjectured that if each family of disjoint open intervals in L is countable, then L is topologically the real line.

It is well known that if we instead require L to be separable, then it is equivalent to the real line. We can therefore rephrase Souslin's conjecture in the following way. We call L a *Souslin line* if we in addition to the properties considered by Souslin also require L to be not separable. The conjecture is now: There is no Souslin line.

The conjecture has an equivalent form in terms of trees. A *Souslin tree* is a tree of cardinality ω_1 such that each chain and each antichain of the tree is countable. The basic fact is: Souslin lines exist iff Souslin trees exist. (For a proof and an elementary survey of the topic, see [17].)

Theorem. AD *implies that there are no Souslin trees.*

The proof uses the fact that ω_1 is measurable. Assume that $\langle T,\leqslant\rangle$ is a Souslin tree. Since the cardinality of T is ω_1, we may assume that T also is measurable, hence carries a two-valued measure μ. For $\rho < \omega_1$ let T_ρ denote the set of elements in the tree of level ρ. Since T is a Souslin tree and each T_ρ is an antichain in T, T_ρ is countable. And since the cardinality of T is ω_1, each T_ρ is non-empty.

Let $\rho < \omega_1$. Define

$$D_\rho = \bigcup_{\gamma<\rho} T_\gamma ,$$

we see that $\mu(D_\rho) = 0$. Let for $t \in T$:

$$f(t) = \{ t' \in T | t \leqslant t' \} .$$

Then $\{ D_\rho \} \cup \{ f(t) | t \in T_\rho \}$ is a countable partition of T, hence there is exactly one $t \in T_\rho$ such that $\mu(f(t)) = 1$. Thus we may define for each $\rho < \omega_1$

$$t_\rho = \text{the unique } t \in T_\rho \text{ such that } \mu(f(t)) = 1.$$

It is not difficult to verify that $\{ t_\rho | \rho < \omega_1 \}$ is an uncountable chain in T, which contradicts the assumption that T is a Souslin tree.

We would like to conclude from this that AD implies that Souslin hypothesis is true. However, the construction of a Souslin tree from a Souslin line requires the uncountable axiom of choice, which we know is inconsistent with AD. Hence there remains a puzzling problem: Is it consistent with AD to have Souslin lines, but not Souslin trees?

On the other hand (as we shall point out in the concluding section of this paper) a decent mathematics on the basis of **ZF** + AD requires that we impose conditions of separability. And, as seen above, adding separability makes Souslin's conjecture trivial.

Remark. The reader will have noticed that what we really proved above, is that if κ is a measurable cardinal, then there are no Aronszajn κ-tree (or fake Souslin tree of cardinality κ). This has been known to the experts on trees for a long time.

4. Which games are determinate?

We hope to have convinced the reader that assumptions of determinateness leads to many interesting results, which have great potential importance for mathematics, – if we can answer the basic questions: Which games are provably determinate? Which games can consistently be assumed to be determinate?

The basic positive result is due to Gale and Stewart [6]. Their main result is:

Theorem. *Let X be either N or $\{0,1\}$. Then the game $G_X(A)$ is determinate if A is open or A is closed.*

This result was extended by Davis [5], whose main result is:

Theorem. *The game $G_N(A)$ is determinate if $A \in F_{\sigma\delta} \cup G_{\delta\sigma}$.*

This is as far as we at present can go within **ZF** + AC. One of the difficulties in extending the result is that the class of determinate sets has no nice closure properties, e.g. it is not closed under unions, intersections, and complementation.

Perhaps Davis' result is optimal? The main open problem is, of course, whether Borelgames are determinate. Dropping the replacement axiom from **ZF** H.Friedman (unpublished) has produced counterexamples. It is also known that $\mathbf{\Delta}^1_1$ represents the limit of what is obtainable in **ZF**. As we shall indicate below there are $\mathbf{\Pi}^1_1$ non-determinate sets in **ZF** + V = L.

The situation is much better understood with respect to games of the type $G^*_X(A)$ and $G^{**}_X(A)$. We shall first state the known relationships between games G, G^*, and G^{**}. To do this we need some notation. Let:

AD	= *Every game $G_N(A)$*	*is determinate*
AD_2	= *Every game $G_2(A)$*	*(i.e. $A \subseteq 2^N$) is determinate*
AD*	= *Every game $G^*_N(A)$*	*is determinate*
AD^*_2	= *Every game $G^*_2(A)$*	*is determinate*
AD**	= *Every game $G^{**}_N(A)$*	*is determinate*
AD^{**}_2	= *Every game $G^{**}_2(A)$*	*is determinate*

The following relationships are known (see [11]):

$$\begin{array}{ccccccc} AD_2 \leftrightarrow AD \rightarrow & AD^* & \rightarrow AD^{**} \leftrightarrow AD_2^{**} \\ & \downarrow & \\ & AD_2^* & \end{array}$$

M.Davis [5] has shown that player I has a winning strategy in games $G_2^*(A)$ if A contains a perfect subset, and that II has a winning strategy if A is countable.

In the Banach-Mazur games $G_N^{**}(A)$ J.Oxtoby [15] (building on previous work of Banach and Mazur) has proved that II wins if A is of the first category, and I wins if A is of the first category in some open subset of N^N.

Restating these results one gets (see [11]):

1. AD_2^* *is equivalent to the assertion that every uncoutable subset of* 2^N *has a perfect subset.*
2. AD^{**} *is equivalent to the asserting that every subset of* N^N *has the property of Baire (i.e. is congruent to an open set modulo sets of first category).*

These are the "classical" results. Recently we have the following remarkable result of D.Martin [8]:

Theorem. *If measurable cardinals exists, then every* $\mathbf{\Sigma}_1^1$ *set is determined.*

Nothing seems to be known about the determinateness of $\mathbf{\Delta}_2^1$ sets. (Note that $\mathbf{\Delta}_2^1$ determinateness is the first non-trivial assumption of determinateness needed for the prewellordering theorem.)

Counterexamples are easier to come by. E.g. a non Lebesgue measurable subset of the real line must be non-determinate.

If we work within **ZF** + V = L we immediately get a $\mathbf{\Delta}_2^1$ counterexample: **ZF** + V = L implies Red($\mathbf{\Pi}_3^1$). If every $\mathbf{\Delta}_2^1$ set were determined, the prewellordering theorem would give Red($\mathbf{\Pi}_3^1$). And as is well known we cannot at the same time have Red($\mathbf{\Sigma}_n^1$) and Red($\mathbf{\Pi}_n^1$).

The following is a $\mathbf{\Pi}_1^1$ counterexample: Using the $\mathbf{\Delta}_2^1$ wellordering of N^N which follows from V = L, we may define a $\mathbf{\Sigma}_2^1$ subset of N^N which contains one code α for each ordinal less than ω_1. This is an uncoutable set, and we claim that it cannot contain a perfect subset. For if so, this subset would also be uncountable and hence cofinal in the given set, and therefore could be used to define a $\mathbf{\Sigma}_1^1$ set WO = $\{\alpha \in N^N | \alpha$ is a wellordering of $N\}$, viz. $\alpha \in$ WO if α is a linear ordering of N and there is a function in the perfect set (which is a closed set) such that α is orderisomorphic to a segment of this function. But this is impossible since WO $\in \mathbf{\Pi}_1^1 - \mathbf{\Sigma}_1^1$.

By the Kondo-Addison uniformization theorem every $\mathbf{\Sigma}_2^1$ set is a 1–1 projection of a $\mathbf{\Pi}_1^1$ - set. And since a 1–1 continuous image of a perfect set is a perfect set, we get a $\mathbf{\Pi}_1^1$ - counterexample.

We shall make some further comments on the relationship between AD and MC. In section 3 we saw that AD implies that ω_1 is measurable, hence that the consistency of **ZF** + AC + MC follows from the consistency of **ZF** + AD. Further results of Solovay were quoted showing that AD is a much stronger assumption than MC. Martin's theorem quoted above is a step in the converse direction, MC implies that every $\mathbf{\Sigma}_1^1$ (or $\mathbf{\Pi}_1^1$) set is determined. This result can be used to obtain different proofs of some results which follows from the existence of measurable cardinals.

Classically one knows that an uncountable $\mathbf{\Sigma}_1^1$ set contains a perfect subset. Unrestricted AD extends this to every uncountable subset of N^N. By Martin's theorem we can conclude that every $\mathbf{\Pi}_1^1$ set is determined, and looking closer at the characterization theorem of M.Davis, it is not difficult to conclude that every uncountable $\mathbf{\Pi}_1^1$ set contains a perfect subset. Using the Kondo-Addison uniformization theorem, the result is lifted to $\mathbf{\Sigma}_2^1$. Thus we have obtained a quite different proof a result of Solovay and Mansfield (see Solovay [18]). (This proof was also noted by Martin in [8].)

The existence of a $\mathbf{\Pi}_1^1$ counterexample, as presented above, depended essentially on the fact that $\omega_1 = \omega_1^L$. Assuming MC, hence determinacy of every $\mathbf{\Pi}_1^1$ set, we are led to conclude that $\omega_1^L < \omega_1$, or more generally that $\omega_1^{L[a]} < \omega_1$ for all $a \subseteq \omega$. (For details see Solovay [18].) Thus we get a rather different proof of a theorem of Rowbottom and Gaifman.

Consistency of AD still remains unsettled. Concerning AD* and AD** the following result is an immediate corollary of Solovay [20]:

Theorem. Con(**ZF**+AC+$\exists\alpha$ (*α inaccessible cardinal*)) *implies* Con(**ZF**+DC+AD_2^*+AD**).

However, AD fails in the model considered by Solovay (see [20] p.2).

5. Concluding remarks

How seriously is AD to be regarded as a new axiom of set theory? In their note [13] Mycielski and Steinhaus are rather cautious. They note that AD has a remarkable deductive power, that it implies many desirable properties such as Lebesgue measurability of every subset of the real line. (And we may add: it implies the prewellordering theorem.) It does contradict the general axiom of choice, but implies a form of the countable axiom of choice which is sufficient for many of the most important applications to analysis. This is particularily so if one is careful to add suitable assumptions of separability and hence will have no need for the most general forms of theorems such as Hahn-Banach, Tychonoff etc.

So if one is willing to judge the credibility of an axiom by its consequences, there are many arguments in favor of AD. However, one may argue that one would like to have a more direct insight into the "true" universe of set theory before one committs oneself to AD. And above all one would like to have consistency results, which are notably lacking in this field.

Perhaps one has not to go all the way to AD in order to obtain a significant strengthening of the current set theoretic foundation. Let PD stand for the assertion that every projective set is determinate, i.e. that the game $G_N(A)$ is determinate for any A belonging to some class Δ_n^1, $n \in N$. The theory **ZF** + AC + PD could be the sought for strengthening.

Many constructions of real analysis and probability theory are initially carried out within the class of Borelsets, Δ_1^1, and one would be perfectly happy to remain there. But the Borel sets are not sufficiently closed with respect to operations analysts like to perform. The full projective hierarchy seems to be the next class beyond the Borel sets which has reasonable closure properties. But in passing from the Borel sets to all of the projective hierarchy one is not able at the same time to extend the nice properties which hold at the lower levels of the hierarchy. The strength of the theory **ZF** + AC + PD is that many of the desirable properties of the first few levels provably extends to the whole hierarchy (e.g. Lebesgue measurability, reduction and separation principles etc.) (And we may add that from this point of view it is a defect of **ZF** + V = L that in this theory we can find counterexamples to many of these properties within the projective hierarchy, even at low levels.)

Is **ZF** + AC + PD consistent? It has been suggested that large cardinal assumptions will do, but not much seems to be known. (See Martin [8] for some further remarks.)

Added after the symposium

Recent results of Solovay and Martin point to the great strength of $\mathbf{\Delta}_2^1$ determinateness. Solovay has shown that $\mathbf{\Delta}_2^1$ determinateness suffices to obtain inner models with many measurable cardinals, and Martin has constructed a hierarchy within $\mathbf{\Delta}_2^1$ and shown among other things that determinateness at low levels of this hierarchy suffices to obtain the existence of $x^\#$ for all $x \subseteq \omega$.

This shows that one really would have to have large cardinal assumptions in order to prove consistency of PD. On the other hand it may very well be that some of the more important applications of PD to the projective hierarchy may be proved consistent on more "reasonable" assumptions. (We already know that Lebesgue-measurability of projective sets are consistent with ZFC [20].)

Further important progress has also been made on the uniformization problem (see end of section 2). Moschovakis has recently shown that if n is odd and every $\mathbf{\Delta}_{n-1}^1$ game is determined, then every $\mathbf{\Pi}_n^1$ relation can be uniformized.

The result of H.Friedman referred to in section 4 has now been published (Annals of Mathematical Logic, vol. 2 (1971) pp. 325-357).

References

[1] J.Addison, Separation principles in the hierarchies of classical and effective set theory, Fund. Math. XLVI (1958) 123–135.

[2] J.Addison, Some consequences of the axiom of constructibility, Fund. Math. XLVI (1959) 337–357.

[3] J.Addison, Y.Moschovakis, Some consequences of the axiom of definable determinateness, Proc. N.A.S. 59 (1968) 708–712.

[4] D.Blackwell, Infinite games and analytic sets, Proc. N.A.S. 58 (1967) 1836–1837.

[5] M.Davis, Infinite games of perfect information, Advances in Game Theory, Annals of Math. Studies 52 (1964) 85–101.

[6] D.Gale, F.M.Stewart, Infinite games with perfect information, Contributions to Game Theory, Vol. II, Annals of Math. Studies 28 (1953) 245–266.

[7] D.Martin, The axiom of determinateness and reduction principles in the analytic hierarchy, Bull. Am. Math. Soc. 74 (1968) 687–689.

[8] D.Martin, Measurable cardinals and analytic games, Fund. Math. LXVI (1970) 287–291.

[9] D.Martin, R.Solovay, A basis theorem for $\mathbf{\Sigma}_3^1$ sets of reals, Annals of Math. 89 (1969) 138–159.

[10] Y.Moschovakis, Determinacy and prewellorderings of the continuum, in: Mathematical Logic and Foundations of Set Theory, ed. Y.Bar-Hillel (North-Holland, Amsterdam, 1970).

[11] J.Mycielski, On the axiom of determinateness, Fund. Math. LIII (1964) 205–224.
[12] J.Mycielski, On the axiom of determinateness II, Fund. Math. LIX (1966) 203–212.
[13] J.Mycielski, H.Steinhaus, A mathematical axiom contradicting the axiom of choice, Bull. Pol. Acad. 10 (1962) 1–3.
[14] J.Mycielski, S.Swierczkowski, On the Lebesgue measurability and the axiom of determinateness, Fund. Math. LIV (1964) 67–71.
[15] J.Oxtoby, The Banach-Mazur game and Banach category theorem, Contributions to the theory of games, Vol. III, Annals of Math. Studies 39 (1957) 159–163.
[16] H.Rogers Jr., Theory of Recursive Functions and Effective Computability (McGraw-Hill, New York, 1967).
[17] M.E.Rudin, Souslin's conjecture, American Math. Monthly 76 (1969) 1113–1119.
[18] R.Solovay, Cardinality of Σ^1_2-sets, in: Foundation of Mathematics, Symposium papers commemorating the sixtieth birthday of Kurt Gödel, ed. Bulloff (Springer, Berlin, 1969) 58–73.
[19] R.Solovay, Measurable cardinals and the axiom of determinateness (Preprint, UCLA Set Theory Conference, 1967).
[20] R.Solovay, A model of set theory in which every set of reals is Lebesgue measurable, Annals of Math. 92 (1970) 1–56.

UNE EXTENSION DE L'INTERPRETATION DE GÖDEL A L'ANALYSE, ET SON APPLICATION A L'ELIMINATION DES COUPURES DANS L'ANALYSE ET LA THEORIE DES TYPES

Jean-Yves GIRARD
(8, Rue du Moulin d'Amboile, 94-Sucy en Brie, France)

Ce travail comprend (Ch. 1–5) une interprétation de l'Analyse, exprimée dans la logique intuitionniste, dans un système de fonctionnelles Y, décrit Ch. 1, et qui est une extension du système connu de Gödel [Gd]. En gros, le système est obtenu par l'adjonction de deux sortes de types (respectivement existentiels et universels, si les types construits avec $\rightarrow$ sont considérés comme implicationnels) et de quatre schémas de construction de fonctionelles correspondant à l'introduction et à l'élimination de chacun de ces types, ainsi que par la donnée des règles de calcul (réductions) correspondantes.

Le système diffère de celui de Spector [Sp] en ce que la signification constructive des termes introduits dans le système considéré ici n'est pour le moins pas familière alors même que les règles de calcul sont relativement simples. Les schémas de Spector admettent une interprétation *extensionnelle* qui est naturelle à partir de la notion de fonctionnelle continue, ce qui n'est pas possible ici, alors que par contre l'interprétation dans le calcul des réductions est simple (il s'agit d'introduction et d'élimination de types) pour le système considéré, mais ne semble pas l'être pour celui de Spector (voir commentaires de Kreisel).

Le point crucial pour la cohérence (relative) du système, et sa signification en tant que calcul est d'après Tait [Tt2] la possibilité de donner une preuve de *réductibilité* univoque des termes. Une telle démonstration de réductibilité, utilisant la notion de "*candidat de réductibilité*" est traitée Ch. 2. Schématiquement, un candidat de réductibilité est une réductibilité *abstraite*, et permet de briser le caractère apparemment circulaire des définitions touchant au système.

D'autre part en utilisant cette notion, et suivant une conjecture de Martin-Löf et Prawitz (formulée aussi par Kreisel), il s'est avéré que l'élimination des coupures dans la logique *intuitionniste* du second ordre G^1LC (d'après la notation de [Tk]) pouvait être démontrée directement (Ch. 6). Cette démonstration est étendue (Ch. 7) à la théorie des types d'ordre fini quelconque dans la déduction intuitionniste $G^\omega LC$, exprimée en vue de concision dans un langage ne comportant que des prédicats monadiques, la généralisation étant évidente.

Ce résultat diffère des travaux précédents sur la question ([Tt1], [Th], [Pr2])

1. Quant à la méthode utilisée qui est ici *syntaxique* et non sémantique.
2. Quant au résultat lui-même: il est montré ici qu'un *processus formel effectif de reconstitution d'une démonstration sans coupure se termine tourjours* et non pas simplement un théorème d'existence d'une telle démonstration. (Théorème de *normalisation* par opposition à Hauptsatz existentiel; voir SPT II de Kreisel dans ce volume.)
3. En conséquence, la démonstration n'utilise pas le tiers-exclu c'est à dire se place (localement) dans l'analyse (resp. la théorie des types) non-prédicative construite sur la déduction intuitionniste(*).

Je remercie M.Reznikoff pour les chaleureux encouragements et l'attention critique qu'il a portée à ce travail dès le début, ainsi que pour l'avoir présente au 2è Symposium Scandinave de Logique Mathématique à Oslo. Je remercie aussi le Professeur Kreisel qui par ses critiques d'une première version de ce travail m'a orienté vers la recherche d'une demonstration de réductibilité des termes du système, exprimable localement dans l'analyse (Ch. 2). D'un autre côté les remarques de M.Martin-Löf sur la possibilité d'une démonstration de normalisation de l'Analyse (Ch. 6) on été déterminantes pour la suite de ce travail; Martin-Löf et Prawitz ont d'ailleurs trouvé une démonstration indépendante du résultat principal, en partant de la notion de candidat de réductibilité du Ch. 2. Je tiens à remercier finalement M.Vidal-Madjar dont les exposés sur les travaux de Howard et Tait au séminaire de théorie de la démonstration de Paris m'ont été très utiles.

(*) En fait, les démonstrations précédentes donnaient aussi un procédé de normalisation, car Kreisel a démontré (Buffalo Conference, pp. 135–136, Technical Note II) que tout énoncé Π_2^0 démontrable à l'aide du tiers-exclu dans l'analyse, est démontrable sans le tiers-exclu; néanmoins, il serait très difficile, pour des raisons techniques évidentes de transformer les théorèmes de *forme normale* cités plus haut en *théorèmes de normalisation*, et d'ailleurs, vraisemblablement on n'obtiendrait pas ainsi un processus "naturel" de normalisation.

1. Description du système Y

Le système Y est un système *intentionnel*; ses éléments sont des assemblages finis, construits récursivement, de manière purement combinatoire. Ces assemblages sont appéles *termes.*

Y est essentiellement une extension du système T de Gödel; cette extension est obtenue par l'adjonction de nouveaux types au système T, et de schémas de formation de termes, correspondant à l'introduction et à l'élimination de ces nouveaux types (voir l'introduction).

Les types de Y contiennent en général des variables; ces variables sont appelées *indéterminées*, par opposition aux *variables* de Y. Un terme de Y dont la construction ne nécessite pas d'indéterminée, peut, à peu de choses près, s'identifier à un terme de T.

Nous conviendrons qu'il n'y a pas de variable ou d'indéterminée muette, ceci, en supposant que la notation de Bourbaki est utilisée systématiquement. Toutes les apparitions d'une même variable, rendues muettes simultanément, sont donc en principe remplacées par des carrés, tous reliés par un trait au symbole mutifiant. Nous supposerons aussi que tous les termes sont écrits en notation "polonaise". Bien entendu, la notation polonaise et les carrés seront abandonnés dans ce qui va suivre, pour un système d'écriture certainement ambigu, mais plus praticable.

La notion spécifique qui permet les constructions de Y est celle d'*indice.* Un symbole A indexé est une expression de la forme $\mathrm{Id}A_r$, où r est un type de Y; une telle expression est abrégée en A_r; r est alors appelé l'indice de l'expression. Si b est un terme dans lequel une expression de la forme A_r apparaît, et si α est une indéterminée qui apparaît dans r, on dit que *α apparaît en indice dans b*, plus précidément, que *α apparaît en indice de A dans b.*

Ce qui est caractéristique de Y, c'est que des indéterminées puissent apparaître en indice de ses termes.

Enfin, une notation pour la substitution: si q est une expression (terme ou type) de Y, si p est une autre expression, on note par $q[p]$, l'expression q^p_x si p est un terme, q^p_α si p est un type, les variables x et α étant sous-entendues.

§ 1. Notion de type.

Les types sont des objets extérieurs au système; ils se comportent, outre leur rôle habituel, qui est de classifier les termes, en opérateurs par rapport à Y; à ce titre, le rapport types/système Y rappelle le rapport corps de base/espace vectoriel.

Définition 1.
1. o est un type.
2. les indéterminées $\alpha, \beta, \alpha', \beta'$, ... sont des types.
3. si r et s sont des types, $r \to s$ est un type.
4. si r et s sont des types, $r \times s$ est un type.
5. si r est un type, α une indéterminée, $\delta\alpha r$ est un type.
6. si r est un type, α une indéterminée, $\sigma\alpha r$ est un type.
7. les seuls types sont donnés par 1–6.

Interprétation des types. Contrairement au système T de Gödel, il n'a a aucun cadre extensionnel qui convienne au système Y; néanmoins, on peut donner une description intuitive de la signification de chaque type:
1. o est le type des entiers.
3. un terme (ou une fonctionnelle) de type $r \to s$ se comprend comme la donnée d'une application qui, à toute fonctionnelle de type r, associe une fonctionnelle de type s.
4. une fonctionnelle de type $r \times s$ se comprend comme la donnée du couple ordonné d'une fonctionnelle de type r et d'une fonctionnelle de type s.
5. une fonctionnelle de type $\delta\alpha r$ se comprend comme la donnée, pour chaque type s, d'une fonctionnelle de type $r[s]$. (Cette donnée s'effectuant "uniformément", dans un sens intuitif qui sera précisé plus tard; en gros celà veut dire que les fonctionnelles en question ont des significations similaires quand s varie: par example le terme $\mathrm{DT}\alpha\lambda x_\alpha x_\alpha$ correspond à la donnée pour chaque type s, de $\lambda x_s x_s$, c'est à dire de toutes les fonctionnelles identiques.)
6. une fonctionnelle de type $\sigma\alpha r$ se comprend comme la donnée d'un type s et d'une fonctionnelle de type $r[s]$.

Calcul des prédicats K1 *correspondant à la construction des types.*
1. o est une formule atomique.
2. les indéterminées α, β, ... sont des variables de formules atomiques.
3–6. $\to, \times, \delta, \sigma$, se comprennent respectivement comme l'implication, la conjonction, les quantifications universelle et existentielle.

Axiome: $$r \vdash r$$

Règles logiques

$$\frac{\Delta, r \vdash s}{\Delta \vdash r \to s} \qquad \frac{\Delta, s \vdash t \quad \Gamma \vdash r}{\Delta, \Gamma, r \to s \vdash t}$$

$$\frac{\Delta \vdash r \quad \Gamma \vdash s}{\Delta, \Gamma \vdash r \times s} \qquad \frac{\Delta, r_i \vdash t}{\Delta, r_1 \times r_2 \vdash t}$$

$$\frac{\Delta \vdash r}{\Delta \vdash \delta\alpha r}(*) \qquad \frac{\Delta, r[s] \vdash t}{\Delta, \delta\alpha r \vdash t}$$

$$\frac{\Delta \vdash r[s]}{\Delta \vdash \sigma\alpha r} \qquad \frac{\Delta, r \vdash t}{\Delta, \sigma\alpha r \vdash t}(*)$$

Règles structurales

$$\frac{\Delta \vdash r \quad \Gamma, r \vdash t}{\Delta, \Gamma \vdash t} \qquad \frac{\Delta \vdash s}{\Delta, r \vdash s}$$

$$\frac{\Delta, r, r \vdash s}{\Delta, r \vdash s} \qquad \frac{\Delta, r, s, \Gamma \vdash t}{\Delta, s, r, \Gamma \vdash t}$$

Remarquons que les sequents sont des sequents intuitionnistes de types; que le type $\delta\alpha\alpha$ peut jouer le rôle de type du faux; enfin, que ce système est équivalent à la formulation intuitionniste de G^1LC ([Tk]), sans variable du premier ordre, les variables du second ordre étant à zéro place. Il est naturel (d'après Howard) de construire Y comme le système de termes attaché à K1.

§ 2. **Définition de** Y.

1. *Schemas faibles.* (Ces schemas sont appeles faibles, car ils ne font pas partie due "systeme de Howard" de K1.)

(i) Pour chaque type r, la constant nulle de type r, 0_r. 0_o est abrégé en $\bar{o}$, et correspond au zéro de l'arithmétique.

(ii) La constante S, de type $o \to o$.

(iii) Pour chaque type r, la constante de récursion de type $(r,(r,o\to r) \to (o \to r))$ notée REC_r.

2. *Schémas forts.*

(i) Une constante, une variable de type r, est un terme de type r.

(ii) Pour chaque type r, les variables de type r: x_r, y_r, z_r ...

(iii) *Abstraction*: si a est un terme de type s, x une variable de type r, λxa est un terme de type $r \to s$ ($\to$ *introd.*).

(iv) *Application*: si b est un terme de type r, a un terme de type $r \to s$, APab est un terme de type s ($\to$ *élim.*). APab est abrégé en $a(b)$.

(v) *Tensorisation*: pour tous types r et s, $\otimes_{rs}$ est une constante de type $(r,s \to r \times s)$ ($\times$ *introd.*).

(*) α n'apparaît pas dans la conclusion.

(vi) *Projection*: Pour tous types r et s, Π^1_{rs} et Π^2_{rs} sont des constantes de types respectifs $(r \times s \to r)$ et $(r \times s \to s)$ ($\times$ *élim.*).
(vii) *Stratification universelle*: soient a un terme de type r, α une indéterminée qui n'apparaît pas en indice d'une variable de a; alors $\mathrm{DT}\alpha a$ est une constante de type $\delta\alpha r$ (δ *introd.*).
(viii) *Extraction*: si a est un terme de type $\delta\alpha r$, si s est un type, $\mathrm{EXT}as$ est un terme de type $r[s]$ (δ *élim.*). $\mathrm{EXT}as$ est abrégé en $a\{s\}$.
(ix) *Injection*: pour tous types $\sigma\alpha r$ et s, $I_{\sigma\alpha rs}$ est une constante de type $(r[s] \to \sigma\alpha r)$ (σ *introd.*).
(x) *Stratification existentielle*: soit a un terme de type $(r \to s)$, α une indéterminée qui n'apparaît pas dans s, et qui n'apparaît pas en indice d'une variable de a; $\mathrm{ST}\alpha a$ est alors une constante de type $(\sigma\alpha r \to s)$ (σ *élim.*).
3. Les seuls termes de Y sont ceux donnés par 1–2.

Exemples. 1. Puisque x_α est un terme de type α, on peut former le terme $\lambda x_\alpha x_\alpha$, de types $\alpha \to \alpha$. Ce terme ne contenant pas de variable, on peut former $\mathrm{DT}\alpha\lambda x_\alpha x_\alpha$, qui est donc de type $\delta\alpha(\alpha\to\alpha)$. Si s est un type quelconque, $\mathrm{DT}\alpha\lambda x_\alpha x_\alpha\{s\}$ est un terme de type $s \to s$.

2. Considérons la variable $x_{\alpha\to\alpha}$, et formons $I_{\sigma\alpha\alpha\to\alpha\ \alpha}(x_{\alpha\to\alpha})$; on peut former alors successivement $\lambda x_{\alpha\to\alpha} I_{\sigma\alpha\alpha\to\alpha\ \alpha}(x_{\alpha\to\alpha})$, et le terme $\mathrm{ST}\alpha\lambda x_{\alpha\to\alpha} I_{\sigma\alpha\alpha\to\alpha\ \alpha}(x_{\alpha\to\alpha})$. Ce dernier terme est de type $(\sigma\alpha\alpha\to\alpha) \to (\sigma\alpha\alpha\to\alpha)$.

Définition 2. On désigne par F le sous-système de Y formé des termes ne contenant ni variable, ni indéterminée; il est facile de vérifier que le type d'un terme de F ne contient pas d'indéterminée.

Calcul des prédicats K2 *correspondant à la construction des termes*. K2 est le "système de Howard" de K1; ses séquents sont des séquents intuitionnistes de termes, et on suppose que la partie gauche de chaque séquent est formée de variables distinctes deux à deux. Toutes les règles sont écrites sous réserve que les variables du séquent conclusion à gauche de $\vdash$ soient toutes distinctes.

Axiome: $$x_p \vdash x_p$$

Règles logiques

$$\frac{\Delta, x_r \vdash a}{\Delta \vdash \lambda x_r a} \qquad \frac{\Delta, x_s \vdash a[x_s] \quad \Gamma \vdash b}{\Delta, \Gamma, x_{r\to s} \vdash a[x_{r\to s}(b)]}$$

$$\frac{\Delta \vdash a \quad \Gamma \vdash b}{\Delta, \Gamma \vdash a \otimes b} \qquad \frac{\Delta, x_r \vdash a[x_r]}{\Delta, x_{r\times s} \vdash a[\Pi^1(x_{r\times s})]} \ \ldots$$

$$\frac{\Delta \vdash a}{\Delta \vdash \mathrm{DT}\alpha a}\,(*) \qquad \frac{\Delta, x_{r[s]} \vdash a[x_{r[s]}]}{\Delta, x_{\delta\alpha r} \vdash a[x_{\delta\alpha r}\{s\}]}$$

$$\frac{\Delta \vdash a}{\Delta \vdash \mathrm{I}_{\sigma\alpha r s}(a)} \qquad \frac{\Delta, x_r \vdash a[x_r]}{\Delta, x_{\sigma\alpha r} \vdash (\mathrm{ST}\alpha\lambda x_r a[x_r])(x_{\sigma\alpha r})}\,(*)$$

Règles structurales

$$\frac{\Delta \vdash a \quad \Gamma, x_r \vdash b[x_r]}{\Delta, \Gamma \vdash b[a]} \qquad \frac{\Delta \vdash a}{\Delta, x_r \vdash a}$$

$$\frac{\Delta, x_r, y_r \vdash a[x_r, y_r]}{\Delta, x_r \vdash a[x_r, x_r]} \qquad \frac{\Delta, x_r, y_s, \Gamma \vdash a}{\Delta, y_s, x_r, \Gamma \vdash a}.$$

Nous verrons plus loin qu'un séquent de K2 $\Delta \vdash a$, peut se comprendre comme l'énoncé "a est réductible"; if ne restera plus qu'a vérifier qu'un arbre de K2 est effectivement une démonstration de réductibilite.

Il est facile de vérifier par induction sur les arbres de K2 que, si $\Delta \vdash a$ est démontrable dans K2, toutes les variables de a sont dans Δ.

§ 3. **Définitions.**

1. *Sous-termes.*

(i) Si a est une constante ou une variable, le seul sous-terme de a est a.

(ii) Si a est $b(c)$, les sous-termes de a sont exactement ceux de b et de c, sans oublier a.

(iii) Si a est $b\{s\}$, les seuls sous-termes de a autres que a lui-même sont exactement ceux de b.

2. *Numéraux*. Le n-ième numéral, noté $\bar{n}$, est le terme de Y écrit avec exactement n signes AP, n signes S, et un signe $\bar{o}$, à l'exclusion de tout autre signe.

3. *Substitutions.* Par substitution, on entend l'opération qui consiste, soit à remplacer une indéterminée par un type, soit celle qui consiste à remplacer une variable par un terme du même type.

4. *Translations.* Par translation, on entend plusieurs substitutions itérées. Par exemple, soit a le terme x_α; si b est un terme de type s, on peut translater s pour α et ensuite b pour x_s; le résultat qui est b est noté $a[b]$.

(*) α n'apparaît pas en indice d'une des variables de Δ.

2. Définition de l'égalité intentionelle dans F

Sauf mention expresse du contraire, toutes les notions et théorèmes de ce chapitre s'appliquent au système F (voir Def. 2, § 2, Ch. 1).

§ 1. **Notion de réduction.**

1. *Axiomes de la reduction immediate.*

$$0_{r\to s}(a) \Rightarrow 0_s$$

$$\pi^i(0_{r_1 \times r_2}) \Rightarrow 0_{r_i} \qquad i = 1, 2$$

$$0_{\delta\alpha r}\{s\} \Rightarrow 0_{r[s]}$$

$$\mathrm{ST}\alpha u(0_{\sigma\alpha r}) \Rightarrow u(0_r)^o_\alpha \tag{1}$$

$$\mathrm{REC}(u,v,\bar{o}) \Rightarrow u$$

$$\mathrm{REC}(u,v,\overline{n+1}) \Rightarrow v(\mathrm{REC}(u,v,\bar{n}),\bar{n}) \tag{2}$$

$$\lambda x a(b) \Rightarrow a[b] \tag{3}$$

$$\pi^i(a_1 \otimes a_2) \Rightarrow a_i \qquad i = 1, 2 \tag{4}$$

$$\mathrm{DT}\alpha u\{r\} \Rightarrow u[r] \tag{5}$$

$$\mathrm{ST}\alpha u(I_{\sigma\alpha rs}(b)) \Rightarrow u^s_\alpha(b) \tag{6}$$

Définition 3. On dit que le terme u de F se *réduit immédiatement* dans le terme v si $u \Rightarrow v$ est un exemple des schémas 1–6.

Par exemple, $\mathrm{DT}\alpha\lambda x_\alpha x_\alpha\{s\}$ se réduit immédiatement en $\lambda x_s x_s$.

Définition 4. Soit a un terme, b un sous-terme de a; on dit que b est *minimal* dans a si il existe un terme c tel que b se réduise immédiatement en c, et si aucun sous-terme de b ne possède la même propriété.

2. *Définition de la réduction.*

Définition 5. On dit que a se *réduit atomiquement* en b, si b résulte de la substitution dans a d'une apparition d'un sous-terme minimal u par un terme v tel que u se réduise immédiatement en v.

Définition 6. On dit que a se *réduit* en b si l'on peut passer de a à b par une suite de réductions atomiques. Celà se note aRb. Remarquons que l'on a toujours aRa.

Définition 7. Un terme qui n'admet pas de sous-terme minimal est dit *réduit*. (L'adjectif normal étant à éviter, puisqu'une forme réduite n'est pas toujours sans coupure.)

Il s'agit, pour la cohérence (relative) du système de montrer, d'après Tait [Tt2], que tout terme admet une forme réduite et une seule.

3. *Théorème de monovalence.*

Lemme 1. *Des apparitions distinctes de sous-termes minimaux b et c dans a ne se recontrent pas, c'est à dire n'ont pas d'apparition commune d'un sous-terme de a. Si* $u \Rightarrow v$ *et* $u \Rightarrow v'$ *sont des réductions immédiates, alors v et v' sont identiques.*

Vérification immédiate.

Theoreme 1. *Si* aRb *et* aRb', *où b et b' sont réduits, alors b et b' sont identiques. On dit alors que b est la forme réduite de a.*

Demonstration. Voir la démonstration de Tait ([Tt2]). En effet, les seules hypothèses sous lesquelles cette démonstration est valable sont celle du lemme 1.

§2. **Définition de la réductibilité.**

En ayant en tête la notion habituelle de réductibilité pour le système T, ([Sh], [Tt2]) on voit clairement comment définir la réductibilité pour les types sans signes δ ni σ. Prenons maintenant l'exemple d'un type $\delta\alpha r$: on voudrait dire que a de type $\delta\alpha r$ est réductible si pour tout types s, $a\{s\}$ est reductible. Prenons l'exemple de $\delta\alpha\alpha \to \alpha$, et soit a le terme $\mathrm{DT}\alpha\lambda x_\alpha x_\alpha$; supposons que $\theta(b)$ exprime le fait que b est reductible de type r. Alors $\lambda x_s x_s$ est réductible, car tous les prédicats θ qui définissent la réductibilité vérifient $[bRa \wedge \theta(a)] \Rightarrow \theta(b)$. Donc a est réductible, puisque $a\{s\}$ se réduit en $\lambda x_s x_s$. Malheureusement, il est clair que nous ne disposons d'aucun procédé pour éliminer le cercle vicieux qui est à la base d'une telle définition de la réductibilité. Remarquons cependant que la "démonstration" qui vient d'être donnée utilisé relativement peu d'informations sur la réductibilité de type r: en fait n'importe quel prédicat θ qui vérifie la condition de stabilité par reduction pourrait faire l'affire. En d'autres termes, pour démontrer que l'identité est réductible, il n'est pas du tout nécessaire de définir la réductibilité pour chaque type. Ceci justifie les définitions suivantes:

1. *Candidats de réductibilité*

Définition 8. Un candidat de réductibilité de type r (en abrégé un c.r.) est un prédicat θ qui vérifie les conditions suivantes:
(i) $\theta(a) \Rightarrow$ "a est de type r"
(ii) $\theta(0_r)$
(iii) $[\theta(b) \wedge aRb] \Rightarrow \theta(a)$
(iv) $\theta(a) \Rightarrow$ "a admet une forme réduite".
Ces conditions sont abrégées en $Z_r(\theta)$.

Un c.r. est une réductibilité abstraite, dans le sens que les propriétés énoncées plus haut sont intuitivement vérifiées par toute définition "convenable" de la réductibilité.

Exemples de c.r. Soit $G \subset F$, tel que: $0_r \in G$ et tel que tous les elements de G soient des termes réduits de type r. Alors le prédicat θ défini par $\theta(a) \Leftrightarrow$ "il existe $b \in G$, aRb" est un c.r. de type r. Ceci montre clairement que la quantification sur les c.r. est une vraie quantification du second ordre, puisque l'ensemble des c.r. de chaque type a en général la puissance du continu.

2. *La quasi-réductibilité, our réductibilité avec paramètres.* Soit $r[\boldsymbol{\alpha}]$ un type de Y, où $\boldsymbol{\alpha}$ est une suite de n indéterminées contenant toutes celles de r, S une suite de n types sans indéterminée $s_1 \ldots s_n$, $\boldsymbol{\theta}$ une suite de prédicats $\theta_1 \ldots \theta_n$ telle que θ_i soit de type s_i.

On définit alors la $\mathbf{S}; \boldsymbol{\theta}/r[\boldsymbol{\alpha}]$ - réductibilité, qui exprime une proprieté des termes de type $r[\mathbf{S}]$. Les éléments de $\boldsymbol{\theta}$ sont appelés paramètres. Le seul cas intéressant est celui où les paramèteres sont des c.r. Bien que ce prédicat dépende de $\mathbf{S}$, $\boldsymbol{\alpha}$ et $\boldsymbol{\theta}$, on dira que a est *quasi-réductible* de type $r[\mathbf{S}]$ si a est $\mathbf{S}; \boldsymbol{\theta}/r[\alpha]$ - réductible. La quasi-réductibilité de type $r[\mathbf{S}]$ (en abrégé q.r.) sera notée $\mathbf{S}; \boldsymbol{\theta}/N(r,\square)$, où l'on ne marque pas les variables de la suite $\boldsymbol{\alpha}$.

Définition 9.

$$\mathbf{S};\boldsymbol{\theta}/N(o,a) \quad \Leftrightarrow \exists n\ aR\bar{n}$$

$$\mathbf{S},s;\boldsymbol{\theta},\theta/N(\alpha,a) \quad \Leftrightarrow \theta(a)$$

$$\mathbf{S};\boldsymbol{\theta}/N(r\times s,\alpha) \quad \Leftrightarrow \mathbf{S};\boldsymbol{\theta}/N(r,\Pi^1(a)) \wedge \mathbf{S};\boldsymbol{\theta}/N(s,\Pi^2(a))$$

$$\mathbf{S};\boldsymbol{\theta}/N(r{\to}s,a) \Leftrightarrow \forall b(S;\boldsymbol{\theta}/N(r,b) \Rightarrow \mathbf{S};\boldsymbol{\theta}/N(s,a(b)))$$

$$\mathbf{S};\boldsymbol{\theta}/N(\delta\alpha r,a) \Leftrightarrow \forall s\forall\theta(Z_s(\theta) \Rightarrow \mathbf{S},s;\boldsymbol{\theta},\theta/N(r,a\{s\}))$$

$$\mathbf{S};\boldsymbol{\theta}/N(\sigma\alpha r,a) \Leftrightarrow (\exists s\exists b\exists\theta(Z_s(\theta) \wedge aRI_{\sigma\alpha r[\mathbf{S}],r[\mathbf{S}]}(b)$$

$$\wedge\, \mathbf{S},s;\boldsymbol{\theta},\theta/N(r,b))) \vee (aR0_{\sigma\alpha r[\mathbf{S}]})\,.$$

A titre d'exemple, écrivons la $\boldsymbol{\phi};\boldsymbol{\phi}/N(\delta\alpha\alpha,a) \Leftrightarrow \forall s\forall\theta(Z_s(\theta) \Rightarrow \theta(a\{s\}))$. Pour s fixé, $a\{s\}$ doit être dans tous les c.r. de type s, soit dans le plus petit de tous, c.a.d. doit se réduire en 0_s: a est donc intentionnellement nul.

3. *La réductibilité.*

(i) Dans le système F (sans variable, ni indéterminée): a est *réductible* si $\boldsymbol{\phi};\boldsymbol{\phi}/N(r,a)$, où r est le type de a.
(ii) Dans le système YF (dont les termes sont ceux de Y qui ne contiennent pas de variable, mais peuvent contenir des indéterminées): soit a un terme de YF, r son type, $\boldsymbol{\alpha}$ l'ensemble des indéterminées qui apparaissent dans a; a est *réductible* (en abrégé red.) si pour toute suite $\mathbf{S}$ de types sans indéterminée de même longueur que $\boldsymbol{\alpha}$, et toute suite $\boldsymbol{\theta}$ de c.r., $a[\mathbf{S}]$ est $\mathbf{S};\boldsymbol{\theta}/r[\boldsymbol{\alpha}]$ - réductible.
(iii) Dans le système Y: soit a un terme de Y, r sont type; $\mathbf{X}$ la suite des variables qui apparaissent dans a; a est red. si pour toute suite B termes de YF réductibles, $a[\mathbf{B}]$ est un terme de YF réductible.

§ 3. Théorème de réductibilité.

Lemme 2. $\mathbf{S};\boldsymbol{\theta}/N(r)$ *est un* c.r. *de type* $r[\mathbf{S}]$, *sous réserve que la suite* $\boldsymbol{\theta}$ *soit formée de* c.r.

Démonstration. Par induction sur la construction des prédicats de q.r.
+ $r = o$, $r = \alpha$: évident.
+ $r = s \times t$:
(i) Si $\Pi^1(a)$ admet une forme réduite, ce ne paur être que parce que a en admet une.
(ii) Si aRb et si b est q.r., $\Pi^i(a)$ se réduit en $\Pi^i(b)$, et est donc q.r., d'après l'hypothèse d'induction; a est alors q.r.
(iii) $\Pi^i(0)$ se réduit en 0; or $0_{s[\mathbf{S}]}$ et $0_{t[\mathbf{S}]}$ sont q.r. ...
+ $r = s \to t$
(i) Par hyp. d'induction, $0_{s[\mathbf{S}]}$ est q.r.; si a est q.r., $a(0)$ l'est aussi, donc admet une forme réduite par hypothèse; a en admet alors nécessairement une.
(ii) Si aRa', on a $a(b)Ra'(b)$; si a' et b sont red., il s'ensuit, grâce à l'hypothèse d'induction, que $a(b)$ est red.

(iii) $0(b)$ se réduit en 0 si b est réductible, car alors b admet une forme réduite.
$+ r = \delta\alpha s$
(i) Si $a\{t\}$ est q.r., il admet une forme réduite; donc a en admet une.
(ii) Si aRa', $a\{t\}R\, a'\{t\}$; si a' est q.r., $a'\{t\}$ l'est, donc il en est de même de $a\{t\}$, pour tout t... (et pour tout c.r. θ).
(iii) 0 est q.r., car $0\{t\}$ l'est, puisque $0\{t\}R0$ ...
$+ r = \sigma\alpha s$
(i) 0 est une forme réduite; d'autre part, si $aRI(b)$, où b est q.r., et admet donc une forme réduite, il est clair que a en admet alors une, ...
(ii) Si aRb et $(bR\, I(c) \vee bR0)$, on a $(aR\, I(c) \vee aR0)$...
(iii) On a $0R0$.

C.Q.F.D.

Dorénavant, les lemmes seront énoncés pour Y, mais démontrés en général seulement pour F, la généralisation $F \to YF \to Y$ étant évidente.

Lemme 3. (*Réductibilité des schémas faibles.*)
1. 0_r *est réductible.*
2. S *est réductible.*
3. REC *est réductible.*

Lemme 4. (*Réductibilité des axiomes.*)
x_r *est réductible.*

Lemme 5. (*Réductibilité de* $\times$.)
1. $\otimes$ *est réductible.*
2. Π^1 *et* Π^2 *sont réductibles.*

Lemme 6. (*Réductibilité de* $\to$.)
1. *Si a est réductible,* λxa *est réductible.*
2. *a et b réductibles* $\Rightarrow a(b)$ *réductible.*

Démonstration. 1. par le lemme 2 et l'axiome $\lambda xa(b)\, Ra[b]$. 2. Par définition.

Lemme 7. (*Substitution.*)
$\mathbf{S};s[\mathbf{T}];\boldsymbol{\theta},(\mathbf{T};\boldsymbol{\theta}'/N(s[\boldsymbol{\alpha}']))/N(r[\boldsymbol{\alpha},\alpha],a) \Leftrightarrow \mathbf{S},\mathbf{T};\boldsymbol{\theta},\boldsymbol{\theta}'/N(r[\boldsymbol{\alpha},s[\boldsymbol{\alpha}']],a)$.

En d'autres termes, la q.r. est stable par substitution. La démonstration est complètement évidente.

Lemme 8. (*Réductibilité de* δ.)
1. *a réductible* $\Rightarrow$ DTαa *réductible.*
2. *a réductible* $\Rightarrow a\{t\}$ *réductible.*

Démonstration. 1. Par définition de la réductibilité pour YF, par le lemme 2 et l'axiome pour DT.
2. Par définition et par les lemmes 2 et 7: si a est red., $a\{t\}$ est q.r. pour tout c.r. θ et tout t; mais la réductibilité de type t est elle-même un c.r., et le resultat de la substitution de $N(t)$ pour θ dans $t;\theta/N(r[\boldsymbol{\alpha}])$ est équivalent à $N(r[t])$. (N abrège $\phi;\phi/N$.)

Lemme 9.
1. $I(b)$ *est réductible.*
2. *a réductible* $\Rightarrow$ STαa *réductible.*

Démonstration. 1. La q.r. est un c.r.; si b est réductible, en appliquant le lemme 7, il s'ensuit donc que $I(b)$ est réductible.
2. Il faut montrer que ST$\alpha a(I(b))$ et ST$\alpha a(0)$ sont réductibles, si $I(b)$ l'est. Alors, b est $s;\theta/r[\alpha]$-réductible pour un certain s et un certain c.r. θ; ST$\alpha a(I(b))$ se réduit en $a[s](b)$; mais $a[s']$ est $s';\theta'/r[\alpha] \to t$-réductible pour tous s et θ'; en particulier $a[s]$ est $s';\theta/r[\alpha] \to t$-red. Donc $a[s](b)$ est $s;\theta/t$-red., soit $\phi;\phi/t$-red., puisque α n'apparaît pas dans t. Le même argument montre que $a[o](0)$ est red.

Théorème 2.
1. Tous les termes de F sont réductibles.
2. Tous les termes de F admettent une forme réduite et une seule.

§ 4. **Définition de l'égalité intentionnelle.**
Dans F, $\vdash a = b$ est une abreviation pour "a et b ont la meme forme reduite". On verifie le

Lemme 10. *L'égalité est réflexive, symétrique, transitive. L'égalité est stable pour* AP *et* EXT. *Si* $\vdash a = b$, *alors* $\vdash u[a] = u[b]$.

Si on introduit l'abreviation $\vdash a \neq b$ pour "a et b ont des formes reduites distinctes", on peut demontrer le lemme:

Lemme 11.
$\vdash a = b \vee \vdash a \neq b$.
$\neg(\vdash a{=}b \wedge \vdash a{\neq}b)$.

§ 5. **Interprétation de la réductibilité dans l'analyse.**
La reductibilite n'est pas globalement interpretable dans l'analyse; on peut cependant interpreter des formes locales du theoreme 2.

1. *Profondeur d'un type.* On definite PF(r) et PF(r,α) par induction sur la construction de r:

$$\mathrm{PF}(o) = \mathrm{PF}(\alpha) = \mathrm{PF}(\alpha,\alpha) = o$$
$$\mathrm{PF}(o,\alpha) = \mathrm{PF}(\beta,\alpha) = -\infty \qquad (\beta \text{ et } \alpha \text{ distincts})$$
$$\mathrm{PF}(r{\to}s) = \mathrm{PF}(r{\times}s) = \sup(\mathrm{PF}(r),\mathrm{PF}(s))$$
$$\mathrm{PF}(r{\to}s,\alpha) = \mathrm{PF}(r{\times}s,\alpha) = \sup(\mathrm{PF}(r,\alpha), \mathrm{PF}(s,\alpha))$$
$$\mathrm{PF}(\delta\beta r,\alpha) = \mathrm{PF}(\sigma\beta r,\alpha) = \sup(\mathrm{PF}(r,\alpha) + 1) \qquad (\alpha \text{ et } \beta \text{ distincts})$$
$$\mathrm{PF}(\delta\beta r) = \mathrm{PF}(\sigma\beta r) = \sup(\mathrm{PF}(r), \mathrm{PF}(r,\beta)+1)) .$$

On apelle profondeur de r l'entier PF(r).

2. *Système F_n.* Les systèmes F_n, YF_n, Y_n, sont définis comme F, YF et Y, mais avec la restriction suivante: dans EXTas et $I_{\sigma\alpha rs}$, $\mathrm{PF}(s) \leqslant n$. Il est clair que F est la réunion des F_n, et que F_n est stable par réduction.

3. *Réductibilité pour F_n.* La $\mathbf{S};\boldsymbol{\theta}/r$-réductibilité se définit comme en § 2-2, sauf que les quantifications sur les types sont bornées par la PF égale a n, et que les définitions pour les types $\delta\alpha r$ et $\sigma\alpha r$ de PF $> n$ sont remplacées par: $N(\delta\alpha r,a) \Leftrightarrow \forall s N(r[s],a\{s\})$; $N(\sigma\alpha r,a) \Leftrightarrow (\exists s \exists b N(r[s],b) \wedge aR\, I(b)) \vee aR0)$ les quantifications sur les types étant toujours bornées par la PF égale a n. Ces définitions ne sont pas vicieuses, puisque $\mathrm{PF}(r[s]) \leqslant \sup(\mathrm{PF}(r),\mathrm{PF}(s))$. Il est inutile de définir la q.r. dans ce cas. On peut définir la red. pour YF_n, comme pour YF, à la différence que si $\mathrm{PF}(r) > n$, et si a est de type n on dira que a est red. si $a[\mathbf{S}]$ est red. pour toute suite $\mathbf{S}$. (On peut même borner les PF des types de $\mathbf{S}$ par n.) On définit la red. pour Y_n comme pour Y.

Il est alors clair que la red. pour Y_n peut s'exprimer par un prédicat hyperarithmétique en Π^1_n, soit Δ^1_{n+1}.

On peut alors démontrer le théorème 2 comme pour F; la différence principale est que le lemme 7 n'est plus valide pour des PF $> n$; mais les seuls cas où le lemme 7 est utilisé dans la démonstration est celui de EXT et de I; si la PF du type $\delta\alpha r$ ou $\sigma\alpha r$ utilisé est $> n$, on peut se servir des nouvelles définitions de la réductibilité, et on n'a pas besoin du lemme 7; si cette PF est $\leqslant$ à n, les PF des autres types sont alors bornées par n, par définition de F_n. Dans ce cas, le lemme 7 est toujours valide.

La démonstration de réductibilité ne met d'ailleurs en oeuvre que des schémas de compréhension utilisés dans les applications du lemme 7, soit sur des prédicats de q.r. de PF $\leqslant n$. *La réductibilité pour F_n est donc formalisable dans l'analyse Δ^1_{n+1}.* Réciproquement, on peut vérifier facilement que la réductibilité pour F_n entraine la non-contradiction de l'analyse Π^1_n, en regardant de plus près l'interprétation de Gödel de l'analyse dans F (voir plus loin).

Soit f un terme de F, de type $o \to o$; il est dans un des F_n:

Théorème 3. *Les fonctions de F sont récursives-prouvables (au sens de* [Sp] *) dans l'analyse.*

§ 6. **Une extension de F non réductible.**

On ajoute a Y et F le schema J_{sr}, pour tous types r et s, de type $r \to s$, avec les axiomes de reduction immediate:

$J_{sr}(a) \Rightarrow a$ si $r = s$

$J_{sr}(a) \Rightarrow 0$ sinon.

Il est facile de montrer, avec nos définitions, que J n'est pas réductible; aussi, dans le lemme suivant, "réductible" signifiera essentiellement : 1) stabilité par réduction, par application des schémas de F. 2) qu'un terme réductible admet une forme normale.

Lemme 12.

1\. *J_{rs} est reductible pour tous types sans variables r et s.*

2\. *J_{rs} n'est pas reductible.*

Démonstration. 1. évident. 2. On considère le terme:

$c = \mathrm{DT}\beta J_{\rho\delta\alpha\alpha\to\delta\alpha\alpha}(\lambda z_{\delta\alpha\alpha}(z_{\delta\alpha\alpha}\{\delta\alpha\alpha\to\delta\alpha\alpha\}(z)))$

alors $c\{\delta\alpha\alpha\to\delta\alpha\alpha\}(c)$ se réduit, en plusieurs étapes, ... en lui-même, et il n'y a pas d'autre réduction possible. *C.Q.F.D.*

Si on considère que J est l'exemple-même de ce que l'on pourrait appeler une "définition par cas sur les types", il est clair qu'une telle définition n'est pas possible(*).

Pourtant, en regardant la démonstration de réductibilité pour le système F, on est frappé par le fait que les seuls schémas de compréhension utilisés portent sur des variétés exprimant la q.r.; le schéma de compréhension restreint aux variétés de q.r. est certainement cohérent, si l'analyse l'est. Cependant, il n'y a aucun modèle du second ordre dans lequel les ensembles sont exactement les variétés de q.r. sans paramètre: dans un tel modèle, vérifier la réductibilité de J reviendrait à vérifier celle de J_{sr}, pour r et s sans indéterminée, et donc J serait réductible: la restriction aux variétés de q.r. n'autorise pas l'adjonction du schéma: $\forall\theta F \Leftrightarrow \bigwedge_V F[V]$, ceci, bien que la q.r. soit stable par substitution. (Bien entendu, la conjonction doit porter sur les variétés de q.r. qui ne contiennent pas de variables n'apparaissant pas dans $\forall\theta F$.) La différence

(*) Je dois la décourerte de cet exemple à une remarque de G.Kreisel sur le "paradoxe de Curry".

est flagrante avec le calcul du premier ordre (on remplace "variété" par "terme";).

3. Notion de validité dans Y

Une équation de Y est une expression de la forme $a = \bar{o}$, où a est un terme de Y de type o. En général, la partie $= \bar{o}$ de l'équation sera sous-entendue, ce qui fait qu'une équation sera identifiée avec la donnée de a de type o. On dit que a est *valide* si pour toute translation de types sans indéterminée pour toutes ses indéterminées et de termes de F pour toutes ses variables, on a $\vdash a[\bar{U}] = \bar{o}$.

On introduit dans F les constantes suivantes:

Ad:	$\mathrm{REC}\lambda x_o x_o \lambda x_1 x_o y_o S(x_1(y_o))$	*Addition*
$\cdot$:	$\mathrm{REC}\lambda x_o \bar{o} \lambda x_1 x_o y_o \mathrm{Ad}(x_1(y_o), y_o)$	*Produit*
P :	$\mathrm{REC}\bar{o}\lambda x_o y_o y_o$	*Prédecesseur*
N :	$\mathrm{REC}S(\bar{o})\lambda x_o y_o \bar{o}$	*Antisigne*
L :	$\mathrm{REC}\lambda x_o x_o \lambda x_1 x_o y_o P(x_1(y_o))$	*Différence*
E :	$\lambda x_o y_o \mathrm{Ad}(L(x_o, y_o), L(y_o, x_o))$	*Distance*

où 1 est une abréviation pour le type $(o \to o)$.

On introduit dans Y les abréviations $\neg$ et $\vee$.
Si A est une abréviation pour a, $\neg A$ est une abréviation pour $N(a)$; Si A et B sont des abréviations pour a et b respectivement, $A \vee B$ est une abréviation pour $a.b$.

Le sens intuitif de $\neg$ et $\vee$ est évident; on peut définir facilement la notion de tautologie, par le biais des valeurs de vérité, par exemple.

Lemme 1. *Si $B_1 \ldots B_n$ sont des équations de Y (écrites avec $\neg$ et $\vee$), si A est conséquence tautologique de $B_1 \ldots B_n$, si enfin $B_1 \ldots B_n$ sont valides, A est valide.*

Démonstration. Par les théorèmes 1 et 2, ...

En particulier, $\neg A \vee A$ est valide; on peut introduire les connecteurs $\Rightarrow$, $\wedge$, de la manière habituelle.

Lemme 2. *Si $A[\bar{o}]$ et $A[x] \Rightarrow A[S(x)]$ sont valides alors $A[x]$ est valide.*

Lemme 3. *Si A est valide, et si b est un terme de Y, $A[b]$ est valide; de même, si s est un type, $A[s]$ est valide si A l'est.*

Quelques abréviations

Par abus de notation, on écrira:

$\mathrm{DT}\alpha\beta a$	pour	$\mathrm{DT}\alpha(\mathrm{DT}\beta a)$
$\mathrm{ST}\alpha\beta a$	pour	$\mathrm{ST}\alpha(\mathrm{ST}\beta a)$
$a\{r,s\}$	pour	$(a\{r\})\{s\}$
$\mathrm{I}_{\sigma\alpha\beta rst}(a)$	pour	$\mathrm{I}_{\sigma\alpha(\sigma\beta r)s}(\mathrm{I}_{\sigma\beta r[s]\,t}(a))$

avec des conventions similaires pour σ et δ.

Formules généralisées

Une formule généralisée est une expression de la forme $\exists x\forall yA\,[x,y,\mathbf{Z}]$, où x et y sont des variables de Y, $\mathbf{Z}$ est une suite de variables de Y telle que toutes les autres "variables" de A soient des indéterminées.

On dit qu'une formule généralisée est valide s'il existe un terme b du type de x, *ne contenant pas* y, et tel que $A[b,y,\mathbf{Z}]$ soit valide.

On peut envisager des formules généralisées à un nombre positif quelconque de quantificateurs, sous réserve que les $\exists$ précèdent les $\forall$; on supposera alors qu'il s'agit d'une abréviation pour une formule de la forme de celles que nous avons décrites: $\exists x\forall y\forall y'A\,[x,y,y',\mathbf{Z}]$ est ainsi une abréviation pour $\exists x\forall YA\,[x,\Pi^1(Y),\Pi^2(Y),\mathbf{Z}]$ ...

4. Formalisation de l'analyse et de la théorie des types

Il s'agit de présenter rapidement la formalisation de Takeuti ([Tk]): divers systèmes sont possibles, suivant le résultat que l'on souhaite démontrer (la déduction est ici intuitionniste).

1. **Le langage**

(i) les variables du premier ordre: w, w'...

(ii) les lettres de fonctions à n places ($n \geqslant o$): f^n, f'^n..., par exemple $\bar{o}$ à 0 places, S à une place.

(iii) les variables de prédicat a n places ($n > o$): θ, θ'...

(iv) les lettres de prédicat à n places ($n>o$): le signe =, à deux places, par exemple.

Termes
(i) une variable du premier ordre est un terme.
(ii) si $d_1 ... d_n$ sont des termes, et si f^n est une lettre de fonction à n places, $f^n d_1 ... d_n$ est un terme.

Formules atomiques
(i) soit R une lettre de prédicat à n places, $d_1 ... d_n$ des termes; alors $Rd_1 ... d_n$ est une formule atomique.
(ii) soit θ une variable de prédicat à n places, $d_1 ... d_n$ des termes; alors $\theta d_1 ... d_n$ est une formule atomique.

Formules
(i) une formule atomique est une formule.
(ii) si A et B sont des formules, w une variable du premier ordre, θ une variable de prédicat, $A \vee B$, $A \wedge B$, $A \Rightarrow B$, $\neg A$, $\forall wA$, $\exists wA$, $\forall \theta A$, $\exists \theta A$, sont des formules. (l'emploi du signe $\neg$ est facultatif; on peut traduire $\neg A$ par $A \Rightarrow \bar{o} = \bar{1}$, par exemple, ou encore plus simplement par $A \Rightarrow \forall \theta \forall w \theta w$, si l'on veut rester dans le calcul des prédicats).

Variétés
Soit A une formule, $w_1 ... w_n$ des variables du premier ordre distinctes deux à deux; alors $\{w_1 ... w_n\}A$ est une variété à n places. ($n>o$, et $w_1 ... w_n$ sont muets dans la variété).

Substitution d'une variété à n places pour une variable de prédicat à n places: si V est la variété $\{w_1 ... w_n\}A$, si θ est à n places, si B est une formule, on note B_θ^V (par abus de notation: $B[V]$), la formule obtenue à partir de B en remplaçant les formules atomiques $\theta d_1 ... d_n$ par $A[d_1 ... d_n]$.

Exemple. Si B est $\forall w(\theta w \Leftrightarrow A[w])$, et si V est $\{w\}A$, $B[V]$ est $\forall w(A[w] \Leftrightarrow A[w])$.

2. Calcul des prédicats du second ordre
(dans le cas où le signe $\neg$ ne fait pas partie du langage).
Les séquents sont alors de la forme $\Gamma \vdash A$, ou Γ est une suite de formules, et A est une formule.

On écrit alors les règles et axiomes habituels du calcul des prédicats *intuitionniste* du premier ordre pour $\vee, \wedge, \Rightarrow, \forall, \exists$, et on rajoute les schémas du second ordre:

$$\frac{\Gamma \vdash A}{\Gamma \vdash \forall\theta A}(*) \qquad \frac{\Gamma, B[V] \vdash A}{\Gamma, \forall\theta B \vdash A}$$

$$\frac{\Gamma \vdash A[V]}{\Gamma \vdash \exists\theta A} \qquad \frac{\Gamma, B \vdash A}{\Gamma, \exists\theta B \vdash A}(*)$$

3. **L'analyse**

(i) formalisation avec le signe =.(En vue du Ch. 5: interpretation de Gödel.) On suppose que les constantes logiques sont =, S, $\bar{o}$. On écrit alors les axiomes et schémas:

$$w = w$$

$$w = w' \wedge w'' = w' \rightarrow w = w''$$

$$w = w' \rightarrow Sw = Sw'$$

$$w = w' \wedge \theta w \rightarrow \theta w'$$

$$\frac{A[\bar{o}] \quad A[w] \rightarrow A[Sw]}{A[w]}$$

$$A \rightarrow A \qquad \frac{B}{A \rightarrow B} \qquad \frac{A \quad A \rightarrow B}{B} \qquad \frac{A \rightarrow B \quad B \rightarrow C}{A \rightarrow C}$$

$$A \vee B \rightarrow A \qquad B \vee A \rightarrow A \qquad \frac{C \rightarrow A \quad C \rightarrow B}{C \rightarrow A \wedge B} \qquad \frac{A \wedge B \rightarrow C}{A \rightarrow (B \rightarrow C)} \qquad \frac{A \rightarrow (B \rightarrow C)}{A \wedge B \rightarrow C}$$

$$A \rightarrow A \vee B \qquad A \rightarrow B \vee A \qquad \frac{A \rightarrow C \quad B \rightarrow C}{A \vee B \rightarrow C}$$

$$Sw = \bar{o} \rightarrow A \ .$$

Pour la quantification du premier ordre, soient w une variable qui n'apparaît pas dans B, et d un terme.

(*) θ n'apparaît pas dans la conclusion (rappelons qu'il n'y a pas de variable muette). On peut démontrer alors le schéma de compréhension sous la forme $\exists\theta\forall w(\theta w \leftrightarrow A)$ en utilisant l'exemple du § précédent.

$$\frac{B \to A}{B \to \forall w A} \qquad \forall x A \to A[d]$$

$$A[d] \to \exists w A \qquad \frac{A \to B}{\exists w A \to B}$$

Pour la quantification du second ordre, soit θ une variable de prédicat à n places qui n'apparaît pas dans B, et soit V une variété à n places.

$$\frac{B \to A}{B \to \forall \theta A} \qquad \forall \theta A \to A[V]$$

$$A[V] \to \exists \theta A \qquad \frac{A \to B}{\exists \theta A \to B}$$

$\neg A$ est interprété comme $A \to \bar{o} = S\bar{o}$; au premier ordre, ce formalisme est exactement celui de Spector ([Sp]).

(ii) formalisation non-égalitaire (en vue du Ch. 6: Elimination des coupures). On suppose que les constantes sont S et $\bar{o}$.

On écrit alors les règles et axiomes due calcul des prédicats du second ordre pour le système dont les seules constantes sont S et $\bar{o}$. Dans quelle mesure peut-on interpréter le système de l'analyse (formalisé comme précedemment) dans G^1LC.

La premiere chose est de choisir un type du faux; on prend $\forall\theta\forall w\theta w$, qui joue ce rôle à merveille, modulo le schéma de compréhension. Tous les axiomes purement logiques de l'analyse (aux deux ordres) se trouvent alors immédiatement interprétés. Il reste cependant à interpreter l'egalite, et le schema d'induction.

On convient que $d = d'$ est une abréviation pour: $\forall\theta(\theta d \to \theta d')$. Visiblement $\forall\theta(\theta d \to \theta d)$; $\forall\theta(\theta d \to \theta d') \wedge \forall\theta(\theta d' \to \theta d'') \to \forall\theta(\theta d \to \theta d'')$; $\forall\theta(\theta d \to \theta d') \wedge \theta' d \to \theta' d'$. De même, en considérant la variété $\{w\}\forall\theta(\theta w \to \theta d)$, de $\forall\theta(\theta d \to \theta d') \to (\forall\theta(\theta d \to \theta d) \to \forall\theta(\theta d' \to \theta d))$, on obtient $d = d' \to d' = d$. En considérant la variété $\{w\}\theta S w$, et le théorème $\forall\theta(\theta d \to \theta d') \to (\theta S d \to \theta S d')$, on obtient $d = d' \to Sd = Sd'$.

On convient que $N(d)$ est une abréviation pour $\forall\theta(\theta\bar{o} \wedge \forall w(\theta w \to \theta S w) \to \theta d)$. On a clairement $N(\bar{n})$ pour tout n; en convenant que toutes les quantifications du premier ordre sont restreintes à N, on peut alors dériver le schéma d'induction.

Les deux formules qui restent à établir sont $\forall w \forall w'(\forall\theta(\theta Sw \to \theta Sw') \to \forall\theta(\theta w \to \theta w'))$ et $\forall w'(\forall\theta(\theta\bar{o} \to \theta Sw) \to \forall\theta\forall w\theta w)$. Notons les par A_1 et A_2. On peut alors rajouter les deux schémas

$$\frac{\Gamma, A_1 \vdash B}{\Gamma \vdash B} \quad \text{et} \quad \frac{\Gamma, A_2 \vdash B}{\Gamma \vdash B}$$

pour pouvoir interpréter tous les schémas de l'analyse.

4. La théorie des types

On se restreint aux conecteurs $\to$ et $\forall$, qui sont suffisants, comme l'a montré Prawitz [Pr1].

Pour plus de simplicité, nous dirons qu'un "type"-nous dirons de préférence "*ordre*", pour ne pas créer de confusion- est un entier n. Pour chaque ordre n, nous supposerons l'existence de variables d'ordre n, appelées *n-indéterminées,* ou en abrégé n-ind. Les n-ind. sont notées θ_n, θ'_n... Nous supposerons aussi l'existence de lettres de fonction $f, g, \ldots,$ susceptibles de se combiner entre elles et avec les o-ind. pour former les *o-termes*, dont l'un au moins dont être sans indéterminée.

Les formules et les termes sont définies par induction, comme suit:

(i) Si T est un n-terme, si θ est une n+1-ind., θT est une *formule,* qui est dite atomique.

(ii) Si A et B sont des formules, si θ_n est une indéterminée, $A \to B$ et $\forall\theta_n A$ sont des formules.

(iii) Si A est une formule, θ_n une indéterminée, $\{\theta_n\}A$ est un n+1-*terme.*

Substituer le n+1-terme T pour θ_{n+1} dans l'expression (terme ou formule) D, c'est dans un premier temps procéder à la substitution *combinatoire* de T pour θ_{n+1} dans D, puis, en commençant par les plus petites sous-formules, remplacer les expressions *formelles* TU par $A[U]$, où A est tel que T soit $\{\theta_n\}A$, la substitution étant supposée définie à l'ordre n. (A l'ordre o, la substitution est bien entendu uniquement combinatoire.)

On peut alors écrire le système séquentiel de déduction, en considérant des séquents intuitionnistes de formules, et les règles habituelles pour le seul connecteur $\to$, les règles pour $\forall$ étant:

$$\frac{\Gamma \vdash A}{\Gamma \vdash \forall\theta_n A}(*) \qquad \frac{\Gamma, A[T] \vdash B}{\Gamma, \forall\theta_n A \vdash B}(**)$$

(*) θ_n n'apparaît pas dans Γ.
(**) T est un n-terme.

Indiquons rapidement comment retrouver les notions habituelles de la théorie des types à partir du calcul des prédicats d'ordre fini que nous venons de décrire:
On introduit le signe =, relation entre o-termes. Comme axiomes, on considère les clôtures par coupures des séquents:

$$T = T,\quad T = U \vdash U = T,\quad T = U,\quad U = V \vdash T = V,\quad ST = SU \vdash T = U\,,$$

$$ST = o \vdash \theta_1 U\,.$$

Si l'élimination des coupures est possible sans le signe =, elle l'est certainement encore après son adjonction et après celle des nouveaux schémas que nous avons pris.

On peut adjoindre l'axiome d'extensionalité de manière cohérente [Tk], par exemple en posant:
$\mathrm{Ext}_o(\theta_o) \Leftrightarrow \theta_o = \theta_o, \theta_o = {}_o\theta_o \Leftrightarrow \theta_o = \theta_o.$

$$\mathrm{Ext}_{n+1}(\theta_{n+1}) \Leftrightarrow \forall\theta_n \forall\theta'_n(\mathrm{Ext}_n(\theta_n) \wedge \mathrm{Ext}_n(\theta'_n) \wedge \theta_n = {}_n\theta'_n \wedge \theta_{n+1}\theta_n \Rightarrow \theta_{n+1}\theta'_n)$$

$$\theta_{n+1} = {}_{n+1}\theta'_{n+1} \Leftrightarrow \forall\theta_n(\mathrm{Ext}_n(\theta_n) \wedge \theta_{n+1}\theta_n \Rightarrow \theta'_{n+1}\theta_n)$$

et en restreignant toutes les ind. à Ext.

5. Interprétation de l'analyse dans Y

(Dans ce qui suit, on désigne par 1_n le type défini par $1_0 = o$, et $1_{n+1} = o \to 1_n$; n'étant sous-entendu, on abrègera 1_n en 1.)

A chaque formule A de l'analyse, on associe une formule généralisée de Y, notée A^*.

(i) Si A est $d = d'$, A^* est $\exists x \forall y E(d,d')$, où x et y sont des variables de type o qui n'apparaissent pas dans d et d'.

(ii) Si A est $\theta d_1 \ldots d_n$, A^* est $\exists x_\alpha \forall y_\beta\, G(x,y,d_1 \ldots d_n)$, où α et β sont des indéterminées distinctes, et G est une variable de type $(\alpha,\beta \to 1_n)$. On suppose α, β et G attachées injectivement à θ par un procédé quelconque. L'interprétation des connecteurs propositionnels et des quantificateurs du premier ordre se fait exactement comme dans [Sp].

Pour définir l'interprétation du second ordre, supposons que A^* est $\exists x \forall y\, B[x,y,G,\mathbf{Z}]$, où α, β, G sont associés à θ. (x de type r, y de type s) $(\exists\theta A)^*$ peut se noter symboliquement $(\exists\alpha\exists\beta)\exists G \exists x \forall y\, B[x,y,G,\mathbf{Z}]$. Ou, d'une manière équivalente, $(\exists\alpha\exists\beta)\ \exists x'\forall y\ B[\Pi^1 x', y, \Pi^2 x', \mathbf{Z}]$. On affaiblit cette formule en proposant

$$(\exists\alpha\exists\beta)\ \exists x'\forall y'\ B[\Pi^1 x, y'(x'), \Pi^2 x', \mathbf{Z}]\ .$$

Cette dernière formule est équivalente à:

$$(\exists\alpha\exists\beta)\ \exists x'\forall Y\ B[\Pi^1 x', Y\{\alpha,\beta\}(x'), \Pi^2 x', \mathbf{Z}]\ .$$

(Y est de type $\delta\alpha\beta(rx(\alpha,\beta\to 1))\to$).

Or, se donner α, β et x' dont le type r' dépend de α et β, c'est se donner X de type $\sigma\alpha\beta r'$. En utilisant l'axiome de réduction pour ST, on aboutit à la formulation suivante:

$$(\exists\theta A)^* : \exists X\forall Y(\mathrm{ST}\alpha\beta(\lambda z \mathrm{B}[\Pi^1 z, Y\{\alpha,\beta\}(z), \Pi^2 z, \mathbf{Z}]))\,(X)\ .$$

On aboutirait par un raisonnement similaire à:

$$(\forall\theta A)^* : \exists X\forall Y(\mathrm{ST}\alpha\beta(\lambda z \mathrm{B}[X\{\alpha,\beta\}(\Pi^2 z), \Pi^1 z, \Pi^2 z, \mathbf{Z}]))\,(Y)\ .$$

Interprétation d'une variété.

Soit $V : \{w_1 \ldots w_n\}A$ une variété; on suppose que A^* est $\exists x\forall y \mathrm{A}'[x,y,\mathbf{Z}]$. On désigne par V^* le terme $\lambda x y w_1 \ldots w_n \mathrm{A}'$.

Lemme. *La translation $A^*[V^*]$ est valide en même temps que $(A[V])^*$; plus précisément, on peut choisir les mêmes fonctionnelles pour réaliser l'une et l'autre.*

Démonstration évidente.

Théorème 4. *Si A est un théorème de l'analyse, A^* est valide.*

Corollaire. 1. La cohérence de l'analyse se ramène à celle du système Y (pour lequel on a le théorème de réductibilité).
2. Les fonctions représentables dans F sont exactement les récursives prouvables de l'analyse.
3. F est équivalent au système de Spector, dans le sens que les mêmes fonctions de type $o \to o$ sont représentables dans les deux systèmes.
4. Il n'y a pas de démonstration de réductibilité pour F globalement formalisable dans l'analyse.

Démonstration. 3. Car les fonctionnelles de Spector sont exactement les récursives-prouvables de l'analyse ([Sp], [H,K]).
4. Par le 1. et le deuxième théorème d'incomplétude, ou par le 2 et le fait que les récursives-prouvables n'ont pas d'énumération récursive-prouvable.

Démonstration du théorème. La plus grande partie de l'interprétation se traitant exactement comme dans [Sp], nous nous bornerons au cas des schémas du second ordre.

$\forall\theta A \to A[V]$
Il faut trouver x et Y tels que $\mathrm{ST}\alpha\beta\lambda z A\,[X\{\alpha,\beta\}(\Pi^2 z),\Pi^1 z,\Pi^2 z]\,(Y(X,y)) \to A\,[x(X),y,V^*]$ soit valide. Pour Y, on prend $\lambda Xy\mathrm{I}(y\otimes V^*)$, et pour x : $\lambda XX\{r,s\}(V^*)$ (r et s sont tels que V^* est de type $r,s\to 1$).

$A[V] \to \exists\theta A$
Il faut interpréter $A\,[x,y(x,Y),V^*] \to \mathrm{ST}\alpha\beta\lambda z A\,[\Pi^1 z, Y\{\alpha,\beta\}(z),\Pi^2 z]\,(X(x))$, en trouvant y et X; on suppose que V^* est de type $(r,s\to 1)$. Il suffit de prendre pour X : $\lambda x\mathrm{I}(x\otimes V^*)$, et pour y, $\lambda xYY\{r,s\}(X)$.

$A \to B \vdash \exists\theta A \to B$
Par hypothèse, il existe a et b tels que $A\,[x,a(x,y'),G] \to B\,[b(x),y']$ soit valide, et il faut trouver Y et x' tels que $\mathrm{ST}\alpha\beta\lambda z A\,[\Pi^1 z, Y(X,y')\{\alpha,\beta\}(z),\Pi^2 z]\,(X) \to B[x'(X),y']$ soit valide. On peut clairement supposer que α et β n'apparaissent pas en indice d'une variable autre que G dans a; car une autre variable qui aurait cette propriété serait inessentielle à l'interprétation, et pourrait donc être remplacée par le 0 du même type. On peut faire une supposition similaire pour b. Pour x', on peut prendre $\mathrm{ST}\alpha\beta\lambda z b(\Pi^1 z)[\Pi^2 z]$; pour Y, on peut prendre $\lambda Xy'\mathrm{DT}\alpha\beta\lambda z a(\Pi^1 z,y')[\Pi^2 z]$.

$B \to A \vdash B \to \forall\theta A$
Par hypothèse, il existe a et b tels que $B\,[x',y)] \to A\,[a(x'),y,G]$ soit valide, et il faut trouver X et y' tels que: $B\,[x',y'(x',Y)] \to \mathrm{ST}\alpha\beta\lambda z A\,[X(x')\{\alpha,\beta\}(\Pi^2 z),\Pi^1 z,\Pi^2 z]\,(Y)$ soit valide. On peut toujours supposer que α et β n'apparaissent pas en indice d'une variable autre que G dans a et b. Pour y', on peut prendre $\lambda x'\mathrm{ST}\alpha\beta\lambda z b(x',\Pi^1 z)[\Pi^2 z]$; pour X, on peut prendre $\lambda x'\mathrm{DT}\alpha\beta\lambda G a(x')$. *C.Q.F.D.*

Remarque: On pourrait donner une interpretation de l'analyse classique (avec le tiers-exclu) dans le système Y, d'une façon analogue à celle de Shoenfield [Sh].

6. Théorème de normalisation pour G^1LC

Dans ce qui suit, il s'agit, à l'aide de la méthode de Howard, de démontrer un théorème d'élimination des coupures pour G^1LC (voir Ch. 4).

Pour plus de simplicité, toutes les variables de prédicat seront supposées monadiques. Pour pouvoir préparer la généralisation du chapitre 7, nous noterons θ... les variables des deux ordres, θ_0 représentant plus particulièrement une variable du premier ordre, et θ_1 une variable du second ordre. Les variables seront appelées *indéterminées* (*ind.*). De même, par le vocable de *terme*, nous entendrons soit un terme (du 1er ordre) soit une variété de G^1LC. Par *type*, nous entendrons une formule de G^1LC, supposé écrit avec les seuls signes $\rightarrow$ et $\forall$, les autres symboles étant dérivables comme l'a montré Prawitz [Pr], et les corollaires standard pour v et E etant toujours derivables(*).

Un élément du système fonctionnel HY sera appelé *fonctionnelle* (en abrégé: *fcl*), pour ne pas créer de confusion.

§ 1. Description de HY

(i) Pour chaque type A, les variables de type A, x_A, y_A sont des *fcl*.
(ii) Si a est une *fcl* de type A, si x est une variable de type B, λxa est une *fcl* de type $B \rightarrow A$.
(iii) Si a et b sont des *fcl* de types respectifs $A \rightarrow B$ et A, APab (en abrégé $a(b)$) est une *fcl* de type B.
(iv) Si a est une *fcl* de type A, si θ_i (i=0,1) est une i-ind. qui n'apparaît pas en indice d'une variable de a, DQ$_i\theta_i a$ est une *fcl* de type $\forall\theta_i A$.
(v) Si a est une *fcl* de type $\forall\theta_i A$, si T est un i-terme (i=0,1) EXT$_i aT$ (abrégé en $a\{T\}$) est une *fcl* de type $A[T]$.

§ 2. Notion de réduction

1. *Sous-fcl*
On dit que b est une *sous-fcl* de a si b est anterieur a a dans sa construction.

2. *Réduction immédiate*

$$\lambda xa(b) \Rightarrow a[b] \tag{1}$$

$$\mathrm{DQ}_i\theta_i a\{T\} \Rightarrow a[T] \qquad (i=0,1) \tag{2}$$

On dit que u se réduit immédiatement à v si $u \Rightarrow v$ est un exemple de (1)-(2).

(*) Je dois cette simplification a Martin-Löf.

Remarque. Pour des raisons techniques, il est commode d'introduire le schéma 0_A pour tout type A; les axiomes de la réduction immédiate pour 0 sont les suivants:

$$0(b) \Rightarrow 0\,, \qquad\qquad 0\{T\} \Rightarrow 0\,. \tag{3}$$

Suivant le contexte, HY comportera, ou ne comportera pas le schéma 0, et il est bien entendu que 0 n'est utile que le temps d'une démonstration de réductibilité.

3. *Réduction*

Une *sous-fcl minimale b* de *a* est une *sous-fcl* telle qu'il existe une *fcl c* telle que *b* se réduise immédiatement à *c*, et telle qu'aucune *sous-fcl* stricte de *b* n'ait la même propriété.

On dit que *a* se réduit atomiquement à *b* si l'on peut passer de *a* à *b* par substitution, pour une apparition d'une *sous-fcl* minimale *c* de *a*, d'une *fcl d* telle que *c* se réduise immédiatement à *d*.

Une *réduction* est une suite de *réductions* atomiques.

On abrège en *aRb* l'énoncé "*a* se réduit en *b*".

Une *fcl* est normale si elle n'a aucune *sous-fcl* minimale. Une *forme normale* de *a* est une *fcl. b* normale telle que *aRb*.

§3. Formes normales et démonstrations sans coupures

La construction de HY paraphrase exactement (du moins sans le 0) un système de déduction naturelle de Prawitz [Pr] ; une *fcl* normale correspond à une démonstration sans coupure au sens de Prawitz. Prawitz a montré [Pr] l'équivalence entre sa notion de démonstration sans coupure et la notion séquentielle. Pour démontrer le

Théorème 6. G^1LC *vérifie le principe de normalisation.*

Il suffit de montrer que toute *fcl* admet une forme normale, d'après ce qui précède.

§ 4. Notion de réductibilité

Dans ce qui suit, sauf mention expresse du contraire, nous nous plaçons dans le sous-système HF, formé des *fcl* sans variables et indéterminées; par terme, nous entendrons terme *clos*; rappelons qu'il y a un *i*-terme clos.

1. *Candidats de réductibilité* (en abrégé: c.r.)

(CR0) (i) Si T est un 0-terme, un c.r..de hauteur T est T lui-même.
(ii) Si T est un 1-terme, un c.r. de hauteur T est un prédicat φ à deux arguments, qui vérifie:

(CR1) $\varphi(U,a) \Rightarrow U$ est un 0-terme et a est de type TU
(CR2) $\varphi(U,0)$
(CR3) $aRb \Rightarrow (\varphi(U,a) \Leftrightarrow \varphi(U,b))$
(CR4) $\varphi(U,a) \Rightarrow a$ admet une forme normale.
On abrège en $Z_T(\varphi)$ l'énoncé "φ est un c.r. de hauteur T".

2. *La quasi-réductibilité* (en abrégé: q.r.)

Soit A un type (resp. T un terme), soit $\boldsymbol{\theta}$ une suite d'indéterminées qui contient toutes celles de A (resp. de T), soit $\mathbf{T}$ une suite de termes de même longueur que $\boldsymbol{\theta}$, $\boldsymbol{\varphi}$ une suite de c.r. de hauteurs respectives $\mathbf{T}$; on définit la $\mathbf{T}$; $\boldsymbol{\varphi}/A$-réductibilité, qui exprime une propriété des *fcl* de type $A[\mathbf{T}]$ (resp. $(\mathbf{T};\boldsymbol{\varphi}/T)^*$ que nous montrerons être un c.r. de hauteur $T[\mathbf{T}]$).

(QR1) $\mathbf{T},T;\boldsymbol{\varphi},\varphi/N(\theta_1 U,a) \Leftrightarrow \varphi(TU[\mathbf{T}],a)$
(QR2) $\mathbf{T};\boldsymbol{\varphi}/N(A\to B,a) \quad \Leftrightarrow \forall b(\mathbf{T};\boldsymbol{\varphi}/N(A,b) \Rightarrow \mathbf{T};\boldsymbol{\varphi}/N(B,a(b)))$
(QR3) $\mathbf{T};\boldsymbol{\varphi}/N(\forall\theta_i A,a) \quad \Leftrightarrow \forall\varphi\forall T(Z_T(\varphi) \quad \Rightarrow \mathbf{T},T;\boldsymbol{\varphi},\varphi/N(A,a\{T\}))$
(QR4) $(\mathbf{T};\boldsymbol{\varphi}/T)^* = T[\mathbf{T}]$ si T est un 0-terme.
(QR5) $(\mathbf{T};\boldsymbol{\varphi}/T)^* = \{U,a\}(\mathbf{T};\boldsymbol{\varphi}/N(TU,a))$ si T est un 1-terme.

3. *La réductibilité*

On la définit à partir de la q.r. exactement comme au ch. 2.

§ 5. **Théorème de réductibilité**

Lemme 1. *Une fcl a au plus une forme normale.*

Lemme 2. $(\mathbf{T};\boldsymbol{\varphi}/T)^*$ *est un c.r. de hauteur* $T[\mathbf{T}]$, *sous réserve que* $\boldsymbol{\varphi}$ *soit une suite de c.r.*

Démonstration. Comme au ch. 2.

Lemme 3. (Substitution).

$$\mathbf{T},T[\mathbf{T}'];\boldsymbol{\varphi},(\mathbf{T}';\boldsymbol{\psi}/T)^*/N(A,a) \Leftrightarrow \mathbf{T},\mathbf{T}';\boldsymbol{\varphi},\boldsymbol{\psi}/N(A[T],a).$$

Ce lemme se démontre simplement (voir ch. 7).

Lemme 4.
1. x_A *est red.*
2. *si a et b sont red., a(b) est red.*
3. *si a est red., a{T} est red.*

Démonstration. 1, 2, 3 sont des conséquences évidentes des définitions; remarquons l'usage du lemme de substitution (et donc du schéma de compréhension) pour 3.

Lemme 5.
1. *si a est red.,* $DQ\theta_i a$ *est red.*
2. *si a est red.,* λxa *est red.*

Démonstration. 1. si $a[T]$ est q.r. pour tout T (il existe un i-terme clos), $a[T]$ admet une forme normale, et il alors rapidement vérifié que a en admet une, disons a'; $DQ\theta_i a\{T\}$ se réduit donc en $a'[T]$ qui est la forme normale de $a[T]$; par CR3 et QR3, $DQ\theta_i a$ est donc réductible.
2. si $a[b]$ est red. pour tout b red., $a[0]$ est red., et il est rapidement vérifié que si $a[0]$ admet une forme normale, a en admet une, disons a'. Si b a la forme normale b', $\lambda xa(b)$ se réduit en $a[b']$, qui a la même forme normale que $a[b]$, comme on le vérifie. Par CR3 et QR2, λxa est donc réductible.

Théorème 7. *Toutes les fcl de* HY *sont réductibles.*

Donc toute *fcl* a une forme normale, ce qui donne le théorème 6.

7. Théorème de normalization pour $G^\omega LC$

Pour obtenir l'analogue du théorème 6 pour $G^\omega LC$, il suffit de considérer un système fonctionnel $H^\omega Y$, donné comme suit:

1. *Description de* $H^\omega Y$
Comme au ch. 6, mais on ne suppose pas que $i = 0, 1$: on se permet i entier quelconque.

2. *Notion de réduction*
Comme au ch. 6, avec i quelconque.

3. *Formes normales et démonstrations sans coupure*
Comme au ch. 6, on montrerait que si toute *fcl* de $H^\omega Y$ admet une forme normale, le

Théorème 8. $G^\omega LC$ *vérifie le principe d'élimination des coupures.*

Est vérifié.

4. *Notion de réductibilité*

(i) Un candidat de réductibilité de hauteur T est défini par les clauses: Si T est un 0-terme, par CRO.
Si T est un n+1-terme par (CR2), (CR3), (CR4), et (C'R1):
(C'R1) $\varphi(\psi,a) \Leftrightarrow$ il existe un n-terme U tel que ψ soit un c.r. de hauteur U, et a est de type TU (ce qui correspond à (CR1) pour $n = 0$).
(ii) La quasi réductibilité est définie par (QR2), (QR3), (QR4), ainsi que par
(Q'R1) $\mathbf{T},T'; \varphi, \varphi/N(\theta_{n+1} U,a) \Leftrightarrow \varphi(\mathbf{T},T';\boldsymbol{\varphi},\varphi/U)^*,a)$
(Q'R5) $(\mathbf{T};\boldsymbol{\varphi}/T)^* = \{\psi,a\}(\exists U(Z_U(\psi) \wedge \mathbf{T},U;\boldsymbol{\varphi},\psi/N(T\theta_n,a))$ si T est un n+1-terme.
(iii) La réductibilité se définit comme d'habitude à partir de la q.r.

5. *Théorème de réductibilité*

On peut reprendre les lemmes 1–5 dans leur formalution exacte. Celà donne le théorème de réductibilité, et du coup le théorème 8. Par exemple, démontrons l'analogue du lemme 3:

$$\mathbf{T},T[\mathbf{T}'] ; \varphi, (\mathbf{T}';\psi/T)^*/N(A,a) \Leftrightarrow \mathbf{T},\mathbf{T}'; \varphi,\psi/N(A[T],a) .$$

Par induction sur longueur (A) + longueur (T). Si A n'est pas de la forme θU, le lemme est consequence evidente de l'hypothese d'induction. Nous supposons dans ce qui suit que $A = \theta U$ et que T est substitué pour θ'.
(i) θ' est distinct de θ; on peut se ramener au cas où θ' apparaît dans U. Si U est un 0-terme, θ' est une 0-ind., et $(\mathbf{T}';\boldsymbol{\psi}/T)^*$ est $T[\mathbf{T}']$, puisque T est alors un 0-terme.

Si U est le n+1-terme $\{\theta''_n\}B$, il nous suffit de prouver l'équivalence $\varphi((\mathbf{T},T[\mathbf{T}'];\boldsymbol{\varphi},(\mathbf{T}';\boldsymbol{\psi}/T)^*/U)^*,a) \Leftrightarrow \varphi((\boldsymbol{\varphi},\boldsymbol{\psi};\mathbf{T},\mathbf{T}'/U[T])^*,a)$, et il est suffisant de montrer que $\mathbf{T},T[\mathbf{T}'],T'';\boldsymbol{\varphi},(\mathbf{T}';\boldsymbol{\psi}/T)^*, \varphi'/N(B,b) \Leftrightarrow$
$\Leftrightarrow \mathbf{T},\mathbf{T}',T'';\boldsymbol{\varphi},\boldsymbol{\psi},\varphi'/N(B[T],b)$, pour tous φ',T'' et tout b, ce qui fait partie de l'hypothèse d'induction.
(ii) θ' est θ; et θ' n'apparaît pas dans T. Puisque T n'est pas un 0-terme, il est de la forme $\{\theta''_n\}B$; il faudrait démontrer: $(\mathbf{T}';\boldsymbol{\psi}/T)^*((\mathbf{T};\boldsymbol{\varphi}/U)^*,a) \Leftrightarrow$
$\Leftrightarrow \mathbf{T},\mathbf{T}';\boldsymbol{\varphi},\boldsymbol{\psi}/N(B[U],a)$ et il suffit de prouver $\mathbf{T}',U[\mathbf{T}];\boldsymbol{\psi},(\mathbf{T};\boldsymbol{\varphi}/U)^*/N(B,a) \Leftrightarrow$
$\Leftrightarrow \mathbf{T}',\mathbf{T};\boldsymbol{\psi},\boldsymbol{\varphi}/N(B[U],a)$. Cette dernière équivalence fait partie de l'hypothèse d'induction.
(iii) θ' est θ et θ apparait dans T: en combinant (i) et (ii) C.Q.F.D.

Références

[Gd] K.Gödel, Über eine bisher noch nicht benützte Erweiterung des finiten Standpunktes, Dialectica 12 (1958).

[H,K] W.A.Howard et G.Kreisel, Transfinite induction and Bar induction of types 0 and one, and the role of continuity in intuitionistic analysis, JSL 31 (1966) 3.

[Pr1] D.Prawitz, Natural deduction (Almqvist and Wiksell, Stockholm, 1965).

[Pr2] D.Prawitz, Some results for intuitionistic logic with second order quantification rules, in: Intuitionism and Proof Theory, eds. A.Kino, J.Myhill and R.E.Vesley (North-Holland, Amsterdam, 1970).

[Sh] J.R.Shoenfield, Mathematical Logic (Addison-Wesley, 1967) Ch. 8.

[Sp] C.Spector, Provably recursive functionals of analysis: a consistency proof of analysis by an extension of principles formulated in current intuitionistic mathematics, Recursive function theory, Proc. Symp. Pure Math., Vol. V (AMS, Providence, 1962).

[Th] M.Takahashi, A proof of cut-elimination theorem in simple type theory, J. Math. Soc. Jap. 19 (1967).

[Tk] G.Takeuti, On a generalised logical calculus, Jap. J. Math. 23 (1953).

[Tt1] W.W.Tait, A non-constructive proof of Gentzen's Hauptsatz for second order predicate calculus, Bull. Amer. Math. Soc. 72 (1966).

[Tt2] W.W.Tait, Intentional interpretation of functionals of finite type, JSL 32 (1967).

A NORMALFORM IN FIRST ORDER ARITHMETIC

Herman R. JERVELL
University of Oslo

1. We work with extensions of the systems of natural deductions NM, NJ, NK introduced by Gentzen [1] and Johansson [3]. The systems are extended by quantifierfree axioms and inductionrule. We call the extended systems NMA, NJA, NKA. Prawitz [5] has shown how to define a normalform for prooftrees in NM, NJ, NK. For the case where the logical symbols are &, $\supset$, $\forall$ he does it by giving certain local reductions in a natural way. A prooftree is in normalform if it has no local reductions. He shows that any prooftree can be brought to a normalform by a finite number of local reductions. In the usual correspondence between NM, NJ, NK and LM, LJ, LK the prooftrees in normalform correspond to cutfree proofs.

In this paper we extend Prawitz's result to NMA, NJA, NKA. It is well known that there can be no full cut-elimination result for elementary number theory (first order arithmetic). We can see this in minimal and intuitionistic elementary number theory as follows: From a cutfree proof of a Π^0_2 formula $\forall x \exists y A(x.y)$ we can read off a primitive recursive function $f(x)$ such that $\forall x A(x,f(x))$ is true. We know that we can prove that the Ackermann-function is total; but since it is not primitive recursive, we cannot give a cut-free proof that it is total.

In spite of this we give an extension of the normalform results to NMA, NJA, NKA. We give in a natural way local reductions of prooftrees. We show that all reduction-sequences starting with a given prooftree terminate after a finite number of reductions in the same normalform. This normalform is strong enough to conclude the consistency of NMA, NJA, NKA. In NMA and NJA we show how to derive the results of Harrop [2].

The proof is influenced by Sanchis [6]. I have been given much help by Dag Prawitz. With his normalform for iterated inductive definitions Per Martin-Løf has since given a theorem stronger than at least some of the results in this paper.

2. As mentioned above NMA, NJA, NKA are the systems NM, NJ, NK extended by quantifierfree axioms and inductionrule.

We have an unlimited list of free variables $a, b, c, \ldots$; and an unlimited list of bound variables $x, y, z, \ldots$. Our connectives and quantifiers are &, v, $\supset$, $\forall$, $\exists$. We have symbols for zero 0, successor $'$, and relations including $=$, S (sum), P (product).

We write ⅄ for $0 = 0'$.

The numerals are $0, 0', 0'', \ldots$.

Terms, atomic formulae, formulae, and closed formulae are defined in the usual way.

Our proofs are written in treeform. We call them prooftrees. The downmost formula (or rather the formula at the downmost node of the tree) is the conclusion of the prooftree. The topmost formulae are either axioms or assumptions. The assumptions are either open or closed. (Prawitz [5] calls a closed assumption discharged.) We read the prooftree as: From the open assumptions $A_1, \ldots A_n$ we get the conclusion B. A closed assumption is written with a squarebracket around.

The axioms are the quantifierfree formulae with true universal closure.

To each connective and quantifier we have rules for introduction and elimination. These are the same as in NM, NJ, NK. In the usual shorthand (see Prawitz [5]) the rules are given by:

&I) $$\frac{A \quad B}{A \,\&\, B}$$

&E) $$\frac{A \,\&\, B}{A} \qquad \frac{A \,\&\, B}{B}$$

vI) $$\frac{A}{A \vee B} \qquad \frac{B}{A \vee B}$$

vE) $$\frac{A \vee B \quad \begin{matrix}[A]\\ C\end{matrix} \quad \begin{matrix}[B]\\ C\end{matrix}}{C}$$

$\supset$I) $$\frac{\begin{matrix}[A]\\ B\end{matrix}}{A \supset B}$$

$\supset$E) $$\frac{A \quad A \supset B}{B}$$

$\forall$I) $$\frac{Aa}{\forall x A x}$$

$\forall$E) $$\frac{\forall x A x}{A t}$$

$\exists$I) $$\frac{A t}{\exists x A x}$$

$\exists$E) $$\frac{\exists x A a \quad \begin{matrix}[Aa]\\ B\end{matrix}}{B}$$

in addition we have an inductionrule

IND)
$$\frac{Ao \quad \begin{matrix}[Aa]\\ Aa'\end{matrix}}{At}$$

We have the usual restriction on the eigenvariable a in ∀I, ∃E, IND. These rules are common for all three systems and are all the rules of NMA. To get NJA we add the rule

$\curlywedge_I$)
$$\frac{\curlywedge}{A}$$

To get NKA we add the more general rule

$\curlywedge_K$)
$$\frac{\begin{matrix}[A \supset \curlywedge]\\ \curlywedge\end{matrix}}{A}$$

In both $\curlywedge_I$ and $\curlywedge_K$ we assume that A is different from $\curlywedge$. In case we have only &, ⊃, ∨ as logical signs, we can assume that A is atomic.

We distinguish between major and minor premisses. In &I, &E, ∨I, ⊃I, ∀I, ∀E, ∃I, $\curlywedge_I$, $\curlywedge_K$ all the premisses are major. In ∨E the one to the left is major, the two to the right minor. In ∃E the one to the left is major, the one to the right is minor. In ⊃E the one to the right is major, the one to the left is minor. In IND both premisses are minor.

A branch in a prooftree which can be traced up from the conclusion to an axiom or an assumption or consequence of IND through major premisses is called a main branch.

Being reasonably careful with the free variables in a prooftree, we can substitute a term for a free variable not used as an eigenvariable.

A main subtree of a prooftree is a subtree with conclusion a minor premiss of a rule with consequence in a main branch of the original prooftree.

3. We can consider an introductionrule as giving a sufficient reason for introducing a connective, and an eliminationrule as an inverse to the introductionrule. If we first apply an introductionrule to introduce a connective and then the eliminationrule, we essentially restore the original situation. It was not necessary to use the two rules. We have another redundancy when the inductionterm in IND is either zero or successor. To each such redundancy we have a reduction.

Definition. A maximal formula in a prooftree is a formula which occurs as either both consequences of an introductionrule and major premiss of an eliminationrule, or consequence of IND with inductionterm either zero or successor.

Definition. A prooftree is in normalform if it does not contain any maximal formula.

Our problem now is to give a systematic transformation of any prooftree to a prooftree in normalform with the same conclusion and not more open assumptions. This will be done by the reductions defined below. We will see that for each maximal formula there is a natural way of getting rid of it, but at the possible expense of creating new maximal formulae. Observe that in the reductions defined below the conclusions remain the same and we do not get new open assumptions. The reductions are as follows:

&-reduction:

$$\begin{array}{c} \Sigma_1 \quad \Sigma_2 \\ \dfrac{\dfrac{A \quad B}{A \,\&\, B}}{A} \\ \Sigma_3 \end{array} \qquad \text{is reduced to} \qquad \begin{array}{c} \Sigma_1 \\ A \\ \Sigma_3 \end{array}$$

$$\begin{array}{c} \Sigma_1 \quad \Sigma_2 \\ \dfrac{\dfrac{A \quad B}{A \,\&\, B}}{B} \\ \Sigma_4 \end{array} \qquad \text{is reduced to} \qquad \begin{array}{c} \Sigma_2 \\ B \\ \Sigma_4 \end{array}$$

∨-reduction:

$$\begin{array}{c} \dfrac{\begin{array}{c}\Sigma_1 \\ \dfrac{A}{A \vee B}\end{array} \quad \begin{array}{c}[A] \\ \Sigma_2 \\ C\end{array} \quad \begin{array}{c}[B] \\ \Sigma_3 \\ C\end{array}}{C} \\ \Sigma_4 \end{array} \qquad \text{is reduced to} \qquad \begin{array}{c} \Sigma_1 \\ A \\ \Sigma_2 \\ C \\ \Sigma_4 \end{array}$$

$$\frac{\dfrac{\begin{array}{c}\Sigma_5\\ B\end{array}}{A\vee B}\quad \begin{array}{c}[A]\\ \Sigma_2\\ C\end{array}\quad \begin{array}{c}[B]\\ \Sigma_2\\ C\end{array}}{\begin{array}{c}C\\ \Sigma_4\end{array}} \qquad \text{is reduced to} \qquad \begin{array}{c}\Sigma_5\\ B\\ \Sigma_3\\ C\\ \Sigma_4\end{array}$$

$\supset$*-reduction*:

$$\frac{\begin{array}{c}\Sigma_1\\ A\end{array}\quad \dfrac{\begin{array}{c}[A]\\ \Sigma_2\\ B\end{array}}{A\supset B}}{\begin{array}{c}B\\ \Sigma_3\end{array}} \qquad \text{is reduced to} \qquad \begin{array}{c}\Sigma_1\\ A\\ \Sigma_2\\ B\\ \Sigma_3\end{array}$$

$\forall$*-reduction*:

$$\frac{\dfrac{\begin{array}{c}\Sigma_1\\ Aa\end{array}}{\forall xAx}}{\begin{array}{c}At\\ \Sigma_2\end{array}} \qquad \text{is reduced to} \qquad \begin{array}{c}\Sigma_1'\\ At\\ \Sigma_2\end{array}$$

where Σ_1' is obtained from Σ_1 by substituting t for a.

$\exists$*-reduction*:

$$\frac{\dfrac{\begin{array}{c}\Sigma_1\\ At\end{array}}{\exists xAx}\quad \begin{array}{c}[Aa]\\ \Sigma_2\\ B\end{array}}{\begin{array}{c}B\\ \Sigma_3\end{array}} \qquad \text{is reduced to} \qquad \begin{array}{c}\Sigma_2\\ At\\ \Sigma_2'\\ B\\ \Sigma_3\end{array}$$

where Σ_2' is obtained from Σ_2 by substituting t for a.

IND-*reduction (zero-case)*:

$$\frac{\begin{array}{c}\Sigma_1\\ Ao\end{array}\quad \begin{array}{c}[Aa]\\ \Sigma_2\\ Aa'\end{array}}{\begin{array}{c}Ao\\ \Sigma_3\end{array}} \qquad \text{is reduced to} \qquad \begin{array}{c}\Sigma_1\\ Ao\\ \Sigma_3\end{array}$$

IND-*reduction (successor-case)*:

$$\frac{\begin{matrix} & [Aa] \\ \Sigma_1 & \Sigma_2 \\ Ao & Aa' \end{matrix}}{\begin{matrix} At' \\ \Sigma_3 \end{matrix}} \quad \text{is reduced to} \quad \frac{\begin{matrix} & [Aa] \\ \Sigma_1 & \Sigma_2 \\ Ao & Aa' \end{matrix}}{\begin{matrix} At \\ \Sigma_2' \\ At' \\ \Sigma_3 \end{matrix}}$$

where Σ_2' is obtained from Σ_2 by substituting t for a.

These are all the reductions.

Definition. A reductionsequence is a sequence of prooftrees such that each prooftree reduces to the next in the sequence.

4. We want to prove that all reductionsequences terminate. Say we would first prove that to each prooftree there is a reductionsequence which terminates in a prooftree in normalform. It is not hard to show that if this is true, we can always do with the particular reductionsequences we get by always reducing one of the downmost maximal formulae in the main branch, and then after the main branches are cleared up go to the main branches in the main subtrees etc. So we concentrate on those reductionsequences. It becomes soon apparent that the major obstacles to a proof are the inductionrules with inductionterm a free variable. To take care of those we add the obvious ω-reduction: Substitute any numeral for a free variable in the inductionterm. We are forced to add two other rather trivial reductions so that the prooftree remains a prooftree after the substitution. There are additional problems when we have $\vee$ or $\exists$. To take care of those we introduce the collapsed prooftrees. We then prove over several lemmata, all obvious except the main lemma, that the relation given by all those extra reductions is well-founded. We can then prove the weaker version of the theorem mentioned above by induction over the well-founded relation. Being a little more clever we can prove that all reductionsequences terminate. The main problem here is that in some reduction we may cut off a whole subtree and will therefore not be able to keep track of what could be going on in that subtree. To take care of this we introduce the associated subtrees of a maximal formula.

Definition. The associated subtree of a prooftree with respect to a maximal formula is the subtree which can be cut off in the reduction. So for example

$$\text{to}\quad \begin{matrix}\dfrac{\dfrac{\begin{matrix}\Sigma_1 & \Sigma_2\\ A & B\end{matrix}}{A \,\&\, B}}{A}\\ \Sigma_3\end{matrix}\qquad \text{we associate}\qquad \begin{matrix}\Sigma_2\\ B\end{matrix}$$

$$\text{and to}\quad \begin{matrix}\dfrac{\begin{matrix}\Sigma_1\\ A\end{matrix}\quad \dfrac{\begin{matrix}[A]\\ \Sigma_2\\ B\end{matrix}}{A \supset B}}{B}\\ \Sigma_3\end{matrix}\qquad \text{we associate}\qquad \begin{matrix}\Sigma_1\\ A\end{matrix}$$

Definition. To each $\vee$E and $\exists$E we define the collapsed prooftrees

$$\begin{matrix}\dfrac{\begin{matrix}\\ \Sigma_1\\ A \vee B\end{matrix}\quad \begin{matrix}[A]\\ \Sigma_2\\ C\end{matrix}\quad \begin{matrix}[B]\\ \Sigma_3\\ C\end{matrix}}{C}\\ \Sigma_4\end{matrix}\qquad \text{is collapsed to}\qquad \begin{matrix}A\\ \Sigma_2\\ C\\ \Sigma_4\end{matrix}\qquad \text{and}\qquad \begin{matrix}B\\ \Sigma_3\\ C\\ \Sigma_4\end{matrix}$$

$$\text{and}\quad \begin{matrix}\dfrac{\begin{matrix}\\ \Sigma_1\\ xAx\end{matrix}\quad \begin{matrix}[Aa]\\ \Sigma_2\\ B\end{matrix}}{B}\\ \Sigma_3\end{matrix}\qquad \text{is collapsed to}\qquad \begin{matrix}Aa\\ \Sigma_2\\ B\\ \Sigma_3\end{matrix}$$

Definition. We define a binary relation $\mathcal{R}$ between prooftrees. $\Sigma_1 \mathcal{R} \Sigma_2$ is defined by cases depending on the free variables in the main branches of Σ_1 and on the downmost formula in the main branches of Σ_1 which is not the consequence of an eliminationrule, of $\curlywedge_{\mathrm{I}}$, nor of $\curlywedge_{\mathrm{K}}$. (Not that it matters, but there is at most one such formula.)

(a) A formula in the main branches contains a free variable a not used as an eigenvariable.

$$\Sigma \mathcal{R} \Sigma'$$

where Σ' is obtained from Σ by substituting any numeral for a.

(b) Case a does not apply and the last rule used is an introductionrule. Depending on whether we have one or two premisses we get

$$\frac{\Sigma}{A} \mathcal{R} \Sigma$$

or

$$\frac{\Sigma_1 \quad \Sigma_2}{A} \mathcal{R} \Sigma_1, \Sigma_2 \quad \text{i.e.} \quad \frac{\Sigma_1 \quad \Sigma_2}{A} \mathcal{R} \Sigma_i \ (i=1,2)$$

(c) Case a and case b do not apply and there is a downmost maximal formula in the main branches. Then

$$\Sigma \mathcal{R} \Sigma_1, \Sigma_2$$

where Σ_1 is the reduction of Σ and Σ_2 is the associated subtree.

(d) Case a and case b do not apply and there is a $\vee$E or $\exists$E in the main branches. Then

$$\Sigma \mathcal{R} \Sigma_1$$

where Σ_1 is the collapsed prooftree.

(e) Case a, b, c do not apply (i.e. all the formulae in the main branch are consequences of eliminationrules or $\curlywedge_I$ or $\curlywedge_K$). Then

$$\Sigma \mathcal{R} \Sigma_1, ..., \Sigma_n$$

where $\Sigma_1, ..., \Sigma_n$ are the main subtrees (i.e. subtrees above a minor premiss with consequence in the main branch). This concludes the definition of $\mathcal{R}$.

Definition. $\succ$ is the transitive closure of $\mathcal{R}$.

Definition. $\mathcal{R}$-sequence is a sequence of prooftrees each in $\mathcal{R}$-relation to the next.

5. We will show that $\succ$ is well-founded, i.e. all $\mathcal{R}$-sequences are finite.

Definition. A prooftree is regular if all $\mathcal{R}$-sequences starting with it are finite.

We have the following obvious lemma:

Lemma 1. (i) *If Σ is regular and $\Sigma\ \mathcal{R}\ \Sigma'$, then Σ' is regular.*
(ii) *If all prooftrees in $\mathcal{R}$-relation to Σ are regular, then Σ is regular.*

Note that we can do induction over the ordering $\succ$ restricted to regular proof trees. We call this $\mathcal{R}$-induction. The following is also obvious.

Lemma 2. (i) *A prooftree consisting of only an axiom or an assumption is regular. (We call such a prooftree trivial).*
(ii) *Regularity is closed under $\curlywedge_{\mathrm{I}}$, $\curlywedge_{\mathrm{K}}$ and introduction rules.*
(iii) *Regularity is closed under* &E *and* $\forall$E.
(iv) *Regularity is closed under* $\supset$E, $\vee$E, $\exists$E *provided there are only trivial prooftrees above the minor premisses.*

Proof. We indicate how to prove first part of (iii). We use $\mathcal{R}$-induction. Assume $\overset{\Sigma}{A\&B}$. Want $\overset{\Sigma}{(A\&B)/A}$ regular. Two cases to consider – either the last rule in $\overset{\Sigma}{A\&B}$ is an introductionrule or it is not. Both cases equally obvious.

Main lemma. *If $\overset{\Pi}{A}$ and $\underset{\Sigma}{A}$ are regular, then also $\overset{\Pi}{\underset{\Sigma}{A}}$. (We may here put Π over more than one open assumption A.)*

Proof. The proof is by a double induction. A primary induction over the length of A and a secondary $\mathcal{R}$-induction over either $\underset{\Sigma}{A}$ with less than or equal $\overset{\Pi}{A}$ or over $\overset{\Pi}{A}$ with less than or equal $\underset{\Sigma}{A}$. To the initial step observe that the least prooftrees in the $\mathcal{R}$-relation consist of a single branch with only &E, $\vee$E, $\curlywedge_{\mathrm{I}}$, $\curlywedge_{\mathrm{K}}$ used as rules. So we use lemma 2 to get $\overset{\Pi}{\underset{\Sigma}{A}}$ regular.
Now to the induction step. Suppose there is an infinite $\mathcal{R}$-sequence starting with $\overset{\Pi}{\underset{\Sigma}{A}}$. We divide up into cases depending on the first $\mathcal{R}$-relation in the sequence.
(i) We use case a in the definition of $\mathcal{R}$.
(ii) We use case b.
(iii) We use case c with either associated subtree or reduction with maximal formula different from A.
(iv) We use case d.
(v) We use case e.
(vi) We use case c and reduction with maximal formula A.

Cases (i) – (v) are obvious. So we go to case (vi). First observe that we can put $\begin{smallmatrix}\Pi\\ A\end{smallmatrix}$ over all the open assumptions A in $\begin{smallmatrix}A\\ \Sigma\end{smallmatrix}$ not in the main branch by an argument as in case (i) – (v) to get the regular prooftree $\begin{smallmatrix}A\\ \Sigma'\end{smallmatrix}$. We want to put $\begin{smallmatrix}\Pi\\ A\end{smallmatrix}$ over the open assumption A in the main branch of $\begin{smallmatrix}A\\ \Sigma'\end{smallmatrix}$. We now have subcases depending on the principal logical symbol in A. We give the argument for $A = B \supset C$, $A = B \vee C$. The remaining subcases are similar.

$$\begin{array}{c} \Pi \\ B \supset C \\ \Sigma' \end{array} = \begin{array}{c} \\ \\ \\ B \end{array}\ \begin{array}{c} [B] \\ \Pi \\ C \\ \hline B \supset C \end{array} \atop {\displaystyle \frac{\qquad}{\begin{array}{c} C \\ \Sigma_2 \end{array}}}$$

Observe that $\begin{smallmatrix}\Sigma_1\\ B\end{smallmatrix}$, $\begin{smallmatrix}B\\ \Pi'\\ C\end{smallmatrix}$, $\begin{smallmatrix}C\\ \Sigma_2\end{smallmatrix}$ are regular. By induction the reduction of

$$\begin{array}{c} \Pi \\ B \supset C \\ \Sigma' \end{array} \qquad \begin{array}{c} \Sigma_1 \\ B \\ \Pi' \\ C \\ \Sigma_2 \end{array}$$

is regular.

$$\begin{array}{c} \Pi \\ B \vee C \\ \Sigma' \end{array} = \dfrac{\dfrac{\begin{array}{c}\Pi' \\ B\end{array}}{B \vee C} \quad \begin{array}{c}[B] \\ \Sigma_1 \\ D\end{array} \quad \begin{array}{c}[C] \\ \Sigma_2 \\ D\end{array}}{\begin{array}{c} D \\ \Sigma_3 \end{array}}$$

We have $\begin{smallmatrix}\Pi'\\ B\end{smallmatrix}$ and $\begin{smallmatrix}B\\ \Sigma'\\ D\\ \Sigma_3\end{smallmatrix}$ regular so by induction the reduction of $\begin{smallmatrix}\Pi\\ B \vee C\\ \Sigma'\end{smallmatrix}\ \begin{smallmatrix}\Pi'\\ B\\ \Sigma_1\\ D\\ \Sigma_3\end{smallmatrix}$ is also regular.

This concludes the proof of the main lemma.

In case our prooftrees contain only formulae built up from &, $\supset$, $\vee$ we can prove that last case in a simpler way. We assume here that in $\curlywedge_I$, $\curlywedge_K$ A is atomic. Let $\begin{smallmatrix}A\\ \Sigma_1\\ A_1\end{smallmatrix}, \ldots, \begin{smallmatrix}A\\ \Sigma_n\\ A_n\end{smallmatrix}$ be the main subtrees of $\begin{smallmatrix}A\\ \Sigma\end{smallmatrix}$.

By induction $\begin{smallmatrix}\Pi\\ A\\ \Sigma_1\\ A_1\end{smallmatrix}, \ldots, \begin{smallmatrix}\Pi\\ A\\ \Sigma_n\\ A_n\end{smallmatrix}$ are regular.

Using the assumptions we see that the lengths of $A_1, \dots, A_n$ are less than the length of A. Cut of $\overset{A}{\Sigma}$ at $A_1, \dots, A_n$ to get the prooftree $A \underset{\Sigma^*}{A_1 \dots A_n}$

Using lemma 2 we get $\overset{\Pi}{A}\, \underset{\Sigma^*}{A_1 \dots A_n}$ regular.

By induction

$$\begin{array}{c}\Pi\\ A\\ \Sigma\end{array} = \begin{array}{c}\Pi\\ A\\ \end{array}\; \underset{\Sigma^*}{\begin{array}{c}\Pi\\ A\\ \Pi_1\\ A_1\end{array} \cdots \begin{array}{c}\Pi\\ A\\ \Pi_n\\ A_n\end{array}}$$

is regular and we are done.

Now using the main lemma and lemma 2 we immediately have

Lemma 3. (i) *Regularity is closed under* $\supset$E, $\vee$E, E.
(ii) *Regularity is closed under* IND *with inductionterm a numeral.*
(iii) *Regularity is closed under* IND.

Theorem 1. *All prooftrees are regular.*

6. We will now prove the normalform theorem. By $\mathcal{R}$-induction it is easy to prove that all prooftrees can be reduced to a prooftree in normalform. We want to show that all reductionsequences terminate.

Definition. The order of a formula in a prooftree is the number of minorpremisses we must go through to get down from the formula to the conclusion of the prooftree.

Definition. Given two formulae A, B in a prooftree. A dominates B if either of the following holds
(i) the order of $A <$ the order of B;
(ii) they have the same order and the branch through A is to the left of the branch through B; or
(iii) they have the same order and are on the same branch and A is below B.

Lemma 4. *A dominates B is a linear well-ordering.*

To each reduction ρ of a prooftree we assign the maximal formula.

Lemma 5. *Let ρ be a reduction of Π to Π' and A the assigned formula in Π. Then the ordering of Π up to but not including A is an initial segment of the ordering in Π'.*

To each reduction we assign the initial segment given by lemma 5.

Lemma 6. *Let ρ_0 be a reduction of Π_0 to Π_1 with segment I_0 and ρ_1 a reduction of Π_1 to Π_2 with segment I_1. Assume I_1 is more than one formula less than I_0. We can then apply ρ_1 to Π_2 to get Π_2' with segment I_1. If Π_2' is different from Π_2, then there are reductions $\sigma_0, \sigma_1, ..., \sigma_n$ such that σ_0 takes Π_2' to Σ_1, σ_1 takes Σ_1 to Σ_2, ..., σ_n takes Σ_n to Π_2. The reductions $\sigma_0, ..., \sigma_n$ have segments larger than I_1 and they are all of the same kind as the reduction ρ_0.*

Definition. A reductionsequence is standard, if the segment of any reduction ρ is not more than one formula shorter than the one of the reduction which precedes ρ in the sequence.

Lemma 7. *If we have a finite reductionsequence which takes Π to Π', then there is another finite standard reductionsequence which takes Π to Π'. All the reductions in the new sequence are of types used in the old sequence.*

Lemma 8. *Given an infinite reductionsequence starting with Π, then there is another infinite standard reductionsequence starting with Π.*

Theorem 2. *All reductionsequences terminate.*

Proof. We prove by $\mathcal{R}$-induction over Π that all reductionsequences starting with Π terminate. Obvious if Π is not in $\mathcal{R}$-relation to any prooftree. Assume we have a standard infinite reductionsequence starting with Π. The proof goes now by cases:

(i) The main branch of Π has a free variable not used as an eigenvariable.
(ii) The last rule in Π is an introductionrule.
(iii) The main branch contains a maximal formula and cases (i), (ii) do not apply.
(iv) Cases (i), (ii) and (iii) do not apply.

Here (i), (ii) and (iv) are immediate. For (iii) either the downmost maximal formula in the main branches is reduced in the first step in the reductionsequence or it is contained in the segment of any reduction in the sequence. (Here we used that the sequence was standard.) The first alternative is obvious.

We give an example of what to do with the second. Say our maximal formula is $A \supset B$, and Π is

$$\dfrac{\begin{matrix}\Pi_1\\ A\end{matrix} \quad \dfrac{\begin{matrix}[A]\\ \Pi_2\\ B\end{matrix}}{A \supset B}}{\begin{matrix}B\\ \Pi_3\end{matrix}}$$

Since $A \supset B$ is included in all the segments, it will separate each prooftree in the reductionsequence in two parts. There must be either an infinite reductionsequence starting with $\begin{smallmatrix}\Pi_1\\ A\end{smallmatrix}$ or one starting with $\begin{smallmatrix}A\\ \Pi_2\\ B\end{smallmatrix}$. In the last case we also get an infinite reductionsequence starting with $\begin{smallmatrix}A\\ \Pi_2\\ B\\ \Pi_3\end{smallmatrix}$. Now $\Pi \mathcal{R} \begin{smallmatrix}\Pi_1\\ A\end{smallmatrix}, \begin{smallmatrix}A\\ \Pi_2\\ B\\ \Pi_3\end{smallmatrix}$ and we are done. Observe that we had to have $\Pi \mathcal{R} \begin{smallmatrix}\Pi_1\\ A\end{smallmatrix}$ since it could happen that there were no assumptions A above B. We do a similar analysis when the maximal formula is $A \& B$, $A \vee B$, $\forall x A x$, or $\exists x A x$. This concludes the proof.

A standard reductionsequence ending in a prooftree in normalform is uniquely determined. One always chooses the reduction with the least segment. Hence:

Theorem.3. *Given a prooftree* Π. *Then all reductionsequences starting with* Π *and ending in a normalform, end in the same normalform.*

Prawitz [5] gives also a stronger normalform.

Definition. A segment in a prooftree Π is a sequence $A_1, \ldots, A_n$ of consecutive formula occurrences in a branch such that

(i) A_1 is not the consequence of $\vee$E or $\exists$E;

(ii) A_i for each $i < n$ is a minor premiss of $\vee$E or $\exists$E; and

(iii) A_n is not the minor premiss of $\vee$E or $\exists$E.

Definition. A maximal segment is a segment that begins with a consequence of an I-rule or $\curlywedge_{\mathrm{I}}$ and ends with a major premiss of an E-rule.

Definition. A redundant application of $\vee$E or $\exists$E is an application which has a minor premiss where no assumption is closed.

Definition. A prooftree is strongly normal if it contains neither maximal segments nor redundant applications of $\vee$E or $\exists$E. (Observe that a maximal formula is a maximal segment so that a strongly normal prooftree is normal.)

Definition. A redundant variable in a prooftree is a free variable not used as an eigenvariable and which does neither occur in the conclusion nor in any open assumption.

Using rendundant variables there are trivial transformations of prooftrees to prooftrees in (strong) normalform. For instance take the prooftree $\begin{matrix}\Pi_1\\ A\\ \Pi_2\end{matrix}$ over into

$$\dfrac{\dfrac{\dfrac{\begin{matrix}\Pi_1\\ A\end{matrix} \quad 0=0}{A \,\&\, 0=0} \qquad \dfrac{\begin{matrix}\Pi_1\\ A\end{matrix} \quad a=a}{A \,\&\, a=a}}{A \,\&\, b=b}}{\begin{matrix}A\\ \Pi_2\end{matrix}}$$

Observe that the reduction of a prooftree without rendundant variables is without redundant variables.

Theorem 4. *To all prooftrees Π we can find a normal prooftree with no redundant variables and with the same conclusion and not more open assumptions as in Π.*

Theorem 5. *To all prooftrees Π we can find a strongly normal prooftree with the same conclusion and not more open assumptions and no redundant variables.*

Proof. By $\mathcal{R}$-induction over Π. Obvious if Π is not in $\mathcal{R}$-relation to any other prooftree. We divide up into cases as usual:

(i) The main branches of Π contain a free variable not used as an eigenvariable.

(ii) The last rule used is an introductionrule.

(iii) In the main branches we have a $⅄_{\mathrm{I}}$ followed by an eliminationrule.

(iv) In the main branches we have a maximal formula.

(v) In the main branches we have a redundant $\vee$E or E.

(vi) In the main branch we have only $⅄_{\mathrm{I}}$, $⅄_{\mathrm{K}}$, &E, $\supset$E, $\vee$E.

(vii) In the main branch we have only $\curlywedge_I$, $\curlywedge_K$ and E-rules but at least one $\vee$E or E, and case (i) does not apply.

Here (i) – (vi) are straightforward. Now to (vii). Take the topmost of the $\vee$E or E in the main branch. Say it was $\vee$E. Our prooftree Π is

$$\begin{array}{c} \begin{array}{ccc} \Pi_1 & \Pi_2 & \Pi_3 \\ A \vee B & C & C \end{array} \\ \hline C \\ \Pi_4 \end{array}$$

By $\mathcal{R}$-induction and the assumption we can get strongly normal prooftrees without redundant variables

$$\begin{array}{c} \Pi_1' \\ A \vee B \end{array}, \quad \begin{array}{c} \Pi_2' \\ \Pi_4' \\ D \end{array}, \quad \begin{array}{c} \Pi_3' \\ \Pi_4' \\ D \end{array}.$$

If $\begin{matrix}\Pi_2'\\ \Pi_4'\\ D\end{matrix}$ has not A as open assumption, take it as the result. Similarly if $\begin{matrix}\Pi_3'\\ \Pi_4'\\ D\end{matrix}$ has not B as open assumption. Else take

$$\begin{array}{c} \begin{array}{ccc} \Pi_1' & \Pi_2' & \Pi_3' \\ & \Pi_4' & \Pi_4' \\ A \vee B & D & D \end{array} \\ \hline D \end{array}$$

where we close the open assumptions A above D in the first minor premiss and the open assumptions B above D in the second. The proof when the topmost of the $\vee$E or $\exists$E in the main branch is $\exists$E, is similar. This concludes the proof.

There are difficulties in getting equivalents to theorem 2 and 3 for the strong normalform. Firstly it is not clear how we should reduce a maximal segment. Secondly there are no reasons why we should get uniqueness. For example

$$\begin{array}{c} \begin{array}{ccc} \begin{array}{c} \Pi_1 \\ A \\ \hline A \vee B \end{array} & \begin{array}{c} [A] \\ \Pi_2 \\ C \end{array} & \begin{array}{c} \\ \Pi_3 \\ C \end{array} \end{array} \\ \hline C \end{array}$$

has both $\begin{matrix}\Pi_3\\C\end{matrix}$ and $\begin{matrix}\Pi_1\\A\\\Pi_2\\C\end{matrix}$ as natural reductions.

7. We will now use the normalform and the strong normalform for prooftrees en NMA, NJA, NKA. The consistency of the systems is obvious since a normal proof without redundant variables of $0 = 0'$ cannot contain free variables, quantifiers, inductionrules. Using the strong normalform we can prove the results of Harrop [2] for NMA and NJA. In fact we can follow step for step the proof of Prawitz [5] of Harrops results for NM and NJ. Of course we do not have the subformulaproperty for normal and strongly normal proofs. The result of Kreisel ([4], page 331) gives hope for improved results in extended systems.

We prove our normalform theorem by use of bar induction. We could also have used ordinalassignments and transfinite induction.

References

[1] G.Gentzen, Untersuchungen über das logische Schliessen, Mathematische Zeitschrift 39 (1934) 176–210.

[2] R.Harrop, Concerning formulas of the type $A \rightarrow B \vee C, A \rightarrow (Ex)B(x)$ in intuitionistic formal systems, JSL 25 (1960) 27–32.

[3] I.Johansson, Der Minimalkalkül, ein reduzierter intuitionistischer Formalismus, Compositio matematica 4 (1936) 119–136.

[4] G.Kreisel, A survey of proof theory, JSL 33 (1968) 321–388.

[5] D.Prawitz, Natural deduction, Stockholm studies in philosophy 3 (Almquist & Wiksell, Stockholm, 1965).

[6] L.Sanchis, Functionals defined by recursion, Notre Dame Journal of Formal Logic 8 (1967) 161–174.

A SURVEY OF PROOF THEORY II

G.KREISEL
Stanford University

Abstract

This paper explains recent work in proof theory from a neglected point of view. Proofs and their representations by formal derivations are treated as principal objects of study, not as mere tools for analyzing the consequence relation. Though the paper is principally expository it also contains some material not developed in the literature. In particular, adequacy conditions on criteria for the identity of proofs (in § 1c), and a reformulation of Gödel's second theorem in terms of the notion of canonical representation (in § 1d); the use of normalization, instead of normal form, theorems for a direct proof of closure under Church's rule of the theory of species [in § 2a(ii)] and the uselessness of bar recursive functionals for (functional) interpretations of systems containing Church's thesis [in § 2b(iii)] ; the use of ordinal structures in a quantifier-free formulation of transfinite induction (in § 3); the irrelevance of axioms of choice to the explicit realizability of existential theorems both for classical and for Heyting's logical rules (in § 4c) and some new uses of Heyting's rules for analyzing the indefinite cumulative hierarchy of sets (in § 4d); a semantics for equational calculi suitable when terms are interpreted as rules for computation [in Appl. Ia(iii)], and, above all, an analysis of formalist semantics and its relation to realizability interpretations (in App. Ic). A less technical account of the present point of view is in [21].

Introduction

The main results reported in [18], which will be referred to as (SPT), concern *proof theory as a tool for studying logical consequence*; specifically, logical consequence from (subsets of) the usual axioms of analysis or set theory. The methods of proof theory are needed to establish the independence of ω-consequences such as various induction principles since, at least at present, we do not have *manageable* models which are non-standard with respect to the integers. Since consequence is a relation between formulae and sets of formulae while proof theory is concerned with derivations, the bulk of the proof theoretic machinery gets "lost" in the statements of theorems. Thus the ratio interest of results/effort involved

is unsatisfactory. In the present complement to (SPT) I shall try to improve this ratio by formulating results that do refer explicitly to the derivations and not only to the consequence relation.

In SPT and particularly [20], I stressed another unsatisfactory aspect of present day proof theory which is also connected with, so to speak, the shady role of derivations; specifically, the lack of a clear explanation of the *choices* of formal rules (studied or used). There I looked at the problem from the point of view of Hilbert's programme or, more generally, of an analysis of different *kinds* of intuitive proof; in short from an epistemological point of view. Here I wish to emphasize formal results and problems concerning *relations* **between** *proofs*, for example the *identity relation between proofs described by formal derivations of a given system* (and related topics, in §1). It must be expected, and it seems to turn out, that this study cuts across epistemological distinctions; specifically, that a formal theory of some of these relations will apply uniformly to proofs of, epistemologically, obviously different kinds. This is of course quite consistent with the impression of mathematicians, who are certainly occupied with the notion of identity of proofs, that (epistemo) logical distinctions between different kinds of proof are not useful to mathematical practice.

The formal results mentioned are mainly about *normalization procedures for natural deductions* first developed systematically by Prawitz [32] and since then also by Martin-Löf, particularly in the present volume. This whole chunk of proof theory was left out of SPT simply because I did not realize its significance. Here it is to be remarked that this part of proof theory is sometimes connected with Gentzen's ideas on the *meaning of the logical operations as rules for their use,* about which I expressed reservations in SPT, bottom of p. 329. I still have reservations which will be explained in App. I with some help from the heuristically useful distinction between *computation* and *inference* tules. But *modulo* certain conjectures in §1, the formal relations treated by Prawitz have significance independently of the possibly problematic ideas that led to them.

§2 and §3 formulate and expand some simple basic points which are hidden in the Technical Notes of SPT, resp. in the very discursive discussion of ordinal structures, pp. 333–339.

In §4 I develop a bit the remark above to the effect that (familiar) logical distinctions are not much used, by going over Heyting's own explanation of the meaning of the logical operations and his formal laws. All this was *intended* for constructive mathematics, to be interpreted in terms of constructive proofs and functions. But what is actually asserted makes little use of any detailed knowledge of constructivity. Needless to say, this fact does not cast doubt on the interest of a closer analysis; on the contrary, I mention the fact to stress the need for discovering sharper requirements on such an analysis.

It goes without saying that a reader of this article will have studied Prawitz' contribution to the present volume where the main ideas of normalization are described. (After all, as mentioned already, SPT II was written principally because the subject of normalization had been neglected in SPT.) Here I surround these main results, in the style of my earlier expositions, with comments on their significance, some more or less obvious consequences, and open problems. Experience suggests that, at least at the present stage of proof theory, there is need for this kind of information to be sure that we are really dealing with "main" results. Actually the text below overlaps a little with Prawitz' [37] in that there are *some* indications of the main ideas; the indications are given not because I thought it necessary (or possible for me) to improve on his exposition of basic principles but because the two papers were written during the same period and so I could not refer to the details of [37].

1. Proof versus consequence

The general nature of our problem is quite clear. Consider *formal rules* which are intended to formalize certain *proofs*; in other words, we have syntactic objects, derivations, d which represent or decribe mental acts $\bar{d}$, the proofs (which carry conviction); cf. [22] p. 196 for an elementary discussion of the relation between d and $\bar{d}$, or the "mapping": $d \to \bar{d}$, which is a particular case of the general relation between words and the thoughts they express. Since we are dealing with a "small" class of words, we can hope for more precise results than are known for the more general (and more familiar!) relation. We must expect more detailed results for formal rules which are intended to codify reasoning about proofs, for example Heyting's systems, than for formal rules, specifically classical ones, whose intended interpretation refers to truth (and not, explicitly, to proofs); cf. §2a(i).

Given a property P of or a relation R between proofs our task is to find relations P_F, resp. R_F such that for all d of our formal system

$$P_F(d) \text{ iff } P(\bar{d}) \quad \text{and} \quad R_F(d,d') \text{ iff } R(\bar{d},\bar{d}') .$$

For exposition, we shall reverse this procedure, and first describe some formal relations P_F, R_F which will then be used to state the facts about the objects of principal interest, namely properties and relations of proofs.

Superficially, the single most striking consequence of the view of proof theory just described, is certainly this. *Different styles of formalization previously judged only by aesthetic criteria of elegance or convenience acquire independent significance*; cf. end of (a) and (c) below.

(a) *Normal derivations and conversions.* Ever since Gentzen's original work there has been stress on special "normal" derivations, with different analyses of what is essential about these derivations (cf. middle of p. 329 of SPT). Here the special role of these normal derivations will be that they serve as *canonical representations* of all proofs represented in the system considered, the way the numerals are canonical notations for the natural numbers.

A minimum requirement is then that *any derivation can be normalized,* that is transformed into a unique normal form by a series of steps, so-called "conversions", each of which preserves the proof described by the derivation. This requirement has a formal and an informal part:
(α) The *formal* problem of establishing that the conversions terminate in a unique normal form (independent of the order in which they are applied).
(βi) The *informal* recognition (by inspection) that the conversion steps considered preserve identity, and the informal problem of showing that
(βii) distinct, that is incongruent normal derivations represent different proofs (in order to have unique, canonical, representations).

For examples of remarkable progress with the formal problem see the work of Martin-Löf and Prawitz in this volume. The particular conversion procedures considered evidently satisfy requirement (βi) since each conversion step merely contracts the introduction of a logical symbol immediately followed by its elimination. Such a contraction clearly does not change the proof described by the two formal derivations (before and after contraction).

Discussion. We can now restate the significance of the distinction described in SPT, p. 329, Ex. 2, between completeness of the normal derivations (in the sense that to each derivation there exists some normal derivation with the same end formula, for short: a normal form theorem) and normalization by explicitly prescribed, deterministic or non-deterministic procedures. *A normal form theorem leaves open the informal requirement* (βi) *above.* Provided of course proper attention is paid to (βi) (as in the remarks on the particular procedure of Prawitz and Martin-Löf), *a normalization theorem is the proper tool for the study of* (βi).

As stressed in SPT, p. 364, contrary to a common misconception the distinction is *not* to be analyzed in terms of constructivity, in the sense that model theoretic proofs of normal form theorems *can* be made constructive. SPT treats first order logic. In the case of higher order logic, if "constructive" is interpreted as meaning: formalized in the theory of species, Prawitz' proof of the normal form theorem in [33] is made constructive in Technical Note II of [19]. (As is well-known, cf. SPT §12, pp. 351, 352, this is not the meaning of "constructive" used in the bulk of existing proof theory.) However, generally speaking, the natural proof of a normalization theorem has turned out to be constructive (in the sense described) as it stands[1].

Naturally the point of view, stressed at the beginning of this subsection concerning the significance of different styles of formalization, requires us to reconsider familiar criteria of "equivalence". Formalizations which we find significantly different from the present point of view, may have the *same set of theorems*, and this fact will in general be proved by quite elementary methods. A fortiori, they are equivalent as far as those subclasses of theorems are concerned which are involved in so-called proof theoretic strength. (This measure, proper to Hilbert's programme, is quite inappropriate here.) As a corollary the point of view opens up new areas of formal work. Consider specifically a calculus of sequents and a system of natural deduction. Inspection shows that many cut elimination procedures for calculi of sequents do not obviously satisfy the informal requirement (βi), and also that the normalization procedure for systems of natural deduction does not correspond to a particularly natural cut elimination procedure. Consequently we shall have to look at the usual formulations of a calculus of sequents, vary the *order* in which different cuts are considered, and see if different orders lead to non-congruent cut-free derivations (or even, for some systems, that the procedure does not terminate at all). In this case the formal requirement (α) would not be fulfilled (in contrast to the case of natural deduction treated by Prawitz and Martin-Löf). Note that (α) follows from (β) since by (βi) all conversions

[1] It often happens when we ask for *more* (information), the *natural* solution is more elementary; for an analysis of Hilbert's ϵ-substitution method from this point of view see [17] p. 168, 3.351. For actual research it would be important to be more specific in order to know which methods are likely to succeed (naturally) with a given kind of problem! But it is hard to analyze the existing evidence. Certainly, "theoretical" results on the existence of a logically more elementary solution are available, but they do not seem relevant to the practical question of discovery. For example, let A be a first order assertion about fields; if A is true for the field Q of real rationals the proof may require transcendental axioms; if A holds for all real fields, not only for Q, there *exists* a first order proof (from the first order axioms for real fields). But the most natural proof may well involve definitions of a real closure and set theoretic operations on it which are not even definable in the (first order) language of fields. Similarly the mere existence of a constructive proof of the normal form theorems does not ensure that the natural, or at least first, proof *is* constructive. (In the first order case it was, in the second order it was not.)

are supposed to preserve identity of proof and by (βii) *must* terminate in congruent normal forms; but (α) alone does not ensure (β). For more detail on these matters, see p. 91 of Prawitz' monograph [32].

The kind of work proposed here is the sort of *Kleinarbeit* which is generally needed to support a genuine hypothesis (here: concerning the *adequacy* of the normalization theorem for identity criteria on proofs) as opposed to a mere mathematical fancy. Specifically it is needed because we can hardly hope that existing formalizations such as those in [32] are *exactly* right for the new applications, for instance those of (b) and (c) below. After all, the systems were developed for other reasons, logical or aesthetic.

Remark. The principal technical tool used by Prawitz and Martin-Löf for normalizing deductions in the theory of species was introduced by Girard [56]. Independently Girard used his ideas to establish the termination of a certain cut-elimination procedure, thus giving a new proof of Takeuti's "fundamental conjecture" for analysis. I have not had an opportunity to study whether Girard's procedure preserves identity of proofs.

(b) *Normal derivations of existential formulae.* Evidently, besides relations on proofs it makes good sense to consider relations between *proofs, assertions* and *definitions*; correspondingly we have formal relations between *derivations, formulae* and *terms*. There is a very natural relation which has been much discussed in the (constructive) literature, namely

the definition $\bar{t}$ is provided by the proof $\bar{d}$ of the existential assertion $\overline{\exists x A}$;

cf. Problem 1 on p. 125 of [19] for an elementary discussion. Though quite special it will turn out that this relation is quite useful.

An important property of *normal derivations* (as defined by Prawitz et al.) is that they allow us *to read off t from a derivation d of* $\exists x A$; more precisely there is a mechanical method of obtaining the term t from d (which term we recognize as defining the realization provided by $\bar{d}$). Obviously there is a mechanical method of deciding whether d is a derivation of an existential formula. For reference below note that t may contain parameters not occurring in $\exists x A$, for instance if the endpart of d derives $\exists x A$ from $\forall x A$ or from $A[x/t_1] \vee A[x/t_2]$.

Note that, by (a), the analysis of the relation above requires genuinely a normalization and not only a normal form theorem.

(c) *Formulating one-sided adequacy conditions on criteria for the identity of proofs.* As stressed by Prawitz [37], his normalization procedures obviously preserve identity of proofs. Our problem here, (βii) in (a), of deciding whether convertibility to congruent normal forms is *equivalent* to identity of proof, is more delicate. I shall formulate a, demonstrably only partial criterion[2] and afterwards go into the general nature of the problem. To repeat from the discussion in (a): it is not claimed that *exactly* the conversion relations studied in the literature are adequate. (*Added in proof*: see also fn. 20.)

We consider deductions in predicate logic, not arbitrary ones, but of formulae of the form

$$B \to \exists x A \,.$$

(i) We suppose that the relation $\equiv$ between formal derivations (with the same end formula) evidently preserves identity of proofs, i.e., in symbols

$$d_1 \equiv d_2 \Rightarrow \bar{d}_1 = \bar{d}_2 \,.$$

(ii) For further progress we try to derive from $\bar{d}_1 = \bar{d}_2$, the primitive relation under study, some mathematically manageable consequence, say $M(d_1,d_2)$, fulfilling the purely mathematical condition:

(iii) $$M(d_1,d_2) \Rightarrow d_1 \equiv d_2 \,.$$

If we succeed we shall have "trapped" our primitive relation and can infer

$$d_1 \equiv d_2 \Leftrightarrow \bar{d}_1 = \bar{d}_2 \,.$$

A candidate for $M(d_1,d_2)$. Let d_1 and d_2 be derivations in predicate logic of $B \to \exists x A$. Consider any formal system F such as the theory of species which includes predicate logic and is normalizable, the normalization steps satisfying (βi) of (a); we do *not* need here that F satisfies (βii) (fortunately, since (βii) for predicate logic is the principal issue here!). For each substitution instance $B^* \to \exists x A^*$ of $B \to \exists x A$, let d_1^* and d_2^* denote the corresponding substitutions in d_1 and d_2 resp. For any derivation d^* of B^*, let d_1^0 and d_2^0 be obtained by joining d_1^*, resp. d_2^* to d^*. Both d_1^0 and d_2^0 are derivations of $\exists x A^*$ in F and, by (b), provide terms t_1 and t_2 as realizations.

$M(d_1,d_2)$ asserts: for all derivations d^* of substitution instances B^* the corresponding terms t_1 and t_2 define *extensionally* equal functions. Then

[2] Prawitz has helped me find the proof that the criterion is partial.

$M(d_1,d_2)$ satisfies (ii), extensional equality being manageable (cf. § 2b below); hence $\neg M(d_1,d_2) \Rightarrow \neg \bar{d}_1 = \bar{d}_2$.

But $M(d_1,d_2)$ does *not* generally satisfy (iii): it provides only a *partial* criterion that is, there are d_1 and d_2 for which $d_1 \not\equiv d_2$, but the use of M described above does not ensure that $\bar{d}_1 \neq \bar{d}_2$ (in other words, at the present stage the exact significance of the relation $\equiv$ is open for such d_1, d_2).

Let B be true (and hence B^* derivable) and take for A a suitable formula $\exists x(x=c \wedge P)$ with P independent of x, e.g.,

$$\exists x(x=c \wedge [(p \wedge \neg p) \rightarrow (p \rightarrow p)]) .$$

Clearly *any* proof will provide the realization c. But we have two clearly different proofs of

$$(p \wedge \neg p) \rightarrow (p \rightarrow p)$$

(and hence of the whole formula); namely one ignores the conclusion (ex falso quodlibet), the other ignores the premise ($p \rightarrow p$ being valid).

Discussion. To get perspective on the proposed (partial) criterion, it seems instructive to consider the familiar analysis of the notion of *logical validity* (from Frege's formulation of rules of inference to Gödel's completeness proof). The primitive notion of identity of proof is to correspond to logical validity, perhaps with the subclass of deductions considered here corresponding to the restriction to *first* order language. Then (i) above corresponds to the fact that Frege's formal rules evidently preserve logical validity. The "manageable" property M in (ii) corresponds to the mathematical property of validity in all countable domains (Skolem-Löwenheim). And the parallel to (iii) is provided by Gödel's completeness proof. For *subclasses* of the first order language, for instance for purely universal formulae, we can replace "validity in countable domains" by "validity in finite domains". For second order formulae we do not have formal rules (as is well-known), but also we do not have an equally manageable property M, second order validity being sensitive to open questions about the existence of large cardinals (cf. [22], pp. 190–191). In the latter case we operate with partial criteria, obtained by reflection on specific matters such as the existence of, say Π_1^1-indescribable cardinals. It is safe to say that proposed adequacy conditions for identity criteria need not be complete (but of course they must settle some interesting open question).

A much more serious objection to the criterion (than its partial character) is this. The proposed proofs of adequacy *evade* rather than solve questions about the nature of the identity of proofs or, indeed, about the nature of proofs. For what we propose to show, for specific derivations, is that questions of the adequacy of $\equiv$ can be settled without closer analysis of the concepts involved. But, at the present time, the criterion above has a pedagogic use: it corrects the common assumption that "nothing" precise (and reasonable) can be done on questions about synonymity of proofs.

Remark. At the risk of trying to explain *obscurum per obscurius*, I should point out a striking analogy between the problem of finding (α) a conversion relation corresponding to identity of proofs and (β) an "equivalence" relation such as that of *combinatorial equivalence* in topology corresponding to a basic invariant in our geometric concepts. Quite often it is difficult to formulate explicit adequacy conditions on (β) in advance (our confidence in a proposed equivalence relation may well depend on the quality of the proposer). The use of different styles of formalization mentioned in (a) above, may be compared to the use of different coordinate systems in geometry, where one system is often particularly suited for the study of a specific geometric relation, "suited" not only in the sense of being manageable, but the passage from one co-ordinate system to another may introduce singularities without geometric meaning such as the indeterminateness of the second polar co-ordinate at the origin.

(d) *Further illustrations: Gödel's second theorem.* The reader who shares my confidence in striking examples (and perhaps also my skepticism about isolating *the* central problem at an early stage of research) may wish to look at familiar material which is most naturally formulated in terms of *proofs* rather than *consequence*. I think Gödel's second theorem is an excellent example.

We shall consider *consistent* formal systems. So, as far as the set of theorems is concerned, the question whether A and $\neg A$ both occur, will not arise at all!

Here a moment's thought shows that, in vivid language, *it is not even sufficient to identify a formal system with its set of deductions, we have to consider the manner in which we verify that a syntactic object is a deduction,* in short we have to consider the formal rules. (I shall take these rules to be given by their production rules.) For, consider any formal system F you know, and define F^* as follows (cf. [17], p. 154, 3.221).

An object d is a deduction of F^* if it is (i) a deduction of F and (ii) for all deductions d', d'' of F (with Godel number) $\leqslant d$, d' does not lead to a formula which is the formal negation of the formula derived by d''.

Now, if F is consistent, F^* has *exactly* the same deductions as F, only the verification of the property of being a deduction is longer, corresponding to step (ii). Evidently there is a perfectly elementary proof of the consistency of F^*. Equally evidently, different (in fact, *not* demonstrably equivalent) formulae *express* the proof relations of F and F^* and hence their consistency. The formal notion of *canonical representation* in 3.222 on p. 154 of [17] gives an *analysis of the concept of* **expressing** *the proof relations of F and F** *which is adequate for the present problem* (of formulating Gödel's second theorem properly). Though not stated in [17], similar conditions determine, up to provable isomorphism, the *canonical* Gödel numbering of finite sequences (of $a_1, ..., a_n$ say) with the following structure: the empty sequence is a distinguished element, and for each a_i, adjunction of a_i and its inverse is an operation; cf. e.g. [23], p. 256, 2.5.3.

Remark. There is an additional point to be observed here which, however, does not involve attention to derivations; consequence is sufficient. It is sometimes said that Gödel's theorem applies to systems which "contain arithmetic" (or, more explicitly, *modus ponens* and are complete for numerical arithmetic). Clearly, in the ordinary sense of the word, F^* contains as much arithmetic as F! The natural formulation runs quite simply as follows.

Given F and formulae A_1, A_2, A_3 of F, one of the following cannot be derived in F:

A_1 expresses (in terms of canonical representations) that F is closed under modus ponens, and A_1 holds.

A_2 expresses that F is complete for numerical arithmetic (in fact complete with respect to a specific primitive recursive predicate, of course canonically represented), and A_2 holds.

A_3 expresses that F is consistent, and A_3 holds.

It is perfectly natural that in Gödel's original paper not much attention was given to a proper formulation. First of all, at the time the importance of normal derivations had not been realized, and hence, for the usual systems, formulae A_1 and A_2 could always be found. Secondly, as far as Hilbert's programme was concerned the absence of A_1 or A_2 constitutes the *same kind of inadequacy* as of A_3: we should have no reason to suppose that F codifies mathematical practice. (I say "the same kind" because of course Hilbert's programme, as he formulated it, does not require the adequacy conditions to be proved within the system studied.)

Summarizing, we see that not only deductions, treated as extensional objects, are relevant here (over and above the set of consequences), but even additional information or "structure", namely the sequence of operations involved in building up the deductions.

(e) *Note on the consistency problem* (supplementing SPT, p. 323 and pp. 360–361). The following points are elementary.

The consistency *results* do not express at all well the mathematical content of the consistency proofs; specifically (by SPT, Technical Note II, on reflection principles, conservative extensions and commuting models) we now have the concepts needed to express their content both elegantly and much more informatively; cf. also the end of b(ii) in App. I. Also (cf. SPT, Technical Note I) some of Hilbert's assumptions connecting consistency proofs with *reliability* seem unjustified. But, to avoid misunderstanding, it should be remembered that we *do* have perfectly genuine consistency proofs in the sense that the metamathematical methods used are *patently* more elementary than the intended interpretation (which led to the formal system studied; and not only in the case where there are simply doubts about the consistency as is SPT, p. 325, l. 12–13). For example, in the case of arithmetic with induction restricted to purely universal formulae, the methods used by Herbrand or Gentzen are evidently more elementary than the set theoretic conception of the structure of arithmetic; equally, we have of course also model theoretic methods, where an ingenious model may use significantly more elementary existential assumptions than the obvious or "standard" model; cf. SPT, Technical Note IV. These observations are quite consistent with the fact that, *in special cases,* for example in Gentzen's consistency proof for arithmetic by ϵ_0-induction, the situation is more delicate. Since, practically speaking, the non-constructive conception of natural number is not genuinely problematic, and also the validity of ϵ_0-induction is certainly not immediately *seen*, the epistemological value of Gentzen's proof depends on a more delicate analysis of kinds of evidence. (Naturally more is written on such open questions which require attention than on the many consistency proofs with a clear-cut epistemological conclusion.) At least at the present stage of analysis the methods developed for his proof seem to me to have led to more interesting results for other application such as those discussed in (a) above than for the original consistency problem.

Remark. The fact that simple-minded problems concerning consistency or, more generally, *reliability* of principles should have led to significant distinctions *among* rèliable principles seems to me typical of a quite general pattern (just as in physics naive problems concerning *reality*, e.g. of light, led to significant distinctions *among* the objects of the real world). Naturally it is not suggested that the uses of these distinctions, specifically between normal and other derivations, have been exhausted! To mention only one example, implicit in (b) above, in connection with *length* or "feasibility" of constructions: the length of a non-normal derivation of $\exists xA$ may be much smaller than the numerical value of the realization which it provides. In short, "*ordinary*" *logical inference spoils feasibility*. (As observed by Takeuti, for normal derivations in his "cut-free" analysis this is not the case.)

2. Operations on derivations: syntactic transformations and functional interpretations

In contrast to §1 which treats matters that were neglected in SPT, the present section is concerned with a familiar distinction (cf. [17], pp. 159–160, 3.31) between the two general methods of proof theory mentioned in its heading. Typical syntactic transformations are normalization and cut-elimination procedures introduced by Gentzen. Typical functional interpretations are the no-counterexample-interpretation [14] or Gödel's [7]; also Herbrand's theorem can be viewed as such an interpretation (cf. [14]) though he himself did not do so (other points of difference are explained at the end of this section). Though implicit in the literature there are some simple general points about *areas of useful application* of these two methods which do not seem to have been stated explicitly. Since we are concerned with uses, the differences are more important than the similarities: given a problem we want a hint on which method is more likely to apply. Similarities will be gone into in App. I in connection with Prawitz' homomorphism between deductions and terms (proofs and functions-as-rules). For expository reasons we shall also defer, to §3, all *quantitative* refinements of these two methods in terms of ordinals (or, more pedantically, ordinal structures); there has been so much work on this aspect that a report on it here would distort the general picture.

Let me state quite briefly three practical conclusions which are formulated more precisely below.

(α) Syntactic transformations concentrate on *proofs* and need only very elementary functions; the interpretations (mentioned above, not realizability which is a hybrid) concentrate on *functions*, that is definition principles, and use only very elementary proofs, for detail, see (aiii) and (biii) below.

(β) Syntactic transformations are specially adapted for obtaining *derived rules*, generally speaking because normal derivations are so simple. Thus normal form theorems are often sufficient for this purpose.

(γ) Interpretations are useful for obtaining independence results from a *schema*. By varying the interpretation principle or the class of functionals considered, a whole schema can be made valid for an interpretation.

(a) *Syntactic transformations* map derivations $\in \mathcal{D}$ into the (sub) class $\mathcal{D}_N$ of *normal* derivations. Naturally the applications may depend merely on structural properties of normal derivations, not on the particular transformation used, in which case a *normal form theorem* is sufficient. Obviously, if a normal form theorem is true for the pair $(\mathcal{D}, \mathcal{D}_N)$ there is always *some* recursive mapping: $\mathcal{D} \to \mathcal{D}_N$ preserving end formulae: given a derivation $d \in \mathcal{D}$, run through $\mathcal{D}_N$ until you find $d' \in \mathcal{D}_N$ with the same end formula as d.

(i) In SPT, p. 329 and particularly p. 348(b) I stressed those normal derivations which possess the *subformula* property. The most striking consequence is that *if* an application of a normal form theorem depends on this particular property, for systems including induction it is an advantage to consider *infinite* normal proof figures[3]. (And even here we have limitations for recursive figures since there are, demonstrably, none satisfying the subformula property if bar induction is included; cf. [17], p. 167, 3.343 and SPT, p. 348(b).) At the present time, as far as I know, applications of normal forms in *classical* systems depend on the subformula property.

Digression on infinite proof figures. As a result of correspondence with Prawitz it seems desirable to expand my earlier remarks on this subject, in SPT, footnote 3 on p. 324 or p. 332(b). Firstly we have the point of principle, the *representation* of our thoughts, that is of proofs, by means of such infinite proof figures. There is no question that the latter are more explicit than finite proof figures, yet manageable enough. The (extensional) proof figures are *not complete* representations; as a minimum one would add a *description* (e.g. at

[3] We say proof *figure* and not proof *tree* because, for comparison with (ii), it is better to allow a formula A as a premise of two or more inferences, we do not require separate proofs for each occurrence of A. (As usual, we suppose the proof figure to be given not merely by a partial ordering relation, but with additional structure associating the premises of a formula to it.)

each node a description of the figure "below" the node) together with a proof *that* the figure is properly built up. This corresponds to a familiar procedure in technical proof theory spelt out in the clearest possible terms in [17], p. 163 bottom; cf. also c(ii) below. From the general point of view stressed in the present article concerning the problematic character of constructive logical operators, it is to be stressed that the proofs to be added to the extensional proof figure (for a more complete representation of our intensions) establish *logic free assertions*. At the time when SPT was written there was not even an attempt in the literature of making explicit a *meaning* of finite derivations. Only in the present volume do we have Prawitz's analysis [37] by use of his *validity predicate* for deductions, albeit in a logically complicated form. (Earlier uses of, formally similar, computability predicates made *no* contribution to the present problem of explaining *what* is being coded by finite derivations.) Secondly we have the mathematical point, in my opinion of paramount importance for the intelligibility of the subject, of giving an *intrinsic meaning to the ordinals used in this part of proof theory*, mentioned in SPT, p. 332 (b). The infinite proof figures were the *only* objects which had an intrinsic connection with ordinals. The situation has changed with normalization problems where *specific* well founded reduction figures are principal objects of study; cf. §3a(ii). Evidently the interest of these figures is contingent on the interest of the *specific* reduction processes, and it was for that reason that I went out on a limb in §1 to search for such an interest. (Here ends the digression.)

Returning now to applications of normal forms, for Heyting's systems (and in contrast to the classical case considered earlier on) the subformula property is not essential. Specifically, for normal forms *derived rules* are evident, generally of the following form: for A of suitable syntactic structure

if $A \to \exists x B$ is derivable so is $A \to B[x/t]$ for some term t

and thus $\exists x(A \to B)$ where x is not free in A; cf. [17], p. 160, 3.322. (They are genuine derived *rules* in the sense that the implication $(A \to \exists x B) \to \exists x(A \to B)$ is not derivable.) Despite massive work in this area it is not generally realized that such *conditional explicit definability results are much more useful than* (the more familiar) *absolute ones*; for the simple reason that the *former extend automatically when axioms of the structure of A are added to the system considered*; cf. [17] loc. cit. or p. 269 of [33]. As mentioned many derived rules have the form above, including Markov's rule, discussed at length in Troelstra's article in the present volume [46]. (It should perhaps be remarked that, in formal arithmetic, $\forall x(A \vee \neg A) \to \neg\neg \exists x A$ may be derivable, even if $\forall x(A \vee \neg A) \to \exists x A$ is not; take $T(e,e,x) \vee \forall y \neg T(e,e,y)$ for A with parameter e; or constant e if $\exists x T(e,e,x)$ is not formally decidable.)

Two remarks seem to me pertinent here. Firstly, about the derived rules specifically, it should be noted that they are *not* linked to the constructive interpretation of Heyting's systems. On the one hand, as will be explained in §4, *not* even the disjunctive property is *required by* a sound interpretation; on the other as seen by adding (constructively) invalid axioms of the structure of A, constructive soundness is *not needed for* the derived rules. Secondly, about normal forms generally: though for some applications the subformula property is not required we do not expect (and do not get) all important properties of normal deductions in the first order case where we do have the subformula property. For example, the *interpolation lemma* can fail. (By SPT, p. 357 (iv) this does not cast doubt on the notion of normal form, but rather on the choice of language.)

(ii) An application which, at present, involves a *normalization* theorem in an interesting way, is the proof of: *closure under Church's rule*. The normal form theorem yields immediately the result: if $\forall x \exists y A(x,y)$ is derivable there is a recursion equation with number e_0 such that, for each numeral n, $A(n, \{e_0\}(n))$ is derivable where $\{e_0\}(n)$ denotes the numerical value of the function defined by e_0 at the argument n. The issue is to show that the universal formula $\forall x A(x, \{e_0\}(x))$ is also derivable in the system considered. (To be precise; I mean here the e_0 corresponding to the mechanical rule: run through the formal derivations till you hit the first one whose end formula has the form $A(n,m)$ with numeral m and associate this m to n.) Note that strictly speaking, we do not need a normalization theorem, but only this: given a proof of $\forall x \exists y A(x,y)$ in S we need a proof in S itself *that*, for each numeral n, $\exists y A(n,y)$ has a normal derivation in a suitable subsystem S_0; "suitable" means that the reflection principle for S_0 can be established in S. In Note II of [19], closure under Church's rule is obtained by combining Prawitz' *classical* proof [33] of the normal form theorem for the theory of species and a corollary to Spector's description [43] in his system Σ_4 of the provably recursive functions of classical analysis namely:

> Classical analysis, with or without axioms of choice ([19], p. 135, 1.17-19), is *conservative* for $\forall$E formulae over the theory of species.

In [19] the corollary is obtained from a *model* (in the theory of species) for Σ_4, which can now be replaced by a (simpler) proof of computability of Σ_4 by use of Girard's work [56] (or directly by [56] without mention of Σ_4).

As mentioned in § 1a, the recent normalization theorems make this detour via [33] unnecessary. More importantly, by § 1b they yield more; namely for a derivation d_n of $\exists y A(n,y)$, a term t_n defining the object $\bar{x}$ provided by the proof $\bar{d}_n$. Since from a given derivation d of $\forall x \exists y A(x,y)$ we obtain d_n canonically by substitution, the normalization procedure also provides a recursion equation e_1 such that

$$\forall x A(x, \{e_1\}(x)) \text{ is derivable } \textit{and } t_n^* = \{e_1\}(n)$$

(where t_n^* is some closed term obtained from t_n if the latter contains parameters; cf. [19] §1). Note that in general $\{e_0\}(n) \neq \{e_1\}(n)$, again by [19] §1; however e_1 cannot be said to be *the* rule provided by $\bar{d}$ as the intended meaning of the quantifier-combination $\forall\exists$ in $\forall x \exists y A$ [cf. App. Ia(i) for the defects of Kleene's T predicate for the present purpose].

(iii) Finally, a word about property (α) mentioned at the beginning of this section. The description of the (infinite) proof figures in (i) and the *immediate* reduction or normalization relation (not its transitive closure) in (ii) can be given by use of Kalmar elementary definitions; not even all primitive recursive ones are needed. This fact is plausible because well-orderings are involved and all recursive well-orderings are embeddable in an order preserving way in *Kalmar elementary ones* [12]; what has to be checked is that the embeddings are elementary too (and can be proved to be so by applying induction to elementary predicates; concerning this last and absolutely basic restriction, cf. [17] p. 165, 3.3322). It is in this sense that *syntactic transformations concentrate on proofs* (of elementary free variable statements) *and do not involve* (more than a minimum of) *functions.*

Though perhaps no more than a remark, the property of syntactic transformations just mentioned provides a useful concrete background for the discussion in §4 of Heyting's meaning of the logical operations[4].

[4] I have often stressed an analogy between set-theoretic and constructive foundations: while *types* (of sets) and *proofs* (at least of identities) are essential to foundations, they do not enter as objects of study into practice. Amusingly, we also have parallel objections! J.P.Serre once complained in conversation about the fuss logicians make about types since nobody uses the axiom of foundation anyway; and, he added, if you want it you simply *define* the collection of those sets which are hereditarily well founded. Scott, in [50], p. 239, l.-10 to l.-9, expresses very clearly similar misgivings about the role of proofs in constructive foundations. Pushed beyond reason, Serre's view blocks any chance of a convincing reason for Zermelo's "restriction" of Frege's inconsistent version of the comprehension principle and Scott's view blocks any chance, at least at present, of a non-circular explanation of implication; cf. also App. Ic(ii).

(b) *Functional interpretations* have the following general form ([17] p. 158, 3.301-3.303 or SPT p. 378–379). We associate with each formula A a formula $\exists s A_0(s)$ such that, if A is true so is $\exists s A_0(s)$ with s ranging over a "large" class F^+ of functions or functionals, and if $\exists s A_0(s)$ is proved by restricted methods, $\exists s A_0(s)$ is true if s ranges over a smaller, usually explicitly generated class F^-. If A_0 is logically complicated, the two statements are not comparable (because the ranges of the quantifiers inside A_0 will generally also be different). But if, for example, A_0 is purely universal, and if the smaller range of s is dense in the large range, for some topology on which the functionals considered are continuous, then $(\exists s \in F^-)A_0^-$ is stronger than $(\exists s \in F^+)A_0^+$. (This condition is satisfied by the interpretations mentioned at the beginning of this section.) In other words, such interpretations show clearly *what more we know when we have proved a theorem than if we only know that it is true.*

Though connections between syntactic transformations and functional interpretations do exist (and will be referred to repeatedly in this text), at the present time the single most important feature of the latter is their *simplicity*, particularly when classes of extensional functionals suffice for one's purpose, for example, for *independence results*. Now, if A is proved we not only have that $(\exists s \in F^-)A_0^-$ is true, but we have a mapping: $d \to s_d$, such that if d derives A in the formal system studied then $A_0(s_d)$ can be derived in the system, say $\mathcal{G}$, which supplies the interpretation. So, for independence of A, it is enough to find *some* class C of functionals satisfying $\mathcal{G}$, such that $A_0(s)$ is *false for all* $s \in C$. If A is independent for, so to speak, brutal reasons, any class C will do provided it satisfies very simple conditions; cf. also (iii) below.

It is not necessary here to go into the use of interpretations for independence results from schemata, i.e., property (γ) mentioned at the beginning of the section, because it is very well illustrated by Troelstra's exposition in [46]. (A reader who wants to compare independence proofs from a schema by means of normal forms with uses of interpretations may consider the independence of the schema M from IP in 5.2 of Troelstra's paper [46].)

(i) The well-known independence proofs of the law of the excluded middle, with variables f for sequences of type $0 \to 0$,

$$\forall f \exists n [fn=0 \vee \forall m(fm \neq 0)]$$

interpreted by

$$\exists N \forall f [f(Nf)=0 \vee \forall m(fm \neq 0)] ,$$

use only continuity of N for the product topology on sequences of natural numbers.

(ii) Again, often only the *recursive* character (in any of the various senses described in Troelstra's article [46]) of the functionals considered need be used; despite the fact that for any formalized $\mathcal{T}$, we shall have realizations (models) by recursively enumerable *subclasses* of the class of recursive functionals.

Of course the same applies to closure under Church's rule discussed in (a) (ii) above: the e's can be found in the recursively enumerable set of *demonstrable* recursion equations, that is equations that can be proved in the system considered to define a (total) function.

(iii) Coming now to *limitations* of functional interpretations we distinguish between those connected with the syntactic form of the interpretation $\exists s A_0$ of the formula A and those connected with the particular range of the variable occurring in A_0. As an example of the former we have formulae A where s does not occur in A_0 at all. This will happen, generally speaking when A is a purely universal formula (and quantifier-free formulae are decidable). In this case, the "brutal" method sketched cannot be expected to help in establishing the independence of A.

An interesting example of the second kind of limitation is provided by the socalled bar recursive functions of finite type introduced by Spector [43]. They demonstrably *satisfy the interpretation* [7] *of the negation of Church's thesis.* Indeed, by [43], p. 19, (12.1.1) they satisfy the interpretation of

$$\neg\neg\forall x \exists y \forall z\, [T(x,x,y) \vee \neg T(x,x,z)]$$

for Kleene's T, but also

$$\neg \exists e \forall x \exists v \forall z\, \{T(e,x,v) \wedge [T(x,x,Uv) \vee \neg T(x,x,z]\}$$

since this formula is a theorem of first order intuitionistic arithmetic. But this conflicts with Church's thesis (indeed with its double negation)

$$\forall x \exists y A(x,y) \rightarrow \exists e \forall x \exists v\, [T(e,x,v) \wedge A(x,Uv)]\ .$$

Recently Professor Gödel has pointed out to me a more elegant proof. The system Σ_2, described [43] p. 6 is *formally inconsistent* with Church's thesis; (added in proof) cf. also chapter IX of [60]. Since T is decidable

$$\neg\neg\exists y\forall z\,[T(x,x,y)\vee\neg T(x,x,z)]$$

is a theorem of arithmetic. But so by axiom F

$$\forall x\neg\neg P\rightarrow\neg\neg\forall xP$$

taking $\exists y\forall z\,[T(x,x,y)\vee\neg T(x,x,z)]$ for P, we get a contradiction with Church's thesis. (However, it seems plausible that Σ_2 is closed under Church's *rule*.)

It would be interesting to see whether the function schemata used by Girard have models (for example the one consisting of the hereditarily computable terms) for which the interpretation of Church's thesis *is* satisfied. This would constitute a clear-cut advantage of the functions in [56] over the bar recursive functions.

Discussion. It cannot be stressed too much that limitations of the kind described do not spoil the *practical value* of interpretations. Quite generally, we must expect interpretations with a *familiar* range of functionals (which makes the interpretation easy to handle) to be *incomplete*, i.e., we must expect that $(\exists s\in F^{\neg})A_0^{\neg}$ can be true even if A is not provable. After all, we know that the full complex of logical relationships is complicated: it would be foolish to expect a method (here: interpretation) which is both generally applicable *and* simple in cases of special interest to us.

Remark. To avoid misunderstanding, in connection with the topic of criteria for the *identity* of proofs, it is perhaps worth mentioning that we can easily introduce *some* equivalence relation between derivations even if we consider only *extensional* equality (between terms). Using the notation above, and an interpretation in $\mathcal{G}$, we define $\underset{\mathcal{G}}{\equiv}$ by:

$$d\underset{\mathcal{G}}{\equiv}d' \text{ if } s_d \text{ and } s_{d'} \text{ are } \textit{extensionally} \text{ equal.}$$

For example, let us take the two derivations, say d and d', of

$$(p\wedge\neg p)\rightarrow(p\rightarrow p)$$

mentioned in the *Discussion* of § 1a. Then, for practically any interpretation $\mathcal{G}$, we find $\neg d\underset{\mathcal{G}}{\equiv}d'$. Of course it would in general be absurd to suppose that

$$d\underset{\mathcal{G}}{\equiv}d' \Leftrightarrow \bar{d}=\bar{d}'\,.$$

We need a separate investigation, in terms of adequacy conditions, as in § 1(c).

(c) *Metamathematical principles* needed for understanding the syntactic transformations and functional interpretations. (More formally, one would speak of the principles needed to prove the assertions: Every derivation $d \in \mathcal{D}$ can be normalized, resp: If d derives A then some derivation d' of $\mathcal{G}$ derives $A_0(s_d)$.)

(i) In the case of *finite* derivations the principal point for syntactic transformations is to show that the *normalization figure* is well founded. As mentioned at the end of § 1a, this figure has derivations d at each node, and the immediate successors are the derivations obtained by applying a *single* normalization step to d, that is contracting any introduction of a logical particle followed in d immediately by its elimination. (The reason why, in general, we do not have a proof tree is that *several* such normalization steps can be applied to a single derivation.) Evidently if the derivations are finite, only finitely many steps can be applied, but a given derivation may be the result of applying a single normalization step to any one of infinitely many derivations, just as 0 is the result of a single computation step applied to $(s^n 0).0$ for $n = 0, 1, \dots$.

(ii) In the case of, possibly, *infinite* derivations there is the additional step of verifying that each (infinite) proof figure involved is well-founded. More explicitly, we give a *description* of a sequence of proof figures; as mentioned in (a) the functions used in this description are elementary. What has to be established, as indeed also in (i) above, is first that the figure described is *locally* correct, that is the formula at a node N of a proof figure is built up according to the rules from the formulae at the immediate successor of N; second in the infinite case, that the whole figure is well-founded; third that the normalization figure described is again locally correct (in the obvious sense) and, lastly, well-founded.

Evidently, *if* these normalization procedures are to be useful for consistency results, this will depend on finding *principles of proof of well-foundedness* which are, in the sense of § 1(e), more elementary than the principles that have led to the formal system studied; cf. also §3 below.

(iii) For the functional interpretations, at least where A_0 is not logically complicated, the principal point is *usually* the existence of functionals satisfying the axioms $\mathcal{G}$; "usually" in the sense that the proof of

$$(d \vdash A) \to d' \underset{\mathcal{G}}{\vdash} A_0(s_d)$$

is quite elementary for the current interpretations: note that "s_d" is the *name* of a term in $\mathcal{G}$; we do not use an enumeration functional for the functionals named in $\mathcal{G}$.

At the present time it seems fair to say that for the systems $\mathcal{G}$ used, such as Gödel's system T in [7], the *existence of the functionals involved is indeed evident*, but *not evident on particularly elementary grounds*. For hereditarily recursive objects (cf. HRO and HEO in Troelstra [46]), their natural definition uses the principles of first order intuitionistic arithmetic; and while the non-extensional operations HRO have more striking properties than HEO, properties which are easy to establish, the *principles* used are no more elementary. If $\mathcal{G}$ is interpreted by more specific computation rules (cf. App. I), the computability predicate has again a logically complicated form.

(d) *Digression* concerning the early work by Herbrand and Gentzen, on interpretations and syntactic transformations. Since I was probably the first person to "resurrect" Herbrand's work 25 years ago, to use its and generalize it [14], I can probably make a reasonable guess at its true and its superficial attractions. (Its limitations are evident to anybody who is not totally ignorant of the main stream of proof theory over the last 20 years; for example, at no place in SPT would it have been profitable to use Herbrand's formulation.) First and foremost, Herbrand's work involves refinements of model theoretic constructions; and since, when applicable, model theoretic reasoning is more easily visualized, Herbrand allows us the best of both worlds: model theoretic clarity and quantitative estimates (for a constructive explicit treatment). No analysis of the logical operations, in particular of the propositional operation of implication, is attempted. As described at the beginning of (b) above, Herbrand allows us to make clear the *content* of a theorem proved by restricted means without going into a detailed analysis of proofs. The true attraction is that often such information on the "constructive content" is all we want, and it is good to have a direct way of getting it. But, as so often, *il faut reculer pour mieux sauter.*

The first place where the striking superiority of Gentzen's analysis is evident is in connection with Heyting's predicate logic. Even if some kind of analogue to Herbrand's theorem can be squeezed out, cf. Minc [28], it is not elegant. Indeed, the basic feature of Herbrand's analysis, the separation of *all* quantifier inferences, is not altogether plausible here[5], since, in contrast to

[5] For footnote, see next page.

classical logic, implication involves much the same kind of abstraction as universal quantification; cf. §4 below. Thus once the intrinsic interest of intuitionistic systems for proof theory is recognized (as it has been by research over the last 40 years), we have here a definite limitation of Herbrand's analysis.

There is also a quite different extension of Herbrand's theorem provided by the *no-counterexample-interpretation* of [14]. Formally it is similar, not to Herbrand's own analysis, but to the proof given in Hilbert-Bernays by means of the ϵ-theorems. Conceptually it is quite different. (The difference is that it uses functionals of lowest type and function *variables* in an essential way, concepts which Herbrand regarded as too abstract[6].) This is quite suitable for arithmetic and ramified systems, but not beyond, in the precise sense explained on top of p. 380 in SPT. And of course nothing corresponding to the normalization or even normal form theorems for full classical analysis have grown out of Herbrand's work.

3. Ordinal structures and formal theories of ordinals

In SPT, pp. 335-339 and 352b and, particularly, in [20] the ordinal structures used in proof theory, that is the orderings of the natural numbers and functions on them, were analyzed from an epistemological point of view. Since the discussions rambled on, let me summarize the main conclusion here.

As described in §2c, the main aim is to give an elementary justification of transfinite induction on (the domains of) our ordinal structures; in particular, more elementary or constructive than induction on abstract well-orderings. The key difference is that our orderings are *built up by* means of specific constructions (such as *addition* or *taking ω copies*); specifically by *iteration of these constructions only along previously introduced ordinal structures.* Consequently, transfinite induction on our ordinal structures can be analyzed explicitly in terms of the specific construction or build-up of our orderings; corresponding to the justification of ordinary, that is ω-,induction in terms of

[5] *Correction.* I did not recognize this state of affairs when I formulated the problem solved by Minc loc. cit. Note that, as usual, contraction of a disjunction $A \vee A \vee B$ to $A \vee B$ is not counted as an "inference". (The whole business of separating different *kinds* of inference by use of Herbrand-style theorems is still obscure; cf. SPT, 379 (iii) and footnote 39.)

[6] *Correction* (of Martin-Löf's [25], p. 12, 1.15). If one disregards this difference the complications of Herbrand's own formulation become quite incomprehensible (which is quite a separate matter from the fact that they can be avoided).

the construction of natural numbers by means of the successor operation. In contrast, in the abstract case, we have the operations *hidden* in the logically complicated assumption of well-foundedness. More formally, the abstract principle of transfinite induction is expressed by:

derive Ax from $[(\forall y<x)Ay \to Ax]$

which contains the logically compound subformula $(\forall y<x)A(y)$, and is therefore unsuited for a *logic-free metatheory,* required by the kind of proof theory here considered, cf. §2a(iii). The moment we have a *complete* set of build-up functions (in the terminology of Feferman [4]) denoted by, say, $f_1, ..., f_k$ we have a *quantifier-free* formulation of transfinite induction corresponding to the build-up of the ordinal structure; cf. [17], p. 172.

Let c_1 be (demonstrably) the *limit* of the segment generated by finite iteration of the f. Then we derive

$$x < c_1 \to Ax \quad \text{from } A0, \quad Ax \to Af_i x \quad \text{for } 1 \leqslant i \leqslant n\,.$$

To infer Ac_1, we need a replacement for the usual formulation $(\forall y<x)\,Ay \to Ax$ (of the progressive character of A) since it contains quantifiers. An evidently sufficient condition is provided by a derivation of

$$(*) \qquad (\tau x < x \to A\tau x) \to Ax$$

for some term τ already introduced. More generally the inference may be justified from the meaning of A, in particular (cf. [17], p. 172, 3.4214) if A is the property: the segment x has been built up by use of the operations $f_1, ..., f_n$; and conclude that the segment c_1 has been so built up. (More precisely, in the terminology of [20], c_1 has been *seen* to be so built up by methods implicit in the operations $f_1, ..., f_n$.) Thus, if the operations: $x \to f_i x$, preserve well-foundedness (in a suitable sense, in particular justifying transfinite iteration of a process along a well-founded ordering) we now permit iteration of the f_i themselves up to c_1 and, for $y < c_1$, denote the yth iterate by f_i^y.

Generally let c_{n+1} be the limit of the segment generated by iterating the f transfinitely often, but $<c_n$ times. Then we derive

$$x < c_{n+1} \to Ax \quad \text{from } (y<c_n \wedge Ax) \to Af_i^y x \quad \text{for } 1 \leqslant i \leqslant n, \text{and } Ac_{n+1}\,.$$

These rules, in contrast to the abstract principle of transfinite induction above, are quantifier-free and hence logic-free if A is decidable. Note that the formulation above provides a more *explicit* analysis of the process of transfinite induction on $<$ than when (*) alone is regarded as sufficient to infer Ax. Here (*) is used only to infer Ac_n from $x < c_n \to Ax$.

In general, we need additional functions besides the build-up functions f, to establish the premises of the rules, in particular to express and establish the defining properties of the c_n. Thus the property *Lim*, of being a limit number, is defined by: $spx \neq x$ where s and p are the successor and predecessor function respectively; but to express in a quantifier-free way *that* this definition expresses the intended meaning we also need an additional binary g and a proof of $(spx{\neq}x \wedge y{<}x) \to y < g(y,x) < x$.

A particularly useful group of additional functions are the *inverses* of the build-up functions, also called *retracing functions*, as the predecessor is the inverse of the successor function. By use of such functions we can express explicitly the *fundamental relation* between

an element and its name built up from $0, f_1, ..., f_k$

that is, between an object x in the ordering and the term (built up from $0, f_1, ..., f_k$) which denotes x. This is fundamental because the term *reflects the construction of the segment up to* x as the numerals $(0, s0, ss0, ...)$, the *standard notations* for integers, reflect the construction of the objects they denote. An obvious consequence is this:

Let O_1 and O_2 be ordinal structures with isomorphic domains of ordinal α; both containing build-up and retracing functions as described above. Then O_1 and O_2 are isomorphic by the mapping *explicitly defined* as follows:

For x_1 in O_1, find its standard notation t by means of the retracing functions in O_1; by means of the build-up functions in O_2, determine the "value", i.e., the denotation x_2 of t in O_2.

In other words, our ordinal structures are determined *uniquely up to the explicit isomorphism above.* The reader may compare this *functorial analysis* of ordinal structures with the analysis of canonical representations discussed in subsection (d) of § 1, an analysis which determines representations uniquely up to demonstrable equivalence.

Remark. People in proof theory, evidently interested in the aims descirbed in § 2c, usually speak of the *ordinal* of a formal system; for example, ϵ_0 of first order arithmetic. Taken literally this conflicts with our discussion which shows beyond a shadow of doubt that, for their aims, not the ordinal nor even the ordering, but the *ordinal structure* is essential. But, practically speaking, no mistakes are likely to be made, just because the relevant ordinal structures are not only determined uniquely in the sense described, but isomorphic to the *familiar* ϵ_0-ordering (which is the ordering that people use without further analysis). The very *definition* of the ordinal ϵ_0 as the limit of $\omega, \omega^\omega, ...$ refers to ordinal *functions*, essentially those needed for the ordinal structure brought out by closer analysis. Here it should be remembered that, at the present time, *we do not have a* **general** *scheme for associating in an intrinsic way an ordinal structure to a formal system* (but we do have one for associating an ordinal: bounds on provable Σ_1^1 - well orderings, induction principles needed for reflection principles; cf. SPT, pp. 340–341). Also, though such an intrinsic characterization would be aesthetically very attractive it is not needed for the specific metamathematical purposes of §2c which require only *some* ordinal structure built up in an elementary way.

In earlier publications ([20] but also SPT §12b) I considered the problem of associating ordinal structures or "natural" well-orderings to given ordinals. I shall not prusue this problem here, but two much more modest formal questions involved in setting up a *logic-free metatheory*, namely (α) and (β) below which were neglected in SPT.

(α) What are minimum *formal* requirements on quantifier-free systems of ordinal functions if they are to serve for formalizing the metamathematical principles discussed in §2(c)?

This question has of course perfectly good meaning if, as is usual in the literature, we have in mind a formal language for arithmetic and consider specific well-orderings of the natural numbers with number theoretic functions representing our ordinal operations. But since we are not concerned with their arithmetic properties and since we have just seen that the ordinal structures to be considered are unique up to a particularly elementary (explicit) kind of isomorphism we may just as well consider *formal theories of ordinals.* Without excluding the possibility that the variables may range over the particular (finite and infinite) sets which von Neumann used in his set theoretic ordinal structures, our theories will also be realized by ordinal structures that are defined by quite elementary (constructive) processes.

(β) Are there elegant formal theories of ordinals corresponding to the systems of arithmetic and analysis which are the principal subject matter of current proof theory?[7]

Remark. Since proof theory has been dominated so far by Hilbert's programme and other constructive aims, most of the few formal theories of ordinals

[7] In (c) we shall consider reasons why questions (α) and (β) were neglected for a long time.

studied in proof theory are constructive; in particular, they have models over "small" segments of the recursive ordinals, the function symbols being realized by (primitive) recursive functions on these ordinals, or, more precisely, their notations. But inasmuch as the requirement of constructivity is not always appropriate, as has been urged throughout this article, also other formal theories will be considered here, particularly in (b) and (c).

Naturally the latter are not directly useful for refining the kind of well-foundedness proofs mentioned in §2 (c); specifically, refining them by eliminating the general notion of wellfoundedness in favour of operations on ordinal structures built-up in a particularly elementary manner. But apart from such an epistemological purpose, an ordinal analysis might be expected to have also technical uses, simply because it replaced the *qualitative* notion of well-foundedness by a *quantitative* formulation. To some extent this quantitative version, like interpretations in §2 (b) could give an answer to the recurring question:

> What more do we know when we know that a theorem can be proved by limited means than if we merely know that it is true?

(a) We consider first question (α) applied to the theory of *syntactic transformations* described in §2(a).

(i) If we are principally concerned with (infinite) proof figures, but not the conversion relation, a minimum requirement is this:

> For the natural coding of formulae the proof figures must be *definable* in the theory of ordinals and their basic properties formally derivable. The basic properties are of course that the proof figures are "locally correct", that is built-up according to the rules of proof under study, and that they are well-founded.

Though the familiar normal form theorems for, say ramified analysis, by use of infinite normal (or cut-free) proofs have not been formalized in any theory of ordinals the method is fairly clear; for instance, we know already that the proof figures themselves have the appropriate order type (SPT, p. 332b). Indeed it was perhaps wise to wait because, as mentioned in (c) below, it is probably more elegant to deal with subsystems in the language of set theory rather than analysis: it would have been frustrating to labour over a formalization of the metamathematics of analysis.

Let me here say a word about technical uses of a quantitative ordinal analysis of normal proof figures though *mutatis mutandis* related considerations also apply to an analysis of the conversion figures considered in (ii) below.

For a sufficiently strong sense of "normal" it turns out that a bound on the *ordinal size* of a normal deduction imposes a significant restriction on the theorem proved; for example ([41], p. 222, concerning normal derivations with the subformula property) a derivation of the well-foundedness of a relation has an ordinal exceeding that of the relation itself. (In the case of ordinary predicate calculus of first order, the necessarily *finite* length of a normal derivation is significant.) Here the order type of the normal form of any given deduction is a useful characteristic even if we do not go into the details of its ordinal structure.

For a genuine practical application, the considerations of §2(b) about "incomplete" interpretations apply. Quite evidently, the ordinal bound itself cannot possibly yield every independence result: as is well known, the addition of any true Σ_1^1 statement to a formal system does not alter its ordinal bound! (though it will in general alter its ordinal structure). But *if* an independence result is so brutal that it can be proved by looking at the ordinal bound only, the independence proof will generally be very easy.

(ii) The problems of formalizing the conversion procedures in §2a(ii) are less well understood; not surprisingly since, as mentioned already, those procedures have been neglected by proof theorists. For example, a satisfactory treatment (at least: satisfactory in the sense of SPT, p. 332(b)[8]) would require, above all, the study of the *computation* or *conversion figures qua* ordered structures. It is still not quite clear whether the *canonical* assignment of ordinals to these figures, say for first order arithmetic, really uses all ordinals $< \epsilon_0$. Of course, we know from §2(c) (i) that a *proof* of well-foundedness in a theory of ordinals (with successor, addition, exponentiation) needs induction $\leqslant \epsilon_0$. But this is a separate question from determining the relational type of the figures themselves or the least ordinal into which they can be embedded; more precisely, embedded by means of mappings which are characterized by *definability* (not also *provability*) conditions.

Evidently the problem of *formalizing normalization theorems in a theory of ordinals* induces minimum requirements on such a theory of ordinals in a way which is exactly analogous to (i) above.

It is perhaps not superfluous to go into the *nature* of "the" problem of formalizing say Gentzen's original consistency proof. This will explain and, I think, even justify people's reluctance so far to work on this problem. - As

[8] Recent experience seems to confirm this dogma: in [9], Howard considers a formally similar situation, namely a computation figure and assigns ordinals (such that the application of a reduction step reduces the ordinal). The assignment is not, explicitly, related to *the order type of anything,* and is certainly not pleasant to check.

somebody said: A formalization is the outward and visible sign of an inward and invisible grace, namely of one's understanding, of knowing what one is talking about. (Formalization shares both the advantages and disadvantages, for a given person, of correct formal manners.) Specifically, a *principal* difficulty is to decide in what terms, in what *language*, the formalization is to be given, a matter which is certainly not decided by the informal argument; and then, to decide to which points special attention should be given. Now, it is fair to say that though it was immediately clear that some striking reduction had been achieved by Gentzen, not even the most fundamental and now very familiar point was clearly realized: that ϵ_0-induction is applied to a quantifier-free, that is logic-free predicate. If one does not have reasons to *look* for a quantifier-free formalization, one will truly end up with the splendid joke: Gentzen proved the consistency of ordinary, that is ω-induction by means of ϵ_0-induction. Equally to the point is an example where somebody stumbles on a formalization, but does not profit from it. As already stressed in SPT, top of p. 332, Schütte [41] formulated explicitly the properties of some ordinal functions needed for the consistency proof. But the significance of these properties did not spring to the eye from the formalization; it was found only when one *looked* for it, in terms of an intrinsic characterization of the natural ordinal structure on ϵ_0.

(b) By §2c (iii), the relation between ordinals or ordinal structures and the functions (of higher type) used in the interpretations of §2b must *in general* be expected to be tenuous. More precisely, the theory of ordinal structures is of course directly relevant if the functions are thought of as rules for applying given computation or reduction procedures; in this case the minimum requirement on such a theory is completely parallel to that of a (ii); the computation figure should be definable (or: computation tree if the rules are deterministic) and its basic properties should be provable. We shall take up this matter in App. I.

But, as a matter of historical fact, the functions one had in mind when introducing the no-counter example-interpretation or Gödel's [7], were not thought of as such computation rules. In other words the existence of the functions involved was evident on other grounds. Certainly, since then, relations between those functions (or at least schemata satisfied by them) and ordinal structures have been established; cf. SPT, pp. 332-333 for the continuous functions used in the no-counter example – interpretation and Howard's assignment mentioned in footnote 8, for Gödel's T. However, by no stretch of the imagination could it be claimed that these relations provided the original reason for introducing the interpretations; indeed Gödel explicitly proposed the principles formulated in T as an *alternative* to Gentzen's use of ϵ_0-induction, and hence independent of the latter (but possibly less elementary, cf. § 2ciii).

The functions of higher type referred to in the last paragraph have the natural numbers as ground type. More recently (cf. (c) below), functions of higher type over the ordinals have been studied; naturally with a very direct relation between functionals and ordinals.

(i) For the case of continuous (and hence of course extensional) functionals of *lowest* type over the integers, with the discrete topology on the integers and the product topology on functions, we do have a close relation, since there is an *inductive generation* of this class of *functionals*[9]. But, as just mentioned, many of the schemata in the literature for such continuous functionals are introduced for other reasons, in particular because their computability is made evident by use of the notion of choice sequence. In such cases, the computation "procedure" we have in mind *does not refer to the inductive generation but to a method of trial and error.* With the usual convention (e.g. [16]) we take a neighbourhood function f_0 on finite sequences of natural numbers, a choice sequence α and try out $f_0(\bar{\alpha}0), f_0(\bar{\alpha}1), f_0(\bar{\alpha}2)$ till we hit an m such that $f_0(\bar{\alpha}m) \neq 0$; cf. computations on those definitions of recursive functions which are given in Kleene's form $U[\mu_y T(e_0,n,y)]$, where, for each n, we try out $T(e_0,n,0)$, $T(e_0,n,1)$, ... till we hit a $T(e_0,n,m)$ which is true. For *these* definitions (not to be confused with the *computational* normal forms in [42] or [44] !) the obvious order type of the computations has a finite ordinal; cf. also App. Ia(i).

The simple general point made in the last paragraph is, perhaps, further supported by detailed work. On the one hand we have the easy proof of computability in [42] pp. 225–227, of the closed terms, actually for higher types, of Gödel's theory T [7], when they are thought of as denoting computation procedures formulated in the theory itself, discussed further in App. I (a). On the other we have the complications (in [44]) arising from bar recursion of type 0, a schema which is suggested by the notion of choice sequence. At the present stage we do not know if the difference is intrinsic, see also the end of Troelstra's paper [46].

[9] In [23] and elsewhere it was overlooked that Kalmar discussed this fact some 15 years ago in [11]. (In the logical literature this relation is more familiar from the order type of the unsecured sequences of such functionals in the socalled Brouwer-Kleene ordering.)

(ii) For familiar functions of higher type (or, more precisely, functions satisfying *topological* conditions such as the socalled continuous ones of [16] or [40]) we do not know any simple connection with ordinals, in particular, no inductive generation similar to (i).

To be precise, by Gödel's theory of constructible sets we have a completely systematic method of connecting *any* theory of functionals which can be developed from the usual axioms of set theory (or additional axioms which hold in L) with a theory of ordinals. We need only restrict ourselves to the constructible functionals and formulate the latter as, e.g., in [48]. But this goes well beyond the principles envisaged in existing proof theory (on the analysis of SPT, p. 351, §12).

(iii) Quite recently Feferman [6] has made very interesting use of suitable *segments* of the constructible hierarchy to establish connections between functionals and ordinals (or more precisely number theoretic functions defined by means of functionals of finite type). The crucial differences are, firstly, that the functionals considered are *not constructive*, not even in the weak sense of having a recursive realization for the *function* symbols (i.e., not even constructive in the sense of the theory of species); secondly, ordinals do not enter in the form of the ordinal structures here described but simply as the *ordinals of hierarchies*.

Since the formal theories of the *particular* hierarchies which he considers, up to ϵ_0 steps, have a proof theoretic analysis by quite elementary means, his work can serve as an *intermediate* stage for constructive proof theory. (From the point of view of method this is to be compared to intermediate uses of model theory described in SPT, Note II and, particularly, his own work in [51]; the difference is that not models of quantification theory, but suitable classes of extensional functionals are introduced.) Nevertheless, in the sense in which I meant the *warning* on p. 334, l.-14 to l.-12 of SPT, it is now necessary to warn against this warning.

(c) *Theories of sets and ordinals.* Traditional proof theory studied mainly formal systems formulated in the language of arithmetic or analysis (with variables for natural numbers and sets of them). This choice was natural when one wanted to use constructive methods and hence to avoid abstract assumptions. Since the most familiar uses of sets and transfinite ordinals were highly abstract, the mere use of the corresponding languages was thought to carry a risk of confusion. Times have changed; we have a better grasp of principles and we are familiar with quite elementary models of axioms in the languages of sets and ordinals. Consequently it makes good sense also in proof theory to use these elegant languages which, in particular, avoid elaborate coding procedures.

(i) Relations between subsystems of the usual set theories and (the usual) systems of analysis were discussed in (SPT), Technical Note VI, pp. 375–376. Some set theories corresponding to subsystems of analysis were considered in (SPT), p. 376(c), but more interesting ones have been studied since then. For example, Feferman's system [5] is intended to provide a set theoretic system corresponding to his system IR of analysis [3] or, equivalently, to his hierarchy of ramified analysis; or [10] where an elegant set theoretic version of "bar-induction" is treated without any (stated) systematic purpose.

(ii) Relations between set theories and theories of ordinals: A non-recursive step. The obvious first step, already mentioned in b(ii), is simply to specialize the theory of constructible sets as formulated in [48] to subsystems of usual set theory. By standard collapsing arguments, we get minimum well-founded models.

In general these minimum models are non-recursive in the following sense. Either the *domain* itself contains non-recursive ordinals, or, if it is a segment α of the recursive ordinals, the *ordinal functions* are not realized by recursive functions on the natural well ordering of α. (Equivalently, the ordering relation is not recursive on the domain made up of the *terms* of the theory.)

As an example of the latter Zucker studied the minimum model of group 1 in [45] (in the course of analyzing the claims of Wette [47] regarding this group of axioms). The domain consists of the ordinals $<\omega^\omega$, but it is easily seen that the functions named in the axioms are *not* realized by recursive functions on (the canonical ordering of) ω^ω; cf. the review of [47]. As an example of the former, Prawitz [35] has given an elegant theory of ordinals (and specific functions on them) which corresponds to full analysis; here the *domain* itself of the ordinals needed goes beyond the recursive ones.

(iii) Relations between set theories and theories of ordinals: recursive models. More explicitly, we now look for theories of ordinals which are realized by segments of the *recursive* ordinals $<|a|$ (where $a \in O$ [12]) such that the ordinal functions on the ordering $\{(x,y){:}x <_O y <_O a\}$ are also recursive. Most of the work along these lines has been done since (SPT) was written though Howard introduced a first example some years ago in Section VI of the privately circulated Stanford Report on the Foundations of Analysis. The methods so far used proceed somewhat indirectly as follows. A quantification theory of ordinals and particular species of ordinals is set up which corresponds to the subsystem of set theory or analysis considered. For example, for theories codifying the familiar principles of *generalized inductive definition* (g.i.d.) we have an absolutely standard reduction to the theory of ordinals: to find the least set X_A satisfying $\forall x\,[A(P,x) \to P(x)]$, for monotone A, we put $P_0(x) \leftrightarrow A(\perp,x)$, and define by transfinite recursion a sequence P_α for ordinals $\alpha > 0$ by

$$P_\alpha(x) \leftrightarrow (\exists\beta{<}\alpha) A(P_\beta,x)$$

where $x \in X_A \leftrightarrow \exists\alpha P_\alpha(x)$.

This quantification theory is *interpreted* in a suitable system of higher type; by Howard *loc.cit.* for non-iterated g.i.d., in the style of Gödel [7], by Zucker [49], for iterated g.i.d., using the modification of 3.5.1. in [16]. "Suitable" means here that the closed terms can be used as the domain of a manageable model. For readers familiar with Gödel's proof that the continuum hypothesis holds for L (the collection of constructible sets), the current methods, first made explicit by Feferman [4], are best described as follows. As in b(ii) we think of the theory of constructible sets formulated in a theory of ordinals [48], with an ordinal theoretic relation $\alpha e \beta$ to mean: the set with number α is a member of the set with number β.

The first step is to set up a quantifier-free system which is evidently satisfied by a "large" (uncountable) segment of the ordinals when the function symbols including constants are realized by familiar ordinal functions: call this structure 0^∞. This corresponds to the step in Gödel's "collapsing" argument where some large ordinal is adjoined to a given segment $<\alpha$ (where α is a cardinal in L), and the "Skolem hull" is formed. The latter does *not* fill up a segment of the ordinals. We may regard the formation of the Skolem hull as the construction of a *term model*, consisting of constants for each ordinal $<\alpha$ and for the adjoined ordinal, and terms formed by means of function symbols f for the Skolem functions used. By definition, the realization $\bar{f}$ of f in a term model (also called: canonical realization) is defined by the action

$$\bar{f}: t_1, \ldots, t_n \to f t_1 \ldots t_n$$

for all n-tuples of terms (if f has n arguments).

The next step in the collapsing argument is to consider the ordering of the terms

$$\{(t_1,t_2) : t_1^s < t_2^s\}$$

where t^s is the realization of t in the Skolem hull, that is the ordinal denoted by t. The two facts essential for Gödel's proof are that the ordinal α_1 of this ordering has cardinal α (in L) and that the ordering is definable in L_α. This ensures that the Skolem hull *together* with its structure is definable since there is an obvious indexing (in L_α) of the terms and hence of the canonical realization of the function symbols; in particular, $\{t_1, t_2 : t_1^s < t_2^s\}$ is also definable. (Evidently, the Skolem hull regarded as a set theoretic object and not only as a structure is not in general definable in L_{α_1}.)

For the present prupose of finding recursive models, analogous but more delicate requirements are needed. Instead of preservation of cardinals we want α_1 to be recursive (for the given α). And instead of (invariant) definability over L_{α_1} we want the relation:

(*) $$\{(t_1, t_2) : t_1^\infty < t_2^\infty\}$$

to be recursive where now t^∞ is the ordinal denoted by t in 0^∞. Evidently, if this is satisfied, once again the function symbols are automatically realized by recursive functions (on these terms).

Feferman [4] gives some useful general conditions on ordinal functions for which (*) is satisfied. Actually in [4] his primary concern is with the more *elementary* parts of proof theory where no collapsing occurs at all (for an application of collapsing see, e.g., Zucker's thesis [49]). We start again with a quantifier-free system which is evidently satisfied by familiar ordinal functions over familiar structures. But now it turns out that the ordinals denoted (in these familiar structures) by the terms fill up a segment anyway, i.e., the systems are *replete* in the notation of [4], and (*) holds too. In short, we have an *absoluteness* or *invariance* property:

The terms have the same value whether the function constants get their intended (familiar) or their canonical realization.

An interesting difference between iterated and non-iterated g.i.d. is just this: in the latter case, the closed terms used in the interpretation [49] do not have this invariance property.

Remarks. Howard's interpretation is quantifier-free and the model is recursive in the strong sense that the $\doteq$ relation (even) between terms of non zero type can be realized by a recursive relation. Zucker's interpretation allows indeed a recursive model for the domain, the functions and even the = relation, but has a *residue of logic* in the form of two species which are not realized by recursive predicates. (This asymmetry between functions and predicates is of course quite familiar.)

From the point of view described at the beginning of this section, of the *build-up* of ordinal structures, the use of functionals of higher type over the ordinals is quite natural. A functional of higher type corresponds to reflection *on* the process of iterating operations of lower type (though it does not make explicit the details of this process). Some *formal* notions and axioms expressing this use of higher types can be found in one of Feferman's articles in the Buffalo volume [52]. A more delicate analysis, which confines itself to operations on ordinal structures (of lowest type), was given by Howard [53], and Zucker [49] in terms of the particular build-up functions employed in Bachmann's hierarchy.

Evidently, depending on one's interest, further work will pursue two, at least *prima facie* diametrically opposite aims. On the one hand the work will be *extended* using, no doubt, principles suggested by familiar set theoretic material such as Mahlo's iteration procedures. So to speak the processes are the same, only the basic operations (taking successors in the constructive case and power sets in the set theoretic case!) are different. Indeed from this point of view, ordinal constructions that are here developed should serve as a *testing ground* for problematic axioms of infinity. In fact it may even turn out that the term "axiom of infinity" is not quite appropriate, that is, that (cardinal) *size* derives essentially from the basic operations, and that the full *complexity* is naturally present in the recursive case; cf. footnote 37 on p. 377 of SPT[10].

On the other hand one will examine the models constructed more carefully and try to find concepts in terms of which essential differences can be analyzed precisely. For example I am not yet persuaded that the difference between iterated and uniterated g.i.d. is negligible even assuming, as seems reasonable, that on interpretation of the logical operations is found which is really appropriate to the use of g.i.d. (as explained e.g. in SPT, §12(a) or p. 352). If this is so, closer inspection of the functionals used in the interpretations by Howard and Zucker may help one find the concepts needed to state the difference.

4. Logical operations: proofs and functions

Nearly 40 years ago Heyting gave a meaning to the basic logical notions (of proposition, species and operations on them) [8]. The meaning was explained, as I read it now, in terms of *two* primitives, namely *judgement* or proof, specifically proofs of identities which are of course "logic free", and *functions*

[10] The qualification "naturally" is essential since size is always eliminable in the sense that there are denumerable elementary submodels.

whose arguments and values are hereditarily pairs (p,π) where p and π denote proofs and functions resp. For example, (p_0,π_0) establishes $A \to B$, for short

$$(p_0,\pi_0) \vdash A \to B$$

means that p_0 is a proof of

$$[(p,\pi) \vdash A] \Rightarrow (\pi_0(p,\pi) \vdash B]$$

for all p and π. Heyting also wrote down formal laws which can be seen to be valid (even) from a very rough understanding of the two primitive notions of proof and function.

Now the single most important point to remember is this.

Though Heyting *intended* p to range over constructive proofs and π over constructive functions, what he *actually* said about these primitives, the laws he actually asserted, made little use of any detailed analysis of the qualification *constructive*. Heyting certainly emphasized the fact that *any* list of formal laws leaves some room for different interpretations; but he failed to stress just how much room was left open by his particular list of formal laws.

(a) As is to be expected, for a more detailed analysis of constructivity, specifically if constructive number theoretic functions are recursive, Heyting's laws are incomplete, and the set of valid laws (for the language of predicate logic) is not recursively enumerable [19] [11].

Though it is very natural to present various kinds of "realizability interpretations" (discussed at this meeting by Troelstra [46]) as variants of Heyting's scheme (cf. [17], p. 128–129, 2.31–2.32) this is not usually done. Also interpretations of the logical operations "in terms of" formal derivability such as Prawitz' [34], fit in here where p now ranges over (proofs described by) derivations in a given system, and π over a (very restricted) class of functions. For yet another variant (used in the first of the recent discussions of Heyting's scheme [15]), the "guiding" model let p range over proofs which are, hereditarily, formalizable in a progression of formal systems, and π over functions such that, in the definition of $\to$ above, the level of (the first element of) $\pi_0(p,\pi)$ was not too far from the level of p; cf. App. Ic(ii).

[11] *Correction.* Contrary to Myhill's facile explanations, [29], p. 327, l.14, incompleteness is not due to lack of analysis of the meaning, but to knowing what we are talking about; cf. the case of higher order logic where we have incompleteness (of formal systems) if we do specify what we are talking about, namely principal models.

Remark. It is fairly easy to generate paradoxes if one tries to set up a formal theory of constructions (i.e., of proofs and functions). But, as usual, this indicates equally that we have too *many* reasonable interpretations as that we have none! Indeed, if we have anything in mind at all when setting up formal laws which are inconsistent, this means that one law is valid or at least plausible for one meaning, another for a different meaning. If we had no meaning in mind the proposed laws would not be plausible at all.

(b) To give a positive turn to the "inadequacies" noted in (a), it is of course necessary to find intrinsically interesting or at least useful examples among the unintended interpretations. The examples mentioned in (a) involve *restrictions* on the notions intended by Heyting since (cf. SPT §13) proof theory has been traditionally interested in particularly *elementary* methods; its aim was to be "reductive" (in the sense of Prawitz [36])[12]. But good use can be made also of non-constructive interpretations. For example, Feferman's work on "predicativity relative to the notion of natural number" or, more simply, on "reducibility to arithmetic" uses the non-constructive meaning of numerical quantification, and thus the functional **E** [13], for function variables α

$$\mathbf{E}\alpha = 0 \leftrightarrow \exists x(\alpha x{=}0)\,, \qquad \mathbf{E}\alpha = 1 \leftrightarrow \neg\exists x(\alpha x{=}0)$$

is quite appropriate. This work in [6], already mentioned in §3(b) is also formally very satisfactory.

(c) *Explicit definitions.* There is one use of Heyting's formal laws which does not come under his scheme at all but is, I believe, much closer to the interests of mathematical practice. The general consideration is this.

In ordinary classical mathematics the operations $\exists$ and $\vee$ are so to speak unemployed. They are explicitly definable in terms of $\neg$ and $\forall$, resp. $\wedge$. So we ask for formal laws that reproduce ordinary classical reasoning for the so-called negative fragment $\neg, \wedge, \forall$, but for existential theorems and disjunctions we have a stronger requirement than truth, i.e., we require (for closed formulae)

$\exists xA$ is derivable (if and) only if, for some term t, $A[x/t]$ is derivable.

$A \vee B$ is derivable (if and) only if either A or B is derivable[13]

[12] It goes without saying that we all know one interpretation which goes *beyond* Heyting's, where provability is identified with truth, the pair (p,π) reduces to the single element π, and *all* functions are considered!

[13] In systems including e.g. arithmetic, the second condition is included in the first since $(A \vee B) \leftrightarrow \exists x[(x{=}0 \to A) \wedge (x{\neq}0 \to B)]$.

NB. These conditions are *not* (even) required by constructive validity, e.g. of predicate logic, contrary to an almost universal misconception! Consider formulae A and B of predicate logic with, say, a single predicate symbol X; suppose X is binary.

$$A \vee B \text{ is valid if and only if}$$

for all species D ("D" for domain) and all $X^* \subset D \times D$, $A^* \vee B^*$ holds when the variables of A and B range over D and X is replaced by X^*; for short

$$\forall D(\forall X^* \subset D^2)(A^* \vee B^*) .$$

But it is certainly not evident that therefore

$$[\forall D(\forall X^* \subset D^2)A^*] \vee [\forall D(\forall X^* \subset D^2)B^*] .$$

The requirement for existential theorems involves an equally if not more startling uniformity

$$\forall D \forall X^* \exists x^* A^* \to \exists t \forall D \forall X^* A'$$

where A' is obtained by replacing x^* in A^* by the value t^* of the term t in (D,X^*). For first order formulae A, t does not contain (a symbol for) D nor X and t^* does not depend on D nor X. For higher order logic using abstraction terms, t^* involves D and X, but t does not contain a symbol for D.

The present "non-logical" use of Heyting's laws is particularly interesting in connection with various formulations of the *axiom of choice*. As has often been remarked there is an almost universal misconception about the relation between the axiom of choice and explicit definability, because of the accident that in the usual formulations of the axioms of set theory all axioms other than the axiom of choice assert the existence of sets for which we have an explicit definition. What is overlooked is that there are existential theorems without explicit realizations which are classical *logical* consequences of these axioms (SPT p. 349 bottom). In other words, *unrestricted use of* (ordinary) *classical logic does not preserve explicit realizability of existential theorems* (more precisely, *demonstrable* realizability; cf. the problem top of p. 372 of SPT).

In contrast, if we use Heyting's rules and even if we add the axiom of choice (and also the negative translation of the axiom of choice! cf. [39]) we have realizations of existential theorems.

Remark. One reason for supposing that these questions of existential realizations are closer to the interests of mathematical practice is simply that the central problem of interpreting $\rightarrow$, which has been discussed very clearly over the last 40 years, has simply not caught "public" attention. Questions of existential realizations have. More theoretically, the latter questions are intelligible without logical preoccupations, the central question is not. It would be interesting to know how one would have set up *discovering* suitable formal laws which ensure realizations of existential theorems (without having in mind Heyting's own interpretation). Amusingly, Heyting's laws are naturally set out in such a way that they are *exactly* the classical laws except for the additional rule

$$\neg\neg A \rightarrow A$$

which does not mention existential quantification at all!

(d) *Other uses.* More problematic, but also more ambitious, applications of Heyting's formal systems rely on Kripke's discovery [34] that they are valid for an interpretation of the logical operations suggested by the idea of a *potential* totality or of an ever *expanding* body of knowledge. I say "suggested by" and not "in terms of" because the *sequence* of models used to represent the expansion of the universe (or of our knowledge) is itself usually treated in the literature as an ordinary set. This procedure provides no epistemological analysis at all. An alternative is to regard the logical operations applied to potential totalities as *primitive*: Kripke's interpretation is not regarded as an explanation or "reduction" but as asserting properties of these logical operations obtained by reflection upon their meaning. From such an impredicative view of these operations it is perfectly proper to use them in formulating their own "semantics".

Several people including Kripke (cf. the reference in Putnam [38, 284]) or Pozsgay [30] have proposed to use Heyting's rules for an analysis of the idea of generating sets by *arbitrary* iterations of the power set operation (cumulative hierarchy of types). Tacitly one assumes in ordinary set theory that one is dealing with a *segment* of the hierarchy since otherwise the classical interpretation of the universal quantifier does not apply here, there being no set of all sets; cf. [17] p. 101, l. 19–22 and footnote 12 on p. 120. The situation is strictly analogous to the simple-minded finitist's idea of generating *all* hereditarily finite sets. Also formally the treatment is parallel provided only one uses heavily *set induction* corresponding to ordinary induction in arithmetic; for example, in arithmetic one proves the decidability of equality by induction from the successor axioms and then goes on to prove the decidability of formulae containing only bounded quantifiers, having introduced suitable arithmetic functions; similarly, by means of set theoretic induction one *proves* the decidability of formulae containing only bounded quantifiers from the decidability of atomic formulae by essential use of the elementary set theoretic operations, corresponding to the "suitable" arithmetic functions in arithmetic.

The *comprehension axiom* must be modified to

$$\forall a \forall x_1 \ldots \forall x_n [\forall x(A \vee \neg A) \rightarrow \exists y \forall x(x \in y \leftrightarrow [x \in a \wedge A])]$$

where the free variables in A are among $x, x_1, \ldots, x_n$ and y does not occur in A. The restriction to decidable A is required because for the present meaning of *set* (the cumulative hierarchy), a set is a well defined unity (in Cantor's words) with a definite extension.

In [54], Note I §2(b), I suggested the *reflection principle* in the form

$$\forall x_1 \ldots \forall x_n [A \rightarrow \exists \alpha(x_1 \in V_\alpha \wedge \ldots \wedge x_n \in V_\alpha \wedge A_\alpha)]$$

for an arbitrary A with free variables $x_1, \ldots, x_n$, where α ranges over the ordinals, V_α denotes the segment of the hierarchy up to α and A_α is obtained from A by restricting all quantifiers to V_α.

It should be noted that these modified schemata imply the corresponding familiar axioms when the "negative" translation is applied (cf. SPT, p. 344 (iii)). Thus *the present interpretation justifies the use of classical logic applied to the axioms listed.* Incidentally, I see no justification (for the present interpretation of the logical operations) of the classically equivalent form of the reflection principle above:

$$\forall x_1 \ldots \forall x_n \exists \alpha [x_1 \in V_\alpha \wedge \ldots x_n \in V_\alpha \wedge (A \leftrightarrow A_\alpha)]$$

that is, of finding α for given values of $x_1, \ldots, x_n$, merely from the form of A without knowing whether A is well determined; only its negative translation is justified. But not even this much is apparent for the "full" principle $\exists \alpha (\forall x_1 \in V_\alpha) \ldots (\forall x_n \in V_\alpha)(A \rightarrow A_\alpha)$; cf. footnote 6 on p. 10 of [57].

The reader of Note I §2 b in [54] will have noticed that an argument for the reflection principle must use specific properties of the concept of *set*, not merely the fact that the ranges of our variables are indefinite. These properties cannot be shared by (the finitist's idea of) the indefinite hierarchy of hereditarily finite sets, since the reflection principle does not hold for the latter. Presumably the essential point is that the finitist can prove A by use of the generation principle: $x, y \to x \cup \{y\}$ (in his language under which no finite V_α is closed. (Here we have another example of an assertion about sets which cannot be said to be "transferred" from our knowledge of finite sets; cf. [54] Note I §1 b, especially footnote 9.)

Remark. What is problematic here is not primarily the validity of Heyting's rules. As has been stressed repeatedly they tend to be valid whenever we speak, even quite vaguely, of processes. The problem is whether, when dealing with a *particular* process, Heyting's schema is fruitful; cf. footnotes 16 and 19 to Note I of [54] or footnote 3 of [20]. For example, Schütte [41], following Ackermann's ideas (cf. [1]), discusses not unreasonable logical laws for "indefinite" properties for which $A \leftrightarrow \neg\neg A$.

Appendix I
Computations and formalist semantics of the logical particles

The topics treated here are not yet ripe for a systematic exposition, though there has been renewed interest in them recently (see [44] or Prawitz' paper in this volume); following related earlier work by Curry and Lorenzen, in particular his operative Logik. At the present stage it seems useful to ask 3 questions which have been neglected in the literature.

(α) What are the *general* aims of this kind of work?

(β) What are the *exact* relations between this work and more familiar material in the literature?

(γ) For which (mathematical) results is this work actually *needed*?
Rules (or functions) are considered in (a) and (b) below, logic in (c).

Ad (α) it seems clear that the general aim is to replace our usual impredicative notions by notions satisfying the basic *formalist requirement*:

All objects involved should be explicitly listed.

This kind of reduction is similar to but more radical than that considered in [19] where the abstract impredicative notions are replaced by *recursive* ones. The difference is that though we have of course a 'listing', we do not have an *internal*, that is recursive, listing of recursive definitions. The steps from the abstract to the recursive versions are given in a(i) and c(i) for computation and logic resp.

Ad (β), the 'familiar' material in question consists of course of the recursive versions above. The general principle for using these, formalistically not acceptable versions is quite commonplace:

> Formulate explicitly the closure properties of the class of recursive operations needed to verify the specific laws considered (which hold for the abstract interpretation).

In other words, explicit formalization is good for a formalist foundation. As a corollary: *some* formalistically acceptable interpretation is usually easy to come by from known work, and the principal fruitful problem for current research is to analyze what further requirements a formalist foundation should satisfy: not the existence of some (coherent) formalist interpretation, but the choice among such interpretations is problematic. This matter will be considered in b(iii) and c(iii) in terms of the *expressive power* (of simple languages) provided by formalist interpretations. Put differently: here we need not adopt the formalist *philosophy*, of mathematical precision and mathematical reasoning generally, which requires formalist interpretations; but we expect the latter to be useful in areas which do have formalist character. For example, the preparation of any mathematical problem for a computer constitutes some kind of formalist reduction; it does not seem unreasonable to expect that there is a useful general theory here comparable to model theory which is a general theory of axiomatic systems and which has turned out to be useful in mathematical practice.

Ad (γ) we compare mainly results for the particular system T (introduced by Gödel [7]) obtained by use of the 'crude' recursive model HRO in [46], already mentioned in §2c(iii), and of the formalist interpretation in [44]; cf. b(ii). In fact the principal fruitful problem here is to *search* for (interesting) problems which do need the more refined formalist interpretation.

Besides these general points (α)–(γ) which have analogues in almost any subject at a corresponding stage of development, two *specific considerations* are introduced:

Firstly, the distinction between those formalist foundations which have an *abstract impredicative residue in the metamathematical explanations* and those which are, roughly speaking, hereditarily *logic-free*; see the introduction of [19] for the corresponding situation with recursive versions, especially the logical residue in the quantifier combination $\forall\exists$ used to define 'recursive'. Here b(i) and particularly c(ii) are relevant.

Secondly, as already mentioned at the very beginning of this article, I propose to use formal relations, which were discovered in work on a formalist foundation, *for the ananlysis of the abstract notions themselves* cf. c(iii). This is not to be regarded as a kind of *tour de force* (prompted by my distrust of formalist philosophy above), but simply as an instance of traditional procedure. For example, when we study the abstract notion of *set*, we also consider the collection L_ω of hereditarily finite sets generated from ϕ by the operation: $x, y \to x \cup \{y\}$, and formulate axioms and definitions valid for L_ω. But once our attention has been drawn to these axioms we make a fresh start and ask if they also hold for the abstract notion; cf. note 13 on p. 146 of [19].

I begin with computations (and not with logic) because here, at least occasionally, our *usual* meaning is formalistic; specifically, when we write down the formula

(*) $$0 + s0 = s0$$

(where s is the successor symbol) we sometimes *mean* that the formula (*) itself is obtained by *applying the defining equations for addition*

$$a + 0 = a \qquad a + sb = s(a + b);$$

here it is tacitly understood that the LHS in a defining equation is replaced by the RHS (and not vice versa) until a closed term is reduced to its *canonical form*, namely a *numeral* 0, s0, ss0, ... Thus the defining equations play a *double role,* as *computation rules* in the sense just described, and as *assertions* about the mapping, from numerals to numerals, determined by these computation rules. The distinction is genuine; for example, the totally undefined function is computed from the rule: replace *fa* by $2fsa$, but the *constant* function $\dot{0}$ satisfies

$$fn = 2f(n + 1) \text{ for all } n.$$

The rest of this Appendix will be quite concentrated, assuming a good knowledge of the literature cited.

(a) *Semantics of T* here, as in [7], regarded as an *equational calculus.* Thus, as is familiar from the reduction of primitive recursive arithmetic to equational form, we need an *equality functional* (here for each finite type σ) and formulate *induction* by the rule:
For terms t_1 and t_2 of type $0 \to \sigma$, derive $t_1 n = t_2 n$ if $t_1 0 = t_2 0$ and $t_1 sn = tnt_1 n$, $t_2 sn = tnt_2 n$ have been derived for some term t of type $0 \to (\sigma \to \sigma)$, with variable n of type 0.

Then an interpretation or 'realization' must give a meaning to the constants, the variables and = only; for a *constructive* treatment it would be natural to require also a specified class of *proofs* (of formulae with free variables) as in [22], p. 202, 1.-11. While at some later stage it will perhaps be useful to consider *all* models of T, for the present purpose of answering questions (α)–(γ) at the beginning of this Appendix, it is crucial to pick out *relevant models.*

The reader is referred to [7] for the meaning which led (Gödel) to the formulation of T, in terms of the abstract impredicative notions of *constructive function of finite* type over the natural numbers and of *definitional equality.* Contrary to the most familiar idea of function of finite type in constructive mathematics, even for $\sigma \neq 0$, an operation of type $\sigma \to \tau$ **does not operate on 'approximations' to the argument (of type** σ) but on a rule (or *definition* of the argument). Thus we do not expect extensionality and, a fortiori, not continuity. Any *general doubts* about the sense of these explanations are quickly dispelled by its recursive version HRO, developed by Troelstra in [46], already mentioned in §2c(iii).

(i) Here the *domain* of the model of T consists of HRO, the *hereditarily recursive operations,* that is (physical) *programmes* of a Turing machine, which are, hereditarily, well-defined; the relation realizing = is *literal identity*. Closed terms are interpreted by a programme in such a way that the axioms of T hold in this model. For reference in (b) below: we can get non-mechanical models too, for example hereditarily hyperarithmetic operations.

Evidently, not every object in HRO has a *name* in T for this interpretation, which is unacceptable in a formalist foundation; HRO is not recursively listable. The following *refinement* is typical of the use of recursive models referred to in the introduction:

Since T is quantifier-free we may cut down HRO to those programmes which *do* have names in T (and inspection shows that we can find a primitive recursive list for each finite type). Since each programme in HRO is well-defined for *all* of HRO it is automatically well-defined for our subclasses.

Discussion. While the results of [46] to which we return in (b) below, show HRO (and more generally, machine programmes) to be an excellent tool for studying T, it is less clear that T, in particular its language, has enough structure to express interesting facts about programmes. Specifically even though T has some non-extensional features and allows us to formulate operations which give different results when applied *to* distinct but extensionally equivalent programmes, it does not say anything about the execution *of* programmes. On a more technical level, even the model HRO is somewhat defective because HRO is introduced by Kleene's T predicate. This provides a good normal form for recursive *functions*, but not for *computation procedures*. As mentioned in §3b(i), Kleene lays out in an ω-order all possible computations, that is (finite) deductions in his particular equation calculus, and a computation 'from' a recursion equation say e consists in going through this list till one hits a deduction which really is such a computation! (Whatever else may be in doubt this is a different procedure from simply carrying out the relevant, last, deduction).

(ii) Models more directly related to T can be defined by means of the concept of *hereditarily computable term* introduced in [44] (where 'convertible' is used for 'computable'). The essential step is to pick out, from among the (equational) axioms, *defining equations* for constants t say, of the form $t = t_1$. They are used as *computation rules*, determined by the immediate reduction relation, say $\circ\!\!\rightarrow$, where $t' \circ\!\!\rightarrow t''$ means:

t'' is the result of replacing the subterm t of t' by t_1.

The relation $\circ\!\!\to$ is primitive recursive and finitary.[14] The terminology is justified because of the strong computability property of $\circ\!\!\to$: Every reduction sequence ρ starting with t terminates in an irreducible term $|t|_\rho$ say, and $|t|_\rho$, $|t|_{\rho'}$, are *unique up to congruence*; this normal form of t is denoted by $|t|$.

The *metamathematical principles* needed are

quite elementary for the proof of *congruence*, i.e., of *consistency of computation rules,*

ϵ_0-recursion for *existence* of normal forms in the sense that for $\alpha < \epsilon_0$ there is a t_α of type $0 \to 0$ such that $|t_\alpha s^n 0| = s^{fn}0$ and f is not α-recursive. (This also shows that the *transitive closure* of $\circ\!\!\to$ is not α-recursive).[15] To be precise one needs sequence variables to *state* that *every* ρ terminates but the proof does not need strong existential axioms on ρ and can be formalized in a conservative extension of ϵ_0-arithmetic; cf. also b(i).

To describe three models of T ($\mathfrak{T}$ for 'term', $\mathfrak{N}$ for 'normal term', $\mathfrak{M}$ for 'mapping') we use $\equiv$ for congruence, t for *closed* terms, t_1 for closed terms of type σ if t is of type $\sigma \to \tau$. Let $\bar{t}$ denote the *mapping* (function): $|t_1| \mapsto |tt_1|$ if t is of type $\sigma \to \tau$, and $|t|$ if t is of type 0, and let $\underset{\circ}{=}$ denote *extensional equality* between such mappings. The *domains* of the models below consist of realizations of (all the) closed terms.

	$\mathfrak{T}$	$\mathfrak{N}$	$\mathfrak{M}$
t	t	$\|t\|$	$\bar{t}$
$t = t'$	$\|t\| \equiv \|t'\|$	$\|t\| \equiv \|t'\|$	$\bar{t} \underset{\circ}{=} \bar{t'}$
(possibly)			
juxtaposition	$t, t_1 \mapsto tt_1$	$\|t\|, \|t_1\| \mapsto \|tt_1\|$	$\bar{t}, \bar{t}_1 \mapsto (\overline{tt_1})$

Thus, = is, essentially, realized by identity in $\mathfrak{N}$ (but not in $\mathfrak{T}$). Usually juxtaposition is treated as a purely syntactic term combinator and not given a realization by some kind of application operation (it is not function *application* itself not even in $\mathfrak{M}$). This matter affects the recursion theoretic complexity of the description of $\mathfrak{N}$, since the set of normal terms and the con-

[14] The notation in [44] is different. Also, for the sake of the particular method of proof used, Tait picks a (more deterministic) subset of these computation rules. Note for reference that the converse of $\circ\!\!\to$ is not finitary since e.g. for all n, $s^n 0.0 \circ\!\!\to 0$.

[15] These questions concerning methods of proof and definition are to be distinguished from those concerning the (extensional order) *type* of this relation; cf. the digression in § 2a(i) and § 3a(iii) of the main text, and b(ii) below.

gruence relation are primitive recursive, but the mapping $|t|, |t_1| \mapsto |tt_1|$ is not.

The *metamathematical principles* needed to establish that these objects are models of T includes ϵ_0-recursion since the mapping: $t \mapsto |t|$ intervenes. (If, in the pedantic fashion of [22], p.202(b), the realization of a formula with variables involves a *proof*, we can take proofs denoted by derivations in T itself.) Evidently the *consistency* of T asserts more than the consistency of the computation rules (determined by the defining equations) of T, because T contains also such *inference rules* as induction and substitution which allow shortcuts; for example we derive $0 + a = a$ and infer $0 + s^n 0 = s^n 0$ by substitution without going through the computation of $0 + s^n 0$ from the defining equations for addition.

Remark. As would be expected from the formalist conception which suppresses type distinctions, both the *data* (the computation relation $\circ\!\!\rightarrow$) to be considered and our *assertions about the data* (formulated in T) are presented by similar formal procedures. But the roles are different; in the language of model theory, $\circ\!\!\rightarrow$ determines (more or less directly) the diagram of *given* models while the axioms and rules of T are *shown* to be valid for them; hence the expression 'inference' rule above. The particular models $\mathfrak{T}$, $\mathfrak{N}$, $\mathfrak{M}$ are *canonical* in the sense that T has a *name* for each element in their domains.

(iii) Leaving to (b) a discussion of the uses of (ii) at the present time, we may mention *routine* generalizations of (ii). Thus, reversing the historical order, instead of selecting defining equations from a given equational calculus, one would start with a suitable class of computation relations $\circ\!\!\rightarrow$, and look for equational calculi valid for them in the sense of a(ii); note that a(ii) makes sense even if $\circ\!\!\rightarrow$ is defined for objects which have no name in the equational calculus. ('Suitable' means that the class is large, yet satisfies lots of, equational, axioms and rules). Or we might look for manageable syntactic conditions on sets of equations which ensure strong computability (of all closed terms built up from the symbols in the equations); in other words, we ask: What are defining equations? As a corollary one would expect information on *general* extensions of classes of defining equations which preserve computability such as the familiar addition of an *equality functional* E with the reduction rules, for closed terms t, t':

$$\text{From } |t| \equiv |t'| \text{ derive } E(t, t') = 1$$

$$\neg |t| \equiv |t'| \text{ derive } E(t, t') = 0.$$

Warning. For sensible conjectures it is necessary to keep a firm grasp of the distinction between computations or conversions on the one hand and proofs on the other (even if within some limited context we may happen to have some extensional equivalence). This is well illustrated by allowing *free variables in the defining equations* of T. Their computability, to normal terms also possibly containing free variables, is shown as for closed terms and, consequently, $\{(t', t''): |t'| \equiv |t''|\}$ is recursive. Inspection shows, for constants t', t'' of type $\sigma \to \tau$ and *variable* a of type σ that

$$|t'| \equiv |t''| \Leftrightarrow |t'a| \equiv |t''a| \,.$$

Also, of course

$$|t'| \equiv |t''| \Rightarrow \vdash_T t' = t'' \,.$$

But while the converse holds for *closed* t', t'', it does not hold, in general, for open terms. In fact, for primitive recursive t', t'' of type $0 \to 0$ the sets

$$\{(t', t''): \vdash_T t'a = t''a\} \text{ and } \{(t', t''): \exists n \vdash_T t's^n 0 \neq t''s^n 0\}$$

are not even recursively separable. Naturally it would be interesting to analyze explicitly the distinction between computation and inference rules involved here but in the mean time one had better respect it implicitly if one wants to work in the field at all.

Model theoretic terminology is suitable to describe the facts above. Thus T is *sound* for its own computation rules, that is, for closed terms t' and t''

$$(\vdash_T t' = t'') \Rightarrow |t'| \equiv |t''|$$

and T is *complete* since

$$(|t'| \equiv |t''| \Rightarrow \vdash_T t' = t'')$$

(the latter even for *open* t' and t'').

(b) *Reviewing the situation.* Without going into the reasons why the models HRO in a(i), $\mathfrak{T}$ or $\mathfrak{N}$ in a(ii) were introduced or why people wanted to assign ordinals to terms of T in (i) below, we shall consider some philosophical and mathematical uses.

(i) Gödel's intention in [7] was to use (the properties of the notion of constructive function of finite type codified in) T for a *consistency proof* of formal arithmetic. The models HRO, $\mathfrak{T}$ or $\mathfrak{N}$ are not suitable because they are, literally, defined in arithmetic terms, with this difference: HRO is even extensionally non-arithmetic, while $\mathfrak{N}$ has at least a primitive recursive domain and = (though not application). The *proof*, e.g. in [44], showing that $\mathfrak{N}$ is a model uses full arithmetic together with the reflection principle for $\forall\exists$ formulae. (It applies induction to the logically complicated computability predicate to show that the latter is primitive recursive! all terms being computable.) This is well known to be proof theoretically equivalent to ϵ_0-recursion, by Gentzen's syntactic transformations discussed in §2.

Alternatively *this* proof theoretic equivalence can now be established by the formal reduction to T in [7] together with the assignment of ordinals $< \epsilon_0$ to terms of T in [9] (or the earlier but neglected work [58]), the metamathematical principles used being identical. The total labour required for the two alternatives is probably much the same in the particular case of formal arithmetic here considered; see §2b and the survey [55] for advantages of the second alternative (the functional interpretation) for *extensions* of arithmetic, when an ordinal analysis is unwieldy. Naturally this route is really attractive if the relevant computation rules are found to have independent interest.

In [7] definitional equality between terms of type $\neq 0$ was mentioned but not used. Tait expressed doubts in [44] about the sense of definitional equality $t = t'$ unless all possible *arguments* of t and t' are listed. Whatever the virtues of such a listing may be, the model HRO shows clearly that those doubts are unfounded (and so do non-canonical models referred to in a(iii) if models more in the style of [44] are preferred).[16]

Finally it is perhaps worth remarking that, in accordance with footnote 6 of [19], the mechanical character of the rules treated is not essential to the notion of definitional equality; cf. a(i).

(ii) The particular mathematical uses of $\mathfrak{N}$ emphasized in [44], for example the *conservative extension* property of T^ω (that is T with decidable = and intuitionistic logic for functions of finite type) over first order arithmetic,

[16] This was stressed in my review of [44]. I take this opportunity to correct an error there when I say that computability of terms is also needed for 1 – consistency: any model of T (over the natural numbers) provides some numerical denotation for each closed term of type 0. So if $\exists x A x$ has been proved in arithmetic for primitive recursive A, by [7] there is a term t for which At is proved in T, and if $\bar{t}$ is the value of t in the given model, $A\bar{t}$ is true and hence derivable in arithmetic. Of course without computability of the numerical term t, its denotations in different models might be distinct.

can also be proved by use of HRO. More simply, as is to be expected from §2b since HRO is a more 'brutal' model.

Presumably $\mathfrak{N}$ is more efficient when the defining equations themselves (and not general models) of T are principal objects of study. But, perhaps, $\mathfrak{N}$ is still the best tool for the following result which does not mention 'defining equations':

There is a *free* model of T, that is for closed terms t_1, t_2

$$t_1 = t_2 \text{ is true in the model iff } \vdash_T t_1 = t_2$$

and this model is *recursive.*

Still taking the interest of T for granted, a more striking use of a(ii) is the connection established between (the functionals of) T and a genuine ordered structure, specifically the (well-founded) *computation relation* induced by the defining equations, read from left to right, and presumably of (order) type ϵ_0 (ω being excluded by the remark in footnote 14). As in footnote 15, ϵ_0 has here an extensional , not an auxiliary metamathematical significance. This connection between the formal principles T and ϵ_0 is certainly not apparent from HRO nor, as already discussed in §3b, from the original interpretation of T.

However, the most fruitful step at the present time is to *look* for significant stronger results. Goodman showed (in unpublished work) that the conservative extension property holds if *axioms of choice* are added to T^ω. Here $\mathfrak{N}$ does not seem to be enough; nor HRO even though one of the most interesting results of [46] asserts that it is consistent to assume that HRO satisfies axioms of choice.

Remark on conservative extension results. Technically they serve to *formulate* explicitly vaguely felt 'differences' between different metamathematical studies; for example the simple $\neg\neg$ translation shows only that classical analysis is conservative over the theory of species for $\forall$ formulae, while Spector's work was used in [19] to extend this to $\forall\exists$ formulae; cf. §2a(ii). But, at the risk of sounding a bit pompous, one can say more: they establish *adequacy or: autonomy properties of languages and principles of inference*. Recall that when we justify axioms in constructive mathematics, say in arithmetic, we refer to *proofs* and *functions* (on proofs), concepts which are not mentioned in the language of formal arithmetic at all. Indeed extending the language (and principles) constitutes the most familiar method of strengthening necessarily incomplete systems of arithmetic, for example when induction is applied to predicates in a wider language. Now conservative extension results establish *adequacy with respect to the addition of certain principles formulated in a wider language.* It may fairly be said that once we drop the doctrinaire elements of Hilbert's programme (cf. SPT, pp. 360–361) *reductive proof theory in its proper sense requires conservative extension and not merely consistency results.*

(iii) Granted an interest in T, (i) and (ii) contain a useful summary of its more delicate formal properties. But as formalists are never tired of saying, the interest of formal systems depends on one's 'purposes'. The only explicitly stated purpose of T, for a consistency proof of arithmetic, is not helped by the formalistic refinements of a (ii); cf. (i) above. So what purposes *are* to be served here?

Though a(i) and a(ii) mention *computation* rules it cannot be claimed that the particular rules of T, operating on terms of higher type, are obviously typical of the actual practice of computer science. A more promising purpose can, perhaps, be found if, as in [44], we think of T as formulated by use of combinators, and of *combinators as providing the language for a systematic theory of formal procedures*; as *set theory* provides the language for *classical* (extensional) *mathematics.* This sensible aim is sometimes obscured by 'glamorous' but far-fetched allusions to paradoxes of self reflection.

The semantics of combinators is more sophisticated than $\mathfrak{T}$ or $\mathfrak{N}$ in a(ii) where each term t in (the equational calculus) T denotes itself or at least its normal form; in short t denotes an object *in* the computation relation. Combinators would express something *about* the computation relation. Or, to use familiar model theory, *combinators would have the role of logical operations.* Equations not containing combinators should correspond to atomic formulae which denote relations *in* the models considered, while logically complicated formulae express something *about* the model denoting objects in the set-theoretic *super structure* over the model (first order formulae denote sub*sets* of the domain of the model). As philosophers sometimes say: the logical operations do not 'represent' (anything *in* the model). And the introduction of combinators, or something like them, suggests itself because the *use of logically complicated formulae has turned out to be marvellously efficient for expressing notions and facts about mathematical structures which we,* that is mathematicians who have studied these structures, *really want to know*! (For example: infinite, convergent, uniformly convergent can all be expressed systematically in the language of first order arithmetic with its usual interpretation).

But here the parallel ends. The *expressive power* of the model theoretic interpretation of our familiar logical languages has been *established.* We have a substantial body of informal mathematics *and* we have *Principia* which verified that this body of notions and results can be formulated in the language of set theory (with its ordinary interpretation). In the projected theory of formal procedures, we do not have the analogue to *Principia*; in fact, we hardly have the analogue to the body of informal mathematics mentioned above. Perhaps before searching for a language (of combinators) proper to a *systematic* theory of computations, we might ask ourselves quite soberly what we really want to know about them at all.

(c) *Formalist semantics.* The impredicative starting point is the Brouwer-Heyting explanation of the logical particles. To be precise, we have two variants, one *using* logic in the explanation itself (cf. also §4(d) in connection with Kripke's models), the other *reducing* all logic to proofs of identities, that is assertions which are not logically compound; cf., e.g., [19], note 11 on p.146 concerning 'operations' and 'judgements'.

The reader is referred to Prawitz' article [37] in this volume for two examples of formalist interpretations (which satisfy Heyting's formal laws.) One, in Chapter IV of [37], is an abstract *functional* scheme using familiar λ-terms. The other, called *operational* in App. A, is more concrete, using (normalization) operations on formal deductions in familiar systems (adjoined to arbitrary Post systems). Both use logic in the metamathematical explanations, as in the first of Heyting's variants above.[17]

There is, by now, no shadow of doubt about the value for current proof theoretic studies of such formalist interpretations which, by Chapter IV of [37], relate terms-cum-computations to derivations-cum-normalizations. Even a quite rough idea of this homomorphism has turned out to be useful! In one direction, normalization procedures for deductions in the theory of species were suggested by Girard's computations of terms [56] and, in the opposite direction, Hinata's assignment of ordinals to terms [58] was suggested by one of Takeuti's ordinal analyses of deductions.

As to the initial questions (α) and (γ) of this Appendix the references above give quite a good idea of the general aims of formalist semantics and its

[17] To avoid (fairly common) oversights the reader should note that Heyting does not treat explicitly the notion of *logical validity*, but rather explains the meaning of the logical operations, tacitly assuming that the *atomic* formulae are interpreted and the domains of the variables are given. A definition of *logical validity* requires us to analyze these tacit assumptions, by considering all possible domains and all possible interpretations, which is done explicitly in §4c above. Evidently Heyting makes the (unstated, but not unreasonable) assumption that we know so little about these possible domains and interpretations that any proof of logical validity must be uniform in them, treat them as parameters. And by [33] existing formal theories of species are consistent with this in the sense that if $\forall X_1 \dots \forall X_n \exists x A$ is derivable, so is $\forall X_1 \dots \forall X_n A[x/t]$ for a term t independent of $X_1, \dots, X_n$.

mathematical uses (It seems plausible that the material on T reported in (a) and (b) can be obtained as some kind of corollary if the *computation rules* of T are construed as suitable Post rules.) It remains to consider question (β) and, of course, corresponding to b(iii), the expressive power of formalist interpretations.

(i) *Logically complex (recursive) realizability.* This is a recursive 'intermediary' between the abstract notion and its formalist substitute. To avoid purely superficial but distracting blemishes, let me begin with some trivial modifications in Kleene's original realizability (for number theory); cf. also Troelstra's exposition in this volume. We write $R(e, \alpha)$ for:

e realizes the (closed) formula α.

For *atomic* formulae α, Kleene puts $R(e, \alpha) \Leftrightarrow \alpha$, which is natural in number theory where all atomic formulae are decidable. If instead we had some Post system for generating atomic formulae we should put

$R(e, \alpha) \Leftrightarrow e$ derives α in the system.

(Indeed, this style of modification is used when Kleene modifies the clauses of his realizability definition by additional requirements of formal derivability or validity of α in order to get suitable *derived* rules.)

Again in the interpretation of the *universal quantifier* for number theory it is natural to hold the domain fixed. When treating general Post systems as 'approximations to our knowledge about atomic sentences' (as in 1.1 of Chapter IV in [37]), approximations to our knowledge of the domain of individuals suggest expanding rather than constant domains (familiar from Kripke's models [24]).

Finally, and quite trivially, Kleene's *type-free* realizations (e can realize different formulae) may be replaced by a typed version where now a formula α is realized by the *pair*, (e, α), where, in Kleene's version, it is realized by e itself; *application* is defined by

$$\{(e', \alpha \to \beta)\}\,(e, \alpha) = (\{e'\}(e), \beta).$$

I want to go into the realizability interpretation of *implication* more carefully because its non-standard character is often (though not always: cf. note 1 on p.143 of [19]) overlooked. It is directly relevant here because it also affects the (logically complex) formalist interpretations in [37]. We are not merely verifying some given formal laws; so we have to make the *intensions of realizability more explicit*. To repeat (from §4d and elsewhere): It would be circular to use logical operations in the definition of realizability if the latter were intended to tell us their meaning. But it is perfectly sensible to use them (if we understand them), to render the meaning of α more explicit. This is done by introducing the relation $R(e, \alpha)$, that is

e realizes α

with (the proposition denoted by) α *equivalent* to $\exists e R(e,\alpha)$. So $\alpha \to \beta$ is rendered by

$$\exists e' R(e', \alpha) \Rightarrow \exists e'' R(e'', \beta),$$

or

$$\forall e' [R(e', \alpha) \Rightarrow \exists e'' R(e'', \beta)] .$$

Despite the fact that $R(e', \alpha)$ is in general undecidable, $R(e, \alpha \to \beta)$ is taken to be

$$(**) \qquad \forall e' [R(e', \alpha) \Rightarrow R(\{e\}(e'), \beta)] .$$

This step is certainly non-standard, for example, the equivalence between (*) and (**) is not a formal theorem of first order arithmetic (though it can be stated in arithmetic language for fixed α and β). If, as in Kleene's original formulation, $\{e\}$ is *partial,* the interpretation means that e'' depends *only* on e' and not on other information about $R(e', \alpha)$. In short, though e'' does not depend extensionally on the function $\{e'\}$, the dependence is 'too' extensional because it ignores differences between possible proofs of $R(e', \alpha)$. The non-standard character becomes even more striking if, instead of partial functions, we consider *total* realizing functions. (This applies directly to Chapter IV of [37] ; and such total 'typed' variants of Kleene's realizability also satisfy Heyting's laws; for a related example worked out in the literature, cf. the modified realizability interpretation by HRO or HEO studied in [46].) Then the passage from (*) to (**) amounts to replacing

$$\forall e' [R(e', \alpha) \Rightarrow \exists e'' R(e'', \beta)] \text{ by } \forall e' \exists e'' [R(e', \alpha) \Rightarrow R(e'', \beta)] ,$$

although $R(e', \alpha)$ *is an undecidable predicate* (of e').

This concludes the comments *about* recursive realizability, and we turn to the *basic refinement* corresponding to that of a(i).

> Use variables for different types and write down
> *explicit closure conditions* (on their ranges) sufficient
> to provide realizations of all formally derivable theorems.

As in b(ii) we may ask for the technical use of such refinements. Clearly they are not needed for 'brutal' results such as the formal independence of

$$\forall x\, \exists y\, \forall z\, [T(x,x,y) \vee \neg T(x,x,z)]$$

for which ordinary recursive realizability is sufficient. On the other hand the first proof of independence of Markov's principle in predicate logic ([16], p.113, 3.52) relied on such a refinement.

Remark. The great number of possible variants of realizability interpretations of the logical operations (in particular of $\forall$ and $\rightarrow$ above, all satisfying Heyting's laws) seem to me to support the view expressed in the introduction to this Appendix: not the existence *of*, but the choice *between*, formalist semantics is the most fruitful issue, at least at the present time.

(ii) *Logic-free formalist semantics*, where in contrast to realizability in (i) the metamathematical explanations do not have a logical residue. One good example is in Gödel's work [7] where an even more obviously non-standard interpretation of $\rightarrow$ is used than in realizability. Gödel's original interpretation is not formalist in the sense of this Appendix although the terms used are explicitly listed, since no *formalist* meaning is given to them. Such a meaning is supplied by [44] but *this* version is not logic-free; cf. b(i) above and also §2c(iii).

A **thoroughly logic free and formalist** semantics (satisfying Heyting's laws) can presumably be obtained by formalizing appropriately the logic-free version of the Brouwer-Heyting explanation mentioned in the first paragraph of the present subsection (c). The particular use of *partial* functions by Goodman [59] does not recommend itself for this purpose because of the, apparently, essential use of the hidden logical operation involved in the concept 'is defined'.

As already mentioned in b(ii) some refinement in this direction seems to be needed for the best formal results to date (concerning the addition of axioms of choice). If this need is genuine, the extra complication introduced by having variables over *judgements* may be tolerable; 'extra' compared to the already complicated formalist refinements of recursive realizability.

Evidently logic-free (formalist) semantics have foundational interest only because the relevant *definition principles can be given an independent justification* (as in §3 or [20]).

Remark. Again the mere existence of such semantics is not problematic, by note 32 on p.513 of [20] applied to logic free progressions (indexed by ordinals σ). The critical point, once more in the interpretation of $\rightarrow$, is the *height restriction* ρ_σ expressing the informal requirement that, at stage σ, the step from σ' to $\rho_\sigma(\sigma')$ is known to be justified; cf. [20], p.498. Writing $P(e, \sigma; \alpha)$ for the relation:

> e, coding a derivation e_1 and a term e_2, both at level σ, realizes the formulae α (at σ),

$P(e, \sigma; \alpha \rightarrow \beta)$ requires e_1 to be a formal derivation at σ of

$$P(e', \sigma'; \alpha) \Rightarrow P[e_2 e', \rho_\sigma(\sigma'); \beta]$$

with variables e' and σ'. Here, and in contrast to (i), P is *decidable.*

(iii) For orientation on *purposes of formalist semantics* it is well to remember common features of all reductionist schemes.[18] They begin with, often doctrinaire, objections to existing notions. The reductions are not uniquely determined. Closer examination shows the objections to be more dubious than the notions in question. At this stage the 'glamour' of the reductionist scheme fades. Nevertheless we may return to the scheme, no longer satisfied with the mere existence of a reduction, but requiring it to help us understand matters of established interest. There are two general directions.

Firstly we may want to know about the objects used in the reductionist scheme. Specifically, if we consider the *operational* semantics in App. A of [37] which is about *formal rules*, we ask ourselves what we want to know about them; cf. b(iii) in connection with computations. The very first question (of any semantics) is:

> What can we express?

in the given language with our interpretation. Here is a possible 'test'. In his book *Beweistheorie* [41] pp.40–46, Schütte treats *zulässige, ableitbare, and*

[18] To avoid misunderstanding: formalist semantics is not *explicitly* needed for Hilbert's programme, that paradigm of reductive proof theory, which does not interpret logically complex formulae at all. But such interpretations are usually needed to *find* consistency proofs and, particularly, to make the syntactic transformations intelligible; for a convincing example see App. A of [37].

direkt ableitbare Regeln, that is rules which are conservative (also called: derived), demonstrably derived by constructive means, respectively derived in a specific uniform way (and conservative for all extensions). These notions are perhaps not central, but they are quite natural. So one could see whether the operational interpretation (of familiar languages) is able to express at least *these* notions 'about' formal operations. More generally, it seems to me we could profit here from experience with Kripke's interpretation [24]. No doubt the original intention was to give a set theoretic *reduction* of some current non-classical notions, among them the (impredicative) meaning of the logical particles introduced by Brouwer-Heyting. It turned out to have weaknesses for this analysis; cf. the view of [24]. But besides having several *unexpected* foundational uses such as those discussed in §4, this interpretation of the usual logical language was also found to have striking *expressive power*; 'striking' because the well-known (and at one time startling) expressive power of first order predicate logic was verified for its *model theoretic* interpretation. As shown (in unpublished work) by D.Gabbay and C.Smorynski, very natural *geometric* properties of trees can here be characterized by formulae of simple syntactic structure. So if one wants a general theory of the kind of models treated in [24] at all, the language of predicate calculus with the interpretation of [24] may fairly be said to have intrinsic (non-doctrinaire) interest. Incidentally for *this* interpretation the restriction to the usual intuitionistic propositional operations is quite artificial; what is usually described as a 'necessity' operator □ is *here* as natural a unary propositional operator as can be desired[19]. Perhaps this point should be kept in mind in work on operational semantics and the *addition of new 'logical' operators* should be envisaged.

The second, somewhat neglected, kind of use for reductionist schemes is as *an aid in the analysis of the abstract notions themselves*! For example, the natural use of formal independence results, by unintended 'elementary' models of the axioms A considered, belongs here. The results should not be regarded as showing some indefiniteness or other defect of the abstract notions, but as a *defect of our present analysis* (of them) codified by A. And

[19] On the other hand the description of □ as a 'necessity' operator is quite unconvinding since no serious analysis of (objective) *possibility* is even attempted: a structure is considered to be possible if it is consistent with the positive diagram of the available information. Nor is it verified that more realistic hypotheses about objective possibility can be expressed in the language of predicate logic. (The fact that the resulting formal laws are similar to *some* 'ordinary' uses of *possible* simply reflects the superficial character of these uses.) Current probability theory and statistics provide a much more sophisticated analysis of: possibility.

independence proofs *pin-point* specific problems about these notions which actually require further analysis. (Experience suggests that one cannot rely on ordinary practice to lead automatically to such problems; after all, even when strong axioms have actually been formulated such as those of set theory, it takes mathematicians a long time to learn to use them efficiently.) Evidently as long as the reductions are used as technical auxiliaries in this way they need not have intrinsic interest.

Another use of the same kind, that is a use which depends on the reductions being more *manageable* than the abstract notions (of primary interest), is this. The study of the reductions *suggests* certain (formal) relations and we then use them, for example conversion relations (in the case of operational semantics), to *analyze, not to replace abstract relations* (such as identity of proofs denoted by derivations). This requires a *separate* investigation, and, as we have seen in § 1a and § 1c, the *exact* significance of the formal relations in the literature is still in doubt. Here it must be remarked that *stability properties* (such as an homomorphism or even isomorphism between two such structures as terms and derivations; cf. Chapter IV of [37]) are not relevant. An independent adequacy condition is needed, of the kind discussed in § 1c. Of course as we have seen, the particular proposal of § 1c was too simple minded[20]. In any case stability results provide no safeguard against a *systematic oversight* (when we overlook intended conversion and computation rules for the *same* reason) nor against *confusion* (when we overlook, say, a conversion rule *because* the corresponding computation rules is not intended).

[20] (Added in proof) More sophisticated proposals might use work on the λ-calculus and the homomorphism between λ-terms and deductions. Specifically, as Mr. Barendregt has pointed out to me, completeness in the sense of Hilbert-Post (of the *relevant* λ-calculus!) would certainly by sufficient. A paradigm of a Hilbert-Post completeness result, for equations between normalizable terms, was established by Bohm [61].

Appendix II
Addenda and Corrigenda to SPT

The major additions made in the present article are not listed. A symbol [SPT n] means reference [n] of SPT, pp. 385–388; for supplements to the incomplete references cf. [20] p. 516.

Pp. 331–332, footnote 8. It has to be remembered that, for cut-free systems, *not all inconsistencies are demonstrably interdeducible,* that is, there is no proof (in the system) of

$$(\vdash A \wedge \vdash \neg A) \leftrightarrow (\vdash B \wedge \vdash \neg B)\,.$$

where the variables A and B range over all formulae. In connection with Hilbert's programme, the relevant inconsistencies are of the form that both A and $\neg A$ are derivable where A is (the translation of) a *real,* that is *numerical* assertion. Perhaps it should be called "Hilbert consistency". Also on p. 349, 1.3, "consistency" (of Takeuti's cut-free analysis) means: Hilbert consistency. Translations of numerical assertions, specifically equations between numerals, in Takeuti's system are first order formulae. To avoid misunderstanding: it is not literally true that Takeuti "observed" the result that I attribute to him, in the sense of actually *stating* it; but he observed a fact (derivations in his system of first order formulae consist only of first order formulae) which implies the result in an elementary way and he gave an elementary proof of this fact. Actually the proof establishes consistency uniformly for all first order formulae.

P. 350. The three questions are solved; cf. [19], p. 136. Question 1 has a positive answer. Questions 2 and 3 are answered by the result:

There are primitive recursive functionals F_1 and F_2 for which the following properties can be established finitistically:

(a) Suppose (the function) ψ maps a derivation with cut into a derivation without cut of the same end formula, then $F_1\psi$ maps any derivation of $\exists x Ax$, for a canonical representation A of a primitive recursive predicate, into a numerical derivation of An for some numeral n; for short, $F_1\psi$ established 1-consistency.

(b) Conversely, if (the function) σ establishes 1-consistency, then $F_2\sigma$ establishes the normal form theorem.

Thus Question 2 has a negative answer. Question 3(i) has a negative answer and (consequently) Question 3(ii) a positive one.

P. 351. All questions and conjectures in (2), i.e., 1. 3 to the end of (SPT §11) are settled.

P. 357, 1.1. The material of [SPT 2] has now appeared in improved form in J.Barwise, Applications of strict Π_1^1 predicates to infinitary logic, JSL 34 (1969) 409–422.

P. 357, 1. 4–6. The question has been settled positively by: J.Gregory, On a finiteness condition for infinitary logic, Dissertation, University of Maryland, 1969.

P. 367 (c) (i). $\mathcal{C}$ should be defined to be the collection of functions which are arithmetic (and not only those which are recursive) in some complete Π_1^1-set. Otherwise Π_1^0-CA *with* set parameters is not satisfied. The rest of the argument is unaffected.

P. 371, 1. 16–17 is false. If A is Π_2^1 and the Σ_3^1 sentence $(\exists X \in 2^\omega)A$ is provable in **ZF**, so is $(\exists X \in L \cap 2^\omega)A$ by SPT Note VI b(i) 1.c. But it is consistent to add to ZF the assumption that all constructible sets of integers are analytic [R.B.Jensen, Notices Am. Math. Soc. 15 (1968) 189, 68T-6]. It seems to be open whether there is an A in Π_2^1 (with a single free variable X) such that $A(X^*)$ is a theorem of **ZF** for some set theoretically defined X^*, but not for any analytic X^*.

P. 375, footnote 34. Friedman's construction has appeared under the title: Bar Induction and Π_1^1-CA, JSL 34 (1969) 353–362. *Correction.* Footnote 1 of this paper is perfectly true because I did make suggestions on writing the paper; only Friedman did not adopt these suggestions, and the interest of his work is not apparent. But the interest exists and, for once, happens to be best described in autobiographical terms. (i) In footnote 25 of [17] p. 139 I mentioned a model of bar induction; what I *said* was true, namely that there is such a model whose elements are of hyper degree $<0'$; what I *meant* was false, namely that *all* such functions constitute a model. (ii) I noticed the error as soon as Thomason's results on hyper degrees were announced because his results show that the model I meant does not satisfy the pairing axiom. (iii) A correction, stating (i) and (ii) explicitly, is in footnote 34 of SPT. (iv) While SPT was in print I prepared [55] where bar recursion of transfinite degree is considered in Problems 2 and 3 on p. 156. I convinced myself that if (i) could be made to work, Problem 2 would certainly have a positive solution (and hence Problem 3 a negative one) because the schema of bar recursion of transfinite degree has a model by socalled continuous or countable functionals of transfinite degree. Specifically, bar induction for $L_{\omega_1\omega}$ would allow us to extend the model of [55] §3 for bar recursion of finite degree by ordinary bar induction. Hence my interest, referred to in Friedman's paper, in the extension to $L_{\omega_1\omega}$. (v) I mentioned (i) – (iv) to him; he not only made sense of (i), but noticed that Problem 2 of [55] has a positive solution even with $\Pi_1^1 - CA$ instead of $\Delta_2^1 - CA$. (vi) The solution was too late to be included in [55], but I added a reference to it in SPT, at the end of footnote 34 ("added in proof").

References

[1] W.Ackermann, Grundgedanken einer typenfreien Logik, in: Essays on the foundations of mathematics (Magnes Press, Jerusalem and North-Holland, Amsterdam, 1961) 143–155.
[2] H.B.Curry and R.Feys, Combinatory logic (North-Holland, Amsterdam, 1958).
[3] S.Feferman, Systems of predicative analysis, JSL 29 (1964) 1–30.
[4] S.Feferman, Systems of predicative analysis II; Representation of ordinals, JSL 33 (1968) 193–220.
[5] S.Feferman, Predicatively reducible systems of set theory, Proc. Symp. Pure Math. 13 (AMS, Providence, 1971).
[6] S.Feferman, Ordinals and functionals in proof theory (ICM, Nice, 1970).
[7] K.Gödel, Uber einer bisher noch nicht benutzte Erweiterung des finiten Standpunktes, Dialectica 12 (1958) 280–287.
[8] A.Heyting, Die formalen Regeln der intuitionistischen Logik, S B Preuss. Akad. Wissenschaften, phys-math. Klasse (1930) 42–56.
[9] W.A.Howard, Assignment of ordinals to terms for primitive recursive functionals of finite type, in: Intuitionism and proof theory, eds. A.Kino, J.Myhill and R.E.Vesley (North-Holland, Amsterdam, 1970) 443–458.
[10] R.B.Jensen and M.E.Schroder, Mengeninduktion und Fundierungsaxiom, Arch f. math. Logik u.Grundlagen 12 (1969) 119–133.
[11] L.Kalmar, Über arithmetische Funktionen von unendlich vielen Variablen, welche an jeder Stelle nur von einer endlichen Anzahl von Variablen abhängig sind, Colloquium mathematicum 5 (1957) 1–5.
[12] S.C.Kleene, Forms of predicates in the theory of constructive ordinals, American Journal of Math. 66 (1944) 41–58; 77 (1955) 405–428.
[13] S.C.Kleene, Recursive functionals and quantifiers of finite types, Trans. A.M.S. 91 (1959) 1–52.
[14] G.Kreisel, On the interpretation of non-finitist proofs, JSL 16 (1951) 241–267.
[15] G.Kreisel, Ordinal logics and the characterization of informal concepts of proof, (ICM, Edinburgh, 1958) 289–299.
[16] G.Kreisel, Interpretation of classical analysis by means of constructive functionals of finite type, in: Constructivity in mathematics, ed. A.Heyting (North-Holland, Amsterdam, 1959) 101–128.
[17] G.Kreisel, Mathematical logic, in: Lectures on modern mathematics, vol. III, ed., Saaty (N.Y., 1965) 95–195.

[18] G.Kreisel, A survey of proof theory, JSL 33 (1968) 321–388.
[19] G.Kreisel, Church's thesis; a kind of reducibility axiom for constructive mathematics, in: Intuitionism and proof theory (North-Holland, Amsterdam, 1970) 121–150, reviewed Zentralblatt. 199 (1971) 300–301.
[20] G.Kreisel, Principles of proof and ordinals implicit is given concepts, in: Intuitionism and proof theory (North-Holland, Amsterdam, 1970) 489–516.
[21] G.Kreisel, The collected works of Gerhard Gentzen, Journal of Philosophy 68 (1971) (to appear).
[22] G.Kreisel and J.L.Krivine, Elements of mathematical logic; model theory (North-Holland, Amsterdam, 1967).
[23] G.Kreisel and A.S.Troelstra, Formal systems for some branches of intuitionistic analysis, Annals of mathematical logic 1 (1970) 229–387.
[24] S.A.Kripke, Semantical analysis of intuitionistic logic I, in: Formal systems and recursive functions, eds. J.N.Crossley and M.A.E.Dummett (North-Holland, Amsterdam, 1965) 92–130.
[25] P.Martin-Löf, Notes on constructive mathematics (Uppsala, 1970).
[26] P.Martin-Löf, this volume.
[27] P.Martin-Löf, Hauptsatz for the simple theory of types (to appear).
[28] G.E.Minc, Analog of the Herbrand's theorem for the non-prenex formulas of the constructive predicate calculus, Sem. in Math., V.A.Steklov Math. Institute, (Leningrad 4, 1969) 47–51, reviewed Zentralblatt 186 (1970) 5–6.
[29] J.Myhill, The formalization of intuitionism, in: Contemporary philosophy, ed., Klibansky (Florence, 1968) 324–341.
[30] L.Pozsgay, Liberal intuitionism as a basis for set theory, Proc. Symp. Pure Math 13 (AMS, Providence, 1971).
[31] D.Prawitz, Angående konstruktiv logik och implikationsbegreppet, in: Sju filosofiska studier tillägnade Anders Wedberg (Stockholm, 1963) 9–32, reviewed JSL 33 (1968) 605.
[32] D.Prawitz, Natural deduction, A proof theoretical study (Almquist & Wiksell, Stockholm, 1965).
[33] D.Prawitz, Some results for intuitionistic logic with second order quantifier-rules, in: Intuitionism and proof theory (North-Holland, Amsterdam, 1970) 259–269.
[34] D.Prawitz, Constructive semantics, Proc. of first Scandinavian logic symposium, Abo 1968 (Uppsala, 1970).
[35] D.Prawitz, On the proof theory of mathematical analysis, in: Logic and Value, Essays dedicated to Thorild Dahlquist on his fiftieth birthday (Uppsala, 1970).
[36] D.Prawitz, The philosophical position of proof theory, in: Contemporary philosophy in Scandinavia (Baltimore, 1970).
[37] D.Prawitz, this volume.
[38] H.Putnam, Foundations of set theory, in: Contemporary philosphy, ed. Klibansky (Florence, 1968) 275–285.
[39] B.Scarpellini, On cut elimination in intuitionistic systems of analysis, in: Intuitionism and proof theory (North-Holland, Amsterdam, 1970) 271–285.
[40] B.Scarpellini, A model for bar recursion of higher types, Compositio Math. 23 (1971) 123–153.
[41] K.Schütte, Beweistheorie (Springer, Berlin, 1960).
[42] J.R.Shoenfield, Mathematical Logic (N.Y., 1967).
[43] C.Spector, Provably recursive functionals of analysis, Recursive Function Theory, Proc. Symp. Pure Maths. 5 (1962) 1–27.

[44] W.W.Tait, Intensional interpretations of functionals of finite type I, JSL 32 (1967) 198–212, reviewed Zentralblatt 174 (1969) 12–13.
[45] G.Takeuti, A formalization of the theory of ordinal numbers JSL 30 (1965) 295–317.
[46] A.S.Troelstra, this volume.
[47] E.Wette, Definition eines (relativ vollständigen) Systems konstruktiver Arithmetik, in: Foundations of Mathematics, eds. J.J.Bulloff, T.C.Holyoke, S.W.Hahn (Springer, Berlin, 1969) 130–195, reviewed JSL 36 (1971).
[48] M.Yasugi, Interpretations of set theory and ordinal number theory, JSL 32 (1967) 145–161.
[49] J.Zucker, Dissertation, Stanford University (1971).
[50] D.Scott, Constructive validity, in: Symposium on automatic demonstration, Springer Lecture Notes 125 (1970) 237–275.
[51] S.Feferman, Formal Theories for transfinite iterations of generalized inductive definitions and some subsystems of analysis, in: Intuitionism and proof theory (North-Holland, Amsterdam, 1970) 303–326.
[52] S.Feferman, Hereditarily replete functionals over the ordinals, in: Intuitionism and proof theory (North-Holland, Amsterdam, 1970) 289–302.
[53] W.A.Howard, Assignment of ordinals to terms for type zero bar recursive functionals (abstract) JSL 35 (1970) 354.
[54] G.Kreisel, Two notes on the foundations of set-theory, Dialectica 23 (1969) 93–114.
[55] G.Kreisel, Functions, ordinals, species, in: Logic, methodology and philosophy of science III (North-Holland, Amsterdam, 1968) 145–159, reviewed Zentralblatt 187 (1970) 265–266.
[56] J.Y.Girard, this volume.
[57] A.Levy, Principles of reflection in axiomatic set theory, FM 49 (1960) 1–10.
[58] Shigeru Hinata, Calculability of primitive recursive functionals of finite type, Science Reports of the Tokyo Kyoiku Daigaku, A, 9 (1967) 218-235.
[59] N.D. Goodman, A theory of constructions equivalent to arithmetic, in: Intuitionism and proof theory (North-Holland, Amsterdam, 1970) 101–120.
[60] H.Luckhardt, Habilitationsschrift, Philipps-Universität, Marburg, 1970.
[61] C.Böhm, Alcune proprieta delle forme β-η-normali nel λ-K-calcolo, Pubblicazioni dell'istituto per le applicazioni del calcolo, no. 696, Consiglio nazionale delle ricerche, Rome, 1968.

DIOPHANTINE REPRESENTATION OF RECURSIVELY ENUMERABLE PREDICATES

Yu.V.MATIJASEVIČ
Leningrad Branch, Steklov Institute of Mathematics, Academy of Sciences of the U.S.S.R.

The tenth problem on David Hilbert's famous list (cf. [1]) is formulated as follows:

Given a diophantine equation with any number of unknown quantities and with rational integral numerical coefficients: To devise a process according to which it can be determined by a finite number of operations whether the equation is solvable in rational integers.

A diophantine equation is an equation of the form

$$P(x_1,...,x_n) = 0$$

where P is a polynomial (all polynomials consided here are polynomials with integer coefficients).

It is well-known (cf. [2]) that an algorithm for determining the solvability in integers would yield an algorithm for determining the solvability in positive integers and conversely. Hence we will limit our discussion to questions of solvability in positive integers. Lower-case Latin letters will always be variables whose range is the positive integers.

A relation $\mathcal{R}(x_1,...,x_n)$ among natural numbers is called *diophantine* if there is a polynomial P such that

$$\mathcal{R}(x_1,...,x_n) \Leftrightarrow \exists y_1...y_k\ [P(x_1,...,x_n,y_1,...,y_k)=0] .$$

Main theorem. *Every recursively enumerable predicate is diophantine.*

Corollary. *Hilbert's tenth problem is unsolvable.*

The first major contribution to the proof of the main theorem has been made by Martin Davis. He has shown in [3] that *every recursively enumerable predicate $\mathcal{R}(x_1,...,x_n)$ can be represented in the form*

$$\mathcal{R}(x_1,\ldots,x_n) \Leftrightarrow \exists w \forall z_{\leqslant w} \exists y_1 \ldots y_k \; [P(x_1,\ldots,x_n,w,z,y_1,\ldots,y_k)=0]$$

where P is a polynomial.

Taking advantage of this representation Martin Davis, Hilary Putnam and Julia Robinson have proved in [4] that *every recursively enumerable predicate $\mathcal{R}(x_1,\ldots,x_n)$ can be represented in the form*

$$\mathcal{R}(x_1,\ldots,x_n) \Leftrightarrow \exists y_1 \ldots y_k \; [P(x_1,\ldots,x_n,y_1,\ldots,y_k)=Q(x_1,\ldots,x_n,y_1,\ldots,y_k)] \tag{1}$$

where P and Q are functions built from variables and particular positive integers by addition, multiplication and exponentiation.

To prove the main theorem it is sufficient to show that the relation given by

$$z = x^y \tag{2}$$

is diophantine. In such a case we can eliminate exponentiation from (1) in the usual way and thus obtain a diophantine representation of $\mathcal{R}$.

The question of whether relation (2) is diophantine has been studied by Julia Robinson in [5]. Among others theorems she has proved the following one:

If there exists a diophantine relation $\mathcal{D}(u,v)$ such that

$$\forall uv [\mathcal{D}(u,v) \Leftrightarrow v \leqslant u^u] \tag{3}$$

and

$$\forall k \exists uv [\mathcal{D}(u,v) \& u^k < v] \tag{4}$$

then relation (2) *is diophantine.*

A relation $\mathcal{D}(u,v)$ is said *to be a relation of exponential growth* if it meets conditions (3) and (4).

Here we point out an example of diophantine relation of exponential growth and outline the proof.

Let φ_n be defined by

$$\varphi_0 = 0\,, \qquad \varphi_1 = 1\,, \qquad \varphi_{k+1} = \varphi_k + \varphi_{k-1}$$

(φ_n is the famous Fibonacci series). The relation given by

$$v = \varphi_{2u} \tag{5}$$

is the above mentioned example.

The sequence

$$\varphi_0, \varphi_2, ..., \varphi_{2n}, ...$$

can be defined as follows:

$$\varphi_0 = 0, \quad \varphi_2 = 1, \quad \varphi_{2(k+1)} = 3\varphi_{2k} - \varphi_{2(k-1)} . \tag{6}$$

It can be easily proved by induction that

$$2^{u-1} \leqslant \varphi_{2u} < 3^u . \tag{7}$$

This implies that relation (5) is a relation of exponential growth.

To prove that relation (5) is diophantine we consider the sequences $\psi_{m,n}$ defined for every $m \geqslant 2$ by

$$\psi_{m,0} = 0, \quad \psi_{m,1} = 1, \quad \psi_{m,k+1} = m\psi_{m,k} - \psi_{m,k-1} .$$

It can be easily proved by induction that

$$\psi_{m,n} \equiv n (\mathrm{mod}\, m-2) ,$$

$$\psi_{m,n} \equiv \varphi_{2n} (\mathrm{mod}\, m-3) . \tag{8}$$

Hence if $d | m-3$ then

$$\mathrm{Rem}(\psi_{m,n}, d) = \mathrm{Rem}(\varphi_{2n}, d) \tag{9}$$

($\mathrm{Rem}(a,b)$ denotes the remainder obtained upon dividing a by b).

Let k be any positive integer and $d = \varphi_{2k} + \varphi_{2(k+1)}$. Let us analyse the sequence

$$\mathrm{Rem}(\varphi_0, d), \mathrm{Rem}(\varphi_2, d), ..., \mathrm{Rem}(\varphi_{2n}, d), ... \tag{10}$$

It is clear that

$$\mathrm{Rem}(\varphi_{2j}, d) = \varphi_{2j} \quad (0 \leqslant j \leqslant k+1) .$$

We can rewrite (6) in the form $\varphi_{2(k-1)} = 3\varphi_{2k} - \varphi_{2(k+1)}$ and prove by induction that

$$\mathrm{Rem}(\varphi_{2j}, d) = d - \varphi_{2(2k+1-j)} \qquad (k \leqslant j \leqslant 2k)\,. \tag{11}$$

Then we can prove by induction that

$$\mathrm{Rem}(\varphi_{2(2k+1+j)}, d) = \mathrm{Rem}(\varphi_{2j}, d)\,.$$

In other words sequence (10) is periodical and $2k + 1$ is the length of the period.

We shall use the following properties of numbers φ_n and $\psi_{m,n}$:

$$x^2 - xy - y^2 = 1 \Leftrightarrow \exists i[x{=}\varphi_{2i+1} \& y{=}\varphi_{2i}]\,, \tag{12}$$

$$m \geqslant 2 \Rightarrow [[x^2{-}myx{+}y^2{=}1 \& x{\leqslant}y] \Leftrightarrow \exists i[x{=}\psi_{m,i} \& y{=}\psi_{m,i+1}]]\,, \tag{13}$$

$$\varphi_s^2 | \varphi_t \Rightarrow \varphi_s | t\,, \tag{14}$$

$$s\varphi_s | t \Rightarrow \varphi_s^2 | \varphi_t\,. \tag{15}$$

It is not very difficult to prove these properties by induction and course-of-values induction.

Main lemma. $v = \varphi_{2u}$ *if and only if there are positive integers* l, z, g, h, m, x, y *such that*

$$u \leqslant v < l\,, \tag{16}$$

$$l^2 - lz - z^2 = 1\,, \tag{17}$$

$$g^2 - 2gh - 4h^2 = 1\,, \tag{18}$$

$$l^2 | g\,, \tag{19}$$

$$m = 3 + (4h+g)h\,, \tag{20}$$

$$x^2 - myx + y^2 = 1\,, \tag{21}$$

$$u = \mathrm{Rem}(x, l)\,, \tag{22}$$

$$v = \mathrm{Rem}(x, 4h+g)\,. \tag{23}$$

Sufficiency. Let numbers $u, v, l, z, g, h, m, x, y$ meet conditions (16)–(23).

By virtue of (12) and (13) it follows from (17), (18) and (21) that there are integers s, k, n such that $l = \varphi_s$, $g = \varphi_{2k+1}$, $2h = \varphi_{2k}$, $x = \psi_{m,n}$. Hence $4h + g = \varphi_{2k} + \varphi_{2(k+1)}$.

By virtue of (14) it follows from (19) that

$$l | 2k + 1 . \tag{24}$$

By virtue of (9) it follows from (20) and (23) that

$$v = \mathrm{Rem}(\varphi_{2n}, \varphi_{2k} + \varphi_{2(k+1)}).$$

We represent n in the form $n = (2k+1)\alpha + \beta$ where α and β are integers and $0 \leqslant \beta < 2k + 1$. In accordance with the periodicity of sequence (10) we have

$$v = \mathrm{Rem}(\varphi_{2\beta}, \varphi_{2k} + \varphi_{2(k+1)}) .$$

If $\beta > k$ then by virtue of (11) we should have

$$v = \varphi_{2k} + \varphi_{2(k+1)} - \varphi_{2(2k+1-\beta)} \geqslant \varphi_{2(k+1)} .$$

But by virtue of (16) and (19)

$$v < l < g = \varphi_{2k+1} < \varphi_{2(k+1)}$$

and hence $\beta \leqslant k$. Then

$$v = \mathrm{Rem}(\varphi_{2\beta}, \varphi_{2k} + \varphi_{2(k+1)}) = \varphi_{2\beta}$$

and by virtue of (7)

$$\beta \leqslant 2^{\beta-1} \leqslant v < l . \tag{25}$$

It follows from (18)–(20) that $l | m - 2$. By virtue of (8) it follows from (22) that $u = \mathrm{Rem}(n, l)$.

It follows from (24) and (25) that

$$u = \mathrm{Rem}(n, l) = \mathrm{Rem}((2k+1)\alpha + \beta, l) = \beta$$

and hence $v = \varphi_{2u}$. The sufficiency is proved.

Necessity. Let u be any positive integer and $v = \varphi_{2u}$. We put $l = \varphi_{24u+1}$, $z = \varphi_{24u}$. It is clear that condition (16) is satisfied.

It can easily be shown that l is odd and $\varphi_{l(24u+1)-1}$ is even. We put $g = \varphi_{l(24u+1)}$, $h = \varphi_{l(24u+1)-1}/2$. By virtue of (12) conditions (17) and (18) are satisfied. By virtue of (15) condition (19) is also satisfied.

We take m in accordance with (20) and put $x = \psi_{m,u}$, $y = \psi_{m,u+1}$. By virtue of (13) condition (21) is satisfied.

It follows from (18), (19) and (20) that $l|m-2$. By virtue of (8) condition (22) is satisfied. Since $4h+g|m-3$ by virtue of (9) condition (23) is satisfied too. The necessity is proved.

It is easy to see that the relations $a < b$, $a \leqslant b$, $a|b$ are diophantine and hence can be eliminated from conditions (16)–(23). A system of diophantine equations can be easily transformed into a single equation (cf. [2]). Hence the relation (5) is diophantine.

The above construction of a diophantine equation of exponential growth is described in more detail in [6]. This work completes the proof of the main theorem.

Combining our main theorem with an earlier result of Hilary Putnam [7], we can obtain an interesting theorem about presentations of resursively enumerable sets. It follows from the main theorem that every recursively enumerable set of positive integers S can be represented in the form

$$a \in S \Leftrightarrow \exists y_1 ... y_n \; [P(a, y_1, ..., y_n) = 0] \; .$$

It is easy to show that

$$a \in S \Leftrightarrow \exists z y_1 ... y_n \; [a = z(1 - (P(z, y_1, ..., y_n))^2)] \; .$$

In other words, *every recursively enumerable set of positive integers* (for example, the set of all prime numbers) *coincides with the set of all positive values of some polynomial with integer coefficients.*

Using Gödel numbering of recursively enumerable sets we can construct a polynomial $M(y_1, ..., y_n, g)$ such that every recursively enumerable set S of positive integers can be represented in the form

$$a \in S \Leftrightarrow \exists y_1 ... y_n \; [a = M(y_1, ..., y_n, g_S)]$$

where g_S is Gödel number of S.

The constructions of such universal polynomials known today have some 200 variables. For the set of all prime numbers we can construct a polynomial with about 30 variables. Of course, these constructions are not the best ones and we can hope they will be essentially improved in future.

References

[1] D.Hilbert, Mathematical problems. Lecture delivered before the International Congress of mathematicians at Paris in 1900, Bull. Amer. Math. Soc. 8, No. 10 (1902) 437–479.

[2] M.Davis, Computability and Unsolvability (N.Y., 1958).

[3] M.Davis, Arithmatical problems and recursively enumerable predicates, Journ. Symb. Logic 18, No. 1 (1953) 33–41.

[4] M.Davis, H.Putnam and J.Robinson, The decision problem for exponential diophantine equations, Ann. of Math. 74, No. 3 (1961) 425–436.

[5] J.Robinson, Existential definability in arithmetic, Trans. Amer. Math. Soc. 72, No. 3 (1952) 437–449.

[6] Yu.V.Matijasevič, Diofantovost perechislimekh miozhestv, Doklady Akad. Nauk USSR, 191, no. 2 (1970) 279–282; English translation: Soviet. Math. Dokl. 11, No. 2 (1970) 354–357.

[7] H.Putnam, An unsolvable problem in number theory, Journ. Symb. Logic 25, No. 3 (1960) 220–232.

HAUPTSATZ FOR THE INTUITIONISTIC THEORY OF ITERATED INDUCTIVE DEFINITIONS

Per MARTIN-LÖF
University of Stockholm

1. Introduction.

1.1. The principle of definition by generalized induction, perhaps best exemplified by the definition of the constructive second number class given by Church and Kleene, and the corresponding principle of proof by generalized induction were first formalized by Kreisel 1963. Also, the idea of iterating generalized inductive definitions, as done by Church and Kleene in their definition of the higher constructive number classes, gives rise to a corresponding principle of proof which was first stated as a formal schema by Kreisel 1964 in his proof of the wellordering of Takeuti's 1957 ordinal diagrams of finite order. A complete formulation of a classical theory of generalized inductive definitions iterated along a primitive recursive wellordering was given by Feferman 1969 whose main object was to establish the relation between his theory and certain subsystems of classical analysis.

1.2. In the present paper I shall give a proof theoretical analysis of the intuitionistic theory of generalized inductive definitions iterated an arbitrary finite number of times. Like the Hilbert type systems of first order predicate logic which were used before Gentzen 1934, the theories of single and iterated generalized inductive definitions formulated by Kreisel and Feferman do not lend themselves immediately to a proof theoretical analysis. My first aim is therefore to reformulate the axioms expressing the principles of definition and proof by generalized induction as rules of inference similar to those introduced by Gentzen 1934 in his system of natural deduction for first order predicate logic. As in Gentzen's case, this reformulation leads to a notable systematization which is interesting already in the case of ordinary inductive definitions, the rules corresponding to the axioms which express the principle of definition by induction appearing as introduction rules for the inductively defined predicates, whereas the axioms which express the principle of proof by induction give rise to the corresponding elimination rules. Moreover, the generalized inductive definitions appear as inductive definitions iterated once and the iterated generalized inductive definitions as inductive definitions iterated twice or more. This explains why I shall omit the attribute generalized in the sequel and talk simply about iterated inductive definitions.

1.3. As soon as the rules for the inductively defined predicates have been separated into introduction and elimination rules, it becomes clear that, in addition to the logical cuts discovered by Gentzen 1934, there arise certain new cuts corresponding to the inductively defined predicates. Also, just as with the logical cuts, there is associated in a natural way with each new form of cut a rule of contraction which shows how to transform the deduction so that the cut becomes eliminated. My main object is to show that, by successive applications of the rules of contraction, every deduction can be reduced to a cut free deduction. This constitutes an extension of Gentzen's 1934 Hauptsatz to the intuitionistic theory of iterated inductive definitions.

1.4. The opinion seems to have been generally accepted that there be no real cut elimination theorem for first order arithmetic and that such a theorem could only be obtained by eliminating the induction schema in favour of the ωrule. However, when arithmetic is formulated as a theory of ordinary inductive definitions, it becomes possible to formulate and prove a cut elimination theorem which is just as natural and basic as the one for pure first order logic, although, like in second order logic, the subformula principle is necessarily lost. This cut elimination theorem for first order arithmetic is just a special case of the Hauptsatz for the theory of iterated inductive definitions and is obtained by allowing no other predicates in that theory than those defined by ordinary induction.

1.5. The method I shall use in order to prove Hauptsatz for the intuitionistic theory of iterated inductive definitions is an extension of the method that Tait 1967 used in his proof of the normal form theorem for the terms of Gödel's 1958 theory of primitive recursive functionals of finite type. That Tait's method can be carried over from terms denoting functionals of finite type to formal intuitionistic proofs is not astonishing, because Gödel 1958 noted that there is a close connection between the notion of computable functional of finite type and the intuitionistic notion of proof, and Curry and Feys 1958 established an isomorphism between two theories that formalize the very simplest properties of these notions, namely, their basic theory of functionality and the positive implicational calculus, respectively.

1.6. Since Hauptsatz implies consistency, it cannot, according to Gödel's second theorem, be proved by exclusive use of principles which are formalizable in the theory itself. Nevertheless, for every specific deduction in the theory of iterated inductive definitions, the proof that it reduces to a cut free deduction may be formalized in the theory itself. Thus, Hauptsatz becomes provable if the theory is slightly strengthened, for example, by adding the reflection principle

if $F(t)$ is provable for all closed terms t, then $\bigwedge x F(x)$.

1.7. A comparison between the method used by Gentzen 1936 in his consistency proof for first order arithmetic and the method I shall use in the present paper may be illuminating. Gentzen's proof can be divided into the following six parts.

1.7.1. Definition of the reduction procedure to be applied to the proof figures.
1.7.2. Definition of an appropriate system of ordinal notations.
1.7.3. Definition of a recursive total ordering between the ordinal notations.
1.7.4. Proof of the wellfoundedness of the order relation. In the case of Takeuti's ordinal diagrams of finite order this proof uses the notion of accessibility which is defined by iterated generalized induction.
1.7.5. Recursive assignment of an ordinal notation to every proof figure.
1.7.6. Proof that a reduction step diminishes the ordinal assigned to a proof figure.

1.8. These six parts of Gentzen's proof have the following counterparts in my proof.

1.8.1. Definition of the rules of contraction.
1.8.2. Disappears, because instead of the ordinal notations I shall use the proof figures themselves.
1.8.3. Definition of a recursive predecessor relation between the proof figures.
1.8.4. Proof of the wellfoundedness of the predecessor relation. This proof uses the notion of computability which is defined by iterated generalized induction.
1.8.5. Disappears.
1.8.6. Disappears, because it is immediately clear that, when the reduction procedure is applied to a proof figure, one obtains a proof figure which precedes the given one.

1.9. I am very grateful to Dag Prawitz who checked in detail an early version of this paper.

2. A canonical form for the iterated inductive definitions.

2.1. The language I shall use is the standard one for first order logic. There may be an arbitrary finite number of function symbols, but, typically, these are just 0 and s, denoting the natural number zero and the successor function, respectively. With each predicate symbol there is associated not only a place index, indicating the number of argument places, but also a nonnegative integer called its *level*. The level of a formula is defined to be the maximum of the levels of the predicate symbols which occur in it.

2.1.1. For the sake of notational simplicity, finite sequences of variables and terms will be denoted by single letters. For example, an atomic formula will be written Pt where P is an $n$ary predicate symbol and t a sequence of n terms.

2.2. An *ordinary production* is a figure of the form

$$\frac{Qq(x) \quad \ldots \quad Rr(x)}{Pp(x)}$$

with zero or more atomic formulae $Qq(x), \ldots, Rr(x)$ as premises of the conclusion $Pp(x)$. I use x to denote the totality of all variables that occur in the production. The level of P must be greater than or equal to the levels of Q, ..., R.

2.3. A *generalized production* is either of the form

$$\frac{H(x) \to Qq(x)}{Pp(x)}$$

called $\to$*production* or of the form

$$\frac{\bigwedge y Qq(x,y)}{Pp(x)}$$

called $\bigwedge$*production*. In the first case the level of P must be greater than or equal to the level of Q and greater than the level of the possibly composite formula $H(x)$ and, in the second case, the level of P must be positive and greater than or equal to the level of Q. In both cases x denotes the totality of all variables that occur free in the production.

2.4. The level of a production is defined to be the level of the predicate symbol which occurs in its conclusion.

2.5. The productions are schemata for defining predicates and are to be understood as they stand once it has been stipulated, first, that the logical constants are to have their constructive meaning, second, that the variables range over the closed terms and, third, that the statement below a horizontal line follows from the statements above the line. For example, the first and second Peano axiom may be written

$$N0 \qquad \frac{Nx}{Nsx}$$

provided the unary predicate symbol N is used to express the property of being a natural number.

2.6. The above interpretation of the productions may be elaborated a bit more so as to conform with the usual intuitionistic interpretation of the logical constants. The productions are then understood as instructions telling us how we are allowed to construct proofs of atomic statements of the form Pt where t is a sequence of closed terms. Consider first a production of level 0. Such a production is necessarily ordinary and tells us that if we have proofs of $Qq(t)$, ..., $Rr(t)$ where t is a sequence of closed terms, then we have a proof of $Pp(t)$. Thus a proof of Pt where P is a predicate symbol of level 0 may be viewed as a finite tree made up by closed substitution instances of the productions of level 0 and may, if so desired, be identified with its symbolic representation. Having defined what constitutes a proof of a closed atomic formula of level 0, we know automatically from the intuitionistic interpretation of the logical constants what constitutes a proof of a closed composite formula of level 0. Consider now a production of level 1. If it is ordinary, it tells us just as before that if we have proofs of $Qq(t)$, ..., $Rr(t)$ then we have a proof of $Pp(t)$. If it is a $\rightarrow$production it tells us that if we have a method of transforming an arbitrary proof of $H(t)$ into a proof of $Qq(t)$ where t is a sequence of closed terms, then we have a proof of $Pp(t)$. Note that, since the level of $H(t)$ equals 0, we are supposed to have understood already what constitutes a proof of $H(t)$. Finally, a Λproduction tells us that if we have a method which allows us for every closed term u to construct a proof of $Qq(t,u)$ where t is a sequence of closed terms, then we have a proof of $Pp(t)$. Now we know we are allowed to prove closed atomic formulae of level 1 and can proceed inductively to define what constitutes a proof of a closed composite formula of level 1, a closed atomic formula of level 2 and so on.

2.6.1. Note that the definition of what constitutes a proof of an atomic statement Pt where t is a sequence of closed terms is itself an iterated inductive definition which after arithmetization can be expressed by means of a finite number of ordinary and generalized productions.

2.7. The productions can also be interpreted by means of the impredicative notion of species. Indeed, the level restrictions ensure that there are minimal species corresponding to the predicate symbols of level 0 that satisfy the productions of level 0 and that, given these, there are minimal species corresponding to the predicate symbols of level 1 that satisfy the productions of level 1 and that, given the species determined by the predicate symbols of level 0 and 1, there are minimal species corresponding to the predicate symbols of level 2 that satisfy the productions of level 2 and so on. The species determined by the predicate symbols of level n are precisely the species which are $\omega_n$recursively enumerable in the sense of alfa recursion theory where $\omega = \omega_0, \omega_1, \ldots, \omega_n, \ldots$ denote the recursively regular ordinals enumerated in increasing order. In particular, the species determined by the predicate symbols of level 0 are precisely the species which are recursively enumerable in the ordinary sense.

3. **The intuitionistic theory of itereated inductive definitions.** This theory formalizes the principles of proof that are implicit in the concepts just introduced together with the usual concepts of first order intuitionistic logic. I shall formulate it as an extension of the system of natural deduction introduced by Gentzen 1934 and studied by Prawitz 1965.

3.1. A *deduction* is started by making some *assumptions* from which conclusions are drawn by repeatedly applying the following *rules of inference.*

3.2. Rules of inference associated with the logical constants.

3.2.1. $\rightarrow$introduction.

$$\dfrac{\begin{array}{c}\not{F}\\ \vdots\\ G\end{array}}{F \to G}$$

The formula F has been crossed out in order to indicate that some occurrences of F as assumption of the deduction of G may have been *cancelled*. This means that the assumptions of the deduction of $F \to G$ are the assumptions of the deduction of G minus the occurrences of F which are cancelled at the inference from G to $F \to G$. When an assumption is cancelled, it must be indicated in some unambiguous way at what inference this happens. For example, Gentzen 1934 marks an assumption that is cancelled by a number and writes the same number at the inference by which it is cancelled.

3.2.2. $\to$elimination or modus ponens.

$$\frac{F \to G \quad F}{G}$$

3.2.3. $\wedge$introduction.

$$\frac{F \quad G}{F \wedge G}$$

3.2.4. $\wedge$elimination.

$$\frac{F \wedge G}{F} \qquad \frac{F \wedge G}{G}$$

3.2.5. $\vee$introduction.

$$\frac{F}{F \vee G} \qquad \frac{G}{F \vee G}$$

3.2.6. $\vee$elimination.

$$\cfrac{F \vee G \quad \begin{matrix} \not{F} \\ \vdots \\ H \end{matrix} \quad \begin{matrix} \not{G} \\ \vdots \\ H \end{matrix}}{H}$$

3.2.7. Λ introduction.

$$\frac{F(x)}{\Lambda x F(x)}$$

This rule is subjected to the restriction that the variable x, whose free occurrences in the deduction of $F(x)$ become bound by the Λintroduction, must not occur free in any assumption of the deduction of $F(x)$.

3.2.8. Λelimination.

$$\frac{\Lambda x F(x)}{F(t)}$$

3.2.9. Vintroduction.

$$\frac{F(t)}{\mathrm{V} x F(x)}$$

3.2.10. Velimination.

$$\cfrac{\mathrm{V} x F(x) \quad \begin{matrix} \not{F(x)} \\ \vdots \\ G \end{matrix}}{G}$$

This rule is subjected to the restriction that the variable x, whose free occurrences in the deduction of G from $F(x)$ become bound by the Velimination, must not occur free in G or in any assumption of the deduction of G other than $F(x)$.

3.3. The *major premise* of an elimination inference is the premise whose outermost logical sign is eliminated by the inference. The other premises of the inference are called *minor premises*. The deduction of the major premise is called the *major deduction* and the deductions of the minor premises are called the *minor deductions* of the elimination inference.

3.4. Rules of inference for the inductively defined predicates.

3.4.1. Ordinary production.

$$\frac{Qq(t) \quad \ldots \quad Rr(t)}{Pp(t)}$$

3.4.2. →production.

$$\begin{array}{c} \cancel{H(t)} \\ \vdots \\ \dfrac{Qq(t)}{Pp(t)} \end{array}$$

The formula $H(t)$ has been crossed out in order to indicate that some occurrences of $H(t)$ as assumption of the deduction of $Qq(t)$ may be cancelled at the inference from $Qq(t)$ to $Pp(t)$.

3.4.3. ⋀production.

$$\frac{Qq(t,y)}{Pp(t)}$$

This rule is subjected to the restriction that the variable y must occur neither in t nor free in any assumption of the deduction of $Qq(t,y)$.

3.4.4. Elimination of an inductively defined predicate.

$$\frac{Pt \quad \begin{array}{c}\text{minor}\\ \text{deductions}\end{array}}{F(t)}$$

A production should be considered as an introduction rule for the predicate which occurs in its conclusion. The rule which has been schematically represented above is the corresponding elimination rule.

3.5. In an application of the elimination rule for an inductively defined predicate the formula Pt is called the major premise. Definition of minor premise, major deduction and minor deduction as for the logical elimination rules.

3.6. Before explaining the elimination rule for an inductively defined predicate which has been schematically represented above, I need to define what it means for a predicate symbol to be *linked* with another predicate symbol. First, every predicate symbol is linked with itself. Second, if P occurs in the conclusion of an ordinary production

$$\frac{Qq(x) \quad \ldots \quad Rr(x)}{Pp(x)}$$

then P is linked with every predicate symbol which is linked with one of $Q, \ldots, R$. Third, if P occurs in the conclusion of a generalized production

$$\frac{H(x) \to Qq(x)}{Pp(x)} \qquad \frac{\bigwedge y Qq(x,y)}{Pp(x)}$$

then P is linked with every predicate symbol which is linked with Q.

3.7. An instance of the elimination rule for an inductively defined predicate P is obtained as follows. Associate with every predicate symbol which is linked with P an abstraction term, that is, a formula and as many variables as indicated by the place index of the predicate symbol in question

$$\begin{array}{cccc} P & Q & R & \ldots \\ \\ \lambda x F(x) & \lambda y G(y) & \lambda z H(z) & \ldots \end{array}$$

For every ordinary production which in its conclusion has a predicate symbol which is linked with P, say

$$\frac{Qq(x) \quad \ldots \quad Rr(x)}{Pp(x)}$$

there should among the minor deductions of the elimination inference be one of the form

$$\begin{array}{ccc} G(q(x)) & \ldots & H(r(x)) \\ \vdots & & \vdots \\ & F(p(x)) & \end{array}$$

satisfying the restriction that a variable in the sequence x, whose free occurrences in the minor deduction become bound by the elimination inference, must not occur free in an assumption other than the indicated $G(q(x))$, ..., $H(r(x))$ which are all cancelled at the inference we are considering. Similarly, for every generalized production which in its conclusion has a predicate symbol which is linked with P, say

$$\frac{H(x) \to Qq(x)}{Pp(x)} \qquad \frac{\bigwedge y Qq(x,y)}{Pp(x)}$$

there should among the minor deductions of the elimination inference be one of the form

$$\begin{array}{ccc} H(x) \to G(q(x)) & \qquad & \bigwedge y G(q(x,y)) \\ \vdots & & \vdots \\ F(p(x)) & & F(p(x)) \end{array}$$

satisfying the restriction that a variable in the sequence x, whose free occurrences in the minor deduction become bound by the elimination inference, must not occur free in an assumption other than the indicated $H(x) \to G(q(x))$ and $\bigwedge y G(q(x,y))$, respectively, which are cancelled at the inference we are considering.

3.8. Examples.

3.8.1. Let $\perp$ be a 0ary predicate symbol of level 0 which does not occur in the conclusion of any of the productions. Thus there is no introduction rule for $\perp$. The elimination rule described above takes the form

$$\frac{\perp}{F}$$

which is nothing but the intuitionistic rule of absurdity.

3.8.2. Suppose we introduce a binary predicate symbol E of level 0 for equality by means of the ordinary production

$$Exx$$

with zero premises. E is not to occur in the conclusion of any other production. The introduction rule for E makes

$$Ett$$

an axiom for every term t, and the corresponding elimination rule takes the form

$$\frac{Etu \quad F(x,x)}{F(t,u)}$$

which is one way of formulating the standard rules for equality as seen by choosing $F(x,y)$ of the form $F(x) \rightarrow F(y)$.

3.8.3. Introduce N of level 0 for the property of being a natural number by means of the productions

$$N0 \qquad \frac{Nx}{Nsx}$$

and the stipulation that N must not occur in the conclusion of any other production. The elimination rule for N then takes the form

$$\frac{Nt \quad F(0) \quad \begin{matrix} \cancel{F(x)} \\ \vdots \\ F(sx) \end{matrix}}{F(t)}$$

which is nothing but the induction schema.

3.9. A deduction all of whose assumptions have been cancelled is said to be a *proof* of its end formula. A formula is *provable* if there exists a proof of it.

4. Rules of contraction.

4.1. If a logical constant or an inductively defined predicate is introduced only to be immediately eliminated we shall say that a *cut* occurs, and a formula which is at the same time the conclusion of an introduction inference and the major premise of an elimination inference will be called a *cut formula*.

4.2. To each possible form of cut there corresponds a *rule of contraction* which tells us how we are allowed to simplify a deduction which ends with an elimination inference whose major premise is the conclusion of an introduction inference by eliminating the cut.

4.2.1. →contraction.

$$
\dfrac{\dfrac{\begin{matrix}\not F\\ \vdots\\ G\end{matrix}}{F\to G}\quad\begin{matrix}\vdots\\ F\end{matrix}}{G}
\quad \text{contr} \quad
\begin{matrix}\vdots\\ F\\ \vdots\\ G\end{matrix}
$$

Before the contraction can be carried out some bound variables in the deduction of G from F may have to be renamed so that no free variable in the deduction of F becomes bound after the contraction.

4.2.2. ∧ contraction.

$$
\dfrac{\dfrac{\begin{matrix}\vdots\\ F\end{matrix}\quad\begin{matrix}\vdots\\ G\end{matrix}}{F\wedge G}}{F}
\quad \text{contr} \quad
\begin{matrix}\vdots\\ F\end{matrix}
$$

The case when G instead of F is inferred from $F\wedge G$ is quite similar.

4.2.3. ∨ contraction.

$$\frac{\dfrac{\overset{\vdots}{F}}{F \vee G} \quad \begin{matrix} F \\ \vdots \\ H \end{matrix} \quad \begin{matrix} G \\ \vdots \\ H \end{matrix}}{H} \quad \text{contr} \quad \begin{matrix} \vdots \\ F \\ \vdots \\ H \end{matrix}$$

Before the contraction can be carried out, some bound variables in the deduction of H from F may have to be renamed so that no free variable in the deduction of F becomes bound after the contraction. The case when $F \vee G$ is inferred from G instead of F is quite similar.

4.2.4. Λ contraction.

$$\dfrac{\dfrac{\overset{\vdots}{F(x)}}{\Lambda x F(x)}}{F(t)} \quad \text{contr} \quad \begin{matrix} \vdots \\ F(t) \end{matrix}$$

The simplified deduction of $F(t)$ is obtained by substituting the term t for all free occurrences of x in the deduction of $F(x)$. Before doing this, however, some of the bound variables of this deduction may have to be renamed so that no variable in t becomes bound after the substitution. In the sequel it will be tacitly assumed that bound variables are renamed whenever necessary in order to avoid undesired ties.

4.2.5. V contraction.

$$\frac{\dfrac{\overset{\vdots}{F(t)}}{\mathsf{V} x F(x)} \quad \begin{matrix} F(x) \\ \vdots \\ G \end{matrix}}{G} \quad \text{contr} \quad \begin{matrix} \vdots \\ F(t) \\ \vdots \\ G \end{matrix}$$

The lower part of the simplified deduction is obtained by substituting the term t for all free occurrences of x in the deduction of G from $F(x)$.

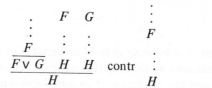

4.2.6. Contraction of an ordinary production.

$$
\dfrac{\dfrac{\begin{matrix}\vdots & & \vdots\\ Qq(t) & \dots & Rr(t)\end{matrix}}{Pp(t)} \qquad \begin{matrix}\text{minor}\\ \text{deductions}\end{matrix}}{F(p(t))}\ \text{contr}
$$

$$
\begin{matrix}
\dfrac{\begin{matrix}\vdots & \\ Qq(t) & \begin{matrix}\text{minor}\\ \text{deductions}\end{matrix}\end{matrix}}{G(q(t))} & \dots & \dfrac{\begin{matrix}\vdots & \\ R(t) & \begin{matrix}\text{minor}\\ \text{deductions}\end{matrix}\end{matrix}}{H(r(t))}\\
& \ddots \quad \vdots \quad .\!\cdot\!{}^{\cdot} & \\
& F(p(t)) &
\end{matrix}
$$

The lower part of the simplified deduction is obtained from that one of the minor deductions of the given deduction which is of the form

$$
\begin{matrix}
G(q(x)) & \dots & H(r(x))\\
& \ddots \quad .\!\cdot\!{}^{\cdot} & \\
& F(p(x)) &
\end{matrix}
$$

by substituting each term in the sequence t for all free occurrences of the respective variable in the sequence x.

4.2.7. Contraction of a $\rightarrow$production.

$$
\dfrac{\dfrac{\begin{matrix}\cancel{H(t)}\\ \vdots\\ Qq(t)\end{matrix}}{Pp(t)} \qquad \begin{matrix}\text{minor}\\ \text{deductions}\end{matrix}}{F(p(t))}\ \text{contr}\qquad
\begin{matrix}
\dfrac{\dfrac{\begin{matrix}\cancel{H(t)} & \\ \vdots & \\ Qq(t) & \begin{matrix}\text{minor}\\ \text{deductions}\end{matrix}\end{matrix}}{G(q(t))}}{H(t) \rightarrow G(q(t))}\\
\vdots\\
F(p(t))
\end{matrix}
$$

The lower part of the simplified deduction is obtained from that one of the minor deductions of the given deduction which is of the form

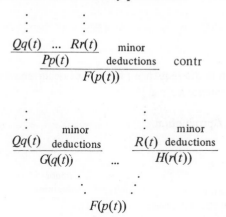

$$\begin{array}{c} H(x) \to G(q(x)) \\ \vdots \\ F(p(x)) \end{array}$$

by substituting each term in the sequence t for all free occurrences of the respective variable in the sequence x.

4.2.8. Contraction of a Λproduction.

$$\dfrac{\dfrac{\begin{array}{c}\vdots\\ Qq(t,y)\end{array}}{Pp(t)} \quad \begin{array}{c}\text{minor}\\ \text{deductions}\end{array}}{F(p(t))} \quad \text{contr} \quad \begin{array}{c} \dfrac{\dfrac{\begin{array}{c}\vdots\\ Qq(t,y)\end{array} \quad \begin{array}{c}\text{minor}\\ \text{deductions}\end{array}}{G(q(t,y))}}{\Lambda y G(q(t,y))} \\ \vdots \\ F(p(t)) \end{array}$$

The lower part of the simplified deduction is obtained from that one of the minor deductions of the given deduction which is of the form

$$\begin{array}{c} \Lambda y G(q(x,y)) \\ \vdots \\ F(p(x)) \end{array}$$

by substituting each term in the sequence t for all free occurrences of the respective variable in the sequence x.

4.3. A deduction *reduces* to another deduction if the latter can be obtained from the former by repeated contractions of subdeductions, where by a subdeduction I mean an initial part of a deduction.

4.4. A deduction which cannot be further reduced is said to be *cut free* or *normal*. We are now prepared to formulate the *Hauptsatz* or *normal form theorem* for the intuitionistic theory of iterated inductive definitions.

5. **Hauptsatz.** *Every deduction reduces to a normal deduction.*

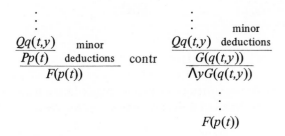

5.1. The structure of my proof of Hauptsatz can be described as follows. First, I shall define by ordinary induction what it means for a deduction to be *normalizable.* Roughly speaking, a deduction is normalizable if it can be brought on normal form by carrying out successive contractions of subdeductions in a specific order which I believe is the most natural one. Second, I shall define what it means for a deduction to be *computable.* The definition of computability, which utilizes iterated inductive definitions of precisely the kind that my theory formalizes, is such that it is immediately clear that a computable deduction is also normalizable. The proof is then completed by showing that every deduction is computable. Once the notion of computability has been defined, this final part of the proof, although involving many cases, is in principle a mere verification.

5.2. Suppose a deduction ends with an elimination inference. Note that an elimination inference always has one and only one major premise. Thus, by always choosing the major premise of an elimination inference, we can in a unique way proceed upwards in the deduction from the end formula until we reach either a cut or a top formula. In the first case, the cut we hit upon will be called the *main cut* and, in the second case, the branch we have proceeded along will be called the *main branch*. Since the main branch never passes through an introduction inference and always through the major premise of an elimination inference, the top formula in the beginning of the main branch cannot have been cancelled. This fact will be crucial when we come to the determination of the form of cut free deductions.

6. **Definition of what it means for a deduction to be normalizable.**

6.1. The deduction consists solely of an assumption. Then it is normalizable outright.

6.2. The last inference of the deduction is an introduction. Then it is normalizable provided the deductions of the premises of this inference are all normalizable.

6.3. The last inference of the deduction is an elimination.

6.3.1. The deduction has a main cut. Then it is normalizable provided the deduction which is obtained from it by eliminating the main cut is normalizable.

6.3.2. The deduction has no main cut. Then it is normalizable provided the minor deductions of the eliminations on the main branch are all normalizable.

6.4. Each clause in the definition of normalizability asserts that a given deduction is normalizable provided certain (finitely many) other deductions, which we may call the predecessors of the given deduction, are all normalizable. Thus, a deduction is normalizable if and only if the tree of its successive predecessors is wellfounded. This finite tree is then called the *normalization* of the deduction.

6.5. If a deduction is normalizable, then it reduces to a normal deduction. This is seen immediately by induction on the normalization of the deduction.

7. Definition of what it means for a deduction to be computable. I proceed by induction on $\omega n + m$ where m is the number of logical signs and n the level of the end formula of the deduction. Thus, in the definition of computability for deductions whose end formula contains m logical signs and is of level n, I assume that computability has already been defined for all deductions whose end formula has a lower value of $\omega n + m$.

7.1. The deduction consists solely of an assumption. Then it is computable outright.

7.2. The last inference of the deduction is an introduction.

7.2.1. →introduction.

$$\begin{array}{c} \not{F} \\ \vdots \\ \dfrac{G}{F \to G} \end{array}$$

is computable provided

$$\begin{array}{c}\vdots\\ F\\ \vdots\\ G\end{array}$$

is computable for every computable deduction

$$\begin{array}{c}\vdots\\ F\end{array}$$

Note that the formula F has a lower value of $\omega n + m$ than $F \to G$.

7.2.2. $\wedge$ introduction.

$$\dfrac{\begin{array}{cc}\vdots & \vdots\\ F & G\end{array}}{F \wedge G}$$

is computable provided

$$\begin{array}{c}\vdots\\ F\end{array} \qquad \begin{array}{c}\vdots\\ G\end{array}$$

are both computable.

7.2.3. $\vee$ introduction.

$$\dfrac{\begin{array}{c}\vdots\\ F\end{array}}{F \vee G}$$

is computable provided

$$\begin{array}{c} \vdots \\ F \end{array}$$

is computable. Similarly when $F \vee G$ is inferred from G instead of F.

7.2.4. Λ introduction.

$$\begin{array}{c} \vdots \\ \dfrac{F(x)}{\Lambda x F(x)} \end{array}$$

is computable provided

$$\begin{array}{c} \vdots \\ F(t) \end{array}$$

is computable for every term t.

7.2.5. V introduction.

$$\begin{array}{c} \vdots \\ \dfrac{F(t)}{\mathsf{V} x F(x)} \end{array}$$

is computable provided

$$\begin{array}{c} \vdots \\ F(t) \end{array}$$

is computable.

7.2.6. Ordinary production.

$$\begin{array}{ccc} \vdots & & \vdots \\ Qq(t) & \ldots & Rr(t) \\ \hline & Pp(t) & \end{array}$$

is computable provided

$$\begin{array}{ccc} \vdots & & \vdots \\ Qq(t) & \ldots & Rr(t) \end{array}$$

are all computable.

7.2.7. →production.

$$\begin{array}{c} \not{H}(t) \\ \vdots \\ Qq(t) \\ \hline Pp(t) \end{array}$$

is computable provided

$$\begin{array}{c} \vdots \\ H(t) \\ \vdots \\ Qq(t) \end{array}$$

is computable for every computable deduction

$$\begin{array}{c} \vdots \\ H(t) \end{array}$$

Note that, because of the level restrictions on a →production, the formula $H(t)$ has a lower value of $\omega n + m$ than $Qq(t)$.

7.2.8. $\bigwedge$ production.

$$\begin{array}{c} \vdots \\ \dfrac{Qq(t,y)}{Pp(t)} \end{array}$$

is computable provided

$$\begin{array}{c} \vdots \\ Qq(t,u) \end{array}$$

is computable for every term u.

7.3. The last inference of the deduction is an elimination.

7.3.1. The deduction has a main cut. Then it is computable provided the deduction which is obtained from it by eliminating the main cut is computable.

7.3.2. The deduction has no main cut. Then it is computable provided the minor deductions of the eliminations on the main branch are all normalizable.

7.4. Each clause in the definition of computability asserts that a deduction is computable provided certain (infinitely many, in general) other deductions, which we may call the predecessors of the given deduction, are all computable. Thus, a deduction is computable if and only if the tree of its successive predecessors is wellfounded. This infinite wellfounded tree is then called the *computation* of the deduction.

7.5. A deduction which is computable is also normalizable. This is seen by comparing clause for clause the definition of normalizability with the definition of computability, thereby remembering that a deduction which consists solely of an assumption is computable. Expressed differently, what we have achieved is an imbedding of the finite tree which we have called the normalization of a deduction into the huge infinite tree which we have called its computation. Therefore, the wellfoundedness of the former follows from the wellfoundedness of the latter.

8. **Theorem.** *Every deduction is computable.* This is proved by induction on the length of the deduction, but we have to make a stronger induction hypothesis, namely, that if we, first, substitute arbitrary terms for its free variables and, second, to the deduction obtained after the substitution attach arbitrary computable deductions of its assumptions, then the resulting deduction is computable. Several cases have to be distinguished depending on how the end formula of the deduction has been inferred.

8.1. The deduction consists solely of an assumption. Trivial.

8.2. $\rightarrow$introduction. We have to show that a deduction of the form

$$\cfrac{\begin{array}{c} \not F \\ \vdots \\ G \end{array}}{F \rightarrow G}$$

is computable. By 7.2.1 this is so if

$$\begin{array}{c} \vdots \\ F \\ \vdots \\ G \end{array}$$

is computable for every computable deduction

$$\begin{array}{c} \vdots \\ F \end{array}$$

which follows immediately from the induction hypothesis.

8.2.2. $\wedge$introduction. We have to show that a deduction of the form

$$\frac{\begin{matrix}\vdots & \vdots \\ F & G\end{matrix}}{F \wedge G}$$

is computable. By 7.2.2 this is so if

$$\begin{matrix}\vdots & \qquad & \vdots \\ F & \qquad & G\end{matrix}$$

are both computable which follows immediately from the induction hypothesis.

8.2.3. $\vee$introduction. We have to show that a deduction of the form

$$\frac{\begin{matrix}\vdots \\ F\end{matrix}}{F \vee G}$$

is computable. By 7.2.3 this is so if

$$\begin{matrix}\vdots \\ F\end{matrix}$$

is computable which follows immediately from the induction hypothesis.

8.2.4. $\bigwedge$introduction. We have to show that a deduction of the form

$$\frac{\begin{matrix}\vdots \\ F(x)\end{matrix}}{\bigwedge x F(x)}$$

is computable. By 7.2.4 this is so if

$$\begin{matrix}\vdots \\ F(t)\end{matrix}$$

is computable for every term t which follows immediately from the induction hypothesis.

8.2.5. $\bigvee$ introduction. We have to show that a deduction of the form

$$\begin{array}{c}\vdots\\ \dfrac{F(t)}{\bigvee xF(x)}\end{array}$$

is computable. By 7.2.5 this is so if

$$\begin{array}{c}\vdots\\ F(t)\end{array}$$

is computable which follows immediately from the induction hypothesis.

8.2.6. Ordinary production. We have to show that a deduction of the form

$$\begin{array}{c}\vdots \qquad\quad \vdots\\ \dfrac{Qq(t)\ \ \dots\ \ Rr(t)}{Pp(t)}\end{array}$$

is computable. By 7.2.6 this is so if

$$\begin{array}{ccc}\vdots & & \vdots\\ & \dots & \\ Qq(t) & & Rr(t)\end{array}$$

are all computable which follows immediately from the induction hypothesis.

8.2.7. $\rightarrow$production. We have to show that a deduction of the form

$$\begin{array}{c}\cancel{H(t)}\\ \vdots\\ \dfrac{Qq(t)}{Pp(t)}\end{array}$$

is computable. By 7.2.7 this is so if

$$\begin{array}{c} \vdots \\ H(t) \\ \vdots \\ Qq(t) \end{array}$$

is computable for every computable deduction

$$\begin{array}{c} \vdots \\ H(t) \end{array}$$

which follows immediately from the induction hypothesis.

8.2.8. $\wedge$production. We have to show that a deduction of the form

$$\begin{array}{c} \vdots \\ \dfrac{Qq(t,y)}{Pp(t)} \end{array}$$

is computable. By 7.2.8 this is so if

$$\begin{array}{c} \vdots \\ Qq(t,u) \end{array}$$

is computable for every term u which follows immediately from the induction hypothesis.

8.3. The last inference of the deduction is an elimination. We use induction on the computation of the major deduction of this elimination inference. This induction is, of course, subordinate to the basic induction on the length of the given deduction. Basis. The major deduction of the final elimination is computable according to 7.1 or 7.3.2. Then the computability of the deduction follows from 7.3.2 by using the fact that, according to the basic induction hypothesis, the minor deductions of the final elimination are computable and a fortiori normalizable. Induction step. If the major deduction of the final elimination is computable according to 7.3.1, then the computability of the deduction follows immediately from the subordinate induction hypothesis and 7.3.1. The crucial case arizes when the last inference of the major deduction of the final elimination is an introduction, that is, when the major premise of the final elimination is a cut formula. Eight subcases have to be distinguished depending on the form of this cut.

8.3.1.

$$\dfrac{\dfrac{\begin{matrix}\not{F}\\ \vdots\\ G\end{matrix}}{F\to G}\quad\begin{matrix}\vdots\\ F\end{matrix}}{G}$$

According to the basic induction hypothesis, the deductions

$$\dfrac{\begin{matrix}\not{F}\\ \vdots\\ G\end{matrix}}{F\to G}\qquad\qquad\begin{matrix}\vdots\\ F\end{matrix}$$

are both computable. By 7.2.1 so is

$$\begin{matrix}\vdots\\ F\\ \vdots\\ G\end{matrix}$$

The computability of the given deduction now follows from 7.3.1.

8.3.2.

$$\cfrac{\cfrac{\begin{array}{cc}\vdots & \vdots \\ F & G\end{array}}{F\wedge G}}{F}$$

According to the basic induction hypothesis

$$\cfrac{\begin{array}{cc}\vdots & \vdots \\ F & G\end{array}}{F\wedge G}$$

is computable. By 7.2.2 so is

$$\begin{array}{c}\vdots \\ F\end{array}$$

The computability of the given deduction now follows from 7.3.1.

8.3.3.

$$\cfrac{\cfrac{\begin{array}{c}\vdots \\ F\end{array}}{F\vee G} \quad \begin{array}{c}\not{F} \\ \vdots \\ H\end{array} \quad \begin{array}{c}\not{G} \\ \vdots \\ H\end{array}}{H}$$

According to the basic induction hypothesis

$$\cfrac{\begin{array}{c}\vdots \\ F\end{array}}{F\vee G}$$

is computable. By 7.2.3 so is

$$\begin{array}{c}\vdots \\ F\end{array}$$

Applying the basic induction hypothesis again, we can conclude that

$$\begin{array}{c}\vdots \\ F \\ \vdots \\ H\end{array}$$

is computable. The computability of the given deduction now follows from 7.3.1.

8.3.4.

$$\begin{array}{c}\vdots \\ \underline{F(x)} \\ \underline{\bigwedge x F(x)} \\ F(t)\end{array}$$

According to the basic induction hypothesis

$$\begin{array}{c}\vdots \\ \underline{F(x)} \\ \bigwedge x F(x)\end{array}$$

is computable. By 7.2.4 so is

$$\begin{array}{c}\vdots \\ F(t)\end{array}$$

The computability of the given deduction now follows from 7.3.1.

8.3.5.

$$\frac{\dfrac{\begin{matrix} \vdots \\ F(t) \end{matrix}}{\vee x F(x)} \quad \begin{matrix} \not{F}(x) \\ \vdots \\ G \end{matrix}}{G}$$

According to the basic induction hypothesis

$$\frac{\begin{matrix} \vdots \\ F(t) \end{matrix}}{\vee x F(x)}$$

is computable. By 7.2.5 so is

$$\begin{matrix} \vdots \\ F(t) \end{matrix}$$

Applying the basic induction hypothesis again, we can conclude that

$$\begin{matrix} \vdots \\ F(t) \\ \vdots \\ G \end{matrix}$$

is computable. The computability of the given deduction now follows from 7.3.1.

8.3.6.

$$\frac{\dfrac{\begin{matrix} \vdots \\ Qq(t) \end{matrix} \quad \ldots \quad \begin{matrix} \vdots \\ Rr(t) \end{matrix}}{Pp(t)} \qquad \begin{matrix} \text{minor} \\ \text{deductions} \end{matrix}}{F(p(t))}$$

By 7.3.1 it suffices to show that

$$
\dfrac{\begin{array}{c}\vdots\\ Qq(t)\end{array}\ \begin{array}{c}\text{minor}\\ \text{deductions}\end{array}}{G(q(t))}
\quad \cdots \quad
\dfrac{\begin{array}{c}\vdots\\ Rr(t)\end{array}\ \begin{array}{c}\text{minor}\\ \text{deductions}\end{array}}{H(r(t))}
\\
\ddots \qquad \qquad \qquad \quad \cdot^{\cdot^{\cdot}}
\\
F(p(t))
$$

is computable. Now, the computability of the deductions of $G(q(t))$, ..., $H(r(t))$ follows from the subordinate induction hypothesis stated in 8.3, and the computability of the whole deduction then follows from the basic induction hypothesis. Remember that the deduction of $F(p(t))$ from $G(q(t))$, ..., $H(r(t))$ is obtained from that one of the minor deductions which is of the form

$$
\begin{array}{c}
G(q(x)) \quad \cdots \quad H(r(x)) \\
\ddots \qquad \cdot^{\cdot^{\cdot}} \\
F(p(x))
\end{array}
$$

by substituting each term in the sequence t for all free occurrences of the respective variable in the sequence x.

8.3.7.

$$
\dfrac{\dfrac{\begin{array}{c}H(t)\\ \vdots\\ Qq(t)\end{array}}{Pp(t)}\ \begin{array}{c}\text{minor}\\ \text{deductions}\end{array}}{F(p(t))}
$$

By 7.3.1 it suffices to show that

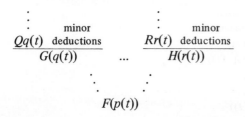

$$
\cfrac{\cfrac{\begin{array}{c}\cancel{H(t)}\\ \vdots\\ Qq(t)\end{array}\quad \begin{array}{c}\text{minor}\\ \text{deductions}\end{array}}{G(q(t))}}{\begin{array}{c}H(t)\rightarrow G(q(t))\\ \vdots\\ F(p(t))\end{array}}
$$

is computable. This follows from the basic induction hypothesis if we can prove the computability of

$$
\cfrac{\cfrac{\begin{array}{c}\cancel{H(t)}\\ \vdots\\ Qq(t)\end{array}\quad \begin{array}{c}\text{minor}\\ \text{deductions}\end{array}}{G(q(t))}}{H(t)\rightarrow G(q(t))}
$$

By 7.2.1 the latter deduction is computable provided

$$
\cfrac{\begin{array}{c}\vdots\\ H(t)\\ \vdots\\ Qq(t)\end{array}\quad \begin{array}{c}\text{minor}\\ \text{deductions}\end{array}}{G(q(t))}
$$

is computable for every computable deduction

$$
\begin{array}{c}\vdots\\ H(t)\end{array}
$$

This, in turn, follows from the subordinate induction hypothesis stated in 8.3.

8.3.8.

$$\dfrac{\vdots \qquad \qquad \qquad \qquad}{\dfrac{\dfrac{Qq(t,y)}{Pp(t)} \quad \begin{array}{c}\text{minor}\\ \text{deductions}\end{array}}{F(p(t))}}$$

By 7.3.1 it suffices to show that

$$\begin{array}{c} \vdots \qquad\qquad\qquad \\ \dfrac{\dfrac{Qq(t,y) \quad \begin{array}{c}\text{minor}\\ \text{deductions}\end{array}}{G(q(t,y))}}{\bigwedge y G(q(t,y))} \\ \vdots \\ F(p(t)) \end{array}$$

is computable. This follows from the basic induction hypothesis if we can prove the computability of

$$\begin{array}{c} \vdots \qquad\qquad\qquad \\ \dfrac{\dfrac{Qq(t,y) \quad \begin{array}{c}\text{minor}\\ \text{deductions}\end{array}}{G(q(t,y))}}{\bigwedge y G(q(t,y))} \end{array}$$

By 7.2.4 the latter deduction is computable provided

$$\begin{array}{c} \vdots \qquad\qquad\qquad \\ \dfrac{Qq(t,u) \quad \begin{array}{c}\text{minor}\\ \text{deductions}\end{array}}{G(q(t,u))} \end{array}$$

is computable for every term u. This, in turn, follows from the subordinate induction hypothesis stated in 8.3.

9. Corollaries which follow from Hauptsatz by combinatorial reasoning.

9.1. *If an atomic formula of level* 0 *is provable, then it has a proof which consists entirely of applications of the productions of level* 0. *Note that these are all ordinary.*

9.1.1. Suppose we are given a proof of an atomic formula of level 0. According to Hauptsatz, it reduces to a normal proof. This normal proof must consist entirely of applications of the productions of level 0, because, otherwise, there would be a lowest formula in the proof which is not the conclusion of a production of level 0. The proof of this formula must end with an elimination inference and, consequently, the assumption in the beginning of its main branch cannot have been cancelled. However, all asumptions of a proof are cancelled. We have reached a contradiction.

9.1.2. We might, using the terminology of Hilbert, say that atomic formulae of lowest level express *real* statements and that composite formulae as well as atomic formulae of higher level express *ideal* statements. Corollary 9.1 may then be interpreted as saying that we can always eliminate the use of ideal statements from a proof of a real statement. However, our proof of this fact uses the full force of the ideal statements which means that, in agreement with Gödel's second theorem, no reduction of the kind Hilbert aimed at is achieved. Nevertheless, something else and important follows from our analysis, namely, that, once we have formalized a proof of a real statement, a proof in which ideal statements may occur as a vehicle, we can find the direct proof, which does not make the excursion via ideal statements, *mechanically*, that is, by symbol manipulation.

9.2. *If* $F \vee G$ *is provable, then either* F *or* G *is provable.*

9.2.1. Suppose we are given a proof of $F \vee G$. According to Hauptsatz, it reduces to a normal proof. This normal proof cannot end with an elimination inference, because in that case the assumption in the beginning of its main branch could never have been cancelled. Thus, it ends with an introduction inference which necessarily must be an application of the $\vee$introduction rule. The proof of the premise of this final $\vee$introduction is either a proof of F or a proof of G.

9.3. *If* $\bigvee xF(x)$ *is provable, then so is* $F(t)$ *for some term* t.

9.3.1. The normal proof of $\bigvee x F(x)$ which we get by applying Hauptsatz must end with an introduction inference, because, otherwise, the assumption in the beginning of its main branch could not have been cancelled. Consequently, it is of the form

$$\frac{\begin{array}{c}\vdots\\ F(t)\end{array}}{\bigvee x F(x)}$$

and the desired proof of $F(t)$ is obtained by deleting the last inference.

10. **Probable wellorderings.** *The precise bound on the provable wellorderings of the intuitionistic theory of iterated inductive definitions equals*

$$\operatorname*{Lim}_n F^1_{F^2_{\cdot_{\cdot_{\cdot_{F^n_2(1)}}}}(1)}(1)$$

in Isles's 1968 *generalized Bachmann notation.*

10.1. Let $O(n)$ denote the least upper bound of Takeuti's 1957 ordinal diagrams of order n. According to Levitz's lecture at the conference in Buffalo 1968

$$O(n) = F^1_{F^2_{\cdot_{\cdot_{\cdot_{F^n_\omega(1)}}}}(1)}(1)$$

and

$$O(n-1) < F^1_{F^2_{\cdot_{\cdot_{\cdot_{F^n_2(1)}}}}(1)}(1) < O(n)$$

for every n. Also, Kreisel 1964 has formalized the proof of the wellfoundedness of $O(n)$ in the intuitionistic theory of iterated inductive definitions with predicates of level n at most. This shows that the least upper bound of the provable wellorderings of the intuitionistic theory of iterated inductive definitions is at least as big as

$$\operatorname{Lim}_n F^1_{F^2_{\ddots_{F^n_2(1)}}(1)}(1)$$

In order to prove the converse inequality we shall consider the intuitionistic theory of iterated inductive definitions based on the productions

$$N0 \qquad \frac{Nx}{Nsx} \qquad \frac{Esxsy}{Exy} \qquad \frac{E0sx}{\bot} \qquad Exx \qquad \frac{Exy}{Esxsy}$$

the productions

$$\frac{Px_1 \ldots x_n \quad Ex_1y_1 \quad \ldots \quad Ex_ny_n}{Py_1 \ldots y_n} \qquad \frac{\bot}{Px_1 \ldots x_n}$$

for every predicate symbol P and defining productions of arbitrarily many further predicates with which neither $\bot$ nor E is to be linked. Replacing every predicate except $\bot$ and E by its least species interpretation as described in 2.7, in particular, N by

$$\lambda x \bigwedge X(X0 \wedge \bigwedge x(Xx \to Xsx) \to Xx)$$

we interpret this theory into intuitionistic second order logic with the axioms for equality, the third and fourth Peano axiom

$$\bigwedge x \bigwedge y(Esxsy \to Exy) \qquad \bigwedge x(E0sx \to \bot)$$

and the comprehension axiom restricted to formulae which are semi isolated in the sense of Takeuti 1967. Now, Takeuti 1967 showed the consistency of his system SJNN, which is equivalent to classical second order logic with the semi isolated comprehension axiom, the axioms for equality and the third and fourth Peano axiom, by using the principle of transfinite induction on

$$\operatorname{Lim}_{n} O(n)$$

as the only non finite method of proof. Consequently, the wellfoundedness of this ordinal cannot be proved in the intuitionistic theory of iterated inductive definitions since, in that case, we could formalize a consistency proof for the theory specified above in the theory itself, contradicting Gödel's second theorem.

10.2. At a seminar in Stanford summer 1969, I conjectured that if we only allow predicates of level less than n in the intuitionistic theory of iterated inductive definitions the precise bound on the provable wellorderings equals

$$F^1_{F^2_{\cdot^{\cdot^{\cdot}}_{F^n_2(1)}\cdot^{\cdot^{\cdot}}}(1)}(1)$$

For $n = 1$ and $n = 2$ this has been proved by Gentzen 1943 and Howard and Gerber 1968, respectively, because

$$F^1_2(1) = \epsilon_0 \qquad F^1_{F^2_2(1)}(1) = \varphi_{\epsilon_{\Omega+1}}(1)$$

Also, Zucker 1969 has, without knowledge of my conjecture, demonstrated its validity for $n = 3$.

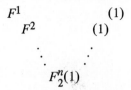

10.3. In the above determination of the ordinal associated with the intuitionistic theory of iterated inductive definitions, all the hard part of the analysis was taken from Takeuti 1967. I believe, however, that it will be possible to carry out the ordinal analysis in a much more perspicuous way directly for the theory of iterated inductive definitions. This belief is based on the following observations. Looking at the definition of computability, one sees that the computation of a deduction with end formula of level n is an $\omega_n$arithmetical tree of deductions and, hence, that its length is dominated by ω_{n+1}. However, once it has been proved that every deduction is computable, it appears that the computations are actually recursive trees of deductions and hence that their lengths are dominated by ω_1 already. (This does not mean, of course, that we have eliminated the use of the higher constructive number classes, because they enter effectively into the proof of the recursiveness of the computations.). Also, since there is a recursive procedure which associates with every deduction its computation, the lengths of the computations will be uniformly bounded by a certain recursive ordinal. I expect that it will be possible to estimate the lengths of the computations by means of the ordinal diagrams of finite order or, equivalently, the generalized Bachmann notations considered above. Conversely, let R be a binary predicate of level 0 and let the unary predicate A of level 1 express accessibility with respect to the relation R. Then it is easy to see that the computation of a proof of At where t is a closed term cannot be shorter than the rank of t with respect to the relation R. Consequently, it is not possible to measure the lengths of the computations by means of a system of ordinal notations which is smaller than

$$\operatorname*{Lim}_n F^1 \, F^2 \cdots F_2^n(1) \cdots (1)\,(1)$$

References

H.B.Curry and R.Feys, Combinatory logic (North-Holland, Amsterdam, 1958).

S.Feferman, Formal theories for transfinite iterations of generalized inductive definitions and some subsystems of analysis (1969). To appear.

G.Gentzen, Untersuchungen über das logische Schliessen, Math. Z. 39 (1934) 176–210, 405–431, Die Widerspruchsfreiheit der reinen Zahlentheorie, Math. Ann. 112 (1936) 493–565, Beweisbarkeit und Unbeweisbarkeit von Anfangsfällen der transfiniten Induktion in der reinen Zahlentheorie, Math. Ann. 119 (1943) 140–161.

H.Gerber, Brouwer's bar theorem and a system of ordinal notations, in: Intuitionism and Proof Theory, eds. A.Kino, J.Myhill and R.E.Vesley (North-Holland, Amsterdam, 1968).

K.Gödel, Über eine bisher noch nicht benützte Erweiterung des finiten Standpunktes, Dialectica 21 (1958) 280–287.

D.Isles, Regular ordinals and normal forms, in: Intuitionism and Proof Theory, eds. A.Kino, J.Myhill and R.E.Vesley (North-Holland, Amsterdam, 1970).

G.Kreisel, Generalized inductive definitions, Reports of the seminar on foundations of analysis, Sect. III, Stanford, 1963, Review, Zentralblatt für Mathematik 106 (1964) 237–238.

D.Prawitz, Natural deduction (Almqvist and Wiksell, Stockholm, 1965).

W.W.Tait, Intentional interpretations of functionals of finite type, J. Symbolic Logic 32 (1967) 198–212.

G.Takeuti, Ordinal diagrams, J. Math. Soc. Japan 9 (1957) 386–394, Consistency proofs of subsystems of classical analysis, Ann. Math. 86 (1967) 299–348.

J.Zucker, Characterizations of the provably recursive ordinals of ID_ν for $\nu \geqslant 2$ (1969). Preliminary report.

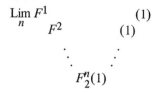

HAUPTSATZ FOR THE THEORY OF SPECIES

Per MARTIN-LÖF
University of Stockholm

1. Introduction.

1.1. The completeness of the cut free rules for the (impredicative) theory of species was proved by Prawitz 1968. However, using his method, it has not been possible to prove that every deduction can be normalized by successive eliminations of cuts. This seems to be due to the fact that, although one is primarily interested in properties of the proof figures, the semantical notions used apply not to the proof figures but to the formulae of the system.

1.2. A semantical notion, specially invented for the purpose of proving normal form theorems, is Tait's 1967 notion of computability (or convertibility as he says). Martin-Löf 1970 showed that the method of computability applies not only to terms but also to formal proofs and extended it to the intuitionistic theory of iterated inductive definitions. Simultaneously, Girard 1970 has extended the method to a system of terms which is so strong that it can be used to interpret full classical analysis.

1.3. The purpose of the present paper is to show that by making use of Girard's idea it is now possible to analyse the theory of species by means of the method of computability(*). It follows from this analysis that every deduction of the theory of species actually reduces to a cut free deduction.

2. Syntax.

2.1. The language we shall consider contains individual variables, possibly function constants, species variables, possibly species constants, and finally,

(*) This possibility has also been realized by Prawitz. See appendix B of his contribution to this volume.

the logical constants $\rightarrow$ and $\bigwedge$. A universal quantifier binds either an individual variable or a species variable. Absurdity, conjunction, disjunction and existential quantification are all defined as in Prawitz 1965, that is, by putting

$$\bot = \bigwedge YY$$

$$F \wedge G = \bigwedge Y((F \rightarrow (G \rightarrow Y)) \rightarrow Y)$$

$$F \vee G = \bigwedge Y((F \rightarrow Y) \rightarrow ((G \rightarrow Y) \rightarrow Y))$$

$$\bigvee x F(x) = \bigwedge Y(\bigwedge x(F(x) \rightarrow Y) \rightarrow Y)$$

$$\bigvee X F(x) = \bigwedge Y(\bigwedge X(F(X) \rightarrow Y) \rightarrow Y)$$

where Y is a 0ary species variable.

2.2. Finite sequences of variables and terms will be denoted by bold face letters. If $\mathbf{x}$ is a sequence of n individual variables and $F(\mathbf{x})$ a formula, then $T = \lambda\mathbf{x}F(\mathbf{x})$ is an $n$ary species term. If $\mathbf{t}$ is a sequence of n individual terms, then $T\mathbf{t}$ denotes the formula $F(\mathbf{t})$.

2.3. Free and bound occurrences of a variable in a formula are defined as usual. If x is one of the variables in the sequence $\mathbf{x}$, then every occurrence of x in $T = \lambda\mathbf{x}F(\mathbf{x})$ is bound. Formulae and species terms which only differ in the naming of their bound variables are identified.

2.4. If T is an $n$ary species term, X an $n$ary species variable and $F(X)$ a formula, then $F(T)$ denotes the formula which is obtained by replacing every part of $F(X)$ of the form $X\mathbf{t}$ for which X is free by $T\mathbf{t}$. Before doing this, however, one may have to rename some bound individual variables in T so that no variable occurrence in $\mathbf{t}$ becomes bound in $T\mathbf{t}$. Likewise, one may have to remane some bound variables in $F(X)$ so that no variable occurrence which is free in T becomes bound in $F(T)$.

3. **Rules of inference.**

3.1. We shall use Prawitz's 1965 system of natural deduction for second order logic in its first version. Thus, deductions are built up from assumptions by means of the following rules of inference.

3.1.1. →introduction.

$$\frac{\begin{matrix} F \\ \vdots \\ G \end{matrix}}{F \to G}$$

3.1.2. →elimination or modus ponens.

$$\frac{F \to G \quad F}{G}$$

3.1.3. ⋀introduction of first order.

$$\frac{F(x)}{\bigwedge x F(x)}$$

3.1.4. ⋀elimination of first order.

$$\frac{\bigwedge x F(x)}{F(t)}$$

3.1.5. ⋀introduction of second order.

$$\frac{F(X)}{\bigwedge X F(X)}$$

3.1.6. ⋀elimination of second order.

$$\frac{\bigwedge X F(X)}{F(T)}$$

3.2. Free and bound occurrences of a variable in a deduction are defined as in Martin-Löf 1970. Deductions which only differ in the naming of their bound variables are identified. It will be tacitly assumed that bound variables are renamed whenever necessary in order to avoid undesired ties.

3.3. The notions of major premise, minor premise, major deduction, minor deduction, cut, main cut and main branch are defined as in Martin-Löf 1970.

4. Rules of contraction.

4.1. →contraction.

$$\frac{\dfrac{\begin{array}{c}\not{F}\\ \vdots\\ G\end{array}}{F\to G}\quad\begin{array}{c}\vdots\\ F\end{array}}{G}\quad \text{contr}\quad \begin{array}{c}\vdots\\ F\\ \vdots\\ G\end{array}$$

4.2. $\wedge$contraction of first order.

$$\frac{\dfrac{\begin{array}{c}\vdots\\ F(x)\end{array}}{\wedge x F(x)}}{F(t)}\quad \text{contr}\quad \begin{array}{c}\vdots\\ F(t)\end{array}$$

4.3. $\wedge$contraction of second order

$$\frac{\dfrac{\begin{array}{c}\vdots\\ F(X)\end{array}}{\wedge X F(X)}}{F(T)}\quad \text{contr}\quad \begin{array}{c}\vdots\\ F(T)\end{array}$$

5. The definition of what it means for a deduction to be normalizable can be carried over word for word from Martin-Löf 1970.

6. Computability predicates.

6.1. Let T be a species term. A predicate α_T which is defined for deductions of the form

$$\begin{array}{c}\vdots\\ Tt\end{array}$$

will be called a computability predicate of type T (candidat de réductibilité in Girard's terminology) if it satisfies the following conditions.

6.1.1. A deduction which consists solely of an assumption satisfies α_T.

6.1.2. A deduction which ends with an elimination inference and has a main cut satisfies α_T if and only if the deduction which is obtained from it by eliminating the main cut satisfies α_T.

6.1.3. A deduction which ends with an elimination inference and has a cut free main branch satisfies α_T if and only if the minor deductions of the applications of modus ponens on the main branch are all normalizable.

6.1.4. If a deduction satisfies α_T, then it is normalizable.

6.2. There are plenty of computability predicates. For example, the predicate which holds precisely for the normalizable deductions with end formula of the form $T\mathbf{t}$ is a computability predicate of type T.

7. Let $\mathbf{X} = X_1, \ldots, X_n$ be a sequence of species variables and let $\mathbf{T} = T_1, \ldots, T_n$ and $\alpha_{\mathbf{T}} = \alpha_{T_1}, \ldots, \alpha_{T_n}$ be corresponding sequences of terms and computability predicates, respectively. Then, if $T(\mathbf{X}) = \lambda \mathbf{x} F(\mathbf{x},\mathbf{X})$ is a species term all of whose free species variables occur in the sequence $\mathbf{X}$, we shall introduce a new predicate $\varphi_{T(\mathbf{X})}(\alpha_{\mathbf{T}})$ which is to be defined for deductions of the form

$$\begin{array}{c} \vdots \\ F(\mathbf{t},\mathbf{T}) \end{array}$$

Such a deduction is to satisfy $\varphi_{T(\mathbf{X})}(\alpha_{\mathbf{T}})$ if and only if it satisfies $\varphi_{F(\mathbf{t},\mathbf{T})}(\alpha_{\mathbf{T}})$ and so it suffices to define $\varphi_{F(\mathbf{X})}(\alpha_{\mathbf{T}})$ for an arbitrary formula $F(\mathbf{X})$. This we do by induction on the number of logical signs in $F(\mathbf{X})$. Basis. $F(\mathbf{X})$ is atomic. If C is a species constant, then a deduction with end formula $C\mathbf{t}$ satisfies $\varphi_{C\mathbf{t}}(\alpha_{\mathbf{T}})$ if and only if it is normalizable. If X is a species variable, then a deduction with end formula $T\mathbf{t}$ satisfies $\varphi_{X\mathbf{t}}(\alpha_T,\alpha_{\mathbf{T}})$ if and only if it satisfies α_T. Induction step. $F(\mathbf{X})$ is composite. Several cases have to be distinguished depending on the last inference of the deduction for which $\varphi_{F(\mathbf{X})}(\alpha_{\mathbf{T}})$ is to be defined.

7.1. The deduction which consists solely of the assumption $F(\mathbf{T})$ satisfies $\varphi_{F(\mathbf{X})}(\alpha_{\mathbf{T}})$.

7.2. The last inference of the deduction is an introduction.

7.2.1. $\rightarrow$introduction.

$$\cfrac{\begin{matrix} \not{F}(\mathbf{T}) \\ \vdots \\ G(\mathbf{T}) \end{matrix}}{F(\mathbf{T}) \rightarrow G(\mathbf{T})}$$

satisfies $\varphi_{F(\mathbf{X}) \rightarrow G(\mathbf{X})}(\alpha_{\mathbf{T}})$ provided

$$\begin{matrix} \vdots \\ F(\mathbf{T}) \\ \vdots \\ G(\mathbf{T}) \end{matrix}$$

satisfies $\varphi_{G(\mathbf{X})}(\alpha_{\mathbf{T}})$ for all

$$\begin{matrix} \vdots \\ F(\mathbf{T}) \end{matrix}$$

that satisfy $\varphi_{F(\mathbf{X})}(\alpha_{\mathbf{T}})$.

7.2.2. $\bigwedge$introduction of first order.

$$\cfrac{\begin{matrix} \vdots \\ F(x,\mathbf{T}) \end{matrix}}{\bigwedge x F(x,\mathbf{T})}$$

satisfies $\varphi_{\bigwedge x F(x,\mathbf{X})}(\alpha_{\mathbf{T}})$ provided

$$\begin{array}{c} \vdots \\ F(t,\mathbf{T}) \end{array}$$

satisfies $\varphi_{F(t,\mathbf{X})}(\alpha_{\mathbf{T}})$ for all individual terms t.

7.2.3. Λintroduction of second order.

$$\begin{array}{c} \vdots \\ \dfrac{F(X,\mathbf{T})}{\Lambda XF(X,\mathbf{T})} \end{array}$$

satisfies $\varphi_{\Lambda XF(X,\mathbf{X})}(\alpha_{\mathbf{T}})$ provided

$$\begin{array}{c} \vdots \\ F(T,\mathbf{T}) \end{array}$$

satisfies $\varphi_{F(X,\mathbf{X})}(\alpha_T,\alpha_{\mathbf{T}})$ for all species terms T and computability predicates α_T.

7.3. The last inference of the deduction is an elimination.

7.3.1. The deduction has a main cut. Then it satisfies $\varphi_{F(\mathbf{X})}(\alpha_{\mathbf{T}})$ provided the deduction which is obtained from it by eliminating the main cut satisfies $\varphi_{F(\mathbf{X})}(\alpha_{\mathbf{T}})$.

7.3.2. The deduction has a cut free main branch. Then it satisfies $\varphi_{F(\mathbf{X})}(\alpha_{\mathbf{T}})$ provided the minor deductions of the applications of modus ponens on the main branch are all normalizable.

8. $\varphi_{T(\mathbf{X})}(\alpha_{\mathbf{T}})$ is a computability predicate of type $T(\mathbf{T})$.

8.1. That $\varphi_{T(\mathbf{X})}(\alpha_{\mathbf{T}})$ satisfies 6.11, 6.12 and 6.13 follows immediately from the definition. To verify 6.14 it clearly suffices to show for an arbitrary formula $F(\mathbf{X})$ that if a deduction satisfies $\varphi_{F(\mathbf{X})}(\alpha_{\mathbf{T}})$ then it is normalizable. This we do by induction on the number of logical signs in $F(\mathbf{X})$. Basis. Immediate from the definition. Induction step. If $F(\mathbf{X})$ is composite, then a deduction satisfies $\varphi_{F(\mathbf{X})}(\alpha_{\mathbf{T}})$ if and only if, by a finite number of eliminations of main cuts, it reduces to a deduction which consists solely of an assumption, has a cut free main branch with normalizable minor deductions or else ends with an introduction inference. In the first two cases we are done immediately and in the third case we have to consider separately each possible form of the introduction inference.

8.1.1. →introduction. If

$$\cfrac{\begin{matrix} \not{F}(\mathbf{T}) \\ \vdots \\ G(\mathbf{T}) \end{matrix}}{F(\mathbf{T}) \to G(\mathbf{T})}$$

satisfies $\varphi_{F(\mathbf{X})\to G(\mathbf{X})}(\alpha_{\mathbf{T}})$, then

$$\begin{matrix} F(\mathbf{T}) \\ \vdots \\ G(\mathbf{T}) \end{matrix}$$

satisfies $\varphi_{G(\mathbf{X})}(\alpha_{\mathbf{T}})$. By induction hypothesis, the latter deduction is normalizable, and, consequently, so is the former.

8.1.2. $\bigwedge$ introduction of first order. If

$$\cfrac{\begin{matrix} \vdots \\ F(x,\mathbf{T}) \end{matrix}}{\bigwedge x F(x,\mathbf{T})}$$

satisfies $\varphi_{\bigwedge x F(x,\mathbf{X})}(\alpha_{\mathbf{T}})$, then

$$\begin{matrix} \vdots \\ F(x,\mathbf{T}) \end{matrix}$$

satisfies $\varphi_{F(x,\mathbf{X})}(\alpha_{\mathbf{T}})$. By induction hypothesis, the latter deduction is normalizable and, consequently, so is the former.

8.1.3. $\wedge$ introduction of second order. If

$$\begin{array}{c}\vdots\\ \dfrac{F(X,\mathbf{T})}{\wedge XF(X,\mathbf{T})}\end{array}$$

satisfies $\varphi_{\wedge XF(X,\mathbf{X})}(\alpha_{\mathbf{T}})$, then

$$\begin{array}{c}\vdots\\ F(X,\mathbf{T})\end{array}$$

satisfies $\varphi_{F(X,\mathbf{X})}(\alpha_X,\alpha_{\mathbf{T}})$ for all α_X. By induction hypothesis, the latter deduction is normalizable and, consequently, so is the former.

9. Consider a deduction

$$\begin{array}{c}F_1(\mathbf{X}) \quad \dots \quad F_n(\mathbf{X})\\ \ddots \quad \dots \quad .\!\cdot\!{}^{\cdot}\\ F(\mathbf{X})\end{array}$$

whose free species variables form the sequence $\mathbf{X}$ and whose assumptions are $F_1(\mathbf{X}), \dots, F_n(\mathbf{X})$. Then, for all individual terms that we substitute for its free individual variables and for all sequences of species terms $\mathbf{T}$ that we substitute for $\mathbf{X}$ and for all $\alpha_{\mathbf{T}}$, if the deductions

$$\begin{array}{ccc}\vdots & & \vdots\\ F_1(\mathbf{T}) & \dots & F_n(\mathbf{T})\end{array}$$

satisfy $\varphi_{F_1(\mathbf{X})}(\alpha_{\mathbf{T}}), \dots, \varphi_{F_n(\mathbf{X})}(\alpha_{\mathbf{T}})$, respectively, then

$$\begin{array}{c}\begin{array}{ccc}\vdots & & \vdots\\ F_1(\mathbf{T}) & \dots & F_n(\mathbf{T})\end{array}\\ \ddots \quad \dots \quad .\!\cdot\!{}^{\cdot}\\ F(\mathbf{T})\end{array}$$

satisfies $\varphi_{F(\mathbf{X})}(\alpha_{\mathbf{T}})$. The proof is by induction on the length of the deduction. Several cases have to be distinguished depending on how the end formula of the deduction has been inferred.

9.1. The deduction consists solely of an assumption. Trivial.

9.2. The last inference is an introduction.

9.2.1. $\rightarrow$introduction. We have to show that a deduction of the form

$$\frac{\begin{matrix}\not{F}(\mathbf{T})\\ \vdots \\ G(\mathbf{T})\end{matrix}}{F(\mathbf{T}) \rightarrow G(\mathbf{T})}$$

satisfies $\varphi_{F(\mathbf{X})\rightarrow G(\mathbf{X})}(\alpha_{\mathbf{T}})$. By 7.2.1 this is so if

$$\begin{matrix}\vdots \\ F(\mathbf{T}) \\ \vdots \\ G(\mathbf{T})\end{matrix}$$

satisfies $\varphi_{G(\mathbf{X})}(\alpha_{\mathbf{T}})$ for all

$$\begin{matrix}\vdots \\ F(\mathbf{T})\end{matrix}$$

that satisfy $\varphi_{F(\mathbf{X})}(\alpha_{\mathbf{T}})$ which follows immediately from the induction hypothesis.

9.2.2. $\bigwedge$introduction of first order. We have to show that a deduction of the form

$$\frac{\begin{matrix}\vdots \\ F(x, \mathbf{T})\end{matrix}}{\bigwedge x F(x, \mathbf{T})}$$

satisfies $\varphi_{\Lambda x F(x,\mathbf{X})}(\alpha_{\mathbf{T}})$. By 7.2.2 this is so if

$$\begin{array}{c} \vdots \\ F(t,\mathbf{T}) \end{array}$$

satisfies $\varphi_{F(t,\mathbf{X})}(\alpha_{\mathbf{T}})$ for all individual terms t which follows immediately from the induction hypothesis.

9.2.3. Λintroduction of second order. We have to show that a deduction of the form

$$\begin{array}{c} \vdots \\ \dfrac{F(X,\mathbf{T})}{\Lambda X F(X,\mathbf{T})} \end{array}$$

satisfies $\varphi_{\Lambda X F(X,\mathbf{X})}(\alpha_{\mathbf{T}})$. By 7.2.3 this is so if

$$\begin{array}{c} \vdots \\ F(T,\mathbf{T}) \end{array}$$

satisfies $\varphi_{F(X,\mathbf{X})}(\alpha_T,\alpha_{\mathbf{T}})$ for all T and α_T which follows immediately from the induction hypothesis.

9.3. The last inference of the deduction is an elimination.

9.3.1. $\rightarrow$elimination. We have to show that a deduction of the form

$$\dfrac{\begin{array}{c} \vdots \\ F(\mathbf{T}) \rightarrow G(\mathbf{T}) \end{array} \quad \begin{array}{c} \vdots \\ F(\mathbf{T}) \end{array}}{G(\mathbf{T})}$$

satisfies $\varphi_{G(\mathbf{X})}(\alpha_{\mathbf{T}})$. By induction hypothesis

$$\begin{array}{c} \vdots \\ F(\mathbf{T}) \rightarrow G(\mathbf{T}) \end{array}$$

satisfies $\varphi_{F(\mathbf{X})\to G(\mathbf{X})}(\alpha_{\mathbf{T}})$. Consequently, by a finite number of eliminations of main cuts, it reduces to a deduction which consists solely of an assumption, has a cut free main branch with normalizable minor deductions or else ends with an introduction inference. In the first two cases we are done since by induction hypothesis

$$\begin{array}{c} \vdots \\ F(\mathbf{T}) \end{array}$$

satisfies $\varphi_{F(\mathbf{X})}(\alpha_{\mathbf{T}})$ and is a fortiori normalizable. In the third case we know that

$$\dfrac{\begin{array}{c} \cancel{F(\mathbf{T})} \\ \vdots \\ G(\mathbf{T}) \end{array}}{F(\mathbf{T})\to G(\mathbf{T})} \qquad \begin{array}{c} \vdots \\ F(\mathbf{T}) \end{array}$$

satisfy $\varphi_{F(\mathbf{X})\to G(\mathbf{X})}(\alpha_{\mathbf{T}})$ and $\varphi_{F(\mathbf{X})}(\alpha_{\mathbf{T}})$, respectively. By 7.2.1

$$\begin{array}{c} \vdots \\ F(\mathbf{T}) \\ \vdots \\ G(\mathbf{T}) \end{array}$$

satisfies $\varphi_{G(\mathbf{X})}(\alpha_{\mathbf{T}})$ and, consequently, so does

$$\dfrac{\dfrac{\begin{array}{c} \cancel{F(\mathbf{T})} \\ \vdots \\ G(\mathbf{T}) \end{array}}{F(\mathbf{T})\to G(\mathbf{T})} \quad \begin{array}{c} \vdots \\ F(\mathbf{T}) \end{array}}{G(\mathbf{T})}$$

which was to be proved.

9.3.2. $\bigwedge$ elimination of first order. We have to show that a deduction of the form

$$\begin{array}{c} \vdots \\ \dfrac{\bigwedge x F(x, \mathbf{T})}{F(t, \mathbf{T})} \end{array}$$

satisfies $\varphi_{F(t,\mathbf{X})}(\alpha_{\mathbf{T}})$. By induction hypothesis

$$\begin{array}{c} \vdots \\ \bigwedge x F(x, \mathbf{T}) \end{array}$$

satisfies $\varphi_{\bigwedge x F(x,\mathbf{X})}(\alpha_{\mathbf{T}})$. Consequently, by a finite number of eliminations of main cuts, it reduces to a deduction which consists solely of an assumption, has a cut free main branch with normalizable minor deductions or else ends with an introduction inference. In the first two cases we are done and in the third case we know that

$$\begin{array}{c} \vdots \\ \dfrac{F(x, \mathbf{T})}{\bigwedge x F(x, \mathbf{T})} \end{array}$$

satisfies $\varphi_{\bigwedge x F(x,\mathbf{X})}(\alpha_{\mathbf{T}})$. By 7.2.2

$$\begin{array}{c} \vdots \\ F(t, \mathbf{T}) \end{array}$$

satisfies $\varphi_{F(t,\mathbf{X})}(\alpha_{\mathbf{T}})$ and, consequently, so does

$$\begin{array}{c} \vdots \\ \dfrac{\dfrac{F(x, \mathbf{T})}{\bigwedge x F(x, \mathbf{T})}}{F(t, \mathbf{T})} \end{array}$$

which was to be proved.

9.3.3. $\bigwedge$ elimination of second order. We have to show that a deduction of the form

$$\begin{array}{c}\vdots\\ \dfrac{\wedge XF(X,\mathbf{T})}{F(T(\mathbf{T}),\mathbf{T})}\end{array}$$

satisfies $\varphi_{F(T(\mathbf{X}),\mathbf{X})}(\alpha_{\mathbf{T}})$. By induction hypothesis

$$\begin{array}{c}\vdots\\ \wedge XF(X,\mathbf{T})\end{array}$$

satisfies $\varphi_{\wedge XF(X,\mathbf{X})}(\alpha_{\mathbf{T}})$. Consequently, by a finite number of eliminations of main cuts, it reduces to a deduction which consists solely of an assumption, has a cut free main branch with normalizable minor deductions or else ends with an introduction inference. In the first two cases we are done and in the third case we know that

$$\begin{array}{c}\vdots\\ \dfrac{F(X,\mathbf{T})}{\wedge XF(X,\mathbf{T})}\end{array}$$

satisfies $\varphi_{\wedge XF(X,\mathbf{X})}(\alpha_{\mathbf{T}})$. By 7.2.3

$$\begin{array}{c}\vdots\\ F(T(\mathbf{T}),\mathbf{T})\end{array}$$

satisfies $\varphi_{F(X,\mathbf{X})}(\alpha_{T(\mathbf{T})},\alpha_{\mathbf{T}})$ for all computability predicates $\alpha_{T(\mathbf{T})}$ and, consequently, so does

$$\begin{array}{c}\vdots\\ \dfrac{\dfrac{F(X,\mathbf{T})}{\wedge XF(X,\mathbf{T})}}{F(T(\mathbf{T}),\mathbf{T})}\end{array}$$

It now only remains to put $\alpha_{T(\mathbf{T})} = \varphi_{T(\mathbf{X})}(\alpha_{\mathbf{T}})$ and use the subsitution property

$$\varphi_{F(X,\mathbf{X})}(\varphi_{T(\mathbf{X})}(\alpha_{\mathbf{T}}),\alpha_{\mathbf{T}}) = \varphi_{F(T(\mathbf{X}),\mathbf{X})}(\alpha_{\mathbf{T}})$$

which is immediately verified by induction on the number of logical signs in the formula $F(X,\mathbf{X})$.

10. **Hauptsatz.** *Every deduction is normalizable.*

10.1. Given an arbitrary deduction, let $\mathbf{X}$ be the totality of its free species variables and $F(\mathbf{X})$ its end formula. From what we have just proved it follows that the deduction satisfies $\varphi_{F(\mathbf{X})}(\alpha_{\mathbf{X}})$ whatever be the choice of the sequence of computability predicates $\alpha_{\mathbf{X}}$. In particular, it is normalizable.

10.2. Inspection of the proof of Hauptsatz shows that for every specific deduction the proof that it is normalizable can be formalized in the theory of species itself.

11. The following three corollaries which follow from Hauptsatz by combinatorial reasoning are due to Prawitz 1968 who derived them from his completeness theorem for the cut free sequent calculus which corresponds to the system of natural deduction we are considering. We provide the proofs since they are somewhat different for the system of natural deduction.

11.1. *From a proof of $F \vee G$ we can find a proof of either F or G.*

11.1.1. The normalized proof of $F \vee G = \Lambda Y((F\to Y) \to ((G\to Y)\to Y))$ must have one of the forms

$$\begin{array}{c} \not{F}\!\!\not{\to}\!\not{Y} \quad \not{G}\!\!\not{\to}\!\not{Y} \\ \vdots \quad \vdots \\ \underline{\not{F}\!\!\not{\to}\!\not{Y} \quad F} \\ \underline{Y} \\ \underline{(G\to Y)\to Y} \\ \underline{(F\to Y)\to((G\to Y)\to Y)} \\ F\vee G \end{array} \qquad\qquad \begin{array}{c} \not{F}\!\!\not{\to}\!\not{Y} \quad \not{G}\!\!\not{\to}\!\not{Y} \\ \vdots \quad \vdots \\ \underline{\not{G}\!\!\not{\to}\!\not{Y} \quad G} \\ \underline{Y} \\ \underline{(G\to Y)\to Y} \\ \underline{(F\to Y)\to((G\to Y)\to Y)} \\ F\vee G \end{array}$$

The left proof contains a deduction of F from the assumptions $F\to Y$ and $G\to Y$. By substituting $F\vee G$ for Y we obtain a deduction of F from the assumptions $F \to (F \vee G)$ and $G \to (F \vee G)$. Attaching proofs of $F \to (F \vee G)$ and $G \to (F \vee G)$ to this deduction we obtain the desired proof of F. If the proof of $F \vee G$ has the form pictured to the right, we obtain a proof of G by the same argument.

11.2. *From a proof of* $\bigvee x F(x)$ *we can find an individual term t and a proof of* $F(t)$.

11.2.1. The normalized proof of $\bigvee x F(x) = \bigwedge Y(\bigwedge x(F(x) \to Y) \to Y)$ must have the form

$$\dfrac{\dfrac{\dfrac{\dfrac{\cancel{\bigwedge x(F(x)\to Y)}}{F(t)\to Y} \qquad \begin{matrix}\cancel{\bigwedge x(F(x)\to Y)}\\ \vdots \\ F(t)\end{matrix}}{Y}}{\bigwedge x(F(x)\to Y)\to Y}}{\bigvee x F(x)}$$

Take the subdeduction of $F(t)$ from the assumption $\bigwedge x(F(x) \to Y)$, substitute $\bigvee x F(x)$ for Y and attach a proof of $\bigwedge x(F(x) \to \bigvee x F(x))$. We then get the desired proof of $F(t)$.

11.3. *From a proof of* $\bigvee X F(X)$ *we can find a species term T and a proof of* $F(T)$.

11.3.1. The normalized proof of $\bigvee X F(X) = \bigwedge Y(\bigwedge X(F(X) \to Y) \to Y)$ must have the form

$$\dfrac{\dfrac{\dfrac{\dfrac{\cancel{\bigwedge X(F(X)\to Y)}}{F(U(Y))\to Y} \qquad \begin{matrix}\cancel{\bigwedge X(F(X)\to Y)}\\ \vdots \\ F(U(Y))\end{matrix}}{Y}}{\bigwedge X(F(X)\to Y)\to Y}}{\bigvee X F(X)}$$

Take the subdeduction of $F(U(Y))$ from $\bigwedge X(F(X) \to Y)$, substitute $\bigvee X F(X)$ for Y and attach a proof of $\bigwedge X(F(X) \to \bigvee X F(X))$. We then get a proof of $F(T)$ where $T = U(\bigvee X F(X))$.

12. The extension of the treatment of second order logic given in the present paper to the full theory of types is rather straightforward and will be published elsewhere.

References

J.Y.Girard, Une extension de l'interpretation de Gödel a l'analyse, et son application a l'elimination des coupures dans l'analyse et la theorie des types (1970). This volume.

P.Martin-Löf, Hauptsatz for the intuitionistic theory of iterated inductive definitions (1970). This volume.

D.Prawitz, Natural deduction (Almqvist and Wiksell, Stockholm, 1965), Some results for intuitionistic logic with second order quantification rules, in: Intuitionism and Proof Theory, eds. A.Kino, J.Myhill and R.E.Vesley (North-Holland, Amsterdam, 1970).

W.W.Tait, Intentional interpretations of functionals of finite type, J. Symbolic Logic 32 (1967) 198–212.

IDEAS AND RESULTS IN PROOF THEORY

Dag PRAWITZ
University of Stockholm

In this lecture I shall give an exposition of certain themes in proof theory. I do not intend to give a general survey of proof theory but shall concentrate on the following topics:

(i) the ideas behind what may be called Gentzen-type analysis in proof theory, where in particular, I want to draw attention to the fact that they constitute the embryo to a general proof theory;

(ii) extensions of the results obtained by Gentzen to more powerful theories;

(iii) the connection between proofs and the terms used in functional interpretations of intuitionistic logic, in particular, the connection between Gentzen-type analysis and the Gödel-type analysis that originated with Gödel's so-called Dialectica interpretation.

In an appendix, I develop a notion of validity of derivations, which may be contemplated as a possible explication of Gentzen's ideas about an operational interpretation of the logical constants.

Proofs of the results are usually left out but in the appendix mentioned, it is shown how this notion of validity may be used as a convenient tool to establish the main result about strong normalization in first order logic. In a second appendix, it is shown how to extend this notion and this result to second order logic.

To start with, I shall make some general comments about proof theory.

To simplify the reading, I list the content in more detail:

I want to mention that many of the view points of this paper evolved during several conversations that I have had with Georg Kreisel and Per Martin-Löf to both of whom I am much indebted. Georg Kreisel also read the draft of the paper and made valuable suggestions.

I. General and reductive proof theory

1. As the name suggests, proof theory studies proofs. In other words, it studies not only the theorems of a theory, *what* we know in the theory, but also *how* we know the theorems.

Such studies may differ considerably with respect to their aims, however. Accordingly, I shall distinguish between *general* and *reductive proof theory.* This is a distinction which (although not called by these names) is in effect made in some of Georg Kreisel's writings.

In *general proof theory*, we are interested in the very notion of proof and its properties and impose no restriction on the methods that may be used in the study of this notion.

In *reductive proof theory*, we are interested in analysing mathematical theories to attain a reduction of them. The study of the proofs of a theory is the tool used to obtain this end, and hence, this study has to use more elementary principles than those occurring in the theory in question.

2. The subject matter of *general proof theory* is thus proofs considered as a process by which we get to know the theorems of a theory or the validity of an argument, and this process is studied here in its own right – the study is not only a tool for another analysis. Obvious topics in general proof theory are:

2.1. The basic question of defining the notion of proof, including the question of the distinction between different kinds of proofs such as constructive proofs and classical proofs.

2.2. Investigation of the structure of (different kinds of) proofs, including e.g. questions concerning the existence of certain normal forms.

2.3. The representation of proofs by formal derivations. In the same way as one asks when two formulas define the same set or two sentences express the same proposition, one asks when two derivations represent the same proof; in other words, one asks for identity criteria for proofs or for a "synonymity" (or equivalence) relation between derivations.

2.4. Applications of insights about the structure of proofs to other logical questions that are not formulated in terms of the notion of proof.

3. *Reductive proof theory* must of course be based upon some conception of an order between different principles with respect to how elementary they are. Typically, one singles out one kind of principles like the finitistic ones or the constructive ones and then tries to interprete a theory which at least on the surface contains also other principles into a theory that contains only the principles in question. An interpretation of this kind may also be obtained by other methods than the proof theoretical ones, i.e. without essentially using the notion of proof, but proof theoretical interpretations often differ radically from interpretations usually considered in logic in some respects (besides the special epistemological status of the theory in which the interpretation is made).

3.1. Firstly, it may not be possible to interprete every sentence in the interpreted theory directly. The sentences in the interpreted theory are thus divided into two groups: the *real sentences* which are directly given a meaning and the *ideal sentences* which lack such a direct meaning. The problem is then to show that the theory as a whole can be understood as a theory about the real sentences in which the ideal sentences only serve (as so-called ideal elements) to facilitate operations within the theory or to round off the theory. To this end, one has to show that every derivable real sentence – i.e. also when the proof proceeds over the meaningless ideal sentences – is true according to the meaning given to the real sentences. A typical proof theoretical demonstration of this kind is obtained when it is shown how to transform a derivation of a real sentence that proceeds over ideal sentences to a derivation containing only real sentences. In reductive proof theory, it is required that this demonstration is given by using only the principles occurring in the theory in which the interpretation is made.

3.2. Secondly, the interpretation itself may depend not only on the form of the sentences but also on their derivations. For instance, there may be a mapping f from formulas in a theory $\mathbf{T}_1$ to formulas in a theory $\mathbf{T}_2$, a mapping g from derivations in $\mathbf{T}_1$ into terms in $\mathbf{T}_2$, and an operation ϕ such that when π is a derivation in $\mathbf{T}_1$ of a sentence A, then $\phi(f(A),g(\pi))$ is a sentence holding in $\mathbf{T}_2$.

4.1. As an early example (perhaps the first one) of an investigation in general proof theory, we may take *Frege's* formal definition of derivability. His definition may be understood as an extensional characterization of logical proofs (i.e. a characterization with respect to the set of theorems) within certain languages: his notion of derivability is such that to every (intuitive) proof of a proposition within a certain domain, there exists a derivation of the corresponding formula; but the characterization is only extensional since the formal derivation may use quite different methods of proof and have a structure different from the intuitive proof.

4.2. The founder of reductive proof theory is of course *Hilbert*. In his various proof theoretical publications, Hilbert considered two main problems. The first one is to give an analysis of mathematical theories which at least on the surface does not seem to go very far, namely, to demonstrate their formal consistency with the use of finitary means. The second one, which is philosophically more mature, is to reduce classical mathematics to finitary mathematics using the idea of a division of mathematical sentences into real and ideal sentences, the real sentences here being the ones that can be given a finitary meaning directly. The two problems are not always distinguished although Hilbert was often careful enough to do so. The second problem is clearly the most interesting one, but under some rather general conditions, the two problems happen to be equivalent: the truth of the derivable real sentences implies the consistency of the theory provided every sentence is derivable from a contradiction (and some real sentence is not true); and conversely, the consistency implies the truth of the derivable real sentences provided each true real sentence is derivable (and the negation of a false real sentence is a true real sentence).

4.3. Later examples of works in reductive proof theory are *Kreisel*'s no counter example interpretation and *Gödel*'s interpretations in terms of computable functionals (the so-called Dialectica interpretation). These two interpretations, which give a constructive meaning to *every* derivable sentence in first order arithmetic, show the second characteristic feature of a proof theoretical interpretation described above where the interpretation depends on the derivations.

4.4. *Gentzen*'s works to which I shall now turn are to a great extent part of both general and reductive proof theory.

II. Gentzen's analysis of first order proofs

A most basic question in general proof theory, which is also of fundamental importance for reductive proof theory, is of coure the question how the notion of logical proof within first order languages is to be analysed. The work by Gentzen (1935) may be viewed as an answer to this question. The answer was given in two steps: In a first analysis, Gentzen showed how the notion could be defined in terms of certain formal systems constructed by him. Then, by a deeper analysis of the structure of these proofs, he showed that they could be written in a very special form, which altogether gave a very satisfactory understanding of these proofs.

The first step was carried out for the so-called systems of natural deduction, while the second step was carried out for the so-called calculi of sequents. There are certain advantages (which will soon become apparent) in carrying out both steps for the systems of natural deduction and I shall briefly do this here.

II.1. Gentzen's systems of natural deduction

1.1. *Main idea*

Gentzen's systems of natural deduction arise from a particular analysis of deductive inferences by which the deductive role of the different logical constants are separated. The inferences are broken down into atomic steps in such a way that each step involves only one logical constant. The steps are of two kinds, and for each logical constant there are inferences of both kinds: steps that allow the *introduction* of the logical constant (i.e., the conclusion of the inference has the constant as outermost symbol) and steps that allow the *elimination* of the logical constant (i.e., the premiss or one of the premisses of the inference has the constant as outermost symbol).

The proofs start from *assumptions*, which at certain steps in the proof may be discharged or *closed*; typically, an assumption A is closed at an introduction of an implication $A \supset B$.

1.2. *Inference rules*

It is suitable to represent the proofs as *derivations* written in tree form. The top formulas of the tree are then the assumptions, and the other formulas of the tree are to follow from the one(s) immediately above by one of the *inference rules* that formalizes the atomic inferences mentioned above. A formula A in the tree is said to *depend* on the assumptions standing above A that have not been closed by some inference preceeding A. The *open assumptions* of a derivation are the assumptions on which the last formula depends.

I state the inference rules in the form of schemata in the usual way. A formula written within square brackets above a premiss is to indicate that assumptions of this form occurring above the premiss are discharged at this inference. An inference rule is labelled with the logical constant that it deals with followed by "I" when it is an introduction and "E" when it is an elimination.

&I) $\dfrac{A \quad B}{A \,\&\, B}$ &E) $\dfrac{A \,\&\, B}{A}$ $\dfrac{A \,\&\, B}{B}$

∨I) $\dfrac{A}{A \vee B}$ $\dfrac{B}{A \vee B}$ ∨E) $\dfrac{A \vee B \quad \begin{matrix}[A]\\ C\end{matrix} \quad \begin{matrix}[B]\\ C\end{matrix}}{C}$

⊃I) $\dfrac{\begin{matrix}[A]\\ B\end{matrix}}{A \supset B}$ ⊃E) $\dfrac{A \quad A \supset B}{B}$

$$\forall\text{I})\quad \frac{A(a)}{\forall x A(x)} \qquad\qquad \forall\text{E})\quad \frac{\forall x A(x)}{A(t)}$$

$$\exists\text{I})\quad \frac{A(t)}{\exists x A(x)} \qquad\qquad \exists\text{E})\quad \frac{\exists x A(x) \quad \begin{matrix}[A(a)]\\ B\end{matrix}}{B}$$

1.2.1. *Restrictions.* Obvious conventions about substitution are to be understood. The rules ∀I and ∃E are with the following further restrictions concerning the parameter a, called the *proper parameter* (or Eigenparameter) of the inference: In ∀I, a is not to accur in the assumtions that $A(a)$ depends on; in ∃E, a is not to accur in B nor in the assumptions that the premiss B depends on except those of the form $A(a)$ (closed by the inference).

1.2.2. *Negation.* We assume that the first order languages contain a constant Λ for absurdity (or falsehood) and that $\sim A$ is understood as shorthand for $A \supset \Lambda$. The obvious introduction and elimination rules for negation

$$\sim\text{I})\quad \frac{\begin{matrix}[A]\\ \Lambda\end{matrix}}{\sim A} \qquad\qquad \sim\text{E})\quad \frac{A \quad \sim A}{\Lambda}$$

are then special cases of ⊃I and ⊃E, respectively.

1.2.3. *Major and minor premisses.* In an inference by an application of an E-rule, the premiss in which the constant in question is exhibited (in the figures above) is called the *major premiss* of the inference and the other premiss(es) if any, we call the *minor premiss(es).*

1.2.4. *Convention about proper parameters.* To simplify certain formal details in the sequel, it shall tacitly be assumed that a parameter in a derivation is the proper parameter of at most one inference, that the proper parameter of an ∀I-inference occurs only above the conclusion of the inference, and that the proper parameter of an ∃E-inference occurs only above the minor premiss of the inference.

1.3. *The systems* **M, I, C**

1.3.1. *Minimal logic.* The rules given above determine the system of natural deduction for (first order) *minimal logic,* abbreviated **M**.

1.3.2. *Intuitionistic logic*. By adding the rule Λ_I (intuitionistic absurdity rule)

$$\frac{\Lambda}{A}$$

where A is to be atomic and different from Λ, we get the system of natural deduction for (*first order*) *intuitionistic logic* (**I**).

1.3.3. *Classical logic*. The system of nautral deduction for (first order) *classical logic* (**C**) is obtained by

(i) considering languages without the constant v and $\exists$ and leaving out the rules for these constants (they become derived rules when v and $\exists$ are defined in the usual way) and

(ii) adding to the rules of **M** the rule Λ_C (classical absurdity rule)

$$\frac{\begin{matrix}[\sim A]\\ \Lambda\end{matrix}}{A}$$

where A is atomic and different from Λ.

1.4. *Derivations and derivability*

We say that Π is a *derivation* in **M**(**I** or **C**) of A from a set of formulas Γ when Π is a tree formed according to the above explanations using the rules of **M**(**I** or **C**) with an end formula A depending on formulas all belonging to Γ. If there is such a derivation, we say that A is *derivable* in the system in question from Γ; in short: $\Gamma \vdash A$. When A is derivable from the empty set of assumptions, we may say simply that A is *derivable*.

1.5. *Extensions by the additions of atomic systems*

It is also of interest to consider extensions of the three systems defined above by adding further rules for atomic formulas. There may also be reason to specify the languages of the systems exactly. By an *atomic system*, I shall understand a system determined by a set of *descriptive constants*, (i.e. individual, operational, and predicate constants) and a set of *inference rules* for atomic sentences with these constants (i.e. both the premisses and the conclusion are to be atomic formulas of this kind). A rule may lack premisses and is then called an *axiom*. Let **S** be an (atomic) system of this kind. By a *formula over* **S**, we shall understand a formula whose descriptive constants are those of **S**. By **M(S)**, we shall understand the system of natural deduction whose language is the first order language determined by the descriptive constants of **S** and whose rules are the rules of **S** and **M**. We define the systems **I(S)** and **C(S)** similarly. Note that **I(S)** is the same as **M(S⁺)** where **S⁺** is obtained from **S** by adding the rule Λ_{I}.

In many contexts, it is not essential how the rules of a system **S** are specified and we make no restriction of that kind. Of special interest, however, are the *Post systems* where the inference rules are determined as the instances of a finite number of schemata of the form

$$\frac{A_1 \quad A_2 \quad \dots \quad A_n}{B}$$

where A_1, A_2, A_n, and B are atomic formulas. One may also require that B contains no parameter that does not occur in some A_i.

1.6. *Remark*

A trivial reformulation of the systems described above is obtained if we make explicit the assumptions that a formula in a derivation depends on by writing these assumptions in a sequence followed by an arrow in front of the formula. The tree of formulas is then replaced by a tree of so-called *sequents* of the form $\Gamma \to A$ where Γ is a sequence of formulas. If the inference rules are now formulated with these sequents as the basic objects, they get a somewhat different look. For instance, ⊃I and ⊃E now become

$$\frac{\Gamma, A \to B}{\Gamma \to A \supset B} \qquad\qquad \frac{\Gamma \to A \quad \Delta \to A \supset B}{\Gamma, \Delta \to B}$$

and the derivations now start not from assumptions but from axioms of the form $A \to A$. Clearly, there is only an inessential notational difference between the first formulation and this reformulation; and the new formulation is not to be confused (as is sometimes done) with the calculus of sequents, which differs more essentially by having, instead of elimination rules, rules for operating on the formulas to the left of the arrow (cf. for instance, the new formulation of ⊃E with the rule for introducing ⊃ in the antecedent in the calculus of sequents). (For a remark concerning the relationship between natural deduction and the calculus of sequents, see sec. 5.1.)

II.2. The significance of Gentzen's systems

The most noteworthy properties of Gentzen's systems of natural deduction seems to be (2.1) the analysis of deductive inferences into atomic steps, by which the deductive role of the different logical constants is separated and (2.2) the discovery that these atomic steps are of two kinds, viz. introductions and eliminations, standing in a certain symmetrical relation to each other.

2.1. This analysis may be understood as an attempt to characterize the notion of proof, not only provability as first done by Frege (sec. I.4.1), in the sense that it is an attempt (2.1.1) to isolate the essential deductive operations and (2.1.2) to break them down as far as possible.

2.1.1. The deductive operations that are isolated are to begin with constructive (or intuitionistic) ones. There is a close correspondence between the constructive meaning of a logical constant and its introduction rule. For instance, an implication $A \supset B$ is constructively understood as the assertion of the existence of a construction of B from A, and in accordance with this meaning $\supset$I allows the inference of $A \supset B$ given a proof of B from A. Of course, a proof of B from A is not the same as a construction of B from A; it is rather a special kind of such a construction (cf. sections 2.2.2 and IV.1). There is thus not a complete agreement but a close correspondence between the constructive meaning of the constants and the introduction rules; sometimes the correspondence is very close: some of Heyting's explanation, see e.g. Heyting (1956) 97–99 and 102, may almost be taken as a reading of Gentzen's introduction rules.

This correspondence between the introduction rules and the constructive interpretation of the logical constants is a strong indication that the essential *constructive* deductive operations have been isolated. By a (first order) *positive proof*, I shall in this paper understand a (first order) proof that uses intuitionistically valid deductive operations but no operation assuming any special properties of Λ; an *intuitionistic proof* is then simply a proof using intuitionistically valid deductive operations. The claim is thus that **M** constitutes an analysis of first order positive proofs and **I**, an analysis of first order intuitionistic proofs.

The *classical* deductive operations are then analysed as consisting of the constructive ones plus a principle of indirect proof for atomic sentences, which may be understood as stating as a special assumption that the atomic sentences are decidable[1]. One may doubt that this is the proper way of analysing classical

[1] In the formulation by Gentzen (1935), one adds instead of the rule Λ_C the axiom of the excluded middle to get classical logic from intuitionistic logic. Our choice of Λ_C is motivated by the subsequent development.

inferences, and it is true that the rules of the classical calculus of sequents or some variants of it (like the one by Schütte (1951) or the one by Tait (1968)) are closer to the classical meaning of the logical constants. But this possibility of analysing classical inferences as a special case of constructive ones (applicable to decidable sentences) provides a way of constructively understanding classical reasoning (which is the essential fact behind Kolmogoroff's (1925) and Gödel's (1932) interpretation of classical logic in intuitionistic logic; see also Prawitz and Malmnäs (1968)) and also explains the success in carrying over to classical logic the deeper results concerning the structure of proofs, which at first sight are evident only for constructive proofs (cf. sec. 2.2.3).

The claim that the essential deductive operations have been isolated is not to be understood as a claim that these operations mirror all informal deductive practices, which would be an unreasonable demand in view of the fact that informal practices may sometimes contain logically insignificant irregularities. What is claimed is that the essential logical content of intuitive logical operations that can be formulated in the languages considered can be understood as composed of the atomic inferences isolated by Gentzen. It is in this sense that we may understand the terminology *natural* deduction.

Nevertheless, Gentzen's systems are also natural in the more superficial sense of corresponding rather well to informal practices; in other words, the structure of informal proofs are often preserved rather well when formalized within the systems of natural deduction. This may seem surprising in view of what was said about the correspondence between the inference rules and the *constructive* meaning of the logical constants. But it is a fact that actual reasoning often makes use of a mixture of constructive and non-constructive principles with predominance of constructive principles, the non-constructive ones typically amounting to an occasional use of the principle of indirect proof. For instance, it is a fact that an implication $A \supset B$ most often is proved by deducing B from A, a procedure that is not singled out by the classical truth functional meaning of $\supset$ as the most natural one.

2.1.2. It seems fair to say that a proof built up from Gentzen's atomic inference is *completely analysed* in the sense that one can hardly imagine the possibility of breaking down his atomic inferences into some simpler inferences.

The separation of the deductive role of the different logical constants was partly achieved already by Hilbert in some of his axiomatic formulations of sentential logic. Gentzen is able to complete this separation by separating also the role of implication from that of the other constants.

We may note in passing that the derivations in Gentzen's systems are completely analysed also in the less important sense that for each formula in the derivation, it is uniquelly determined from what premisses and by which inference rule it is inferred; these are properties that Gentzen's systems share also with certain other logical calculi.

2.1.3. From what has been said above, it should be clear that Gentzen's systems of natural deduction are not arbitrary formalizations of first order logic but constitutes a significant analysis of the proofs in this logic[1].

The situation may be compared to the attempts to characterize the notion of computation where e.g. the formalism of μ-recursive functions or even the general recursive functions may be regarded as an extensional characterization of this notion while Turing's analysis is such that one may reasonably assert the thesis that every computation when sufficiently analysed can be broken down in the operations described by Turing.

2.2. What makes Gentzen's systems especially interesting is the discovery of a certain symmetry between the atomic inferences, which may be indicated by saying that the corresponding introductions and eliminations are *inverses* of each other. The sense in which an elimination, say, is the inverse of the corresponding introduction is roughly this: the conclusion obtained by an elimination does not state anything more than what must have already been obtained if the major premiss of the elimination was inferred by an introduction. For instance, if the premiss of an &E was inferred by introduction, then the conclusion of the &E must already occur as one of the premisses of this introduction. Similarly, if the major premiss $A \supset B$ of an $\supset$E was inferred by an introduction, then a proof of the conclusion B of the $\supset$E is obtained from the proof of the major premiss of the $\supset$E by simply replacing its assumption A by the proof of the minor premiss.

2.2.1. In other words, a proof of the conclusion of an elimination is already "contained" in the proofs of the premisses when the major premiss is inferred

[1] It seems fair to say that no other system is more convincing in this respect. The axiomatic systems introduced by Frege and continued by Russell, Hilbert, and others clearly do not usually have this aim at all. There exists other systems that have been called systems of natural deduction, often proposed for didactical pruposes. To the extent that they are not to be considered as mere notational variants of Gentzen's systems, it must be said that they do not even approximately match Gentzen's analysis. (Their alleged pedagogical merits also seem doubtful, see Prawitz (1965) 103–105 and Prawitz (1967).) Gentzen's calculi of sequents may be considered as (and were historically) derived from his systems of natural deduction.

by introduction. We shall refer to this by saying that the pairs of corresponding introductions and eliminations satisfy the *inversion principle*. We shall see very soon how to make this principle more precise, but let us first consider another aspect of the principle.

2.2.2. The inversion principle seems to allow a *reinterpretation* of the logical symbols. With Gentzen, we may say that the introductions represent, as it were, the "definitions" of the logical constants. An introduction rule states a sufficient condition for introducing a formula with this constant as outermost symbol (which, as we saw, was in very close agreement with the constructive meaning of the constant but did not express this meaning completely), and this condition may now be taken as the "meaning" of the logical constant. For instance, $A \supset B$ is now to mean that there is a deduction of B from A. The eliminations, on the other hand, are "justified" by this very meaning given to the constants by the introductions. As guaranteed by the inversion principle, the conclusion of an elimination only states what must hold in view of the meaning of the major premiss of the elimination. The examples with &E and $\supset$E given above already illustrates this. As a further illustration, consider the inference

$$\frac{\sim\forall x A(x)}{\exists x \sim A(x)}$$

This inference is clearly not justified by the meaning given to the constants by the introductions: The sufficient condition for introducing $\sim\forall xA$ i.e. a proof of Λ from the assumption $\forall xA$, in no way guarantees that $\exists x \sim A$ holds (in the sense of the introductions rules) since such a proof may not at all contain a proof of $\sim A(t)$ for some term t.

These ideas of Gentzen's are of course quite vague since it is not meant that the introductions are literally to be understood as "definitions". In appendix A, I shall consider one possible way of making the ideas precise.

2.2.3. Here, I shall consider a more direct way of making the inversion principle precise. Since it says that nothing new is obtained by an elimination immediately following an introduction (of the major premiss of the elimination), it suggests that such sequences of inferences can be dispensed with. From this observation, it is possible to obtain quite simply Gentzen's results about the structure of proofs, the second step in his analysis. Indeed, the whole idea of this analysis is contained in the observations made above. Note, however, that only the rules of minimal logic are governed by the inversion principle; both the rule Λ_I and the rule Λ_C clearly fall outside the pattern of introductions and eliminations. Note in particular that the principle of indirect proof when not restricted to atomic formulas constitute quite a new principle for inferring compound formulas (which is not at all justified in the terminology of sec. 2.2.2 by the meaning given to the constants by the introduction rules). Our restriction that the conclusions of applications of the rules Λ_I and Λ_C are to be atomic (1.3.1 and 1.3.2) are motivated by these considerations. It is by this restriction that these extra rules do not disturb the pattern of introductions and eliminations or the development in the next section (cf. what was said in sec. 2.1.1 about the value of reducing classical logic in this way).

II.3. **Normal derivations and the reducibility relation**

3.1. *Definition of normal derivation*

3.1.1. *Maximum formulas.* A formula occurrence in a derivation that stands at the same time as the conclusion of an introduction and as the major premiss of an elimination is called a *maximum formula*. As is seen by inspecting the inference rules, such a formula is of greater complexity than the surrounding formulas; it constitutes a local maximum (in its path as defined in sec. 3.2.1). The inversion principle implies that a maximum formula is an unnecessary detour in a derivation which can be removed.

3.1.2. *Maximum segments.* Note: at applications of the rules for vE and ∃E, formulas of the same form occur immediately below each other. A sequence of formula occurrences $A_1, A_2, ..., A_n$ in a derivation is said to be a *maximum segment* in the derivation when they are of the same form, A_{i+1} stands immediately below A_i, A_1 is the conclusion of an introduction, and A_n is the major premiss of an elimination (A_i, for $i < n$, is then a minor premiss of an ∨E or ∃E). Also maximum segments constitutes detours that can be removed. When ∨ and ∃ are not present (as in our formulation of classical logic) no such segments can appear.

3.1.3. *Normal derivations.* A derivations in any of the systems considered above is now defined as *normal* or said to be in *normal form* when it contains no maximum formula and no maximum segment.

3.1.4. *Fully normal derivations.* Also a normal derivation may contain certain redundancies that one wants to remove. An application of ∨E is said to be *redundant* if the two minor premisses do not stand below assumptions that are closed by the inference. Similarly, an application of ∃E is said to be *redundant* if no assumption is closed by the inference. An application of Λ_C is said to be *redundant* if there is an assumption $\sim A$ closed by the inference that is major premiss of an elimination and all of the assumptions on which the minor premiss A depends are assumptions on which also the conclusion A of the application of Λ_C depends. Redundant applications of ∨E, ∃E, and Λ_C constitute unnecessary complications and are easily removed (see sec. 3.4). A derivation is said to be *fully normal* or to be in *full normal form* when it is normal and contains no such rendundant application of vE, ∃E, or Λ_C.

3.2. *The form of normal derivations*

A normal derivation has quite a perspicuous form: it contains two parts, one *analytical part* in which the assumptions are broken down in their components by use of the elimination rules, and one *synthetical part* in which the final components obtained in the analytical part are put together by use of the introduction rules. Between the analytical and the synthetical part there is a *minimum part* in which operations on atomic formulas may occur. To state this form of the normal derivations in a more precise way, we introduce a certain terminology.

3.2.1. *Branches and paths.* A *branch* in a derivation is a sequence $A_1, A_2, ..., A_n$ of formula occurrences in the derivation where A_1 is an assumption not discharged by ∨E or ∃E, A_{i+1} is the formula occurrence immediately below A_i, and A_n is either the end formula of the derivation or the minor premiss of an ⊃E but no A_i with $i < n$ is such a minor premiss. A *path* is like a branch except that the formula occurrence immediately succeeding the major premiss of an ∨E or ∃E is not the formula occurrence immediately below but one of the assumptions discharged by the inference in question.

3.2.2. For derivations not containing any ∨E or ∃E, we can now state the form of normal derivations in the following

Theorem. *A branch in a normal derivation in* **M(S)**, **I(S)**, or **C(S)** *not containing* ∨E *or* ∃E *can be divided into three unique parts:*
(i) one *analytical part*, $A_1, A_2, ..., A_{m-1}$, in which each formula is the major premiss of an elimination and contains the immediately succeeding formula as a subformula;
(ii) one *minimum part*, $A_m, A_{m+1}, ..., A_{m+k}$, in which each formula except the last one is premiss of Λ_I, Λ_C, or a rule of **S**;

(iii) one *synthetical part*, $A_{m+k}, A_{m+k+2}, ..., A_n$, in which each formula is the conclusion of an introduction and is a subformula of the immediately preceding one.

Both the analytical and the synthetical part may be empty ($m = 1$ or $m + k = n$, respectively). In the case of the system **M**, the minimum part contains exactly one formula A_m, called the *minimum formula* of the branch. The minimum formula is the conclusion of an elimination, the premiss of an introduction, and a subformula of both A_1 and A_n, and is the only formula of the branch with all these properties. In the case of the other systems, the minimum part may contain more than one formula, which then all have to be atomic. When all the minima formulas in a fully normal derivation are atomic, I shall say that the derivation is in *expanded normal form*.

3.2.3. For derivations containing ∨E or ∃E, we consider paths instead of branches. The paths in such a derivation are divided into *segments* consisting of all the consecutive formula occurrences of the same form. The statement of the form of normal derivations in sec. 3.2.2 then extends literally to the case when ∨E and ∃E are present if we replace "branch" by "path" and "formula" by "segment" and agree to the following conventions: a *segment* is said to be the *conclusion* (*(major) premiss*) of the inference of which the first (last) occurrence in the segment is the conclusion ((major) premiss); if the first occurrence in the segment is an assumption closed by an inference ∨E or ∃E, the segment is said to be the conclusion of this inference; one segment is said to be a *subsegment* of another segment, if the formula occurring in the first segment is a subformula of the formula occurring in the second segment. In order that every formula in a derivation is to belong to one path, we have to require that no ∨E or ∃E is redundant and therefore, we consider fully normal derivations.

3.2.4. From this detailed description of the normal derivations, we easily obtain some more specific corollaries:

3.2.4.1. **Corollary**. *The last inference in a fully normal derivation in* **M**, **I**, *or* **C** *without open assumptions is an introduction.*

3.2.4.2. **Corollary**. *A fully normal derivation in* **M(S)**, **I(S)**, *or* **C(S)** *of an atomic formula from a set of atomic formulas is a derivation in* **S**.

3.2.4.3. *Subformula principle for* **M** *and* **I**: Each formula in a fully normal derivation in **M** or **I** of A from Γ is a subformula of A or of some formula of Γ.

3.2.4.4. *Subformula principle for* **C**: Each formula in a normal derivation in **C** of A from Γ either is a subformula of A or of some formula of Γ or is an assumption $\sim B$ closed by Λ_C (in which case B is a subformula of the kind mentioned or is an occurrence of Λ immediately below such an assumption).

3.2.4.5. The subformula principle also holds when the logical systems are extended by the addition of the rules of a system **S** for atomic formulas but then with an exception for the atomic formulas. The principle may furthermore be strengthened by saying somewhat more about how the different formula occurrences are related to A or Γ (see Prawitz (1965) 43–44 and 53–54).

3.3. *Reductions, immediate simplifications and expansions*

3.3.1. We shall now show how to remove maximal formulas from a derivation. This means simply that we shall make the inversion principle explicit for the different cases that can arise. The derivation obtained from a derivation Π by removing (in the way already exemplified in sec. 2.2) a maximum formula whose outermost symbol is α we shall call an *α-reduction* of Π. Below we state the five reductions corresponding to the five possible forms of a maximum formula. These five reductions are said to be *proper reductions*. To be able to remove also maximal segments, we add two *permutative reductions*, viz. $\vee$E- and $\exists$E-*reductions*, which decrease the length of maximal segments.

To state the reductions in a convenient way, I shall use Π (with or without indices) to range over derivations and Σ to range over finite sequences of derivations. Furthermore, I shall use a *concatenation operation* $(\Sigma/\Gamma/\Pi)$ where Γ is a set of top formulas in Π to denote the result obtained from Π by writing the deductions in Σ above each of top formulas in Γ (i.e., in such a way that the top formulas in question come immediately below the end formulas of the derivations in Σ in the given order). When Γ is a set of top formulas of the form A, I often denote the set by $[A]$ and write $(\Sigma/[A]/\Pi)$ in the more graphic notation

$$\frac{\Sigma}{\begin{matrix}[A]\\ \Pi\end{matrix}}$$

When this notation is used, it is always tacitly assumed that the proper parameters in Π do not occur in the formulas in Σ.

In the cases below, the right derivation is a reduction (of the kind in question) of the derivation to the left.

3.3.1.1. *&-reductions*

$$\dfrac{\dfrac{\dfrac{\Sigma_1}{A_1} \quad \dfrac{\Sigma_2}{A_2}}{A_1 \,\&\, A_2}}{A_i} \qquad\qquad \dfrac{\Sigma_i}{A_i} \qquad\qquad i = 1 \text{ or } 2\,.$$

3.3.1.2. v*-reductions*

$$\dfrac{\dfrac{\dfrac{\Sigma}{A_i}}{A_1 \vee A_2} \quad \begin{matrix}[A_1]\\ \dfrac{\Sigma_1}{B}\end{matrix} \quad \begin{matrix}[A_2]\\ \dfrac{\Sigma_2}{B}\end{matrix}}{B} \qquad\qquad \dfrac{\begin{matrix}\dfrac{\Sigma}{[A_i]}\\ \Sigma_i\end{matrix}}{B}$$

Here $[A_i]$ denotes the set of assumptions in Σ_i that are closed by the $\vee$E in question (i=1 or 2).

3.3.1.3. $\supset$*-reductions*

$$\dfrac{\dfrac{\Sigma_1}{A_1} \quad \dfrac{\begin{matrix}[A_1]\\ \dfrac{\Sigma_2}{A_2}\end{matrix}}{A_1 \supset A_2}}{A_2} \qquad\qquad \dfrac{\begin{matrix}\dfrac{\Sigma_1}{[A_1]}\\ \Sigma_2\end{matrix}}{A_2}$$

Here $[A]$ denotes the set of assumptions in Σ_2 that are closed by the $\supset$I.

3.3.1.4. $\forall$*-reductions*

$$\dfrac{\dfrac{\dfrac{\Sigma(a)}{A(a)}}{\forall x A(x)}}{A(t)} \qquad\qquad \dfrac{\Sigma(t)}{A(t)}$$

We write $\Sigma(a)$ to indicate that the formulas in the part of the derivation above $A(a)$ may contain the parameter a. The deduction $\Sigma(t)$ is to be obtained from $\Sigma(a)$ by replacing every occurrence of a by the term t. Note that the restriction on ∀I and the tacit assumption about the proper parameters (sec. 1.2.4) together guarantee that the right derivation is correct.

3.3.1.5. ∃-*reductions*

$$\dfrac{\dfrac{\dfrac{\Sigma_1}{A(t)}}{\exists x A(x)} \quad \dfrac{\begin{matrix}[A(a)]\\ \Sigma_2(a)\end{matrix}}{B}}{B} \qquad\qquad \dfrac{\begin{matrix}\dfrac{\Sigma_1}{[A(t)]}\\ \Sigma_2(t)\end{matrix}}{B}$$

The remark made above in connection with the ∀-reduction applies also here mutatis mutandis. $[A(a)]$ denotes the set of assumptions in $\Sigma_2(a)$ which are closed by the ∃E.

3.3.1.6. ∨E-*reductions*

$$\dfrac{\dfrac{\dfrac{\Sigma_1}{A\vee B} \quad \dfrac{\Sigma_2}{C} \quad \dfrac{\Sigma_3}{C}}{C} \quad \Sigma_4}{D} \qquad\qquad \dfrac{\dfrac{\Sigma_1}{A\vee B}\quad \dfrac{\dfrac{\Sigma_2}{C}\ \Sigma_4}{D} \quad \dfrac{\dfrac{\Sigma_3}{C}\ \Sigma_4}{D}}{D}$$

The lowest occurrence of C in the left deduction is to be the last occurrence in a maximum segment. Σ_4 is thus a sequence of deductions of the minor premisses of the (elimination) inference of which the C mentioned is major premiss; hence, Σ_4 may be empty (viz., in the case of &E and ∀E) and (to be quite correct) may have to be written to the right of C (viz., in the case of ⊃E).

3.3.1.7. ∃E-*reductions*

$$\dfrac{\dfrac{\dfrac{\Sigma_1}{\exists x Ax} \quad \dfrac{\Sigma_2}{C}}{C} \quad \Sigma_4}{D} \qquad\qquad \dfrac{\dfrac{\Sigma_1}{\exists x Ax} \quad \dfrac{\dfrac{\Sigma_2}{C}\ \Sigma_4}{D}}{D}$$

The remark above in connection with ∃E-reductions applies also here.

3.3.1.8. *Remark*: It has been remarked by Martin-Löf that it is only necessary to require in the ∨E- and ∃E-reductions that the lowest occurrence of C is the major premiss of an elimination. A reduction of this kind can then always be carried out and we can sharpen the requirements as to the normal form accordingly.

3.3.2. *Immediate simplifications*. To bring a derivation to full normal form, we also have to get rid of redundant applications of $\vee$E, $\exists$E, and Λ_C. I shall say that Π_2 is an *immediate simplification* of Π_1 if Π_2 can be obtained from Π_1 by replacing a subtree Π in one of the following three ways:

3.3.2.1. Π has the form shown to the left below where no assumption in Σ_i ($i = 1$ or 2) is closed by the $\vee$E in question and Π is replaced by the derivation shown to the left below

$$\dfrac{\dfrac{\Sigma}{A_1 \vee A_2} \quad \dfrac{\Sigma_1}{B} \quad \dfrac{\Sigma_2}{B}}{B} \qquad\qquad \dfrac{\Sigma_i}{B}$$

3.3.2.2. Π has the form shown to left below where no assumption in Σ' is closed by the $\exists$E in question and Π is replaced by the derivation shown to the right below

$$\dfrac{\dfrac{\Sigma}{\exists x A(x)} \quad \dfrac{\Sigma'}{B}}{B} \qquad\qquad \dfrac{\Sigma'}{B}$$

3.3.2.3. Π has the form shown to the left below where no assumption in Σ is closed in Σ' and Π is replaced by the derivation shown to the right below.

$$\dfrac{\dfrac{\dfrac{\dfrac{\Sigma}{A} \quad \sim A}{[\Lambda]}}{\overset{\Sigma'}{\Lambda}}}{A} \qquad\qquad \dfrac{\Sigma}{A}$$

3.3.3. *Immediate expansions*. There is an obvious way of bringing a derivation in full normal form to expanded normal form (i.e. so that all the minima formulas are atomic, see 3.2.2). I shall say that Π_2 is an *immediate* expansion of Π_1 if Π_2 is obtained from Π_1 by applying one of these obvious operations. For instance, if Π_1 contains a minimum formula $A \& B$ and the derivation to the left below is the subtree of Π_1 that ends with this formula, we may replace this subtree by the derivation shown to the right below

$$\frac{\Sigma}{A \,\&\, B} \qquad\qquad \dfrac{\dfrac{\dfrac{\Sigma}{A \,\&\, B}}{A} \quad \dfrac{\dfrac{\Sigma}{A \,\&\, B}}{B}}{A \,\&\, B}$$

3.4. *Reducibility, equivalence, and convertibility*

3.4.1. *Immediate reducibility*. A derivation Π is said to *reduce immediately* to Π' if Π' is obtained from Π by replacing a subtree of Π by a reduction of it.

3.4.2. *Reducibility*. A derivation Π is said to *reduce* to Π' if there is a sequence $\Pi_1, \Pi_2, \ldots, \Pi_n$, $n \geqslant 1$, where $\Pi_1 = \Pi$, Π_i reduces immediately to Π_{i+1}, for each $i < n$, and $\Pi_n = \Pi'$.

A sequence $\Pi_1, \Pi_2, \ldots$ where for each i, Π_i reduces immediately to Π_{i+1} and the last derivation of the sequence if any is normal is said to be a *reduction sequence starting from* Π_1.

An *irreducible* derivation is one to which there is an immediate reduction, in other words, a derivation that reduces only to itself. A derivation is clearly irreducible if and only if it is in normal form.

3.4.3. *Equivalence*. Equivalence between derivations is defined in the same way as reducibility but allowing also Π_{i+1} to reduce to Π_i. This relation is clearly reflexive, transitive, and symmetric.

3.4.4. *Convertibility*. A derivation Π_1 is said to *convert* to Π_2 if there is a derivation Π' such that Π_1 reduces to Π' and Π_2 is obtained from Π' by successive immediate simplifications. When we want to consider derivations in expanded normal form, we redefine this notion by requiring instead that Π_2 is obtained from Π' by successive immediate simplifications or expansions.

3.5. *Results and conjecture*

We shall distinguish two kinds of theorems, normal form theorems and normalization theorems[1], of which the last kind is a strengthening of the first kind.

3.5.1. **Normal form theorem.** *If A is derivable in* **M(S)**, **I(S)**, *or* **C(S)** *from* Γ, *then there is a (fully, expanded) normal derivation in the system in question of A from* Γ.

[1] This terminology was suggested by Kreisel (where I used the less felicitous terminology weak and strong normal form theorem).

Thus, the normal form theorem asserts that to every derivation there exists one in normal form (of the same formula from the same assumptions) but does not say anything about how the normal derivation is related to the given one. There are also proofs of the normal form theorem, (viz. well-known semantical completeness proofs) which does not give any information of this kind either. Such information is however supplied by the following theorem.

3.5.2. **Normalization theorem.** *Every derivation in* **M(S)**, **I(S)**, *or* **C(S)** *reduces (converts) to (full, expanded) normal form.*

The theorem can be proved by the following observation: When Π is immediately reduced to Π' by a proper reduction, there is at least one maximum formula that disappears although other ones may arise, and when one of the two permutative reductions are used, the length of at least one maximum segment is decreased. Although it is true that new maximal formulas and maximal segments may arise by a reduction, it can be seen that the reductions always can be choosen so that the formulas occurring as new maximal formulas or occurring in new maximal segments are of less degree than the removed one. Thus, we can use an induction over these measures.

The normalization theorem may be strengthened further as follows.

3.5.3. **Strong normalization theorem.** *Every derivation* Π *in* **M(S)**, **I(S)**, *or* **C(S)** *reduces to a unique normal derivation* Π' *and every reduction sequence starting from* Π *terminates (in* Π'*).*

3.5.4. **Corollary about** $\vee$ **and** $\exists$. *$A \vee B$ is derivable in* **M(S)** *or* **I(S)** *only if either A or B is derivable in* **M(S)** *or* **I(S)**, *respectively.* $\exists x A(x)$ *is derivable in* **M(S)** *or* **I(S)** *only if for some term t, $A(t)$ is derivable in* **M(S)** *or* **I(S)**, *respectively.*

The corollary follows immediately from the normal form theorem together with corollary 3.2.4.1.

3.5.5. **Corollary about atomic formulas.** *If an atomic formula A is derivable in* **M(S)**, **I(S)** *or* **C(S)** *from a set of atomic formulas* Γ, *then A is derivable from* Γ *already in* **S**.

The corollary is an immediate consequence of the normal form theorem and corollary 3.2.4.2.

3.5.6. *Identity between proofs*. Each derivation clearly represents a proof (we have also argued for the converse of this, see sections 2.1 and 4.1.1). But when do two derivations represent the same proof? A first possible answer to this question is the following

Conjecture. *Two derivations represent the same proof if and only if they are equivalent.*

That two equivalent derivations represent the same proof seems to be a reasonable thesis. It seems evident from our discussion above of the inversion principle that a proper reduction does not effect the identity of the proof represented. There may be some doubts concerning the permutative ∨E- and ∃E-reductions in this connection, and there may be reasons to consider a more direct way of removing maximal segments than the one choosen above. With this reservation, one half of the conjecture seems unproblematic.

It is more difficult to find facts that would support the other half of the conjecture; the possibility of finding adequacy conditions for an identity criteria such as the one above is recently discussed by Kreisel (1970) in this volume.

It should be noted that the strong normalization theorem gives a certain coherence to the conjecture. It implies that two derivations are equivalent only if the normal derivations to which they reduce are identical, and hence, that two different normal derivations are never equivalent. As an example of two derivations in **M** of the same formula that are not equivalent, we may thus consider the following two derivations:

$$\dfrac{\dfrac{\dfrac{A}{A \supset A}}{B \supset (A \supset A)}}{(A \supset A) \supset (B \supset (A \supset A))} \qquad \dfrac{\dfrac{A \supset A}{B \supset (A \supset A)}}{(A \supset A) \supset (B \supset (A \supset A))}$$

The proofs that they represent are clearly based on different ideas and are hence different, which is thus in agreement with the conjecture.

Nevertheless, the conjecture as stated above is clearly in need of certain refinements. Firstly, derivations that only differ with respect to proper parameters should obviously be counted as equivalent. Secondly, one may ask whether not also the expansion operations preserve the identity of the proofs represented. It seems unlikely that any interesting property of proofs is sensitive to differences created by an expansion.

II.4. A summary of the analysis

To connect the analysis presented above with the introductory remarks about general and reductive proof theory, we may try to summarize what seem to be the most significant aspects of the analysis.

4.1. The examples of topics in general proof theory given in sec. I.2.1.-I.2.4 are all exemplified here.

4.1.1. We have argued at length (sec. 2.1) for the claim that Gentzen's systems of natural deduction constitutes a *characterization* (cf. I.2.1) of (different kinds of) first order proofs. We may summarize this claim in the thesis:

Every first order positive, intuitionistic, or classical proof can be represented in **M**, **I**, *or* **C**, *respectively.*

4.1.2. The second step in Gentzen's analysis (presented in sec. 3) clearly constitutes a further significant analysis of the *structure* (cf. I.2.2) of first order proofs inasmuch as the normal form (sec. 3.1) has quite distinctive features (sec. 3.2). With Gentzen, we may say that the proof represented by a normal derivation makes no detours ("*es macht keine Umwege*"); or, having formulated the normal form for natural deductions, we may say somewhat more pregnantly: the proof is *direct* in the sense that it proceeds from the assumptions to the conclusions by first only using the meaning of the assumptions by breaking them down in their components (the analytical part), and then only veryfying the meaning of the conclusions by building them up from there components (the synthetical part)[1].

4.1.2.1. If we accept the thesis in 4.1.1 and also accept as a thesis what was called the unproblematic part of the conjecture about the identity of proofs, viz., that two equivalent derivations represent the same proof, we may give the normalization theorem the following formulation:

Every first order proof can be written in normal form, i.e. can be represented by a normal derivation.

4.1.2.3. If we accept Gentzen's ideas about a reinterpretation of the logical constants in which the elimination rules are justified by the meaning given to

[1] As "conclusions", we must here count also the hypothesis of a premiss, and as "premisses" also the hypothesis of a conclusion; a more precise statement can be obtained by the use of the notion of positive and negative subformula (cf. Prawitz (1965) 43).

the logical constants by the introduction rules (sec. 2.2.2), we may note another aspect of the normalization (or normal form) theorem; lacking a more precise formulation of Gentzen's ideas, we have to remain somewhat vague (but cf. appendix A):

A derivation proceeding via introductions followed by eliminations (i.e., with a structure opposite that of a normal deduction) may leave some doubts about whether the conclusion obtained is really valid (in the sense here discussed), i.e., one may question whether the condition for introducing the conclusion by introduction is satisfied. The inversion principle states that each *particular* elimination following an introduction is justified since by a reduction, the conclusion can also be obtained directly without *this* detour; but of course, new maximum formulas may arise by this reduction. The normalization theorem strengthens this by showing that *all* maximum formulas can be removed from a derivation and thus *justifies the logical system as a whole.*

4.1.2.3.1. The corollary 3.5.4 about disjunction and existential quantification may be seen as just an expression of this, showing that a derivation of $A \vee B$ is justified since it can be transformed either to a derivation of A or to a derivation of B as required by the meaning of $\vee$ and that a derivation of $\exists x A(x)$ is justified since it can be transformed to a derivation of $A(t)$ for some term t as required by the meaning of $\exists$.

4.1.2.3.2. Similarly, the corollary 3.5.5 can also be seen in terms of this justification, showing as it does that the logical rules are not creative: they do not allow derivations of atomic formulas that cannot also be obtained directly without the use of the logical rules.

4.1.3. The equivalence relation obtained in the analysis (sec. 3.4) seems to allow also an approach to the problem of when two derivations represents the same proof (cf. I.2.3). As we saw (sec. 3.5.6), certain considerations strengthened by the strong normalization theorem makes it reasonable to propose a *conjecture stating an identity criterion for proofs.*

4.1.4. Not surprisingly, the analysis allows also *applications* to problems in other areas, i.e., problems not formulated in terms of proofs (cf. I.2.4). As an illustration, we have quoted the corollary about disjunction and existential quantification (cf. also 4.1.2.3.1). Many other applications, e.g. the interpolation theorem to mention one, could have been quoted.

4.2. For reductive proof theory, the analysis allows a certain reduction of the logical part of first order systems **M(S)**, **I(S)**, and **C(S)**. Suppose that we accept the atomic sentences in these systems as real sentences (cf. sec. I2.1) with the meaning given to them by **S** and thus consider an atomic sentence as true if and only if it is derivable in **S**. Corollary 3.5.5 (obtained just in the way suggested in sec. I.2.1 by transforming derivations that proceed over ideal sentences to derivations that use only real sentences) then asserts:

every derivable real sentence is true;

in other words, the systems in question are conservative extensions of the system **S** (cf. also 4.1.2.3.2). To be a complete reduction, one also has to show that the proof of this corollary uses something essentially less than the whole system of first order logic.

II.5. Historical remarks

5.1. Gentzen presented his analysis of first order proofs in 1935. The systems of natural deduction were stated at this time, but as already remarked above, the analysis of the structure of proofs (here presented in sec. 3) was carried out for his calculi of sequents. It is clear from his writings, however, that he discovered the analysis by reflecting upon his systems of natural deduction. Although the inversion principle was not stated explicitly by Gentzen, its idea was clearly recognized as the basic idea underlying his results for the calculus of sequents (see especially Gentzen (1938) 26–27). Here we have used this idea to obtain the results directly in a very natural way. According to what he says, Gentzen preferred to formulate and prove his results for the calculus of sequents because the axiom of the excluded middle (which he used instead of Λ_C) presented special problems (Gentzen (1935) 177). As we have presented it here, the classical case presents no special difficulties but comes out rather as a special case of minimal logic; however, this is at the cost of taking ∨ and ∃ in classical logic as defined symbols, and it is true that some complications in the proof arise when one wants to have them as primitives.

In the way Gentzen presented his analysis, it was technically summed up in his so-called Hauptsatz, which states that all applications of the so-called cut rule can be eliminated from the proofs. This Hauptsatz and our normal form theorem are equivalent in the sense that one can be obtained from the other by a suitable translation between the two kinds of systems (as described in some detail in Prawitz (1965) 90–93, where also some other comments about the relations between the systems are made).

There are certain advantages in carrying out the analysis for natural deduction besides the fact that the development (including the proofs of the theorems) flows very natural from the underlying idea. The main advantages is that the significance of the analysis, as I have tried to describe it above, seems to become more visible[1]. Furthermore it has recently been possible to extend the analysis of first order proofs to the proofs of more comprehensive systems when they are formulated as systems of natural deduction (as will be described in III), while an analogous analysis with a calculus of sequents formulation does not suggest itself as easily. Finally, the connection between this Gentzen-type analysis and functional interpretations such as Gödel's Dialectica interpretation becomes very obvious when the former is formulated for natural deduction (as will be seen in IV).

5.2. The approach used above was introduced in Prawitz (1965) to which I may refer for further details. A somewhat weaker version of the normal form theorem was independently obtained by Raggio (1965).

The extension of the logical systems with the rules of an atomic system **S** is a minor present addition, which gives a convenient way to state certain points systematically; it covers also such an extension of pure predicate logic as is obtained by the addition of rules for identity.

The theorems in Prawitz (1965) are stated as normal form theorems but their proofs give also the corresponding normalization theorems; however, this viewpoint is not sufficiently stressed. The strong normalization theorems are a later addition. Theorems of a similar kind were originally obtained for terms such as those used in connection with the functional interpretation of intuitionistic logic. The uniqueness property corresponds to the so-called Church-Rosser property for reductions in the λ-calculus. For results for terms to the effect that all reduction sequences terminates, see e.g. Sanchis (1967) and Howard (1970).

The conjecture about identity between proofs (3.5.6) is due to Martin-Löf and is also influenced by similar ideas in connection with terms (see Tait (1967)).

[1] It is an historical fact that Gentzen's result when technically summed up in the Hauptsatz has given rise to many misunderstandings. Since the cut rule may be looked upon as a generalization of modus ponens or as stating a transitive law of implication, there has been a not to infrequent misconception that the significance of the result was that modus ponens or the transitive law could be eliminated from proofs. As Kreisel remarked in his lecture at this symposium, one has then to explain what is dubious about these old, respectable principles. Clearly, this belief is not only superficial but quite mistaken: modus ponens is present also in normal derivations in the systems of natural deduction (and it is a triviality that the principle of transitivity holds in these systems although it does not occur as a primitive rule); it is really also present in cut-free derivations in the calculus of sequents in the form of introduction of $\supset$ in the antecedent.

III. Extensions to other systems

III.1. First order Peano arithmetic

1.1. *Definition of the system* **P**

Let $\mathbf{S^A}$ be the Post system (sec. I.1.5) determined by

(i) the descriptive constants 0, $'$, =, Q, and R where 0 is an individual constant (denoting zero), $'$ is an 1-place operational constant (denoting the successor function), = is a 2-place predicate constant (denoting identity), and Q and R are 3-place predicate constants to express addition and multiplication, and

(ii) the usual rules for identity, rules corresponding to Peano's third and fourth axioms, rules corresponding to the recursive definitions of addition and multiplication, and rules expressing the functional property of Q and R; e.g., the rule corresponding to Peano's fourth axiom is

$$\frac{a' = b'}{a = b}\ ;$$

note that all the axioms of first order arithmetic except the induction axioms can be written as rules of a Post system.

Let $\mathbf{P_M}$, $\mathbf{P_I}$, and $\mathbf{P_C}$ be the system obtained from $\mathbf{M(S^A)}$, $\mathbf{I(S^A)}$, and $\mathbf{C(S^A)}$, respectively, by the addition of the *rule of induction*:

$$\frac{A(0) \quad \begin{matrix}[A(a)] \\ A(a')\end{matrix}}{A(t)}$$

whose applications are with the restriction that a, the proper parameter of the application, is not to occur in other assumptions that $A(a')$ depends on except those of the form $A(a)$, which are closed by the application of the rule.

I shall use **P** ambiguously for $\mathbf{P_M}$, $\mathbf{P_I}$, or $\mathbf{P_C}$. Note that if Λ is defined as $0 = 1$, then $\mathbf{P_M}$ and $\mathbf{P_I}$ have the same set of theorems and the theorems of $\mathbf{P_C}$ coincide with the theorems of $\mathbf{P_M}$ that do not contain $\vee$ or $\exists$.

The system **P** thus constitutes a formalization of first order Peano arithmetic. I shall not discuss to what extent proofs of first order arithmetic can be represented in such a system.

In the next sections, I shall instead describe how some of the results about the structure of first order proofs can be extended to **P**.

1.2. *The status of the rule of induction*

If one is to extend the analysis of the structure of first order proofs to the proofs represented by derivations in the system **P**, one has to account for how the rule of induction fits into the pattern of introductions and eliminations. Since the validity of the rule depends on the understanding that the individual domain consists of the natural numbers, it would be natural to reformulate the rule as an introduction rule for $\forall$:

$$\dfrac{A(0)\qquad \begin{matrix}[A(a)]\\ A(a')\end{matrix}}{\forall x A(x)}$$

with the same restrictions as before. (The introduction rule for $\forall$ in first order logic can be derived from this rule.)

One may then hope to obtain a normal form theorem where normal derivations are defined literally as in II.3.1. Indeed, when an application of the introduction rule for $\forall$ formulated above is followed by an $\forall$E where the term t is a numeral representing the number n, i.e. in the situation shown to the left below, we have a reduction as shown to the right below

$$\dfrac{\dfrac{\dfrac{\Sigma_1}{A(0)} \qquad \dfrac{\begin{matrix}[A(a)]\\ \Sigma_2(a)\end{matrix}}{A(a')}}{\forall x A(x)}}{A(t)} \qquad\qquad \begin{array}{c} \Sigma_1 \\ \hline [A(0)] \\ \Sigma_2(0) \\ \hline [A(0')] \\ \Sigma_2(0') \\ \hline [A(0'')] \\ \vdots \\ A(t) \end{array} \qquad n \text{ times}$$

If we call this an $\forall$-reduction, we may define the notion of reducibility exactly as in II.3.4. However, when t contains a parameter, a maximum formula of the kind shown to the left above cannot be eliminated in this way, and in fact, it can be shown that there is no normal form theorem of this kind for **P**; see Kreisel (1965) 163. (This confirms the well-known situation where one feels that one has to prove a stronger theorem than the theorem one is interested in to be able to carry out the induction step.)

1.3. *Gentzen's result*

Gentzen's (1938) result for first order Peano arithmetic can be described in our present terminology as a proof by finitistic means enlarged by induction up to ϵ_0 of the theorem: Every proof of an atomic sentence in **P** reduces to normal form. Since a normal derivation of an atomic sentence in **P** is a derivation already in $\mathbf{S}^{\mathbf{A}}$, this entails a result of the kind sought for in reductive proof theory (provided the induction up to ϵ_0 is accepted as sufficiently elementary), and as we see, it is a direct extension of the result described in II.3.5.5 or II.4.2.

Gentzen's own formulation is in terms of a calculus of sequents.

An earlier result by Gentzen (1936) is in terms of a natural deduction system for arithmetic but is of a different character.

Formally, the present formulation for natural deduction is a considerable simplification. It also suggests a stronger result that will be described below.

1.4. *A weak normal form for derivations in* **P**

Although all maximal formulas that arise by applications of the induction rule cannot be eliminated, one may consider the derivations obtained by carrying out the reduction described above in 1.2 and the reductions defined in II.3.3 as far as possible. These derivations will be said to be in normal form but it should be remembered that this normal form is considerably weaker than the one suggested above in section 1.2.

Since all maximal formulas cannot be avoided, it is better to keep the rule of induction in its first formulation in section 1.1. We shall thus regard this rule as falling outside the pattern of introductions and eliminations, and in a normal derivation, applications of this rule is restricted to diminish its disturbance of this pattern.

More precisely, we define a derivation in **P** as *normal* when it contains no maximal formulas and no maximal segments and the term t in an application of the induction rule is not 0 or of the form u' (it follows that t is then a parameter). A derivation in **P** is said to be in *full normal form* when it (i) is in normal form, (ii) satisfies the conditions in section II.3.1.4, and (iii) contains only parameters that are either proper parameters or have occurrences in open assumptions or the end-formula.

To the reductions described in II.3.3, we now add induction-reductions, which are of two forms. In both cases, the right derivation below is said to be an (*induction-*) *reduction* of the derivation to the left.

$$\frac{\dfrac{\Sigma_1}{A(0)} \quad \dfrac{\Sigma_2}{A(a')}}{A(0)} \qquad\qquad \frac{\Sigma_1}{A(0)}$$

$$\frac{\dfrac{\Sigma_1}{A(0)} \quad \dfrac{\begin{array}{c}[A(a)]\\ \Sigma_2(a)\end{array}}{A(a')}}{A(t')} \qquad\qquad \begin{array}{c}\dfrac{\dfrac{\Sigma_1}{A(0)} \quad \dfrac{\begin{array}{c}[A(a)]\\ \Sigma_2(a)\end{array}}{A(a')}}{[A(t)]}\\ \dfrac{\Sigma_2(t)}{A(t')}\end{array}$$

$[A(a)]$ is the set of assumptions closed by the application of the induction rule. Repeated applications of these induction-reductions cover the reduction described above in section 1.2.

Reducibility and *equivalence* between derivations in **P** is now defined as in II.3.4 (including the induction-reductions among the reductions). Note that a derivation is in normal form if and only if it is irreducible. A derivation Π_1 in **P** is said to *convert* to Π_2 if there is a derivation Π' obtained from Π_1 by substituting 0 for all parameters in Π_1 that do not satisfy condition (iii) in the definition of full normal form above and Π' converts to Π_2 in the sense defined in section II.3.4.4.

Many of the results in section II.3 can now be extended to **P**. In particular, we can prove the (strong) normalization theorem as formulated in II.3.5.3.

In a normal derivation, we have thus normalized all applications of the logical rules and reduced the applications of the induction rule as far as possible. In this respect, we have strengthened Gentzen's result as formulated in 1.3, which was concerned only with derivations of atomic sentences.

It should be noted that the theorem about the form of normal derivations in section II.3.2 does not extend to **P** (unless the paths are defined so that they end at premisses of applications of the induction rule and may start at the conclusions of such applications). Also the subformula principle fails in **P**. However, the corollary II.3.2.4.1 about the last inference in a derivation in full normal form extends to **P** (replacing **S** by $\mathbf{S}^{\mathbf{A}}$). Hence, besides the corollary II.3.5.5 about atomic formulas (which is the result by Gentzen already noted above), the corollary II.3.5.4 about disjunction and existential quantification extends to **P**. In addition, we note the following *corollary*: If $\forall x \exists y A(x,y)$ is derivable in $\mathbf{P_I}$, then there is a mechanically computable function f such that for each natural number n, $A(n^*,f(n)^*)$ is derivable in $\mathbf{P_I}$ where n^* and $f(n)^*$ are the numerals that denote n and $f(n)$. The proof is immediate from the results above: We can first mechanically convert the derivation of

$\forall x \exists y A(x,y)$ to full normal form. By a corollary referred to above, its last inference is then $\forall$I whose premiss is of the form $\exists y \forall(a,y)$. Omitting the last formula of the derivation and substituting n^* for a, we have a derivation of $\exists y A(n^*,y)$, which again may be converted to full normal form. By the same corollary, the last inference of the derivation is now $\exists$I, whose premiss is of the form $A(n^*,m^*)$. The value m of f for the argument n can thus be read off from this derivation.

The normalization theorem for **P**, which was suggested by Per Martin-Löf, is proved by Jervell (1970) in this volume; or rather, a certain weaker variant of the normalization theorem as formulated above is proved by Jervell. The notion of validity described in appendix A seems to provide the most convenient way of proving the (strong) normalization theorem. For applications in reductive proof theory, one would have to use more elementary methods, however.

The corollaries mentioned above have also been obtained by Scarpellini (1969) using somewhat similar methods. They were obtained earlier by other methods, e.g. by Kleene's notion of realizability.

III.2. **First order arithmetic with infinite induction**

Schütte (1951b) seems to have been the first one to realize that by replacing the rule of induction by an infinite rule for the introduction of $\forall$, so-called infinite induction, one obtains a formulation of arithmetic that allows a normal form for derivations without the weakness noted above. I shall briefly describe how this may be done in the present framework. To keep the description short, I consider only languages without $\exists$.

P$^{\mathbf{i}}$ is to be a system that is like **P** except for the following two differences:
(i) the individual parameters are left out, and hence, the numerals are the only individual terms;
(ii) the $\forall$I-rule of II.1.2 and the rule of induction are replaced by an infinite $\forall$I-rule (or a rule of infinite induction) indicated by the following schema

$$\frac{A(0) \quad A(1) \quad A(2) \quad \ldots}{\forall x A(x)}$$

If $\Pi_1, \Pi_2, \Pi_3, \ldots$ or more compactly, $\{\Pi_i\}_i$ is an infinite sequence of derivations such that for each n, Π_n is a derivation of $A(n^*)$, then the new $\forall$I-rule allows us to combine these trees by writing $\forall x A(x)$ immediately below all the end-formulas of the derivations in $\Pi_1, \Pi_2, \Pi_3, \ldots$ to get the derivation

$$\frac{\Pi_1 \quad \Pi_2 \quad \Pi_3 \quad \ldots}{\forall x A(x)} \qquad \text{or} \qquad \frac{\{\Pi_i\}_i}{\forall x A(x)}$$

where $\forall x A(x)$ depends on the union of all the sets Γ_i of open assumptions in Π_i. The derivation in $\mathbf{P^i}$ may thus consist of infinite trees but in minimal and intuitionistic $\mathbf{P^i}$ and for applications in constructive proof theory, the new $\forall$I-rule is restricted by the requirement that the sequence $\{\Pi_i\}_i$ is to be constructively given.

It is easily verified that all the sentences derivable in **P** are also derivable in $\mathbf{P^i}$.

Note that the inversion principle holds also for the new pair of $\forall$I and $\forall$E. We may thus formulate a new *$\forall$-reduction* for $\mathbf{P^i}$: The derivation to the right below is said to be an ($\forall$-) reduction of the derivation to the left

$$\cfrac{\cfrac{\cfrac{\Sigma_1}{A(0)} \quad \cfrac{\Sigma_2}{A(1)} \quad \cfrac{\Sigma_3}{A(2)} \quad \ldots}{\forall x A(x)}}{A(n)} \qquad\qquad \frac{\Sigma_n}{A(n)}$$

If $\exists$ is also present, we only have to replace the finite $\exists$E by an obvious infinite one and modify the $\exists$-reductions accordingly.

With this change in the definition of $\forall$- (and $\exists$-) reductions, the whole of section II.3 can be carried over to $\mathbf{P^i}$. In particular, we note that in contrast to **P**, the normal derivations have the form described in II.3.2 and satisfy the subformula principle.

Infinite systems of this kind are clearly of significance for reductive proof theory. In contrast to the case of **P**, there is no effort in verifying that the proof of the normalization theorem requires only induction up to ϵ_0 in addition to ordinary finitary arguments.

It is less clear whether these systems are of any great interest for general proof theory. Kreisel (1967) and (1968) argues that infinite thoughts seem to be much better represented by infinite objects than by the words we use to communicate them. On the other hand, it must be remembered that an infinite derivation of the kind described above is in certain respects an incomplete representation of an argument. In order to be conclusive, each application of $\forall$I in such a derivation should be supplemented by an argument showing that for each n, Π_n is a derivation of $A(n^*)$. It is by leaving out this supplementary argument in the representations of the proofs that the derivations get such a simple structure.

III.3. **Infinite sentential logic**

Tait (1968) showed that Schütte's results for first order arithmetic with infinite induction as well as the results for some other systems could be considered as special cases of results for a system for infinite sentential logic. His results were formulated for a calculus of sequents (or rather for a variant of such a calculus where Gentzen's sequents are simplified so that they contain only a succedent). A natural deduction formulation was given by Martin-Löf (1969), who also (in contrast to Schütte and Tait) considers intuitionistic (or minimal) infinite sentential logic.

The formulas of Martin-Löf's infinite sentential logic are built up from sentential parameters with the help of implications and one operation that allows us to form infinite conjunctions. We may also add an operation allowing the formation of infinite disjunctions. The *formulas* can then be defined as follows:

(1) A sentential parameters is a formula.

(2) If A and B are formulas, then so is $(A \supset B)$.

(3) If $\{A_i\}_i$ is an infinite sequence of formulas, then $\underset{i}{\&} A_i$ and $\underset{i}{\vee} A_i$ are formulas.

In reductive proof theory and in intuitionistic or minimal infinite sentential logic, clause (3) is restricted by requiring that $\{A_i\}_i$ is a constructive sequence.

Inferences with these infinite formulas may, as in first order logic, be analysed in introductions and eliminations for the three operations that build up the formulas. As in first order arithmetic, the inferences may contain infinitely many premisses and the derivations may thus consist of infinite trees. The rules for $\supset$I and $\supset$E are exactly as in first order logic. The other four rules are indicated by the following figures:

$$\underset{i}{\&}\text{I)} \quad \frac{\{A_i\}_i}{\underset{i}{\&} A_i} \qquad\qquad \underset{i}{\&}\text{E)} \quad \frac{\underset{i}{\&} A_i}{A_j} \quad \text{for any } j$$

$$\underset{i}{\vee}\text{I)} \quad \frac{A_j}{\underset{i}{\vee} A_i} \quad \text{for any } j \qquad\qquad \underset{i}{\vee}\text{E)} \quad \frac{\underset{i}{\vee} A_i \quad \left\{\begin{matrix}[A_i] \\ B\end{matrix}\right\}_i}{B}$$

The $\underset{i}{\&}$I-rule allows the inference of the infinite conjunction $\underset{i}{\&} A_i$ given a sequence $\{\Pi_i\}_i$ of derivations such for each i, Π_i is a derivation of A_i (cf. infinite induction in section 2).

The $\underset{i}{\&}$E-rule allows the inference of any A_j from $\underset{i}{\&} A_i$.

The $\bigvee_i$I-rule allows the inference of $\bigvee_i A_i$ from any A_j.

The $\bigvee_i$E-rule allows assumptions to be closed as follows: given a derivation of $\bigvee_i A_i$ depending on (the formulas of) Γ and a sequence $\{\Pi_i\}_i$ of derivations such that for each i, Π_i is a derivation of B depending on Δ_i, we may infer B that now depends on the union of Γ and the union of all sets $\Delta_i - \{A_i\}$.

As before, we restrict in certain contexts the $\&_i$I- and $\bigvee_i$E-rules by requiring that the sequences of derivations in question are constructive.

The natural deduction system for *minimal infinite sentential logic*, $\mathbf{M^i}$, is determined by these six inference rules. To get corresponding intuitionistic and classical system, $\mathbf{I^i}$ and $\mathbf{C^i}$, we may add the Λ_I- and Λ_C-rules, respectively. However, if Λ is defined as the conjunction of all sentential parameters, the Λ_I-rule holds as a derived rule in $\mathbf{M^i}$.

It is easily seen that also the new pairs of introductions and eliminations satisfy the inversion principle and accordingly we can define $\&_i$- and $\bigvee_i$-reductions as shown below where the right derivation is a reduction of the kind in question of the left derivation:

$\&_i$-reductions

$$\dfrac{\dfrac{\left\{\dfrac{\Sigma_i}{A_i}\right\}_i}{\&_i A_i}}{A_j} \qquad\qquad \dfrac{\Sigma_j}{A_j}$$

$\bigvee_i$-reductions

$$\dfrac{\dfrac{\dfrac{\Sigma}{A_j}}{\bigvee_i A_i} \quad \left(\begin{matrix}[A_i]\\ \Sigma_i\\ \hline B\end{matrix}\right)_i}{B} \qquad\qquad \begin{matrix}\Sigma\\ \hline [A_j]\\ \Sigma_j\\ \hline B\end{matrix}$$

The results of section II.3 can now be carried over to $\mathbf{M^i}$, $\mathbf{I^i}$, and $\mathbf{C^i}$.

III.4. Theories of (iterated) inductive definitions

If the rules of a Post system **S** are understood as completely determining the predicates (as the sets of terms for which the predicates can be proved to hold), i.e. if the rules of **S** are understood as inductive definitions of the predicates in question, then there are certain valid inferences that are not allowed in any of the systems **M(S)**, **I(S)**, and **C(S)**. Let us e.g. make the assumption that a certain formula $A(a)$ satisfies as a value of a one-place predicate constant P all the rules of **S** in which P occurs; i.e., we assume that if we replace every occurrence of the form Pt in these rules by $A(t)$ (possibly replacing also other predicate symbols by other formulas throughout), then for each rule, we can infer the formula obtained from the conclusion (by this replacement) from the formulas obtained from the premisses (by this replacement). For instance, if we have a rule

$$\frac{Pa}{Pa{+}2}$$

then the assumption is that we can infer $A(a{+}2)$ from $A(a)$. Under this assumption, we can infer $A(t)$ from Pt.

We can formulate an inference rule for inferences of this kind. There is one major premiss Pt and the minor premisses express the fact that $A(a)$ satisfies as a value of P all the rules in which P occurs (and if other predicate constants are replaced by formulas, the minor premisses are also to express the corresponding thing for these formulas and predicates). This rule may naturally be thought of as an *elimination rule for the predicate constant P* while the rules in **S** in which P occurs in the conclusion may be thought of as *introduction rules for P.*

It can be seen that the inversion principle holds for these new pairs of introductions and eliminations and we can thus add additional reductions accordingly.

The system that arise from **M(S)** by the additions of these elimination rules may be called the *first order minimal theory of inductive definitions based on* **S**, abbreviated $\mathbf{M(S)}^{\mathrm{ind}}$. As indicated above, Gentzen's analysis of first order proofs can be extended to these theories of inductive definitions. This extension is due to Martin-Löf (1970), who in particular proves the normalization theorem for the systems $\mathbf{M(S)}^{\mathrm{ind}}$. By starting from **I(S)** or **C(S)**, we obtain corresponding intuitionistic or classical system, respectively[1].

Let $\mathbf{S}^{\mathbf{N}}$ be the Post system that is like $\mathbf{S}^{\mathbf{A}}$ (sec. 1.1) except that it contains an additional one-place predicate constant **N** (for the property of being a natural number) and rules corresponding to Peano's first and second axioms, i.e. the rule consisting of just the conclusion $N0$ (or the axiom $N0$) and the rule

[1] It should be noted however that the subformula principle fails for all these systems.

$$\frac{Na}{Na'}$$

The elimination rule for N thus allows inferences of the form

$$\frac{Nt \quad A(0) \quad \overset{[A(a)]}{A(a')}}{A(t)}$$

which is just another formulation of mathematical induction. (Note that induction inferences are here eliminations because they depend on the meaning of N, while in **P** they may be thought of as introductions depending on the intended restriction of the individual domain (cf. sec. 1.2).) $\mathbf{M}(\mathbf{S}^{\mathbf{P}})^{\mathrm{ind}}$ thus constitutes an alternative formulation of $\mathbf{P}_{\mathbf{M}}$ and similarly for the intuitionistic and classical variants.

Martin-Löf further shows how to extend this analysis to theories of iterated inductive definitions by starting from certain generalized Post systems. Rather strong mathematical theories, viz. subsystems of second order arithmetic, can be formulated in this way.

These results, which are presented in Martin-Löf's paper in this volume, are of considerable interest for general proof theory.

III.5. **Second order logic**

5.1. *The second order systems*

Introduction and elimination inferences can also be formulated for second order quantification as was done in Prawitz (1965). It is sometimes convenient to extend the formalism by the addition of a logical constant λ, used in second order (or abstraction) terms

$$\{\lambda x_1 x_2 \ldots x_n A(x_1, x_2, \ldots, x_n)\}$$

to denote the relation that holds between the $x_1, x_2, \ldots, x_n$ such that $A(x_1, x_2, \ldots, x_n)$. The following rules (where X is an n-ary predicate variable and P is an n-ary predicate parameter, $n = 0, 1, 2, \ldots$) can then be stated

$\forall_2$I) $\dfrac{A(P)}{\forall X A(X)}$ $\qquad\qquad$ $\forall_2$E) $\dfrac{\forall X A(X)}{A(T)}$

$\exists_2$I) $\dfrac{A(T)}{\exists XA(X)}$ $\exists_2$E) $\dfrac{\exists XA(X) \quad \begin{matrix}[A(P)]\\ B\end{matrix}}{B}$

$$\lambda\text{I)} \quad \frac{A(t_1,t_2,...,t_n)}{\{\lambda x_1x_2...x_nA(x_1,x_2,...,x_n)\}\ t_1t_2...t_n}$$

$$\lambda\text{E)} \quad \frac{\{\lambda x_1x_2...x_nA(x_1,x_2,...,x_n)\}\ t_1t_2...t_n}{A(t_1,t_2,...,t_n)}$$

In an inference by $\forall_2$I, P, the proper parameter of the inference, is not to occur in any assumption on which $A(P)$ depends. In an inference by $\forall_2$E or $\exists_2$I, T is an n-ary second order term, i.e. either an n-ary predicate parameter or constant or an abstraction $\{\lambda x_1x_2...x_nB(x_1,x_2,...,x_n)\}$ where $B(x_1,x_2,...,x_n)$ is a formula. In an inference by $\exists_2$E, P, which is called the proper parameter of the inference, is not to occur in B nor in any assumption that the premiss B depends on except those of the form $A(P)$ that are closed by the inference.

The system of natural deduction for second order minimal, intuitionistic, and classical logic, denoted $\mathbf{M}^2$, $\mathbf{I}^2$, and $\mathbf{C}^2$, arise from **M**, **I**, and **C**, respectively, by the addition of these rules. However, conjunction, disjunction and existential quantification turn out to be definable by implication and universal quantification also in minimal and intuitionistic second order logic why these constants and their rules can be left out. Absurdity is definable as $\forall XX$ (where X is a 0-place predicate variable), which makes the Λ_I-rule derivable in $\mathbf{M}^2$; hence there is no interesting distinction between intuitionistic and minimal second order logic. $\mathbf{M}^2$ is also referred to as (the natural deduction system for) the (intuitionistic) *theory of species.*

5.2. *Mathematical analysis*

Let $\mathbf{S}^\mathbf{P}$ be the Post system determined by the descriptive constants 0, $'$, and =, the ordinary rules for =, and the rules corresponding to Peano's third and fourth axioms, i.e. $\mathbf{S}^\mathbf{P}$ is like $\mathbf{S}^\mathbf{A}$ in section 1.1 except for not containing the addition and multiplication predicates and their rules. $\mathbf{C}^2(\mathbf{S}^\mathbf{P})$, i.e. the system whose language is the second order language determined by the descriptive constants of $\mathbf{S}^\mathbf{P}$ and whose rules are the rules of $\mathbf{S}^\mathbf{P}$ and $\mathbf{C}^2$, is then a formulation of classical second order Peano arithmetic, also written $\mathbf{P}^2_\mathbf{C}$. The system $\mathbf{M}^2(\mathbf{S}^\mathbf{P})$ or $\mathbf{P}^2_\mathbf{M}$ is the intuitionistic analogue to that theory, i.e. Peano arithmetic built upon the theory of species. As in the first order case, I shall use $\mathbf{P}^2$ ambiguously for $\mathbf{P}^2_\mathbf{M}$ and $\mathbf{P}^2_\mathbf{C}$. (Note however that $\mathbf{P}^2_\mathbf{C}$ is not a subtheory of $\mathbf{P}^2_\mathbf{M}$.)

In $\mathbf{P}^2$, we may in a well-known manner define the notion of natural number and then prove all the Peano axioms, including the induction axiom. Recursively definable functions such as additions and multiplication are explicitly definable in $\mathbf{P}^2$. Furthermore, real numbers are definable in $\mathbf{P}^2$ as certain sets (or relations) of natural numbers after which the existence of a least upper bound to each bounded set of real numbers is provable in $\mathbf{P}^2$ as a theorem schemata. In this way, theorems in traditional mathematical analysis can be proved in $\mathbf{P}^2$.

Thus, unlike the first order case where additional considerations are necessary to extend results for the logical systems to the arithmetical ones, proof theoretical results for second order logic (extended with atomic systems) carry over directly to second order arithmetic and mathematical analysis. This seems first to have been realized by Takeuti (1954) (although in a much more complicated way by what he calls a theory of restrictions). He formulated a calculus of sequents for second (and higher) order logic and conjectured that Gentzen's Hauptsatz could be extended to that system.

5.3. *Normal form and normalization in second order logic*

We note that also the new introductions and eliminations satisfy the inversion principle, which allows us to formulate the following additional reductions below, where the derivation to the right is a reduction of the kind in question of the derivation to the left:

$\forall_2$*-reduction*

$$\dfrac{\dfrac{\dfrac{\Sigma(P)}{A(P)}}{\forall X A(X)}}{A(T)} \qquad\qquad \dfrac{\Sigma(T)}{A(T)}$$

$\exists_2$*-reduction*

$$\dfrac{\dfrac{\dfrac{\Sigma_1}{A(T)}}{\exists X A(X)} \quad \dfrac{\begin{matrix}[A(P)]\\ \Sigma'(P)\end{matrix}}{B}}{B} \qquad\qquad \dfrac{\dfrac{\dfrac{\Sigma_1}{[A(T)]}}{\Sigma'(T)}}{B}$$

λ*-reduction*

$$\dfrac{\dfrac{\dfrac{\Sigma}{A(t_1,t_2,\ldots,t_n)}}{\{\lambda x_1 x_2 \ldots x_n A(x_1 x_2,\ldots,x_n)\}\ t_1 t_2 \ldots t_n}}{A(t_1,t_2,\ldots,t_n)} \qquad\qquad \dfrac{\Sigma}{A(t_1,t_2,\ldots,t_n)}$$

We may thus define the notions of normal derivations, reducibility etc. in the same way as in first order (section II.3). Note also that a second order normal derivation has the same form as a first order normal derivation, i.e. the theorem in II.3.2 holds also here, and the corollaries (in II.3.4) about normal derivations extend thus directly to second order. The subformula principle, however, is of no interest in second order logic since if the subformula notion is defined for second order formulas in analogy with the way it is defined for first order formulas, every formula is a subformula of $\forall XA(X)$ and $\exists XA(X)$. But e.g. the corollary II.3.2.4.2 about atomic formulas is just the fact noted by Takeuti (but formulated by him in a different terminology) as already remarked in the preceding section and means that a sufficiently elementary proof of the normal form theorem for $\mathbf{M}^2$ or $\mathbf{C}^2$ contains a reductive analysis (and thus a consistency proof) of $\mathbf{P}^2$.

However, although the inversion principle and the notions in section II.3 extends to second order logic, the proof of the normalization theorem as outlined in II.3.5.2 does not. The impredicativity of second order logic clearly turns up in $\forall_2$- and $\exists_2$-reductions: a maximum formula $\forall XA(X)$, say, in a derivation Π_1 may be replaced by a new maximum formula $A(T)$ in Π_2 when Π_1 reduces immediately to Π_2 by one of these reductions, and $A(T)$ may be considerably more complex than $\forall XA(X)$; in particular, T may contain $\forall XA(X)$ as a part, in which case a series of immediate reductions may again present us with a maximum formula $\forall XA(X)$. Hence, no measure of the complexity of the maximum formulas (considered isolated) can show that all of them will disappear after a finite number of immediate reductions.

Takeuti's conjecture has, however, been proved by three different semantical methods, viz. (i) by Tait (1966), (ii) by Prawitz (1967a), and (iii) by Takahashi (1967) and Prawitz (1968); the method (iii) was developed for classical higher order logic (i.e. simple type theory). All these proofs established a certain semantical completeness of a cut-free calculus of sequents for classical second order logic from which the normal form theorem for $\mathbf{C}^2$ follows as a corollary.

A similar result was proved for a calculus of sequents of intuitionistic second order logic by Prawitz (1968a) (and was recently extended to higher order intuitionistic logic by Takahashi (1970)) from which the normal form theorem for $\mathbf{M}^2$ (or $\mathbf{I}^2$) follows.

Since all these proofs use methods that are in no way more elementary than those formalized in $\mathbf{P}^2$ (for a discussion of the three methods, see Prawitz (1970)), they are of no immediate interest for reductive proof theory (except that one may be more optimistic about finding a constructive proof of the normal form theorem once an abstract proof has been given). Takeuti (1967) was able to prove the Hauptsatz for a subtheory of classical second order logic, which corresponds roughly to restricting $\forall_2$I and $\exists_2$E to terms T that contain essentially only one second order quantifier, by using an induction over certain recursive ordinals. However, the interest of this result for reductive proof theory is limited by the fact that the arguments needed to establish the well-ordering of the ordering in question is not very elementary.

For general proof theory, these results leaves a great deal to be desired. In particular, they establish only a normal form theorem and not a normalization theorem, i.e. they leave open the question whether there is a reduction sequence for every derivation that terminates; indeed, these semantical proofs give no information about how a normal derivation is obtained from a given derivation. Takeuti's proof for the subtheory of second order logic mentioned above gives some information of this kind. But although he shows how the cuts can be successively removed, the removal of the cuts involves an essential rebuilding of the derivations. Therefore, also his proof leaves open the question whether the derivations in his subsystem reduce to normal derivations.

Added after the Symposium in Oslo: Ideas presented by Girard (1970), for a system of terms intended for an interpretation of $\mathbf{P}^2$ (cf. chapter IV) have changed this situation. It has been shown independently by Girard (1970), Martin-Löf (1970a), and myself (appendix B) that these ideas can be carried over to derivations which yields the normalization theorem for $\mathbf{M}^2$. By some additions, one can also prove the strong normalization theorem and extend the result to $\mathbf{C}^2$ (see appendix B). This extends thus the whole analysis of section III.3 to second order logic. The result yields also other applications (see appendix B.3). For applications in reductive proof, it should be noted, however, that these new proofs use essentially the principles formalized in $\mathbf{P}^2$, and there is thus still no reduction of e.g. the impredicative character of second order logic.

IV. Functional interpretations

IV.1. An interpretation of positive and intuitionistic logic

1.1. *Introductory considerations*

The operational interpretation of the logical constants suggested by Gentzen (section II.2.2.2) is, as remarked above (II.2.1.1), partly narrower than the usual constructive interpretation. For instance, constructively, $A \supset B$ is interpreted as asserting the existence of a construction by which any construction of A can be transformed to a construction of B, which is weaker than asserting the existence of a proof of B from A; such a proof gives a particular kind of a uniform construction transforming constructions of A to constructions of B, which is not required by the usual constructive interpretation.

A systematic account of the constructive interpretation of the logical constants, along the lines of the explanations by Heyting (1956) e.g., can be given by defining inductively when something is a construction of a sentence. As a starting point for such a definition, we may consider the clauses:

(i) k is a construction of $A \supset B$ if and only if k is a constructive function such that for each construction k' of A, $k(k')$ (i.e. the value of k for the argument k') is a construction of B;

(ii) k is a construction of $\forall x A(x)$ if and only if k is a constructive function such that for each term t, $k(t)$ is a construction of $A(t)$.

A definition of this kind has of course to be based or relativized to something that determines the constructions of atomic formulas. In accordance with constructive intentions, I shall assume that the constructions of atomic formulas are recursively enumerable, and the notion of a construction can then be relativized conveniently to Post systems (II.1.5).

Below, I shall tacitly assume that the Post systems contain at least one individual constant.

I shall thus speak of a construction k of a sentence A relative or *over* a Post system **S**. When A is atomic such a construction k will simply be a derivation of A in **S**. In accordance to clause (i) when relativized to **S**, a construction k of $A_1 \supset A_2$ over **S** where A_1 and A_2 are atomic will be a constructive (or with Church's thesis: recursive) function that transforms every derivation of A_1 in **S** to a derivation of A_2 in **S**. However, a consequence of such a definition would be that if A_1 is not constructible over **S** (i.e. not derivable in **S**), $A_1 \supset A_2$ is automatically constructible over **S** since any constructive function would vacously satisfy the condition in clause (i). In particular, provided Λ is not constructible over **S** and $\sim A$ is a shorthand for $A \supset \Lambda$ as usual, it follows that there is no system **S** over which $\sim\sim A \supset A$ is not constructible (hence, classically, $\sim\sim A \supset A$ is constructible in every **S**), which is clearly contrary to the constructive interpretation of implication and negation.

The notion of implication described by (i) is thus quite weak. Note also that an implication in the sense of (i) relativized to Post systems may be constructible over a system **S** but not over an *extension* **S**$'$ of **S** obtained by adding some new inference rules to **S** (e.g., if $A \supset B$ was constructible over **S** just because A was not constructible over **S** but A is constructible over **S**$'$). A stronger notion of implication is obtained by requiring that the construction k transforms not only constructions of A over **S** to constructions of B over **S** but also all constructions of A over extensions $\mathbf{S}'$ of $\mathbf{S}$ to constructions of B over $\mathbf{S}'$. This stronger requirement is particularly appropriate if the Post systems are thought of as approximations of our knowledge about the atomic sentences and not as a complete description of it (as in the theory of inductive definitions in III.4).

I shall adopt these ideas in the definitions below. As a further explanation of these ideas, note that constructions of iterated implications require constructive functions of higher type. For instance, when A and B are atomic, a construction of $(A \supset B) \supset C$ has to be a constructive functional defined for certain constructive functions. We have thus to consider a hierarchy of constructive objects.

1.2. *Definitions*

1.2.1. *Finite types*. The finite types are defined by the following induction:

(i) 0 is a type and i is a type.

(ii) If τ and σ are types and $\sigma \neq i$, then (τ,σ) is a type.

1.2.2. *Constructive objects of finite types*. To simplify the situation, I shall assume that all the symbols of Post systems are drawn from a common stock of symbols so that the totality of *names*, i.e. terms without parameters, in Post systems and the totallity of derivations in Post systems are limited. We can then define the constructive objects of finite types by the following induction:

(i) The derivations in Post systems are the constructive objects of type 0.

(ii) The names in Post systems are the constructive objects of type i.

(iii) The constructive functions from objects of type τ to objects of type σ are the constructive objects of type (τ,σ).

General constructive (or computable) functions of finite types seem first to have been considered by Gödel (1958).

1.2.3. *Types of formulas*. For simplicity, we restrict ourselves to the fragments of first order languages containing only the logical constants $\wedge$, $\supset$, and $\forall$. The type of a formula in these languages are defined by the following induction:

(i) Atomic formulas have the type 0.

(ii) If $A(a)$ is of type τ, then $\forall x A(x)$ is of type (i,τ).

(iii) If A is of type τ and B is of type σ, then $A \supset B$ is of type (τ,σ).

1.2.4. *Constructions of sentences*. Still restricting ourselves to the $\wedge$-, $\supset$-, $\forall$-fragment of first order languages, we define the notion of a construction of a sentence over a Post system **S** by the induction:

(i) k is a construction of an atomic sentence A over **S** if and only if k is a derivation of A in **S**.

(ii) k is a construction of a sentence $A \supset B$ over **S** if and only if k is a constructive object of the type of $A \supset B$ and for each extension **S**$'$ of **S** and for each construction k' of A over **S**$'$, $k(k')$ is a construction of B over **S**$'$.

(iii) k is a construction of a sentence $\forall x A(x)$ over **S** if and only if k is a constructive object of the type of $\forall x A(x)$ and for each name t in **S**, $k(t)$ is a construction of $A(t)$ over **S**.

1.2.5. *Construction of formulas from formulas*. Let $a_1, a_2, ..., a_m$ be the individual parameters that occur in the formulas $A_1, A_2, ..., A_n$, and A (ordered e.g. after their first occurrence). k is said to be a construction of A from A_1, $A_2, ..., A_n$ over **S** if k is an n+m-ary constructive function with the following property: if **S**$'$ is an extension of **S**, if $t_1, t_2, ..., t_m$ are names in **S**, and if $k_1, k_2, ..., k_n$ are constructions of $A_1^*, A_2^*, ..., A_r^*$ over **S**$'$ respectively where A_i^* is the result of replacing every a_j in A_i by t_j, then $k(t_1,t_2,...,t_m,k_1,k_2,...,k_n)$ is a construction of A^* over **S**$'$ where A^* is again the result of replacing every a_j in A by t_j.

1.2.6. *Truth and validity*. We may define a sentence A as *positively true in* a Post system **S** when there is a construction of A over **S** and define a formula A as a *positive consequence* of formulas $A_1, A_2, ..., A_n$ in **S** when there is a construction of A from $A_1, A_2, ..., A_n$ over **S**. A may be defined as *positively valid* when it is positively true in every Post system **S** over which it is a formula. If in all the definitions above we consider only consistent Post systems, i.e. Post systems in which Λ is not derivable, then we may speak about *intuitionistic constructions, truth*, etc.

1.3. *Remarks*

1.3.1. The definitions above were suggested by Prawitz (1968b) (concerning their relation to Kleene's notion of realizability see this paper) where also the other logical constants were considered, and it was shown that A is positively or intuitionistically valid if A is derivable in **M** or **I**, respectively. It was also seen that the axioms of first order arithmetic are positively and intuitionistically true in the Post system $\mathbf{S}^{\mathbf{A}}$ (or, to be quite correct, the Post system that is like $\mathbf{S}^{\mathbf{A}}$ except for containing operational constants instead of predicates for addition and multiplication).

Although classically valid formulas such as $\sim\sim A \supset A$ are not in general positively or intuitionistically valid, it should be noted that minimal and intuitionistic logics are not complete with respect to this interpretation.

1.3.2. We may note that there is a simpler interpretation of intuitionistic (or minimal) logic where we define "$A \supset B$ is true" as simply meaning "if A is true, then B is true", understanding the phrase "if..., then..." intuitionistically. The interpretation in 1.2 above has a richer structure than this simple interpretation but it is nevertheless not reductive: we do not avoid the use of implication and universal quantification in clauses 1.2.4(ii) and 1.2.4(iii). An interpretation with a still richer structure which is reductive is obtained if we demand that a construction of $A \supset B$ is to consist not only of a function k as described above but also of a proof demonstrating that k has the properties required in clause 1.2.4(ii). Such an interpretation was first suggested by Kreisel (1960) and has later been developed by Goodman (1968). This interpretation is superior to the one described here also in other essential respects. The main purpose of the present chapter is to establish a connection between derivations and terms in certain λ-calculi and the present section is only to serve as an introduction to that.

IV.2. **Terms that define constructions**

The functions needed as constructions of derivable formulas are of a very simple kind and can be defined in a certain λ-calculus, which I shall call **K** and which is described below. I shall also consider certain extensions of this calculus.

2.1. *The calculus* **K**

2.1.1. *Types and symbols in* **K**. The *types* are the same as those defined in 1.2.1.

The *symbols* of **K** are *variables*, viz. for each type τ there are denumerably many variables of type τ, denoted $\alpha^\tau, \beta^\tau, \ldots$, the *abstraction operator* λ, and parenthesis.

2.1.2. *Terms in* **K**. The terms in **K** are defined by the following induction:

(i) Variables of type τ are terms of type τ.

(ii) If Φ is a term of type τ and α is a variable of type σ, then $\lambda\alpha\Phi$ is a term of type (σ,τ).

(iii) If Φ is a term of type (τ,σ) and Ψ is a term of type τ, then $\Phi(\Psi)$ is a term of type σ.

λ binds the variable in question in the usual way.

2.1.3. *Interpretation of the terms in* **K**. A closed term of type τ can then be interpreted as a constructive object of type τ in the following way. By a *valuation*, we understand a function V from the variables in **K** such that $V(\alpha^\tau)$ is a constructive object of type τ. We define W_V, viz. the *value* of the terms in **K** with respect to a valuation V, by induction over the length of the terms:

2.1.3.1. $W_V(\alpha) = V(\alpha)$.

2.1.3.2. $W_V(\lambda\alpha^\tau\Phi)$ is the function f such that f is defined for all constructive objects of type τ and when k is such an object, $f(k) = W_{V'}(\Phi)$ where V' is the valuation that is like V except for assigning k to α.

2.1.3.3. $W_V(\Phi(\Psi))$ is the value of the function $W_V(\Phi)$ for the argument $W_V(\Psi)$.

The value of a closed term with respect to V is clearly independent of V and is a constructive object of the same type as the term. A closed term is said to *denote* this value.

An open term Φ with the free variables $\alpha_1^{\tau_1}, \alpha_2^{\tau_2}, \ldots, \alpha_n^{\tau_n}$ is said to *denote* the n-ary function f such that $f(k_1,k_2,\ldots,k_n)$ is defined when each k_j is an object of type τ_j and in this case, $f(k_1,k_2,\ldots,k_n) = W_{V'}(\Phi)$ where V' is like V except for assigning k_j to $\alpha_j^{\tau_j}$ $(j=1,2,\ldots,n)$.

2.1.4. *Result*. Let A be a sentence without operational constants that is derivable in **M** (or **I**). Then, there is a closed term Φ in **K** that denotes an (intuitionistic) construction of A over every Post system over which A is a formula.

2.1.5. *A mapping of derivations on terms.* The result stated above is in effect proved in Prawitz (1968b) by defining a function F from derivations and showing that if Π is a derivation of A from $A_1, A_2, ..., A_n$ then $F(\Pi)$ is a construction of A from $A_1, A_2, ..., A_n$.

2.2. *The calculi* **K(S)**

The results stated above can be extended to systems **M(S)** by extending the calculus **K**. Given a Post system **S**, we define an extension **K(S)** of **K** as follows.

The calculus **K(S)** contains above the symbols of **K** the individual and the operational constants in **S** as symbols. In addition, for each rule in the system **S**, there is a *rule constant r* in **K(S)**.

The terms in **K(S)** are formed as in **K** but with the following additional clauses: The individual constants in **S** are terms in **K(S)** of type i. If $t_1, t_2, ..., t_n$ are terms in **K(S)** of type i and f is an n-ary operational constant in **S**, then $f(t_1,t_2,...,t_n)$ is a term in **K(S)** of type i. If r is the rule constant corresponding to a rule in **S** with n parameters and m premisses and $t_1, t_2, ..., t_n$ are terms in **K(S)** of type i and $\Phi_1, \Phi_2, ..., \Phi_m$ are terms in **K(S)** of type 0, then $r(t_1,t_2,...,t_n,\Phi_1,\Phi_2,...,\Phi_m)$ is a term in **K(S)** of type 0.

The definition of the value (with respect to a valuation) of a term is extended so that the individual constants in **S** have themselves as values and the value of a term $f(t_1,t_2,...,t_n)$ (of type i) is the term obtained by writing f followed by the value of the terms $t_1, t_2, ..., t_n$. If r is the rule constant corresponding to the rule defined by the schema

$$\frac{A_1 \quad A_2 \quad \cdots \quad A_m}{A}$$

then the value of $r(t_1,t_2,...,t_n,\Phi_1,\Phi_2,...,\Phi_m)$ is the tree

$$\frac{\Pi_1 \quad \Pi_2 \quad \cdots \quad \Pi_m}{A^*}$$

where Π_j is the value of Φ_j (j=1,2,...,m) and A^* is the result of simultaneously replacing the jth parameter in A (the parameters being ordered after their first occurrences) by the value of t_j (j=1,2,...,n).

The mapping F in 2.1.5 above can then be extended so that for each derivation Π in **M(S)**, $F(\Pi)$ is a construction with respect to **S** of the end-formula of Π from the open premisses in Π.

2.3. *The calculus* **T**

The calculus **T** is an extension of the calculus $\mathbf{K}(\mathbf{S}^{\mathbf{A}})$ (where $\mathbf{S}^{\mathbf{A}}$ is the Post system described in III.1), which for each type $\tau \neq i$ contains an additional constant I^{τ} such that if Φ is a term of type τ in **T**, if Ψ is a term of type $(i,(\tau,\tau))$ in **T**, and if t is a term of type i in **T**, then $I^{\tau}(\Phi,\Psi,t)$ is a term of type τ in **T**.

In connection with **T**, we may modify the definition of constructive objects so that the objects of type i are just the numerals and the objects of type 0 are just the derivations in $\mathbf{S}^{\mathbf{A}}$ without parameters.

The value $W_V(\Phi)$ of a term Φ in **T** with respect to a valuation V that assigns constructive objects of this modified kind to the variables, is then defined as above with the additional clause:

If $W_V(t) = 0$, then $W_V(I^{\tau}(\Phi,\Psi,t)) = W_V(\Phi)$; if $W_V(t)$ is a numeral of the form u', then $W_V(I^{\tau}(\Phi,\Psi,t))$ = the value of the function $W_V(\Psi)(u)$ for the argument $W_V(I^{\tau}(\Phi,\Psi,u))$.

The mapping F in 2.1.5 can then be extended so that for each derivation Π in **P**, $F(\Pi)$ is a construction with respect to $\mathbf{S}^{\mathbf{A}}$ of the end-formula of Π from the open assumptions in Π.

2.4. *Reductions and normal terms in* **K**, **K(S)**, *and* **T**

The calculus **K** differs from Church's λ-calculus only by having a certain type-structure. As in Church's λ-calculus, we have also here obvious reductions and a normal form. We shall say for terms in **K** or **K(S)** that $\Phi(\Psi)$ is a (λ-) *reduction* of $\lambda\alpha\Phi(\alpha)(\Psi)$, that Φ *reduces immediately* to Ψ if Ψ is obtained from Φ by replacing one of its subterms by its reduction, that Φ *reduces* to Ψ if Ψ is obtained from Φ by a series of immediate reductions, and that Φ is in *normal form* when it contains no reducible subterm, i.e. no subterm of the form $\lambda\alpha\Phi(\alpha)(\Psi)$.

We make the same definitions for **T** except that we add two more reductions: Φ is said to be a reduction of $I^{\tau}(\Phi,\Psi,0)$ and $\Psi(t)(I^{\tau}(\Phi,\Psi,t))$ is a reduction of $I^{\tau}(\Phi,\Psi,t')$.

2.5. *A connection between derivations and terms*

There is an obvious similarity between the definitions for derivations in sections II.3 and III.1.4 and the definitions for terms in **K** and **T** in section 2.4 above. More precisely, it can be seen that the mapping F mentioned in 2.1.5 is an homomorphism (onto its range) with respect to immediate reducibility, i.e. if Π_1 reduces immediately to Π_2, then $F(\Pi_1)$ reduces immediately to $F(\Pi_2)$, furthermore, if $F(\Pi_1)$ reduces immediately to Φ, then there is a Π_2 such that $F(\Pi_2) = \Phi$ and Π_1 reduces immediately to Π_2. From results about normalization for terms in **K**, **K(S)** or **T**, we may thus infer corresponding results for derivations in **M**, **M(S)** and **P**.

Conversely, one can easily define an homomorphism with respect to immediate reducibility from terms in **K** onto a subset of derivations in **M**, and hence from the results about derivations in II.3, we can infer corresponding results about terms in **K**. It does not seem to be known at present whether there is such an homomorphism from terms in **T** onto a subset of derivations in **P**.

Curry and Feys (1958) seem first to have noted the similarity between derivations in propositional logic and terms in certain λ-calculi. Howard (1969) extended their observations to predicate logic and Martin-Löf (1969) made a further extension to infinite sentential logic (see III.3). All these observations are made for λ-calculi with infinitely many ground types (one for each atomic formula in the logical system in question). It is then possible to establish an isomorphism (instead of the homomorphism) between terms and derivations.

IV.3. **Gödel's functional interpretation**

3.1. *The general form of Gödel's interpretation*

The interpretation of intuitionistic logic by Gödel (1958) (referred to in I.4.3) is an example of a reductive proof theoretical analysis of the kind described in section I.3.2. The general form of Gödel's result may be described as follows: With every formula $A(\bar{a})$ in **P** where $\bar{a}$ is a list of the parameters in the formula, there is associated a formula $\overline{A}$ of the form $\overline{\exists y}\overline{\forall z}B(\bar{y},\bar{z},\bar{a})$ where $\overline{\exists y}$ and $\overline{\forall z}$ are abbreviations of sequences of ∃- and ∀-quantifiers, respectively, and $\bar{y}$ and $\bar{z}$ are abbreviations of the variables quantified by these quantifiers, and $B(\bar{y},\bar{z},\bar{a})$ is built up by sentential connectives from equations between terms which may contain in addition to ordinary arithmetical operators variables for constructive functions of finite types (cf. sec. 1.1.2). It is then shown that if $A(\bar{a})$ is provable in $\mathbf{P_I}$, then there is a sequence of functions abbreviated $\bar{F}$ which is definable in a calculus **T** and for which $B(\bar{F}(\bar{a}),\bar{b},\bar{a})$ is provable in **T**. The calculus **T** is here like the one defined in section 2.3 except that there is no type i and no rule constants, i.e. the language are the same with these differences and the axioms are obvious quantifier free axioms which are in harmony with the interpretation stated in section 2. The functions $\bar{F}$ are obtainable uniformly from the proof of $A(\bar{a})$ in $\mathbf{P_I}$. (Thus, the functions

f and g in section I.3.2 may be written $f(A(\bar{a})) = B(\bar{c},\bar{b},\bar{a})$ and $g(\Pi) = \bar{F}$. The operation Φ in I.3.2 is then simply the operation of substituting the second argument for certain variables in the first argument.

3.2. *Tait's and Howard's analysis of* **T**

Since the proof of Gödel's result is strictly finitary, it constitutes a reduction of **P** provided the theory **T** is admitted as a more elementary theory than **P**. However, Tait (1965) and (1967) has suggested that also the theory **T** should be analysed. In particular, Tait (1967) shows that every term in **T** is what he calls convertible (see appendix A.5) and reduces to the normal form defined above in 2.4, which among other things establishes the consistency of **T**.

Howard (1968) shows that the proof of this result can be given by the strictly finitary means of Skolem arithmetic extended with induction up to ϵ_0. One obtains thus the same epistemological reduction as Gentzen (sec. III. 1.3).

But as noted above in 2.4 and 2.5, not only are the same principles needed to carry out Gentzen's analysis of **P** and this analysis of Gödel's **T**, the result is essentially of the same structure.

Appendix A. Validity of derivations

A.1. Validity based on the introduction rules

1.1. *Introductory discussion*

Gentzen's idea that the introduction rules may be looked upon as a kind of definitions that give the meaning of the logical constants in terms of which the elimination rules are justified (section II.2.2.2) is very suggestive, it seems to me. Of course, as already remarked, the introduction rules are not literal definitions and the question thus arises how to make Gentzen's idea precise.

Since the premiss(es) of a first order introduction rule is (are) subformula(s) of the conclusion, a natural idea would be to try to use the condition for inferring a formula A by introduction as a clause in a definition by induction of a notion "A is valid". One may then be able to verfy that the elimination rules preserve this validity.

The basic idea in this definition of validity would thus be that A is valid if A can be built up or constructed by introductions, in other words, if there is a *construction* of A by the use of introductions; note, however, that the constructions considered here are quite different from the ones in section IV.1. Instead of defining the validity of A directly, we may thus define inductively what constitutes a construction of A.

Such an inductive definition would have to be based on some given constructions of the atomic formulas (since the conclusions of Gentzen's I-rules are all compound formulas). These constructions can be given by an atomic system **S** (sec. II.1.5) and as in IV.1, we may thus relativize the notion of a construction to such systems.

Inductive clauses defining constructions of conjunctions, disjunctions, universal quantifications, and existential quantifications relative an atomic system **S** do not offer any difficulties. Constructions of formulas that contain only &, v, $\forall$, and $\exists$ as logical constants will thus consist simply of derivations of these formulas using only the introduction rules for these constants and the rules of **S**.

But implication constitutes a problem since the condition for inferring $A \supset B$ by introduction is a derivation of B from A and this derivation may have to use not only successive introductions constructing B but also eliminations operating on A, which are the very rules that we want to justify on the basis of the meaning given to the constants by the introductions; it would of course be circular to define a construction of $A \supset B$ as simply a derivation of B from A.

The brief discussion by Gentzen (1934) does not give any hint as to how implication is to be handled. A natural idea, which seems to be consonant with the general idea that we are trying to explicate, is to understand by a construction of $A \supset B$ a derivation of B from A *that togehter with a construction of A yields a construction of B.*

To make this idea precise, we have to specify what "yield" is to mean here. Remembering the conjecture about identity between proofs (sec. I.3.5.6), it seems natural to require that the derivation together with a construction of A *reduces* to a construction of B and to take this as the meaning of "yield".

However, one modification of this idea seems desirable. The condition on a construction of $A \supset B$ as formulated above would be vacuously satisfied if there is no construction of A relative to the system **S** in question. The conditions is thus quite weak and can be strengthened as in IV.1 by requiring that the condition above is satisfied also relative to every extension of the system in question.

I shall summarize these ideas in a definition below. I shall then say that a derivation of A that constitutes a construction in the above sense is *valid*; however, in view of the conjecture about identity between proofs, a derivation that reduces to such a construction shall also be counted as valid. Rather than defining the notion of construction discussed above, I shall define this notion of validity inductively. In this definition of validity of derivations, we shall thus require in all the clauses (not only the clause for implication) that the derivation reduces to a derivation of a particular kind.

1.2. *Definitions*

1.2.1. *Validity of closed derivations*. Let Π be a *closed* derivation in a system **M(S)** of a sentence A, i.e. Π has no open assumptions and no parameters that are not proper. We assume that **S** contains at least one individual constant. We define: Π is *valid in* **S** if and only if

1.2.1.1. A is atomic and Π reduces to a derivation in **S**; or

1.2.1.2. A is of the form $A_1 \& A_2$ and Π reduces to a derivation of the form

$$\frac{\Pi_1 \quad \Pi_2}{A_1 \& A_2}$$

and for $i = 1$ and 2, Π_i is a derivation of A_i and is valid in **S**; or

1.2.1.3. A is of the form $A_1 \vee A_2$ and Π reduces to a derivation of the form

$$\frac{\Pi'}{A_1 \vee A_2}$$

where Π' is a derivation of A_1 or A_2 and is valid in **S**; or

1.2.1.4. A is of the form $A_1 \supset A_2$ and Π reduces to a derivation of the form

$$\frac{\Pi_2}{A_1 \supset A_2}$$

such that for each extension **S**$'$ of **S** and for each closed derivation

$$\frac{\Sigma_1}{A_1}$$

in **M(S$'$)** that is valid in **S**$'$, it holds that

$$\begin{array}{c}\underline{\Sigma_1} \\ [A_1] \\ \Pi_2\end{array}$$

is a derivation of A_2 and is valid in **S**$'$ ($[A_1]$ is here the set of open assumptions in Π_2 of the form A_1); or

1.2.1.5. A is of the form $\forall x B(x)$ and Π reduces to a derivation of the form

$$\frac{\Pi'(a)}{\forall x B(x)}$$

whose last inference is an $\forall$I with a as proper parameter and for each name t (i.e. individual term without parameters), $\Pi'(t)$ obtained from $\Pi(a)$ by substituting t for a is (a derivation of $B(t)$) valid in **S**, or

1.2.1.6. A is of the form $\exists x B(x)$ and Π reduces to a derivation of the form

$$\frac{\Sigma'}{\exists x B(x)}$$

where Σ' is a derivation of $B(t)$ for some name t in **S** and is valid in **S**.

1.2.2. *Validity of open derivations.* A derivation Π in **M(S)** (with open assumptions or not proper assumptions) is valid in **S** if and only if for each result Π' of substituting names in **S** for not proper parameters in Π it holds: if **S**$'$ is an extension of **S** and Π^* is the result of replacing every assumption A in Π' by a closed derivation of A in **M(S**$'$**)** that is valid in **S**$'$, then Π^* is valid in **S**.

1.3. *Discussion*

1.3.1. Does the notion of validity defined above capture Gentzen's idea about an operational interpretation of the logical constants (as discussed in section II.2.2.2)? Clearly, it follows immediately from the definition that a derivation whose last inference is an introduction is valid (in **S**) if the derivation(s) of the premiss(es) is (are) valid (in **S**). Furthermore, it can be seen by just the kind of argument that Gentzen had in mind that eliminations preserve validity. More precisely, we may first note as a lemma (proved by induction over the degree of the end formula) that if Π_1 reduces to Π_2 and Π_2 is valid, then Π_1 is valid. Assume now that Π is a derivation whose last inference is an elimination and that the derivation(s) of the premiss(es) of this elimination is (are) valid. From the definition of validity, it follows that the derivation of the major premiss reduces to a derivation whose last inference is an introduction. Hence, the derivation Π as a whole reduces to a derivation Π' with the same elimination as last inference and the major premiss of this elimination is now a maximum formula. It can then be seen that the reduction of Π' is valid, which is just a precise version of Gentzen's informal argument. From the lemma it now follows that Π is valid.

It seems thus fair to say that the notion of validity defined above constitutes one possible explication of Gentzen's idea. But of course, this does not exclude the possibility that there exist other and more interesting ways of developing this idea.

1.3.2. Although the notion of validity defined above may explicate Gentzen's idea about an operational interpretation of the logical constants, one may ask whether such an interpretation is at all reasonable. As remarked in section IV.1.1, the operational interpretation of implication is much stronger than the usual constructive interpretation. And the same holds for universal quantification. It must be admitted that such a strong meaning of $\supset$ and $\forall$ is seldom used. The interest of this operational interpretation is rather that the rules of minimal (or intuitionistic, see 1.3.3 below) logic are sound also for this very strong interpretation. In this context, we may say that a formula A is valid in a system **S** if there is a derivation of A that is valid in **S** and that A is logically valid if it is valid in every **S** over which it is a formula. The proof outlined in 1.3.1 above then shows that every derivable formula in **M** is logically valid in this strong sense. However, this notion of validity of a formula in a system does not have natural mathematical applications. For instance, the induction axioms are not generally valid in the system $\mathbf{S^A}$ (defined in III.1.1): Although a derivation of $A(0)$ valid in $\mathbf{S^A}$ and a derivation of $\forall x(A(x) \supset A(x'))$ valid in $\mathbf{S^A}$ guarantee together the existence of a derivation of $A(t)$ valid in $\mathbf{S^A}$ for every numeral t, there may be no uniformly valid derivation of this kind, i.e. no derivation of $A(a)$ valid in $\mathbf{S^A}$, as required if $\forall x A(x)$ is to be valid in $\mathbf{S^A}$.

In section 2 below, I shall consider a variant of the validity notion, which in contrast to the one above will allow an interpretation of the axioms of first order arithmetic.

1.3.3. The validity notion is defined above only for derivations in systems **M(S)**. But intuitionistic logic is of course also covered since a system **I(S)** is identical to the system $\mathbf{M(S^+)}$ where $\mathbf{S^+}$ is the extension of **S** obtained by adding the rule $\Lambda_{\mathbf{I}}$. However, if we add derived rules to **M(S)** involving compound formulas and want to extend the validity notion to such a system, we have also to extend the notion of reducibility. Such an extension seems always possible also when the added rule only preserves derivability (from null assumptions). For instance, the rule $\Lambda_{\mathbf{C}}$ (principle of indirect proof for atomic formulas) is such a rule and by adding the simplification defined in II.3.3.2.3 as a new reduction, we can extend the notion to systems **C(S)**. But note that the notion cannot be extended in this fashion to systems containing the rule mentioned in II.2.2.2. It would be desirable to define a more general notion of validity which is applicable without changes to extensions of **M(S)** by the addition of derived rules and by which the invalidity of a rule such as the one mentioned in II.2.2.2 could be demonstrated.

1.3.4. Not surprisingly, the above notion of validity is strongly connected with the notion of normalizability. Although the validity of every derivation was easily shown in I.3.1 above, it also follows directly from the normalization theorem (by an induction over the degree of the end formulas). But certain aspects of the normalization theorem, in particular the one discussed in II.4.1.2.2, are better expressed by saying that each derivation is valid. Note also that the corollaries about atomic formulas, disjunctions and existential quantifications also follow immediately from the validity of derivations (cf. II.4.1.2.2.1 and II.4.1.2.2.2).

Conversely, if we strengthen the notion of validity by requiring not only that Π reduces to a derivation of a certain kind but that every sequence of immediate reductions if continued far enough reduces Π to a derivation of this kind, we get a notion that may be called strong validity and that provides a convenient tool for proving the strong normalization theorem. In section 3 below, I shall modify this notion slightly to make it even more convenient for this purpose.

A.2. Validity based on the elimination rules

Since the introductions and eliminations are inverses of each other, Gentzen's idea to justify the eliminations by the meaning given to the constants by the introductions may be reversed. Instead of interpreting the constants in the way above as asserting the existence of certain construction that build up formulas with these constants, we may interprete them as stating the performability of certain operations. A derivation will then be valid when it can be used to obtain certain valid derivations of the subformulas.

Hence, while the clause 1.2.1 would be left unchanged, a derivation Π of $A_1 \& A_2$ would now be defined as valid in **S** if

$$\frac{\Pi}{A_i}$$

is valid in **S** for $i = 1$ and 2.

A derivation Π of $A_1 \supset A_2$ would be defined as valid in **S** if for each extension **S**′ of **S** and for each derivation Π′ of A_1 that is valid in **S**′,

$$\frac{\Pi' \quad \Pi}{A_2}$$

is valid in $\mathbf{S}'$.

Similarly, a derivation Π of $\forall x A(x)$ would be defined as valid when for each name t in $\mathbf{S}$

$$\frac{\Pi}{A(t)}$$

is valid in $\mathbf{S}$.

One may say that while a valid derivation in the sense of the preceding section 1 guarantees the existence of a certain construction of the end formula, a valid derivation in the sense of this section constitutes a rule for inferring certain formulas.

The validity of a derivation whose last inference is an elimination is now immediate from the definition. But to show that validity is preserved by the introductions, we have now essentially to show that a construction of the kind considered in section 1 also constitutes a rule for obtaining valid derivations (in the sense of this section) of other formulas. This is again shown by essential use of the reductions, and the basic idea is thus the same in the two cases.

We may note however that the universal quantifier is now not interpreted as narrowly as in section 1 since we do not require a uniformly valid derivation of $A(a)$ to have a valid derivation of $\forall x A(x)$. In particular, we note that every derivation in the system **P** for first order arithmetic is valid in the sense of this section.

However, disjunctions and existential quantifications seem impossible to handle in this way since the induction over the complexity of the end formulas used in the definition of validity breakes down in these cases.

A.3. Validity used in proofs of normalizability

3.1. *Introductory remarks*

The clauses 1.2.2 – 1.2.6 in the definition 1.2 of validity can be changed without affecting the meaning of the notion by separating two cases, viz. (i) the case when the last inference of Π is an introduction and (ii) the case when the last inference of Π is an elimination. In case (i) we may require in the different cases not that Π reduces to a derivation of a certain kind but that Π is already of this kind. In case (ii), we may simply require that Π reduces to a valid derivation.

When the validity notion is used as a tool in proving normalizability, it is suitable to make this separation and to define the notion directly for all derivations, i.e. not only for the closed ones. Furthermore, when case (ii) applies it is suitable to define also the normal derivations as valid. This agrees with the definition 1.2 when the end formula of the derivation is atomic but is a deviation when the end formula is not atomic. It is then not necessary to relativize the validity notion to atomic systems. Note also that with this modification, there will always exist a normal derivation of each formula and hence we do not get the problem noted in connection with implication in section 1.1 that led us to consider extensions of atomic systems.

To prove the strong normalization theorem, we strengthen the notion of validity to strong validity by requiring when case (ii) applies that *every* derivation to which the given derivation immediately reduces is valid.

3.2. *Definitions*

3.2.1. *Strong validity*. Let Π be a derivation of A in any system **M(S)**, **I(S)**, or **C(S)**. We define: A is strongly valid if and only if one of the following cases applies:

3.2.1.1. The last inference of Π is an &I, ∨I, or ∃I and the derivation(s) of the premiss(es) of the introduction is (are) strongly valid;

3.2.1.2. The last inference of Π is an ⊃I, in which case Π is of the form

$$\frac{\begin{matrix}[A_1]\\ \Pi_2\end{matrix}}{A_1 \supset A_2}$$

with $[A_1]$ as the set of assumptions closed by the ⊃I, and for each strongly valid derivation

$$\frac{\Sigma_1}{A_1}$$

it holds that

$$\begin{matrix}\dfrac{\Sigma_1}{[A_1]}\\ \Pi_2\end{matrix}$$

is strongly valid;

3.2.1.3. The last inference of Π is $\forall$I with proper parameter a and for each individual term t, it holds that the result of substituting t for a in the derivation of the premiss of the $\forall$I is strongly valid;

3.2.1.4. The last inference of Π is not an introduction and the following conditions hold:

(i) Π is normal or each derivation Π' to which Π immediately reduces is strongly valid;

(ii) if Π is of the form

$$\frac{\dfrac{\Sigma}{B_1 \vee B_2} \quad \dfrac{\begin{matrix}[B_1]\\ \Sigma_1\end{matrix}}{A} \quad \dfrac{\begin{matrix}[B_2]\\ \Sigma_2\end{matrix}}{A}}{A}$$

where $[B_i]$ is the set of assumptions in Σ_i closed by this vE (i=1 and 2), then the derivation of the minor premisses of the vE are strongly valid and for each derivation

$$\frac{\Sigma_i'}{B_i}$$

which is a part of a derivation Π' to which the derivation of the major premiss $B_1 \vee B_2$ reduces and where B_i is a formula immediately above either the end formula of Π' or an end segment of Π', it holds that

$$\frac{\dfrac{\Sigma_i'}{[B_i]}}{\begin{matrix}\Sigma_i\\ \hline A\end{matrix}}$$

is strongly valid;

(iii) if Π is of the form

$$\frac{\dfrac{\Sigma_1}{\exists x B(x)} \quad \dfrac{\begin{matrix}[B(a)]\\ \Sigma(a)\end{matrix}}{A}}{A}$$

where a is the proper parameter of this $\exists$E and $[B(a)]$ is the set of assumptions closed by the $\exists$E, then the derivation of the minor premiss of the $\exists$E is strongly valid and for each derivation

$$\frac{\Sigma'}{B(t)}$$

which is a part of a derivation Π' to which the derivation of the major premiss $\exists x B(x)$ reduces and where $B(t)$ is a formula immediately above either the end formula of Π' or an end segment of Π', it holds that

$$\frac{\dfrac{\Sigma'}{[B(t)]}}{\dfrac{\Sigma(t)}{A}}$$

is strongly valid.

The definition is to be understood as a generalized inductive definition, i.e., it proceeds by induction over the complexity of the end formula of the derivation and for each fixed complexity, a derivation is valid if this follows by a finite number of applications of the clauses 3.2.1.1 – 3.2.1.4.

3.2.2. *Strong validity under substitution*. We define: A derivation Π is strongly valid under substitution if and only if for each substitution of terms for not proper parameters in Π and for each way of replacing open assumptions in the derivation after this substitution by strongly valid derivations of the assumptions (not necessarily replacing each open assumption) it holds that the resulting derivation is strongly valid.

3.3. *Results*

We can now state the two main results:

3.3.1. **Theorem.** *Every derivation in* **M(S)**, **I(S)** *or* **C(S)** *is strongly valid under substitution.*

3.3.2. **Theorem.** *Every reduction sequence starting from a strongly valid derivation terminates (in a normal derivation).*

From these two theorems follow the strong normalization theorem in II.3.5.3 if we also verify the more trivial property (similar to the so-called

Church-Rosser property in the λ-calculus) that two reduction sequences that start from the same derivation and terminate always terminate in the same derivation.

3.4. *Proofs*

We first state two lemmata concerning reducibility, which follow immediately from the definitions.

3.4.1. **Lemma.** *If the last inference of* Π *is an introduction and is thus of the form*

$$\frac{\Pi'}{A} \qquad or \qquad \frac{\Pi' \quad \Pi''}{A}$$

and $\Pi_1, \Pi_2, \ldots$ *is a reduction sequence starting from* Π, *then each* Π_i *ends with the same introduction and is thus of the form*

$$\frac{\Pi_i'}{A} \qquad or \qquad \frac{\Pi_i' \quad \Pi_i''}{A}$$

respectively, and $\Pi_1', \Pi_2', \ldots$ *and* $\Pi_1'', \Pi_2'', \ldots$ *with omissions for possible repetitions are also reduction sequences.*

3.4.2. **Lemma.** *If* $\Pi_1(a)$ *reduces to* $\Pi_2(a)$, a *is not a proper parameter in* $\Pi_1(a)$, *and* $[A(a)]$ *is a set of open assumptions in* $\Pi_1(a)$, *then every derivation*

$$\begin{array}{c}\Sigma \\ \hline [A(t)] \\ \Pi_1(t)\end{array} \qquad reduces\ to \qquad \begin{array}{c}\Sigma \\ \hline [A(t)] \\ \Pi_2(t)\end{array}$$

By the use of these two lemmata and an induction over the definition of strong validity, we prove

3.4.3. **Lemma.** *If* Π_1 *reduces to* Π_2 *and* Π_1 *is strongly valid, then so is* Π_2.

3.4.4. *Proof of theorem* 3.3.2. We can now prove theorem 3.3.2 by an induction over the definition of strong validity. When the last inference of the derivation is not an introduction, the assertion follows immediately from the induction hypothesis. When the last inference of the derivation is an introduction, it can be seen that the derivation(s) of the premiss(es) of this introduction is (are) also strongly valid and that the induction hypothesis can be applied to them. The assertion then follows from lemma 3.4.1.

3.4.5. *Proof of theorem* 3.3.1. We prove theorem 3.3.1 by an induction over the length of the derivation. The base of the induction is trivial. Also the induction step is immediate in the case when the last inference of the derivation is an introduction: the induction assumption implies immediately the defining clause of strong validity in question. When the last inference is not an introduction, we make use of the following

Lemma. *A derivation* Π *whose last inference is not an introduction is strongly valid when the following conditions are satisfied:*

(i) *every reduction sequence starting from a derivation of a premisss of the last inference of* Π *terminates;*

(ii) *if the last inference of* Π *is* &E, ⊃E, *or* ∀E, *then the derivation(s) of the premiss(es) of this inference is (are) strongly valid;*

(iii) *if the last inference is* ∨E *or* ∃E, *then condition* (ii) *or* (iii), *respectively, in clause* 3.2.1.4 *in the definition of strong validity is satisfied.*

We shall see that this lemma implies that a derivation Π of the form

$$\frac{\Pi_1 \quad \Pi_2 \quad \dots \quad \Pi_n}{A}$$

whose last inference is not an introduction is strongly valid under substitution if the derivations Π_1, Π_2, ..., and Π_n are strongly valid under substitution. We have thus to show that each result Π* of substituting individual terms for individual parameters and derivations for assumptions in Π as described in the definition of strong validity under substitution (3.2.2) is strongly valid. Π* has the form

$$\frac{\Pi_1^* \quad \Pi_2^* \quad \dots \quad \Pi_n^*}{A^*}$$

where Π_i^* is the result of carrying out the substitution in Π_i (i=1,2,...,n), and hence, each Π_i^* is strongly valid. Condition (ii) of the lemma is thus satisfied by Π*. In view of theorem 3.2.2, condition (i) is also satisfied. Too see that also condition (iii) is satisfied, we use the fact the derivation(s) of the minor premiss(es) of the last inference of Π was (were) strongly valid under substitution and apply lemma 3.4.2. We can thus apply the lemma to Π* and conclude that Π* is strongly valid. It remains only to prove the lemma.

Proof of the lemma. To prove the lemma, we shall use an induction over the length of reduction trees of derivations. The reduction tree of a derivation Π is the tree whose threads are the reduction sequences starting from Π (we may also represent them as a graph but that is immaterial here). The reduction tree of an n-tuple of derivations is the tree consisting of n roots, the ith root being the end node of the reduction tree of the ith derivation.

We shall assign an *induction value* to each derivation Π of the kind described in the lemma. It will consist of a triple (α,β,γ) where α is the length of the reduction tree of the derivation of the major premiss of the last inference of Π and β is the length of the derivation of this premiss if there is such a premiss, otherwise $\alpha = \beta = 0$, and γ is the length of the reduction tree of the n-tuple of derivation(s) of the premiss(es) of the last inference of Π (taken in order from the left to the right). Because of clause (i) in the lemma, α and γ are finite. The induction values are ordered lexicographically, and we shall prove the lemma assuming that it has been proved for all derivations with lower induction value.

To prove that Π of the kind described in the lemma is strongly valid, we only need to verify clause (i) in the clause 3.2.1.4 of the definition of strong validity since the other clauses are satisfied according to condition (iii) of the lemma. If Π is normal there is thus nothing to prove. If Π is not normal, we have to show that each Π' to which Π immediately reduces is strongly valid. We consider three cases.

Case (a). Π' is obtained from Π by replacing a proper subtree of Π by its reduction. If Π is

$$\frac{\Pi_1 \quad \Pi_2 \quad \ldots \quad \Pi_n}{A}$$

then Π' is in this case of the form

$$\frac{\Pi_1' \quad \Pi_2' \quad \ldots \quad \Pi_n'}{A}$$

where for one i ($\leqslant n$), Π_i reduces immediately to Π_i' and for other j ($i \neq j \leqslant n$), $\Pi_j' = \Pi_j$. Hence, the reduction value (α',β',γ') of Π' is lower than the induction value (α,β,γ) of Π since either $\alpha' < \alpha$ or $\alpha' = \alpha$, $\beta' = \beta$ but $\gamma' < \gamma$. Π' obviously satisfies condition (i) of the lemma. Conditions (ii) and (iii) are satisfied because of lemma 3.4.3; in the case of condition (iii), we have also to apply lemma 3.4.2 and the fact that reducibility is transitive. By the induction hypothesis, it thus follows that Π' is strongly valid.

Case (b). Π' is a proper reduction of Π. Then the major premiss B of the last inference of Π is the conclusion of an introduction. When B is a conjunction, implication, or universal quantification, we can then (because of clause (ii) in the lemma) apply the definition of strong validity for derivations whose last inference is an introduction and conclude that Π' is strongly valid. When B is a disjunction or existential quantification, the strong validity of Π' follows from clause (iii) of the lemma (and the reflexivity of reducibility).

Case (c). Π' is a commutative reduction of Π. We consider the case of vE-reductions, the case of $\exists$E-reductions being similar. Π and Π' are then of the form shown to the left and right below, respectively, wheren $[B_i]$ is the set of assumptions in Σ_i closed by the $\vee$E:

$$\dfrac{\dfrac{\dfrac{\Sigma}{B_1 \vee B_2} \quad \dfrac{\begin{matrix}[B_1]\\ \Sigma_1\end{matrix}}{C} \quad \dfrac{\begin{matrix}[B_2]\\ \Sigma_2\end{matrix}}{C}}{C} \qquad \Sigma_3}{A} \qquad\qquad \dfrac{\dfrac{\Sigma}{B_1 \vee B_2} \quad \dfrac{\dfrac{\begin{matrix}[B_1]\\ \Sigma_1\end{matrix}}{C} \quad \Sigma_3}{A} \quad \dfrac{\dfrac{\begin{matrix}[B_2]\\ \Sigma_2\end{matrix}}{C} \quad \Sigma_3}{A}}{A}$$

The induction value $(\alpha', \beta', \gamma')$ of Π' is less than the induction value (α, β, γ) of Π since $\alpha' \leqslant \alpha$ and $\beta' < \beta$. To see that the lemma can be applied to Π' it is now sufficient to verify that condition (iii) is satisfied by Π': this together with theorem 3.3.2 implies that condition (i) is satisfied for the derivation of the minor premisses of the last inference of Π'; for the major premiss this is obvious in view of assumptions about Π.

We have thus to show that

$$\dfrac{\dfrac{\Sigma_i}{C} \qquad \Sigma_3}{A} \quad \text{and} \quad \dfrac{\dfrac{\begin{matrix}\dfrac{\Sigma_i'}{[B_i]}\\ \Sigma_i\end{matrix}}{C} \quad \Sigma_3}{A} \tag{1}$$

are strongly valid, the latter under the assumption that

$$\dfrac{\Sigma_i'}{B_i}.$$

is a part of a derivation to which

$$\frac{\Sigma}{B_1 \vee B_2}$$

reduces and B_i is the formula immediately above either the end formula or an end segment of this derivation.

To show this, we shall first apply the induction hypothesis to these derivations in (1). The induction value $(\alpha_1, \beta_1, \gamma_1)$ of any of these derivations in (1) is lower than the induction value (α, β, γ) of Π because if the derivation is of the kind shown to the left in (1) then $\alpha_1 \leqslant \alpha$ and $\beta_1 < \beta$ and in the other case $\alpha_1 < \alpha$. Furthermore, these derivations obviously satisfy condition (i) of the lemma since Π satisfies this condition. If C is a conjunction, implication, or universal quantification, then because of the assumptions about Π, viz. condition (ii) of the lemma, the derivation of the major premiss C of the last inference of Π is strongly valid, and hence, by clause (ii) in 3.2.1.4 in the definition of strong validity, the derivation of the major premiss C of a derivation in (1) is strongly valid. In other words, the derivations in (1) satisfy also condition (ii) of the lemma. It remains to see that they also satisfy condition (iii) of the lemma. This condition concerns Σ_3 and from the fact that this condition is satisfied by Π, one can infer that it is also satisfied by the derivations in (1).

We can thus apply the lemma to the derivations in (1) to conclude that they are strongly valid and then apply the lemma to Π' to conclude that also Π' is strongly valid.

We have thus shown that Π is strongly valid and have hence proved the lemma.

3.5. *Historical remark*

Although we have developed the validity notion here as an explication of Gentzen's idea about an operational interpretation of the logical constants and have shown how this notion slightly modified can be used in proofs of normalization theorems, a notion of this kind, called convertibility, was originally developed by Tait (1967) as a tool in establishing normalizations for terms in the calculus **T**, among other things (cf. IV.2.2).

The notion was carried over to derivations by Martin-Löf (1970) and was used by him in establishing a normalization theorem for the theory of iterated inductive definitions (cf. III.4). His notion and the use he makes of it differ from ours in this section 3 in the following two respects: firstly, Marin-Löf does not consider permutative reductions and shows thus that maximal formulas but not maximal segments can be removed from a derivation; secondly, he considers a particular reduction sequence and shows that it terminates where we show that all reduction sequences terminate. Certain complications that arise in the proof of theorem 3.3.1 (particularly in the lemma) as compared to Martin-Löf's proof are due to the first difference; the second difference does not essentially complicate the proof.

Appendix B. Proof of the strong normalization theorem in 2nd order logic

B.1. Intuitive idea

Attempts to extend the ideas of Appendix A to second order logic immediately encounters the following difficulty: the induction of the definition of validity in A1 or A2 or of strong validity in A3 breaks down at formulas $\forall XA(X)$ and $\exists XA(X)$ since $A(T)$ may be a more complex formula than $\forall XA(X)$ and $\exists XA(X)$. In other words, if we put down clauses defining the validity of derivations ending with $\forall XA(X)$ in analogy with the clauses for $\forall xA(x)$ and ask whether a derivation with $\forall XA(X)$ is valid, then it is true that in a finite number of steps, we can resolve this question into questions concerning the validity of derivations ending with formulas of the form $Tt_1t_2...t_n$; but when T is an abstraction term $\{\lambda x_1x_2...x_nB(x_1,x_2,...,x_n)\}$ we have thus to ask questions concerning derivations ending with $B(t_1,t_2,...,t_n)$ and B may contain the formula $\forall XA(X)$ (cf. III.5.3).

Girard's idea is now, when carried over to the present framework, that we assign an arbitrary meaning to the assertion that a derivation ending with $Tt_1t_2...t_n$ is valid: it is to be valid if and only if it belongs to an arbitrarily choosen set N. The formula $Tt_1t_2...t_n$ may thus be considered as a formula with lowest complexity since we shall never have to break down this formula to answer questions about validity.

In other words, we can define a notion of validity of derivations *relative* an assignment $\mathcal{N}$ to second order terms T of sets $\mathcal{N}(T)$ determining the meaning of the notion for derivations ending with $Tt_1t_2...t_n$.

A derivation

$$\cfrac{\cfrac{\Sigma(P)}{A(P)}}{\forall XA(X)}$$

is then defined as valid when for each term T and for (almost) each such assignment $\mathcal{N}$ to T,

$$\frac{\Sigma(T)}{A(T)}$$

is valid relative $\mathcal{N}$. In order to ensure that validity relative such assignments $\mathcal{N}$ implies normalizability, we will have to put certain requirements on $\mathcal{N}$ and therefore we consider only "almost" all assignments; more precisely, we consider all assignments that assign *regular sets* as defined below.

The definition of validity will thus contain a quantification over all regular sets. We shall prove that the set of valid derivations is such a regular set. In other words, when we define the notion of validity for the case when the derivation ends with a formula $\forall XA(X)$, there will be a quantification over sets among which is the very notion that we are defining. We have thus here a splendid example of an impredicativity. And this impredicativity will be used in the proof that each derivation is valid, where we shall consider in particular the assignment that assigns the set of valid derivations to a second order term T.

B.2. **Formal development**

We shall develop the idea described above in more detail in the same general way as in Appendix A.3. For the sake of shortness, we leave out existential quantification of second order variables; the reader should have no difficulty in extending the treatment of first order existential quantification to second order in the same general way as we shall here extend the treatment of first order universal quantification to second order.

2.1. *Definitions*

2.1.1. *Regular sets*. We define: A set N of second order derivations is regular if and only if the following two conditions are satisfied:

2.1.1.1. if $\Pi \in N$, then every reduction sequence starting with Π terminates;

2.1.1.2. if $\Pi \in N$ and Π reduces to Π', then $\Pi' \in N$.

2.1.2. *Strong validity relative assignments* $\mathcal{N}$. Let Π be a derivation of A in **M(S)** and let $\mathcal{N}$ be an assignment of regular sets to occurrences of second order terms in A; different occurrences of the same term may be assigned different sets and all occurrences need not have an assignment[1]. We shall define

[1] For footnote, see next page.

the notion: Π is strongly valid relative $\mathfrak{N}$. The definition is by a main induction on the "degree of A relative $\mathfrak{N}$" by which we understand the measure we get if the degree of A is calculated in the usual way except that occurrence of $Tt_1t_2...t_n$ where T is in the domain of $\mathfrak{N}$ is given the same measure as the atomic formulas. For each such complexity, we define the notion by inductive clauses in exactly the same way as in A.3.2.1 except that we replace "strong validity" by "strong validity relative $\mathfrak{N}$" (with the understanding in clauses A.3.2.1.1 – 3 that $\mathfrak{N}$ is to assign to an occurrence of a second order term in the immediate subformulas of A in question the same value (if any) that $\mathfrak{N}$ assigns to the corresponding occurrence in A) and add the following clauses:

2.1.2.1. the last inference of Π is λI, A is of the form $Tt_1t_2...t_n$ where this occurrence of T is in the domain of $\mathfrak{N}$ and $\Pi \in \mathfrak{N}(T)$;

2.1.2.2. the last inference of Π is λI, A is of the form $Tt_1t_2...t_n$ where T is not in the domain of $\mathfrak{N}$, and the derivation of the premiss of the last inference of Π is strongly valid relative $\mathfrak{N}$;

2.1.2.3. the last inference of Π is $\forall_2$I in which case Π is of the form

$$\cfrac{\cfrac{\Sigma(P)}{A(P)}}{\forall XA(X)}$$

where P is an n-ary predicate parameter, and it holds for each n-ary second order term T and for each regular set N that

$$\frac{\Sigma(T)}{A(T)}$$

[1] Since we must allow assignments of different sets to different occurrences of the same term, one may prefer to describe the relativization of validity of a derivation Π to an assignment $\mathfrak{N}$ as a relativization to a triple $(A,\mathfrak{T},\mathfrak{N}')$ instead. $\mathfrak{T}$ is here an assignment of predicate terms to predicate parameters, $A^{\mathfrak{T}}$, i.e. the result of simultaneously substituting these terms for these parameters in A, is the end formula of Π, and $\mathfrak{N}'$ is an assignment of regular sets to the same predicate parameters to which $\mathfrak{T}$ assigns terms. For instance, if $\mathfrak{N}$ is an assignment that assigns N_1 to certain occurrences of T and N_2 to other occurrences of T, then A is formed from the end formula of Π by replacing the first occurrences of T by a predicate parameter P and the other occurrences by a different parameter Q. $\mathfrak{T}$ then assigns T to both P and Q but $\mathfrak{N}'$ assigns N_1 to P and N_2 to Q.

is strongly valid relative $\mathfrak{N}+\binom{T}{N}$, by which is meant the assignment that assigns N to the occurrences of T in $A(T)$ that is substituted for P in $A(P)$ and assigns to other occurrences of second order terms in $A(T)$ the same value (if any) that $\mathfrak{N}$ assigns to the corresponding occurrence in $\forall XA(X)$.

2.1.3. *Strong validity under substitution.* We define for derivations in any system $\mathbf{M}_2(\mathbf{S})$: Π is strongly valid under substitution if and only if for each substitution of individual terms for individual variables in Π, for each substitution of n-ary (n=0,1,...) second order terms for n-ary second order parameters in Π, and for each assignment $\mathfrak{N}$ of regular sets to occurrences of these substituted terms in the open premisses and end formula of the derivation after the substitution, where the same set is assigned to occurrences that replace the same parameters, it holds: if Π^* is obtained from Π by carrying out these substitutions and then simultaneously replacing open assumptions by derivations in $\mathbf{M}_2(\mathbf{S})$ of the same assumptions that are strongly valid relative $\mathfrak{N}$, then Π^* is strongly valid relative $\mathfrak{N}$.

2.2. *Results*

The results in A.3.3 can now be extended to second order:

2.2.1. **Theorem.** *Each derivation in* $\mathbf{M}_2(\mathbf{S})$ *is strongly valid under substitution.*

2.2.2. **Theorem.** *If* Π *is a strongly valid derivation in* $\mathbf{M}_2(\mathbf{S})$ *relative as assignment* $\mathfrak{N}$ *of regular sets, then each reduction sequence from* Π *terminates.*

The strong normalization theorem now follows for $\mathbf{M}_2(\mathbf{S})$ in the same way as for $\mathbf{M}(\mathbf{S})$.

2.3. *Proofs*

The lemmata A.3.4.1 – A.3.4.3 hold also for second order logic; in lemma 3.4.3, we replace "strong validity" by "strong validity relative $\mathfrak{N}$". When proving this last lemma by induction over the definition of strong validity relative $\mathfrak{N}$, we note that condition 2.1.1.2 in the definition of regular sets is needed.

We prove theorem 2.2.2 by induction over the definition of strong validity relative $\mathfrak{N}$ in the same way as we proved theorem A.3.3.2 in A.3.4.4 except that in the new case corresponding to clause 2.1.2.1, we have to use condition 2.1.1.1 in the definition of regular set, and in the new case corresponding to clause 2.1.2.3, we note that there exists regular sets (e.g. the empty set) and hence that strong validity relative $\mathfrak{N}$ also of derivations whose last inference is $\forall_2$I implies strong validity of the derivation of the premiss of the inference relative $\mathcal{N}+\binom{P}{N}$ for some N.

The proof of theorem 2.2.2 has the same structure as the proof of theorem A.3.3.1 in A.3.4.5. The base and the induction step in the case when the last inference is an introduction are again immediate. The lemma in the proof is stated in the same way except that we add λE and $\forall_2$E to condition (ii). There is essentially only one new case that arises, viz. in case (b) in the proof of the lemma, we have to consider the case of $\forall_2$-reductions. In this case, we know that the derivation of the premiss of the last inference of Π, which is of the form

$$\cfrac{\cfrac{\cfrac{\Sigma(P)}{C(P)}}{\forall X C(X)}}{C(T)}$$

is strongly valid relative $\mathcal{N}$ and hence by definition that

$$\frac{\Sigma(T)}{C(T)}\ ,$$

which is just the reduction Π′ of Π, is strongly valid relative $\mathcal{N}+\binom{T}{N}$ for any regular N. Since the set of valid derivations relative $\mathcal{N}$ is regular according to theorem 2.2.2 and the analogue to lemma A.3.4.3, we may set N equal to this set. We then apply the following lemma and conclude that Π′ is strongly valid also relative $\mathcal{N}$.

Lemma. *Let N be the set of strongly valid derivations relative* $\mathcal{N}$. *Then,* Π *is strongly valid relative* $\mathcal{N}$ *if and only if* Π *is strongly valid relative* $\mathcal{N}+\binom{T}{N}$, *where* $\mathcal{N}+\binom{T}{N}$ *is an extension of* $\mathcal{N}$ *that assigns N to certain occurrences of T in the end formula of* Π.

The lemma is proved by a trivial induction over the definition of strong validity relative $\mathcal{N}$.

B.3. Extensions to other systems

Unlike the situation in first order logic, the results for minimal (or intuitionistic) logic in section 2 do not immediately extend to classical logic. The reason for this is that by an $\forall_2$-reduction or an $\exists_2$-reduction, an application of the Λ_C-rule may not any longer satisfy the restriction that we have imposed on this rule, viz. that the conclusion is atomic (I.1.3.3). However, by a simple, separate argument one can show that the derivation can be transformed so that this restriction becomes satisfied (cf. Prawitz (1965), 40–41, 70–71). Alternatively, we can add these transformations as new reductions and then proceed as in section 2. The results thus hold also for classical second order logic.

If we stay in minimal (or intuitionistic) second order logic, we can apply the results of section 2 to show that a rule corresponding to an axiom of choice holds as a rule that preserves derivability (from null assumptions). The rule is

$$\frac{\forall x \exists X A(x,X)}{\exists Y \forall x A(x, \lambda x_1 x_2 \ldots x_n Y x x_1 x_2 \ldots x_n)}$$

where X is an n-ary and Y is an $(n+1)$-ary predicate variable. To see that this rule preserves derivability, assume that the premiss is derivable. From the analogue of lemma II.3.5.4 for second order logic, we can conclude that $A(a, T(a))$ is derivable for some $T(a)$ where $T(a)$ is an n-ary second order term which may contain the parameter a. By use of the λ-rules, we may infer the formula

$$A(a, \lambda x_1 x_2 \ldots x_n \{\lambda x x_1 x_2 \ldots x_n T(x) x_1 x_2 \ldots x_n\} a x_1 x_2 \ldots x_n)$$

from which the conclusion follows by an $\forall$I and $\exists$I.

In agreement with the remark made in A.1.3.3, it is possible to add this rule, which is to be counted as an elimination rule, to the system $\mathbf{M}^2$, define a new reduction, and extend the results of section 2 to this system. The reduction in question is shown below where the second derivation is a reduction of the first derivation:

$$\cfrac{\cfrac{\cfrac{\cfrac{\Sigma}{A(a, T(a))}}{\exists X A(a,X)}}{\forall x \exists X A(x,X)}}{\exists Y \forall x A(x, \lambda x_1 x_2 \ldots x_n Y x x_1 x_2 \ldots x_n)}$$

$$\cfrac{\cfrac{\cfrac{\Sigma}{A(a, \lambda x_1 x_2 \ldots x_n \{\lambda x x_1 x_2 \ldots x_n T(x) x_1 x_2 \ldots x_n\} a x_1 x_2 \ldots x_n)}}{\forall x A(x, \lambda_1 x_2 \ldots x_n \{\lambda x x_1 x_2 \ldots x_n T(x) x_1 x_2 \ldots x_n\} x x_1 x_2 \ldots x_n)}}{\exists Y \forall x A(x, \lambda x_1 x_2 \ldots x_n Y x x_1 x_2 \ldots x_n)}$$

where X is an n-ary and Y an $(n+1)$-ary predicate variable and $T(a)$ is an n-ary second order term that may contain the parameter a. In order that the second figure is to be a correct derivation, the abstraction terms should be understood as abbreviations on the meta-level, i.e. $A(\{\lambda x_1 x_2 ... x_n B(x_1,x_2,...,x_n)\} t_1 t_2 ... t_n)$ is to be understood as denoting $A(B'(t_1,t_2,...,t_n))$ where $B'(t_1,t_2,...,t_n)$ is obtained from $B(t_1,t_2,...,t_n)$ by renaming bound variables if necessary to avoid conflicts (cf. version 1 of the second order systems in Prawitz (1965)).

The proofs in section 2 may be extended without difficulties to this new system with this new reduction. The result is of interest since it shows that in an intuitionistic framework, the axiom of choice does not destroy definability, i.e. the property that $A(T)$ is derivable for some term T if $\exists X A(X)$ is derivable.

References

H.B.Curry and R.Feys (1958), Combinatory logic (North-Holland, Amsterdam).

G.Gentzen (1935). Untersuchungen über das logische Schliessen, Mathematische Zeitschrift, vol. 39, 176–210, 405–431.

G.Gentzen (1936), Die Widerspruchsfreiheit der reinen Zahlentheorie, Mathematische Annalen, vol. 112, 493–565.

G.Gentzen (1938), Neue Fassung des Widerspruchsfreiheitsbeweises für die reine Zahlentheorie, Forschungen zur Logik und zur Grundlegung der exakten Wissenschaften, new series, no. 4 (Leipzig) 19–44.

J.Y.Girard (1970), Une extension du système de fonctionelles recursives de Gödel et son application aux fondements de l'analyse, this volume.

K.Gödel (1932), Zur intuitionistischen Arithmetik und Zahlentheorie, Ergebnisse eines mathematischen Kolloquiums, Heft 4 (for 1931–32, published 1933) 34–38.

K.Gödel (1958), Uber eine bisher noch nicht benutzte Erweiterung des finiten Standpunktes, Dialectica, vol. 12, 290–287.

N.Goodman (1968), A theory of constructions equivalent to arithmetic, in: Intuitionism and proof theory, eds. A.Kino, K.Myhill and R.E.Vesley (North-Holland, Amsterdam, 1970) 101–120.

A.Heyting (1956), Intuitionism (North-Holland, Amsterdam).

W.Howard (1968), Assignment of ordinals to terms for primitive recursive arithmetic, in: Intuitionism and proof theory, eds. A.Kino, J.Myhill and R.E.Vesley (North-Holland, Amsterdam, 1970) 443–458.

W.Howard (1969), The formulae-as-types notion of construction, privately circulated manuscript.

H.Jervell (1970), A normalform in first order arithmetic, this volume.

A.Kolmogoroff (1925), O principé tertium non datur (sur le principe de tertium non datur), Mat. Sb. (Recueil mathématique de la Société de Mathématique de Moscou) 32, 646–667.

G.Kreisel (1960), Foundations of intuitionistic logic, Logic, methodology and philosophy of science (Stanford University Press, Stanford, 1962) 192–210.

G.Kreisel (1965), Mathematical logic, in: Lectures on modern mathematics, ed. Saaty, vol. III (New York) 95–195.

G.Kreisel (1967), Mathematical logic: what has it done for the philosophy of mathematics? in: Philosopher of the century, ed. Bertrand Russell (London) 201–272.

G.Kreisel (1968), A survey of proof theory, The journal of symbolic logic 33, 321–388.

G.Kreisel (1970), A survey of proof theory II, this volume.

P.Martin-Löf (1969), Infinite terms and a system of natural deduction, mimeographed manuscript.

P.Martin-Löf (1970), Hauptsatz for the intuitionistic theory of iterated inductive definitions, this volume.

P.Martin-Löf (1970a), Hauptsatz for the theory of species, this volume.

D.Prawitz (1965), Natural deduction, A proof-theoretical study (Almquist & Wiksell, Stockholm).

D.Prawitz (1967), A note on existential instantiation, The journal of symbolic logic 32, 81–82.

D.Prawitz (1967a), Completeness and Hauptsatz for second order logic, Theoria 33, 246–258.

D.Prawitz (1968), Hauptsatz for higher order logic, The journal of symbolic logic 33, 452–457.

D.Prawitz (1968a), Some results for intuitionistic logic with second order quantification rules, in: Intuitionism and proof theory, eds. A.Kino, J.Myhill and R.E.Vesley (North-Holland, Amsterdam, 1970) 259–270.

D.Prawitz (1968b), Constructive semantics, Proceedings of the first Scandinavian logic symposium (Uppsala, 1970).

D.Prawitz (1970), On the proof theory of mathematical analysis, Logic and Value, Essays dedicated to Thorild Dahlquist on his fiftieth birthday (Uppsala).

D.Prawitz and P.-E.Malmnäs (1968), A survey of some connections between classical, intuitionistic and minimal logic, in: Contributions to mathematical logic, eds. A.Schmidt, K.Schütte and H.J.Thiele (North-Holland, Amsterdam) 215–229.

A.Raggio (1965), Gentzen's Hauptsatz for the systems NI and NK, Logique et analyse 30, 91–100.

L.E.Sanchis (1967), Functionals defined by recursion, Notre Dame journal of formal logic 8, 161–174.

B.Scarpellini (1969), Applications of Gentzen's second consistency proof, Mathematische Annalen 181, 325–354.

K.Schütte (1951), Schlussweisen-Kalküle der Prädikatenlogik, Mathematische Annalen 122, 47–65.

K.Schütte (1951a), Beweistheoretische Erfassung der unendlichen Induktion in der Zahlentheorie, Mathematische Annalen 122, 369–389.

W.Tait (1965), Infinite long terms of transfinite type I, in: Formal systems and recursive functions, eds. J.N.Crossley and M.A.E.Dummet (North-Holland, Amsterdam).

W.Tait (1966), A nonconstructive proof of Gentzen's Hauptsatz for second order predicate logic, Bulletin of the American mathematical society 72, 980–983.

W.Tait (1967), Intentional interpretation of functionals of finite type I, The journal of symbolic logic 32, 198–212.

W.Tait (1968), Normal derivability in classical logic, in: The syntax and semantics of infinitary languages, Lecture notes in mathematics, ed. J.Barwise 72 (Springer, Berlin). 204–236.

M.Takahashi (1967), A proof of cut-elimination theorem in simple type theory, The journal of the mathematical society of Japan 19, 399–410.

M.Takahashi (1970), Cut-elimination theorem and Brouwerian-valued models for intuitionistic type theory, Mathematicorum universitatis Sancti Pauli, Tokyo 1–18.

G.Takeuti (1953), On a generalized logical calculus, The japanese journal of mathematics 23, 39–96 (errata, ibid. 24 (1953) 149–156).

G.Takeuti (1967), Consistency proofs of subsystems of classical analysis, Annals of mathematics 86, 299–348.

PREDICATE-FUNCTOR LOGIC(*)

W.V.QUINE
Harvard University

Logic in its adolescent phase was algebraic. There was Boole's algebra of classes and Peirce's algebra of relations. But in 1879 logic came of age, with Frege's quantification theory. Here the bound variable, so characteristic of analysis rather than of algebra, became central to logic. This new logic came to constitute even a basic theory of the bound variable; for, all the other desired uses of bound variables can be so paraphrased as to cause the bound variables to figure solely as variables of quantification.

Once this smooth-running theory is at hand, there is some interest in translating it back into algebraic form. For, the logic of quantification excels the old algebras of classes and relations not only in flexibility, but in scope; and so it seems worth while to see what it would add up to when couched in just the blocklike sort of constants and connectives and free variables that are the stock in trade of elementary algebra. Such a translation need have no practical advantages, but it would be an algebraic explanation of the bound variable – an algebraic analysis of analysis.

Schönfinkel achieved such a translation in 1924. He dispensed even with free variables. He made do with just three constant names and a single binary connective. The names were names of three functions, and the connective was functional application. The functions were applied to one another as arguments, to yield further functions as values. In particular the function thus yielded could be a zero-place function, or truth value; and then the formula expressing it counted as a sentence and sometimes as a truth of logic. Such is the theory that was investigated and developed in the subsequent decades by Curry under the name of combinatory logic.

But if we want merely to distill the algebraic essence of the bound variable, or of quantification, then combinatory logic is too strong; for it suffices for

(*) Condensed from my "Algebraic logic and predicate functors" with the kind permission of Bobbs-Merrill and Professors Rudner and Scheffler. The work was supported in part by a grant from the National Science Foundation.

expressing not just logic but also set theory and hence mathematics generally. It is heir to all the quandaries of doctrine and proof procedure that plague general set theory.

In 1936, I presented the primitive ideas and definitions for what I called a calculus of concepts. It used free variables whose values were truth values and classes and relations of all finite degrees – that is, all finite numbers of argument places. Its power of expression was limited to roughly the scope of the logic of quantification and identity, thus shunning the outer space of general set theory. But its scope was not exactly that of the logic of quantification and identity. The discrepancy had to do with the degrees of relations. I kept my scheme somewhat abstract on that score, and this prevented full translation of quantificational schemata into it. This limitation could easily have been removed by introducing numerical indices, but I had a different interest at the time.

In 1952 and later years there appeared papers by Tarski and his pupils on what they called cylindrical algebras. One of these algebras had about the same scope of expression as my calculus of concepts. Nominally it treated only of relations of infinite degree, but for each of these relations there was a point beyond which all further argument places were vacuous; so in effect the degrees were finite and various. Moreover this algebra preserved the same abstractness, regarding degrees in this sense, as did my calculus of concepts; and thus the scope of expression of this algebra deviated from that of the logic of quantification and identity in just the same small way as did that of the calculus of concepts.

Tarski's algebras differed from my calculus of concepts in presupposing an underlying logic of truth functions and identity; my scheme was autonomous, and the truth functions and identity were definable within it. Tarski's algebras were fully axiomatized; I had left my calculus of concepts in a programmatic state, without axioms.

Bernays, in 1959, presented an algebra which took Tarski's as its point of departure but resolved the abstractness of degree by use of numerical indices. He showed that his algebra is exactly equal in power of expression to the logic of quantification and identity; the two are intertranslatable. Also he presented axioms and proved them complete. His algebra, like Tarski's, was rested upon a prior logic of truth functions and identity.

All these systems – Bernays's, Tarski's, and my early scheme – were presented as algebras whose elements were classes of sequences. A denumerable universe of such classes – finite for each length of sequence – is rich enough for these systems. But in point of fact there is no need here to think in set-theoretic terms at all, however modest. This is not to say that these algebras can be disinterpreted and treated as abstract algebras; that would be a trivial remark. My point is rather that we can treat these so-called free class variables simply as schematic predicate letters, on a par with those of the ordinary logic of quantification.

So much by way of historical background. Now I want to sketch a system which departs from that of Bernays in the following ways. Rather than presupposing a logic of truth functions and identity, it is autonomous. Rather than treating of classes, it operates with schematic predicate letters in the manner of the logic of quantification. These letters still carry indices, however, like Bernays's class variables, to indicate degree; for we cannot determine degree simply by counting the argument variables, as in quantification theory, there being no longer any such variables. There are also other departures from Bernays, having to do only with economy; I shall not indicate them, but merely describe my system as it turns out. It is an improvement of one that I published in 1960.

There are six functors on predicates, and one constant two-place predicate. Using extraneous notation I can explain them thus:

Complementation $-F^n x_1 .. x_n \equiv \sim (F^n x_1 .. x_n)$ (1)

Intersection $(F^m \cap G^n) x_1 .. x_{\max(m,n)} \equiv F^m x_1 .. x_m \cdot G^n x_1 .. x_n$ (2)

Major permutation $\mathrm{P} F^n x_2 .. x_n x_1 \equiv F^n x_1 .. x_n$ (3)

Minor permutation $\mathrm{p} F^n x_2 x_1 x_3 .. x_n \equiv F^n x_1 .. x_n$ (4)

Padding $[F^n x_0 .. x_n \equiv F^n x_1 .. x_n$ (5)

Cropping $] F^n x_2 .. x_n \equiv (\exists x_1) F^n x_1 .. x_n$ (6)

Identity $Ixy \equiv x = y$. (7)

Where $m = n = 0$, complementation and intersection provide the truth functions; for predicates of degree 0 are sentences.

$$-F^0 \equiv \sim F^0 , \qquad F^0 \cap G^0 \equiv F^0 \cdot G^0 .$$

The notation proper contains no 'x's; no variables, free or bound, apart from the schematic predicate letters.

The notation of this logic, which I call *predicate-functor logic,* is *just* adequate to the ordinary logic of quantification and identity. Let us see first how to translate any formula of this notation step by step into ordinary logical notation. An example will suffice:

$$\rceil(G^1 \cap \rceil -\mathrm{p}(H^2 \cap \rceil K^2)), \tag{8}$$

$$(\exists x)(G^1 \cap \rceil -\mathrm{p}(H^2 \cap \rceil K^2))x, \qquad \text{(by (6); } n{=}1\text{)}$$

$$(\exists x)(G^1 x \cdot \rceil -\mathrm{p}(H^2 \cap \rceil K^2)x), \qquad \text{(by (2); } m{=}n{=}1\text{)}$$

$$(\exists x)(G^1 x \cdot (\exists y) -\mathrm{p}(H^2 \cap \rceil K^2)yx), \qquad \text{(by (6); } n{=}2\text{)}$$

$$(\exists x)(G^1 x \cdot (\exists y) \sim \mathrm{p}(H^2 \cap \rceil K^2)yx), \qquad \text{(by (1); } n{=}2\text{)}$$

$$(\exists x)(G^1 x \cdot (\exists y) \sim (H^2 \cap \rceil K^2)xy), \qquad \text{(by (4); } n{=}2\text{)}$$

$$(\exists x)(G^1 x \cdot (\exists y) \sim (H^2 xy \cdot \rceil K^2 x)), \qquad \text{(by (2); } m{=}2, n{=}1\text{)}$$

$$(\exists x)(G^1 x \cdot (\exists y) \sim (H^2 xy \cdot (\exists z) K^2 zx)). \qquad \text{(by (6); } n{=}2\text{)}$$

Toward showing, conversely, how to translate closed formulas of ordinary logic into predicate-functor logic, it is convenient to adopt the following three abbreviations. Parenthetical exponents mean iteration.

Cartesian product	$'F^m \times G^n'$ for $'F^m \cap \lceil^{(m)} G^n'$.	
Reflection	$'\mathrm{S}F^n'$ for $'\rceil(I \cap F^n)'$.	
i-th permutation	$'\mathrm{p}_i F^n'$ for $'(\mathrm{Pp})^{(n-i)}\mathrm{P}^{(i-1)}F^n'$.	

It is clear from (2) and (5) that the definition of Cartesian product has this effect:

$$(F^m \times G^n)x_1 \ldots x_m y_1 \ldots y_n \equiv F^m x_1 \ldots x_m \cdot G^n y_1 \ldots y_n \,. \tag{9}$$

By (2) and (7), moreover,

$$(I \cap F^n)x_1 \ldots x_n \equiv x_1 = x_2 \cdot F^n x_1 \ldots x_n \,, \qquad (n>1) \tag{10}$$

so, by (6), the definition of reflection has this effect:

$$\mathrm{S}F^n x_2 \ldots x_n \equiv F^n x_2 x_2 \ldots x_n \,. \tag{11}$$

Finally it can be verified from (3) and (4) that the definition of the i-th permutation has this effect:

$$\mathrm{p}_i F^n x_i x_1 x_2 \ldots x_{i-1} x_{i+1} \ldots x_n \equiv F^n x_1 \ldots x_n \,. \tag{12}$$

To translate any closed formula of ordinary logic, we begin by translating all universal quantifiers into existential quantification and negation. Then we translate the scope of each innermost existential quantifier into alternational normal form and distribute the quantifier through the alternation. Thereupon each innermost quantifier comes to govern, at worst, a conjunction of atomic formulas with or without negation signs attached to them. Here is a typical innermost quantification at this stage:

$$(\exists y)(\sim(y=z) \cdot F^3 zyz \cdot \sim F^3 xyz) \,.$$

Then we proceed to translate each such innermost quantification. The present example goes through these stages:

$$(\exists y)(-Iyz \cdot F^3 zyz \cdot -F^3 xyz) \,, \qquad \text{(by (1) and (7))}$$

$$(\exists y)((-I \times F^3 \times -F^3) yzzyzxyz) \,, \qquad \text{(by (9))}$$

$$(\exists y)(\mathrm{p}_4(-I \times F^3 \times -F^3) yyzzzxyz) \,, \qquad \text{(by (12))}$$

$$(\exists y)(\mathrm{p}_7 \mathrm{p}_4(-I \times F^3 \times -F^3) yyyzzzxz) \,, \qquad \text{(by (12))}$$

$$(\exists y)(\mathrm{SSp}_7 \mathrm{p}_4(-I \times F^3 \times -F^3) yzzzxz) \,, \qquad \text{(by (11))}$$

$$\text{Ɉ}\mathrm{SSp}_7 \mathrm{p}_4(-I \times F^3 \times -F^3) zzzxz \,. \qquad \text{(by (6))}$$

This is how we eliminate each innermost quantifier. Applying this method then to each surviving quantifier as it becomes innermost, we eliminate all quantifiers and hence all bound variables. In particular a closed formula of ordinary logic thus goes over into a formula purely of predicate-functor logic, devoid of individual variables altogether.

Since the predicate-functor approach to logic differs so radically from the quantificational approach, one wonders how a simple proof procedure for it might look, and what new light it might shed on logic. What is wanted here, in contradistinction to the algebras of Tarski and Bernays, is an autonomous proof procedure presupposing no prior logic.

Instead of seeking as theorems only schemata of degree 0 whose instances are true sentences, it is convenient to welcome as theorems all schemata of any degree n that are *valid* in this extended sense: their instances are predicates satisfied by all n-length sequences. As an infinite initial stock of axioms, then, we may accept all tautologous Boolean functions; that is, all compounds built of '$-$' and '$\cap$' after the pattern of a truth-table tautology in '$\sim$' and '$\cdot$'. A natural rule of inference to adopt is the analogue, in these Boolean terms, of *modus ponens*; viz.,

$$\text{If} \vdash \zeta \text{ and} \vdash \ulcorner \zeta \mathbin{\text{ɔ}} \eta \urcorner \text{ then} \vdash \eta$$

where the *implex* $F^m \mathbin{\text{ɔ}} G^n$ is defined as $-(F^m \cap - G^n)$. Further there is this quadruple rule:

$$\text{If} \vdash \zeta \text{ then} \vdash \ulcorner \mathrm{P}\zeta \urcorner, \vdash \ulcorner \mathrm{p}\zeta \urcorner, \vdash \ulcorner \mathbf{[}\zeta \urcorner, \text{ and } \vdash \ulcorner - \mathbf{]} - \zeta \urcorner .$$

Also a rule of substitution for predicate letters is wanted, allowing substitution of schemata of any degree for predicate letters of that degree. This rule presupposes a rule for computing the degree of a schema: padding adds 1, cropping subtracts 1, and intersection takes the higher of two degrees.

Some of the axioms that suggest themselves, in addition to the Boolean tautologies, are these:

$$\mathbf{]}I , \qquad F^n \mathbin{\text{ɔ}} \mathbf{[}\,\mathbf{]} F^n , \qquad (I \cap F^n) \mathbin{\text{ɔ}} \mathrm{p}F^n .$$

To understand the last of these three, recall (10).

It is convenient to adopt as an abbreviation one more Boolean functor along with 'ɔ'. The *concourse* or symmetric quotient $F^m \# G^n$ is defined as $(F^m \mathbin{\text{ɔ}} G^n) \cap (G^n \mathbin{\text{ɔ}} F^m)$; thus it is $(F^m \cap G^n) \cup (-F^m \cap -G^n)$(*). Just as 'c' as main connective in an axiom does the work of '$\supset$', so '#' does the work of '$\equiv$' or '$=$'. Provision would be made for a metatheorem allowing replacement, anywhere, of one side of a proved concourse by the other.

Here are some likely further axioms.

(*) The names "implex" and "concourse" and their symbols are from my *System of Logistic.*

$$F^n \# \mathrm{pp}F^n , \qquad F^n \# \mathrm{p}^{(n)}F^n , \qquad F^n \#]\,[\,F^n , \qquad F^n \# \mathrm{P}[\,F^n .$$

To understand this last schema, we must consider how the generality of (2) affects the concourse. We get:

$$(F^n \# \mathrm{P}[\,F^n)x_1 ... x_{n+1} \equiv F^n x_1 ... x_n \equiv \mathrm{P}[\,F^n x_1 ... x_{n+1} .$$

Also there are these distribution laws:

$$\mathrm{p} - F^n \# -\mathrm{P}F^n , \qquad \mathrm{P}(F^m \cap G^n) \# (\mathrm{P}F^m \cap \mathrm{P}G^n) ,$$

$$\mathrm{p} - F^n \# -\mathrm{p}F^n , \qquad \mathrm{p}(F^m \cap G^n) \# (\mathrm{p}F^m \cap \mathrm{p}G^n) .$$

A straggler to notice, among perhaps others, is '$\mathrm{P}F^2 \# \mathrm{p}F^2$'. A major agendum is a proof of the completeness of some such proof procedure, or, better, of some other and more instructively unified sort of proof procedure for predicate-functor logic.

References

[1] P.Bernays, Ueber eine natürliche Erweiterung des Relationenkalküls, in: Constructivity in Mathematics, ed. A.Heyting (North-Holland, Amsterdam, 1959) pp. 1–14.

[2] H.B.Curry and R.Feys, Combinatory Logic (North-Holland, Amsterdam, 1958).

[3] L.Henkin, The representation theorem for cylindrical algebras, in: Mathematical Interpretation of Formal Systems, T.Skolem et al. (North-Holland, Amsterdam, 1955).

[4] W.V.Quine, A System of Logistic (Harvard University Press, Cambridge, 1934).

[5] W.V.Quine, Toward a calculus of concepts, Journal of Symbolic Logic 1 (1936) 2–25.

[6] W.V.Quine, Variables explained away, Proceedings of the American Philosophical Society 104 (1960) 343–347. Reprinted in Selected Logic Papers (Random House, New York, 1966).

[7] W.V.Quine, Algebraic logic and predicate functors, in: Logic and Art: Essays in Honor of Nelson Goodman, eds. R.Rudner and I.Scheffler (Bobbs-Merrill, Indianapolis) at press.

[8] M.Schönfinkel, Ueber die Bausteine der mathematischen Logik, Mathematische Annalen 92 (1924) 305–316. Translated and discussed in: From Frege to Gödel, ed. J.van Heijenoort (Harvard University Press, Cambridge, 1966).

[9] A.Tarski, A representation theorem for cylindrical algebras, Bulletin of the American Mathematical Society 58 (1952) 65–66.

INFINITE FORCING IN MODEL THEORY

Abraham ROBINSON(*)
Yale University

1. Introduction

The present paper is one of a series which is concerned with the application of the forcing concept to Model Theory [1], [5]. Here we concentrate on the consideration of infinite forcing conditions. We obtain results which are analogous to several of those obtained previously for finite forcing but also find significant differences. Next we establish a new link between the forcing relation and the classical concepts of Model Theory, and this leads us to a kind of compactness theorem for forcing and to the axiomatization of classes of generic structures by infinitary sentences. Some of these results are developed also for finite forcing.

Although this is not essential for our purposes we shall adopt an approach which is fundamentally different from that used earlier, in that we shall identify forcing conditions with *structures* rather than with sets of basic sentences.

2. Foundations

Let Σ be a class of *similar* first order structures (i.e., "the same" or more precisely, corresponding, relations and functions are defined in all elements of Σ). In addition, Σ may include also the empty set, $\emptyset$, but should include at least one structure in the usual sense.

Our formal language will be the Lower Predicate Calculus with equality, to be interpreted always as the identity. We shall take it for granted that equality is included in the vocabulary of any set of axioms K under consideration and hence, is included in the diagram of every model of K. A well formed formula (wff) is said to be *defined* in a structure M if all individual constants, relation

(*) Research supported in part by the National Science Foundation Grant No. GP-8625.

symbols, and function symbols of X are interpreted in M. In general, we shall not mention the correspondence which provided this interpretation explicitly but shall take it for granted that if a number of wff are considered simultaneously in relation to a number of structures then their extralogical constants denote the same individuals or "the same" relations or functions in all of these structures. Different individual constants may denote the same individual.

We define a ranking of wff as follows. If X is atomic then it is of rank 1, $r(X) = 1$. Also

$$r(X \wedge Y) = r(X \vee Y) = r(X) + r(Y)$$

$$r(\neg X) = r((\exists y)X) = r(X) + 1 .$$

Only the connectives $\vee, \wedge$, and $\neg$ and only the existential quantifier will be regarded as basic so that these rules provide a unique ranking for all wffs.

For a given Σ we define a relation $M \Vdash X$, M *forces* X between elements $M \neq \emptyset$ of Σ and sentences X *which are defined in* M, as follows.

2.1. For an atomic sentence X, $M \Vdash X$ if and only if $M \models X$, M satisfies X; $M \Vdash X$ where $X = Y \wedge Z$ if and only if $M \Vdash Y$ and $M \Vdash Z$; $M \Vdash X$ where $X = Y \vee Z$ if and only if M forces at least one of Y and Z; $M \Vdash X$ where $X = (\exists y)\sigma(y)$ if and only if $M \Vdash Q(a)$ for some constant a. Finally (as the only but crucial departure from the satisfaction relation) $M \Vdash X$ where $X = \neg Y$ if and only if there is no $M' \in \Sigma$ which is an extension of M such that $M' \Vdash Y$.

If Σ contains only a single proper structure, M, then it is not difficult to see that if a sentence X is defined in M then $M \Vdash X$ if and only if $M \models X$. Thus, in this case, the forcing relation and the satisfaction relation coincide. We may therefore regard the forcing relation more generally as a generalization of the relation of satisfaction. We shall refrain from entering into a discussion of the philosophical significance of these matters.

The following lemmas, which are familiar from earlier theories [2], [5], [1] are immediate consequences of the definition 2.1.

2.2. **Lemma.** $M \in \Sigma$ *cannot force both* X *and* $\neg X$.

2.3. **Lemma.** *If* $M, M' \in \Sigma$, $M \subset M'$ *and* $M \Vdash X$ *then* $M' \Vdash X$.

Now let K be a non-empty and consistent set of sentences. We define $\Sigma = \Sigma_K$ as the class of all structures which are consistent with K, i.e. which are substructures of models of K, together with the empty set. (It is understood that if functions are present, a substructure is closed under their application.) Then Σ_K is closed under union of chains (inductive). That is to say, if $S = \{M\}$ is a monotonic subset of Σ (M, M$' \in S$ entails M $\subset$ M$'$ or M$' \subset$ M) then $\bigcup S \in \Sigma$.

An element M of Σ_K is called K-generic if all sentences of K are defined (but do not necessarily hold) in M and if for every sentence X which is defined in M, M forces either X or $\neg X$ (but not both, by 2.2). Our conditions imply that M $\neq \emptyset$, M is a proper structure.

2.4. **Theorem.** *Let* M $\in \Sigma$. *Then* M *is contained in a* K-*generic structure* M* $\in \Sigma$.

Proof. For a given M, let $M_0 \supset M$ be a model of K. Range all sentences which are defined in M_0, in a vocabulary which includes constants for all elements of M (and which is compatible with the interpretation by which M_0 is a model of K, see above), in a well-ordered set $\{X_{0\nu}\}_{\nu<\alpha}$ where α is an initial ordinal (i.e. a cardinal) $\geqslant \omega$. Define a well-ordered set of elements of Σ, $\{M_{0\nu}\}_{\nu<\alpha}$, as follows. Put $M_{00} = M_0$. For any successor ordinal $\nu = \mu^+$, consider $X_{0\mu}$. If $M_{0\mu} \Vdash X_{0\mu}$ and also if $M_{0\mu} \Vdash \neg X_{0\mu}$, define $M_{0\nu} = M_{0\mu}$. If neither of these relations holds there exists an $M' \supset M_{0\mu}$ such that $M' \Vdash X_{0\mu}$. Choose one of these M$'$ and call it $M_{0\nu}$. For every limit ordinal ν, put $M_{0\nu} = \bigcup_{\mu<\nu} M_{0\mu}$. Having thus defined the sequence $\{M_{0\nu}\}$ put $M_1 = \bigcup_{\nu<\alpha} M_{0\nu}$. Then for all $X_{0\nu}$, $\nu<\alpha$, either $M_1 \Vdash H_{0\nu}$ or $M_1 \Vdash \neg X_{0\nu}$.

Next, extend the vocabulary introduced previously for M_0, so as to include symbols for all the individuals of M_1. Range all sentences which are formulated in this vocabulary and, hence, are defined in M_1, as a well ordered set $\{X_{1\nu}\}_{\nu<\beta}$ where β is an initial ordinal $\geqslant\omega$. Then all elements of $\{X_{0\nu}\}$ appear also in $\{X_{1\nu}\}$. Apply the same procedure as before to obtain an $M_2 \in \Sigma$, $M_2 \supset M_1$ such that for all $X_{1\nu}$, $\nu < \beta$, either $M_2 \Vdash X_{1\nu}$ or $M_2 \Vdash \neg X_{1\nu}$. Continuing in this way, obtain a sequence of structures of Σ, $M \subset M_0 \subset M_1 \subset M_2 \subset \ldots$. Finally, put $M^* = \bigcup M_n$. Since every sentence X defined in M* in the vocabulary introduced step by step must be defined already in some M_n we then have either $M_{n+1} \Vdash X$ or $M_{n+1} \Vdash \neg X$ and hence, either $M^* \Vdash X$ or $M^* \Vdash \neg X$. Although this conclusion was obtained in the first instance only for sentences X defined in M* in terms of a particular vocabulary, it will be seen that, for any X, the forcing relation with respect to M really depends only on the individuals denoted by the individual constants of X, and not on the particular notation. Accordingly, either $M^* \Vdash X$ or $M^* \Vdash \neg X$ for any X defined in M^* consistently with the interpretation of the extralogical symbols of K. This completes the proof of 2.4.

2.5. **Theorem.** *In order that a structure* M *of* Σ *be* K*-generic it is necessary and sufficient that the sentences of* K *be defined in* M *and that for every sentence* X *defined in* M, $M \models X$ *if and only if* $M \Vdash X$.

Proof. The condition is sufficient. For since, for any sentence X defined in M either $M \models X$ or $M \models \neg X$ we then have either $M \Vdash X$ or $M \models \neg X$.

For necessity, we suppose that M is K-generic and we carry out the proof by induction on the rank of X. If X is atomic, $r(X) = 1$, then the assertion follows immediately from 2.1. Suppose $r(X) = n > 1$ and suppose that the assertion has been proved for sentences of rank less than n.

If $X = Y \wedge Z$, then $r(Y) < n$, $r(Z) < n$, hence if $M \models X$ then $M \models Y$, $M \models Z$, $M \Vdash Y$, $M \Vdash Z$, $M \Vdash X$. Also, if $M \Vdash X$ then $M \Vdash Y$, $M \Vdash Z$, $M \models Y$, $M \models Z$, $M \models X$. The proof is similar if X is of one of the forms $X = Y \vee Z$ or $X = (\exists y)Q(y)$. If $X = \neg Y$, so that $r(Y) = n - 1$, then if $M \models X$, it cannot be true that $M \models Y$. Hence it cannot be true that $M \Vdash Y$, hence $M \Vdash \neg Y$, $M \Vdash X$. If $M \Vdash X$ then $M \models X$. For if not $M \models X$ then $M \models Y$, hence $M \Vdash Y$ which is incompatible with $M \Vdash X$, by 2.2. This completes the argument.

Thus, the condition of 2.5 may also be used as an alternative definition for the notion of a K-generic structure. It says that a proper structure M is K-generic if and only if K is defined in M and the relations of satisfaction and forcing on M coincide. We may also replace "$M \models X$ if and only if $M \Vdash X$" by "$M \models X$ entails $M \Vdash X$".

Let $M \in \Sigma$ and let X be any sentence with relation and function symbols from K but whose individual constants are not necessarily defined in M. Then we say that M *forces* X *weakly*, in symbols, $M \Vdash^* X$ if and only if there is no $M' \in \Sigma$, $M' \supset M$ such that $M' \Vdash \neg X$. If X is defined in M then $M \Vdash^* X$ if and only if $M \Vdash \neg\neg X$. This will be the case, more particularly, if $M \Vdash X$. Also if X is defined in M and $M \Vdash^* \neg X$ then $M \Vdash \neg X$. If $M \Vdash^* X$ and $M' \supset M$ for $M' \in \Sigma$ then $M' \Vdash^* X$. Also, no $M \in \Sigma$ can force weakly both X and $\neg X$ for if $M \Vdash^* \neg X$ and $M' \supset M$ is an element of Σ_K in which X is defined then M' cannot force $\neg\neg X$. Accordingly, $M'' \Vdash \neg X$ for some $M'' \supset M'$ and so M cannot force X weakly. It follows from 2.4 and 2.5 that $M \Vdash^* X$ if and only if X holds in all K-generic structures $M' \supset M$ in which it is defined.

3. The forcing operator

Let K be a non-empty and consistent set of sentences, as before. For any $M \in \Sigma_K$, we define $K^F(M)$ as the set of all sentences which are defined in K and which are forced weakly by M. In particular, we put $K^F = K^F(\emptyset)$ and we call K^F the *forcing companion* of K, and F the *forcing operator*. We may qualify "forcing" by "infinite" if we have to distinguish these concepts from corresponding ones in the theory of forcing by finite conditions [1], [5]. It follows from the remark at the end of section 2 that K^F consists of all sentences which are defined in K and which hold in all K-generic structures of Σ_K. We shall regard it as one of the central aims of our theory to investigate the properties of K^F and of its models, for given K. *We assume throughout that* K *is non-empty and consistent.*

3.1. **Theorem.** *Let* M *and* M′ *be* K*-generic structures in* Σ_K *such that* $M' \supset M$. *Then* M′ *is an elementary extension of* M.

Proof. Let X be defined in M such that $M \models X$. Then $M \Vdash X$, hence $M' \Vdash X$, hence $M' \models X$. This proves the assertion.

A well formed formula is existential if it is either (i) free of quantifiers or (ii) a conjunction or a disjunction of existential formulae or (iii) of the form $(\exists y)X$ where X is existential. An existential formula is logically equivalent to a prenex existential formula. If an existential formula holds in a structure M then it holds in all extensions of M.

Similarly, a wff is *universal* if it is either (i) free of quantifiers, or (ii) a conjunction or disjunction of universal formulae, or (iii) of the form $(\forall y)X$ (i.e. $\neg[(\exists y)[\neg X]]$) where X is universal. A universal formula is logically equivalent to a prenex universal formula.

3.2. **Theorem.** *Let* M *be a* K*-generic structure and let* $M' \supset M$ *be a model of* K. *Let X be any existential sentence which is defined in* M *and holds in* M′. *Then X holds also in* M.

Proof. Let M″ be a K-generic structure in Σ_K which is an extension of M′. Such an M″ exists, by 2.4. Then $M'' \models X$, since X is existential, and $M \models X$ by 3.1.

X is *an* $\forall E$*-sentence* if it is of the form

3.3. $$X = (\forall y_1)...(\forall y_m)(\exists z_1)...(\exists z_n)Q(y_1,...,y_m,z_1,...,z_n),$$

$$m \geqslant 0, n \geqslant 0$$

where Q does not contain any quantifiers.

3.4. **Theorem.** *Let* M *be a* K*-generic structure and let* $M' \supset M$ *be a model of* K. *Let* X *be any* $\forall\exists$*-sentence which is defined in* M′. *Then* X *holds also in* M.

Proof. Suppose that X is given by 3.3. Then we have to show that, for any $a_1, ..., a_m$ denoting elements of M, $Y = (\exists z_1)...(\exists z_n)Q(a_1,...,a_m,z_1,...,z_n)$ holds in M. But this follows immediately from 3.2 and the fact that Y holds in M′.

3.5. **Corollary.** *Let* X *be an* $\forall\exists$ *sentence or a universal sentence or an existential sentence which is defined in (the vocabulary of)* K *and deducible from it. Then* $X \in K^F$.

Proof. For any $\forall\exists$ sentence X the assertion follows from 3.4. For let $M \in \Sigma_K$, M generic, then M is a substructure of a model M′ of K, and $M' \models X$, and so $M \models X$, as required. For X universal or existential, the result follows from the fact that X is then logically equivalent to a sentence of class $\forall\exists$ (with $n = 0$ or $m = 0$). For X universal we can also argue directly from the fact that a universal sentence persists under passage to substructures.

3.6. **Theorem.** *The class of* K*-generic structures in* Σ_K *is inductive (closed under union of chains).*

Proof. Let S be a monotonic set of K-generic structures in Σ_K. We have to show that $M = \cup S$ is a K-generic structure. Let X be any sentence which is defined in M. Then X is defined also in some $M' \in S$. Since M′ is K-generic, either $M' \Vdash X$, entailing $M \Vdash X$ or $M' \Vdash \neg X$, and so $M \Vdash \neg X$. This proves the assertion.

Let $K_\forall$ be the set of the universal sentences which are defined in, and deducible from, K. $K_\forall$ will be called the *universal part* of K. Two sets of sentences with the same universal part may be called universally equivalent.

A structure is consistent with K if and only if it is consistent with $K_\forall$, $\Sigma_K = \Sigma_{K_\forall}$. Moreover, since $K_\forall$ is universal, every substructure of a model of K satisfies all sentences of $K_\forall$ which are defined in it. Thus, Σ_K consists of all structures which satisfy the sentences of $K_\forall$ defined in them.

The K-generic structures are determined directly from Σ_K without reference back to K. Hence

3.7. **Theorem.** $K^F = (K_\forall)^F$.

Next, we prove

3.8. **Theorem.** $(K^F)_\forall = K_\forall$.

Proof. Let X be a universal sentence in the vocabulary of K or, which is the same, of K^F, such that $K^F \vdash X$. Suppose that X is not deducible from K then $\neg X$ (which is logically equivalent to an existential sentence) holds in some model M of K and, hence, holds in some K-generic structure $M' \supset M$. But M' is a model of K^F, and so $M' \models X$, a contradiction. This proves $(K^F)_\forall \subset K_\forall$. On the other hand, if the universal sentence X is deducible from K then (by 3.5, or directly) X is deducible also from K^F or, more precisely, belongs to it. This proves 3.8.

3.9. **Corollary.** $K^{FF} = K^F$.

This follows immediately from 3.8.

3.10. **Theorem.** For any K_1 and K_2, $K_1^F = K_2^F$ if and only if $K_{1\forall} = K_{2\forall}$.

Proof. 3.7. shows that the condition is sufficient. It is also necessary since $K_1^F = K_2^F$ entails $(K_1^F)_\forall = (K_2^F)_\forall$ or, which is the same, $K_{1\forall} = K_{2\forall}$.

The equation $K_{1\forall} = K_{2\forall}$ has a simple model-theoretic interpretation.

3.11. **Theorem.** *Let* K_1 *and* K_2 *be two non-empty and consistent sets of sentences which are formulated in the same vocabulary. Then* $K_{2\forall} \subset K_{1\forall}$ *if and only if* K_2 *is model-consistent relative to* K_1, *i.e. if and only if every model of* K_1 *can be embedded in a model of* K_2.

Suppose that M is a model of K_1 which cannot be embedded in a model of K_2. Then there exists an existential sentence, X, which is defined in K_2 such that $M \models X$ but $K_2 \vdash \neg X$. Rewriting $\neg X$ as a universal sentence Y we then have $Y \in K_{2\forall}$. But M does not satisfy Y, hence $Y \notin K_{1\forall}$, $K_{2\forall}$ is not a subset of $K_{1\forall}$. This shows that the condition is necessary.

Conversely, suppose that $K_{2\forall}$ is not a subset of $K_{1\forall}$ and let $Y \in K_{2\forall} - K_{1\forall}$. Then there exists a model M of $K_{1\forall}$ which satisfies $\neg Y$, and since $\neg Y$

is logically equivalent to an existential sentence, it follows that $\neg Y$ holds in all extensions of M. Hence, no such structure can be a model of K_2.

3.12. **Corollary.** *Let* K *and* K_2 *be two non-empty and consistent sets of sentences which are formulated in the same vocabulary. Then* $K_{2\forall} = K_{1\forall}$ *if and only if* K_1 *and* K_2 *are mutually model-consistent.*

4. The joint embedding property

Let K be a non-empty and consistent set of sentences, as before, and Let M_1 and M_2 be two structures whose relations and functions are denoted by symbols of K. When is there a model M of K which is an extension both of M_1 and of M_2? Before answering this question, we observe that, in practice, it may be taken for granted that certain elements of M_1 and M_2 are mapped on the same element in M. This requirement may be due to the fact that the elements in question have the same name, i.e. are denoted by the same symbol, for example if that symbol belongs to K. Thus, let $A \to M_1$ and $A \to M_2$ be mappings of a set of individual constants A into M_1 and M_2 respectively. Then our precise question is, whether there exist injections $M_1 \to M$, $M_2 \to M$ such that

$$\begin{array}{ccccc} & & M_1 & & \\ & \nearrow & & \searrow & \\ A & & & & M \\ & \searrow & & \nearrow & \\ & & M_2 & & \end{array}$$

is commutative. It is understood that at the same time, the constants of A which occur also in K are mapped on the same elements of M as they are in the interpretation of K in M.

4.1. **Theorem.** *For given* K, A, M_1 *and* M_2, *there exists a joint embedding of* M_1 *and* M_2 *in a model* M *of* K, *as detailed above, if and only if for any existential sentences* X_1 *and* X_2 *whose individual constants belong to* A *or to* K *and such that* $M_1 \models X_1$, $M_2 \models X_2$, *the set* $K \cup \{X_1, X_2\}$ *is consistent.*

Remarks. In the statement of the above theorem, "existential" may be replaced by "primitive", where we recall that an existential sentence is primitive if it is prenex and if its matrix is a conjunction of basic wff, i.e. of atomic wff and (or) the negations of atomic wff.

Proof of 4.1. Choose diagrams D_1 and D_2 of M_1 and M_2 respectively such that both D_1 and D_2 include A but have no other individual constants in common with each other. Then any model M of $K \cup D_1 \cup D_2$ provides embeddings $M_1 \to M$, $M_2 \to M$, as required and, conversely, any M which satisfies the stated conditions for a joint embedding is a model of $K \cup D_1 \cup D_2$. Accordingly, such a joint embedding exists if and only if $K \cup D_1 \cup D_2$ is consistent.

Suppose first that $K \cup D_1 \cup D_2$ is not consistent. Then there exist basic sentences $Y_1, ..., Y_k \in D_1$, $Z_1, ..., Z_m \in D_2$ such that $K \cup \{Y_1, ..., Y_k, Z_1, ..., Z_m\}$ is inconsistent. Put $Y_1 \wedge ... \wedge Y_k = Y(a_1,...,a_l)$, $Z_1 \wedge ... \wedge Z_m = Z(b_1,..., b_l)$ where the constants that have been displayed are those that do not belong to A or K, and introduce

$$X_1 = (\exists x_1) ... (\exists x_l) Y(x_1,...,x_l),\ X_2 = (\exists x_1) ... (\exists x_n) Z(x_1,...,x_n) .$$

Then a simple application of the predicate calculus shows that $K \cup \{X_1, X_2\}$ is inconsistent, the condition of the theorem is sufficient (even if we assume it only for *primitive* X_1, X_2).

Conversely, suppose that there always exist embeddings of M_1 and M_2 into a structure M as detailed above. Let X_1 and X_2 be existential sentences whose individual constants belong to A or K such that $M_1 \models X_1$, $M_2 \models X_2$. Then both X_1 and X_2 hold in M, with the same interpretation of the individual constants which appear in them. But M is a model of K, with the same interpretation for the individual constants of A and so $K \cup \{X_1, X_2\}$ is consistent.

We shall say that the set K has the *joint embedding property* if any two models M_1 and M_2 of K can be embedded in a model M of K as detailed above, where A is the set of individual constants in K.

4.2. **Theorem.** *In order that the set* K *have the joint embedding property, it is necessary and sufficient that for any two existential sentences* X_1 *and* X_2 *which are defined in, and consistent with* K, $\{X_1, X_2\}$ *also is consistent with* K.

Proof. The condition is sufficient. Taking for A in 4.1 the set of individual constants of K, we have to show that if $M_1 \models X_1$ and $M_2 \models X_2$ for two models M_1 and M_2 of K then $K \cup \{X_1, X_2\}$ is consistent. But $M_1 \models X_1$ entails that X_1 is consistent with K and, similarly, X_2 is consistent with K. The condition of 4.2 now ensures that $K \cup \{X_1, X_2\}$ is consistent.

The condition is also necessary. For suppose that it is satisfied and let M_1 and M_2 be models of $K \cup \{X_1\}$ and $K \cup \{X_2\}$ respectively. Then M_1 and M_2 can be jointly embedded in a model M of K, and M satisfies both X_1 and X_2, with the same interpretation for the constants of these sentences. It follows that $K \cup \{X_1, X_2\}$ is consistent.

Passing to the negations of existential sentences, and writing them in universal form, it is not difficult to see that 4.2 is equivalent to the following.

4.3. **Theorem.** *In order that the set* K *possess the joint embedding property, it is necessary and sufficient that for any two universal sentences* X_1 *and* X_2 *which are defined in* K *and such that* $X_1 \vee X_2 \in K_\forall$ *(or, equivalently, such that* $K \vdash X_1 \vee X_2$*) at least one of* X_1 *and* X_2 *belongs to* $K_\forall$.

In the language of the metamathematical theory of ideals, the condition 4.3 states that $K_\forall$ is *irreducible* in the domain of universal sentences.

4.4. **Theorem.** *For* K^F *to be complete, it is necessary and sufficient that* K *possess the joint embedding property.*

See [5] foı the corresponding result in the theory of forcing by finite conditions.

Proof. Suppose that K possesses the joint embedding property. Let X be any sentence in the vocabulary of K. We have to show that either $\emptyset \Vdash^* X$ or $\emptyset \Vdash^* \neg X$. If this is not the case then there exist structures $P_1 \in \Sigma_K, P_2 \in \Sigma_K$ such that $P_1 \Vdash \neg X$, $P_2 \Vdash \neg\neg X$. Also, by the definition of Σ_K there exist models M_1, M_2 of K which are extensions of P_1 and P_2 respectively. Then $M_1 \Vdash \neg X$, $M_2 \Vdash \neg\neg X$. By the joint embedding property, there exists a model M of K in which M_1 and M_2 can be embedded simultaneously. Hence $M \Vdash \neg X$, $M \Vdash \neg\neg X$, which is impossible.

Suppose next that K^F is complete and let X_1 and X_2 be two universal sentences which are defined in K. Assume that $X_1 \notin K_\forall$, $X_2 \notin K_\forall$. But $K_\forall = (K^F)_\forall$ and K^F is complete, consistent, and deductively closed. Hence $\neg X_1 \in K^F$, $\neg X_2 \in K^F$, $\neg(X_1 \vee X_2) \in K^F$, $X_1 \vee X_2 \notin K^F$, $X_1 \vee X_2$ cannot be contained in $(K^F)_\forall = K_\forall$. This shows that K possesses the joint embedding property, by 4.3.

To sum up, the forcing operator selects one set K^F from every class of mutually model-consistent sets K. The set K^F is complete if and only if K possesses the joint embedding property.

5. Forcing companions and model companions

Let K be a non-empty and consistent set of sentences, as before. The set K* will be called a model companion of K if K* has the same vocabulary as K, is mutually model-consistent with K and is model-complete. In particular, if K* has the same vocabulary as K, is an extension of K, and is model-consistent and model-complete relative to K, then it is called a model completion of K (compare [1], [5], [6]). Up to logical equivalence, K cannot possess more than one model companion (and hence, cannot possess more than one model completion) as is shown by the following theorem.

5.1. **Theorem.** *Let* K_1^* *and* K_2^* *be two model companions of a set of sentences* K. *Then* $K_1^* \equiv K_2^*$, *i.e. every sentence of* K_2^* *is deducible from* K_1^*, *and vice versa.*

Proof. Let M_1 be any model of K_1^*. Since K_1^* and K_2^* are mutually model-consistent with K they are model-consistent with each other. Accordingly there exists a structure $M_2 \supset M_1$ which is a model of K_2^* and, similarly, there exist structures $M_3, M_4, M_5, \ldots$ such that $M_1 \subset M_2 \subset M_3 \subset M_4 \subset M_5 \subset \ldots$ and such that $M_1, M_3, M_5, \ldots$ are models of K_1^* while $M_2, M_4, M_6, \ldots$ are models of K_2^*. But K_1^* and K_2^* are both model-complete and so $M_1 \prec M_3 \prec M_5 \prec \ldots$ and $M_2 \prec M_4 \prec M_6 \prec \ldots$ where the symbol $\prec$ stands for elementary extension. It follows that $M = \bigcup_n M_n = \bigcup_k M_{2k} = \bigcup_k M_{2k+1}$ is an elementary extension of both M_1 and M_2.

Now let X be any sentence of K_2^*. Then X holds in M_2, hence, in M, hence, in M_1. This shows that $K_1^* \vdash X$ and proves the theorem. Accordingly, by abuse of language, we may talk of *the* model companion or *the* model completion of a set K. Evidently, among all the model-companions of a set K (if there are any) there is one that is largest, i.e. the deductive closure of all of them.

5.2. **Theorem.** *Suppose* K *is model-complete. Then the class of* K*-generic structures is just the class of models of* K.

Proof. We show first that for every model M of K and for every sentence X defined in M, $M \models X$ if and only if $M \Vdash X$. This is obvious, if X is atomic. Suppose X is of rank $n > 0$ and that the assertion has been proved for sentences of rank less than n. The assertion for X can then be proved in a straightforward manner if X is a conjunction, or a disjunction, or if it has been obtained by existential quantification. Suppose now that $X = \neg Y$, and that $M \Vdash X$. Then $M \models X$, for otherwise $M \models Y$ and hence, by our inductive assumption, $M \Vdash Y$. Conversely, if $M \models X$ then we have to show that $M \Vdash X$. If this is not the case, then there exists an $M' \supset M$, $M' \in \Sigma_K$ such that $M' \Vdash Y$ where we may assume that M' is a model of K. But then $M' \models Y$ by the inductive assumption, and $M \models Y$, since M is an elementary substructure of M'. This contradicts $M \models X$. Reference to 2.5 now shows that every model of K is K-generic.

Now let M be K-generic. Then we have to show that M is a model of K. At any rate, we can embed M in a model M' of K. Then M' is K-generic, by what has been proved already, and M' is an elementary extension of M, by 3.1. Hence M is a model of K. This proves 5.2.

5.3. **Corollary**. *Suppose* K *is model-complete. Then* K^F *is the deductive closure of* K.

5.4. **Theorem**. *Suppose* K *possesses a model companion,* K*. *Then* K^F *is the deductive closure of* K*.

Proof. K* is mutually model consistent with K, so $K^F = (K^*)^F$ by 3.10 and 3.12. K* is model-complete, so $(K^*)^F = K^F$ is the deductive closure of K*. This proves the assertion.

Thus (compare [1] and [5]) whenever K possesses a model companion, $K^F = K^f$. By contrast, let K = N be the set of all true sentences of Arithmetic in a vocabulary which consists of addition and multiplication as well as equality. Then $N^f = N$, as shown in [1]. However, $N^F \neq N$. For let N_0 be any non-standard model of N. Then N_0 is included in a K-generic structure N_1 which is a model of N^F. By 3.2, N_1 satisfies all existential sentences defined in it which are true in some $N_2 \supset N_1$ which is a model of N. But if N^F were equal to N then, on the contrary, a theorem of M.Rabin [4] would ensure that there does exist an existential sentence X which is defined in N_1 and holds in some $N_2 \supset N_1$ which is a model of N but does not hold in N_1 itself. This shows that $N^F \neq N$.

N^F is a remarkable object. Although different from N, it includes many theorems of standard Arithmetic, in particular all $\forall\exists$-sentences which are true for the natural numbers. It also includes the system of axioms Q of R.M.Robinson [7] and since Q is essentially undecidable it follows that N^F also is undecidable. Moreover, N^F is complete since N is complete and, therefore, had the joint embedding property. It follows that N^F is not even recursively enumerable.

Another case which is of some interest is provided by K = P where P is a set of axioms for Peano Arithmetic. Then $P^F \neq N^F$ since by a theorem of Matijasevič [3] P_A is a proper subset of the set of all true universal sentences of Arithmetic. Moreover, as M.Rabin has shown (oral communication), by an argument which involves an application of Matijasevič theorem, P does not possess the joint embedding property and so P^F cannot be complete. However, P^F still includes the set of axioms Q of R.M.Robinson and, accordingly is essentially undecidable.

6. Some subclass of Σ_K

The most obvious subclass of Σ_K is given by the K-generic structures. We denote it by G_K. As we have seen (3.6 above) G_K is closed under union of chains. Also (3.1 above) if $M' \supset M$ for two elements M and M′ of G_K then M′ is an elementary extension of M, $M < M'$.

6.1. **Theorem.** *Suppose* G_K *is an arithmetical class (variety). Then* K^F *is a model companion of* K.

Proof. Let H be a set of sentences in the vocabulary of K such that G_K is the class of models of H. Then H is mutually model-consistent with K. Also, H is model-complete, by 3.1. Hence, H is a model companion of K. The theorem now follows from 3.4.

All elements of G_K are models of K^F. But if K does not possess a model companion then 6.1 shows that K^F possesses models which do not belong to G_K.

$M \in \Sigma_K$ is said to be K-*pregeneric* if all constants of K are interpreted in K, and if for every sentence X defined in M either $M \Vdash^* X$ or $M \Vdash^* \neg X$. The class of K-pregeneric structures will be denoted by P_K.

$M \in \Sigma_K$ is called *existentially complete* in Σ_K (sometimes also *existentially closed* or *algebraically closed* in Σ_K) if for every existential sentence X which is defined in M and for every $M' \supset M$, $M' \in \Sigma_K$, $M' \models X$ entails $M \models X$. 3.2 shows that any K-generic structure is existentially complete in Σ_K. We denote by E_K the class of all structures of Σ_K which are existentially complete and such that all constants of K are interpreted in them. Then $G_K \subset E_K$. We shall show in due course (7.8) that $E_K \subset P_K$.

6.2. **Theorem.** *For* $M \in \Sigma_K$ *to be* K-*pregeneric it is necessary and sufficient that the constants of* K *be interpreted in* M *and that any two* K-*generic extensions of* M, M_1 *and* M_2, *be elementarily equivalent in the vocabulary of* M.

Proof. Let M be K-pregeneric and let X be defined in M and $M_1 \models X$. Then $M_1 \Vdash X$. But then $M \Vdash \neg\neg X$ (for otherwise $M \Vdash^* \neg X$ or, equivalently, $M \Vdash \neg X$). Hence $M_2 \Vdash \neg\neg X$, $M_2 \models X$, the condition is necessary. Suppose now that the condition is satisfied but that for some X defined in M neither $M \Vdash^* X$ nor $M \Vdash^* \neg X$ (i.e. $M \Vdash \neg X$). Then there exist extensions M_1 and M_2 of M such that $M_1 \Vdash \neg X$ and $M_2 \Vdash X$. Let $M_1' \supset M_1$ and $M_2' \supset M_2$ be K-generic. Then $M_1' \Vdash \neg X$, $M_2' \Vdash X$, and hence $M_1' \models \neg X$, $M_2' \models X$, contrary to assumption. This complete the proof.

6.3. **Theorem.** *Let* $M \in \Sigma_K$ *be* K-*pregeneric and let* M_1 *and* M_2 *be two* K-*generic extensions of* M. *Then* M_1 *and* M_2 *can be embedded in a* K-*generic structure* M' *such that the diagram*

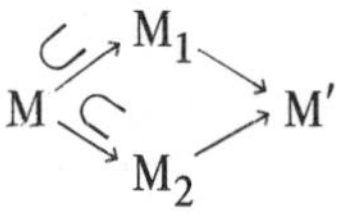

is commutative.

For the proof, we only have to show that there exists *some* $M' \in \Sigma_K$ such that the above diagram is commutative, since such M' can then be embedded further in a K-generic model. In particular, we may require that this M' be a model of K. To show that such an M' exists, we only have to verify (see the discussion in section 4 above) that if X_1 and X_2 are two existential sentences in the vocabulary of M and $M_1 \models X_1$, $M_2 \models X_2$, then $K \cup \{X_1, X_2\}$ is consistent. But this is obvious since $M_2 \models X_2$ implies $M_1 \models X_2$, by 6.2, and M_1 can be embedded in a model of K, which then satisfies both M_1 and M_2.

We may ask whether we obtain a new subclass of Σ_K if we replace forcing by weak forcing in the condition of Theorem 5. The answer to this question is negative as is shown by the following theorem, which is due to C.W.Coven.

6.4. **Theorem.** *Suppose that all constants of* K *are interpreted in* $M \in \Sigma_K$ *and suppose that for every sentence* X *which is defined in* M, $M \models X$ *entails* $M \Vdash^* X$. *Then* M *is* K-*generic.*

Proof. We have to show that for every X which is defined in M, either $M \Vdash X$ or $M \Vdash \neg X$. Suppose that this is not the case for some particular X. At any rate, we have either $M \models X$ or $M \models \neg X$. In the latter case $M \Vdash^* \neg X$ and so $M \Vdash \neg X$, contrary to assumption. Hence, we may assume that $M \models X$ but neither $M \Vdash X$ nor $M \Vdash \neg X$. Suppose that X is of lowest possible rank. Then

X cannot be atomic, by 2.1, and it cannot be a negation, for if $X = \neg X$ then $M \Vdash^* \neg Y$ and $M \Vdash \neg Y$, as before. We are left with the possibilities that X is a conjunction, or a disjunction, or that it is obtained by existential quantification.
(i) Suppose $X = Y \wedge Z$ so that the ranks of Y and Z are lower than the rank of X. Hence, by our inductive assumption, either $M \Vdash Y$ or $M \Vdash Y$ and, either $M \Vdash Z$ or $M \Vdash Z$. At the same time $M \models X$ and so $M \models Y$ and $M \models Z$. If $M \Vdash Y$ and $M \Vdash Z$ then $M \Vdash X$, and we have finished. Hence we may suppose, without loss of generality, that $M \Vdash \neg Y$. But $M \models Y$ entails $M \Vdash \neg\neg Y$, by the condition of the theorem, and so X cannot be a conjunction.
(ii) Suppose $X = Y \vee Z$. Then $M \models X$ and we may suppose, without loss of generality, that $M \models Y$. Hence $M \Vdash \neg\neg Y$, so M cannot force $\neg Y$, M forces Y, by the inductive assumption. Hence, M forces X.
(iii) Suppose $X = (\exists y)Q(y)$. Since $M \models X$, $M \models Q(a)$ for some a denoting an object of M, and so $M \Vdash \neg\neg Q(a)$. But then $M \Vdash \neg Q(a)$ is impossible, and so (by our induction) $M \Vdash Q(a)$, $M \Vdash X$. This completes the proof of 6.3.

However, the classes G_K, E_K, P_K are, in general, distinct. Indeed, $G_K \neq E_K$ if K = N, the set of sentences true in Arithmetic (see 5 above) for then the standard model of Arithmetic is existentially complete but not generic. On the other hand, if K possesses a model completion K*, then we claim that all models of K are K-pregeneric. For let M be any model of such a K, and suppose that for some X which is defined in M neither $M \Vdash^* X$ nor $M \Vdash^* \neg X$. Then there exist extensions M_1 and M_2 of M which belong to Σ_K such that $M_1 \Vdash \neg X$, $M_2 \Vdash X$. Hence, there exist K-generic extensions M_1' of M_1 and M_2' of M_2 such that $M_1' \Vdash \neg X$, $M_1' \models \neg X$, $M_2' \Vdash X$, $M_2' \models X$. But this is impossible since M_1' and M_2' are models of K* and K* is model-complete relative to K and, hence, M_1' and M_2' are elementarily equivalent in the vocabulary of M. This completes our argument.

For example, for K- the theory of fields, all fields are K-pregeneric although only the algebraically closed fields are existentially complete. Thus, in general, $E_K \neq P_K$.

7. A compactness theorem for infinite forcing

We define the *modified rank* of a well formed formula X as follows. For X atomic, or X a negation, $X = \neg Y$, the modified rank of X is 1, $m.r.(X) = 1$. Also, $m.r((\exists y)X) = m.r(X) + 1$ and

$$m.r(Y \wedge Z) = m.r(Y \vee Z) = m.r(Y) + m.r(Z)\,.$$

We define the *existential degree* ($e.d$) of a wff X as the number of its existential quantifiers which are not in the scope of a negation. Thus, if $m.r(X) = 1$ then $e.d(X) = 0$ and $e.d((\exists y)X) = e.d(X) + 1$, $e.d(Y \wedge Z) = e.d(Y \vee Z) = e.d(Y) + e.d(Z)$.

Let K be given, as before, and let $Q(x_1,...,x_n)$, $n \geqslant 0$ be any wff of modified rank 1 which is defined in K.

7.1. **Theorem.** *There exists a set* S_X *of sets* $\{Q_\nu(x_1,...,x_n)\}$ *of existential wff which are defined in* K *such that for any* $a_1, ..., a_n$ *and denoting individuals dividuals of an element* M *of* Σ_K, $M \Vdash Q(a_1,...,a_n)$ *if and only if* $M \models Q_\nu(a_1,...,a_n)$ *for all* $Q_\nu(x_1,...,x_n)$ *which are contained in one and the same element of* S_X.

Proof. The elements of S_X will be defined as follows. Consider any mapping of constants $a_1, ..., a_n$, on individuals of some $M \in \Sigma_K$ (consistently with the denotation of the constants of K). If $M \Vdash Q(a_1,...,a_n)$ then we construct a particular element $T_{M \leftarrow a}$ of S_X as the set of all existential wff $Q_\nu(x_1,...,x_n)$ which are defined in K such that $Q_\nu(a_1,...,a_n)$ holds in M under the specified mapping of the a_j. S_X shall be the set of all $T_{M \leftarrow a}$ obtained in this way. It follows immediately that if $M \Vdash Q(a_1,...,a_n)$ in a particular instance then all $Q_\nu(a_1,...,a_n)$ hold in M for one particular element of S_X, i.e. for the $T_{M \leftarrow a}$ which was constructed expressly for this case. Thus, the condition of the theorem is necessary (for the specified S_X).

To see that the condition is also sufficient, suppose first that $X = Q(x_1,...,x_n)$ is atomic. (Notice that X may still contain individual constants of K.) Then any $T_{M \leftarrow a}$ for $M \Vdash Q(a_1,...,a_n)$ must contain $Q(x_1,...,x_n)$ since $Q(a_1,...,a_n)$ holds in M. Suppose now that $Q_\nu(a_1,...,a_n)$ holds in some $M' \in \Sigma_K$ for all $Q_\nu(x_1,...,x_n) \in T_{M \leftarrow a}$. Then $M' \models Q(a_1,...,a_n)$ and so $M' \Vdash Q(a_1,...,a_n)$, as required.

Suppose next that $X = Q(x_1,...,x_n) = \neg R(x_1,...,x_n)$ is a negation. Let $M \in \Sigma_K$ such that (for a particular interpretation of $a_1,...,a_n$) $M \Vdash \neg R(a_1,...,a_n)$ and let M'' be any other element of Σ_K such that, for a particular interpretation of $a_1, ..., a_n$, $M'' \Vdash R(a_1,...,a_n)$. Then there cannot exist a joint embedding of M and M'' in a model of K as explained in section 4 above, for a set A which consists of $a_1, ..., a_n$ and of the constants of K which occur in both M and M''. Thus (Theorem 4.1) there exist existential sentences X_0, X'' with individual constants from A or K such that $M \models X_0$, $M'' \models X''$ but $K \vdash \neg(X_0 \wedge X'')$. Also, there exist existential predicates

$Q_0(x_1,...,x_n), Q''(x_1,...,x_n)$ which are defined in K such that $X_0 = Q_0(a_1,...,a_n)$, $X'' = Q''(a_1,...,a_n)$, and it then follows from the definition of S_X that the element of S_X that we have denoted by $T_{\mathrm{M}\leftarrow a}$ contains the predicate $Q_0(x_1,...,x_n)$. Suppose now that $\mathrm{M}' \models Q_\nu(a_1,...,a_n)$ for all $Q_\nu(x_1,...,x_n) \in T_{\mathrm{M}\leftarrow a}$ in a particular assignment of the constants $a_1, ..., a_n$ to elements of a structure $\mathrm{M}' \in \Sigma_{\mathrm{K}}$. Then we have to show that $\mathrm{M}' \Vdash Q(a_1,...,a_n)$ or, which is the same, $\mathrm{M}' \Vdash \neg R(a_1,...,a_n)$. Now if this were not the case then there would exist a structure $\mathrm{M}'' \supset \mathrm{M}'$ such that $\mathrm{M}'' \Vdash R(a_1,...,a_n)$. Moreover, we may always extend M'' to a model of K, so we may as well suppose that $\mathrm{M}'' \models \mathrm{K}$ from the outset. But, for this M'', there exist the predicates $Q_0(x_1,...,x_n) \in T_{\mathrm{M}\leftarrow a}$ and $Q''(x_1,...,x_n)$ introduced above such that $\mathrm{K} \vdash \neg [Q_0(a_1,...,a_n) \wedge Q''(a_1,...,a_n)]$ and, at the same time, $\mathrm{M}'' \models Q''(a_1,...,a_n)$ (and $\mathrm{M} \models Q_0(a_1,...,a_n)$). But $Q_0(x_1,...,x_n) \in T_{\mathrm{M}\leftarrow a}$ and so $\mathrm{M}' \models Q_0(a_1,...,a_n)$, by assumption and $\mathrm{M}'' \models Q_0(a_1,...,a_n)$ since Q_0 is existential. This shows that M'' is a model of $Q_0(a_1,...,a_n) \wedge Q''(a_1,...,a_n)$ although it is also a model of K. Since this contradicts $\mathrm{K} \vdash \neg [Q_0(a_1,...,a_n) \wedge Q''(a_1,...,a_n)]$ we may conclude that $\mathrm{M}' \Vdash \neg R(a_1,...,a_n)$. This completes the proof.

Now let $X = Q(x_1,...,x_n)$, $n \geqslant 0$ be a well formed formula of arbitrary modified rank which is defined in K. Let m be the existential degree of X, $m \geqslant 0$. Generalizing 7.1, we are going to prove

7.2. **Theorem.** *There exists a set S_X of sets $\{Q_\nu(x_1,...,x_n,y_1,...,y_m)\}$ of existential wff which are defined in* K *such that for any $a_1,..., a_n$ and denoting individuals of an element* M *of Σ_{K}, $\mathrm{M} \Vdash Q(a_1,...,a_n)$ if and only if there exist elements of* M, *to be denoted by $b_1, ..., b_m$, such that for at least one particular element T of S_X,* M *satisfies $Q_\nu(a_1,...,a_n,b_1,...,b_m)$ for all $Q_\nu(x_1,...,x_n,y_1,...,y_m)$ in T.*

The proof is by induction on the modified rank of X. For $m.r(X) = 1$, 7.2 reduces to 7.1. Suppose $m.r(X) > 1$ and that the assertion of the theorem has been proved for all formulae whose modified rank is lower than that of X. We have to consider three cases.

(i) $X = Y \wedge Z$. Then Y and Z have modified rank smaller than the modified rank of X, and there exist sets of predicates $S_Y = \{T'\}$, $S_Z = \{T''\}$ which satisfy the conditions of the theorem. We now define S_X as the set of all sets of predicates $Q'_\nu(x_1,...,x_n,y_1,...,y_m) \wedge Q''_\nu(x_1,...,x_n,y_{m+1},...,y_{m+l})$ as Q'_ν ranges over the elements of an arbitrary $T' \in S_Y$ and Q''_ν ranges over an arbitrary $T'' \in S_Z$. (As our notation shows, it is assumed here that the existential degree of Y is m and the existential degree of Z is l so that the existential degree of X is $m + l$.)

Now suppose that $Y = Q'(x_1,...,x_n)$, $Z = Q''(x_1,...,x_n)$, so that $X = Q'(x_1,...,x_n) \wedge Q''(x_1,...,x_n)$ and let M be an element of Σ_K such that $M \not\Vdash Q(a_1,...,a_n)$, $M \Vdash Q'(a_1,...,a_n) \wedge Q''(a_1,...,a_n)$. Then $M \Vdash Q'(a_1,...,a_n)$, $M \not\Vdash Q''(a_1,...,a_n)$ and so, by the inductive assumption, there exist $T' \in S_Y$, $T'' \in S_Z$, and element $b_1, ..., b_m, b_{m+1}, ..., b_l$ such that $Q'_\nu(a_1,...,a_n,b_1,...,b_m)$ and $Q''_\nu(a_1,...,a_n,b_{m+1},...,b_{m+l})$ hold in M for all the elements Q'_ν and Q''_ν of T' and T'' respectively. But then the condition of the theorem is satisfies for the element of S_X which was obtained by our construction from T' and T''. Conversely, if the condition of the theorem is satisfies for the set of predicates obtained from $T' \in S_Y$ and $T'' \in S_Z$ then it is also satisfied for the predicates of T' and of T'' separately. Hence $M \Vdash Q'(a_1,...,a_n)$, $M \Vdash Q''(a_1,...,a_n)$ and so $M \Vdash Q(a_1,...,a_n)$. This completes the consideration of the first case.

(ii) $X = Y \vee Z$. For any $T' \in S_Y$, $T'' \in S_Z$, we define an element of S_X, as before, except that we replace $\wedge$ everywhere by $\vee$. With $Y = Q'(x_1,...,x_n)$, $Z = Q''(x_1,...,x_n)$, as before, we then have $X = Q'(x_1,...,x_n) \vee Q''(x_1,...,x_n)$. Suppose $M \Vdash Q'(a_1,...,a_n) \vee Q''(a_1,...,a_n)$, then we may assume without loss of generality that $M \Vdash Q'(a_1,...,a_n)$. Hence, there exist elements $b_1,...,b_m$ of M such that $M \models Q'_\nu(a_1,...,a_n,b_1,...,b_m)$ for all Q'_ν which belong to a particular $T' \in S_Y$. Let T be the element of S_X obtained by the specified procedure from this particular T' and from any $T'' \in S_Z$. Choosing $b_{m+1}, ..., b_{m+l}$ arbitrarily in M, we then find that $M \models Q_\nu(a_1,...,a_n,b_1,...,b_{m+l})$ for all $Q_\nu \in T$.

Conversely, if $M \models Q_\nu(a_1,...,a_n,b_1,...,b_{m+l})$ for all elements Q_ν of a particular $T \in S_X$ then it is not difficult to see that either $M \models Q'_\nu(a_1,...,a_n, b_1,...,b_m)$ for *all* $Q'_\nu \in T'$ or $M \models Q''_\nu(a_1,...,a_n,b_{m+1},...,b_{m+l})$ for all $Q''_\nu \in T''$, where T' and T'' are the elements of S_Y and S_Z, respectively, which are involved in the construction of T. Hence, either $M \Vdash Q'(a_1,...,a_n,b_1,...,b_m)$ or $M \Vdash Q''(a_1,...,a_n,b_{m+1},...,b_{m+l})$ (or both) and this implies $M \Vdash Q(a_1,...,a_n, b_1,...,b_{m+l})$ in either case.

(iii) $X = (\exists y)Q(x_1,...,x_n,y)$. Put $Y = Q(x_1,...,x_n,x_{n+1})$ and suppose that Y is of existential degree m. Let $S_Y = \{T'\}$ be a set of sets of predicates which belongs to Y in accordance with the conditions of our theorem. For any $T' \in S_Y$ we now define a corresponding set of predicates $T \in S_X$ simply by replacing the variable x_{n+1} in any $Q'_\nu(x_1,...,x_{n+1},y_1,...,y_m) \in T'$ by the variable y_{m+1}, so $Q_\nu(x_1,...,x_n,y_1,...,y_m,y_{m+1}) = Q'_\nu(x_1,...,x_n,y_{m+1},y_1,...,y_m)$.

Now suppose that $M \Vdash (\exists y)Q(a_1,...,a_n,y)$. Then, for some individual of M, to be denoted by a constant b_{m+1} $M \Vdash Q(a_1,...,a_n,b_{m+1})$. Hence, by the assumption of our induction, there exists a $T' \in S_Y$ such that $M \models Q'_\nu(a_1,...,a_n,b_{m+1},b_1,...,b_m)$ for all $Q'_\nu \in T'$. But this means that $M \models Q_\nu(a_1,...,a_n,b_1,...,b_{m+1})$ for all Q_ν in the corresponding $T \in S_X$ and shows that the condition of the theorem is necessary for case (iii). Conversely, suppose that for some $T \in S_X$, there exist $b_1,...,b_{m+1}$ denoting elements of $\mathrm{M} \in \Sigma_\mathrm{K}$ such that $\mathrm{M} \models Q_\nu(a_1,...,a_n,b_1,...,b_{m+1})$ for all $Q_\nu \in T$. Then $\mathrm{M} \models Q'_\nu(a_1,...,a_n,b_{m+1},b_1,...,b_m)$ for all Q'_ν in the corresponding T' and hence, by the assumption of induction, $\mathrm{M} \Vdash Q_\nu(a_1,...,a_n,b_{m+1})$ and, furthermore, $\mathrm{M} \Vdash (\mathrm{E}y)Q(a_1,...,a_n,y)$.

This proves 7.2. Observe that the proof provides a canonical construction of S_X. However, other sets may do as well. For example, if $X = Q(x_1,...,x_n)$ is atomic it is clearly sufficient to assume that S_X contains the single $T = \{Q(x_1,...,x_n)\}$.

For any set A of cardinal $[A]$ we define the *modified cardinal* of A by $\|A\| = \max(|A|,\omega)$. If $\|\mathrm{K}\| = \alpha$ then the number of wff which are definable in K also must be α. Hence, for any $T \in S_X$ as defined above $|T| \leqslant \alpha$.

By analogy with notions introduced elsewhere in Logic, Σ will be called α-compact, for any cardinal α, if for any sentence X and for any $\mathrm{M} \in \Sigma$ which forces X, there exists an $\mathrm{M}' \subset \mathrm{M}$, $|\mathrm{M}'| \leqslant \alpha$ such that $\mathrm{M}' \Vdash X$.

7.3. **Compactness theorem for infinite forcing.** *Suppose* K *has the modified cardinal* α, $\|\mathrm{K}\| = \alpha$. *Then* Σ_K *is* α-*compact.*

Proof. Let $\mathrm{M} \Vdash Z$, and suppose that Z contains in addition to the individual constants of K, the constants $a_1, ..., a_n$, $Z = Q(a_1,...,a_n)$. Put $X = Q(x_1,...,x_n)$ and let $S_X = \{T\}$ be a set of sets of wff as mentioned in 7.2. Let m be the existential degree of X. Then there exist m elements of M, to be denoted by $b_1, ..., b_m$, such that $\mathrm{M} \models Q_\nu(a_1,...,a_n,b_1,...,b_m)$ for all elements Q_ν of a particular $T \in S_X$. But each Q_ν is existential, and so it is satisfied already in a finite substructure M_ν of M. More precisely, if Q_ν contains l existential quantifiers then we may obtain M_ν by adding to the elements denoted by $a_1, ..., a_n, b_1, ..., b_m$ not more than l elements of M. Let M′ be the substructure of M which is obtained by restriction to the individuals of the various M_ν and to the elements obtained from these by operating on them the functions of M (if any). Since $\|\mathrm{K}\| = \alpha$, the number of these functions cannot exceed α, and since $|T| \leqslant \alpha$, $\Sigma|\mathrm{M}_\nu| \leqslant \alpha$. We conclude that $|\mathrm{M}'| \leqslant \alpha$, proving the theorem.

7.4. **Theorem.** *Let* $\mathrm{M} \in \Sigma_\mathrm{K}$. *Then* M *is contained in a* K-*generic structure* $\mathrm{M}' \in \Sigma_\mathrm{K}$ *such that* $|\mathrm{M}'| \leqslant \max(|\mathrm{K}|,|\mathrm{M}|,\omega)$. *Moreover,* M′ *can be constructed as the union (inductive limit) of a monotonic sequence of models of* K, $\mathrm{M}_0 \subset \mathrm{M}_1 \subset \mathrm{M}_2 \subset ..., \mathrm{M}' = \cup \mathrm{M}_n$.

Proof. We refer to the proof of 2.4. There, M_0 was selected as a model of K and an extension of M. By the theorem of Löwenheim-Skolem, we may suppose that $\|M_0\| \leqslant \beta = \max(|K|, |M|, \omega)$. Accordingly, the set of sentences defined in M_0, $\{X_{0\nu}\}_{\nu<\alpha}$ also has a cardinal which does not exceed β. For each $X_{0\nu}$, either itself or its negation is forced by the structure M_1 constructed in the proof of 2.4, and in each case, this is equivalent to the satisfaction by M_1 of at most $\|K\|$ conditions which are obtained from a corresponding S_X. The total number of these conditions thus cannot exceed β. Accordingly, we may find a structure which satisfies all these conditions, is an extension of M_0 and a model of K and whose cardinality does not exceed β. This structure can be used to replace the M_1 of the proof of 2.4 and we call it again M_1. Continuing in this way, we obtain a sequence $M_0 \subset M_1 \subset M_2 \subset \dots$ which satisfies the conditions of 2.4, and whose cardinality does not exceed β. Then $M' = \bigcup M_n$ is a K-generic structure, and its cardinality does not exceed β either.

In particular, for K = N, we may thus obtain a K-generic structure which is countable and which is the inductive limit of a monotonic sequence of non-standard models of Arithmetic.

We shall now show that G_K can be axiomatized (not necessarily recursively) by sentences taken from certain infinitary languages.

Let $\alpha = \|K\| = \max(|K|, \omega)$ and let $\beta = (2^\alpha)^+$, the successor cardinal of 2^α. In standard notation, $L_{\beta,\omega}$ is the language which permits the formation of conjunctions and disjunctions up to, and including, length 2^α, while the quantifiers are still prefixed only one by one, as in the Lower Predicate Calculus.

Now let $X = Q(x_1,\dots,x_n)$ be any wff defined in K, as before and let m be the existential degree of X. Let S_X be the set of sets of existential formulae attached to X by the canonical construction used in the proof of 7.2. Then every $T \in S_X$ consists of wff $Q_\nu(x_1,\dots,x_n,y_1,\dots,y_m)$ which are defined in K, and $|T| \leqslant \alpha$. It follows that $|S| \leqslant 2^\alpha$.

For any $T \in S_X$ let $Q(x_1,\dots,x_n,y_1,\dots,y_m)$, be the conjunction of all the $Q_\nu(x_1,\dots,x_n,y_1,\dots,y_m)$ in T, and let $Q_X(x_1,\dots,x_n,y_1,\dots,y_m)$ be the disjunction of all Q_T as T ranges over S_X. Then Q_X belongs to $L_{\beta,\omega}$. We now define a set of axioms K_G as the union of $K_\forall$ and of the sentences

7.5. $$(\forall x_1)\dots(\forall x_n)(\exists y_1)\dots(\exists y_m)[Q_X(x_1,\dots,x_n,y_1,\dots,y_m) \vee Q_{\neg X}(x_1,\dots,x_n)]$$

where X ranges over the wff defined in K. Then every model of K_G belongs to Σ_K, since $K_G \supset K_\forall$ and for every $Q(a_1,\dots,a_n)$ defined in M, M forces either

$Q(a_1,...,a_n)$ or $\neg Q(a_1,...,a_n)$, by 7.5. It follows that all models of K_G are K-generic structures and the converse is even more obvious. Equivalent sets of axioms are obtained if we replace 7.5 by

7.6. $$(\forall x_1)...(\forall x_n)[Q(x_1,...,x_n) \supset (\exists y_1)...(\exists y_m)Q_X(x_1,...,x_n, y_1,...,y_m)]$$

or by

7.7. $$(\forall x_1)...(\forall x_n)[\ (x_1,...,x_n) \supset Q_{\neg\neg X}(x_1,...,x_n)]$$

where $X = Q(x_1,...,x_n)$ ranges again over the wff which are defined in K (see Theorems 2.5 and 6.4, above).

7.8. **Theorem.** *If* M *is existentially complete in* Σ_K *and all constants of* K *are interpreted in* M *then* M *is* K*-pregeneric.*

Proof. Accepting the assumptions of the theorem, let Y be defined in M. Displaying the constants which do not occur in K, we may write $Y = Q(a_1,...,a_n)$, where $X = Q(x_1,...,x_n)$ is defined in K. Unless $M \Vdash^* Y$, we have $M' \Vdash \neg Y$ for some extension M′ of M. Introduce a set $S_{\neg Y}$ as considered in Theorem 7.2. Then the existential sentences $Q_\nu(a_1,...,a_n)$ hold in M′ for all Q_ν belonging to some element of $S_{\neg X}$. But then they also hold in M and so $M \Vdash \neg Y$ or, equivalently, $M \Vdash^* \neg Y$.

A similar argument leads to

7.9. **Theorem.** *Let* M *be an elementary substructure of a* K*-generic structure* M′ *such that all constants of* K *are interpreted in* M. *Then* M *is* K*-generic.*

Proof. Suppose that for $X = Q(x_1,...,x_n)$ which is defined in K, and for $a_1, ..., a_n$ denoting elements of M, $Q(a_1,...,a_n)$ holds in M. Then $Q(a_1,...,a_n)$ holds in M′ and hence, by 7.7. $Q_{\neg\neg X}(a_1,...,a_n)$ also holds in M′. But $Q_{\neg\neg X}(a_1,...,a_n)$ is a disjunction of conjunctions of existential sentences which are defined in M and so we may conclude that $Q_{\neg\neg X}(a_1,...,a_n)$ is satisfied already by M. We conclude that all the appropriate instances of 7.7 hold in M, M is K-generic.

It is natural to consider what happens as one replaces the class of substructures of models of K, Σ_K, by the class of models of K itself, $\Sigma = \Sigma'_K$, say.

However, this modification does not introduce anything essentially new. It is in fact easy to verify that a structure $M \in \Sigma'_K$ forces a sentence K defined in it according to the rules of 2.1. if and only if M forces X within Σ_K. Naturally we cannot now expect the generic structures to be elements of Σ. We therefore call a structure M *K-generic'* if M is consistent with K and if for every sentence X which is defined in M there exists a model M′ of K which is a substructure of M and which forces either X or $\neg X$. In particular, M may be the union (inductive limit) of a monotonic sequence of models of K. We see from 7.4 that every $M \in \Sigma'_K$ is contained in a K-generic′ structure.

8. Finite forcing

To discuss the uses of our present approach for finite forcing, we find it convenient to assume that the number of relation symbols in K is finite and that there are no function symbols in K. It follows that if M′ is the restriction of a model M of K to a finite set of individuals in M then M′ must be finite. Thus, our present approach in this case is roughly equivalent to the condition used in refs. [1] and [5] to sets of basic sentences which are diagrams of finite substructures of models of K. This again does not change the forcing relation for the conditions which are retained and does not make any difference to the supply of K-generic structures.

Thus, let Σ_K be the set of finite substructures of models of K and define the forcing relation again by 2.1. We may then develop the analogue of Theorem 7.2 above for finite forcing. However, we now have a significant simplification, as appears from the following theorem.

8.1. **Theorem.** *Let $X = Q(x_1,...,x_n)$ be any wff which is defined in* K. *Then there exists a set $\bar{S}_X$ of existential formulae $\bar{Q}(x_1,...,x_n)$ which are defined in* K *such that for any $a_1,...,a_n$ not in* K *and denoting individuals of an element* M *of Σ_K, $M \Vdash Q(a_1,...,a_n)$ if and only if for at least one $\bar{Q} \in \bar{S}_X$, $M \models \bar{Q}(a_1,...,a_n)$.*

Proof. In order to be able to adapt the successive steps involved in the proof of 7.2, we replace 8.1 by

8.2. *Let $Q(x_1,...,x_n)$ be a wff of existential degree $m \geqslant 0$ which is defined in* K. *Then there exists a set $\bar{\bar{S}}_X$ of existential formulae $\bar{\bar{Q}}(x_1,...,x_n,y_1,...,y_m)$ which are defined in* K *such that for any $a_1, ..., a_n$ denoting individuals of an element* M *of Σ_K, $M \Vdash Q(a_1,...,a_n)$ if and only if there exist ele-*

ments of M, *to be denoted by* $b_1, ..., b_m$, *such that for at least one particular* $\bar{\bar{Q}} \in \bar{\bar{S}}_X$, $M \models \bar{\bar{Q}}(a_1,...,a_n,b_1,...,b_m)$.

The passage from 8.2 to 8.1 is immediate. Indeed, supposing that we have determined $\bar{\bar{S}}_X$ as described in 8.2, we may obtain the corresponding $\bar{S}_X$ by replacing each $\bar{\bar{Q}}(x_1,...,x_n,y_1,...,y_m) \in \bar{\bar{S}}_X$ by the formula $\bar{Q}(x_1,...,x_n) = (\exists y_1)...(\exists y_m)\bar{\bar{Q}}(x_1,...,x_n,y_1,...,y_m)$.

To prove 8.2, suppose first that X is of existential degree 0 (see 7.1 and its proof). If $X = Q(x_1,...,x_n)$ is atomic then (as pointed out already for the case of infinite forcing) we may take simply $\bar{\bar{Q}}(x_1,...,x_n) = Q(x_1,...,x_n)$. Suppose now that X is a negation, $X = Q(x_1,...,x_n) = \neg R(x_1,...,x_n)$. Construct first the elements $T = T_{M \leftarrow a}$ of the set S_X as in the proof of 7.1 and let $Q'(x_1,...,x_n)$ be any element of $T_{M \leftarrow a}$. For given M and for a given mapping of $a_1, ..., a_n$ into M, a particular element of $T_{M \leftarrow a}$ is obtained as follows. Let D be the diagram of M, where it is understood that D contains $a_1, ..., a_n$ with the specified interpretation in M. Let Y be the conjunction of the elements of D, $Y = Y(a_1,...,a_n,c_1,...,c_k)$ where $c_1, ..., c_k$ are the constants other than $a_1, ..., a_n$ and the constants of K, which occur in Y. Then $\bar{\bar{Q}}(x_1,...,x_n) = (\exists z_1)...(\exists z_k)Y(x_1,...,x_n,z_1,...,z_k)$ is an element of $T_{M \leftarrow a}$. Also, if $\bar{\bar{Q}}(a_1,...,a_n)$ is satisfied by a structure M′ then M′ is isomorphic to an extension of M and therefore satisfies $Q'(a_1,...,a_n)$, i.e. $\vdash \bar{\bar{Q}}(a_1,...,a_n) \supset Q'(a_1,...,a_n)$. It follows that we may replace the set $T_{M \leftarrow a}$ by the single formula $\bar{\bar{Q}}(x_1,...,x_n)$.

Consider next the cases (i), (ii), (iii) discussed in the proof of 7.2. For case (i), we define $\bar{\bar{S}}_X$ as the set of conjunctions $Q'(x_1,...,x_n,y_1,...,y_m) \wedge Q''(x_1,...,x_n,y_{m+1},...,y_{m+l})$ where Q' ranges over the elements of $\bar{\bar{S}}_Y$ and Q'' ranges over the elements of $\bar{\bar{S}}_Z$. For case (ii), we take $\bar{\bar{S}}_X$ as the corresponding set of disjunctions. Finally, for case (iii), if $X = (\exists y)Q(x_1,...,x_n,y)$ and $Y = Q(x_1,...,x_n,x_{n+1})$ is of existential degree m then we obtain $\bar{\bar{S}}_X$ from $\bar{\bar{S}}_Y$ by replacing x_{n+1} in the wff $\bar{\bar{Q}}(x_1,...,x_n,x_{n+1},y_1,...,y_m)$ which belong to $\bar{\bar{S}}_Y$, by y_{m+1}. This completes the argument.

Evidently, for all X, $|\bar{S}_X| = |\bar{\bar{S}}_X| \leqslant \alpha = \|K\|$. We define $\bar{Q}_X(x_1,...,x_n)$ as the disjunction of the elements of $\bar{S}_X$. Then $\bar{Q}_X$ belongs to $L_{\alpha^+,\omega}$ and so do the sentences.

$$8.3. \qquad (\forall x_1)...(\forall x_n)[Q_X(x_1,...,x_n) \vee \bar{Q}_{\neg X}(x_1,...,x_n)]$$

where $X = Q(x_1,...,x_n)$, as before.

The appropriate definition of a K-generic structure M, for the case under consideration, is as follows. M is K-generic if

8.4. M *is consistent with* K *and all sentences of* K *are defined in it,* and

8.5. *For every sentence* Y *which is defined in* M *either* Y *or* $\neg Y$ *is forced by a finite substructure of* M.

Any sentence X which is defined in M holds in M if and only if it is forced by a finite substructure of M. If K is countable then every $M \in \Sigma_K$ can be extended to a K-generic structure M′ while the situation for general uncountable K is not yet clear.

Finally, $K_\forall$ together with all appropriate instances of 8.3 provides a set of axioms for the notion of a K-generic structure for finite forcing. Adapting the method of proof of Theorem 7.9, we obtain, in view of the fact that, in 8.3, both $\bar{Q}_X$ and $\bar{Q}_{\neg X}$ are disjunctions of conjunctions of existential sentences, the following theorem.

8.6. **Theorem.** *Let* M *be a substructure of a structure* M′ *which is* K*-generic for finite forcing and suppose that all constants of* K *are interpreted in* M *and that for all existential sentences* X *which are defined in* M, $M' \models X$ *entails* $M \models X$. *Then* M′ *is* K*-generic.*

I am indebted to Carol Coven for permitting me to include Theorem 6.3 in the present paper.

References

[1] J.Barwise and A.Robinson, Completing theories by forcing, Annals of Mathematical Logic 2 (1970) 119–142.
[2] P.J.Cohen, Set Theory and the Continuum Hypothesis (Benjamin, New York, 1966).
[3] Y.B.Matijasevič, Recursively enumerable sets are diophantine, (in Russian) Proceedings of the Academy of Science of the USSR, 1970.
[4] M.O.Rabin, Diophantine equations in non-standard models of Arithmetic, Proceedings of the International Congress of Logic, Methodology and Philosophy of Science (Stanford University Press, Stanford, 1962) 151–158.
[5] A.Robinson, Forcing in Model Theory, to be published in the Proceedings of the Colloquium on Model Theory, Rome, November 1969.
[6] A.Robinson, Introduction to Model Theory and to the Metamathematics of Algebra (North-Holland, Amsterdam, 1963).
[7] A.Tarski, A.Mostowski and R.M.Robinson, Undecidable Theories (North-Holland, Amsterdam, 1953).

QUALITATIVE PROBABILITY IN A MODAL SETTING

Krister SEGERBERG
Åbo Akademi

In this paper we shall study a family of propositional calculi which are obtained by adding to modal propositional calculi a binary operator $\gtrsim$ carrying the intuitive meaning of "at least as probable as". Extending ideas due to Kripke we present a semantic modelling suitable for this kind of logic. Most of the paper is devoted to showing that filtration theory can be modified in such a way that completeness can be established by using the following wellknown theorem from measurement theory:

Theorem (Kraft, Pratt, Seidenberg). *Let B be a finite Boolean algebra with* 1 *the unit element and* 0 *the zero element. Let* $\geqslant$ *be a binary relation on B. Then there is a probability measure M on B such that for all* α, β *of B*,

$$M\alpha \geqslant M\beta \text{ if and only if } \alpha \geqslant \beta ,$$

if and only if the following four conditions are satisfied
(i) *Not* $0 \geqslant 1$.
(ii) *For all* α *in B*, $\alpha \geqslant 0$.
(iii) *For all* α, β *in B*, $\alpha \geqslant \beta$ *or* $\beta \geqslant \alpha$.
(iv) *For all positive integers m and all* $\alpha_1, ..., \alpha_m, \beta_1, ..., \beta_m$ *in B, if every atom of B belongs to exactly as many* α*'s as* β*'s, then* $\alpha_i \geqslant \beta_i$ *for all i such that* $1 \leqslant i \leqslant m$ *only if* $\beta_i \geqslant \alpha_i$ *for all i such that* $1 \leqslant i \leqslant m$.

We assume that the reader has some familiarity with Kripke type semantics for modal logic and with filtration theory; study of [2] would provide the necessary background. A lucid exposition of the Kraft/Pratt/Seidenberg theorem and its proof is found in [1]. The results of the present paper were announced in [3].

In addition to propositional letters $\mathbf{P}_0, \mathbf{P}_1, ..., \mathbf{P}_n, ...$ and classical connectives $\bot$ (falsity) and $\rightarrow$ (material implication), our language contains a unary operator $\Box$ ("it is necessary that ...") and a binary operator $\gtrsim$ ("that ... is at least as probable as that ..."). Everything built up from these primitives in the usual way is a formula provided that it does not contain nestings of the $\gtrsim$-operator. We use $\neg, \wedge, \vee$, and $\leftrightarrow$ as abbreviatory devices. $\top$ is short for $(\bot \to \bot)$. We define

$$\mathbf{A} > \mathbf{B} = (\mathbf{A} \gtrsim \mathbf{B}) \wedge \neg(\mathbf{B} \gtrsim \mathbf{A}) .$$

We also introduce this admittedly formidable abbreviation schema:

$$\mathbf{A}_1 ... \mathbf{A}_m \ \mathbb{E}\ \mathbf{B}_1 ... \mathbf{B}_m = \Box(\mathbf{C}_0 \vee ... \vee \mathbf{C}_m) ,$$

where $m \geqslant 1$ and, for $0 \leqslant p \leqslant m$, $\mathbf{C}_p$ is the disjunction of all conjunctions

$$\delta_1 \mathbf{A}_1 \wedge ... \wedge \delta_m \mathbf{A}_m \wedge \epsilon_1 \mathbf{B}_1 \wedge ... \wedge \epsilon_m \mathbf{B}_m$$

such that exactly p of the δ's and p of the ϵ's are the empty symbol string, the rest of them being the negation sign.

By a *Kripke model* we understand any structure $\langle U,R,V \rangle$ where U is a set, R a binary relation on U, and V a function such that, for every $n \in N = \{0,1,2,...\}$ and every $x \in U$, $V(n,x)$ is defined and equal to 0 or 1. By a *probability model*, or *model* for short, we understand any structure $\langle U,R,V,B,M \rangle$ where

(i) $\langle U,R,V \rangle$ is a Kripke model;

(ii) B and M are functions on U;

(iii) for every $x \in U$, B_x is a Boolean σ-algebra of subsets of $\{y{:}xRy\}$ with $\emptyset$ as zero element and $\{y{:}xRy\}$ as unit element;

(iv) for every $x \in U$, M_x is a probability measure on B_x.

We define the concept of a formula $\mathbf{A}$ being true at a point x in a model $\mathcal{U} = \langle U,R,V,B,M \rangle$, written $\models^{\mathcal{U}}_{x} \mathbf{A}$, as follows:

$$\models^{\mathcal{U}}_{x} \mathbf{P}_n \text{ iff } V(n,x) = 1 \text{ (for all } n \in N) ; \tag{1}$$

$$\text{Not } \models^{\mathcal{U}}_{x} \bot . \tag{2}$$

$$\models^{\mathcal{U}}_{x} \mathbf{A} \to \mathbf{B} \text{ iff if } \models^{\mathcal{U}}_{x} \mathbf{A} \text{ then } \models^{\mathcal{U}}_{x} \mathbf{B} . \tag{3}$$

$$\models^{\mathcal{U}}_{x} \Box \mathbf{A} \text{ iff, for every } y \text{ such that } xRy, \models^{\mathcal{U}}_{y} \mathbf{A} . \tag{4}$$

$$\models^{\mathcal{U}}_{x} \mathbf{A} \gtrsim \mathbf{B} \text{ iff } M_x(\{y{:}xRy \text{ and } \models^{\mathcal{U}}_{y} \mathbf{A}\}) \geqslant M_x(\{y{:}xRy \text{ and } \models^{\mathcal{U}}_{y} \mathbf{B}\}) .^{*} \tag{5}$$

* The condition to the right of "iff" is regarded as false if M_x is not defined for both arguments.

If we introduce the notation

$$\|\mathbf{C}\|_x^{\mathfrak{U}} = \{y{:}xRy \text{ and } \models_y^{\mathfrak{U}} \mathbf{C}\},$$

then clause (5) is more perspicuously rendered as

$$\models_x^{\mathfrak{U}} \mathbf{A} \gtrsim \mathbf{B} \text{ iff } M_x(\|\mathbf{A}\|_x^{\mathfrak{U}}) \geqslant M_x(\|\mathbf{B}\|_x^{\mathfrak{U}}).$$

With some patience one can verify that

$$\models_x^{\mathfrak{U}} \mathbf{A}_1 \ldots \mathbf{A}_m \;\mathbb{E}\; \mathbf{B}_1 \ldots \mathbf{B}_m$$

holds if and only if every y such that xRy belongs to precisely as many of the sets $\|\mathbf{A}_1\|_x^{\mathfrak{U}}, \ldots, \|\mathbf{A}_m\|_x^{\mathfrak{U}}$ as of the sets $\|\mathbf{B}_1\|_x^{\mathfrak{U}}, \ldots, \|\mathbf{B}_m\|_x^{\mathfrak{U}}$. Thus, in particular, $\models_x^{\mathfrak{U}} \mathbf{A} \;\mathbb{E}\; \mathbf{B}$ if and only if $\models_x^{\mathfrak{U}} \Box(\mathbf{A} \leftrightarrow \mathbf{B})$, so $\mathbb{E}$ is a generalization of strict equivalence. (From now on we shall drop the superscript referring to the model when this can be done without endangering the understanding.)

We say that **A** is true in model $\mathfrak{U}$ if and only if **A** is true at every point in $\mathfrak{U}$. If Σ is a set of formulas every formula of which is true in $\mathfrak{U}$, then $\mathfrak{U}$ is a model for Σ. **A** is valid in a class C of models if and only if **A** is true in all models in C. If Σ is exactly the set of formulas valid in C, then we say that Σ is determined by C. Our main problem in this paper will be to find the set of formulas determined by the class of all models.

Our basic logic will be called *PK*–*P* for probability and *K* for Kripke – and it is axiomatized by the following axiom system. The rules are two,

$$\frac{\mathbf{A} \quad \mathbf{A} \to \mathbf{B}}{\mathbf{B}} \text{ (modus ponens)}; \qquad \frac{\mathbf{A}}{\Box \mathbf{A}} \text{ (necessitation)}.$$

The axioms are first of all the tautologies of classical propositional logic; secondly the instances of the characteristic schema of the modal logic *K*,

#0. $\Box(\mathbf{A} \to \mathbf{B}) \to (\Box \mathbf{A} \to \Box \mathbf{B})$;

and thirdly all instances of the following schemata:

#1. $\Box(\mathbf{A} \leftrightarrow \mathbf{A}') \wedge \Box(\mathbf{B} \leftrightarrow \mathbf{B}') \to (\mathbf{A} \gtrsim \mathbf{B} \to \mathbf{A}' \gtrsim \mathbf{B}')$.

#2. $\bot \gtrsim \bot$.

#3. $A \gtrsim A \wedge B \gtrsim B \rightarrow (A \rightarrow B) \gtrsim (A \rightarrow B)$.

#4. $A \gtrsim B \rightarrow A \gtrsim A$.

#5. $A \gtrsim B \rightarrow B \gtrsim B$.

#6. $A \gtrsim A \wedge B \gtrsim B \rightarrow A \gtrsim B \vee B \gtrsim A$.

#7. $A_1 \ldots A_m \; \mathbb{E} \; B_1 \ldots B_m \rightarrow (A_1 \gtrsim B_1 \wedge \ldots \wedge A_m \gtrsim B_m$

$\rightarrow B_1 \gtrsim A_1 \wedge \ldots \wedge B_m \gtrsim A_m)$, for all $m \geqslant 1$.

#8. $\top > \bot$.

#9. $A \gtrsim A \rightarrow A \gtrsim \bot$.

We say that a set L of formulas is a normal extension of *PK* if $PK \subseteq L$ and L is closed under modus ponens, necessitation and substitution. Note this replacement rule derivable for any normal extension L of *PK*: if $\vdash_L A \leftrightarrow B$ and $\mathbf{C}'$ is like $\mathbf{C}$ except for containing $\mathbf{B}$ in some place where $\mathbf{C}$ has $\mathbf{A}$, then $\vdash_L \mathbf{C} \leftrightarrow \mathbf{C}'$.

Consistency theorem for *PK*. *The theorems of PK are true in all models.*

Proof. We omit the inductive proof, the only difficulty of which is to show that all instances of #7 are true in all models. This difficulty is removed as follows. Let x be any element in some arbitrary model $\mathfrak{U} = \langle U, R, V, B, M \rangle$, and assume that for some formulas $\mathbf{A}_1, \ldots, \mathbf{A}_m, \mathbf{B}_1, \ldots, \mathbf{B}_m$,

$$\models_x A_1 \ldots A_m \; \mathbb{E} \; B_1 \ldots B_m \; ; \tag{1}$$

$$\models_x A_i \gtrsim B_i, \text{ for all } i \text{ such that } 1 \leqslant i \leqslant m . \tag{2}$$

Let the symbols δ and ϵ be used to stand for either the empty string of symbols or the negation sign. We call a set

$$\|\delta_1 A_1 \wedge \ldots \wedge \delta_m A_m \wedge \epsilon_1 B_1 \wedge \ldots \wedge \epsilon_m B_m \|_x$$

a cell if and only if, for some p such that $0 \leqslant p \leqslant m$, exactly p of the δ's and p of the ϵ's are the empty string. Let C be a variable running over the set of cells. If

$$C = \|\delta_1 \mathbf{A}_1 \wedge \ldots \wedge \delta_m \mathbf{A}_m \wedge \epsilon_1 \mathbf{B}_1 \wedge \ldots \wedge \epsilon_m \mathbf{B}_m\|_x$$

and δ_i (ϵ_i) is the empty string, then we say that δ_i (ϵ_i) is empty in C. Because of (1), for $1 \leqslant i \leqslant m$,

$$\|\mathbf{A}_i\|_x = \bigcup\{C : \delta_i \text{ is empty in } C\}\,;$$

$$\|\mathbf{B}_i\|_x = \bigcup\{C : \epsilon_i \text{ is empty in } C\}\,.$$

The cells are pairwise disjoint. Thus, since M_x is a probability measure,

$$M_x(\|\mathbf{A}_i\|_x) = \sum_{\delta_i \text{ empty in } C} M_x(C)\,;$$

$$M_x(\|\mathbf{B}_i\|_x) = \sum_{\epsilon_i \text{ empty in } C} M_x(C)\,.$$

Let

$$S = \sum_{i=1}^{m} M_x(\|\mathbf{A}_i\|_x)\,;$$

$$T = \sum_{i=1}^{m} M_x(\|\mathbf{B}_i\|_x)\,.$$

Then

$$S = \sum_{i=1}^{m} \sum_{\delta_i \text{ empty in } C} M_x(C)\,;$$

$$T = \sum_{i=1}^{m} \sum_{\epsilon_i \text{ empty in } C} M_x(C)\,.$$

It is easy to see that, for any fixed C, $M_x(C)$ will occur as many times in S as in T, and vice versa. Hence,

$$S = T\,. \tag{3}$$

It follows from (2) that, for $1 \leqslant i \leqslant m$,

$$M_x(\|\mathbf{A}_i\|_x) \geqslant M_x(\|\mathbf{B}_i\|_x)\,. \tag{4}$$

The combination of (3) and (4) implies that, for $1 \leqslant i \leqslant m$,

$$M_x(\|\mathbf{A}_i\|_x) = M_x(\|\mathbf{B}_i\|_x)\,.$$

Hence, for all i such that $1 \leqslant i \leqslant m$,

$$\models_x \mathbf{B}_i \gtrsim \mathbf{A}_i\,,$$

which is what we wanted to establish.

We now turn to the task of proving the converse of the Consistency Theorem – that the formulas true in all models are theorems of *PK*. We begin by introducing several new concepts.

Suppose θ is a set of formulas such that θ is closed under subformulas and $\bot \in \theta$. Let

$$\Delta = \{\mathbf{A}\text{: for some } \mathbf{B},\ \mathbf{A} \gtrsim \mathbf{B} \in \theta \ \text{ or } \mathbf{B} \gtrsim \mathbf{A} \in \theta\}\,,$$

and let Δ' be the closure of Δ under Boolean compounds. If θ satisfies also the condition that $\mathbf{A} \gtrsim \mathbf{B} \in \theta$, for all $\mathbf{A}, \mathbf{B} \in \Delta'$, then we shall say that θ is *stuffed*. The formulas in Δ' will be called the *value formulas* of θ. Note that there can be no occurrence of $\gtrsim$ in a value formula.

Let L be any normal extension of *PK*. We say that a formula set Ψ_0 is a *base* (with respect to L) for a set Ψ if for every $\mathbf{A} \in \Psi$ there is some $\mathbf{A}_0 \in \Psi_0$ such that $\vdash_L \mathbf{A} \leftrightarrow \mathbf{A}_0$. We say that Ψ is *logically finite* (with respect to L) if there is a finite base for Ψ. Note that a set has a finite base if it has a logically finite one.

Lemma 1. *If Ψ is a finite set of formulas closed under subformulas, and if θ is the smallest stuffed superset of Ψ, then θ is logically finite.*

Proof. Let $\Delta = \{\mathbf{A}\text{: for some } \mathbf{B},\ \mathbf{A} \gtrsim \mathbf{B} \in \Psi \text{ or } \mathbf{B} \gtrsim \mathbf{A} \in \Psi\}$, and let Δ' be the closure of Δ under Boolean compounds. Δ is finite, and, even though Δ' is infinite as soon as Δ is non-empty, Δ' is logically finite (as can be seen, for example, by using a normal form argument). Let Δ^* be a finite base for Δ' and define θ_0 as the closure under subformulas of the finite set

$$\Psi \cup \{\mathbf{A} \gtrsim \mathbf{B} : \mathbf{A}, \mathbf{B} \in \Delta^*\} .$$

Clearly θ_0 is finite. We shall show that θ_0 is a base for θ. Take any $\mathbf{A} \in \theta$. If $\mathbf{A}$ does not contain the $\gtrsim$-operator, then either $\mathbf{A} \in \Psi$ or $\mathbf{A}$ is a Boolean compound of formulas in Ψ. In the former case $\mathbf{A} \in \theta_0$, and certainly $\vdash_L \mathbf{A} \leftrightarrow \mathbf{A}$. In the latter case $\mathbf{A} \in \Delta'$, and hence there is some $\mathbf{A}' \in \Delta^*$ such that $\vdash_L \mathbf{A} \leftrightarrow \mathbf{A}'$; and $\Delta^* \subseteq \theta_0$. On the other hand, if $\mathbf{A}$ contains the $\gtrsim$-operator, then there are $\mathbf{B}$ and $\mathbf{C}$, Boolean compounds of formulas in Δ, such that $\mathbf{A} = \mathbf{B} \gtrsim \mathbf{C}$. Thus there are $\mathbf{B}^*, \mathbf{C}^* \in \Delta^*$ such that $\vdash_L \mathbf{B} \leftrightarrow \mathbf{B}^*$ and $\vdash_L \mathbf{C} \leftrightarrow \mathbf{C}^*$. Consequently, $\vdash_L \mathbf{B} \gtrsim \mathbf{C} \leftrightarrow \mathbf{B}^* \gtrsim \mathbf{C}^*$; and $\mathbf{B}^* \gtrsim \mathbf{C}^* \in \theta_0$. This ends the proof.

We assume now that L is an arbitrary fixed normal extension of PK. We let X_L denote the set of all L-maximal sets of formulas, and define the relation R_L and the function V_L as follows:

$$xR_Ly \text{ iff, for all } \mathbf{A},\ \Box\mathbf{A} \in x \text{ only if } \mathbf{A} \in y ;$$

$$V_L(n,x) = \begin{cases} 1, & \text{if } \mathbf{P}_n \in x , \\ 0, & \text{if } \mathbf{P}_n \notin x ; \end{cases}$$

for all $x, y \in X_L$ and all $n \in N$. Furthermore, assume that X is a fixed subset of X_L, either all of X_L or else $\{x : t{=}x \text{ or } tR_L^{*}x\}$, for some $t \in X_L$ (where R_L^{*} is the ancestral of R_L). We assume that R and V are the restrictions of R_L and V_L to X. A fact worth noting is that, for all $\mathbf{A}$ and for all $x \in X$, if $\mathbf{A} \in y$ for all y such that xRy then $\Box\mathbf{A} \in x$.

Let θ be a stuffed set of formulas, logically finite with respect to L. We define, for $x, y \in X$,

$$x \sim y \text{ iff } x \cap \theta = y \cap \theta .$$

Clearly $\sim$ is an equivalence relation in X. We write $[x]$ for the equivalence class of x, and $X^{\sim}$ for the set of all equivalence classes. Let $R^{\sim}$ be a binary relation on $X^{\sim}$ such that

(i) if xRy, then $[x]R^{\sim}[y]$;

(ii) if $[x]R^{\sim}[y]$ and $\Box\mathbf{A} \in x \cap \theta$, then $\mathbf{A} \in y$.

(It is easily verified that these conditions are meaningful and that there are relations $R^{\sim}$ that satisfy them.) Let $V^{\sim}$ be any function such that for every $\mathbf{P}_n \in \theta$,

$$V^{\sim}(n,[x]) = V(n,x)\,.$$

(Again the condition is meaningful and satisfiable.) We observe that $\mathcal{M}^{\sim} = \langle X^{\sim}, R^{\sim}, V^{\sim}\rangle$ is a Kripke model. Thus, for every $\xi \in X^{\sim}$, the set

$$\|\mathbf{A}\|_{\xi}^{\mathcal{M}^{\sim}} = \{\eta : \xi R^{\sim} \eta \text{ and } \models_{\eta}^{\mathcal{M}^{\sim}} \mathbf{A}\}$$

is well defined for every $\mathbf{A}$ which does not contain $\gtrsim$. (Strictly speaking, this is to make new use of $\|\ \|$ and $\models$, for $\mathcal{M}^{\sim}$ is a Kripke model and not a probability model. However, no confusion should result.)

Lemma 2. *If* $\mathbf{A} \in \theta$ *and* $\mathbf{A}$ *does not contain* $\gtrsim$*, then, for all* $x \in X$,

$$\models_{[x]}^{\mathcal{M}} \mathbf{A} \textit{ iff } \mathbf{A} \in x\,.$$

The proof goes by induction on the length of $\mathbf{A}$ and is omitted.

We shall try to supplement the Kripke model $\mathcal{M}^{\sim}$ with functions B and M so as to obtain a probability model $\mathcal{M}'$ for which the Lemma 2 holds for *all* formulas in θ. Doing this solves the completeness problem, at least for *PK*, as is explained later.

For $\xi \in X^{\sim}$ we define B_{ξ} as the set of all $\alpha \subseteq \{\eta : \xi R^{\sim} \eta\}$ such that for some value formula $\mathbf{A} \in \theta$, $\mathbf{A} \gtrsim \mathbf{A} \in x$, for any $x \in \xi$, and $\alpha = \|\mathbf{A}\|_{\xi}$. We observe that if $\mathbf{A} \in \theta$ is a value formula then $\mathbf{A} \gtrsim \mathbf{A} \in \theta$, so that $\mathbf{A} \gtrsim \mathbf{A}$ belongs to some $x \in \xi$ if and only if $\mathbf{A} \gtrsim \mathbf{A}$ belongs to every $x \in \xi$.

Lemma 3. *For each* $\xi \in X^{\sim}$, B_{ξ} *is a Boolean algebra with* $\emptyset$ *as zero element and* $\{\eta : \xi R^{\sim} \eta\}$ *as unit element.*

We omit the proof, which is straightforward. It may be mentioned that it uses both the fact that L contains all instances of ## 2–3, and the fact that replacement holds for L.

For $\xi \in X^{\sim}$ we define $\alpha \geqslant_{\xi} \beta$ to hold between elements α, β of B_{ξ} if and only if there are value formulas $\mathbf{A}, \mathbf{B} \in \theta$ such that $\alpha = \|\mathbf{A}\|_{\xi}$, $\beta = \|\mathbf{B}\|_{\xi}$, and $\mathbf{A} \gtrsim \mathbf{B} \in x$, for any $x \in \xi$.

Lemma 4. *For all value formulas* $\mathbf{A}, \mathbf{B} \in \theta$ *and all* $\xi \in X^{\sim}$, $\|\mathbf{A}\|_{\xi} \geqslant_{\xi} \|\mathbf{B}\|_{\xi}$ *if and only if, for any* $x \in \xi$, $\mathbf{A} \gtrsim \mathbf{B} \in x$.

Proof. Assume that $\|\mathbf{A}\|_{\xi} \geqslant_{\xi} \|\mathbf{B}\|_{\xi}$. Then there are value formulas $\mathbf{A}', \mathbf{B}' \in \theta$ such that $\|\mathbf{A}\|_{\xi} = \|\mathbf{A}'\|_{\xi}$, $\|\mathbf{B}\|_{\xi} = \|\mathbf{B}'\|_{\xi}$, and $\mathbf{A}' \gtrsim \mathbf{B}' \in x$, for any $x \in \xi$. Take any $x \in \xi$ and any y such that xRy. By Lemma 2, $\mathbf{A} \leftrightarrow \mathbf{A}' \in y$ and $\mathbf{B} \leftrightarrow \mathbf{B}' \in y$. Hence $\Box(\mathbf{A}' \leftrightarrow \mathbf{A}) \wedge \Box(\mathbf{B}' \leftrightarrow \mathbf{B}) \in x$. Since every instance of schema # 1 is contained in L, it follows that $\mathbf{A} \gtrsim \mathbf{B} \in x$.

Conversely, assume that for all $x \in \xi$, $\mathbf{A} \gtrsim \mathbf{B} \in x$. From the fact that L contains all instances of schemata ## 4–5 we infer that, for all $x \in \xi$, $\mathbf{A} \gtrsim \mathbf{A}$, $\mathbf{B} \gtrsim \mathbf{B} \in x$. Hence $\|\mathbf{A}\|_\xi$, $\|\mathbf{B}\|_\xi \in B_\xi$, and $\|\mathbf{A}\|_\xi \geqslant_\xi \|\mathbf{B}\|_\xi$. The proof is complete.

Lemma 5. *For every $\xi \in X^{\sim}$, B_ξ and $\geqslant_\xi$ satisfy conditions (i)–(iv) of the Kraft/Pratt/Seidenberg theorem.*

Proof. Given Lemma 4 we are content to remark that the proofs that conditions (i)–(iii) are satisfied are easy and follow from the presence of schemata ## 8, 9, and 6, respectively. Somewhat more complicated is the proof of condition (iv): Assume that, for some positive integer m, $\alpha_1, \ldots, \alpha_m, \beta_1, \ldots, \beta_m$ are elements of B_ξ such that every atom of B_ξ belongs to exactly as many α's as β's. Assume, furthermore, that $\alpha_i \geqslant_\xi \beta_i$, for all i such that $1 \leqslant i \leqslant m$. Let $\mathbf{A}_1, \ldots, \mathbf{A}_m, \mathbf{B}_1, \ldots, \mathbf{B}_m$ be value formulas such that, for $1 \leqslant i \leqslant m$,

$$\alpha_i = \|\mathbf{A}_i\|_\xi\,, \qquad \beta_i = \|\mathbf{B}_i\|_\xi\,.$$

Let x be any element of ξ. It follows from Lemma 4 that, for all i such that $1 \leqslant i \leqslant m$, $\mathbf{A}_i \gtrsim \mathbf{B}_i \in x$. We claim that

$$\mathbf{A}_1 \ldots \mathbf{A}_m \;\mathbb{E}\; \mathbf{B}_1 \ldots \mathbf{B}_m \in x\,.$$

Let $\mathbf{C}_0, \ldots, \mathbf{C}_m$ be as in the definition, on p.342, of $\mathbb{E}$. We wish to prove that $\Box(\mathbf{C}_0 \vee \ldots \vee \mathbf{C}_m) \in x$. Let y be any element such that xRy. By the definition of $R^{\sim}$, condition (i) $\xi R^{\sim} [y]$. The atoms of B_ξ are the one-element subsets of $\{\eta : \xi R^{\sim} \eta\}$. Hence, by our hypothesis, $[y]$ belongs to the same number of α's as of β's. Say that that number is r (where, of course, $0 \leqslant r \leqslant m$); then $\models_{[y]} \mathbf{C}_r$. Since the $\mathbf{A}$'s and $\mathbf{B}$'s are value formulas, we know by Lemma 2 that $\models_{[y]} \mathbf{A}_i$ iff $\mathbf{A}_i \in y$ and $\models_{[y]} \mathbf{B}_i$ iff $\mathbf{B}_i \in y$, for $1 \leqslant i \leqslant m$. Therefore $\mathbf{C}_r \in y$, whence $\mathbf{C}_0 \vee \ldots \vee \mathbf{C}_m \in y$. This proves that $\Box(\mathbf{C}_0 \vee \ldots \vee \mathbf{C}_m) \in x$. Since L contains every instance of schema # 7 we conclude that, for all i such that $1 \leqslant i \leqslant m$, $\mathbf{B}_i \gtrsim \mathbf{A}_i \in x$ and hence, by Lemma 4, that $\beta_i \geqslant_\xi \alpha_i$. This ends the proof.

Since we assumed at the outset that θ is logically finite, $X^{\sim}$ is finite. Hence for every $\xi \in X^{\sim}$, B_ξ is finite, so it follows from Lemmata 3 and 5 that the Kraft/Pratt/Seidenberg theorem can be applied. In other words, for each $\xi \in X^{\sim}$ there is a probability measure M_ξ on B_ξ such that

$$M_\xi \alpha \geqslant M_\xi \beta \text{ iff } \alpha \geqslant_\xi \beta .$$

Let B and M be the functions on $X^\sim$ which for $\xi \in X^\sim$ take as values B_ξ and M_ξ, respectively. We define

$$\mathfrak{M}' = \langle X^\sim, R^\sim, V^\sim, B, M\rangle .$$

$\mathfrak{M}'$ is a probability model.

Lemma 6. *For all* $\mathbf{A} \in \theta$ *and all* $x \in X$

$$\models^{\mathfrak{M}}_{[x]} \mathbf{A} \text{ iff } \mathbf{A} \in x .$$

This is the announced improvement of Lemma 2. The proof goes by induction on the length of **A**, and in view of Lemma 4 it offers no problems.

We shall now, at long last, explain how the results obtained relate to the completeness problem. Suppose that $\mathbf{A}_0$ is a certain formula which cannot be derived in L (where L is still some normal extension of PK). Then $\{\mathbf{A}_0 \to \bot\}$ is an L-consistent set, and by Lindenbaum's Theorem it admits of an L-maximal extension, t say. Evidently $\mathbf{A}_0 \notin t$. Let Ψ be the set of subformulas of $\mathbf{A}_0$ – clearly a finite set – and let θ be the smallest stuffed extension of Ψ. By Lemma 1 θ is logically finite with respect to L. Let X be as above, either X_L itself or equal to $\{x : t = x \text{ or } tR_L^* x\}$. If $\mathfrak{M}'$ is constructed as above it follows from Lemma 6 that $\mathbf{A}_0$ is false at $[t]$ in $\mathfrak{M}'$. Thus, from the Consistency Theorem for PK, along with the fact that PK is a normal extension of itself, we infer:

Completeness theorem for *PK*. *PK is determined by the class of all models.*

However, there is more in our construction than this. In fact, using terminology not explained in this paper (but see, for example, [2]), suppose that L is a normal modal logic such that whenever Ψ is a finite set of formulas closed under subformulas then the canonical model for L has a filtration through Ψ which is a Kripke model for L. Let PL be L augmented with schemata ## 1–9 and closed under substitution, modus ponens and necessitation. Then our completeness argument works for PL. Not all, but the majority of modal logics described in the literature are of this sort. In particular many of the famous ones are – for example, the deontic logic D, von Wright's M, Lewis's $S4$ and $S5$, and Prior's Dioderean system. Thus, PD is determined by the class of all serial probability models, *PT* by the class of all reflexive probability models, etc.

We end the paper with three remarks. Directly they concern *PK*, but they are equally valid for the other systems just mentioned.

Remark 1. As our argument shows, *PK* is determined, not only by the class of models, but also by the class of all finite models. Thus it would have made no difference if in the definition of "probability model" we would have given up the conditions that B_x be a σ-algebra and M_x countably additive. Roughly speaking, the object language studied in this paper is too poor to allow the distinction between the two varieties of probability models.

Remark 2. *PK* has the finite model property, in the sense that every non-theorem of *PK* fails in a probability model with only finitely many elements. It may be noted that, although *PK* is axiomatizable, it does not *immediately* follow that *PK* is decidable; the reason is that, for every positive integer other than 1, there are non-denumerably many probability models of that cardinality. For if we are looking for a counter-model with at most a certain number of elements, how do we know that by examining probability models of the right cardinalities one by one we will find one, even if we know that one exists? However, *PK* is decidable, and one way to see it is this. Suppose a certain formula is not demonstrable in *PK*. We know then that it fails in some probability model with at most a certain number of elements. If we take a domain with at most that number of elements there are essentially but finitely many ways in which accessibility relations and valuations can be defined, and there are also but finitely many ways to define the function B. Finally, for each B_x, there are but finitely many ways in which a relation $\geqslant_x$ can be defined, and we know, by the Kraft/Pratt/Seidenberg theorem, which of these definitions will give us definitions of M_x that are probability measures on B_x. And to decide, of a given relation $\geqslant_x$, whether it satisfies conditions (i)–(iv) of the Kraft/Pratt/Seidenberg theorem can be done in finitely many steps. Thus we are sure to find, in at most a finite number of steps, a counter-model of the unprovable formula; in fact, we could compute an upper bound to the number of steps needed. Thus *PK* is decidable.

Remark 3. The requirement that formulas do not contain nestings of the $\gtrsim$-operator can be abandoned with no change in the formulation of the Completeness Theorem. More precisely, let formulas of the latter kind be called unrestricted, and let PK^* be the smallest set of unrestricted formulas that is closed under substitution, modus ponens and necessitation and contains all instances of ## 1–9. Then PK^* is determined by the class of all models (as well as by the class of all finite models). Technically what one must do is to build up the model $\mathcal{M}'$ in several steps corresponding to the degree of nestedness of the formulas of θ. The problem is solved in Jan-Henrik Johansson's unpublished thesis for the degree of *filosofie licentiat* at Åbo Akademi (May, 1970).

References

[1] D.Scott, Measurement structures and linear inequalities, Journal of mathematical psychology, Vol. 1 (1964) 233–247.

[2] K.Segerberg, Decidability of S4.1, Theoria, Vol. 34 (1968) 7–20.

[3] K.Segerberg, Kripke-type semantics for preference logic, in: Logic and value, Essays dedicated to Thorild Dahlquist on his fiftieth birthday (Uppsala, 1971).

NORMAL FORM THEOREM FOR BAR RECURSIVE FUNCTIONS OF FINITE TYPE

W.W.TAIT
University of Illinois at Chicago Circle

1. **Introduction**

1.1. We will prove a Normal Form Theorem for the bar recursive functions of finite type, which were introduced in Spector 1962. These functions will be represented by the bar recursive terms, which are built up from constants denoting the basic operators of explicit definition, primitive recursion and bar recursion. Rules of conversion will be introduced to express the action of these operators. The Normal Form Theorem asserts that every bar recursive term reduces, by means of a finite sequence of conversions, to a unique *normal* term. A normal term is one with no convertible subterms. The normal numerical terms (i.e. of type 0) are the numerals; and so, in particular, the theorem asserts that every numerical bar recursive term has a unique and computable value. The proof that, when t reduces to a normal term, the normal term is unique, is elementary (see 3.4). When such a normal term exists, it is called the *normal form* or *value* of t.

1.2. The proof of the Normal Form Theorem will involve a modified version of the notion of *convertible term,* used in Tait 1967 to prove the normal form theorem for Gödel's 1958 primitive recursive functions of finite type, with and without bar recursion of type 0. In each case, the notion of convertibility is defined for a class of terms which includes, but may extend, the class we are interested in. The uniqueness of normal form (when it exists) will hold for this more extensive class, too. The form of the definition of convertibility is always this:

1.2.1. A term is 0 *convertible* iff it reduces to a numeral.

1.2.2. A term s is $\sigma \to \tau$ *convertible* iff it has a value and, for all σ convertible t, (st) is τ convertible. Sometimes, as in this paper (see 8.2, below), it is possible to so restrict the rules of conversion that the condition in 1.2.2, that *s* have a value, is redundant. However that may be, convertibility always implies the existence of a normal form; and we prove the normal form theorem for a class of terms by proving that they are convertible (relative to the possibly more extensive class of terms). The difference in the treatments of the primitive recursive functions and their extensions by adding bar recursion of various types lies in what we are required to include among the terms in the definition of convertibility, in order to prove that the terms we are interested in are convertible.

1.3. In the case of the primitive recursive functions, we have two natural choices as to the class of terms we include in the definition of convertibility. We could choose just the primitive recursive terms themselves, as in Tait 1967. I will refer to the resulting notion of convertibility as *minimum* convertibility for primitive recursion, since this is the least class of terms relative to which all primitive recursive terms are convertible. Alternatively, we could regard the primitive recursive terms as embedded in the (type-free) theory of combinators, and let the terms include all of the terms of this theory, as was suggested in Tait 1968. I will refer to the resulting notion of convertibility as *general* convertibility. The general convertible terms are essentially the *effective operations* of finite type, introduced in Kreisel 1959; but with this difference: The effective operations were introduced in terms of the equational calculus; and in these terms, Gödel's notion of *definitional equality* has no natural analysis. In terms of combinator theory (of equivalents, such as the calculus of lambda conversion), definitional equality has the natural meaning: have the same normal form. Of course, we have proved more when we prove that the primitive recursive terms are general convertible, rather than simply minimum convertible. E.g. *s* is of type $\sigma \to 0$, we have proved that (st) has a numerical value for all general computable t, and not merely for primitive recursive t. On the other hand, minimum convertibility provides a minimum model for the theory T of primitive recursive functions (Gödel 1958). Note that, in either case, the definition of convertibility is formalizable in artithmetic; and, for each primitive recursive *s*, the proof that *s* is convertible can be carried out in intuitionistic arithmetic. This leads to an interpretation of T in arithmetic, complementing Gödel's interpretation of arithmetic in T. (See Tait 1967 for details.)

1.4. In the case of bar recursion, the terms in which we are ultimately interested, the bar recursive terms, are still combinatorial objects (i.e., strings of symbols). But, to prove them convertible, we must extend the class of terms in the definition of convertibility to include certain "abstract" terms. In the case of bar recursion of type 0, we must consider terms built up, not only from constants, but also from free choice sequences of numerals, where the conversion rule for such a sequence α is

$$\alpha\bar{n} \to \alpha(n)$$

(where $\bar{n}$ is the numeral for n). The reason for this is that bar recursion of type 0 is recursion on the well-founded ordering of unsecured sequences of a function s of type $(0\to 0) \to 0$. But, for this ordering to be well-founded, we need more than that (st) have a value for each general recursive t: we must know that $(s\alpha)$ has a value for each free choice sequence of numbers α. Aside from the introduction of free choice sequences, it should be noted that we still have a choice between the *minimum* convertibility for bar recursion of type 0, in which we restrict the constants to those of the bar recursive terms (with bar recursion only of type 0), and *general* convertibility with free choice sequences of numerals, in which we allow terms from the general theory of combinators. In either case, the terms can be coded by sequences of numbers, σ-convertibility is expressed by an analytic formula for each σ, and the proof that a given bar recursive term, involving only bar recursion of type 0, is convertible can be carried out in intuitionistic analysis (with the axioms of choice and bar induction). This yields the result that Spector's theory Σ_4 of bar recursive functions can be interpreted in intuitionistic analysis when bar recursion is restricted to type 0. Using the Gödel interpretation, the converse is also true: Intuitionistic analysis can be interpreted in the restricted Σ_4.

1.5. Our aim here is to extend the above ideas to the treatment of bar recursion of arbitrary finite type, i.e. recursion on the unsecured sequences of a function of any type of the form $(0\to\sigma) \to 0$. The purpose is not so much to present as constructive a proof of the normal form theorem as possible, as it is to cast the proof in what seems now to be a very general form (see Martin-Löf 1970a, 1970b, and Girard 1970) of the convertibility method. It is certainly reasonable to believe that the study of the appropriate notion of convertibility will be a good way to look for a more direct understanding of the computation of bar recursive functions. The appropriate notion of convertibility in this case is a straight-forward generalization of the case of bar recursion of type 0: we must admit as terms free choice sequences of normal terms of any given type. The main difference lies in the fact that, for type 0, the normal terms are numerals, which are combinatorial objects. But, for $\sigma \neq 0$, the normal terms may themselves contain choice sequences; and so, we need to consider choice sequences whose elements are themselves abstract. There is no difficulty in making this notion precise; and having done so, the proof of convertibility is essentially like the proof in Tait 1967 for bar recursion of type 0 – at least, from the classical point of view. However, because I would like to reformulate the treatment in the earlier paper more explicitly along the lines described in 1.4, the details will be given in full here. But, we will restrict ourselves to the minimum convertibility for bar recursion. (The corresponding general convertibility offers no new problems.)

1.6. For each bar recursive term s, the proof that it is convertible can be carried out in classical analysis with the axiom of dependent choice. Just as in the case of primitive recursion and bar recursion of type 0 in Tait 1967, this leads to a interpretation of Σ_4 in analysis with dependent choice. This latter system is interpretable in analysis without choice, since dependent choice holds in analysis with the analytic version of $V = L$. The circle is completed by Spector's interpretation of analysis in Σ_4. One can also interpret Σ_4 in analysis with dependent choice by interpreting the bar recursive terms as *continuous* (or *countable*) functions of finite type, in the sense of Kleene 1959 and Kreisel 1959. However, although this interpretation works for Σ_4, which only contains numerical equations, it does not work for T, which contains equations of arbitrary type with the axioms $s = t \vee \neg s = t$. For, as in the case of the effective operations, no notion of definitional equality is defined for the continuous functions.

2. The terms of finite type

2.1. The *finite types* are inductively defined by

2.1.1. 0 is a finite type.

2.1.2. If σ and τ are finite types, then so is $(\sigma \to \tau)$. We will write $\rho \to \ldots \to \sigma \to \tau$ for $(\rho \to \ldots \to (\sigma \to \tau) \ldots)$. Thus, each finite type has a unique expression in one of the forms $0, \sigma \to 0, \rho \to \sigma \to 0$, etc.

The intended interpretation of the finite types is this: The objects of type 0 are the natural numbers. The objects of type $\sigma \to \tau$ are certain functions defined for all objects of type σ and whose values are of type τ. We have several choices as to which such functions we take as objects of type $\sigma \to \tau$, corresponding to the different notions of convertability discussed in 1.

2.2. We introduce some *constants* for the basic operations by means of which the bar recursive functions are built up.

2.2.1. $\bar{0}$ is a constant of type 0, intended to denote the number 0.

2.2.2. S is a constant of type $0 \to 0$, intended to denote the *successor* operation.

2.2.3. P is a constant of each type of the form $\sigma \to \tau \to \sigma$, and is intended to denote a *projection* operation.

2.2.4. K is a constant of each type of the form $(\rho{\to}\sigma{\to}\tau) \to (\rho{\to}\sigma) \to \rho \to \tau$, and is intended to denote a *composition* operation.

2.2.5. R is a constant of each type of the form $\tau \to (0{\to}\tau{\to}\tau) \to 0 \to \tau$, and is intended to denote the *primitive recursion* operation.

2.2.6. B is a constant of each type of the form $\tau \to ((\sigma{\to}\tau){\to}\tau) \to ((0{\to}\sigma){\to}0) \to (0{\to}\sigma) \to 0 \to \tau$, and is intended to denote the *bar recursion* operation. The precise meaning of these constants will be given by their conversion rules, below.

2.3. *Terms of finite type.*

2.3.1. The terms of finite type are inductively defined by

2.3.1.1. Each constant of type τ is a term of type τ.

2.3.1.2. If φ is a numerical function, i.e. if $\varphi(n)$ is a number for each number n, then the pair (τ,φ) is a term of type $0 \to \tau$.

2.3.1.3. If s and t are terms of types $\sigma \to \tau$ and σ, resp., then (st) is a term of type τ.

2.3.2. The terms denoting bar recursive functions, the *bar recursive terms*, are those built up using 2.3.1.1 and 2.3.1.3. But, in order to prove these terms computable, we will need to consider the wider class of terms involving 2.3.1.2. We will assume that the terms are coded by numerical functions in such a way that it is decidable whether φ is the code for a term; and if it is, we can decide what types it has and can compute its subterms.

2.3.3. Intended meaning of terms of the form (τ,φ). When f is a numerical functions, define f_m by $f_m(n) = f(\langle m,n\rangle)$, where $\langle m,n\rangle$ is some standard one-to-one pairing operation for the natural numbers. When f is the code for a term of type τ, then $f^{(\tau)}$ denotes that term; otherwise, $f^{(\tau)}$ will denote the term $\bar{0}_\tau$ of type τ, which we will define below in 4.6. The term (τ,φ) is intended to denote the sequence $\varphi_0^{(\tau)}, \varphi_1^{(\tau)}, \varphi_2^{(\tau)}, \ldots$ of terms of type τ.

2.3.4. When r is of type $\rho \to \ldots \to \sigma \to \tau$ and $s, \ldots, t$ are of types $\rho, \ldots, \sigma$, resp., then $rs\ldots t$ denotes the term $(\ldots(rs)\ldots t)$ of type τ.

2.3.5. The *numerals* are the terms $\bar{0}$, $\bar{1} = S\bar{0}$, $\bar{2} = S\bar{1}$, etc., of type 0. Thus, in accordance with the intended meaning, $\bar{n}$ denotes the number n.

2.3.6. The notion of a *subterm* of a term is inductively defined by

2.3.6.1. Every term is a subterm of itself.

2.3.6.2. Every subterm of s or of t is a subterm of st. A *proper* subterm of t is a subterm of t other than itself. A proper subterm of t may have more than one occurrence in t.

2.3.7. A term is called *normal* if it has no subterms of the form *Prs, Krst, Rrst, Brstuv* or $(\tau,\varphi)t$. It will turn out, after we have introduced all the rules of conversion, that the normal terms are precisely the terms which cannot be reduced by means of conversions. The only normal terms of type 0 are the numerals.

3. Reduction of terms

3.1. In sections 4, 5 and 6, we will introduce a system of conversions $u \to v$, where u and v are terms of the same types. This system will have the property that

3.1.1. If $u \to v$ is a conversion, then all proper subterms of u are normal – and consequently are not themselves the left hand terms of conversions; and

3.1.2. If $u \to v$ and $u \to w$ are conversions, then $v = w$.

3.2. If s is obtained by replacing one occurrence of the subterm u of r by v, and $u \to v$ is a conversion, then s is called an *immediate reduct* of r. If each member of the sequence $r, s, \ldots, t$, other than the first, is an immediate reduct of its predecessor, then the sequence is called a *reduction* of r to t, t is called a *reduct* of r and we write $r \mathrel{=\!\!|} t$. The one element sequence r is a reduction of r to r; and so $r \mathrel{=\!\!|} r$. If $r \mathrel{=\!\!|} t$, then r and t are terms of the same types.

3.3. *If there are reductions of r to s and t of lengths m and n, resp., then there are reductions of s and t to a common term of lengths n and m, resp.*

The proof is by induction on $m + n$.

3.3.1. If $m = 1$, then $r = s$ and the result is immediate. Similarly if $n = 1$. So, we will assume that $m > 1$ and $n > 1$.

3.3.2. Let $m = n = 2$. Then s and t are immediate reducts of r. Thus, s is obtained by replacing an occurrence of u by v in r and t is obtained by replacing an occurrence of u' by v' in r, where $u \to v$ and $u' \to v'$ are conversions. If the occurrence of u and the occurrence of u' overlap, then one of these terms must be a subterm of the other. By 3.1.1, it would follow that $u = u'$; and so by 3.1.2, $v = v'$ and $s = t$. Hence, we can assume that the occurrences of u and u' have no symbol occurrences in common. So, we can write $r = p(u,u')$, $s = p(v,u')$ and $t = p(u,v')$. It follows that $p(v,v')$ is an immediate reduct of both s and t.

3.3.3. Let $m > 2$. Then there is a reduction of r to some s' of length $m - 1$, where s' is an immediate reduct of s. By the induction hypothesis, since $m - 1 + n < m + n$, there are reductions of s' and t to some term p of lengths n and $m - 1$, resp. s' has reductions to s and p of lengths 2 and n, resp., and $2 + n < m + n$. So, again, by the induction hypothesis, s and p have reductions of lengths n and 2, resp., to some term q. Since t has a reduction to p of length $m - 1$, it has a reduction to q of length m.

3.3.4. The case $n > 2$ (and m=2) is covered in 3.3.3 by renaming s and t.

This completes the proof.

3.4. Uniqueness of normal form. If r reduces to s and to t, and t is normal, then s reduces to t, by 3.3. If s is also normal, then $s = t$. Thus, there is at most one normal term to which r can reduce. This normal term, when it exists, is called the *normal form* or the *value* of r.

3.5. The following lemma will be needed for our analysis in 9.7 of bar recursion.

3.5.1. *Let $t(u)$ denote a term of type* 0 *containing* 0 *or more designated occurrences of the normal term u of type $0 \to \sigma$. ($t(u)$ may also contain some undesignated occurrences of u.) $t(u')$ denotes the result of replacing each designated occurrence of u in $t(u)$ by the term u' of type $0 \to \sigma$. Assume that $t(u)$ reduces to $\overline{m}$, and that, for each n such that $u\overline{n}$ occurs in the reduction, $u\overline{n}$ and $u'\overline{n}$ have the same value u_n. Then $t(u')$ reduces to $\overline{m}$.*

The proof is by induction on the length k of the reduction of $t(u)$ to $\overline{m}$.

3.5.1.1. $k = 1$. Then $t(u) = t(u') = \overline{m}$.

3.5.1.2. $k > 0$ and the result holds for all shorter reductions.

3.5.1.2.1. Assume that the first step in the reduction does not involve a conversion $u\overline{n} \to s$ on a designated occurrence of u. Then, since u is normal, the first step of the reduction is of the form $t(u) =\!| \; t'(u)$, where $t'(u')$ is an immediate reduct of $t(u')$. By the induction hypothesis, $t'(u') =\!| \; \overline{m}$.

3.5.1.2.2. Assume that the first step of the reduction of $t(u)$ to $\overline{m}$ does involve a conversion $u\overline{n} \to s$ on a designated occurrence of u. Then the first step has the form $t(u) = t_0(u,u\overline{n}) =\!| \; t_0(u,s)$. By the induction hypothesis, $t_0(u',s) =\!| \; \overline{m}$. But $s =\!| \; u_n$ and $u'\overline{n} =\!| \; u_n$; and so $t(u') = t_0(u',u'\overline{n})$ reduces to $\overline{m}$, by 3.4.

This completes the proof.

3.5.2. We can express 3.5.1 by saying that the value of $t(u)$ does not depend on u but only on a finite number of its values $u\overline{n}$.

4. Explicit definition

4.1. The conversion rules for P and K are

4.1.1. $\quad Prs \to r$.

4.1.2. $\quad Krst \to rt(st)$.

r, s and t are to be normal terms of suitable types.

4.2. We will apply Curry's method (Curry and Feys 1958) of reducing explicit definition to the theory of combinators. This can be done even though our terms have type structure and we have chosen to use a restricted notion of reduction. (If $u \to v$ is a conversion, then the proper subterms of u are normal.)

4.3. Let $x, y, \ldots, z$ be distinct new symbols called *variables of types* $\rho, \sigma, \ldots, \tau$, resp. When we want to indicate the type of x, we write it as x^ρ. The definition of *term form in* $x, y, \ldots, z$ is obtained by regarding $x, y, \ldots, z$ as constants of types $\rho, \sigma, \ldots, \tau$ in the definition 2.3.1 of the terms.

4.4. Let t be a term form of type π in $x, y, \ldots, z$. We define the term form $\lambda x.t$ of type $\rho \to \pi$ in $y, \ldots, z$ by induction on t:

4.4.1. If t is a constant, one of $y, \ldots, z$ or of the form (x,φ), then $\lambda x.t = Pt$. Since P has type $\pi \to \rho \to \pi$, this has the required type.

4.4.2. If t is x, then $\lambda x.t$ is KPP. K has type $(\rho\to(0\to\rho)\to\rho) \to (\rho\to 0\to\rho) \to \rho \to \rho$, and P has the types $\rho \to (0\to\rho) \to \rho$ and $\rho \to 0 \to \rho$; and so KPP has type $\rho \to \rho$, which is what is required, since $\pi = \rho$ in this case.

4.4.3. If t is rs, set $\lambda x.t = K(\lambda x.r)(\lambda x.s)$.

This completes the definition.

4.5. *Let* $t(x^\rho)$ *be a term form in* x. *Then* $\lambda x.t(x)$ *is a normal term, and for each normal term* s *of type* ρ,

$$(\lambda x.t(x))s \;=\!\!\mid\; t(s)\,.$$

The proof is straightforward, by induction on $t(x)$.

4.6. The term $\bar{0}_\sigma$ is defined by induction on σ.

4.6.1. $\bar{0}_0 = \bar{0}$.

4.6.2. $\bar{0}_{\sigma\to\tau} = \lambda x^\sigma.\bar{0}_\tau$.

So, $\bar{0}_\sigma$ is a normal term of type σ.

5. Primitive recursion

5.1. The conversion rules for R are

5.1.1. $$Rrs\bar{0} \to r\,.$$

5.1.2. $$Rrs\overline{n+1} \to s\bar{n}(Rrs\bar{n})\,.$$

r and s are to be normal terms.

5.2. In terms of $\bar{0}$, S, P, K and R, we can define any primitive recursive function of finite type, in the sense of Gödel 1958. In particular, we can find:

5.2.1. A term F of type $0 \to 0 \to 0$ such that

$$F\bar{m}\bar{n} \mathrel{=\!|} \begin{cases} \bar{1}, \text{ if } m < n\,. \\ \bar{0}, \text{ if } n \leqslant m\,. \end{cases}$$

5.2.2. A term G of type $(0 \to \sigma) \to 0 \to 0 \to \sigma$ such that, if s is normal

$$Gs\bar{m}\bar{n} \mathrel{=\!|} \begin{cases} s\bar{n}, \text{ if } n < m\,. \\ \bar{0}_\sigma, \text{ if } m \leqslant n\,. \end{cases}$$

5.2.3. A term H of type $(0 \to \sigma) \to 0 \to \sigma \to 0 \to \sigma$ such that, if s and t are normal

$$Hs\bar{m}t\bar{n} \mathrel{=\!|} \begin{cases} t, \quad \text{if } m = n\,. \\ s\bar{n}, \text{ if } m \neq n\,. \end{cases}$$

5.2.4. A term J of type $0 \to \tau \to (0 \to \tau) \to 0 \to \tau$ such that if r and s are normal,

$$J\bar{1}rs\bar{m} \mathrel{=\!|} r\,, \qquad J\bar{0}rs\bar{m} \mathrel{=\!|} s\bar{m}\,.$$

The terms F, G, H and J are needed to express the conversion rule for bar recursion, in the next section. It is important to notice that these terms do not involve B or any subterms of the form (τ,φ): They are *primitive recursive terms.*

6. Bar recursion

6.1. We define

6.1.1. $\langle u;q \rangle \; = Guq$.

6.1.2. $\langle u;q,v \rangle = H\langle u;q \rangle qv$

when u, q and v are of types $0 \to \sigma$, 0 and σ, resp. Thus, if u is the sequence $(u_0,u_1,...)$ – i.e. $u\bar{n} =\!\mid u_n$ for each n – then $\langle u;\bar{n} \rangle$ represents $(u_0,...,u_{n-1}, \bar{0}_\sigma,\bar{0}_\sigma,...)$ and $\langle u;\bar{n},v \rangle$ represents $(u_0,...,u_{n-1},v,\bar{0}_\sigma,\bar{0}_\sigma,...)$.

6.2. The conversion rule for P is

$$Brstu\bar{n} \to J(F(t\langle u;\bar{n}\rangle)\bar{n})r(\lambda x^0 .s(\lambda z^\sigma .Brst\langle u;\bar{n},z\rangle \overline{n+1})\bar{n} .$$

Thus, for each σ and τ, this rule holds for normal r, s, t and u of types τ, $(\sigma\to\tau) \to \tau$, $(0\to\sigma) \to 0$ and $0 \to \sigma$, resp.

6.3. Let $t\langle u;\bar{n}\rangle$ reduce to $\bar{m}$. Then

$$Brstu\bar{n} =\!\mid \begin{cases} r, \text{ if } m < n \\ s(\lambda z^\sigma .Brst \langle u;\bar{n},z\rangle \overline{n+1}), \text{ if } n \leqslant m . \end{cases}$$

Write $v = \lambda x^0 .s(\lambda z^\sigma .Brst \langle u;\bar{n},z\rangle \overline{n+1})$.

v is normal, since every term of the form $\lambda x.p$ is. Thus, the right hand side of the conversion 6.2 reduces to

$$J(F\bar{m}\bar{n})rv\bar{n} .$$

If $m < n$, this reduces to $J\bar{1}rv\bar{n}$, by 5.2.1; and so to r, by 5.2.4. If $n \leqslant m$, it reduces to $J\bar{0}rv\bar{n}$ by 5.2.1; and so to $v\bar{n}$ by 5.2.4. But $v\bar{n}$ reduces to $s(\lambda z^\sigma .Brst \langle u;\bar{n},z\rangle \overline{n+1})$. This shows that B expresses bar recursion in the sense of Spector 1962.

7. Choice sequences

7.1. The conversion rule for (σ,φ) is

$$(\sigma,\varphi)\bar{n} \to \varphi_n^{(\sigma)} .$$

8. Convertible terms (see 1.2.)

8.1. The species C_σ of *convertible terms of type* σ, is defined by induction on σ:

8.1.1. $s \in C_0$ if and only if s is of type 0 and has a value, i.e. $s =\!| \ \bar{n}$ for some n.

8.1.2. $s \in C_{\sigma\to\tau}$ if and only if, for all $t \in C_\sigma$, $st \in C_\tau$.

8.2. *If* $s \in C_\sigma$, *then* s *is of type* σ *and has a value* $\bar{0}_\sigma \in C_\sigma$.

We prove these assertions simultaneously by induction on σ.

8.2.1. $\sigma = 0$. This case is immediate.

8.2.2. Assume 8.2 holds for $\sigma = \rho$ and $\sigma = \tau$, and let $\sigma = \rho \to \tau$. Let $s \in C_\sigma$. Since $\bar{0}_\rho \in C_\rho$ and $\bar{0}_\rho$ is of type ρ, $s\bar{0}_\rho$ is in C_τ, and so, is of type τ. This implies that s is of type σ and that $s\bar{0}_\rho$ has a value. But, any reduction of $s\bar{0}_\rho$ to a normal term clearly involves a reduction of s to normal form. Finally, if $t \in C_\rho$, then t has a value u; and so $\bar{0}_\sigma t =\!| \ \bar{0}_\sigma u =\!| \ \bar{0}_\tau$. Since $\bar{0}_\tau \in C_\tau$, it follows that $\bar{0}_\sigma \in C_\sigma$.

This completes the proof.

8.3. Let $\sigma = \pi \to \ldots \to \rho \to \tau$. Then $s \in C_\sigma$ if and only if, for all $r \in C_\pi$, ..., $t \in C_\rho$, we have $sr\ldots t \in C_\tau$. This follows immediately from the definition of C_σ.

8.4. *If* r *reduces to* s, *then* $r \in C_\sigma$ *if and only if* $s \in C_\sigma$.

We prove this by induction on σ.

8.4.1. If $\sigma = 0$, it follows by 3.4.

8.4.2. Let $\sigma = \rho \to \tau$. By the induction hypothesis, $rt \in C_\tau$ if and only if $st \in C_\tau$, for all $t \in C_\rho$. This completes the proof.

9. **Theorem.** *Every bar recursive term is convertible.*

The bar recursive terms are those which have no subterms of the form (τ,φ); i.e. they are built up from constants using the operation (st).

9.1. If $s \in C_{\sigma\to\tau}$ and $t \in C_\sigma$, then $st \in C_\tau$. This is immediate from the definition of $C_{\sigma\to\tau}$. So, to complete the proof of the theorem, we need only show that each constant is convertible.

9.2. P is convertible.
By 8.3, we need to prove Prs convertible for convertible r and s (of suitable types).
By 8.2 and 8.4, we can assume that r and s are normal. But then, Prs reduces to r, by 4.1.

9.3. K is convertible.
Let r, s and t be convertible and normal. Then $Krst$ reduces to $rt(st)$, by 4.12. rt and st are convertible by 9.1; and hence, so is $rt(st)$.

9.4. The proofs of 9.1–3 are carried out using only inferences from predicate logic.

9.5. R is convertible.
Let r, s and t be convertible and normal. We need to show that $Rrst$ is convertible. t is a numeral $\bar{m}$. We prove $Rrs\bar{m}$ convertible by induction on m.

9.5.1. $m = 0$. $Rrs\bar{m}$ reduces to r, by 5.1.1.

9.5.2. $m = n + 1$. $Rrs\bar{m}$ reduces to $s\bar{n}(Rrs\bar{n})$, by 5.1.2. s, $\bar{n}$ and, by the induction hypothesis, $Rrs\bar{n}$ are all convertible; and hence, so is $s\bar{n}(Rrs\bar{n})$.

9.6. Note that, up to this point, the proof has not used the fact that terms may include subterms of the form (σ,φ). Indeed, the proof is the same as the proof of minimum convertibility (1.3) for the primitive recursive terms in Tait 1967.

9.7. B is convertible.

Let r, s and t be convertible and normal terms of type τ, $(\sigma\to\tau)\to\tau$ and $(0\to\sigma)\to 0$, resp. We have to show that $Q = Brst$ is convertible.

9.7.1. Let u be a convertible term of type $0\to\sigma$; and let $u' = (\sigma,\varphi)$, where $\varphi_n^{(\sigma)} = u\bar{n}$ for each n. By 3.5.1, tu' has the same value as tu. By 6.3, it is easily follows from this that $Qu\bar{n}$ is convertible just in case $Qu'\bar{n}$ is; and they have the same value.

9.7.2. Let v_i be of type σ for $i<n$. $\langle v_0,\ldots,v_{n-1}\rangle$ is the term (σ,φ) where

$$\varphi_i^{(\sigma)} = \begin{cases} v_i, & \text{if } i<n\,. \\ \bar{0}_\sigma, & \text{if } n\leqslant i\,. \end{cases}$$

9.7.3. If $Q\langle v_0,\ldots,v_{n-1}\rangle\,\bar{n}$ is not convertible, and v_i is convertible for each $i<n$, then there is a convertible v of type σ such that $Q<v_0,\ldots,v_{n-1},$ $v>\overline{n+1}$ is not convertible. Since $\langle v_0,\ldots,v_{n-1}\rangle$ is convertible, $t\langle v_0,\ldots,v_{n-1}\rangle$ reduces to some $\bar{m}$. We must have $m\geqslant n$, since otherwise $Q\langle v_0,\ldots,v_{n-1}\rangle\,\bar{n}$ would reduce to r, according to 6.3. So, by 6.3, $Q\langle v_0,\ldots,v_{n-1}\rangle\,\bar{n}$ reduces to $s(\lambda z^\sigma.Q\langle v_0,\ldots,v_{n-1},z\rangle\,\overline{n+1})$. Thus, this term is not convertible, although s is. So, $\lambda z^\sigma.Q\langle v_0,\ldots,v_{n-1},z\rangle\,\overline{n+1}$ is not convertible. I.e., for some convertible v, $Q\langle v_0,\ldots,v_{n-1},v\rangle\,\overline{n+1}$ is not convertible.

9.7.4. We need to prove that $Qu\bar{n}$ is convertible for each n and each convertible u of type $0\to\sigma$. If not, it follows from 6.3 and 9.7.1 that $Q\langle u\bar{0},\ldots,u\overline{n-1}\rangle\,\bar{n}$ is not convertible. By 9.7.3, using the axiom of dependent choice, there is a sequence $v_0, v_1, \ldots$ of convertible terms of type σ such that $v_i = u\bar{i}$ for $i<n$ and, for all $p\geqslant n$, $Q\langle v_0,\ldots,\tau_{p-1}\rangle\,\bar{p}$ is not convertible. Let $w = (\sigma,f)$, where $f_k^{(\sigma)} = v_k$ for all $k\geqslant 0$. Then w is convertible; and so tw has a value $\bar{m}$. By 3.5.1, it follows that $t\langle v_0,\ldots,v_{p-1}\rangle =\!\mid \bar{m}$ for all sufficiently large p. But, choosing such a $p>m$, we obtain a contradiction, since in that case, $Q\langle v_0,\ldots,v_{p-1}\rangle\,\bar{p}$ reduces to r, by 6.3.

This completes the proof of 9.7; and so, we have completed the proof of 9.

10. **Normal Form Theorem.** *Every bar recursive term reduces to normal form.*

This follows from 8.2 and 9.

References

H.B.Curry and R.Feys, Combinatory logic (North-Holland, Amsterdam, 1958).

J.Y.Girard, Une extension de l'interpretation de Gödel a l'analyse, et son application a l'elimination des coupures dans l'analyse et la theorie des types, 1970, these Proceedings.

K.Gödel, Uber eine bisher noch nicht benützte Erweiterung des finiten Standpunktes, Dialectica 12 (1958) 280–287.

S.C.Kleene, Countable functionals, in: A.Heyting (ed.), Constructivity in Mathematics, (North-Holland, Amsterdam, 1959).

G.Kreisel, Interpretation of classical analysis by means of constructive functionals of finite type, in: A.Heyting (ed.), Constructivity in Mathematics (North-Holland, Amsterdam, 1959).

P.Martin-Löf, Hauptsatz for the intuitionistic theory of itereated inductive definitions, 1970a, these Proceedings, Hauptsatz for the theory of species, 1970b, these Proceedings.

C.Spector, Provably recursive functionals of analyses, Recursive function theory (Proc. of symposia in pure mathematics, American Math. Soc.), Providence, R.I. (1962) 1–27.

W.W.Tait, Intensional interpretations of functionals of finite type I, Journal of symbolic logic 32 (1967) 198–212.

W.W.Tait, Constructive reasoning, in: B.Van Rootselaar and J.F.Staal (eds.), Logic, Mathodology and Philosophy of Science III (North-Holland, Amsterdam, 1968) 185–199.

NOTIONS OF REALIZABILITY FOR INTUITIONISTIC ARITHMETIC AND INTUITIONISTIC ARITHMETIC IN ALL FINITE TYPES

A.S.TROELSTRA
University of Amsterdam

§ 1. Introduction

The present paper discusses properties of realizability and modified realizability interpretations for intuitionistic arithmetic **HA** and intuitionistic arithmetic in all finite types $\mathbf{HA}^\omega$. Not all results are new. In such cases we made an attempt to give adequate references to the literature.

In section 2 we describe the formal systems studied, and present the models *HRO* (hereditarily recursive operations) and *HEO* (hereditarily effective operations) for the intensional and the extensional version of $\mathbf{HA}^\omega$ respectively.

In sections 3, 4, 5 we characterize axiomatically the formulae which can be proved in **HA**, resp. $\mathbf{HA}^\omega$ to be realizable, resp. modified realizable, resp. Dialectica interpretable.

Sections 6 – 9 use these results and the models *HRO, HEO* for conservative extension results and consistency results (e.g. consistency of **HA** with Markov's schema and Church's thesis, $\mathbf{HA}^\omega$ is conservative over **HA**, consistency of certain "axioms of choice" for *HRO, HEO*) and proof theoretic-closure conditions (e.g. closure under Church's rule, Markov's rule, $\vdash A \vee B \Leftrightarrow \vdash A$ or $\vdash B$ for closed A, B). Once the basic results in §3 – 5 are available these proof-theoretic closure properties require very little additional effort. (Some of them, sometimes even in a strengthened form, can also be obtained via relatively complete cut-free systems.)

Acknowledgements. This paper owes much to G.Kreisel's constant encouragement and positive criticisms and suggestions. Some of the applications (notably 8.5, 8.6) found their immediate origin in Kreisel's questions, others were suggested by his remarks (especially 6.3).

Frequent discussions with D.H.J.de Jongh also have contributed substantially to this paper. For example, the closure of **HA** under the rule ECR_0 (7.2(i)) was found in a discussion with him.

§ 2. Formal systems and the models HRO, HEO

2.1. In this section we describe the formal systems for intuitionistic arithmetic in all finite types and the models *HRO* (hereditarily recursive operations) and *HEO* (hereditarily effective operations).

In all formal systems considered the logical operations are denoted by $\wedge, \vee, \rightarrow, \neg, \forall, \exists$. For metamathematical implication, equivalence, existential and universal quantification we use $\Rightarrow, \Leftrightarrow, (E\ ), (\ )$ respectively. A, B, C, P, Q are used as metavariables for formulae.

2.2. *Intuitionistic first-order arithmetic* **HA** is supposed to be formalized in one of the usual ways (see e.g. Kleene 1952 or Spector 1962). Our specific conventions are described below.

We use x, y, z, u, v, w to denote number variables, t, s to denote terms. The successor function is denoted by Succ. We find it convenient to assume that there is a constant for every primitive recursive function available, with the corresponding recursion equations as axioms. Numerals are denoted by $\mathbf{n}, \mathbf{m}$.

j is a primitive recursive pairing function of type $N^2 \rightarrow N$, which maps pairs of natural numbers bi-uniquely onto the natural numbers; j_1, j_2 are its inverses, also primitive recursive.

ν_p is a primitive recursive coding of p-tuples of natural numbers onto the natural numbers; $j_1^p, ..., j_p^p$ are its (primitive recursive) inverses. We assume $\nu_2 = j, j_1^2 = j_1, j_2^2 = j_2; \nu_1, j_1^1$ are the identity.

T denotes Kleene's T-predicate (e.g. Kleene 1969, p. 69) and U is the result-extracting function. Any partial recursive function ψ can be represented as

$$U \min_z T(x,y,z) \simeq \psi(y)$$

for a suitable x. We shall assume

$$T(x,y,z) \wedge T(x,y,z') \rightarrow z = z'.$$

Since we assumed that the language of **HA** contains a constant for every primitive recursive function, and since T can be constructed as a primitive recursive predicate, we are free to regard $T(x,y,z)$ as an abbreviation for

$$c_T(x,y,z) = 0\ ,$$

where c_T is a constant for the characteristic function of the T-predicate.

We adopt Kleene's notation $\{x\}(y)$, $\simeq$, Λ; for Kleene's $\{x\}(y_1,...,y_n)$, $n>1$ we write $\{x\}^n(y_1,...,y_n)$ (Kleene 1952, §65, p. 340, §63, p. 327, §65, p. 344). The partial recursive functions themselves we sometimes denote by $\{x\}$, $\{x\}^n$. Expressions involving $\{x\}^n(y_1,...,y_n)$, $\{x\}(y)$ represent in general partially defined functions. As such they are not terms of our formal language for **HA**, but it is possible to treat them systematically as abbreviations. For a formal treatment in **HA** of such "pseudo-terms" and for formal proofs of the basic results of recursion theory we rely on Kleene 1969, where $\{\alpha\}[\beta]$, $\Lambda\alpha$, $\simeq$ are formalized and discussed and the theory of partial recursive functionals has been formalized. (See especially Kleene 1969, 2.4, 2.5 for the discussion of p-terms.) The treatment of $\{x\}(y)$ etc. can be extracted from Kleene 1969 by parallelling his development. Compare also Nelson 1947.

We also adopt abbreviations from Kleene 1969, nl. $!\varphi$ and $!\varphi \wedge A\varphi$:

$$!\varphi \equiv_{\text{def}} \exists x(\varphi \simeq x)\,,$$

$$!\varphi \wedge A(\varphi) \equiv_{\text{def}} \exists x(\varphi \simeq x \wedge A(x))\,.$$

Here φ is a "pseudo-term", i.e. an expression in which $\{.\}.$ occurs.

We denote by $\mathbf{HA}^c$ the formal system for classical first-order arithmetic obtained by adding $A \vee \neg A$ as a schema to **HA**.

2.3. *Type structure.*

The type structure of all (monadic) finite types $\mathbf{T}$, to be used below in the description of intuitionistic arithmetic in all finite types, is defined inductively as follows:

(i) $0 \in \mathbf{T}$,

(ii) $\sigma, \tau, \in \mathbf{T} \Rightarrow (\sigma)\tau \in \mathbf{T}$.

The pure types are denoted by natural numbers and defined inductively by $n+1 = (n)0$.

2.4. *Description of* $\mathbf{E\text{-}HA}^\omega$, $\mathbf{WE\text{-}HA}^\omega$.

There are two versions of intuitionistic arithmetic in all finite types, an extensional version ($\mathbf{E\text{-}HA}^\omega$) and an intensional version ($\mathbf{I\text{-}HA}^\omega$). We write $\mathbf{HA}^\omega$ when the discussion applies to both versions.

$\mathbf{E\text{-}HA}^\omega$ contains variables for all finite types (to be denoted by x^σ, y^σ, z^σ, u^σ, v^σ, w^σ). We shall often omit type superscripts when irrelevant.

$\mathbf{E\text{-}HA}^\omega$ contains the usual logical constants, all the constants of **HA**, and certain constants S, $\Pi_{\sigma,\tau}$, $\Sigma_{\rho,\sigma,\tau}$, R_σ for all $\rho, \sigma, \tau \in \mathbf{T}$. Terms are defined as usual (cf. Spector 1962) and we adopt the associative notation for application: $t_1...t_n$ abbreviates $(...(((t_1)t_2)t_3)...t_n)$.

Prime formulas are equations between terms of type 0, formulas are constructed from prime formulas by means of the logical operations.

E-HA$^\omega$ is based on many-sorted intuitionistic predicate logic, equality axioms for objects of type 0

$$x^0 = y^0 \to y^0 = x^0 , x^0 = z^0 \wedge y^0 = z^0 \to x^0 = y^0$$

and an axiom of extensionality

$$x^\sigma = y^\sigma \to z^{(\sigma)\tau} x^\sigma = z^{(\sigma)\tau} y^\sigma$$

where equality between objects of type σ is defined by

$$x^\sigma = y^\sigma \equiv_{\text{def}} \forall z_1 ... \forall z_n (x^\sigma z_1 ... z_n = y^\sigma z_1 ... z_n) \ ;$$

here $z_1 ... z_n$ is a sequence of variables such that $x^\sigma z_1 ... z_n , y^\sigma z_1 ... z_n$ are terms of type 0. (This defined notion of equality is called *extensional* equality.)

E-HA$^\omega$ contains all axioms and axiom-schemata of **HA**, and the induction schema with respect to all formulas of the extended language.

For the constants S, $\Pi_{\sigma,\tau}$, $\Sigma_{\rho,\sigma,\tau}$, R_σ we adopt the following axioms (all applications are assumed to be meaningful):

$$Sx = \text{Succ}(x) \ ,$$

$$\Pi xy = x \ (x \in \sigma, y \in \tau) \ ,$$

$$\Sigma xyz = xz(yz) \ (x \in (\sigma)(\tau)\rho, y \in (\sigma)\tau, z \in \sigma) \ ,$$

$$\left. \begin{array}{l} Rxy0 = x \ , \\ Rxy(Sz) = y(Rxyz)z \end{array} \right\} (x \in \sigma, y \in (\sigma)(0)\sigma) \ .$$

(Note that Π, Σ enable us to define a λ-abstraction operator; cf. Tait 1967.)

WE-HA$^\omega$ is similar to **E-HA**, but instead of the axiom of extensionality we have the weaker rule of extensionality of Spector 1962:

$$t_1^\sigma = t_2^\sigma \Rightarrow t^{(\sigma)\tau} t_1^\sigma = t^{(\sigma)\tau} t_2^\sigma \ .$$

Note that in **WE-HA**$^\omega$ finite sequences of types of **T** can be reduced to a single type (see e.g. Kleene 1959).

2.5. *Description of* **I-HA**$^\omega$.

We limit ourselves to indication of the differences between **I-HA**$^\omega$ and **E-HA**$^\omega$. Instead of equality between objects of type 0 we now have equality (denoted by =) between objects of type σ, for all $\sigma \in \mathbf{T}$, as a primitive notion.

R_σ is replaced by sets of constants $R^i_{\sigma_1,...,\sigma_p}$, $i = 1, ..., p$ for each p and each p-tuple $\sigma_1, ..., \sigma_p$, $\sigma_i \in \mathbf{T}$ $(i=1,...,p)$. For each $\sigma \in \mathbf{T}$ an equality functional $E_\sigma \in (\sigma)(\sigma)0$ is added.

The equality axioms are replaced by

$$x^\sigma = y^\sigma \to y^\sigma = x^\sigma \;, \qquad x^\sigma = z^\sigma \wedge y^\sigma = z^\sigma \to x^\sigma = y^\sigma \;,$$

$$x^\sigma = y^\sigma \vee \neg x^\sigma = y^\sigma \;, \qquad x^\sigma = y^\sigma \to z^{(\sigma)\tau} x^\sigma = z^{(\sigma)\tau} y^\sigma \;,$$

$$x^{(\sigma)\tau} = y^{(\sigma)\tau} \to x^{(\sigma)\tau} z^\sigma = y^{(\sigma)\tau} z^\sigma \;.$$

For $R^i_{\sigma_1,...,\sigma_p}$, $i = 1, ..., p$ we adopt the axioms

$$R^i \mathfrak{x}\mathfrak{y} 0 = x_i \;,$$

$$R^i \mathfrak{x}\mathfrak{y}(Sz^0) = y_i(R^1 \mathfrak{x}\mathfrak{y} z^0)...(R^p \mathfrak{x}\mathfrak{y} z^0) z^0$$

(we omitted the subscripts $\sigma_1, ..., \sigma_p$). Here $\mathfrak{x}, \mathfrak{y}$ denote the sequences $x_1, ..., x_p$ and $y_1, ..., y_p$ respectively, with $x_i \in \sigma_i, y_i \in (\sigma_1)...(\sigma_p)(0)\sigma_i$. For E_σ we adopt the axioms

$$E_\sigma x^\sigma y^\sigma = 0 \leftrightarrow x^\sigma = y^\sigma \;,$$

$$E_\sigma x^\sigma y^\sigma = 0 \vee E_\sigma x^\sigma y^\sigma = 1 \;.$$

2.6. *Remark.* **WE-HA**$^\omega$ corresponds to the arithmetical part of Spector 1962.

I-HA$^\omega$ is an extension of $\mathbf{T}_0$ in Tait 1967. The extension by the equality functional is necessary if we wish to give a modified realizability and a Dialectica interpretation of **I-HA**$^\omega$ in itself.

Instead of using sequences of terms or variables, we might have adopted a device of Howard A, nl. the introduction of pairing operators $D_{\sigma_1,\sigma_2} \in (\sigma_1)(\sigma_2)\sigma_1 \times \sigma_2$, with inverses $D^1_{\sigma_1,\sigma_2}$, $D^2_{\sigma_1,\sigma_2}$.

In **WE-HA**$^\omega$ the R^i are definable from the R_σ, because of the reduction of sequences of types to a single type.

W.W.Tait (in a letter dated June 22nd, 1970) communicated to the author a method for coding pairs of types of **T** by types of **T** such that the pairing functions and their inverses preserve intensional equality, provided the notion of intensional equality is compatible with a strong form of λ-conversion. A similar remark has been made by S.Stenlund. The problem of constructing such pairing functions is still open w.r.t. weaker forms of conversion.

2.7. *The model of the hereditarily recursive operations HRO.*
We define classes V_σ of natural numbers for each $\sigma \in \mathbf{T}$ as follows:

$$x \in V_0 \quad \equiv_{\text{def}} (x=x) ,$$

$$x \in V_{(\sigma)\tau} \equiv_{\text{def}} \forall y \in V_\sigma \exists u\, [T(x,y,u) \wedge Uu \in V_\tau] .$$

The model *HRO* for $\mathbf{I}\text{-}\mathbf{HA}^\omega$ may be described as follows. The objects of type σ are the pairs (x,σ) with $x \in V_\sigma$. Application is defined by

$$(x,(\sigma)\tau)(y,\sigma) \equiv_{\text{def}} (\{x\}(y),\tau) .$$

Equality is interpreted as

$$(x,\sigma) = (y,\sigma) \equiv_{\text{def}} x = y .$$

S is interpreted as $(\Lambda x.x+1,(0)0)$, $\Pi_{\sigma,\tau}$ as

$$(\Lambda x \Lambda y.x,(\sigma)(\tau)\sigma) ,$$

and $\Sigma_{\rho,\sigma,\tau}$ as

$$(\Lambda x \Lambda y \Lambda z.\, \{\{x\}(z)\}(\{y\}(z)),((\sigma)(\tau)\rho)((\sigma)\tau)\sigma) .$$

The interpretation of $R^i_{\sigma_1,\ldots,\sigma_p}$ is found as follows. Let $\tau_i = (\sigma_1)\ldots(\sigma_p)(0)\sigma_i$, $\rho_i[\sigma_1,\ldots,\sigma_p] = (\sigma_1)\ldots(\sigma_p)(\tau_1)\ldots(\tau_p)(0)\sigma_i$, $i = 1, \ldots, p$. By the s-m-n-theorem there exist primitive recursive $\varphi_{p,i}$ such that

$$\{\varphi_{p,i}x\}^2(y,z) \simeq \{\{\ldots\{\{j^p_i x\}(j^p_1 y)\}(j^p_2 y)\ldots\}(j^p_p y)\}(z) .$$

By the recursion theorem we can find a partial recursive ψ_p such that

$$\psi_p(x,y,0) \simeq x ,$$

$$\psi_p(x,y,Sz) \simeq \nu_p(\{\varphi_{p,1}y\}^2(\xi,z),\ldots,\{\varphi_{p,p}y\}^2(\xi,z)) ,$$

where $\xi \equiv_{\text{def}} \psi_p(x,y,z)$. Let

$$r_p^i = \Lambda x_1 ... \Lambda x_p \Lambda y_1 ... \Lambda y_p \Lambda z. j_i^p \psi_p(\nu_p(x_1,...,x_p), \nu_p(y_1,...,y_p), z) .$$

Then $R^i_{\sigma_1,...,\sigma_p}$ is interpreted by

$$(r_p^i, \rho_i[\sigma_1,...,\sigma_p]) .$$

E_σ is interpreted by

$$(\Lambda x \Lambda y. \operatorname{sg}|x-y|, (\sigma)(\sigma)0)$$

(here $\operatorname{sg}(x) = 0$ if $x = 0$; 1 otherwise).

For any formula $A \in$ **I-HA**$^\omega$ there is an interpretation in *HRO*, represented by an arithmetical formula $[A]_{HRO}$, defined in a natural way as follows. Let Γ indicate a bi-unique mapping of all variables of finite type onto the numerical variables. $[A]_{HRO}$ is obtained from A by replacing any variable x^σ occurring in an equation between terms by Γx^σ; S, Π, Σ, $R^i_{\sigma_1,...,\sigma_p}$, E are replaced by $\Lambda x.x + 1$, $\Lambda x \Lambda y.x$, $\Lambda x \Lambda y \Lambda z.\{\{x\}(z)\}(\{y\}(z))$, r_p^i, $\Lambda x \Lambda y. \operatorname{sg}|x-y|$; application by $\{.\}.$; $\forall x^\sigma$, $\exists x^\sigma$ by $\forall x \in V_\sigma$, $\exists x \in V_\sigma$ respectively; constants of **HA**, =, and propositonal operators are left unchanged.

Note that Church's thesis holds in *HRO* in the following version:

CT $\quad \forall x^1 \exists y^0 \forall z^0 \exists u^0 (T(y,z,u) \wedge Uu = xz)$.

2.8. *The model of the hereditarily effective operations HEO.*

We define inductively classes W_σ of natural numbers, and equivalence relations I_σ between natural numbers for each $\sigma \in \mathbf{T}$ as follows

$$W_0 = V_0,\ I_0(x,y) \equiv_{\text{def}} x \in W_0 \wedge y \in W_0 \wedge x = y ,$$

$$x \in W_{(\sigma)\tau} \equiv_{\text{def}} \forall y \in W_\sigma \exists u [T(x,y,u) \wedge Uu \in W_\tau] \wedge$$

$$\wedge \forall y \forall z \forall v \forall w [I_\sigma(y,z) \wedge T(x,y,v) \wedge T(x,z,w) \to I_\tau(Uv, Uw)] ,$$

$$I_{(\sigma)\tau}(x,y) \equiv_{\text{def}} x \in W_{(\sigma)\tau} \wedge y \in W_{(\sigma)\tau} \wedge$$

$$\wedge \forall z \in W_\sigma \forall v \forall w [T(x,z,v) \wedge T(y,z,w) \to I_\tau(Uv, Uw)] .$$

The model *HEO* for **E-HA**$^\omega$ may be described as follows. The objects of type

σ are the pairs (x,σ) with $x \in W_\sigma$. Application, S, Π, Σ are defined as for *HRO*; R_σ is interpreted as R^1_σ in *HRO*. Exactly in the same manner as for *HRO* we define an interpretation $[A]_{HEO}$ in arithmetic for any formula A of **E-HA**$^\omega$.

Note that *HEO* also satisfies CT.

2.9. *The systems* **HRO, HRO⁻**.

HRO is an extension of **I-HA**$^\omega$ in which it is asserted that the objects of type σ coincide with the hereditarily recursive operations of type σ.

The language of **HRO** is obtained by adding constants $\Phi_\sigma \in (\sigma)0$, $\Phi'_{\sigma,\tau} \in ((\sigma)\tau)(\sigma)0$ for all $\sigma, \tau \in \mathbf{T}$ to the language of **I-HA**$^\omega$. **HRO** is axiomatized by adding the axioms

G1 $\qquad \Phi_0 x^0 = x^0$,

G2 $\qquad \Phi_\sigma x^\sigma = \Phi_\sigma y^\sigma \leftrightarrow x^\sigma = y^\sigma$,

G3 $\qquad T(\Phi_{(\sigma)\tau} x^{(\sigma)\tau}, \Phi_\sigma y^\sigma, \Phi'_{\sigma,\tau} x^{(\sigma)\tau} y^\sigma)$,

G4 $\qquad \Phi_\tau x^{(\sigma)\tau} y^\sigma = U(\Phi'_{\sigma,\tau} x^{(\sigma)\tau} y^\sigma)$,

G5 $\qquad \forall x \in V_\sigma \exists y^\sigma (\Phi_\sigma y = x)$.

HRO⁻ is obtained from **HRO** by omitting G5. G1–4 express that all objects of finite type are hereditarily recursive operations; G5 expresses that every hereditarily recursive operation is an object of finite type.

A corresponding system **HEO⁻** has no special interest, since it does not admit a modified realizability interpretation.

HRO is a model for **HRO**. To see this we only have to interpret Φ_σ by

$$(\Lambda x.x, (\sigma)0)$$

and $\Phi'_{\sigma,\tau}$ by

$$(\Lambda x \Lambda y. \min_z T(x,y,z), ((\sigma)\tau)(\sigma)0) \ .$$

2.10. *Historical note.* The definition of *HRO* was given by G.Kreisel in his course notes of a course on constructive mathematics (Stanford University 1958–1959). As far as we know, the applications of *HRO* in this paper are new.

W.W.Tait described (Tait 1967) a model for a theory $\mathbf{T}_0$ (which is a subtheory of $\mathbf{I\text{-}HA}^{\omega}$), consisting of the closed terms of $\mathbf{T}_0$. His treatment may be extended to $\mathbf{I\text{-}HA}^{\omega}$. Tait proved with the help of this model that $\mathbf{T}_0$ is conservative over **HA**; extension of this methods to $\mathbf{I\text{-}HA}^{\omega}$ would yield that $\mathbf{I\text{-}HA}^{\omega}$ is conservative over **HA**. We obtain the same results with *HRO* (6.1), but the proof is easier. (On the other hand, Tait's methods may be exploited to obtain other results, e.g. computability properties of $\mathbf{I\text{-}HA}^{\omega}$, which are not so easily obtained via *HRO*.) In Tait 1968 (p. 191, lines −10 to −2) a model is described which is very similar to *HRO*, but defined in terms of combinators.

HEO is already described in Kreisel 1959, p. 117 (for pure types only).

§ 3. Numerical realizability

3.1. In this section we discuss Kleene's realizability by numbers (Kleene 1945, 1952) in a formal version (Kleene 1945; the first elaborate treatment in Nelson 1947). We shall refer to this notion as **r**-realizability. We also introduce a variant, **q**-realizability (analogous to the functional **q**-realizability in Kleene 1969).

3.2. **Definition.** With every formula A of **HA** we associate a formula $x \mathbf{\ r\ } A$, x not occurring in A; $x \mathbf{\ r\ } A$ contains only x and the variables free in A free. The definition of $x \mathbf{\ r\ } A$ is by induction on the construction of A, according to the following clauses:

r(i) $x \mathbf{\ r\ } A \equiv A$ for A prime ,
r(ii) $x \mathbf{\ r\ } (A \wedge B) \equiv (j_1 x \mathbf{\ r\ } A \vee j_2 x \mathbf{\ r\ } B)$,
r(iii) $x \mathbf{\ r\ } (A \vee B) \equiv ((j_1 x=0 \to j_2 x \mathbf{\ r\ } A) \wedge (j_1 x \neq 0 \to j_2 x \mathbf{\ r\ } B))$,
r(iv) $x \mathbf{\ r\ } (A \to B) \equiv \forall u (u \mathbf{\ r\ } A \to \exists v (T(x,u,v) \wedge Uv \mathbf{\ r\ } B))$,
r(v) $x \mathbf{\ r\ } \neg A \equiv x \mathbf{\ r\ } (A \to 1=0)$,
r(vi) $x \mathbf{\ r\ } \forall y A(y) \equiv \forall y \exists z (T(x,y,z) \wedge Uz \mathbf{\ r\ } A(y))$,
r(vii) $x \mathbf{\ r\ } \exists y A(y) \equiv j_2 x \mathbf{\ r\ } A(j_1 x)$.

Note that $x \mathbf{\ r\ } \neg A$ if $\forall y (\neg y \mathbf{\ r\ } A)$.

3.3. **Definition.** We obtain a definition of a similar relation $x \mathbf{\ q\ } A$, if we replace in the definition of $x \mathbf{\ r\ } A$ **r** by **q** in the clauses **r**(i), **r**(ii), **r**(v), **r**(vi) (call the new clauses **q**(i) etc.) and replace **r**(iii), **r**(iv), **r**(vii) by
q(iii) $x \mathbf{\ q\ } (A \vee B) \equiv [(j_1 x=0 \to j_2 x \mathbf{\ q\ } A \wedge A) \wedge (j_1 x \neq 0 \to j_2 x \mathbf{\ q\ } B \wedge B)]$,
q(iv) $x \mathbf{\ q\ } (A \to B) \equiv \forall u (u \mathbf{\ q\ } A \wedge A \to \exists v (T(x,u,v) \wedge Uv \mathbf{\ q\ } B))$,
q(vii) $x \mathbf{\ q\ } \exists y A(y) \equiv j_2 x \mathbf{\ q\ } A(j_1 x) \wedge A(j_1 x)$.

3.4. **Definition.** Let **H** be any formal theory. We call a formula **H**-**r**-realizable, or **r**-realizable in **H**, if $\mathbf{H} \vdash \exists x(x \mathbf{\ r\ } A)$. Similarly we define **H**-**q**-realizable, or **q**-realizable in **H**.

3.5. **Theorem.** *For closed formulae A*:

$$\mathbf{HA} \vdash A \Rightarrow (\mathrm{En})[\mathbf{HA} \vdash \mathrm{n} \mathbf{\ r\ } A \text{ and } \mathbf{HA} \vdash \mathrm{n} \mathbf{\ q\ } A] .$$

Proof. For **r**-realizability we find this result in Nelson 1947 for a slightly different formalization of **HA** and $x \mathbf{\ r\ } A$. A more elegant approach is obtained by adaptation of the proof of theorem 50 for functional **r**- and **q**-realizability in Kleene 1969, with help of the informal proof in Kleene 1952 (theorem 62), to the case of arithmetic and numerical realizability.

3.6. **Definition.** A formula of $\mathbf{HA}^\omega$ is said to be *negative* if it does not contain $\vee$, $\exists$. A formula of $\mathbf{HA}^\omega$ is said to be *almost negative* if it does not contain $\vee$, and no $\exists$ except in front of sub-formulae of the form $t = s$.

3.7. **Lemma.** *For each A, $x \mathbf{\ r\ } A$ is equivalent to an almost negative formula w.r.t.* **HA**.

Proof. We have to show that $x \mathbf{\ r\ } A$ can be rewritten as an almost negative formula; this is done by induction on the logical complexity of A.

For example, assuming the lemma for A, B, we can rewrite $x \mathbf{\ r\ } (A \to B)$ as an almost negative formula by $x \mathbf{\ r\ } (A \to B) \leftrightarrow \forall u(u \mathbf{\ r\ } A \to \exists v T(x,u,v) \wedge \forall w(T(x,u,w) \to Uw \mathbf{\ r\ } B))$. Similarly, assuming the induction hypothesis for $A(x)$, we can rewrite $y \mathbf{\ r\ } \forall x A(x)$ as an almost negative formula by $y \mathbf{\ r\ } \forall x A(x) \leftrightarrow \leftrightarrow \forall x(\exists u T(y,x,u) \wedge \forall w(T(y,x,w) \to Uw \mathbf{\ r\ } A(x)))$. Etc. etc.

3.8. **Lemma.** *Let $A(\mathfrak{a})$ be an almost negative formula of* **HA**, *and let $\mathfrak{a}$ be a non-empty string of number variables, containing all variables free in A. Then there is a partial recursive function ψ_A (with gödelnumber n_A say) such that in* **HA**

(i) $\exists u(u \mathbf{\ r\ } A) \to A$,

(ii) $A(\mathfrak{a}) \to\ !\psi_A(\mathfrak{a}) \wedge \psi_A(\mathfrak{a}) \mathbf{\ r\ } A(\mathfrak{a})$,

(iii) $u \mathbf{\ r\ } A \leftrightarrow u \mathbf{\ q\ } A$.

Proof. (Adaptation of the proof of lemma 8.4b in Kleene and Vesley 1965.) (i), (ii), (iii) are proved simultaneously by induction on the construction of A. We describe the construction of ψ_A, the proof of (i), (ii), (iii) is then routine.

(a) $\psi_{t=s}(\mathfrak{a}) = 0$.
(b) Let $A \equiv \exists y(t{=}s)$. Take $\psi_A(\mathfrak{a}) = j(\min_y [t{=}s], 0)$.
(c) Let $A \equiv B \wedge C$. Take $\psi_A(\mathfrak{a}) = j(\psi_B(\mathfrak{a}), \psi_C(\mathfrak{a}))$.
(d) Let $A \equiv B \rightarrow C$. Take $\psi_A(\mathfrak{a}) = \Lambda u. \psi_C(\mathfrak{a})$.
(e) Let $A \equiv \neg B$. Take $\psi_A(\mathfrak{a}) = 0$.
(f) Let $A \equiv \forall x B(x)$. Take $\psi_A(\mathfrak{a}) = \Lambda x. \psi_{B(x)}(\mathfrak{a}, x)$.

3.9. **Lemma.** *Let* $\mathfrak{a}$ *be a non-empty sequence of variables, containing all the variables occurring free in A. Then A is provably equivalent to an almost negative formula iff there exists a partial recursive function* ψ_A *such that* (i), (ii) *of Lemma* 3.8 *are provable.*

Proof. (a) Assume $\mathbf{HA} \vdash A(\mathfrak{a}) \leftrightarrow B(\mathfrak{a})$, $B(\mathfrak{a})$ almost negative. By 3.5 it follows that there is a recursive function ψ such that

$$\mathbf{HA} \vdash \forall \mathfrak{a}(\psi(\mathfrak{a}) \ \mathbf{r} \ A \leftrightarrow B) ,$$

hence

$$\mathbf{HA} \vdash \forall \mathfrak{a}(j_1 \psi(\mathfrak{a}) \ \mathbf{r} \ (A \rightarrow B) \wedge j_2 \psi(\mathfrak{a}) \ \mathbf{r} \ (B \rightarrow A)) .$$

Let ψ_B be the partial recursive function constructed according to 3.9. Then if A, B holds, so

$$\{j_2 \psi(\mathfrak{a})\} \psi_B(\mathfrak{a}) \ \mathbf{r} \ A .$$

Conversely, if $u \ \mathbf{r} \ A$, then $\{j_1 \psi(\mathfrak{a})\}(u) \ \mathbf{r} \ B$, so B holds, hence A holds. This establishes (i), (ii) with $\{j_2 \psi(\mathfrak{a})\} \psi_B(\mathfrak{a})$ for $\psi_A(\mathfrak{a})$.

(b) Now assume (i), (ii) to hold for a certain ψ_A. For simplicity let $\mathfrak{a} \equiv x$, and let ψ_A have a gödelnumber $\mathbf{n}_A$. Then by (i), (ii)

$$A(x) \leftrightarrow \, !\psi_A(x) \wedge \psi_A(x) \ \mathbf{r} \ A(x)$$

and therefore

$$A(x) \leftrightarrow \exists y T(\mathbf{n}_A, x, y) \wedge \forall z (T(\mathbf{n}_A, x, z) \rightarrow Uz \ \mathbf{r} \ A(x)) .$$

Together with lemma 3.8 this yields the "only if" part of the lemma.

3.10. *Remark.* Note that $\mathbf{HA} \vdash A \leftrightarrow \exists x(x \ \mathbf{r} \ A)$ holds for formulae which are equivalent to almost negative formulae preceded by a (possibly empty) string of existential numerical quantifiers.

3.11. In **HA** we can express the following version of Church's thesis

$$\mathrm{CT}_0 \qquad \forall x \exists y A(x,y) \to \exists z \forall x \exists u [T(z,x,u) \wedge A(x, Uu)] \ .$$

By means of **r**-realizability we can prove CT_0 to be consistent relative to **HA**. Note that CT_0 is not derivable in **HA**, since it is false in $\mathbf{HA}^c$. In fact we can prove a stronger result:

3.12. **Theorem.** *Let* ECT_0 *(extended thesis of Church) denote the following schema (A an almost negative formula of* **HA**, *B an arbitrary formula of* **HA***):*

$$\mathrm{ECT}_0 \qquad \forall x [Ax \to \exists y B(x,y)] \to \exists z \forall x [Ax \to \exists u (T(z,x,u) \wedge B(x, Uu))] \ .$$

Then for any universal closure F of an instance of ECT_0, $\mathbf{HA} \vdash \mathbf{n}\ \mathbf{r}\ F$, $\mathbf{HA} \vdash \mathbf{n}\ \mathbf{q}\ F$ *for a suitable numeral* **n**.

Proof. Let Ax be almost negative, and assume for simplicity that there are no additional parameters in Ax and $\exists y B(x,y)$, and let

$$u\ \mathbf{q}\ \forall x [Ax \to \exists y B(x,y)] \ , \ \forall x [Ax \to \exists y B(x,y)] \ .$$

By 3.8 it follows that, if we abbreviate $\{u\}(\psi_A(x))$ by t

$$\forall x [Ax \to !t \wedge t\ \mathbf{q}\ \exists y B(x,y)]$$

or equivalently

$$\forall x [Ax \to !t \wedge j_2 t\ \mathbf{q}\ B(x, j_1 t) \wedge B(x, j_1 t)] \ .$$

Put

$$\varphi_1 = \Lambda x. j_1 t \ ,$$

$$\varphi_2 \simeq \min_u T(\varphi_1, x, u) \ ,$$

$$\varphi(u) = j(\varphi_1, \Lambda x \Lambda w. j(\varphi_2, j(0, j_2 t))) \ ,$$

then it follows that

$$\varphi(u)\ \mathbf{q}\ \exists z \forall x\,[Ax \rightarrow \exists v(T(z,x,v) \wedge B(x,Uv))]\ .$$

Therefore $\Lambda u.\varphi(u)$ realizes $\forall x\,[Ax \rightarrow \exists y B(x,y)] \rightarrow \exists z \forall x\,[Ax \rightarrow \exists v(T(z,x,v) \wedge$ $\wedge B(x,Uv))]$.

Similarly for **r**-realizability.

3.13. **Corollary.** **HA** + ECT_0 *is consistent relative* **HA.**

Proof. Immediate from the theorem, since the **r**-realizable formulae are closed under deduction.

Remark. ECT_0 cannot be generalized to arbitrary formulas A, as is illustrated by the following counterexample. Obviously,

$$\forall x\,[(\exists y T(x,x,y) \vee \neg \exists y T(x,x,y)) \rightarrow$$

$$\rightarrow \exists z((z>0 \wedge T(x,x,z \dot{-} 1)) \vee (z=0 \wedge \neg \exists y T(x,x,y)))]\ .$$

On the other hand there exists no partial recursive function with Gödelnumber u such that

$$\forall x\,[(\exists y T(x,x,y) \vee \neg \exists y T(x,x,y)) \rightarrow \exists w(T(u,x,w) \wedge$$

$$\wedge \{(Uw>0 \rightarrow T(x,x,Uw \dot{-} 1)) \wedge (Uw=0 \rightarrow \neg \exists y T(x,x,y))\})]\ .$$

For it is intuitionistically true that

$$\forall x(\neg\neg(\exists y T(x,x,y) \vee \neg \exists y T(x,x,y))\ ,$$

therefore (1) would imply

$$\forall x(\neg\neg \exists w T(u,x,w) \wedge$$

$$\wedge\ \{(Uw>0 \wedge T(x,x,Uw \dot{-} 1)) \vee (Uw=0 \wedge \neg \exists y T(x,x,y))\})\ .$$

Let v_0 be such that $\exists w T(v_0,x,w) \leftrightarrow \{u\}(x) \simeq 0$, then $\exists w T(v_0,v_0,w) \leftrightarrow \{u\}(v_0)$ $\simeq 0 \leftrightarrow \neg \exists y T(v_0,v_0,y)$ which is contradictory. Hence (1) is false.

3.14. **Theorem.** *(Axiomatization of* **HA**-$\mathbf{r}$*-realizability.)*
(i) $\mathbf{HA}+\mathrm{ECT}_0 \vdash \exists x(x\ \mathbf{r}\ A) \leftrightarrow A$,
(ii) $\mathbf{HA}\vdash \exists x(x\ \mathbf{r}\ A) \Leftrightarrow \mathbf{HA}+\mathrm{ECT}_0 \vdash A$,
(iii) $\mathbf{HA}+\mathrm{ECT}_0 \vdash x\ \mathbf{r}\ A \leftrightarrow x\ \mathbf{q}\ A$.

Proof. (i) is proved by induction w.r.t. the logical complexity of A. For example, assume (i) to be proved for A, B, then it follows in $\mathbf{HA}+\mathrm{ECT}_0$ that $(A\to B) \leftrightarrow (\exists x(x\ \mathbf{r}\ A)\to\exists y(y\ \mathbf{r}\ B)) \leftrightarrow \forall x(x\ \mathbf{r}\ A\to\exists y(y\ \mathbf{r}\ B))$; with ECT_0 $(A\to B)\leftrightarrow$ $\leftrightarrow \exists u\forall x(x\ \mathbf{r}\ A\to !\{u\}(x)\wedge\{u\}(x)\ \mathbf{r}\ B)\leftrightarrow\exists u(u\ \mathbf{r}\ (A\to B))$. The other clauses in the inductive step may be dealt with similarly.

(ii) Assume $\mathbf{HA}\vdash \exists x(x\ \mathbf{r}\ A)$, then with (i) immediately $\mathbf{HA}+\mathrm{ECT}_0 \vdash A$. Conversely, if $\mathbf{HA}+\mathrm{ECT}_0 \vdash A$, then there are formulae $F_1, ..., F_n$, which are universal closures of instances of ECT_0, such that $\mathbf{HA}\vdash F_1 \wedge ... \wedge F_n \to A$. Since $F_1, ..., F_n$ are realizable, it follows that $\mathbf{HA}\vdash \exists x(x\ \mathbf{r}\ A)$.

(iii) is proved by a straightforward induction on the logical complexity of A, using (i).

Note that (ii) characterizes the **HA**-realizable formulae: they are axiomatized by $\mathbf{HA}+\mathrm{ECT}_0$.

Note also that CT_0 is obtained as a special case of ECT_0 by taking $x = x$ for Ax.

3.15. **Theorem.** *Let F be the universal closure of an instance of Markov's schema:*

M $$\forall x(Ax\vee\neg Ax)\wedge\neg\neg\exists xAx \to \exists xAx\ .$$

Then there exists a numeral $\mathbf{n}$ *such that* $\mathbf{HA}+\mathrm{M}\vdash \mathbf{n}\ \mathbf{q}\ F$, $\mathbf{HA}+\mathrm{M}\vdash \mathbf{n}\ \mathbf{r}\ F$.

Proof. Let us assume for simplicity that Ax contains no other parameters, and assume

$$u\ \mathbf{r}\ \forall x(Ax\vee\neg Ax)\wedge\neg\neg\exists xAx\ .$$

Hence

$$\forall x(!\{j_1u\}(x)\wedge([j_1\{j_1u\}(x)=0\wedge j_2\{j_1u\}(x)\ \mathbf{r}\ Ax]\vee$$
$$\vee[j_1\{j_1u\}(x)\neq 0\wedge j_2\{j_1u\}(x)\ \mathbf{r}\ \neg Ax]))\wedge j_2u\ \mathbf{r}\ \neg\neg\exists xAx\ .$$

Let

$$\varphi(u) \simeq \min_x [j_1\{j_1 u\}(x)=0] \; .$$

Since $\forall x(j_1\{j_1 u\}(x)\neq 0)$ would imply $\forall x \exists w(w \mathbf{\ r\ } \neg Ax)$, it follows from M and $j_2 u \mathbf{\ r\ } \neg\neg \exists x A x$ (which implies $\neg\neg \exists x \exists w(w \mathbf{\ r\ } Ax)$) that $\exists x(j_1\{j_1 u\}(x)=0)$. Therefore $!\varphi(u)$, and thus

$$j(\varphi(u), j_2\{j_1 u\}(\varphi(u))) \mathbf{\ r\ } \exists x A x \; .$$

So $\Lambda u.j(\varphi(u), j_2\{j_1 u\}(\varphi(u)))$ realizes $\forall x(Ax \vee \neg Ax) \wedge \neg\neg \exists x A x \rightarrow \exists x A x$. For $\mathbf{q}$-realizability the argument is only slightly more complicated.

3.16. **Corollaries.** (i) $\mathbf{HA} + \mathrm{M} + \mathrm{ECT}_0$ *is consistent relative* **HA**. (ii) $\mathbf{HA} + \mathrm{M} + \mathrm{ECT}_0 \vdash A$ *iff* $\mathbf{HA} + \mathrm{M} \vdash \exists x(x \mathbf{r} A)$.

Proof. Immediate from 3.13, 3.16 and the fact that $\mathbf{HA}^c$ is consistent relative **HA**. (ii) Immediate from 3.17, 3.18.

3.17. **Theorem.** *(Axiomatization of* $\mathbf{HA}^c$-$\mathbf{r}$*-realizability.)*

$$\mathbf{HA}^c \vdash \exists x(x \mathbf{\ r\ } A) \Leftrightarrow \mathbf{HA} + \mathrm{M} + \mathrm{ECT}_0 \vdash \neg\neg A \; .$$

Proof. Assume $\mathbf{HA}^c \vdash \exists x(x \mathbf{\ r\ } A)$. Then this is equivalent to $\mathbf{HA}^c \vdash \neg\neg \exists x Bx$, where Bx is a negative formula obtained by replacing every subformula $\exists y(t{=}s)$ of $x \mathbf{\ r\ } A$ by $\neg \forall y \neg(t{=}s)$. Then $\mathbf{HA} \vdash \neg\neg \exists x Bx$ (because of the properties of the well-known translation of $\mathbf{HA}^c$ into the negative fragment of **HA**), so $\mathbf{HA} + \mathrm{M} \vdash \neg\neg \exists x(x \mathbf{\ r\ } A)$. Therefore $\mathbf{HA} + \mathrm{ECT}_0 + \mathrm{M} \vdash \neg\neg A$.

Conversely, if $\mathbf{HA} + \mathrm{ECT}_0 + \mathrm{M} \vdash \neg\neg A$, then $\mathbf{HA}^c \vdash \exists x(x \mathbf{\ r\ } \neg\neg A)$, so $\mathbf{HA}^c \vdash \neg\neg \exists x(x \mathbf{\ r\ } A)$, hence $\mathbf{HA}^c \vdash \exists x(x \mathbf{\ r\ } A)$.

3.18. **Lemma.** *Let* IP *denote the following schema*

IP $\qquad (\neg A \rightarrow \exists x B) \rightarrow \exists x(\neg A \rightarrow B)$

(A not containing x free). There is a specific instance of IP *such that for its universal closure F*

$$\mathbf{HA}^c \vdash \neg \exists u(u \mathbf{\ r\ } F) \; .$$

Proof. See Kleene 1965, §2.

3.19. **Corollary.** **HA** + M + ECT_0 + IP *is inconsistent.*

Proof. Immediate from 3.17, 3.18. We can improve on this corollary however.

3.20. **Theorem.** **HA** + M + CT_0 + IP *is inconsistent.*

Proof. In **HA** + M + CT_0 + IP

$$\forall x[\neg\neg\exists yT(x,x,y) \to \exists yT(x,x,y)] \qquad \text{(M)}$$

$$\Rightarrow \forall x\exists z[\neg\neg\exists yT(x,x,y) \to T(x,x,z)] \qquad \text{(IP)}$$

$$\Rightarrow \exists u\forall x[!\{u\}(x) \wedge (\neg\neg\exists yT(x,x,y) \to T(x,x,\{u\}(x))] \,. \qquad (\mathrm{CT}_0)$$

This would imply recursiveness of $\exists yT(x,x,y)$, since $c_T(x,x,\{u\}(x))$ is recursive in x. This is obviously contradictory.

§ 4. Modified realizability

4.1. Modified (or generalized) realizability was first introduced in Kreisel 1959 (3.52); it is also used in Kreisel 1962. Below we shall define a version of modified realizability (to be called **mr**-realizability) which corresponds to Kreisel's definition, and a notion of **mq**-realizability, which is related to **mr**-realizability in the same way as **q**-realizability is related to **r**-realizability.

4.2. **Definition.** In the remainder of this section we shall use german letters $\mathfrak{x},\mathfrak{y},\mathfrak{z},\mathfrak{u},\mathfrak{v},\mathfrak{w},\mathfrak{X},\mathfrak{Y},\mathfrak{Z},\mathfrak{U},\mathfrak{V},\mathfrak{W}$ to denote finite, possibly empty sequences of variables of finite types. Lower case letters $x^\sigma, y^\sigma, z^\sigma, u^\sigma, v^\sigma, w^\sigma$ denote as before variables of type σ; the type superscript is sometimes omitted.

Similarly s, t, T denote terms of finite types; $\mathfrak{s}, \mathfrak{t}, \mathfrak{T}$ are used for finite sequences of terms of finite types.

We extend the notation for application to sequences of terms according to the convention of Spector 1962; if $\mathfrak{s} = (s_1,\ldots,s_n)$, $\mathfrak{t} = (t_1,\ldots,t_m)$ then $\mathfrak{s}\mathfrak{t} = (s_1t_1\ldots t_m,\ldots,s_nt_1\ldots t_m)$. $\mathfrak{R}$ is used for a sequence $(R^1_{\sigma_1,\ldots,\sigma_p},\ldots,R^p_{\sigma_1,\ldots,\sigma_p})$.

In using the applicative notation, types are always assumed to be "fitting".

We now define a translation ^{0} which associates to every formula A of $\mathbf{HA}^\omega$

a formula A^0 of the form $\exists \mathfrak{x} A_0 \mathfrak{x}$, A_0 a negative formula of $\mathbf{HA}^\omega$. The translation is defined inductively, according to the following clauses (in clause **mr**(ii) – **mr**(vii) we assume $A^0 \equiv \exists \mathfrak{x} A_0 \mathfrak{x}$, $B^0 \equiv \exists \mathfrak{y} B_0 \mathfrak{y}$):

mr(i) $A^0 \equiv A$ for a negative formula A.
mr(ii) $[A \wedge B]^0 \equiv \exists \mathfrak{x}\mathfrak{y}(A_0 \mathfrak{x} \wedge B_0 \mathfrak{y})$.
mr(iii) $[A \vee B]^0 \equiv \exists z^0 \mathfrak{x}\mathfrak{y}\,[(z=0 \to A_0 \mathfrak{x})) \wedge (z \neq 0 \to B_0 \mathfrak{y}))]$.
mr(iv) $[A \to B]^0 \equiv \exists \mathfrak{Y} \forall \mathfrak{x} [A_0 \mathfrak{x} \to B_0(\mathfrak{Y}\mathfrak{x})]$.
mr(v) $[\neg A]^0 \equiv [A \to 1=0]^0$.
mr(vi) $[\forall z A z]^0 \equiv \exists \mathfrak{X} \forall z A_0(\mathfrak{X} z, z)$.
mr(vii) $[\exists z A z]^0 \equiv \exists z \mathfrak{x} A_0(\mathfrak{x}, z)$.

4.3. **Definition.** We define a translation ^{1} which associates with every formula A of $\mathbf{HA}^\omega$ a formula A^1 of the form $\exists \mathfrak{x} A_1 \mathfrak{x}$ as follows. Let $A^1 \equiv \exists \mathfrak{x} A_1 \mathfrak{x}$, $B^1 \equiv \exists \mathfrak{y} B_1 \mathfrak{y}$.

mq(i) $A^1 \equiv A$ for negative A.
mq(ii) $[A \wedge B]^1 \equiv \exists \mathfrak{x}\mathfrak{y}\,[A_1 \mathfrak{x} \wedge B_1 \mathfrak{y}]$.
mq(iii) $[A \vee B]^1 \equiv \exists z^0 \mathfrak{x}\mathfrak{y}\,[(z=0 \to A_1 \mathfrak{x} \wedge A) \wedge (z \neq 0 \to B_1 \mathfrak{y} \wedge B)]$.
mq(iv) $[A \to B]^1 \equiv \exists \mathfrak{Y} \forall \mathfrak{x}\,[A_1 \mathfrak{x} \wedge A \to B_1(\mathfrak{Y}\mathfrak{x})]$.
mq(v) $[\neg A]^1 \equiv [A \to 1=0]^1$.
mq(vi) $[\forall z A z]^1 \equiv \exists \mathfrak{X} \forall z A_1(\mathfrak{X} z, z)$.
mq(vii) $[\exists z A z]^1 \equiv \exists z \mathfrak{x}\,[A_1(\mathfrak{x}, z) \wedge A z]$.

4.4. **Definition.** If $\mathbf{H} \vdash \exists \mathfrak{x} A_0 \mathfrak{x}$, A is said to be **H-mr**-realizable. Let $\mathfrak{M}$ be a model for $\mathbf{HA}^\omega$, and let **H** be a formal theory in which $\mathfrak{M}$ can be defined, then A is said to be **H-**$\mathfrak{M}$**-mr**-realizable, if $\mathbf{H} \vdash [\exists \mathfrak{x} A_0 \mathfrak{x}]_{\mathfrak{M}}$ (here $[B]_{\mathfrak{M}}$ denotes the formula obtained from a formula B of $\mathbf{HA}^\omega$ by relativizing all quantifiers to $\mathfrak{M}$). Similarly one defines **H-mq**-realizable, **H-**$\mathfrak{M}$**-mq**-realizable.

4.5. *Remark.* Note that $A^{00} \equiv A^0$, and that $(\neg A)^0$ is a negative formula for every A.

4.6. **Theorem.** *Let A be a closed formula of* $\mathbf{HA}^\omega$. **H** *is one of the systems* $\mathbf{HA}^\omega$, $\mathbf{HA}^\omega + \mathrm{IP}^\omega$, $\mathbf{HA}^\omega + \mathrm{AC}$, $\mathbf{HA}^\omega + \mathrm{IP}^\omega + \mathrm{AC}$, *where* AC *denotes the union of all choice-axioms* $\mathrm{AC}_{\sigma,\tau}$:

$$\mathrm{AC}_{\sigma,\tau} \qquad \forall x^\sigma \exists y^\tau A(x,y) \to \exists z^{(\sigma)\tau} \forall x^\sigma A(x, zx)$$

and where IP^ω *denotes the schema obtained by generalizing* IP *to all finite types:*

IP$^\omega$ $(\neg A \to \exists x^\sigma B) \to \exists x^\sigma(\neg A \to B)$ (*σ arbitrary, x^σ not free in A*).

Then

$$\mathbf{H} \vdash A \Rightarrow \mathbf{HA}^\omega \vdash A_0\mathfrak{s} \textit{ and } \mathbf{H} \vdash A_1\mathfrak{s} \textit{ for suitable closed terms } \mathfrak{s}.$$

Proof. For $\mathbf{HA}^\omega$ and **mr**-realizability the theorem is stated e.g. in Kreisel 1962, without proof. The proof however, is rather similar to the proof of 3.5 and is mainly routine, proceeding by induction on the length of a derivation in **H**. We have to verify the assertion of the theorem for the closures of the axioms, and we have to show that the realizability of the universal closures of the premisses of a rule implies the realizability of the universal closure of the conclusion. We may adopt e.g. Spector's axiomatization of intuitionistic logic as our basis for the verification (Spector 1962). Let us check some examples.

(a) Assume the theorem for $A \to C$, $B \to C$. Then

$$\forall \mathfrak{x}[A_1\mathfrak{x} \wedge A \to C_1(\mathfrak{T}\mathfrak{x})] ,$$

$$\forall \mathfrak{y}[B_1\mathfrak{y} \wedge B \to C_1(\mathfrak{T}'\mathfrak{y})] .$$

Also $[A \wedge B \to C]^1 \equiv \exists \mathfrak{z} \forall z^0 \mathfrak{x}\mathfrak{y}[(z=0 \to A_1\mathfrak{x} \wedge A) \wedge (z \neq 0 \to B_1\mathfrak{y} \wedge B) \to C_1(\mathfrak{z}z\mathfrak{x}\mathfrak{y})]$. We use definition by cases:

$$\mathfrak{T}''z\mathfrak{x}\mathfrak{y} = \begin{cases} \mathfrak{T}\mathfrak{x} & \text{if } z = 0 , \\ \mathfrak{T}'\mathfrak{y} & \text{if } z \neq 0 \end{cases}$$

or explicitly $\mathfrak{T}'' = \lambda z\mathfrak{x}\mathfrak{y}.\mathfrak{R}(\mathfrak{T}\mathfrak{x})(\lambda \mathfrak{u}\mathfrak{v}.\mathfrak{T}'\mathfrak{y})z$. We may take $\mathfrak{T}''$ for $\mathfrak{z}$.

(b) Induction. Let $[A(0)]^1 \equiv \exists \mathfrak{x} A_1(\mathfrak{x},0)$, $[\forall y(Ay \to A(Sy))]^1 \equiv \exists \mathfrak{z} \forall y \mathfrak{x}[A_1(\mathfrak{x},y) \wedge A(y) \to A_1(\mathfrak{z}y\mathfrak{x},Sy)]$, $[\forall y Ay]^1 \equiv \exists \mathfrak{X} \forall y A_1(\mathfrak{X}y,y)$. Assume $\vdash A(0)$, $\vdash \forall y[Ay \to A(Sy)]$, then by the induction hypothesis for suitable $\mathfrak{t}, \mathfrak{T}$

$$A_1(\mathfrak{t},0),\ \forall y\mathfrak{x}(A_1(\mathfrak{x},y) \wedge Ay \to A_1(\mathfrak{T}y\mathfrak{x},Sy)) .$$

We define $\mathfrak{T}'$ by primitive recursion

$$\mathfrak{T}'0 = \mathfrak{t}, \qquad \mathfrak{T}'(Sy) = \mathfrak{T}y(\mathfrak{T}'y) .$$

Finally one proves by induction $\forall y A_1(\mathfrak{T}'y,y)$.

(c) (For **I-HA**$^\omega$ only). $[\forall x^\sigma y^\sigma(x=y \vee x\neq y)]^1 \equiv \forall x^\sigma y^\sigma \exists z^0[(z=0\to x=y)\wedge \wedge(z\neq 0\to x\neq y)]^1 \equiv \exists Z^{(\sigma)(\sigma)0}\forall x^\sigma y^\sigma[(Zxy=0\to x=y)\wedge(Zxy\neq 0\to x\neq y)]$. We may take E_σ for Z. Etc. etc.

4.7. **Corollary.** **HA**$^\omega$ + IP$^\omega$ + AC *is consistent relative* **HA** *(use* 2.7 *and* 2.8*).*

4.8. **Theorem** *(analogue of* 3.14, *axiomatization of* **mr**-*realizability).*

(i) $\mathbf{HA}^\omega + \mathrm{IP}^\omega + \mathrm{AC} \vdash A \leftrightarrow \exists \mathfrak{x} A_0\mathfrak{x}$,

(ii) $\mathbf{HA} + \mathrm{IP}^\omega + \mathrm{AC} \vdash A \Leftrightarrow \mathbf{HA}^\omega \vdash \exists \mathfrak{x} A_0\mathfrak{x}$,

(iii) $\mathbf{HA} + \mathrm{IP}^\omega + \mathrm{AC} \vdash A_1\mathfrak{x} \leftrightarrow A_0\mathfrak{x}$.

Proof. (i) is proved by induction on the construction of A. For example, assume (i) to be proved for A, B, then $(A\to B)\leftrightarrow(\exists\mathfrak{x}A_0\mathfrak{x}\to\exists\mathfrak{y}B_0\mathfrak{y})\leftrightarrow\forall\mathfrak{x}(A_0\mathfrak{x}\to \to\exists\mathfrak{y}B_0\mathfrak{y})\leftrightarrow\forall\mathfrak{x}\exists\mathfrak{y}(A_0\mathfrak{x}\to B_0\mathfrak{y})\leftrightarrow\exists\mathfrak{Y}\forall\mathfrak{x}(A_0\mathfrak{x}\to B_0(\mathfrak{Y}\mathfrak{x}))\leftrightarrow(A\to B)^0$. Here we made use of the fact that for negative formulae $A\leftrightarrow\neg\neg A$, hence we could apply IP$^\omega$ to $\forall\mathfrak{x}(A_0\mathfrak{x}\to\exists\mathfrak{y}B_0\mathfrak{y})$. Etc. etc.

(ii) follows from (i) with the help of 4.6.

(iii) is proved by induction on the construction of A.

4.9. **Theorem.** *Markov's schema is not modified realizable w.r.t. HRO or HEO. In fact, let*

$$A \equiv \forall x[\neg\neg\exists y T(x,x,y) \to \exists y T(x,x,y)] .$$

Then A is not **HA**-*HRO*-**mr**-*realizable nor* **HA**-*HEO*-mr-*realizable.*

Proof. (Cf. Kreisel 1958A) $A^0 \equiv \exists Y \forall x[\neg\forall y \neg T(x,x,y)\to T(x,x,Yx)]$. Assume A^0 to hold for *HRO* or *HEO*. Then for some recursive function f:

$$\forall x[\neg\forall y\neg T(x,x,y)\to T(x,x,fx)] .$$

This would imply the recursiveness of $\exists y T(x,x,y)$ (as in the proof of 3.20), which is contradictory.

4.10. **Corollary.** $\mathrm{M_{PR}}$, *i.e.* $\neg\neg\exists x^0 Ax \to \exists x^0 Ax$ *for primitive recursive predicates A is not derivable in* **HA**$^\omega$ + IP$^\omega$ + AC. *(Compare* 9.4 (ii).*)*

4.11. **Theorem.** **HRO⁻** + IP^ω + AC $\vdash A \Rightarrow$ **HRO⁻** $\vdash A_0\mathfrak{s}$ *and* **HRO⁻** $\vdash A_1\mathfrak{s}$ *for an appropriate sequence of closed terms* $\mathfrak{s}$.

Proof. We only have to verify the additional axioms G1–4, which is trivial.

4.12. **Remark.** We cannot extend our method to G5, for it can be shown that the ^{0}-translation of G5 does not hold in *HRO*. Consider the simplest case of G5:

$$\forall x^0 [\forall y^0 \exists z^0 T(x,y,z) \to \exists u^1 (\Phi u = x)] \ .$$

The ^{0}-translation is

$$\exists U^{(0)(1)1} \forall x^0 z^1 [\forall y^0 T(x,y,zy) \to \Phi(Uxz) = x] \ . \qquad (1)$$

Assume (1) to hold in *HRO*; then there would exist a number u such that

$$z \in V_1 \wedge x \in V_0 \to !\{\{u\}(x)\}(z) \wedge \forall y T(x,y,\{z\}(y))$$

$$\to \{\{u\}(x)\}(z) \simeq x \ .$$

Let

$$\varphi(y) = \Lambda x.j_1 \min_w [j_1 w = 0 \wedge T(y,y,j_2 w)] \ .$$

$\{\varphi(y)\} = \lambda x.0$ when $\exists z T(y,y,z)$, otherwise $\{\varphi(y)\}$ is nowhere defined. Let $z = \Lambda y.\min_w T(\Lambda x.0,y,w)$. Then $!\{\{u\}(\varphi(y))\}(z)$ for all y. $\{\{u\}(\varphi(y))\}(z')$ $= \varphi(y) \Rightarrow \varphi(y) \in V_1, \Rightarrow \exists z T(y,y,z)$. $\{\{u\}(\varphi(y))\}(z') \neq \varphi(y)$, then $\varphi(y) \notin V_1$, $\Rightarrow \neg \exists z T(y,y,z)$. This would imply $\exists z T(y,y,z)$ to be a recursive predicate of y, which is contradictory.

4.13. **Theorem.** *Let* ECT_1 *denote the schema*

ECT_1 $\quad \forall x [\neg Ax \to \exists y B(x,y)] \to \exists z \forall x \exists u [T(z,x,u) \wedge (\neg Ax \to B(x,Uu))] \ .$

ECT_1 *is consistent relative* **HA**.

Proof. ECT_1 is a consequence of CT_0 and IP; then the theorem follows with 4.11.

§ 5. The Dialectica translation

5.1. The Dialectica translation ^{D} associates to every formula A of **HA** a formula A^D of the form $\exists\mathfrak{x}\forall\mathfrak{y}A_D(\mathfrak{x},\mathfrak{y})$, A_D quantifier-free. For the definition, see Gödel 1958 or Spector 1962.

5.2. **Notation.** Let IP_0^ω denote the following schema

$$IP_0^\omega \qquad \forall\mathfrak{x}[A\mathfrak{x}\vee\neg A\mathfrak{x}] \wedge [\forall\mathfrak{x}A\mathfrak{x}\rightarrow\exists\mathfrak{y}B\mathfrak{y}] \rightarrow \exists\mathfrak{y}[\forall\mathfrak{x}A\mathfrak{x}\rightarrow B\mathfrak{y}]$$

($\mathfrak{y}$ not free in A, $\mathfrak{x}$ not free in B). Let M^ω denote Markov's schema for all finite types

$$M^\omega \qquad \forall\mathfrak{x}[A\mathfrak{x}\vee\neg A\mathfrak{x}] \wedge\neg\neg\exists\mathfrak{x}A\mathfrak{x} \rightarrow \exists\mathfrak{x}A\mathfrak{x} .$$

(Note that M is the restriction of M^ω to the language of **HA**.) Let IP′, M′ denote the restrictions of IP_0^ω, M^ω respectively to quantifier-free A.

5.3. **Lemma.** *For* $\mathbf{H} = \mathbf{WE\text{-}HA}^\omega, \mathbf{I\text{-}HA}^\omega, \mathbf{HRO}^-$ *we have* $\mathbf{H} + \mathrm{IP}' + \mathrm{M}' + \mathrm{AC} \vdash A \Rightarrow \mathbf{H} \vdash A_D(\mathfrak{s},\mathfrak{y})$ *for a suitable sequence of terms* $\mathfrak{s}$, *for any formula* A *of* **H**.

Proof. In Spector 1962 it is proved that

$$\mathbf{WE\text{-}HA}^\omega \vdash A \Rightarrow \mathbf{WE\text{-}HA}^\omega \vdash A_D(\mathfrak{s},\mathfrak{y})$$

(In fact, Spector shows that $A_D(\mathfrak{s},\mathfrak{y})$ can be proved in the quantifier-free part of $\mathbf{WE\text{-}HA}^\omega$, but this is more than is required for our purpose.)

It is also easily seen that for any instance F of either IP′, or M′, or AC we can find terms $\mathfrak{s}$ such that $\mathbf{WE\text{-}HA}^\omega \vdash F_D(\mathfrak{s},\mathfrak{y})$ (compare Yasugi 1963, Kreisel 1959, 2.11).

In the case $\mathbf{H} = \mathbf{I\text{-}HA}^\omega$, the proof is almost completely similar. The equality functional E_σ is used to show that every quantifier-free formula can be replaced by an equation, and for the interpretation of $\forall x^\sigma y^\sigma(x=y \vee x\neq y)$.

The case $\mathbf{H} = \mathbf{HRO}^-$ is treated similarly.

5.4. **Theorem.** *For* $\mathbf{H} = \mathbf{WE\text{-}HA}^{\omega}, \mathbf{I\text{-}HA}^{\omega}, \mathbf{HRO}^{-}$ *we have*

$$\mathbf{H} + \mathrm{IP}' + \mathrm{M}' + \mathrm{AC} \vdash A \leftrightarrow A^{\mathrm{D}}$$

for any formula A *in the language of* $\mathbf{H}$.

Proof. By induction on the construction of A (cf. Yasugi 1963.)

5.5. **Theorem.** *(Axiomatization of the Dialectica translation). For* $\mathbf{H} = \mathbf{WE\text{-}HA}^{\omega}, \mathbf{I\text{-}HA}^{\omega}, \mathbf{HRO}^{-}$:
(i) $\mathbf{H} + \mathrm{IP}_0^{\omega} + \mathrm{M}^{\omega} + \mathrm{AC} \vdash A \Rightarrow \mathbf{H} \vdash A_{\mathrm{D}}(\mathfrak{s}, \mathfrak{y})$ *for suitable terms* $\mathfrak{s}$,
(ii) $\mathbf{H} + \mathrm{IP}_0^{\omega} + \mathrm{M}^{\omega} + \mathrm{AC} \vdash A \leftrightarrow A^{\mathrm{D}}$ *for every formula* A *in the language of* $\mathbf{H}$.

Proof. It suffices to derive $\mathrm{IP}_0^{\omega}, \mathrm{M}^{\omega}$ in $\mathbf{H} + \mathrm{IP}' + \mathrm{M}' + \mathrm{AC}$; then the assertions (i), (ii) follow by 5.3, 5.4.

In $\mathbf{H} + \mathrm{IB}' + \mathrm{M}' + \mathrm{AC}$ we have $\forall \mathfrak{x}(A\mathfrak{x} \vee \neg A\mathfrak{x}) \leftrightarrow [\forall \mathfrak{x}(A\mathfrak{x} \vee \neg A\mathfrak{x})]^{\mathrm{D}} \leftrightarrow$ $\leftrightarrow \exists X \mathfrak{Y} \mathfrak{Z} \forall \mathfrak{x} \mathfrak{y} \mathfrak{z} [(X\mathfrak{x}=0 \rightarrow A_{\mathrm{D}}(\mathfrak{x}, \mathfrak{Y}\mathfrak{x}, \mathfrak{z})) \wedge (X\mathfrak{x} \neq 0 \rightarrow \neg A_{\mathrm{D}}(\mathfrak{x}, \mathfrak{y}, \mathfrak{Z}\mathfrak{x}\mathfrak{y}))]$. Thus we may assume the existence of an X such that

$$X\mathfrak{x} = 0 \leftrightarrow A\mathfrak{x} \ .$$

Replacing $A\mathfrak{x}$ by $X\mathfrak{x} = 0$ in $\mathrm{M}^{\omega}, \mathrm{IP}_0^{\omega}$ reduces these schemata to instances of $\mathrm{M}', \mathrm{IP}'$.

§6. Conservative extension results

6.1. **Theorem.** $\mathbf{HA}^{\omega} + \mathrm{CT}$, $\mathbf{HRO}$ *are conservative extensions of* $\mathbf{HA}$.

Proof. Immediate from the fact that *HRO, HEO* can be proved in **HA** to be models for **HRO**, $\mathbf{E\text{-}HA}^{\omega}$, and that $[A]_{HRO} \equiv [A]_{HEO} \equiv A$ for arithmetical A (2.7,2.8). For $\mathbf{E\text{-}HA}^{\omega}$ the result occurs as theorem 3 in Kreisel 1959B.

6.2. **Definition.** $\Gamma_0(\Gamma_1, \Gamma_2)$ is the class of formulae of $\mathbf{HA}^{\omega}$ such that in all their subformulae of the form $A \rightarrow B$ or $\neg A$, A is an almost negative formula (negative formula, purely universal formula) preceded by existential quantifiers.

Note that, modulo logical equivalence, $\Gamma_2 \subseteq \Gamma_1 \subseteq \Gamma_0$. Let $\Gamma_{\mathrm{n}}, \Gamma_{\mathrm{an}}, \Gamma_{\mathrm{pr}}$ denote the negative, almost negative and prenex formulae respectively. $\mathbf{H}$ is conservative over $\mathbf{H}' \cap \Gamma$ where Γ is a class of formulae, is an abbreviation for: "$\mathbf{H}$ is an extension of $\mathbf{H}'$ which is conservative w.r.t. formulae of Γ".

6.3. **Theorem.** *(Conservative extensions.)*
(i) $(\mathbf{HA}+\mathbf{ECT}_0) \cap \Gamma_0 = \mathbf{HA} \cap \Gamma_0$;
$(\mathbf{HA}+\mathbf{M}+\mathbf{ECT}_0) \cap \Gamma_0 = (\mathbf{HA}+\mathbf{M}) \cap \Gamma_0$;
(ii) $(\mathbf{HA}^\omega+\mathbf{IP}^\omega+\mathbf{AC}) \cap \Gamma_1 = \mathbf{HA}^\omega \cap \Gamma_1$;
(iii) $(\mathbf{HRO}^-+\mathbf{IP}^\omega+\mathbf{AC}) \cap \Gamma_1 = \mathbf{HRO}^- \cap \Gamma_1$;
(iv) $\mathbf{I\text{-}HA}^\omega + \mathbf{IP}^\omega + \mathbf{AC} + \mathbf{CT}$ *is conservative over* $\mathbf{HA} \cap \Gamma_1$;
(v) $\mathbf{I\text{-}HA}^\omega + \mathbf{IP}_0^\omega + \mathbf{AC} + \mathbf{M}^\omega$, $\mathbf{WE\text{-}HA}^\omega + \mathbf{IP}_0^\omega + \mathbf{AC} + \mathbf{M}^\omega$ *are conservative over* $\mathbf{I\text{-}HA}^\omega \cap \Gamma_2$, $\mathbf{WE\text{-}HA}^\omega \cap \Gamma_2$ *respectively, hence conservative over* $\mathbf{HA} \cap \Gamma_2$;
(vi) $(\mathbf{HRO}^-+\mathbf{IP}_0^\omega+\mathbf{AC}+\mathbf{M}^\omega) \cap \Gamma_2 = \mathbf{HRO}^- \cap \Gamma_2$;
(vii) $\mathbf{I\text{-}HA}^\omega + \mathbf{IP}_0^\omega + \mathbf{AC} + \mathbf{M}^\omega + \mathbf{CT}$ *is conservative over* $\mathbf{HA} \cap \Gamma_2$.

Proof. Ad (i). We note that Γ_0 may be defined inductively by the following clauses:
(a) Prime formulae are in Γ_0 .
(b) $A, B \in \Gamma_0 \Rightarrow A \wedge B, A \vee B, \forall xA, \exists xA \in \Gamma_0$.
(c) Let A be almost negative, $B \in \Gamma_0 \Rightarrow$
$\neg\exists x_1...x_nA \in \Gamma_0$, $\exists x_1...x_nA \to B \in \Gamma_0$.
Now we prove by induction over Γ_0

$$\mathbf{HA} \vdash \exists x(x \mathbf{\ r\ } A) \to A \tag{1}$$

for all $A \in \Gamma_0$.

(A) For prime formulae (1) is immediate.

(B) Assume (1) for Ay. Let $\exists x(x \mathbf{\ r\ } \forall yAy)$, then $\exists x \forall y(!\{x\}(y) \wedge \wedge \{x\}(y) \mathbf{\ r\ } Ay)$, hence $\forall y \exists x(x \mathbf{\ r\ } Ay)$, which implies $\forall yAy$ by the induction hypothesis. Similarly for $A \wedge B$.

If we assume $\exists x(x \mathbf{\ r\ } \exists yAy)$, then $\exists x(j_2x \mathbf{\ r\ } A(j_1x))$, so $\exists x \exists y(x \mathbf{\ r\ } Ay)$, and thus by the induction hypothesis $\exists yAy$. Similarly for $A \vee B$.

(C) If A is almost negative, then $\exists x_1...x_nA \leftrightarrow \exists y(y \mathbf{\ r\ } \exists x_1...x_nA)$ since $\exists xBx \leftrightarrow \exists x \exists y(y \mathbf{\ r\ } Bx) \leftrightarrow \exists z(j_2z \mathbf{\ r\ } B(j_1z)) \leftrightarrow \exists y(y \mathbf{\ r\ } \exists xBx)$ for almost negative B. Therefore, if $\exists y(y \mathbf{\ r\ } (\exists xA \to B))$, it follows that $\exists xA \to \exists z(z \mathbf{\ r\ } B)$. By the induction hypothesis $\exists xA \to B$.

The case of $\neg A$ is reduced to the case of implication.

From 3.5 we know that

$$\mathbf{HA} \vdash A \Rightarrow \mathbf{HA} \vdash \exists x(x \mathbf{\ r\ } A) . \tag{2}$$

From (1) and (2) we conclude

$$\mathbf{HA} \vdash A \Leftrightarrow \mathbf{HA} + \mathrm{ECT}_0 \vdash A$$

for $A \in \Gamma_0$. The second half of (i) is proved similarly, using 3.15.

Ad (ii). The proof is very similar to the proof of (i), but now instead of (1) we have to prove

$$\mathbf{HA}^\omega \vdash \exists \mathfrak{x} A_0 \mathfrak{x} \to A \tag{3}$$

for all $A \in \Gamma_1$; instead of (2) we now use

$$\mathbf{HA}^\omega \vdash A \Rightarrow \mathbf{HA}^\omega \vdash \exists \mathfrak{x} A_0 \mathfrak{x} \,. \tag{4}$$

(iii) is proved similarly to (ii); (iv) is an immediate corollary to (iii).

Ad (v). Proof similar to (i), (ii). Instead of (1) we have to use

$$\mathbf{HA}^\omega \vdash \exists \mathfrak{x} \forall \mathfrak{y} A_D(\mathfrak{x},\mathfrak{y}) \to A \,, \tag{5}$$

for $A \in \Gamma_2$ etc. etc.

(vi) is proved similarly to (ii), (iii); (vii) is an immediate corollary to (vi).

6.4. **Corollary**. *We formulate some immediate consequences for* **HA**.

(i) $\mathbf{HA} + \mathrm{ECT}_0$, $\mathbf{HA} + \mathrm{IP} + \mathrm{CT}_0$ *are conservative over* $\mathbf{HA} \cap \Gamma_n$.
$\mathbf{HA} + \mathrm{ECT}_0$, $\mathbf{HA} + \mathrm{IP} + \mathrm{CT}_0$, $\mathbf{HA} + \mathrm{IP}_0 + \mathrm{M} + \mathrm{CT}_0$ *are conservative over* Γ_{pr}.

(ii) $\mathbf{HA} + \mathrm{ECT}_0 + \mathrm{M}$ *is conservative over* $(\mathbf{HA}+\mathrm{M}) \cap \Gamma_{an}$, $(\mathbf{HA}+\mathrm{M}) \cap \Gamma_{pr}$.

6.5. *Remark.* From results from Kreisel (Kreisel 1965, 2.3332, which is less clearly stated in Kreisel 1959, 5.1; Kreisel 1959, 4.141, 4.21) it can be concluded that $\mathbf{WE\text{-}HA}^\omega + \mathrm{M}^\omega + \mathrm{IP}_0^\omega + \mathrm{AC}$ is conservative over $\mathbf{HA} \cap \Gamma_n$.

6.6. In 8.5 we shall prove that $\mathbf{I\text{-}HA}^\omega + \mathrm{AC} + \mathrm{CT}$, $\mathbf{I\text{-}HA}^\omega + \mathrm{ECT}_0 + \mathrm{AC}$ are conservative over $\mathbf{HA} \cap \Gamma_0$.

6.7. *Remark.* An immediate consequence of 6.3 (i) is that the realizability of M cannot be proved in **HA**, since this would imply $\mathbf{HA} + \mathrm{ECT}_0 \vdash \forall x [\neg \forall y \neg T(x,x,y) \to \exists y T(x,x,y)]$. Now this instance of M is a formula of Γ_{an}, hence a fortiori of Γ_0, so then $\mathbf{HA} \vdash \forall x [\neg \forall y \neg T(x,x,y) \to \exists y T(x,x,y)]$, which is impossible as we have seen (4.10).

§7. Proof-theoretic closure properties, rule of choice, Church's rule

7.1. This section is devoted to various proof-theoretic closure properties for **HA**, $\mathbf{HA}^\omega$ and extensions of these systems. The closure properties to be discussed are

(I) $\vdash \exists x Ax \Rightarrow (\text{E}n) \vdash A\mathbf{n}$ ($\exists x Ax$ closed).

(II) $\vdash \exists x^\sigma Ax \Rightarrow (\text{E}s^\sigma) \vdash As^\sigma$ ($\exists x^\sigma Ax$ closed, s^σ a closed term of type σ).

(III) $\vdash A \vee B \Rightarrow \vdash A$ or $\vdash B$ ($A \vee B$ closed).

IPR $\vdash A \to \exists x Bx \Rightarrow \vdash \exists x(A \to Bx)$ (A not containing x free, A negative, x a numerical variable).

IPR^ω $\vdash A \to \exists x^\sigma Bx \Rightarrow \vdash \exists x^\sigma(A \to Bx)$ (A not containing x^σ free, A negative).

ACR $\vdash \forall x^\sigma \exists y^\tau A(x,y) \Rightarrow \exists z^{(\sigma)\tau} \forall x^\sigma A(x,zx)$.

CR_0 $\vdash \forall x \exists y A(x,y) \Rightarrow \vdash \exists z \forall x \exists v(T(z,x,v) \wedge A(x,Uv))$.

ECR_0 $\vdash \forall x(Ax \to \exists y B(x,y)) \Rightarrow \vdash \exists u \forall x(Ax \to \exists v(T(x,u,v) \wedge B(x,Uv)))$ (A almost negative).

Note that (I) is a special case of (II), and that (I) implies (III) by $A \vee B \leftrightarrow \exists x[(x=0 \to A) \wedge (x \neq 0 \to B)]$. Obviously ECR_0 includes CR_0, and IPR^ω includes IPR.

CR_0, ECR_0 are called "Church's rule" and "extended Church's rule" respectively.

7.2. **Theorem.** *Assume* $\mathbf{HA} + \mathfrak{A}$ $(\mathbf{HA}^\omega + A)$ *to be conservative over* $\mathbf{HA}(\mathbf{HA}^\omega)$ *w.r.t.* Σ_1^0*-formulae.*

(i) *Let* $\mathfrak{A}$ *be a collection of closed formulae such that*

$$F \in \mathfrak{A} \Rightarrow (\text{E}n)[\mathbf{HA} + \mathfrak{A} \vdash \mathbf{n} \ \mathbf{q} \ F] .$$

Then the system axiomatized by $\mathbf{HA} + \mathfrak{A}$ *satisfies* (I), (III), ECR_0, CR_0.

(ii) *Let* $\mathfrak{A}$ *be a collection of closed formulae such that*

$$F \in \mathfrak{A} \Rightarrow (\text{E}\mathfrak{s})[\mathbf{HA}^\omega + \mathfrak{A} \vdash F_1 \mathfrak{s}]$$

($\mathfrak{s}$ *a meta-variable for sequences of closed terms*). *Then* $\mathbf{HA}^\omega + \mathfrak{A}$ *satisfies* (II), (III), ACR, IPR^ω.

Proof. Ad (i). Assume $\mathbf{HA} + \mathfrak{A} \vdash A$, A closed. Then there are $F_1, \ldots, F_n \in \mathfrak{A}$ such that

$$\mathbf{HA} \vdash F_1 \wedge \ldots \wedge F_n \to A . \tag{1}$$

Assuming $\mathfrak{A}$ to satisfy the condition required under (i), we have

$$\mathbf{HA}+\mathfrak{A}\vdash \mathbf{m}\ \mathbf{q}\ (F_1\wedge\ldots\wedge F_n) \tag{2}$$

for some numeral $\mathbf{m}$. By 3.5 and (1) there is a numeral $\mathbf{m}'$ such that

$$\mathbf{HA}\vdash \mathbf{m}'\ \mathbf{q}\ (F_1\wedge\ldots\wedge F_n\to A)\ .$$

Then there is also a numeral $\mathbf{n}$ such that (since $\mathbf{HA}+\mathfrak{A}$ is conservative over $\mathbf{HA}$ w.r.t. Σ^0_1 formulae)

$$\mathbf{HA}\vdash \mathbf{n}\simeq\{\mathbf{m}'\}(\mathbf{m})$$

and therefore

$$\mathbf{HA}+\mathfrak{A}\vdash \mathbf{n}\ \mathbf{q}\ A\ .$$

Now we can derive (I) for $\mathbf{HA}+\mathfrak{A}$ as follows: assume $\mathbf{HA}+\mathfrak{A}\vdash\exists xAx$, $\exists xAx$ closed. Then there is a numeral $\mathbf{n}$ such that $\mathbf{HA}+\mathfrak{A}\vdash\mathbf{n}\ \mathbf{q}\ \exists xAx$, i.e. $\mathbf{HA}+ +\mathfrak{A}\vdash j_2\mathbf{n}\ \mathbf{q}\ A(j_1\mathbf{n})\wedge A(j_1\mathbf{n})$. Since we can find a numeral $\mathbf{n}'$ such that $\mathbf{HA}\vdash j_1\mathbf{n}=\mathbf{n}'$, it follows that $\mathbf{HA}+\mathfrak{A}\vdash A\mathbf{n}'$.

$\mathbf{ECR}_0$ is derived as follows. Assume

$$\mathbf{HA}+\mathfrak{A}\vdash\forall x(Ax\to\exists yB(x,y))$$

and assume that A, B do not contain free variables besides those shown. (The more general case of additional parameters is reduced to this case by contraction of variables.) Then for some numeral $\mathbf{m}$

$$\mathbf{HA}+\mathfrak{A}\vdash\mathbf{m}\ \mathbf{q}\ \forall x(Ax\to\exists yB(x,y))$$

so

$$\mathbf{HA}+\mathfrak{A}\vdash\forall x\forall u[u\ \mathbf{q}\ Ax\wedge Ax\to !\{\{\mathbf{m}\}(x)\}(u)\wedge$$
$$\wedge\ j_2\{\{\mathbf{m}\}(x)\}(u)\ \mathbf{q}\ B(x,j_1\{\{\mathbf{m}\}(x)\}(u))\wedge B(x,j_1\{\{m\}(x)\}(u))]\ .$$

By 3.8 $u\ \mathbf{q}\ Ax\to Ax$ for almost negative A, and therefore

$$\mathbf{HA}+\mathfrak{A}\vdash\forall x[Ax\to !t\wedge B(x,j_1t)]\ ,$$

where $t=\{\{\mathbf{m}\}(x)\}(\psi_A(x))$. Now we can find a numeral $\mathbf{n}$ such that $\Lambda x.j_1\{\{\mathbf{m}\}(x)\}(\psi_A(x)=\mathbf{n}$, hence $\mathbf{HA}+\mathfrak{A}\vdash\exists u\forall x[Ax\to !\{u\}(x)\wedge B(x,\{u\}(x))]$.

Ad (ii). The proof is very similar to the proof of (i).

7.3. **Remark.** For closure under ECR_0, ACR we might have weakened our conditions on $\mathfrak{A}$ to

$$F \in \mathfrak{A} \Rightarrow \mathbf{HA} + \mathfrak{A} \vdash \exists y (y \ \mathbf{q}\ F)$$

and

$$F \in \mathfrak{A} \Rightarrow \mathbf{HA} + \mathfrak{A} \vdash \exists \mathfrak{x} F_1 \mathfrak{x}$$

respectively.

7.4. **Corollary to 7.2.**
(i) **HA, HA** + CT_0, **HA** + ECT_0, **HA** + M, **HA** + M + CT_0, **HA** + M + ECT_0, *satisfy* (I), (III), CR_0, ECR_0.
(ii) $\mathbf{HA}^\omega$, $\mathbf{HA}^\omega$ + IP^ω, $\mathbf{HA}^\omega$ + AC, $\mathbf{HA}^\omega$ + IP^ω + AC, $\mathbf{HRO}^-$ *satisfy* (II), (III), ACR, IPR^ω.
(iii) **HA** *is closed under* IPR.

Proof. (i) is immediate by 3.12, 3.15, (ii) follows from 4.6, (iii) is obtained by combining 6.1 with the fact that $\mathbf{HA}^\omega$ is closed under IPR.

7.5. **Lemma.** *In* $\mathbf{HA}^\omega$ *we can establish the following rule*

CR $\qquad (s^1)(\mathrm{E}n)[\mathbf{HA} \vdash s^1 y^0 \simeq \{\mathbf{n}\}(y^0)]$

(s^1 *a meta-variable for a closed term of type* 1).

Proof. We construct a mapping Φ which assigns to any closed term a certain numeral such that

$$\vdash \Phi \mathbf{n} = \mathbf{n}, \vdash \Phi(s^{(\sigma)\tau} t^\sigma) \simeq \{\Phi s^{(\sigma)\tau}\}(\Phi t^\sigma)\,. \tag{1}$$

This can be done by assigning to each closed term its gödelnumber as a hereditarily recursive operation, as indicated in 2.7 and proving (1) by induction over the set of closed terms.

7.6. **Theorem.** $\mathbf{HA}^\omega$, $\mathbf{HA}^\omega$ + IP^ω, $\mathbf{HA}^\omega$ + AC, $\mathbf{HA}^\omega$ ± AC + IP^ω *are closed under* CR_0.

Proof. The four systems mentioned are closed under ACR. Combination with lemma 7.5 yields closure under CR_0.

7.7. **Corollary. HA, $\mathbf{HA}^\omega$, $\mathbf{HA}^\omega$ + IP^ω, $\mathbf{HA}^\omega$ + AC, $\mathbf{HA}^\omega$ + AC + IP^ω** *are closed under the following rule* ECR_1 *(A negative)*

$$ECR_1 \qquad \vdash \forall x(Ax \to \exists y B(x,y)) \Rightarrow \vdash \exists u \forall x \exists v [T(u,x,v) \wedge (Ax \to B(x, Uv))] \ .$$

Proof. The systems mentioned are closed under IP and CR_0, and ECR_1 is an immediate consequence of IP, CR_0.

7.8. **Historical note.** Properties (I), (III) are well known for **HA** (see e.g. Kleene 1962). Kleene obtained for **HA** closure under a rule $\vdash A \to \exists x Cx \Rightarrow \vdash \exists x(A \to Cx)$, for closed $A \to \exists x Cx$, under a condition on A which is weaker than A being equivalent to a negative formula (Kleene 1962). In Kreisel 1958A a method is sketched how to generalize this to the case with free variables. Kleene devised the functional variant of **q**-realizability and used it to obtain (I), (III) and a form of Church's rule for his system of intuitionistic analysis, and for various subsystems of this system (see Kleene 1969, theorem 50, and §5.9, 5.10). We have adapted the definition of **q**-realizability to obtain an analogue to **r**-realizability for number theory (which itself goes back on Kleene 1945), and we used it to prove closure properties for **HA** and various extensions of **HA**. The resemblance between realizability and modified realizability suggested the notion of modified **q**-realizability (**mq**-realizability) as a means to derive closure properties for $\mathbf{HA}^\omega$ and various extensions of $\mathbf{HA}^\omega$.

§8. Axioms of choice for HRO, HEO

8.1. $AC_{\sigma,\tau}$, AC have already been introduced in 4.6. Let $AC_{\sigma,\tau}!$ denote the schema (A a formula of $\mathbf{HA}^\omega$)

$$AC_{\sigma,\tau}! \qquad \forall x^\sigma \exists ! y^\tau A(x,y) \to \exists z^{(\sigma)\tau} \forall x^\sigma A(x,zx) \ .$$

Let $\text{QF-AC}_{(\sigma_1,\ldots,\sigma_m),(\tau_1,\ldots,\tau_n)}$ denote the schema (A a formula of $\mathbf{HA}^\omega$)

$$\forall x_1^{\sigma_1} \ldots x_m^{\sigma_m} \exists y_1^{\tau_1} \ldots y_n^{\tau_n} A(x_1,\ldots,x_m, Y_1,\ldots,Y_n) \to$$

$$\to \exists Y_1 \ldots Y_n \forall x_1 \ldots x_m A(x_1,\ldots,x_m, Y_1 x_1 \ldots x_m, \ldots, Y_n x_1 \ldots x_m) \ ,$$

where $Y_i \in (\sigma_1)\ldots(\sigma_m)\tau_i$, $i = 1, \ldots, n$.

AC! denotes $AC_{\sigma,\tau}!$ for all σ, τ; QF-AC denotes $\text{QF-AC}_{(\sigma_1,\ldots,\sigma_m),(\tau_1,\ldots,\tau_n)}$ for all $\sigma_1, \ldots, \sigma_m, \tau_1, \ldots, \tau_n$ respectively.

8.2. **Lemma.** *$x \in V_\sigma$, $x \in W_\sigma$, $I_\sigma(x,y)$ are equivalent to almost negative formulas.*

Proof. By induction over the type structure. For $\sigma = 0$ the truth of the assertion is immediate. Assume the lemma to hold for σ, τ. Then $x \in V_{(\sigma)\tau}$, $x \in W_{(\sigma)\tau}$, $I_{(\sigma)\tau}(x,y)$ may be rewritten as

$$\forall y \in V_\sigma [\exists u T(x,y,u) \wedge \forall v(T(x,y,v) \to Uv \in V_\tau)] \ ,$$

$$\forall y \in W_\sigma [\exists u T(x,y,u) \wedge \forall v(T(x,y,v) \to Uv \in W_\tau)] \wedge$$
$$\forall yzvw [I_\sigma(y,z) \wedge T(x,y,v) \wedge T(x,z,w) \to I_\tau(Uv,Uw)] \ ,$$

$$x \in W_{(\sigma)\tau} \wedge y \in W_{(\sigma)\tau} \wedge$$
$$\wedge \forall z \in W_\sigma \forall vw [T(x,z,v) \wedge T(y,z,w) \to I_\tau(Uv,Uw)]$$

respectively. With the induction hypothesis the assertion of the lemma for type $(\sigma)\tau$ follows.

8.3. **Theorem.** $\text{QF-AC}_{(\sigma_1,\ldots,\sigma_n),0}$ *holds for HRO.*

Proof. For simplicity we restrict ourselves to $\text{QF-AC}_{\sigma,0}$ without parameters. Assume $[\forall x^\sigma \exists y^0 A(x,y)]_{HRO}$, A a quantifier-free formula of $\mathbf{I\text{-}HA}^\omega$. Let $A^*(x,y) \equiv [A(x,y)]_{HRO}$, then

$$\forall x \in V_\sigma \exists y A^*(x,y) \ ,$$

$$\mathbf{HA} \vdash x \in V_\sigma \to A^*(x,y) \vee \neg A^*(x,y)$$

or equivalently

$$\mathbf{HA} \vdash \forall xy (x \in V_\sigma \to \exists z [(z=0 \to A^*(x,y)) \wedge (z \neq 0 \to \neg A^*(x,y))] \ .$$

Apply now lemma 7.2 and the closure of **HA** under ECR_0 (7.4), in combination with (I), then it follows that for a certain numeral **n**

$$\mathbf{HA} \vdash x \in V_\sigma \to \exists u (T(\mathbf{n}, j(x,y), u) \wedge (Uu=0 \leftrightarrow A^*(x,y))) \ .$$

Therefore

$$\forall x \in V_\sigma \exists yu(T(\mathbf{n},j(x,y),u) \wedge Uu{=}0)\,.$$

Let $z = \Lambda x.j_1 \min_w [T(\mathbf{n},j(x,j_1 w)j_2 w) \wedge Uj_2 w{=}0]$. Then $\forall x \in V_\sigma A^*(x,\{z\}(x))$. So $z \in V_{(\sigma)0}$, and thus $\exists z \in V_{(\sigma)0} \forall x A^*(x,\{z\}(x))$.

8.4. It is still open whether QF-AC holds generally for *HRO*. By Kreisel 1959, 4.14, 4.21, QF-AC holds (classically) for *HRE*.

8.5. **Theorem.** $[\mathrm{AC}]_{HRO}$ *is provable in* $\mathbf{HA}+\mathrm{ECT}_0$, *so it is consistent to assume* AC *for HRO.*

Proof. We derive $[\mathrm{AC}]_{HRO}$ in $\mathbf{HA}+\mathrm{ECT}_0$. Assume

$$\forall x \in V_\sigma \exists y \in V_\tau A(x,y)\,.$$

$x \in V_\sigma$ is equivalent to an almost negative predicate by 8.2, therefore with ECT_0

$$\exists u \forall x \in V_\sigma \exists v(T(u,x,v) \wedge A(x,Uv) \wedge Uv{\in}V_\tau)\,,$$

hence

$$\exists u \in V_{(\sigma)\tau} \forall x \in V_\sigma \exists v(T(z,x,v) \wedge A(x,Uv))\,.$$

8.6. **Theorem.** $[\mathrm{AC!}]_{HEO}$ *is provable in* $\mathbf{HA}+\mathrm{ECT}_0$, *so it is consistent to assume* AC! *for HEO.*

Proof. Assume

$$\forall x \in W_\sigma \exists y \in W_\tau A(x,y)\,,$$

$$I_\sigma(x,x') \wedge A(x,y) \wedge A(x',y') \to I_\tau(y,y')\,. \tag{1}$$

$x \in W_\sigma$ is equivalent to an almost negative formula (7.2), so by ECT_0 there is a u such that

$$\forall x \in W_\sigma \exists v(T(u,x,v) \wedge A(x,Uv) \wedge Uv \in W_\tau)\,.$$

Assume $I_\sigma(x,x')$, then there are v,v' such that

$$T(u,x,v),\ T(u,x',v'),\ A(x,Uv),\ A(x',Uv'),\ Uv \in W_\tau,\ Uv' \in W_\tau\ .$$

By (1) $I_\tau(Uv,Uv')$. Therefore $u \in W_{(\sigma)\tau}$, and thus

$$\exists u \in W_{(\sigma)\tau} \forall x \in W_\sigma \exists v(T(u,x,v) \wedge A(x,Uv))\ .$$

8.7. **Theorem.** $\mathrm{AC}_{1,0}$ *is false for HEO.*

Proof. Consider

$$\forall x^1 \exists y^0 \forall z^0 \exists v^0 (T(y,z,v) \wedge Uv{=}xz)\ .$$

This assertion is evidently valid for *HEO*, as has been remarked before (2.8). $\mathrm{AC}_{1,0}$ would imply

$$\exists w^2 \forall x^1 z^0 \exists v^0 (T(wx,z,v) \wedge Uv{=}xz)\ .$$

This is obviously false, since there exists no effective operation w such that $\forall x^1 z^0 \exists v^0 (T(wx,z,v) \wedge Uv{=}xz)$.

8.8. *Remark.* Theorem 4.11 yields a result which may be formulated as follows: it is consistent (relative **HA**) to assume that all objects of finite type are hereditarily recursive operations and satisfy AC, IP^ω (relative the language of $\mathbf{I\text{-}HA}^\omega$).

8.9. It is open whether $[\mathrm{AC}]_{HRO}$ implies ECT_0. The premiss $x \in V_\sigma$ is far from being an "arbitrary" almost negative predicate: every V_σ contains infinitely many elements for example. It is immediate that $[\mathrm{AC}]_{HRO}$ implies CT_0. CT does not imply $\mathrm{AC}_{0,0}$.

§9. Markov's schema and Markov's rule

9.1. In this section we bring together some results concerning Markov's schema and Markov's rule.

$\mathrm{M_{PR}}$, M, M^ω have already been introduced. A rule corresponding to M is

MR $\qquad \forall x(Ax \vee \neg Ax), \vdash \neg\neg \exists x Ax \Rightarrow \vdash \exists x Ax\ ,$

and a rule corresponding to M^ω is

$$\mathrm{MR}^\omega \qquad \forall x^\sigma(Ax \vee \neg Ax), \vdash \neg\neg\exists x^\sigma Ax \Rightarrow \vdash \exists x^\sigma Ax\ .$$

In 4.10 it has been shown that M_{PR} is not derivable in $\mathbf{HA}^\omega + \mathrm{IP}^\omega + \mathrm{AC}$, and it has been shown to be contradictory w.r.t. $\mathbf{HRO}^- + \mathrm{IP}^\omega + \mathrm{AC}$.

The next two theorems give additional information regarding almost negative formulae and M_{PR}.

9.2. **Theorem.** *There exists a formula* $\neg A$, *A almost negative, such that for no negative formula B* $\mathbf{HA} \vdash \neg A \leftrightarrow B$.

Proof. Let A be $\forall x[\neg\neg\exists y T(x,x,y) \to \exists y T(x,x,y)]$. Assume $\mathbf{HA} \vdash \neg A \leftrightarrow B$, B negative, then also $\mathbf{HA} \vdash \neg\neg A \leftrightarrow \neg B$ and therefore a fortiori $\mathbf{HA}^c \vdash \neg\neg A \leftrightarrow$ $\leftrightarrow \neg B$. Since $\mathbf{HA}^c \vdash \neg\neg A$, it follows that $\mathbf{HA}^c \vdash \neg B$, and therefore, since B is negative, $\mathbf{HA} \vdash \neg B$. Thus $\mathbf{HA} \vdash \neg\neg A$. Since $(\neg A)^0 \equiv \neg A^0$, and since $\neg A^0$ holds in *HRO*, it follows that $\mathbf{HA} + \neg A$ is consistent. This yields a contradiction with $\mathbf{HA} \vdash \neg\neg A$. Therefore the assumption $\mathbf{HA} \vdash \neg A \leftrightarrow B$ is false.

9.3. **Theorem.** *Let* $\mathbf{HA} \subseteq \mathbf{H} \subseteq \mathbf{HA}^c$. *Then the following two assertions are equivalent:*

(i) *In* $\mathbf{H}$ *every almost negative formula is provably equivalent to a negative formula.*

(ii) M_{PR} *is derivable in* $\mathbf{H}$.

Proof. (ii) ⇒ (i) is immediate. Assume (i), and consider an instance of M_{PR}, say

$$\neg\neg\exists x Ax \to \exists x Ax\ , \tag{1}$$

A primitive recursive. If c_A is the characteristic function of A, (i) is equivalent to

$$\neg\neg\exists x(c_A(x)=0) \to \exists x(c_A(x) = 0)\ . \tag{2}$$

Call the formula (2) F and assume $\mathbf{H} \vdash F \leftrightarrow B$, B negative. Then also $\mathbf{HA}^c \vdash F \leftrightarrow B$, and since $\mathbf{HA}^c \vdash F$, also $\mathbf{HA}^c \vdash B$. Hence $\mathbf{HA} \vdash B$ and thus $\mathbf{H} \vdash F$. This proves (ii).

9.4. Theorem.

(i) *In* $\mathbf{HA}^\omega$ *we have* $\vdash Ax^\sigma \vee \neg Ax^\sigma, \vdash \neg\neg\exists x^\sigma Ax \to \exists x^\sigma Ax \Rightarrow \vdash \forall x^\sigma \neg Ax \vee \exists x^\sigma Ax$. *Similarly for* **HA** (Kreisel 1958A).

(ii) *Not every closed instance of* $\mathrm{M_{PR}}$ *is derivable in* **HA**. (Kreisel 1958A).

(iii) *In* **I-HA**$^\omega$, **WE-HA**$^\omega$ MR^ω *holds. Similarly for* **HA** (Kreisel 1959B).

Proof. (i) Let us assume that A contains the variables x^σ, y^τ free. Then

$$\mathbf{HA}^\omega \vdash \forall x^\sigma y^\tau \exists z^0 [(z=0 \to A) \wedge (z \neq 0 \to \neg A)] \ .$$

Then also, by 7.4 (ii)

$$\mathbf{HA}^\omega \vdash \forall x^\sigma y^\tau [(t_A xy=0 \to A) \wedge (t_A xy \neq 0 \to \neg A)] \ ,$$

t_A a closed term of type $(\sigma)(\tau)0$ of $\mathbf{HA}^\omega$. Then $\neg\neg\exists x^\sigma Ax \to \exists x^\sigma Ax$ is equivalent to

$$\neg\neg\exists x^\sigma (t_A xy=0) \to \exists x^\sigma (t_A xy=0) \ .$$

Therefore

$$\mathbf{HA}^\omega \vdash \neg\neg\exists x^\sigma (t_A=0) \to \exists x^\sigma (t_A=0) \ .$$

By 4.6 it follows that

$$\mathbf{HA}^\omega \vdash \exists z^{(\tau)\sigma} \forall y^\tau (\neg\neg\exists x^\sigma (t_A xy=0) \to t_A (zy)y=0) \ .$$

Since $\mathbf{HA}^\omega \vdash t_A(zy)y = 0 \vee t_A(zy)y \neq 0$ it follows that

$$\mathbf{HA}^\omega \vdash \forall x^\sigma (\neg t_A xy=0) \vee \exists x^\sigma (t_A xy=0) \ ,$$

hence

$$\vdash \forall x^\sigma \neg A(x,y) \vee \exists x^\sigma A(x,y) \ .$$

The corresponding result for **HA** follows from this result together with the fact that **I-HA**$^\omega$ is a conservative extension of **HA**.

(ii) In Kreisel 1958A a counterexample is given with the help of (i) and Gödel's "diagonal formula" for **HA**. Here we present another counterexample. Consider the following closed instances of $\mathrm{M_{PR}}$:

$$F_n \equiv \neg\neg\exists y T(\mathrm{n},\mathrm{n},y) \to \exists y T(\mathrm{n},\mathrm{n},y)\,, \quad n = 0, 1, 2, \ldots$$

Assume

$$(n)[\mathbf{HA} \vdash F_n]\ .$$

Then by the preceding result and closure condition (III) for **HA** (7.4 (i))

$$(\mathrm{n})[\mathbf{HA} \vdash \forall y \neg T(\mathrm{n},\mathrm{n},y) \text{ or } \mathbf{HA} \vdash \exists y T(\mathrm{n},\mathrm{n},y)]\ .$$

On assumption of consistency of **HA** it follows (by a meta-mathematical application of Markov's schema) from the recursive enumerability of the set of theorems of **HA** that $\{n: \exists y T(n,n,y)\}$ is recursive. This is contradictory, hence

$$\text{not } (\mathrm{n})\,[\mathbf{HA} \vdash F_n]\ .$$

(iii) For simplicity assume A to contain free x^σ, y^τ only. As under (i) we construct a term t_A such that

$$\vdash t_A xy = 0 \leftrightarrow A(x,y)\ . \tag{1}$$

Then $\vdash \neg\neg\exists x^\sigma A(x,y)$ is equivalent to $\vdash \forall y^\tau \neg\neg\exists x^\tau (t_A xy{=}0)$. The Dialectica translation of this assertion is the same as the Dialectica translation of $\forall y^\tau \exists x^\sigma (t_A xy{=}0)$. Therefore we can find a closed term $s \in \mathfrak{r}(\sigma)$ such that $\vdash \forall y^\tau (t_A(sy)y{=}0)$ (7.4 (ii)). Therefore, utilizing (1) again, $\vdash \exists x^\sigma A(x,y)$.

9.5. **Corollary to 9.4 (iii).** *(See 9.6). In* **HA** *and* $\mathbf{HA}^c$ *the same gödelnumbers can be proved to represent total recursive functions.*

Proof. Assume $\mathbf{HA}^c \vdash \exists u T(\mathrm{n},x,u)$. Then $\mathbf{HA} \vdash \neg\forall u \neg T(\mathrm{n},u,x)$, or equivalently $\mathbf{HA} \vdash \neg\neg\exists u T(\mathrm{n},x,u)$. Hence by 9.5 (iii) $\mathbf{HA} \vdash \exists u T(\mathrm{n},x,u)$.

9.6. *Historical note.* Theorem 9.4 (i), (iii) are slight strengthenings of the results of Kreisel mentioned; the improvement consists in replacing the condition "A is quantifier-free" by "$\vdash \forall x(Ax \vee \neg Ax)$". 9.5 is proved in Kreisel 1958, §6. A generalization of 9.4 (iii) can be obtained by combining it with conservative extension results (see e.g. Kreisel 1959B, corollary 3).

§10. Extension of results and methods to intuitionistic analysis

10.1. In this section we briefly indicate how many of our results and methods can be extended to intuitionistic analysis. A detailed exposition must await another paper.

It is necessary to distinguish between

(a) Systems of analysis for choice sequences (e.g. the system of Kleene and Vesley 1965). Such systems contain one or more continuity schemata and/or the bar theorem.

(b) Systems of analysis for lawlike sequences e.g. the system **IDB** of Kreisel and Troelstra 1970 (§3), where instead of the bar theorem, a class K of neighbourhood functions is introduced by means of a generalized inductive definition.

10.2. In case (a), the natural analogues of **r**- and **q**-realizability as defined in §3 are functional **r**- and **q**-realizability as defined in Kleene 1969.

Kleene's notion of application $\{\alpha\}[\beta]$ (Kleene 1969) replaces $\{x\}(y)$. The role of ECT_0 with respect to the axiomatization of the provably realizable formulae is taken over by a generalized continuity principle, which in the notation of Kleene 1969 may be stated as follows

$$\forall\alpha[A\alpha\to\exists\beta B(\alpha,\beta)] \to \exists\gamma\forall\alpha[A\alpha\to !\{\gamma\}[\alpha] \wedge B(\alpha,\{\gamma\}[\alpha])] .$$

Brouwer's principle for functions (Kleene and Vesley 1965, $^{\times}27.1$) corresponds to CT_0.

With respect to the same formal theories $\mathbf{HA}^{\omega}$ there are natural analogues to *HRO* and *HEO* which satisfy continuity for type 2 objects, namely the intensional continuous functionals (*ICF*) (Kreisel 1962, remark 10) and the extensional continuous functionals (*ECF*) (Kreisel 1959 and Kleene 1959; Kleene uses the term "countable functional") respectively.

Kleene's "special realizability" (Kleene and Vesley 1965, §10) is equivalent or at least very close to modified realizability with respect to intensional continuous functionals.

Functional **r**-realizability may be used to prove consistency of AC for *ICF*, and consistency of AC! for *ECF* (analogous to 8.5, 8.6 of this paper).

10.3. In case (b) the analogy with the case of **HA** is in some respects even more pronounced. Let us restrict our attention to the system **IDB** of Kreisel and Troelstra 1970.

The definition of (numerical) **r**- and **q**-realizability is extended to **IDB** by interpreting quantifiers $\forall a$, $\exists a$ as ranging over general recursive functions (see Kreisel and Troelstra 1970, 3.7.1). Then, with the same definition of almost negative as for **HA**, results like 3.14 carry over literally, replacing **HA** by **IDB**.

A type structure generated by two basic types 0 and K (the type of the neighbourhood functions) may be defined similarly to **T** (this idea goes back to Howard 1963).

Relative to this type structure we can define, in analogy to **I-HA**$^\omega$, **E-HA**$^\omega$, **WE-HA**$^\omega$, extensions **I-IDB**$^\omega$, **E-IDB**$^\omega$, **WE-IDB**$^\omega$ of **IDB**.

In addition to the schemata of **HA**$^\omega$, **IDB**$^\omega$ contains a schema for defining functionals by induction over K.

The models *HRO, HEO* may be extended to models *K-HRO, K-HEO* for **I-IDB**$^\omega$, **E-IDB**$^\omega$ respectively, etc. etc.

From the detailed treatment it becomes clear that theories of type (b) are in many respects easier to handle than the corresponding theories with continuity and bar-induction.

Bibliography

K.Gödel, Ueber eine bisher noch nicht benützte Erweiterung des finiten Standpunktes, Dialectica 12 (1958) 280–287.

W.A.Howard, Transfinite induction and transfinite recursion, in: Stanford report on the foundations of analysis (Stanford University, 1963) (mimeographed).

Ordinal analysis of bar-recursion of type zero. Unpublished (cited as Howard A).

S.C.Kleene, On the interpretation of intuitionistic number theory, Jour. symbolic logic 10 (1945) 109–124.

Introduction to metamathematics (North-Holland, Amsterdam, P.Noordhoff, Groningen, 1952).

Countable functionals, in: Constructivity in mathematics, ed. A.Heyting (North-Holland, Amsterdam, 1959) 81–100.

Disjunction and existence under implication in elementary intuitionistic formalisms, Jour. Symbolic Logic 27 (1962) 11–18.

Logical calculus and realizability, Acta Philosophica Fennica 18 (1965) 71–80.

Formalized recursive functionals, and formalized realizability, Memoirs of the American Mathematical Society 89 (1969) (American Mathematical Society, Providence, Rh.I.).

S.C.Kleene and R.E.Vesley, The foundations of intuitionistic mathematics, especially in relation to recursive functions (North-Holland, Amsterdam, 1965).

G.Kreisel, Mathematical significance of consistency proofs, Jour. symbolic logic 23 (1958) 155–182.

The non-derivability of $\neg(x)A(x) \rightarrow (Ex)\neg A(x)$, A primitive recursive, in intuitionistic formal systems (abstract), Journal of Symbolic Logic 23 (1958A) 456–457.

Interpretation of analysis by means of constructive functionals of finite type, in: Constructivity in mathematics, ed..A.Heyting (North-Holland, Amsterdam, 1959) 101–128.

Reflection principle for subsystems of Heyting's arithmetic (abstract), Jour. symbolic logic 24 (1959A) 322.

Inessential extensions of Heyting's arithmetic by means of functionals of finite type (abstract), Jour. symbolic logic 24 (1959B) 284.

On weak completeness of intuitionistic predicate logic, Jour. symbolic logic 27 (1962) 139–158.

Mathematical logic, in: Lectures on modern mathematics, ed. T.L.Saaty, Vol. 3 (Wiley, New York, 1965) 95–195.

G.Kreisel and A.S.Troelstra, Formal systems for some branches of intuitionistic analysis, Annals of mathematical logic 1 (1970) 229–387.

D.Nelson, Recursive functions and intuitionistic number theory, Trans. American Mathematical Society 61 (1947) 307–368.

C.Spector, Provably recursive functionals of analysis: a consistency proof of analysis by an extension of principles formulated in current intuitionistic mathematics, in: Proceedings of the symposia in pure mathematics, Vol. 5, ed. J.C.E.Dekker (American Mathematical Society, Providence, Rh.I., 1962) 1–27.

W.W.Tait, Intensional interpretations of functionals of finite type I, Jour. Symbolic Logic 32 (1967) 198–212.

Constructive reasoning, in: Logic, methodology and philosophy of science III, eds. B.van Rootselaar and J.F.Staal (North-Holland, Amsterdam, 1968) 185–199.

M.Yasugi, Intuitionistic analysis and Gödel's interpretation, Jour. of the Mathematical Society of Japan 15 (1963) 101–112.